The Roles of International Law in Development

The Roles of International Law in Development

Edited by

SIOBHÁN MCINERNEY-LANKFORD
ROBERT MCCORQUODALE

OXFORD
UNIVERSITY PRESS

Great Clarendon Street, Oxford, OX2 6DP,
United Kingdom

Oxford University Press is a department of the University of Oxford.
It furthers the University's objective of excellence in research, scholarship,
and education by publishing worldwide. Oxford is a registered trade mark of
Oxford University Press in the UK and in certain other countries

© The several contributors 2023

The moral rights of the authors have been asserted

First Edition published in 2023

All rights reserved. No part of this publication may be reproduced, stored in
a retrieval system, or transmitted, in any form or by any means, without the
prior permission in writing of Oxford University Press, or as expressly permitted
by law, by licence or under terms agreed with the appropriate reprographics
rights organization. Enquiries concerning reproduction outside the scope of the
above should be sent to the Rights Department, Oxford University Press, at the
address above

You must not circulate this work in any other form
and you must impose this same condition on any acquirer

Public sector information reproduced under Open Government Licence v3.0
(http://www.nationalarchives.gov.uk/doc/open-government-licence/open-government-licence.htm)

Published in the United States of America by Oxford University Press
198 Madison Avenue, New York, NY 10016, United States of America

British Library Cataloguing in Publication Data

Data available

Library of Congress Control Number: 2023944952

ISBN 978-0-19-287290-6

DOI: 10.1093/oso/9780192872906.001.0001

Printed and bound by
CPI Group (UK) Ltd, Croydon, CR0 4YY

Links to third party websites are provided by Oxford in good faith and
for information only. Oxford disclaims any responsibility for the materials
contained in any third party website referenced in this work.

To Joan and the memory of Marcus
(Siobhán)
To the memory of Lex
(Robert)

Foreword

Development is—increasingly—a multinational endeavour. At its core, it involves cooperation and collaboration among states, institutions, and people: it is an enterprise undertaken in different ways and at various levels, nationally and in collaboration with the international community. Nowhere is this more evident than in the Sustainable Development Goals (SDGs), adopted unanimously in 2015 under the aegis of the UN General Assembly in the resolution 'The Future We all Want'. The SDGs are directed at all states, and envisage long-term, harmonized policies and strategies at global, national, and local levels. They are also premised on the importance of cooperation and partnerships, and the roles of technology, financial resources, and capable national institutions. They conceive of sustainable development as a complex goal, underpinned by national policies and enabling laws, with several interconnected spheres: economic, social, and environmental. This is reflected in the fact that the SDGs are interdependent, where action (or inaction) in one area will affect outcomes in others. It is against that backdrop that this book emerges as an investigation into the international law underpinnings and parameters of the complex international endeavour that is sustainable development.

This book explores the question of how development is governed and shaped by international law—whether general international law or specialized areas of international law. It explores the influence of, and interplay between, development on international law. It also explores how development actors, including international financial institutions, contribute to the creation, interpretation, or evolution of international law, as well as how international law could and should be used more often by development actors and in development national policy and law-making. Indeed, a recurring theme is the need for all development actors to be aware of the relevance of international law in their specialized roles and fields.

This is an ambitious project—it spans a broad range of subject matter areas and tackles complex structural questions of international law and national development policy. A singular contribution of this book is to remind development practitioners, lawyers, and financiers that their work does not occur in a vacuum isolated from these other critically connected areas and perspectives. This collection also tells cautionary tales about the risks of legal and policy silos, and the risks of the fragmentation of international laws as these play out in various areas of development cooperation. The book as a whole therefore implicitly argues in favour of the importance of international policy and legal coherence to enable the international community to tackle the myriad challenges facing developing countries. Understanding the relevance and applicability of international law to development exemplifies where global thinking is today in terms of the expectations on international actors about how they manage legal and reputational risk.

I think that this book crystallizes and raises the stakes for development actors: underscoring the importance of harmonizing international law and development and challenging them to integrate them in their own spheres of policy, local law, and operations. In this respect, it reminds us of the aim of international law to encompass a sense of collective legal accountability for international commitments to global standards. I hope that a more coherent, consistent, and integrated approach to international law in development policy and practice may eventually help make development cooperation more effective and sustainable, and ultimately facilitate better outcomes.

Christopher Stephens
Senior Vice President and World Bank Group General Counsel
August 2023

Preface

This book grew out of a panel at the American Society of International Law in April 2020, for which we are thankful. That panel considered the central role of international law in the attainment of the Sustainable Development Goals. The discussion by the panel, and from the engaged audience, indicated that a more consistent and coherent approach to international law in development policy and practice, and a less fragmented approach by international law concerning development could yield greater accountability in development and more sustainable and equitable development outcomes. Indeed one clear conclusion of the panel was that the relevant and applicable rules of international law should be incorporated more systematically into development policy, rejecting the notion that development policy or development law constitute a 'self-contained' regime that operates outside international law.

As the ideas from that panel continued to flourish, it became clear that there was very limited literature on these issues. Despite the growth in sustainable development as an area of study and practice, few books have examined it from an international legal perspective. Yet there is an increasing interest across many disciplines about the nexus between development and international law, and a sustained interest in accountability of all development actors. Work in this area can have significant practical consequences for international institutions and governments, as well as for stakeholders.

The chapters explore the relevance and applicability of international law to particular sectors and issues in development activities. It analyses how international law rules and processes can influence procedural and substantive aspects of development policies as these regulate various forms of financial support, trade, technical assistance, and policy dialogue. We were fortunate to gather excellent and insightful contributors to offer their expertise across a wide range of topics and applications. This diversity of backgrounds and perspectives adds significant depth to this collection. Our warmest thanks to them for their chapters, as well as their dedication and patience, as the ideas transformed into the book. Our thanks to Oxford University Press for seeing the potential in the book and for their encouragement throughout the process. Our deep thanks to our families, who supported us with love and kindness when our focus was on this book.

This book began during the difficult times of the COVID-19 pandemic. Yet that pandemic reinforced the real need for international law, especially international human rights law, to be directly considered in development policy decision-making and the central role of international law in building back better and ensuring just transitions. Our hope is that this book underscores that international law is a key pillar in sustainable development policies and practice.

Siobhán McInerney-Lankford and Robert McCorquodale
December 2022

Contents

List of Abbreviations   xiii
List of Contributors   xix

PART I: CONTEXT

1. The Role of International Law in Development: An Introduction   3
   Robert McCorquodale

2. The Case for International Law Due Diligence in the Development Context   14
   Siobhán McInerney-Lankford

3. The Role of International Law in Development Practice   46
   Arnold N Pronto

PART II: THE ROLE OF HUMAN RIGHTS LAW

4. The Triangle of Human Rights, International Law, and Sustainable Development   59
   Jan Wouters and Michiel Hoornick

5. United Nations Human Rights Treaty Bodies' Approaches   80
   Anganile Willie Mwenifumbo, Harumi Fuentes Furuya, and Marie-Joseph Ayissi

6. The ILO's Dialogical Standards-Based Approach to International Labour Law   110
   Katerina Tsotroudi and Jordi Agustí Panareda

7. Achieving Gender Equality   139
   Sandra Fredman

8. Race and Discrimination   162
   Harum Mukhayer

9. The Right to Water   196
   Laurence Boisson de Chazournes, Mara Tignino, and Haoua Savadogo

PART III: THE ROLE OF ENVIRONMENTAL, HUMANITARIAN, AND REFUGEE LAW

10. Environmental Law and Climate Change: A Perspective from Africa   221
    Bakary Kanté

11. Forced Displacement, International Law, and the World Bank   243
    Duygu Çiçek, Paige Casaly, and Vikram Raghavan

12. Problematizing the Role of the World Bank in Latin America Mining Reforms   273
    Ximena Sierra-Camargo

PART IV: THE ROLE OF INTERNATIONAL ECONOMIC LAW

13. International Investment Law   305
    Ursula Kriebaum

14. International Trade and Foreign Investment   339
    Chin Leng Lim

15. The Adequacy of Financing for the Development Agenda   363
    Thomas F McInerney

16. Responsibilities and Public-Private Partnerships in Infrastructure   391
    Humberto Cantú Rivera

17. The Rule of Law in Investment—A Condition for Development?   411
    Farouk El-Hosseny

PART V: CONCLUSIONS

18. The Relevance of International Law to Sustainable Development   431
    Siobhán McInerney-Lankford and Robert McCorquodale

Index   439

List of Abbreviations

AAAA	Addis Ababa Action Agenda
ABNJ	Areas Beyond National Jurisdiction
ACHPR	African Charter on Human and Peoples' Rights
ACHR	Inter-American Convention on Human Rights
ADB	Asian Development Bank
ADWA	Advancing the Decent Work Agenda in North Africa
AfDB	African Development Bank
AIIB	Asian Infrastructure Investment Bank
ARIO	Articles on Responsibilities of International Organisations
AVAT	African Vaccine Acquisition Trust
AVATT	African Vaccine Acquisition Task Team
AWS	Alliance for Water Stewardship
BEPS	Base Erosion and Profit Shifting project (OECD/G20)
BIT	Bilateral Investment Treaty
BLM	Black Lives Matter
BRIC	Brazil, Russia, India, and China countries
C2A	Call to Action for Human Rights
CAC	Collective Action Clause
CAS	Committee on the Application of Standards
CAT	Convention against Torture and other Cruel, Inhuman or Degrading Treatment or Punishment
CBD	Convention on Biological Diversity
CDM	Clean Development Mechanism
CEACR	Committee of Experts on the Application of Conventions and Recommendations
CED	Committee on Enforced Disappearances
CEDAW	Convention on the Elimination of All Forms of Discrimination against Women (UN)
CEPI	Coalition for Epidemic Preparedness Innovations
CERD	Committee on the Elimination of Racial Discrimination
CESCR	Committee on Economic Social and Cultural Rights
CETA	Comprehensive Economic and Trade Agreement
CF	cooperation framework
CFA	Committee on Freedom of Association
CFCs	Chlorofluorocarbons
CH	Methane
CMLV	Cambodia, Myanmar, Lao People's Democratic Republic, and Vietnam
CMW	Committee on the Protection of the Rights of All Migrant Workers and Members of Their Families

List of Abbreviations

CO2	Carbon Dioxide
COP	Conferences of Party
COP17	2009 Copenhagen Accord
COVAX	COVID-19 Vaccines Global Access
CPO	Country Programme Outcome
CRBP	Child Rights and Business Principles
CRC	Committee on the Rights of the Child
CRPD	Committee on the Rights of Persons with Disabilities
CRW	Crisis Response Window
CTD	Committee on Trade and Development (WTO)
DAC	Development Assistance Committee
DC	Development Cooperation
DFI	Development Finance Institutions
DIHR	Danish Institute for Human Rights
DSSI	Debt Service Suspension Initiative
DWCPs	Decent Work Country Programme
E&S	Environmental and Social
EBRD	European Bank for Reconstruction and Development
EC	European Commission
ECHR	European Convention on Human Rights and Fundamental Freedoms
ECLAC	Economic Commission for Latin America and the Caribbean (UN) (also known as CEPAL for its acronym in Spanish)
ECOSOC	Economic and Social Council (UN)
EFO	Economic and Financial Organisation
EHSGs	Environmental Health and Safety Guidelines
EIA	Environmental Impact Assessment
ELI	Environmental Law Institute
EPIC	Equal Pay International Coalition
ESCP	Environmental and Social Commitment Plan
ESF	Environmental and Social Framework (World Bank)
ESG	Environmental, Social, and Governance
ESS	Environmental and Social Standard (World Bank Environmental and Social Framework)
FAO	Food and Agricultural Organization
FCTC	Framework Convention on Tobacco Control (WHO)
FCV	Fragility, Conflict, and Violence
FET	Fair and Equitable Treatment
FPRW	Fundamental Principles and Rights at Work
GATS	General Agreement on Trade in Services
GATT	General Agreement on Tariffs and Trade
GB	Governing Body
GB	ICCPR International Covenant on Civil and Political Rights
GC22	General Comment 22 on reproductive rights (CESCR)
GCF	Green Climate Fund
GCFF	Global Concessional Financing Facility

LIST OF ABBREVIATIONS xv

GEF	Global Environmental Facility
GEP	Global Economic Prospects Report (2022)
GHG	Greenhouse Gases
GPFD	Global Program on Forced Displacement
GSP	Generalized Scheme of Preferences
HIPC	Highly-Indebted Poor Countries
HLPE	High Level Panel of Experts
HLPF	High-level Panel Forum on Sustainable Development
HRBA	Human Rights-based Approach
HRC	Human Rights Committee
HRCt	Human Rights Committee
ID4D	Identification for Development
IDA	International Development Association
IACHR	Inter-American Commission on Human Rights
IADB	Inter-American Development Bank
IAEG-SDGs	Inter-Agency and Expert Group on SDG Indicators
IBHR	International Bill of Human Rights
IBRD	International Bank for Reconstruction and Development
ICCPR	International Covenant on Civil Political Rights
ICERD	International Convention on the Elimination of Racial Discrimination
ICESCR	International Covenant on Economic, Social and Cultural Rights
ICJ	International Court of Justice
ICMA	International Capital Markets Association
ICME	International Council on Metals and the Environment
ICPED	International Convention for the Protection of All Persons from Enforced Disappearance
ICRC	International Committee of the Red Cross
ICSID	International Centre for Settlement of Investment Disputes
IDP	Internally Displaced Person
IO	International Organization
IFC	International Finance Corporation
IFI	International financial institution
IGPRA	Pakistan Income Generating Project for Refugee Areas
IHRB	Institute for Human Rights and Business
IHRL	International Human Rights Law
IIAs	International Investment Agreements
IIED	International Institute for Environment and Development
ILC	International Labour Conference/International Law Commission
ILS	International Labour Standards
IMF	International Monetary Fund
IPCC	Intergovernmental Panel on Climate Change
IPEC	International Programme on the Elimination of Child Labour
IPEC+	International Programme on the Elimination of Child Labour and Forced Labour
IPF	Investment Project Financing

IRO	Refugee Organization
ISDS	Investor-State Dispute Settlement
ITLOS	International Tribunal for the Law of the Sea
ITO	International Trade Organization
ITU	International Telecommunications Union
IUCN	International Union for Conservation of Nature
IWRM	Integrated Water Resources Management
JDZs	Joint Development Zones
JI	Joint Implementation
JMP	Joint Monitoring Programme (WHO/UNICEF)
LDCs	Least Developed Countries
LNOB	Leave No One Behind
M&E	Monitoring and Evaluation
MAA	Mutual Administrative Assistance
MAI	Multilateral Agreement on Investment
MDB	Multilateral Development Bank
MDG	Millennium Development Goal
MEA	Multilateral Environmental Agreement
MEP	Member of the European Parliament
MERCOSUR	Southern Common Market (abbreviation in Spanish)
MIA	Multilateral Investment Agreement
MIGA	Multilateral Investment Guarantee Agency
MNC	Multinational Corporation
MOPAN	Multilateral Organisation Performance Assessment Network
MTBE	Methyl Tertiary Butyl Ether
NAFTA	North American Free Trade Agreement
NAMA	Non-Agricultural Market Access
NDC	Nationally Determined Contributions
NHRI	National Human Rights Institutions
NIEO	New International Economic Order
NOx	Nitrous Oxide
OAU	Organization of African Unity
ODA	Official Development Assistance
OECD	Organization for Economic Cooperation and Development
OHA	Office of Hawaiian Affairs
OHCHR	Office of the High Commissioner on Human Rights
OIOS	Office for Internal Oversight Services
OPEC	Organisation of the Petroleum Exporting Countries
P&B	Programme and Budget
PO	Policy Outcomes
PPP	Polluter Pays Principle/Public-Private Partnerships
PSAC	Programmatic Structural Adjustment Credits
PSAL	Programmatic Structural Adjustment Loan
RPRF	Refugee Policy Review Framework
RTA	Regional Trade Agreement

SCM	Agreement on Subsidies and Countervailing Measures (WTO)
SDG	Sustainable Development Goals
SIFCA	Sustainable Investment Facilitation & Cooperation Agreement
SLARIE	Strengthening Labour Relations and its Institutions in Egypt
SMH	Special Mandate Holder
SOE	State-Owned Mining Enterprise
SPRP	Strategic Preparedness and Response Program (COVID-19)
SPT	Subcommittee on Prevention of Torture
SRM	Standards Review Mechanism
TB	Treaty Body
TC	Technical Cooperation
TRIPs	Agreement on Trade-related Aspects of Intellectual Property Rights
TTIP	Transatlantic Trade and Investment Partnership
TWG	Tripartite Working Group
UDHR	Universal Declaration on Human Rights
UN	United Nations
UNCAC	UN Convention against Corruption
UNCED	United Nations Conference on Environment and Development
UNCITRAL	UN Commission on International Trade Law
UNCLOS	UN Convention on the Law of the Sea
UNCTAD	United Nations Conference on Trade and Development
UNDP	United Nations Development Programme
UNDRIP	United Nations Declaration on the Rights of Indigenous Peoples
UNEA	United Nations Environment Assembly
UNEP	United Nations Environment Programme
UNESCO	United Nations Educational, Scientific and Cultural Organization
UNFCCC	United Nations Framework Convention on Climate Change
UNGA	United Nations General Assembly
UNGPs	United Nations Guiding Principles on Business and Human Rights
UNHCHR	United Nations High Commissioner for Human Rights
UNHCR	UN High Commissioner for Refugees
UNICEF	United Nations International Children's Emergency Fund
UNODC	United Nations Office on Drugs and Crime
UNRRA	United Nations Relief and Rehabilitation Administration
UNSC	United Nations Security Council
UNSD	United Nations Statistics Division
UNSG	United Nations Secretary-General
UNTBs	United Nations Treaty Bodies
UNWG	United Nations Working Group (on Business and Human Rights)
UPR	Universal Periodic Review
UPU	Universal Postal Union
USMCA	United States-Mexico-Canada Agreement
VCLT	Vienna Convention on the Law of Treaties
VIRAT	Vaccine Introduction Readiness Assessment Tool (WHO)
VNRs	Voluntary National Reviews

VRAF	Vaccination Readiness Assessment Framework (World Bank)
WASH	Water Supply, Sanitation and Hygiene
WB	World Bank
WBG	World Bank Group
WHO	World Health Organization
WHR	Window for Host Communities and Refugees (IDA)
WMO	World Meteorological Organization
WTO	World Trade Organisation
WWAP	World Water Assessment Programme (UNESCO)

List of Contributors

Jordi Agustí-Panareda, a senior official at the International Labour Organization, where he serves as Ethics Officer, after having held the positions of Head of Unit at the Freedom of Association Branch of the International Labour Standards Department, and of Senior Legal Officer at the Office of the Legal Advisor. Previously he worked as an associate at the New York law firm Sullivan & Cromwell, and as legal counsel at the World Bank. He holds a Master in Laws from the London School of Economics and Political Science and a Masters and a Doctorate of the Science of Law from Stanford University. His areas of research include international labour standards (and their interaction with other rule systems, eg trade), the law and practice of international organizations (both internal functioning and international rulemaking and supervisory activities), organizational ethics and axiologies, conflict management and decision-making processes.

Marie-Joseph Ayissi, Human Rights Officer and Secretary of the Committee on the Elimination of Racial Discrimination at the UN Office of the High Commissioner for Human Rights in Geneva, where he also worked with the Secretariat of the Human Rights Council and the Human Rights Treaties Bodies Division. Previously, Marie-Joseph worked with ILO and the Permanent Mission of the Francophonie in Geneva. From 2016-2017, he was a Visiting Researcher with the Georgetown University Law Center in Washington DC. Marie-Joseph is a dual national of Cameroon and Switzerland.

Laurence Boisson de Chazournes, Professor of International Law at the University of Geneva. She is currently the Director of the LLM in International Dispute Settlement and also serves as the Director of the Geneva Water Hub's Platform for International Freshwater Law. She is a member of the Institute of International Law and previously was a member of the Advisory Committee of the UN Human Rights Council. She is a counsel and advocate before the International Court of Justice, the International Tribunal for the Law of the Sea, and other courts and tribunals. She also acts as an arbitrator in international disputes and as an expert for international organizations. She has advised on several negotiations involving international watercourses.

Humberto Cantú Rivera, Professor at the Faculty of Law and Director of the Human Rights and Business Institute of the University of Monterrey (UDEM, Mexico). He holds a LLD from Université Panthéon-Assas Paris II, and is a member of the Editorial Board of the Business and Human Rights Journal and of the review Droits fondamentaux. He has published widely on business and human rights and has extensive experience working with and advising States, international organizations, businesses and civil society on business and human rights in international, regional and domestic standard-setting processes, and in the implementation of responsible business conduct standards.

Paige Marie Casaly, Counsel in the Operations Policy practice group of the Legal Department of the World Bank. She provides specialized advice on the development, implementation, and application of the Bank's operational policies, with a focus on the Bank's engagement in situations of fragility, conflict, and violence. She served as a member of the core team that developed the *World Development Report 2023: Migrants, Refugees, and Societies*. Paige previously worked for the United Nations High Commissioner for Refugees and the International Criminal Tribunal for the former Yugoslavia, and is a member of the American Society of International Law, where she is a member of the International Refugee Law, International Organizations, and Migration Law interest groups. She received her Juris Doctor (JD) from New York University School of Law and is a member of the Bar of the State of New York.

Duygu Çiçek, Counsel at the World Bank Legal Department, Environment and International Law Unit. She co-chairs the Human Rights and Sustainable Development Working Group under the Global Forum on Law, Justice, and Development and serves as a member of the International Law Association Committee on International Law and Sea Level Rise. Previously, she worked with the ABA Rule of Law Initiative, the UN High Commissioner for Refugees, and the Council of Europe Office of the Commissioner for Human Rights. She holds an LLM in human rights (University of Edinburgh) and an LLM in international law (George Washington University).

Farouk El-Hosseny, Senior associate in the London office of Three Crowns LLP, specialising in arbitrations governed by the ICC, ICSID and UNCITRAL rules, with a focus on complex commercial and investor-state disputes. He is also a Visiting Assistant Professor at Leiden University's Grotius Center for International Legal Studies. In addition, Farouk acts as arbitrator under the ICC and PCA rules. He is a member of the ICC Bulletin Editorial Board. Farouk holds a PhD degree in public international law from Leiden University and was also educated at the University of Ottawa and the University of Montreal.

Sandra Fredman, Professor of Law, Oxford University, and Director, Oxford Human Rights Hub. She is a Fellow of the British Academy and King's Council (honoris causa). She has numerous peer-reviewed publications. Books include Discrimination Law (3rd edn 2022); Comparative Human Rights (2018); Human Rights Transformed (2008) and Women and the Law (1997). Edited books include Exponential Inequalities (2022) with Shreya Atrey; and Feminist Frontiers on Climate Justice (2023) with Albertyn, Campbell, Alviar and Machado. She helped draft the Abidjan Principles on the Right to Education. Current research includes fair work for gigworkers and the right to Early Childhood Education.

Harumi Fuentes Furuya, Human Rights Officer at the UN Office of the High Commissioner for Human Rights (OHCHR) in Geneva, and has supported several UN treaty bodies as the substantive secretariat. She is currently working in the Economic, Social and Cultural Rights Section of OHCHR. Before joining OHCHR, she worked with UNDP, and she has previously held several NGO positions. Harumi has a background in International Relations, Development Economics and Human Rights. Harumi is a national of Mexico.

Michiel Hoornick, PhD candidate in International Law at the Geneva Graduate Institute on International and Development Studies (IHEID), Switzerland. Previously, he worked as a researcher at the Leuven Centre for Global Governance Studies in Belgium and as programme officer at the Institute on Statelessness and Inclusion, where he coordinated its engagement with the Geneva-based UN human rights mechanisms. This followed traineeships with the UNHCR in Geneva and the Netherlands Permanent Mission to the UN in New York, as well as Master degrees in International and European Law from IHEID and Tilburg University, the Netherlands.

Bakary Kanté, Founder and Chairman of the Africa Sustainability Centre, and he is a leading African thinker-practitioner on sustainability, rule of law and environmental justice at global and national levels. From his early professional life as Director of the Environment, in his native Senegal, he has been imbued with a deep passion for helping to lift Africa from its technology, sustainability, environmental justice deficit, shaped largely by the Continent's colonial history. Dr Kante has over 35 years of experience in diplomacy and high level political negotiations at international and national levels towards promoting international environmental governance, environmental justice and the rule of law.

Ursula Kriebaum, Professor of Public International Law at the University of Vienna, member of the Permanent Court of Arbitration, member of the Panel of Arbitrators under the Agreement on the Withdrawal of the UK from the EU, member of the Panel of Conciliators maintained by the International Centre for Settlement of Investment Disputes, member of the Arbitration panel for the Protocol on Cultural Cooperation to the Free Trade Agreement between the European Union and its Member States and the Republic of Korea, as well as legal expert in various investment arbitrations and human rights cases.

Chin Leng Lim, Choh-Ming Li Professor of Law at the Chinese University of Hong Kong. He is an associé of the Institut de droit international and has lectured at the Hague Academy of International Law. He is a visiting professor at King's College London and an honorary senior fellow at the British Institute of International and Comparative Law.

Harumi McCorquodale, Member of the United Nations Working Group on Business and Human Rights, a five-member group of independent experts. He is Emeritus Professor of International Law and Human Rights at the University of Nottingham, and a barrister and mediator at Brick Court Chambers in London. He has a LLB and BEc from the University of Sydney and a LLM and PhD from the University of Cambridge. Robert undertakes research and publishes in international law and is also a legal practitioner, with his main current focus being on business and human rights. He has advised business of all sizes and assisted governments and civil society around the world. He has appeared as an advocate before the International Court of Justice and the United Kingdom Supreme Court, and as a legal expert before United Nations bodies.

Thomas F McInerney, Executive Director of the Rule of Law for Development Program and Senior Lecturer at Loyola University Chicago School of Law. Previously, he was Director of Research, Policy, and Strategic Initiatives with the International Development Law Organization. He holds a BA in philosophy and government from the College of William and Mary, a MA in philosophy from Loyola University Chicago, a JD from DePaul University, and a PhD in development studies from the Institute of Development Studies, University of Sussex.

Siobhán Mcinerney-Lankford, Head of Unit (Equality, Roma and Social Rights) at the EU Fundamental Rights Agency. Between 2002 and 2023 she worked at the World Bank Legal Vice-Presidency serving as an operational lawyer and legal advisor on human rights law, international law and environmental and social policy. She has taught and published widely on human rights law. She holds an LLB from Trinity College, Dublin, an LLM from Harvard Law School, and a BCL and DPhil from Oxford University. She is admitted to practice law in Rhode Island and the District of Columbia.

Harum Mukhayer, Legal Counsel with the World Bank's Legal Department. She is a public international lawyer who has been working in international development and the inclusion of those most often excluded. specialising in environmental and natural resources law with a focus on international boundary and territorial disputes, for over a decade. She has been mainly working with the UN in Sudan, South Sudan and Somalia. She has a PhD from the University of Cambridge, as a Gates-Cambridge Scholar. Harum brings 10 years of field experience working with international organisations, on issues relating to territorial sovereignty, natural resources law, land law and customary rights, and the rights of border communities between two or more States. Harum's commitment to inclusion was inspired by the Winimum Wintu and Pit River Tribes, and transboundary communities in Sudan, South Sudan and Somalia. Harum traces her ancestral descent from Sudan and identifies as a global nomad.

Anganile Willie Mwenifumbo, Human Rights Officer at the UN Office of the High Commissioner for Human Rights (OHCHR) and works for the Field Operations and Technical Division, Africa Branc, where he focuses on African Union matters among other things. He has previously worked for the Human Rights Council and Treaty Mechanisms Division and OHCHR's Regional Office for Southern Africa. Before joining OHCHR, Anganile worked as a Legal Officer for the African Court on Human and Peoples' Rights and as Head of Litigation for a private law firm in Malawi. He is Malawian.

Arnold Pronto, Principal Legal Officer in the Codification Division of the Office of Legal Affairs of the United Nations, working primarily in the field of the codification and progressive development of public international law. He is a member of the Secretariats of the Sixth Committee of the United Nations General Assembly and of the International Law Commission.

Vikram Raghavan, Lead Counsel in the environmental and international practice group of the World Bank's Legal Department. For two decades, he was the Bank's legal advisor for conflict, refugees, and macroeconomics. His experience includes working on projects across Africa, Asia, and the Middle East, the Bank's development mandate, loan conditionality, conflict and fragility, refugees and forced displacement, humanitarian crises and disasters, military coups, sanctions, and sovereign debt.

Haoua Savadogo, Research and teaching assistant, and a PhD candidate, at the University of Geneva. Her thesis focuses on the responsibility of transnational companies in international law. She holds a Master's degree in Economic Law and an LLM in International Dispute Resolution from the University of Geneva and the Graduate Institute of International and Development Studies. She worked with the Geneva Water Hub on the UNDP/UNAMI project to train government officials from various Iraqi ministries in international water law. She previously worked as a legal assistant at the International Court of Justice and in law firms in Paris.

Ximena Sierra-Camargo, Catalyst Fellow at Osgoode Hall Law School, York University. PhD in Law (Rosario University, Colombia), MA in Socio-legal studies (La Plata National University, Argentina), and BA in Law (Externado de Colombia University). Visiting Research Fellow at the Transnational Law Institute (TLI), King's College London, and the Centre for Critical International Law (CeCIL), Kent Law School. She has performed as an attorney and consultant in NGOs, public entities, and International Organizations and as a lecturer and researcher in Transnational Mining, Public International Law, Human Rights, Law and Development, and Socio-legal studies. Her research interests are in International Law, Transnational Law, Law and Development, Socio-legal studies, and Political Ecology.

Mara Tignino, Reader at the Faculty of Law and the Institute for Environmental Sciences at the University of Geneva and Lead Legal Specialist of the Platform for International Water Law at the Geneva Water Hub. She has been Visiting Professor at Renmin University of China, the University of Barcelona, the Libera Università Internazionale degli Studi Sociali and the Catholic University of Lille. She was also a Visiting Scholar at the George Washington University Law School in Washington D.C. Dr Tignino acts as an expert and legal adviser for States and international organisations. She holds a Ph.D. in international law from the Graduate Institute of International and Development Studies in Geneva and an Habilitation à diriger des recherches from the Faculty of Law of the University Jean Moulin Lyon 3.

Katerina Tsotroudi, Senior official at the International Labour Organisation (ILO) where she currently serves as Global Programming and Collaboration Coordination in the International Labour Standards Department. She holds an LLM from the University of Edinburgh and a Diplôme d'études supérieurs (DES) and PhD from the Graduate Institute of International and Development Studies in Geneva. Her areas of research and publications range from the relationship between international labour standards and development, including in the context of financial crises and the reform of the international financial architecture, to freedom of association and transnational social dialogue.

Jan Wouters, Full Professor of International Law and International Organizations, Jean Monnet Chair ad personam EU and Global Governance, and founding Director of the Institute for International Law and of the Leuven Centre for Global Governance Studies. He studied law and philosophy at Antwerp University, obtained an LL.M. at Yale University and was Visiting Researcher at Harvard University. As Visiting Professor at Sciences Po, Paris-2 (Panthéon-Assas), LUISS and the College of Europe he teaches EU external relations law. As Adjunct Professor at Columbia University he teaches on the EU and human rights. Prof. Wouters is a Member of the Royal Academy of Belgium for Sciences and Arts and practices law as Of Counsel at Linklaters, Brussels.

PART I
CONTEXT

1
The Role of International Law in Development: An Introduction

Robert McCorquodale[*]

1. Context

International law and the rule of law are the foundations of the international system. Clear and foreseeable rules and a system to prevent or sanction violations of these rules are essential preconditions for lasting peace, security, economic development and social progress.[1]

This book aims to explore the ways in which international law could regulate development and influence development policy and approaches, as well as assessing the degree to which that influence could be systematic and explicit. Each chapter will assess how development policies and activities in various substantive areas address or reflect the relevant international law, and the extent to which the applicable international treaties guide the actions of development actors (of which states are the primary actors) in those areas. This book seeks to do so in the context of the need for clear and foreseeable rules within a system, as is provided by international law, and as set out in the quotation above.

This book will examine when and how international law governs aspects of development and when it does not, including in the development policy of multilateral institutions, the structure of particular technical assistance operations, and the provision of various forms of financial assistance. While it does not explore the Sustainable Development Goals[2] (SDGs) in detail, it does touch on them where relevant. Rather, it seeks to explore whether development policy and activities

---

[*] Robert McCorquodale is Emeritus Professor of International Law and Human Rights at the University of Nottingham, a barrister and mediator at Brick Court Chambers, London, and a member of the United Nations Working Group on Business and Human Rights.

[1] Simon Chesterman, *UN Security Council and the Rule of Law* (Institute for International Law and Justice 2008) <unsc_and_the_rule_of_law.pdf (iilj.org)> accessed 17 May 2023, Preface.

[2] UN General Assembly, *Transforming our World: the 2030 Agenda for Sustainable Development* (A/Res/70/1, 2015) (which include the 17 Sustainable Development Goals) <Transforming our world: the 2030 Agenda for Sustainable Development | Department of Economic and Social Affairs (un.org)> accessed 17 May 2023.

Robert McCorquodale, *The Role of International Law in Development: An Introduction* In: *The Roles of International Law in Development*. Edited by: Siobhán McInerney-Lankford and Robert McCorquodale, Oxford University Press.
© Robert McCorquodale 2023. DOI: 10.1093/oso/9780192872906.003.0001

could be more effective, coherent, and sustainable if the relevant and applicable rules of the international legal framework were better understood, acknowledged, and consistently incorporated within decisions about the content, interpretation, and application of development policies. In this respect it suggests that such an approach would advance greater international policy coherence and support greater accountability in development.

In addition, it highlights how international law might be relevant to development given the general neglect, or only selective acknowledgement, of the relevance of international law in development policies and activities. Thus the book challenges the idea that development occurs in a legal vacuum, or that generally applicable law in a variety of fields can be ignored when donors or partners are engaged in development activities. Many of the chapters provide concrete illustrations of the challenges and best practices in sustainable development and the role of international law in these matters. This book aims to place international law as a foundational element in development policies and activities. It generally seeks to do so in the awareness that states are the primary duty bearers under international law. While international organizations, as well as other development actors, such as corporations, do have accountability in this area which requires close consideration, those actors operate within the context of the state as the primary creator, developer, enforcer, and duty bearer under international law, especially under multilateral treaties.

2. International Law

For most of the first part of the twentieth century, the prevailing view was that international law[3] was only about the relations between states.[4] The creation of the United Nations (UN) and the rapid increase in the number of other international organizations comprised of states challenged this view, with the International Court of Justice (ICJ) stating:

> In the opinion of the Court, the [UN] Organisation was intended to exercise and enjoy, and is in fact exercising and enjoying, functions and rights which can only be explained on the basis of the possession of a *large measure of international personality and the capacity to operate upon an international plane* ... That is not the same thing as saying that it is a State, which it certainly is not, or that its legal personality and rights and duties are the same as those of a State.... What it does

---

[3] Often called 'public international law' to distinguish it from 'private international law', the latter of which concerns transactions, such as personal or commercial transactions, across states by those other than states.

[4] For example, Lassa Oppenheim, *International Law* (Longman 1905), vol. 1.

mean is that *it is a subject of international law and capable of possessing international rights and duties, and that it has capacity to maintain its rights by bringing international claims.*[5]

This inclusion of international organizations within the scope of international law is now generally accepted, even though the implications of this remain a subject to debate.[6] This is important in terms of development, where many of the activities are undertaken by states or through state agencies. Further, a significant percentage of the funding of development and development activities worldwide are channelled through and generated by international organizations, such as the World Bank and other multilateral development banks (MDBs), as well as the International Monetary Fund (IMF) and other international financial institutions (IFIs).[7] Of course, each international organization will have different powers and capacities (express and implied) depending on the organization's objects, purposes, and functions. These are usually set out in its constitutive instrument,[8] though the quotation from the ICJ at the start of this section would be expected to apply to international organizations.

In addition, there has been a gradual acknowledgement by commentators that international law now includes other actors, such as non-state armed groups[9] and non-governmental organizations,[10] within its scope. This is also seen in UN Security Council Resolutions which, for example, have stated that terrorist activities by non-state actors are directly a breach of international law.[11] A particular aspect relevant to development is the participation of corporations in international law. There are now a range of mechanisms under international economic law (covering global investment, trade, and financial issues) by which corporations can

---

[5] 'Reparation for Injuries Suffered in the Service of the United Nations', Advisory Opinion, *ICJ Reports 1949*, 174, 178–79 (emphasis added).

[6] For example, Jan Klabbers and August Reinisch, 'Sources of International Organizations' Law' in Samantha Besson and Jean d'Aspremont (eds), *Oxford Handbook on the Sources of International Law* (OUP 2017) 987–1006.

[7] Homi Kharas and Charlotte Rivard, Brookings Institute, 'Financing for Sustainable Development is Clogged' (May 2022), <Financing for sustainable development is clogged (brookings.edu)> accessed 18 May 2023.

[8] WHO, 'Legality of the Threat or Use of Nuclear Weapons Opinion' (WHO Advisory Opinion, ICJ Reports 1996) 66.

[9] Sandesh Sivakumaran, *The Law of Non-International Armed Conflict* (OUP 2012), especially concerning international agreements between states and non-state armed groups: 124–32.

[10] In relation to the International Committee of the Red Cross (ICRC), see (I) Protocol Additional to the Geneva Conventions of 12 August 1949, and Concerning the Protection of Victims of International Armed Conflict (Geneva, 1125 UNTS 3, 8 June 1977) art 97; (II) Protocol Additional to the Geneva Conventions of 12 August 1949, and relating to the Protection of Victims of Non-International Armed Conflicts (Geneva, 1125 UNTS 609, 8 June 1977) art 24. See generally François Bugnion, *The International Committee of the Red Cross and the Protection of War Victims* (ICRC 2003).

[11] Security Council Resolution 1373 [2001] 28 September 2001, para 5: 'Declares that acts, methods, and practices of terrorism are contrary to the purposes and principles of the United Nations and that knowingly financing, planning and inciting terrorist acts are also contrary to the purposes and principles of the United Nations.'

bring claims against states.[12] These mechanisms include institutional bodies (both treaty based and non-treaty based) with established procedures, legally binding decision-making bodies, and enforcement procedures.[13] Thus, an international investment tribunal has held that 'it can no longer be admitted that companies operating internationally are immune from becoming subjects of international law'.[14]

At the same time, there is concern about how international law has applied to those in the Global South. This has included critiques as to how economic power imbalances are accentuated by the formation of international law, the lack of effective representation of the Global South in development decision-making, and the Global North's infusion of market-based approaches to development.[15] As Luis Eslava and Sundhya Pahuja comment:

> [I]t is possible to understand the relationship between states and international law differently, particularly if we concentrate on how that dynamic has played out in the Global South from colonial times to today.... This new order operates via a 'formal' parity among states, and a technicized developmental discourse in which formerly imperial relations were transformed into a renovated vision of global multilateralism and cooperation. From this perspective, states became the vehicles of emancipation and the attainment of well-being and containers of 'intractable' social, political, or economic problems, themselves often generated by the colonial project ... [hence] the promise of global development continues to enable international interventions that encourage a particular kind of global integration, one in which states are reshaped in ways which promote and protect the gains of the (transnational) few.[16]

As a consequence, some writers have argued that development policies can 'facilitate the globalization of production and finance through creating and protecting global property rights, codifying the rights of transnational corporations, and limiting the economic autonomy of sovereign states'.[17] There may be an argument that,

---

[12] Campbell McLachlan, Laurence Shore, and Matthew Weiniger, *International Investment Arbitration* (2nd edn, OUP 2017); Ursula Kriebaum, Christoph Schreuer, and Rudolf Dolzer, *Principles of International Investment Law* (3rd edn, OUP 2022).

[13] Muthucumaraswamy Sornarajah, 'Power and Justice in Foreign Investment Arbitration' (1997) 14 J Int'l Arb 103.

[14] *Urbaser SA and Consorcio de Aguas Bilbao Bizkaia, Bilbao Biskaia Ur Partzuergoa v The Argentine Republic* [2016] ICSID Case No ARB/07/26 [decided 8 December 2016] [1195].

[15] For example, B S Chimni, 'International Institutions Today: An Imperial Global State in the Making' (2004) 15 EJIL 1; Antony Angie, *Imperialism, Sovereignty and the Making of International Law* (CUP 2005); Penelope Simons, 'International Law's Invisible Hand and the Future of Corporate Accountability for Violations of Human Rights' (2012) 3 JHRE 5.

[16] Luis Eslava and Sundhya Pahuja, 'The State and International Law: A Reading from the Global South' (2020) 11 Humanity 118, 136.

[17] B S Chimni, 'Prolegomena to a Class Approach to International Law' (2010) 21 EJIL 71–72.

in so doing, these development policy practices mirror some of the Global South concerns about international law. Some of our chapters take up this challenge.

While the main focus of the book is on international law as contained within treaties, which are legally binding on the state parties to them, there is some relevance of customary international law. Customary international law is legally binding on all states irrespective as to whether they have ratified a relevant treaty. In relation to the relevance of customary international law on international organizations, it has been argued:

> [I]t is increasingly recognized that international organisations are bound by customary international law. Not just 'in certain cases', but in general. Of course, many rules of customary international law simply do not apply to international organisations, as they normally have no territory, no territorial waters, no nationals, etc. But in the areas in which powers have been given to international organisations, it is increasingly recognized that these organisations are bound by the relevant rules of customary international law that are applicable in these areas.[18]

In relation to peremptory norms of international law from which no state can derogate, otherwise known as *jus cogens*,[19] these are, in effect, a binding constitutional law of the international community. The general view is that they are binding on international organizations, not least as an act of an international organization that was contrary to *jus cogens* would be without legal effect.[20] Article 26 of the International Law Commission's (ILC's) Articles on Responsibilities of International Organisations 2011 (ARIO) provides that: 'Nothing ... precludes the wrongfulness of any act of an international organisation which is not in conformity with an obligation arising under a peremptory norm of general international law.' While there are competing views of the legal status of ARIO, no state disputed the above position.[21]

On additional aspect of international law which needs to be clarified is the use of 'soft international law'. One definition of this term is that it usually refers to 'any written international instrument, other than a treaty, containing principles, norms, standards, or other statements of expected behavior'.[22] Thus this term is

---

[18] Niels Blokker, 'International Organizations and Customary International Law' (2017) 14 IOLR 1, 10.
[19] The Vienna Convention on the Law of Treaties 1969, art 53.
[20] In Alexander Orakhelashvili, 'The Impact of Peremptory Norms on the Interpretation and Application of United Nations Security Council Resolutions' (2005) 16 EJIL 59, 60, he argues that the obligation to comply with peremptory norms would constitute 'an inherent limitation on any [international] organization's powers'.
[21] For example, the comments by the United Nations Educational, Scientific and Cultural Organization on behalf of a number of other international organizations, UN Doc AIC6/66SR2, para 93; Jean d'Aspremont, 'The Articles on the Responsibility of International Organizations: Magnifying the Fissures in the Law of International Responsibility' (2012) 9 IOLR 15.
[22] Dinah Shelton, 'Soft Law', in Dinah Shelton, *Handbook on International Law* (Routledge 2008).

used to contrast international law which is clearly legally binding, such as treaties and customary international law, with international law which may not be legally binding either in its formulation or intention. Soft law would appear to include, for example, some UN General Assembly resolutions,[23] the SDGs, and the United Nations Guiding Principles on Business and Human Rights (UNGPs),[24] which are all referred to in this book. Using the terminology of 'soft' international law, though, can be misleading as to its influence:

> [W]idespread acceptance of soft law instruments will tend to legitimise conduct and make it harder to sustain the legality of opposing positions. They may additionally acquire binding legal character as elements of a treaty-based regulatory regime, or constitute a 'subsequent agreement between the parties regarding the interpretation of the treaty or the application of its provisions', or otherwise assist in the development and application of general international law'.[25]

For example, the recommendations of the ILC, being a global body of experts in international law, and as such are 'soft law', have led to customary international law on areas such as state responsibility,[26] and the UNGPs have directly influenced international and national regulation in the area of corporate responsibility for human rights abuse.[27] Therefore, the key aspects of soft international law are that it is law which may become legal binding and/or be used as a source for judging behaviour at the international level.

Overall, it is evident that international law has significantly changed its scope and depth in the past decades. No longer is it solely about the rights and obligations of states as it now extends to international organizations and to non-state actors. This has an impact in terms of the development activities by many actors within the international legal system. Nevertheless, the state remains the primary actor and, if states implemented effectively their obligations under international law, it would enhance the accountability of other development actors, especially international organizations.

---

[23] Some General Assembly Resolutions can be evidence of customary international law, see, for example, International Court of Justice, 'Advisory Opinion on the Chagos Archipelago' [2019] ICJ Reports, para 152.
[24] OHCHR, 'Guiding Principles on Business and Human Rights' <http://guidingprinciplesbusinesshr_en.pdf (ohchr.org)> accessed 17 May 2023.
[25] Alan Boyle and Christin Chinkin, *The Making of International Law* (OUP 2007) 212.
[26] Arman Savarian, 'The Ossified Debate on a UN Convention on State Responsibility' (2021) 70 Int Comp Law Q 769.
[27] Robert McCorquodale, 'Human Rights Due Diligence Instruments: Evaluating the Current Legislative Landscape' in Axel Marx, Geert Van Calster, and Jan Wouters (eds), *Global Governance, Business and Human Rights* (Elgar 2022) 121.

3. Development

Development has been defined in a number of ways over many decades. It used to be equated solely with economic growth and industrialization.[28] In the 1960s and 1970s, 'the literature on economic development is generally categorized by different degrees of attachment to the "market" and mechanisms for creating "just prices", different approaches to the international economy, and, above all, different evaluations of the role of state in the economic life.'[29] In regard to the latter, it appears that the approach was one where the state was meant to be strong and active in promoting economic growth, with subsidies and price intervention, which was often done through trade agreements and direct actions in the Global South by the Global North states and IFIs.[30]

In 1987, the World Commission on Environment and Development provided a report called 'Our Common Future', in which they reimagined development to be 'sustainable development', which they defined as:

> The concept of sustainable development provides a framework for the integration of environment policies and development strategies.... Sustainable development is development that meets the needs of the present without compromising the ability of future generations to meet their own needs. It contains within it two key concepts:
> - the concept of 'needs', in particular the essential needs of the world's poor, to which overriding priority should be given; and
> - the idea of limitations imposed by the state of technology and social organization on the environment's ability to meet present and future needs.[31]

Subsequently, the terminology used has largely been 'sustainable development'. This has also been linked with human development.[32] For example, a former President of the World Bank stated:

> The Bank has long recognized that sustainable development requires both economic growth and social equity. There is, moreover, widespread recognition of the strong link between human rights and development.... The Bank's work

---

[28] For example, Hilary Charlesworth, 'The Public/Private Distinction and the Right to Development in International Law' (1992) 12 Aust YBIL 190.
[29] Ryszard Piasecki and Miron Wolnicki, 'The Evolution of Development Economics and Globalization' (2004) 31 Int J Soc Econ 300, 301.
[30] ibid.
[31] World Commission on Environment and Development, *Our Common Future* (UN 1987), ch 1, para 48 and ch 2, para 1.
[32] For example, Amartya Sen, *Development as Freedom* (OUP 1993) (hereafter 'Development as Freedom'); Martha Nussbaum, *Creating Capabilities: The Human Development Approach* (Harvard UP 2011).

substantially contributes to the realization of rights of people in a number of areas, such as health, education, gender, participation, accountability, environment, and institutional reform activities and, above all, the fight against poverty itself as a fundamental denial of human rights. Other Bank activities also contribute to the realization of human rights: these include fighting corruption, increasing transparency and accountability in governance.[33]

Indeed, the General Assembly Resolution that proclaimed the 2030 Agenda for Sustainable Development and the SDGs have explicitly recognized the linkages between human rights and sustainable development.[34] These SDGs are not legally binding, but are soft law (as noted above) which are intended to change behaviours, through implementation in policies and activities.[35]

There are critiques of the focus on sustainable development. As Margot Salomon comments:

> 'Sustainable development' still presupposes capitalist development. 'Development' thus presupposes fealty to the constitutive features of contemporary capitalism: private property and privately owned and controlled means of production, growth, along with production for global markets and dedication to boosting foreign investor confidence. Production is oriented to *capital accumulation* i.e. to profit rather than to the satisfaction of human needs. People sell their labour power to make a living—a racialized and gendered feature essential to capitalism globally and within countries. 'Sustainability' then, whatever it currently means, is 'sustainability' necessarily wed to class-based profit and accumulation; 'sustainability' within the parameters of (transnational) market dependence.[36]

Others argue that the SDGs are premised on increasing international trade and investment as drivers of sustainable development with consequent human dislocation and corporate concentration[37] and that export-oriented growth is predicated on gender inequality.[38]

---

[33] Note by the President of the World Bank, James Wolfensohn, to the Development Committee, 'Statements Submitted to the Seventy-First Meeting of the Development Committee' (World Bank, DC2005-0011, 25 May 2005) 14. See also Siobhán McInerney-Lankford, 'International Financial Institutions and Human Rights: Select Perspectives on Legal Obligations' in Daniel Bradlow and Daniel Hunter (eds), *International Financial Institutions and International Law* (Kluwer 2010) 239.

[34] *Transforming Our World: The 2030 Agenda for Sustainable Development* (UN Doc A/RES/70/1) paras 10, 18, and 19.

[35] On the SDGs generally, see UN, '17 Goals to Transform Our World' <Home—United Nations Sustainable Development> accessed 17 May 2023.

[36] Margot Salomon, 'Culture as an Alternative to "Sustainable Development"' (*TWAIL Review*, 7 July 2022) <https://twailr.com/culture-as-an-alternative-to-sustainable-development/> accessed 17 May 2023.

[37] For example, Michael Fakhri, 'Report of the UN Special Rapporteur on the Right to Food: The Right to Food in the Context of International Trade Law and Policy' (UN Doc A/75/219, 2020).

[38] Shahra Razavi, 'The 2030 Agenda: Challenges of Implementation to attain Gender Equality and Women's Rights' (2016) 24 GAD 25.

It is also of note that sustainable development was not the only terminology used when understanding development. Amartya Sen argued that the focus of economic and social development should be on 'capabilities', being what people are actually able to do and be.[39] For example, Sen argues that the capabilities approach provides a more accurate and ethically satisfactory way of considering equality than human rights, as it has particular importance for disadvantaged groups worldwide.[40] Indeed, the World Bank provided an excellent clarification of the experiences of those who are in poverty in its report on 'Voices of the Poor'.[41] The human rights aspects of development were clarified by Martha Nussbaum:

> The language of rights still plays, I believe ... important roles in public discourse, despite its unsatisfactory features.... It imports the idea of an urgent claim based upon justice. This is important particularly for women, who may lack political rights. However, the capabilities approach can make this idea of a fundamental entitlement clear in other ways, particularly ... by operating with a list of capabilities which are held to be fundamental entitlements of all citizens based upon justice. Rights language also has value because of the emphasis it places on people's choice and autonomy.[42]

The use of human rights to inform development is an example of what international law can provide in relation to development.

It is international law as a framework for decision-making, process, and outcomes in sustainable development which is the focus of the analysis in this book. In so doing, many of the contributors explore the SDGs, and social and environmental frameworks of key institutions, such as the MDBs, IFIs, and state development agencies, to determine the degree of influence of (sometimes soft) international law within them.

4. Structure

The book is structured into four parts and a conclusion. Part I provides the context to the book, with this introduction, and then chapters by Siobhán McInerney-Lankford and Arnold Pronto. Each of these provide insightful analysis as to the

---

[39] Development as Freedom (n 32).
[40] ibid. Sen's capabilities approach was adopted by a high official of the International Monetary Fund: Sérgio Leite, 'The International Monetary Fund and Human Rights' *Le Monde* (Paris, 4 September 2001).
[41] World Bank, *Voices of the Poor* (World Bank and Poverty Net 2000).
[42] Martha Nussbaum, 'Capabilities as Fundamental Entitlements: Sen and Social Justice' (2011) 9 Feminist Econs 33, 39–40.

role of international law in development, and what international law offers in terms of accountability and clarity for sustainable development.

Part II focuses on the interactions between international human rights, law, and development. This arises out of the comments above about human rights linkages with sustainable development, and are reflected in the statement by the former Secretary-General of the UN, Kofi Annan:

> [S]ustainable development is impossible without the full participation of the people; that it is impossible in the absence of full human rights. Human rights are integral to peace and security, economic development and social equity. That is because human life and human development are at the heart of every mission and every programme that we pursue.[43]

In this part, there are chapters by Jan Wouters and Michiel Hoornick, by Anganile Mwenifumbo, Harumi Fuentes Furuya and Marie Joseph Ayissi, and by Katerina Tsotroudi and Jordi Agustí Panareda, which set out the foundational issues about development in international human rights law (including labour rights) and its treaty bodies. This is followed by chapters looking at specific human rights. These are on gender equality (Sandra Fredman), race discrimination (Harum Makhayer), and the right to water (Laurence Boisson de Chazournes, Mara Tignino, and Haoua Savadogo). The breadth of this coverage indicates the wide range of human rights legal issues of relevance to development.

The chapters in Part III explore international law in relation to environmental, refugee, and humanitarian areas affected by development. These types of concern can be seen in the Joint Statement by the Multilateral Development Banks at the World Humanitarian Summit in May 2016:

> To focus on prevention and preparedness measures through increased resilience to shocks for countries and regions which are most exposed to fragility, MDBs are committed to *provide continued and strengthened support in fragile countries and regions where there is a recognized risk of escalation into a crisis situation* and to help strengthen resilience of home countries. In particular this can be achieved by stepping up technical assistance including for early warning systems, joint financing of private and public investments in an effective and innovative way, enhancing conflict and crises management skills capacities of national and sub-national institutions and supporting policy and governance reforms to strengthen economic resilience.[44]

---

[43] 'Statement by Kofi Annan, Secretary-General of the United Nations, at the opening of the fifty-fourth session of the Commission on Human Rights, Office of the High Commissioner on Human Rights' (United Nations 1998).
[44] World Bank, 'Joint Statement by the Multilateral Development Banks at the World Humanitarian Summit Responding to the Forced Displacement Crisis' (Press Release, 23 May 2016) <https://www.

This part includes chapters on international environmental law and climate change (Bakary Kanté) and on forced displacement (Duygu Çiçek, Paige Casaly, and Vikram Raghavan). In addition, there is a specific focus on the World Bank and mining reforms in the Global South by Ximena Sierra-Camargo, who examines it from a critical development perspective.

Part IV explores the area of international investment and finance, law, and development. With the large role which foreign direct investment by states and private investors have in development financing, it is necessary to consider these issues in relation to their impact on investment. There are also impacts of international law on the role of the state receiving the development funding, as Ursula Kriebaum notes in her chapter, where she includes this statement by an international investment tribunal:

> In order to avoid abuse of the host State's regulatory powers, their exercise must be *bona fide* and in line with principles of international investment law, such as good faith, non-discrimination, and the prohibition of arbitrariness, and result in measures whose impact on investments is proportionate to the interest(s) protected.[45]

Other chapters in this part include considerations of the role of trade law and foreign investment (Chin Leng Lim), financial law (Thomas McInerney), infrastructure and corporate accountability (Humberto Cantú Rivera) and about the rule of law in development, with case studies on international investment law (Farouk El-Hosseny).

The final part seeks to draw the analysis and ideas across the book together in the Conclusions. In so doing, it demonstrates that the contributors to this book have diverse expertise (though primarily with a legal knowledge) and different methodological approaches. They also have diverse personal and professional backgrounds, as is reflected in their summary biographies. This makes their views compelling to read.

---

worldbank.org/en/news/press-release/2016/05/23/joint-statement-by-the-multilateral-development-banks-at-the-world-humanitarian-summit> > accessed 23 September 2023 (emphasis added). See also 'The Forced Displacement Crisis: A Joint Paper by Multilateral Development Banks' (2016) <http://pubdocs.worldbank.org/en/870431464026133311/Joint-MDB-paper-displacement-final.pdf> accessed 18 May 2023.

[45] *Casinos Austria v Argentina* Award (5 November 2021) para 336.

2
The Case for International Law Due Diligence in the Development Context

Siobhán McInerney-Lankford[*]

1. Introduction

This book focuses on the relationship between public international law and sustainable development. It explores the idea that public international law is of central importance to sustainable development,[1] contending that sustainable development depends upon international law and should be grounded in it more systematically. The book considers the relevance and applicability of international law norms to particular sectors and issues implicated in development activities. It analyses how international law rules and processes can influence procedural and substantive aspects of development policies as these regulate various forms of financial support, trade, technical assistance, and policy dialogue.

It is submitted that development law and practice pay insufficient attention to binding rules of international law and that this results in accountability deficits that are filled, to varying degrees, by a patchwork of development policies and mechanisms. A foundational premise of this collection is therefore that development law and practice ought to acknowledge the relevance of international law and reflect greater coherence with the substantive rules of international law because these anchor international legal accountability. The book explores whether, and how, development could be more effective and yield more equitable and sustainable outcomes if the relevant and applicable rules of international law were better understood, consistently incorporated, and appropriately applied in development activities.

---

[*] Head of Unit, Equality, Roma and Social Rights, EU Fundamental Rights Agency (FRA); formerly Senior Counsel, World Bank Legal Department. The views expressed in this chapter are those of the author and should not be attributed to the European Union, the FRA, or European Union Member States, or to the World Bank, its Board of Executive Directors, or the Governments represented thereon.

[1] Sustainable development is generally understood as 'meet[ing] the needs of the present without compromising the ability of future generations to meet their own needs'. United Nations, 'Report of the World Commission on Environment and Development: Our Common Future' (1987) ch 2, para 1; see World Commission on Environment and Development, 'Report of the World Commission on Environment and Development' (G A Res 42/187, The Brundtland Report, 11 December 1987).

The fragmentation of international law[2] and international policy coherence[3] are recurring themes of this book. As this chapter will clarify, fostering linkages between international law and development more explicitly and systematically would promote greater policy coherence and thereby enhance legal accountability in development processes and outcomes. This would help ensure that public actors (particularly states and institutions controlled by states) are held accountable for their acts or omissions in the context of development processes and outcomes, as these would be assessed against international law.

This book seeks to highlight the formative influence and continuing relevance of international law rules in areas of sustainable development, despite the fact that there is only occasional acknowledgement of their relevance of international law in development policies and no systematic approach to their integration in development policies or interpretation in the context of development policies, projects, and programmes. It challenges the idea that development occurs in a legal vacuum or that international law can be ignored when states engage in development activities. It posits international law as an indispensable foundation of sustainable development and rejects the notion that development policy or development law is a 'self-contained' regime that operates outside international law.[4]

2. Legal Accountability in Development

a. Accountability

In its broadest sense, accountability is 'the justification of an actor's performance vis-a-vis others, the assessment or judgment of that performance against certain standards and the possible imposition of consequences if the actor fails to live up to applicable standards.'[5] To be accountable means to be required to answer for one's

---

[2] Martti Koskenniemi and Päivi Leino, 'Fragmentation of International Law? Postmodern Anxieties' (2002) 15 Leiden JIL 553, 560–61 (hereafter 'Fragmentation of International Law?'); see also Bruno Simma, 'Self-Contained Regimes' (1985) 15 NYIL 111, 135 ('The question whether treaty subsystems on the protection of human rights constitute "self-contained regimes", is a very controversial one.... [T]he views put forward in favor of such a qualification are both unconvincing and dangerous for the effectiveness of international human rights law.').

[3] For example, the 2008 Accra Agenda for Action provided 'Gender equality, respect for human rights, and environmental sustainability are cornerstones for achieving enduring impact on the lives and potential of poor women, men, and children. It is vital that all our policies address these issues in a more systematic and coherent way.' The 2011 United Nations Guiding Principles on Business and Human Rights (UNGPs) also emphasize the need to ensure policy coherence (e.g. Principles 8, 9, and 10).

[4] Fragmentation of International Law? (n 2); see also Bruno Simma, 'Self-Contained Regimes' (1985) 15 NYIL 111, 135 ('The question whether treaty subsystems on the protection of human rights constitute "self-contained regimes", is a very controversial one.... [T]he views put forward in favor of such a qualification are both unconvincing and dangerous for the effectiveness of international human rights law.').

[5] Jutta Brunnée, 'International Legal Accountability Through the Lens of the Law of State Responsibility', in Deirdre M Curtin and André Knollkaemper (eds), *Netherlands Yearbook of*

action or inaction and to be exposed to potential sanctions where such action or inaction falls short of the requirements of particular rules or norms. According to Ruth Grant and Robert Keohane:

> [Accountability] implies that some actors have the right to hold other actors to a set of standards, to judge whether they have fulfilled their responsibilities in light of these standards, and to impose sanctions if they determine that these responsibilities have not been met. Accountability presupposes a relationship between power-wielders and those holding them accountable where there is a general recognition of the legitimacy of (1) the operative standards for accountability and (2) the authority of the parties to the relationship (one to exercise particular powers and the other to hold them to account). The concept of accountability implies that the actors being held accountable have obligations to act in ways that are consistent with accepted standards of behavior and that they will be sanctioned for failures to do so.[6]

b. Legal accountability

The term 'legal accountability' has a distinct meaning because 'legal accountability refers to the requirement that agents abide by *formal rules* and be prepared to justify their actions in those terms, in courts or quasi-judicial arenas'.[7] Furthermore, legal norms are different from other norms since 'law can be found, defined and labeled'.[8] Thus the unique nature of legal accountability has its roots in 'certain internal characteristic of law, notably that rules must be compatible with one another, that they must ask reasonable things and that they are transparent and relatively predictable and that known rules actually guide official discretion'.[9] While legal accountability presents challenges and limitations in practice and is by no means a perfect panacea to every global challenge, it is contended that its unique quality adds value in a way that other forms of accountability cannot. Jutta Brunnée rightly argues that these traits infuse legal norms with a particular legitimacy and enhance their ability to shape arguments and to persuade and promote adherence.[10] It is

---

International Law (CUP 2005) 21–56, 24 (hereafter 'International Legal Accountability')) (citing Ruth Grant and Robert Keohane, 'Accountability and Abuses of Power in World Politics' (2005) 99 Am Political Science Rev 29, 29–30 (hereafter 'Accountability and Abuses of Power')).

[6] ibid (Accountability and Abuses of Power) 29–30.
[7] International Legal Accountability (n 5) 22; see also Suzanne Egan, *Extraordinary Rendition and Human Rights Examining State Accountability and Complicity* (Springer Press 2018) 1–17, discussing different definitions of legal accountability.
[8] International Legal Accountability (n 5) 22.
[9] ibid 7 (quoting Lon Fuller, *The Morality of Law* (1965) Yale Univ Press 39, 46–91).
[10] Jutta Brunnée and Stephen Toope, 'Persuasion and Enforcement: Explaining Compliance with International Law' (2002) XIII Finnish YIL 273.

these traits rather 'than formal legal status alone [that] are central to international law's ability to force justification, assessment or judgment and thus to facilitate international legal accountability'.[11]

The definition of legal accountability espoused here is derived from international law.[12] It is situated in the classical paradigm of international law which is mostly 'horizontal'[13] in structure and with obligations owed primarily by one state to another or by all states to one another (e.g. obligations *erga omnes*).[14] More particularly, the definition of legal accountability relied upon in this book is the legal accountability underpinning international treaties.[15] The sources of international law[16] are enumerated in article 38 of the International Court of Justice (ICJ) Statute,[17] the definitive basis of legal accountability in international law.[18] The exponential growth of international law over the past century is evident in the proliferation of international treaties. Thousands of multilateral treaties[19] have been adopted to respond to social injustice, environmental destruction, disease, discrimination, and violent conflict; they span every area of global concern, including arms control, labour, environment, health, human rights, and transnational crime.[20] As Campbell McLachlan observes, 'the general architecture of international law today is dominated by the great structures of the multilateral treaties'.[21]

---

[11] International Legal Accountability (n 5) 7.
[12] Vaughan Lowe, *International Law* (Clarendon Law series, OUP 2007) ('the framework within which international co-operation takes place').
[13] International Legal Accountability (n 5) 21.
[14] The concept of *erga omnes* obligations refers to obligations that states have towards the international community as a whole; these include the outlawing of acts of aggression; the outlawing of genocide; protection from slavery; and protection from racial discrimination. The concept appears for the first time in the *Barcelona Traction, Light and Power Company Limited (New Application, 1962), Belgium v Spain, Judgment, Merits, Second Phase*, ICJ GL No 50, [1970] ICJ Rep 3, (1970).
[15] Defined as (a) an international agreement, (b) among states, (c) that is recorded in a way that evidences, (d) a shared and manifest intent that the agreement be governed by international law, and (e) without regard as to its form. Duncan Hollis, *Oxford Guide to Treaties* (OUP 2012) 1, 31 (hereafter 'Oxford Guide to Treaties').
[16] Ian Brownlie, *Principles of Public International Law* (OUP 2012) 6, 8 ('the normative system of international law is derived from four sources enumerated in Article 38(1) of the Statue of the ICJ').
[17] 'The Court, whose function is to decide in accordance with international law such disputes as are submitted to it, shall apply: international conventions, whether general or particular, establishing rules expressly recognized by the contesting states; international custom, as evidence of a general practice accepted as law; the general principles of law recognized by civilized nations; subject to the provisions of Article 59, judicial decisions and the teachings of the most highly qualified publicists of the various nations, as subsidiary means for the determination of rules of law.'
[18] Geir Ulfstein (ed), *Making Treaties Work: Human Rights, Environment, and Arms Control* (CUP 2007) 3 (hereafter 'Making Treaties Work').
[19] Anthony Aust, *Modern Treaty Law and Practice* (CUP 2000) (in which a multilateral treaty is defined as a treaty to which three or more states are party).
[20] Thomas McInerney, *Strategic Treaty Management: Practice and Implications* (CUP 2015) 1 (citing The Legal Framework of Sustainable Development (n 15) 8).
[21] Campbell McLachlan, 'The Evolution of Treaty Obligations in International Law' in Georg Nolte (ed), *Treaties and Subsequent Practice* (OUP 2013) 72.

This is so despite well-known challenges related to their general effectiveness and poor compliance,[22] analysis of which lies beyond the scope of this book.

The primary function of a treaty is to establish substantive obligations of the parties and, increasingly, to design mechanisms to induce compliance with such obligations.[23] It is submitted that the enshrining of a standard in an international treaty obligation makes a significant difference, including for sustainable development. Writing about the international human rights framework, United Nations (UN) Special Rapporteur on Extreme Poverty opined:

> Human rights provides a context and a detailed and balanced framework; it invokes the specific legal obligations that States have agreed upon in the various human rights treaties; it emphasizes that certain values are non-negotiable; it brings a degree of normative certainty; and it brings into the discussion the carefully negotiated elaborations of the meaning of specific rights that have emerged from decades of reflection, discussion and adjudication. Even more importantly, the language of rights recognizes the dignity and agency of all individuals (regardless of race, gender, social status, age, disability or any other distinguishing factor) and it is intentionally empowering.... Human rights are inseparable from the notion of accountability. Where rights are ignored or violated, there must be accountability.[24]

Thus, international treaties bring with them a particular form of accountability: '[I]nternational legal accountability ... involves the justification of an international actor's performance vis-à-vis others, the assessment or judgment of that performance against binding international law standards and the possible imposition of consequences if the actor fails to live up to the applicable legal standards.'[25] Brunnée explains that:

> legal accountability rests upon certain assumptions about international law. The central assumption is that law emerges from the interaction of the participants in the legal system and an increasingly fixed pattern of expectations about appropriate behaviour. In the international legal order, norms may settle into custom or may be enshrined through treaties.[26]

---

[22] Louis Henkin, *How Nations Behave* (2nd edn, Columbia University Press 1979); Harold Koh, 'Why Do Nations Obey International Law?' (1997) 106 Yale LJ 2599; Abram Chayes, Antonia Chayes, and Ronald Mitchell, 'Managing Compliance: A Comparative Perspective' in Edith Brown Weiss and Harold Jacobson (eds), *Engaging Countries: Strengthening Compliance with International Environmental Accords* (MIT Press 1998) 39–62; International Legal Accountability (n 5).

[23] Making Treaties Work (n 18) 6.

[24] Human Rights Council, *Special Rapporteur on Extreme Poverty and Human Rights* (31st Session 26/3A/70/274, 17 February 2016) para 65 (explaining the World Bank's approach to human rights).

[25] International Legal Accountability (n 5) 24.

[26] ibid.

The international legal accountability under treaties is also undergirded by the principle of *pacta sunt servanda* reflected in article 26 of the Vienna Convention on the Law of Treaties.[27] This principle means that 'every treaty in force is binding upon the parties to it and must be performed by them in good faith'.[28] It establishes a fundamental rule of international law that requires all subjects of international law to exercise in good faith their rights and duties under that law. It means that subjects of international law are legally bound to implement what the law prescribes.[29] The proposition of this chapter is that they are legally bound to do so in the context of development activities as well.

c. Legal accountability and development

Treaties constitute relevant and applicable standards in the context of sustainable development and states' general obligation to comply with their specific treaty obligations is not suspended or deferred in the context of development. Treaties offer a legal accountability standard grounded in existing international legal obligations that continue to apply when states engage in development activities.[30] Citing the examples of the European Convention on Human Rights and Fundamental Freedoms (ECHR) and the International Covenant on Civil and Political Rights (ICCPR), Brunnée observes that 'human rights treaties enable individuals to complain about violations of their treaty-based rights by states parties'. Although the pronouncements of the supervisory bodies of many of the global human rights treaties are not legally binding upon the states concerned, she observes that 'once a state is subject to the system, a degree of accountability is generated by publicly measuring the state party's conduct against the international standards and by the attendant pressure on it to comply'.[31] Legal accountability rooted in international law enjoys the legitimacy of the operative standard derived from international treaties which have been negotiated by states that then sign and ratify them, thereby voluntarily undertaking the obligations they contain. As Peter Malanczuk notes in a discussion of legal aspects of sustainable development: '[i]n a heterogenous, culturally, economically and politically divided society, such as the international community, which lacks sufficient institutional structures to develop a specific

---

[27] The Vienna Convention on the Law of Treaties' (VCLT's) preamble also notes that the principles of free consent and of good faith and the *pacta sunt servanda* rule are universally recognized. Vienna Convention on the Law of Treaties (1155 UNTS 331) (opened for signature 23 May 1969; entered into force 27 January 1980).
[28] Igor Lukashuk, *The Principle of Pacta Sunt Servanda and the Nature of Obligation Under International Law* (1989) 83 AJIL 513–18.
[29] ibid.
[30] On human rights accountability in development (within the UN system), see Mac Darrow and Amparo Tomas, 'Power, Capture and Conflict: A Call for Human Rights Accountability in Development Cooperation' (2005) 27(2) Hum Rts Q 471–538.
[31] International Legal Accountability (n 5) 31.

consensus on subjective issues, such as morality, justice, or equity, the *legitimacy* of rules, principles and institutions is of central importance'.[32]

Thus it is argued that international legal accountability derived from treaties can add value to sustainable development. According to the International Law Commission (ILC),[33] international legal accountability can help focus on the legal consequence of a breach, which triggers responsibility for the responsible state for acts or omissions in the context of development activities. It can help determine whether the relevant obligation is owed to an individual state, several states, or the international community as a whole—in all cases, the responsible state must cease the violation,[34] offer necessary assurances of non-repetition,[35] and make full reparation for the injury caused.[36] Accordingly, the proposal put forward here is that states are legally bound to implement, abide by, and remain accountable for their international legal obligations in development activities.

3. The Challenge of Regime Interaction and Fragmentation in the Context of Development

Regime interaction and fragmentation writ large are challenges in the context of development. Here too lawyers and policy makers must tackle the fundamental question of 'how different elements of international law and governance interact'.[37] The ILC defines 'special regime'[38] as 'a group of rules and principles concerned with a particular subject matter may form a special regime ("self-contained regime") and be applicable as *lex specialis*. Such special regimes often have their own institutions to administer the relevant rules'.[39] Such special regimes may be functional, regional, or national and they usually reflect a functional specialization or teleological orientation, such as environmental law or trade law; they will 'primarily interpret and apply international law within the framework of that particular

---

[32] Peter Malanczuk, 'Sustainable Development: Some Critical Thoughts in the Light of the Rio Conference', in Konrad Ginther, Erik Denters, and Paul J I M de Waart (eds), *Sustainable Development and Good Governance*, 23–52 (Martinus Nijhoff 1995) 51 (hereafter 'Sustainable Development: Some Critical Thoughts') (citing Oscar Schachter, *International Law in Theory and Practice* (Martin Nijhoff Publishers 1991) 20 (on the distinction between 'rules, principles and ends')).

[33] *Draft Articles on Responsibility of States for Internationally Wrongful Acts, with Commentaries* (vol 2, part 2, 2001) (hereafter 'Draft Articles').

[34] ibid art 30(a).

[35] Draft Articles (n 33) art 30(b).

[36] Draft Articles (n 33) art 31.

[37] Margaret Young, *Regime Interaction in International Law: Facing Fragmentation* (CUP 2015) 11.

[38] *Fragmentation of International Law: Difficulties arising from the Diversification and Expansion of International Law, Conclusions of the Work of the Study Group* (CAN4/L702, 18 July 2006) 11–12, para 12 (hereafter 'Fragmentation of International Law').

[39] ibid para 11.

regime'.[40] For the purposes of this analysis, development law can be understood as one such special regime.[41] For its part, fragmentation can be understood as:

> both a process and its result, namely a (relatively) fragmented state of the law. The term has a predominantly negative connotation; it is a pejorative term (rather than diversity, specialization, or pluralism). The diagnosis of fragmentation refers to the dynamic growth of new and specialized subfields of international law after 1989, to the rise of new actors beside states (international organizations, non-governmental organizations (NGOs), and businesses), and to new types of international norms outside the acknowledged sources.[42]

The fragmentation of international law is neither a new nor static phenomenon, and has been the subject of extensive analysis and comment. It can be attributed to a range of factors, including 'sovereign equality of states, the lack of centralized organs, specialization of law, different structures of legal norms (for example hierarchy and non-hierarchical), parallel and sometimes competing regulations, an expanding scope of international law and different dynamics for rule development'.[43] In the context of the present chapter, one may also add the expanding scope of development activities. Fragmentation and the ensuing normative conflicts arise for various reasons: 'sometimes due to the ignorance of lawyers and policy makers "unaware of the legislative and institutional activities it the adjoining fields and the general principles of international law"'.[44] In substantive terms problems arise because of the emergence of 'special regimes' and 'special rules or laws' covering overlapping subject matter that lead to questions about the relationship between these special regimes or between the special regimes and general international law.[45] These in turn result in potential problems across special regimes relating to conflicting obligations, divergent standards, or in substantive inconsistencies between the interpretations of the same rules and norms in the jurisprudence emanating from different special regimes.

Writing about the interaction of international economic law and international human rights law, Siobhán McInerney-Lankford and Aaron Fellmeth identify

---

[40] Ole Kristian Fauchald and André Nollkaemper, *The Practice of International and National Courts and the (De-) Fragmentation of International Law* (Hart Publishing 2012) 3 (hereafter 'The Practice of International and National Courts').

[41] See e.g. Ramu Sarkar, *International Development Law: Rule of Law, Human Rights and Global Finance* (Springer 2020) 2.

[42] Anne Peters, 'The Refinement of International Law: From Fragmentation to Regime Interaction and Politicization' (2017) 15(3) Int'l J Const L 671–704.

[43] The Practice of International and National Courts (n 40) 4.

[44] Christopher Borgen, *Treaty Conflicts and Normative Fragmentation*, in D Hollis (ed), *Oxford Guide to Treaties* (OUP 2012) 448–71, 451 (quoting Fragmentation of International Law (n 38)).

[45] ILC Study Group (n 38) para 489.

three types of international legal fragmentation[46] in the context of development law and general international law:[47]

> [S]ubstantive fragmentation with different regimes or disciplines laying claim to autonomy or where the rules or principles of a special regime conflicts with those of another special regime, or with those of the general law;[48] institutional fragmentation is associated with the lack of formal hierarchy between international courts and tribunals and consequent potential for conflicting decisions with no supervening authority to reconcile them; and methodological fragmentation with respect to sources of law.[49]

At some level, the fragmentation of international law is inevitable,[50] because of the decentralized nature of the international legal system and the fact that the normative baselines and political priorities of special or functional regimes are defined within those regimes. Inevitability notwithstanding, the phenomenon is worthy of analysis in the development context. What this chapter argues for is an acknowledgement of the phenomenon in the development context and an appraisal of potential conflicts in order to mitigate the risks of an erosion of relevant and applicable international law norms and the consequent undermining of accountability, particularly that of state parties.

This book addresses fragmentation and regime interaction between development law and other special regimes of international law, as well as between development law and general international law: in this respect its analysis is confined to 'horizontal fragmentation' between institutions and special or functional regimes of the international legal order.[51] It addresses the substantive, procedural, methodological, and institutional dimensions of fragmentation. While it is acknowledged that understandings of fragmentation differ, that the extent of

---

[46] Fauchald and Nollkaemper identify the following three types of fragmentation if international law: institutional, procedural, and substantive; The Practice of International and National Courts (n 40) 4.

[47] Siobhán McInerney-Lankford and Aaron Fellmeth, 'International Human Rights Law, Normative Hierarchy and Development Policy' (2022) 54(2) NYU J L&POL 311–77, 367.
Others have distinguished functional from geographic fragmentation; or institutional fragmentation from ideational fragmentation. See Anne Peters, 'A Refinement of International Law: From Fragmentation to Regime Interaction and Politicization' (2017) 15 Int'l J Const L 671, 675 (emphasizing the productive uses of multiplicity in refining international law).

[48] The ILC Study Group also identifies a third type of conflict, in the emergence of a special law as exception to the general law. ILC Study Group Report (n 38) paras 53–54.

[49] See Mads Andenas and Eirik Bjorge, 'Introduction: From Fragmentation to Convergence in International Law', in Mads Andenas and Eirik Bjorge (eds), *A Farewell to Fragmentation: Reassertion and Convergence in International Law* (CUP 2015) 16 (discussing types of fragmentation (see pp 4–8) and the different types of conflict).

[50] The Practice of International and National Courts (n 40) 343.

[51] It does not therefore cover vertical forms of fragmentation between domestic and international law or the engagement of national courts with the international legal order. Fauchald and Nollkaemper (n 40) 10.

fragmentation is debated and that the assessment of its impacts (positive, negative, or neutral)[52] is contested, there is little doubt that it exists and that it can be discerned in the context of development.

4. Development Law

The challenge analysed here is that of regime interaction and fragmentation in the context of sustainable development.[53] The central focus of the analysis is development law, even if it does not share all of the attributes of other international law regimes.

Sustainable development is a global imperative. As evidenced in the Millennium Development Goals (MDGs) adopted in 2000, and in the 2030 Agenda and the Sustainable Development Goals (SDGs) adopted in 2015, the pursuit of sustainable development is endorsed by the international community, international organizations and development actors, and individual states. According to the United Nations:

> the 2030 Agenda for Sustainable Development, adopted by all United Nations Member States in 2015, provides a shared blueprint for peace and prosperity for people and the planet, now and into the future. At its heart are the SDGs, which are an urgent call for action by all countries—developed and developing—in a global partnership.[54]

The SDGs consist of seventeen interrelated policy goals which were conceived as 'a blueprint to achieve a better and more sustainable future for all people and the world by 2030'. They cover: ending poverty and hunger, and promoting health, education, gender equality, clean energy, decent work, climate change, and peace, justice, and strong institutions. The SDGs recognize that ending poverty and other deprivations must go hand in hand with strategies that improve health and education, reduce inequality, and spur economic growth—all while tackling climate change and working to preserve our oceans and forests.[55]

---

[52] The Practice of International and National Courts (n 40) 8.
[53] UNDP <https://mail.google.com/mail/u/0/#search/male/FMfcgzGmvpJVKbvhtwBBxpvvqvJMwbbW?projector=1&messagePartId=0.1>.
[54] UN Department of Economic and Social Affairs, 'The 17 Goals' <https://sdgs.un.org/goals> accessed 20 May 2023.
[55] UN Department of Economic and Social Affairs, 'The 17 Goals' <https://sdgs.un.org/goals> accessed 20 May 2023. The SDGs were preceded by other influential policy agendas, declarations, and outcome documents; see Agenda 21 proclaimed at the United Nations Conference on Environment and Development, Rio de Janeiro, Brazil, 3–14 June 1992 http://www.sustainabledevelopment.un.org/content/documents/Agenda21.pdf accessed 20 May 2023. See also Rio +20 (2012). <https://sustainabledevelopment.un.org/rio20A/RES/66/288-Rio+20 Outcome Document>.

The following analysis begins by distinguishing the objective of sustainable development and the means by which it is pursued. From there it assesses the legal pedigree of those means and the nature of 'development law'. In this regard, Malanczuk observes:

> From a methodological point of view, it is necessary to make a clear distinction between objectives of sustainable development and means of achieving the objectives. Furthermore, it is advisable to make a distinction between sustainable development as a concept, on the one hand, and legal principles and legal rules aiming at normative clarification and advancement with regard to certain aspects of the concept, on the other. As a concept, sustainable development is still only a very general notion which formulates a socio-political goal or programme.[56]

Agenda 2030, which includes the SDGs, was proclaimed in a resolution of the United Nations General Assembly (UNGA). The resolution references international law and human rights, confirming that the new Agenda is: (1) guided by the purposes and principles of the Charter of the United Nations, including full respect for international law, and (2) grounded in the Universal Declaration of Human Rights and international human rights treaties (*inter alia*). Nevertheless, the 2030 Agenda is not a treaty and the SDGs are not themselves the subject of international legal obligation. Many had criticized the MDGs for failing to integrate existing obligations, relating to both human rights and development, and some had even charged that the MDGs deviated substantially from sustainable development and international legal agreements that were already in place.[57] Similar criticisms could be levelled against the SDGs because they include neither a human rights goal nor a mention of human rights or human rights legal obligations.[58]

With sustainable development as its overarching goal, development law encompasses 'the complex network of arrangements and undertakings for the benefit of the lesser developed countries. These arrangements range from declarations and final acts adopted at international conferences to more solemn obligations binding on various combinations of states or other international law persons.'[59]

---

[56] Sustainable Development: Some Critical Thoughts (n 32) 51.

[57] Elena Pribytkova, 'Global Obligations for Sustainable Development: Harmonizing the 2030 Agenda for Sustainable Development and International Human Rights Law' (2020) 41 Penn J Int'l L 1031, 1044 (hereafter 'Global Obligations for Sustainable Development').

[58] The goals do not mention human rights, but a number of targets mention of the term 'right': target 1.4 on women's equal rights to economic resources; target 4.7 by 2030 ensures all learners acquire knowledge and skills needed to promote sustainable development, including, among others, through education on sustainable development and sustainable lifestyles, and human rights; target 5.6 ensures universal access to sexual and reproductive health and reproductive rights; target 5.a undertake reforms to give women equal rights to economic resources, as well as access to ownership and control over land and other forms of property, financial services, inheritance and natural resources, in accordance with national laws; target 8.8 protects labour rights.

[59] Peter Mutharika, 'International Law of Development' in Clive Parry and others (eds), *Parry and Grant's Encyclopedic Dictionary of International Law* (Oceana Publications Inc 1986) 91.

Development law consists of informal measures such as international declarations, frameworks, and soft law[60] commitments that establish or elaborate upon development goals. However, development law also includes more traditional sources of international law, such as treaties establishing international organizations (IOs) and international financial institutions (IFIs),[61] and treaties and international agreements[62] concluded between: (i) IOs and Member Countries, (ii) IOs and non-Member Countries, and (iii) IOs and other IOs.[63] Prominent examples of treaties concluded between IOs and states are the financing agreements for loans or guarantees concluded between IFIs and their member countries.

Writing about the World Bank in 1956, former World Bank General Counsel Aron Broches opined, '[the Bank] regularly concludes international agreements with its members embodying the terms of loans and guarantees. These loans and guarantees are international agreements. Thus, these instruments are international treaties and, except as otherwise provided, will be governed by international law.'[64] Elsewhere he confirmed 'The Bank's loan and guarantee agreements with its members are international agreements, "treaties" in the broad sense of the term, as a matter of international law.'[65] Finally, development law includes the policies, procedures, and directives that IOs and IFIs adopt, in addition to any other internal or administrative rules they may elaborate. In this respect, 'development policy' refers to a subset of development law, albeit a sizeable, diverse, and influential one.

In this respect, development law occupies a slightly ambiguous position: it includes treaties and agreements, but is not primarily the purview of

---

[60] In contrast to the sources of law established by article 38 of the Statute of the International Court of Justice, there exists a body of measures and instruments that lack binding legal force. Soft law comprises 'norms that are not themselves legally binding but form part of the broader normative context within which expectations of what is reasonable or proper State behaviour are formed'. Vaughan Lowe, *International Law* (Clarendon Press 2007) 95–96; see also Dinah Shelton, 'Soft Law' in Dinah Shelton (ed), *Handbook of International Law* (Routledge Press 2008).

[61] Constitutive instruments such as the Articles of Agreement of the International Bank for Reconstruction and Development (World Bank), 7 December 1945 (2 UNTS 134).

[62] In order to make the distinction between binding law and soft law, this chapter relies primarily on the term 'treaty', although it is submitted that the terms 'treaty' and 'international agreement' can be used interchangeably and the definitions of each can be tautological. Article 2(a) of the VCLT defines a treaty as 'an international agreement concluded between States in written form and governed by international law, whether embodied in a single instrument or in two or more related instruments and whatever its particular designation'. Article 102 of the UN Charter refers to both: 'every treaty and every international agreement entered into by any Member State of the United Nations after the present Charter comes into force shall as soon as possible be registered with the Secretariat and published by it'. Similarly, article 1 of the General Assembly Regulations to Give Effect to Article 102 of the Charter of the United Nations provides that the obligation to register applies to every treaty or international agreement 'whatever its form and descriptive name'. See also Aron Broches, 'International Legal Aspects of the Operations of the World Bank' (1959) Hague Academy Lectures 405.

[63] Olufemi Elias, 'Who can make Treaties? International Organizations', in Duncan Hollis (ed), *Oxford Guide to Treaties* (OUP 2012) 87.

[64] Aron Broches, 'International Legal Aspects of Operations of the World Bank' (1959) 98 Recueil des Cours 301–409, 405, reproduced in Aron Broches, *Selected Essays World Bank, ICSID and Other Subjects of Public and Private International Law* (Martinus Nijhoff 1995) 22.

[65] Aron Broches, 'The Hague Lectures', 405.

binding international law, being dominated instead by soft law and institutional policy frameworks. The treaties and agreements that predominate in the development space operate more at the operational level to confirm the particular terms of financing rather than setting overarching legal frameworks or defining global normative goals. As a threshold matter, the concept of sustainable development defies precise definition. As Malanczuk notes, there is no agreement on the substance of the concept and a variety of conflicting definitions exist.[66]

In addition, the concept of 'sustainable development' has no overarching treaty basis in international law.[67] Assessing the meaning of sustainable development in international legal discourse, some observers have expressed scepticism that the concept has any legal content at all. This is because it is rarely the subject of legal definition or formulation[68] and because it lacks sufficient clarity for any inference to be drawn in international law.[69] Others note that 'legislating for sustainable development is difficult. The concept does not lend itself well to prescriptive requirements and one size does not always "fit all".'[70] Speaking of the legislative issuances of development actors, de Rivero comments that, '[a]lthough these recommendations and decisions and the principles of economic and social policy embodied in them are not, strictly speaking, legal rules, they do constitute a set of provisions which the international community is recommending to Governments as policy measures'.[71] Such measures are not legally binding: 'political commitments do not have any legal force, while treaty commitments are, by definition binding under international law (*pacta sunt servanda*)'.[72] The SDGs offer an illustrative example of this: they are proclaimed in a UNGA resolution that extolled the virtue of international law and treaties, but neither the resolution nor the Goals constitute binding international law.[73]

An important distinction should therefore be drawn between treaty-based obligations and sustainable development commitments. As Pribytkova has written with respect to human rights obligations and the SDGs, the normative basis lies in legal instruments for the former and in political agreements for the latter:[74] '[n]ot all international agreements are treaties; other possibilities include political

---

[66] Sustainable Development: Some Critical Thoughts (n 32) 25.
[67] Priscilla Schwarz, 'Sustainable Development in International Law' (2005) 5 Non-State Actors & Int'l L 127, 138.
[68] Antonia Layard, 'The Legal Framework of Sustainable Development', in Sue Batty, Simin Davoudi, and Antonia Layard (eds), *Planning for a Sustainable Future* (Spon Press 2001) 33–52, 33 (hereafter 'The Legal Framework of Sustainable Development').
[69] Sustainable Development: Some Critical Thoughts (n 32) 26.
[70] The Legal Framework of Sustainable Development (n 68) 45.
[71] Oswaldo de Rivero, 'New Economic Order and International Development Law' (1982) 60 ILA Rep 122, 194.
[72] The Legal Framework of Sustainable Development (n 15).
[73] Carlo Focarelli, *International Law* (Edward Elgar 2019) 506.
[74] Global Obligations for Sustainable Development (n 57) 1052.

commitments, which are not governed by law'.[75] According to some commentators, the move away from more traditional international law approaches which give pre-eminence to a looser form of agreement reflects a deliberate decision on the part of states. Commenting on the diversity of policy formulations that emanate from IOs, Philip Alston suggests that this may be explained by the desire to maintain as much flexibility as possible.[76] As a number of chapters of this volume illustrate, that trend away from formal legal agreements towards frameworks, global pacts, and goals appears to be increasing.

Development law potentially calls the international law framework into question when it diverges significantly from it in order to mitigate the excessive formalism and rigidity which characterize classical international law, or when its objectives and requirements modify the hierarchy of sources. Yet from an international law perspective, treaties continue to be a source of jurisprudence even if they no longer constitute the principal one.[77] 'Treaties are an essential vehicle for organizing international cooperation and coordination. [...] From a qualitative perspective treaties dictate the content (and contours) of every field of international law. [...] They now occupy, in whole or in part, most areas of international relations.'[78] This is a reality that should be reflected in development law, policy and practice: relevant international treaties should be systematically recognized in corresponding areas affected or regulated by sustainable development policies and activities.

In light of the foregoing, a number of specifications are apposite with respect to development law as a special regime:[79]

(i) not all regimes have the same legal pedigree and are not all measures in each regime are at the same stage of legal development (e.g. compare the International Convention on the Elimination of All Forms of Racial Discrimination and a development policy directive on discriminated or vulnerable groups);[80]

(ii) different special regimes are qualitatively different in the degree to which they contain binding norms (certain special regimes or general

---

[75] The Legal Framework of Sustainable Development (n 15) 31. This definition takes a broad view of the term 'agreement' which is included here without prejudice to the clarifications offered in n 54.

[76] Philip Alston, 'What's in a Name? Does it Really Matter if Development Policies Refer to Goals, Ideals or Human Rights?', in Henny Helmich and Elena Borghese (eds), *Human Rights in Development Cooperation* Special edition No 22 (SIM 1998) 95–108, 97.

[77] Ahmed Mahiou, 'International Law of Development', in Petra Minnerop, Rudiger Wolfrum, and Fauke Lachemann (eds), *International Development Law* (Max Planck Encyclopedia of Public International Law, Thematic Series 3, OUP 2019) 353–61, 356.

[78] The Legal Framework of Sustainable Development (n 15) 8.

[79] According to the ILC Study Group, special regimes can be understood in the following terms: 'A group of rules and principles concerned with a particular subject matter may form a special regime ("Self-contained regime") and be applicable as *lex specialis*. Such special regimes often have their own institutions to administer the relevant rules', ILC Study Group Report (n 38) A/61/10, para 11.

[80] Margaret Young, *Regime Interaction in International Law: Facing Fragmentation* (CUP 2015) 9.

international law will comprise more binding rules than others): compare human rights law with development law and the comparatively higher number of treaties and customary norms in the former compared with the latter;
(iii) the consequence of a regime's rule or norm being grounded in a treaty versus a political declaration means is that there is an identifiable obligation and duty-bearer in the former and not for the latter;
(iv) international law, and international treaties in particular, primarily involve the direct horizontal legal undertakings between sovereign states, while development law includes undertakings between states and development actors, including IFIs, and other non-state actors; and
(v) general international law is the realm of formal adjudicative processes before international courts and tribunals, while development law is dominated by non-judicial accountability mechanisms and policy compliance mechanisms.

Two preliminary conclusions can be offered here on the nature and import of development law.

First, its impact, in terms of pursuing the SDGs effectively and accountably, is likely to be limited unless it is legally binding: '[p]romoting sustainable development ... will only form international binding rules of custom if they have consistency and if countries behave in a certain way because they believe that they are legally required to act in the way they do. Voluntary examples of good practice will not be enough.'[81]

Second, given its substantive reach and its direct implications for a range of multilateral treaties, sustainable development and the SDGs can and should be pursued within the parameters of existing international law. Development activities are not undertaken in a legal vacuum, and yet, development policies and frameworks recognize international law rules in an ad hoc manner, if they do at all. The legal landscape of development activities is a fragmented one which does not speak to a systematic or coherent engagement with international law.

5. Development Law and International Legal Regimes

The nature of the interaction between development law and other international law regimes is itself complex: it has both factual and policy dimensions—it may arise though day-to-day development activities as well as through the formulation, interpretation, and application of development policy. The scale of regime

---

[81] The Legal Framework of Sustainable Development (n 68) 40.

interaction is also increasing, primarily because of the growing reach of development policy and activities[82] into areas governed by pre-existing international treaties. The extent of that reach is significant also because the application of development policy is often accompanied by large volumes of financing, resulting in an outsized influence on the legal and regulatory frameworks of developing countries.

One challenge addressed in this book is fragmentation of international law in the context of development and the failure of states and international organizations to adopt a systematic approach to relevant and applicable norms of international law in the context of development. This is an important challenge to address given the substantial and increasing reach of development activities into most areas of human and social development and the concomitant adoption of environmental and social (E&S) policies, imposing requirements to undertake E&S due diligence and comply with environmental health and safety guidelines (EHSGs).[83]

The latter set of norms, policies, procedures, and guidelines (which arguably belong to the special regime of development law) have been developed and interpreted in parallel with international treaties and standards, but have not been systematically or explicitly grounded in those treaties or standards. The fragmentation, disconnects, and lack of policy coherence in this sphere is problematic and presents legal risk because of the haphazard interaction of legal and policy norms, and, as Ian Brownlie observed, 'the risks of serious conflicts and tensions between the various programmes and principles concerned'.[84] Such conflicts or disconnects could have the consequence of duplicating, diluting, subverting, contradicting,[85] or undermining international law through the proliferation of analogous norms in policy frameworks in areas already governed by international law.

The adoption of norms and principles in development law and policy in lieu of binding rules of international law, and independently of existing international law is common, as is analysed throughout this book. However, these new norms and principles cannot supplant the existing relevant and applicable international law rules or replace the specific legal accountability provided by binding international law. Furthermore, the due diligence required by each is different; some involving legal requirements, some non-legal. They are moreover interpreted by different bodies: international law is interpreted by courts, tribunals, and expert monitoring

---

[82] See Benedict Kingsbury, Nico Kirsch, and Richard Stewart, 'The Emergence of Global Administrative Law' (2005) 68 L & Contemp Probs 15, 16 ('Underlying the emergence of global administrative law is the vast increase in the reach and forms of transgovernmental regulation and administration designed to address the consequences of globalized interdependence').
[83] See e.g. World Bank, 'Environmental and Social Framework' (2016) <https://www.worldbank.org/en/projects-operations/environmental-and-social-framework> accessed 20 May 2023.
[84] Ian Brownlie, 'The Rights of Peoples in Modern International Law' in James Crawford and Hans Kruuk (eds), *The Rights of Peoples* (Clarendon Press 1988) 15.
[85] Brownlie (n 77).

bodies, while development law and policy is interpreted by development institutions and their compliance functions and accountability mechanisms.[86]

Others have commented on how specialized regimes can exacerbate fragmentation if each regime also uses its own dispute resolution forum, as

> [t]his can also lead to each dispute resolution forum favoring its own substantive regime over obligations stemming from other specialized regimes or from general rules of international law.... the proliferation of tribunals may lead to a proliferation of parochial—and potentially conflicting—interpretations of the legal obligations of States parties to more than one treaty regime.[87]

As Georges Abi-Saab noted,

> [c]omplexification creates a need for specialized tribunals to accommodate normative diversification and specialization. [...] which generates a parallel need, equally important and demanding, for a common understanding, interpretation and application of the overarching principles by this widening spectrum of tribunals in order to keep the system together and prevent it from exploding into a multitude of small particles. It requires, in turn, a certain coordination or harmonization between the diverse tribunals.[88]

With different dispute settlement bodies exercising overlapping jurisdictions, there is a clear possibility that they provide divergent interpretations of the same norm, rule, or principle emanating from a special regime (or even a substantive rule of general international law), which in turn risks generating confusion among states about their legal obligations and a weakening of the legal protection provided by international law.[89] They might even adjudicate differently on the same set of facts or in the same dispute. There is also a risk of an entire special regime, such as human rights law, being co-opted or redefined to be compatible with the economic focus of a development institution.[90]

The fragmentation and resultant policy incoherence in the context of development may be harmful for international law. As Ian Brownlie once opined, fragmentation and policy incoherence threaten 'the quality and coherence of international law as a whole and resulting in serious conflicts and tensions between programmes

---

[86] On the proliferation of international tribunals and the substantive fragmentation of international law, see Fragmentation of International Law? (n 2).

[87] Christopher Borgen, 'Treaty Conflicts and Normative Fragmentation', in Duncan Hollis, *Oxford Guide to Treaties* (OUP 2012) 453.

[88] Georges Abi-Saab, 'Fragmentation or Unification: Some Concluding Remarks' (1999) 31 NYU J Int'l L & Pol 919, 926 (hereafter 'Fragmentation or Unification').

[89] See generally, Martti Koskenniemi and Päivi Leino, 'Fragmentation of International Law? Postmodern Anxieties' (2002) 15 Leiden JIL 553, 560–61 (hereafter 'Fragmentation of International Law?') (discussing the spectrum of views on the risks of fragmentation).

[90] Fragmentation of International Law? (n 2) 570 (noting the use of rights discourse by economic institutions like the EU and World Bank).

and principles'.[91] The ILC has warned that such fragmentation may lead to the 'erosion of international law, emergence of conflicting jurisprudence, forum shopping and the loss of legal security'.[92] The issue to assess is therefore how development law and the practice emerging around it evidence such fragmentation, and contribute to incoherence and an erosion of the international rule of law upon which development itself depends.

This fragmentation may also be harmful for sustainable development and may negatively affect people and communities in developing countries. A potential for harm lies in the absence of a governing standard of international law, including through the substituting of an international law standard with an analogous norm in development policy, or through development policy and international law generating conflicting rules or principles in response to the same issue or problem.[93] An example could be development actors' introducing inclusion and non-discrimination requirements in countries' development projects or programmes without linking these to binding equality norms in national, regional, or international human rights instruments, and the relevant interpretations by competent courts or monitoring bodies. There is the risk of harm without effective recourse, redress, or remedy, and a lack of accountability.[94] A great deal has been written about the need for more accountability in development and greater accountability for development actors and IFIs.[95]

It is submitted that the fragmentation of international law in the context of development exacerbates the risk of accountability deficits. That is not to say that development actors, including IFIs and the activities they finance, are not subject to certain forms of accountability[96] through their boards, independent accountability mechanisms, grievance redress services, or project level grievance mechanisms—but these do not uphold international legal accountability anchored explicitly in treaties and they are not a substitute for such accountability.[97] Many

---

[91] Ian Brownlie, 'The Rights of Peoples in Modern International Law', in James Crawford and Hans Kruuk (eds), *The Rights of Peoples* (Clarendon Press 1988).

[92] International Law Commission, 'Fragmentation of International Law: Difficulties Arising from the Diversification and Expansion of International Law' (Fifty-eighth session, Geneva, 1 May–9 June and 3 July–11 August 2006, A/CN4/L702, 18 July 2006).

[93] Definition of 'conflict' proposed by the ILC Study Group Report (n 38) 29.

[94] There is a growing body of literature on the theme of accountability in the context of global governance and constitutionalism. See e.g. Gráinne de Búrca and Joanne Scott (eds), *Law and New Governance in the EU and the US* (Hart Publishing 2006) (charting the spread of new forms of global coordination in governance in the US and EU).

[95] Mac Darrow, *Between Light and Shadow Between Light and Shadow: The World Bank, the International Monetary Fund and International Human Rights Law* (Bloomsbury Press 2003); Jessica Evans, 'The Record of International Financial Institutions on Business and Human Rights' (2016) 1 BHRJ 327–32; Antonio Morelli, 'International Financial Institutions and Their Human Rights Silent Agenda: A Forward-Looking View on the "Protect, Respect and Remedy" Model in Development Finance' (2020) 36(1) Am Univ Int'l L Rev 52–103. Jan Wouters, Eva Brems, Stefan Smis, and Pierre Schmitt, *Accountability for Human Rights Violations by International Organisations* (Intersentia 2010).

[96] Accountability and Abuses of Power (n 5) 37.

[97] Were they to purport to uphold international legal accountability, they would have to do so explicitly and based on a systematic assessment of the relevant and applicable international law rules, presumably based on some form of international law due diligence (discussed in Section 2).

are concerned primarily with assessing compliance with a development actor's policy framework.[98]

This fundamental distinction is rooted in the special quality of international law and the unique nature of international legal accountability discussed in section 2 (b) above. This is grounded in 'a central assumption that law emerges from the interaction of the participants in the legal system and an increasingly fixed pattern of expectations about appropriate behaviour'.[99] In describing the difference between legal norms from broader social norms, Brunnée notes that they are distinguished by certain internal characteristics of law – transparency, reasonableness, and predictability.[100] These features are central to international law's ability to force justification, assessment, or judgement, and thereby facilitate legal accountability.[101] According to Grant and Keohane, the criticisms of these organizations (including IFIs) on grounds of accountability refer not to lack of accountability *per se*, but to weaknesses in democratic accountability.[102] It is contended that international legal accountability could help remedy some of these weaknesses by contributing a measure of transparency, predictability, and legitimacy, which would in turn help advance sustainable development. Indeed, it is widely recognized that development risks not being sustainable if the governing decision-making processes are not transparent, accountable, and free from corruption.[103]

6. Towards International Legal Coherence in Sustainable Development

a. Legal basis

Based on the foregoing and anchored in the unique nature of legal accountability underpinning international legal norms, the following is a proposal for international law due diligence based on an international policy coherence imperative. The proposal does not rely specifically on whether the treaties (or the primary rules they contain) generate a due diligence obligation,[104] whether legal requirement to

---

[98] e.g. World Bank Inspection Panel.
[99] International Legal Accountability (n 5) 9 (citing Jutta Brunnée and Stephen J. Toope, *International Law and Constructivism: Elements of an International Theory of International Law* (2000) 39 Columbia JTL 19).
[100] International Legal Accountability (n 5) 7 (citing Lon Fuller, *The Morality of Law* (Yale University Press 1969) 39, 46–91.
[101] International Legal Accountability (n 5) 7 (citing ibid (Fuller) 46–91).
[102] Citing Robert Dahl, 'Can International Organizations be Democratic? A Skeptic's View', in Ian Shapiro and Casiano Hacker-Cordon (eds), *Democracy's Edges* (CUP 1999) 33–34.
[103] Konrad Ginther, Erik Denters, and Paul J I M de Waart (eds), *Sustainable Development as a Matter of Good Governance: An Introductory View* (Martinus Nijhoff 1995) 8.
[104] See e.g. *Application of the Convention on the Prevention and Punishment of the Crime of Genocide (Bosnia and Herzegovina v Serbia and Montenegro)* (2007) ICJ Judgment ICJ Rep 43 which addressed

exercise due diligence is a component part of a primary rule of international law, or whether such a requirement might be implied in order for a state party to be acting in conformity with the primary rule; these are questions separate from the present discussion. The proposal presented here is more general in nature, rooted in the binding nature of international law, and international treaties in particular—undergirded by the principle of *pacta sunt servanda*—that agreements must be kept. States ought to act consistently with their international legal obligations and such obligations ought to be taken into account when they are participating in development activities as either donor or partner countries. The overlap of development activities and binding international law norms is a structural feature of the international regulatory landscape that must be factored into understanding the relevance and role of international law in sustainable development. The requirement to undertake international law due diligence would therefore itself be anchored in international law[105] and the principle of *pacta sunt servanda* (discussed in Section 2).

Such a requirement of general legal due diligence can be traced to the due diligence principle identified in international law by courts and scholars:[106] 'states have a negative obligation to refrain from breaching their international duties ... and a positive obligation to take reasonable measures to prevent harmful activities by non-state actors'. This due diligence requirement can therefore also be conceived in terms of a 'duty to do no harm'. Both the 1938 *Trail Smelter Arbitration*[107] and the ICJ's 1996 *Nuclear Weapons* Advisory Opinion[108] recognized the existence of an environmental and transboundary duty to 'do no harm' as 'part of the corpus of international law relating to the environment'. In its judgment in *Pulp Mills*,[109] the Court confirmed the existence of a 'duty of vigilance' and a requirement under general international law to undertake an environmental impact assessment where there is a risk that the proposed industrial activity may have a significant adverse impact in a transboundary context.[110] Due diligence obligations have a long history in international environmental law, and they now extend to other areas such

---

the general obligation enunciated in article 1 of the 1948 Genocide Convention requiring states parties to prevent genocide, the primary rule itself generating a legal due diligence requirement.

[105] See Due Diligence in International Law (n 119) 2–3 (concluding that 'due diligence is an evolving principle of international law').

[106] Marian Monnheimer, *Due Diligence in International Human Rights Law* (CUP 2021) 3 (hereafter 'Due Diligence in International Human Rights Law') (citing Robert Barnridge, *The Due Diligence Principle Under International Law* (2006) 8 Int'l Comm L Rev 81–121, 91; Riccardo Pisillo-Mazzeschi, *The Due Diligence Rule and the Nature of International Responsibility of States* (1992) 35 GYIL 9–51, 22 (hereafter 'The Due Diligence Rule').

[107] *Trail Smelter Case (United States of America, Canada) Award*, vol. 3, Reports of Arbitral International Awards, 1905–1982 (16 April 1938).

[108] *Legality of the Threat or Use of Nuclear Weapons*, Advisory Opinion, ICJ Reports 226 (8 July 1996).

[109] *Pulp Mills on the River Uruguay (Argentina v Uruguay)*, ICJ Reports 14 (20 April 2010).

[110] The duty is also manifest in the Rio Declaration and in Principle 21 of the Stockholm Declaration of the United Nations Conference on the Human Environment.

as alien protection and human rights, including in the area of business and human rights. Certain primary rules impose a due diligence standard on state conduct.[111]

Thus, due diligence is paired with a wide array of international obligations across different areas of international law.[112] It may be argued that due diligence is incorporated into primary rules and in obligations that define the required conduct of states in international law—thus as part of their international obligations.[113]

b. Purpose

The purpose of such international law due diligence would be to promote international policy coherence and mitigate the risk associated with fragmentation, including conflicts or contradiction, and the potential for development activities to undermine international law obligations. The UNGPs may be cited by analogy. The Human Rights Council unanimously endorsed the UNGPs in 2011: they are the global standard for preventing and addressing the risk of adverse impacts on human rights linked to business activity, and they provide the internationally-accepted framework for enhancing standards and practices with regard to business and human rights.[114] Principle 10 provides that states, when acting as members of multilateral institutions that deal with business-related issues, should: seek to ensure that those institutions neither restrain the ability of their Member States to meet their duty to protect, nor hinder business enterprises from respecting human rights.

Alice Olino notes that:

> the 'rise' of due diligence has gone hand in hand with the appraisal of risk under international law. Due diligence is indeed perceived as one of the fundamental legal tools to regulate, manage and anticipate risks in international society.... one of the principal functions of due diligence obligations is to prevent harms to other states, to avoid or minimize risk to international public interests and global commons and to regulate the conduct of non-state actors when the latter may commit into national harmful acts or carry out violations of international human rights law.[115]

---

[111] Robert Barnidge, 'The Due Diligence Principle under International Law' (2006) 8 Int'l Comm L Rev 81, 91.

[112] Alice Olino, *Due Diligence Obligations in International Law* (CUP 2022) 6 (hereafter 'Due Diligence Obligations in International Law').

[113] ibid 8.

[114] See e.g. UN Human Rights Council Resolution 17/4, *Guiding Principles on Business and Human Rights: Implementing the United Nations "Protect, Respect and Remedy" Framework* (A/HRC/17/31, 21 March 2011) <https://www.ohchr.org/documents/publications/guidingprinciplesbusinesshr_en.pdf> accessed 20 May 2023 (hereafter 'UNGPs').

[115] Due Diligence Obligations in International Law (n 112) 6, 98–105.

Efforts to mitigate risk would therefore be explicitly grounded in international law.

Thus, international law governs and should guide efforts to ensure international policy coherence, including in the sphere of development.[116]

The UNGPs commentary is apposite here:

> Greater policy coherence is also needed at the international level, including where States participate in multilateral institutions that deal with business-related issues, such as international trade and financial institutions. States retain their international human rights law obligations when they participate in such institutions.[117]

The proposal presented here would therefore involve assessing development policies and projects systematically and holistically in light of relevant and applicable rules of existing international law. As Vaughan Lowe has argued: fundamental principles underlying the international system as a whole'.[118] At its heart therefore, this proposal for international law due diligence aims to promote accountability.

On the connection between due diligence and accountability, the International Law Association (ILA) Study Group on Due Diligence has confirmed that: '[t]he resort to due diligence as a standard of conduct should be seen against the backdrop of general approaches to accountability in international law'.[119] Elsewhere, the Study Group has noted, '[t]he ILA's 2004 Report on Accountability of International Organisations makes clear links to due diligence and utilizes both constituent documents and general international law as sources of accountability'.[120]

c. Definition of 'international law due diligence'

What is 'international law due diligence'? What are its contours and content? Before describing the proposal for human rights due diligence in the context of

---

[116] Philip Alston has argued for *policy coherence in development policy to be anchored directly in IHRL*. See Philip Alston, 'Ships Passing in the Night: The Current State of the Human Rights and Development Debate Seen Through the Lens of the Millennium Development Goals' (2005) 27 HRQ 755, 827 (detailing 'the key elements in a new approach to ensuring effective complementarity between human rights and the Millennium Development Goals').

[117] See UNGPs (n 114) Principles 8, 9, 10.

[118] Campbell McLachlan, 'After Baghdad: Conflict or Coherence in International Law' (2003) 1 NZJPIL 25, 47 (citing Vaughn Lowe, 'The Iraq Crisis: What Now?' (2003) 52(4) ICLQ 859–73.

[119] Tim Stephens and Duncan French, *Due Diligence in International Law: Second Report* (The ILA Study Group on Due Diligence in International Law, July 2016) <https://ila.vettoreweb.com/Storage/Download.aspx?DbStorageId=1427&StorageFileGuid=ed229726-4796-47f2-b891-8cafa221685f> accessed 20 May 2023.

[120] ibid 40 (citing the ILA Committee on the Accountability of International Organisations, Final Report (2004) < https://brill.com/view/journals/iolr/1/1/article-p221_15.xml?language=en,> accessed 20 May 2023.

sustainable development, a brief analysis of due diligence in international law is apposite.

Due diligence can be viewed as emanating from international legal responsibility. As Barnidge observes, 'international law recognizes a number of principles of responsibility. One of them is the due diligence principle, applies across many areas of international law.' Citing Luigi Condorelli, he concludes that the due diligence principle is 'a basic principle of international law'.[121]

According to the ILA Study Group:

> [t]he core content of the due diligence principle was articulated in the *Corfu Channel* case,[122] namely 'every State's obligation not to allow knowingly its territory to be used for acts contrary to the rights of other States.' This principle has developed over a lengthy period, is now clearly a part of customary international law, and reflects cornerstone concepts of international law (including State sovereignty, equality, territorial integrity, and non-interference).

The ILA Study Group went on to identify three constituent elements of the due diligence principle:

(i) a sovereign State is obligated to ensure;
(ii) that in its jurisdiction (which includes all those spaces where the sovereign exercises formal jurisdiction or effective control); and
(iii) other states' rights and interests (including those with respect to the protection of their citizens and companies) are not violated.

According to Riccardo Pisillo-Mazzeschi, due diligence is objective in nature: 'what counts is the breach of an objective standard of conduct by the State as a whole'.[123] It is, moreover, primarily an obligation of conduct rather than result.[124]

Despite being based on an objective standard, due diligence has 'an elastic and relative nature'.[125] It is also likely to vary depending on the area of international law involved: the ILA Study Group has noted, '[d]ue diligence is imbued with differing content according to the specific area of international law in which it is invoked'.[126] As the International Tribunal for the Law of the Sea (ITLOS) stated in the Seabed Mining Advisory Opinion, ' "due diligence" is a variable concept. It may change

---

[121] Barnidge (n 111) (citing Luigi Condorelli, 'The Imputability to States of Acts of International Terrorism' (1989) 19 ISR YBHR 233, 240).
[122] *Corfu Channel Case (United Kingdom of Great Britain and Northern Ireland v. Albania)*, ICJ Rep 4 (1949).
[123] The Due Diligence Rule (n 106) 42.
[124] Due Diligence Obligations in International Law (n 112) 105.
[125] The Due Diligence Rule (n 106) 44.
[126] Due Diligence in International Law: Second (n 119) 4.

over time.'[127] It is likely to vary also according to the state party in question and be subject to certain subjective variation. There may be differences based on the nature of the obligation or primary rule involved[128] and the nature and levels of risk implicated.[129] Riccardo Pisillo-Mazzeschi identifies three other variables: (i) the degree of effectiveness of the State's control over certain areas of its territory; (ii) the importance of the interest to be protected; and (iii) the degree of predictability of the harm.[130] The scope and content of the due diligence will likely vary due to the particular circumstances of each specific case,[131] specific facts, and features of the context.[132]

Building on the work of Alice Olino and that of the ILA,[133] one may characterize the purpose of the proposed international law due diligence in the development context as follows: to evaluate risk in terms of whether development programming or specific development activities will increase 'the probability that the object or result set by a primary rule or international obligation will not be attained'.[134] Put differently, such due diligence would have as its objective to assess whether development policies or programs will result in the breach of an international obligation or harm to a state's rights.

The specific contours of such due diligence require further analysis and would have to be defined case by case, following a detailed analysis of the legal obligations in play and the legal and policy context of its application in development. However, in broad terms it would involve an assessment or screening of the relevant and applicable international law rule(s) and concomitant state obligation(s); it would also require that the assessment or screening be carried out *ex ante* as systematic review and analysis of any relevant or applicable legal norms in the particular development sector(s). It would be limited to a requirement to screen, identify, analyse, and consider relevant and applicable *existing* international law obligations,[135] placing international treaties at the centre of development; but it would not involve the creation of new legal obligations or necessarily imply any form of legal conditionality.

---

[127] The Seabed Disputes Chamber of the International Tribunal for the Law of the Sea (ITLOS) Advisory Opinion in Responsibilities and Obligations of States Sponsoring Persons and Entities with Respect to Activities in the Area (1 February 2011) (hereafter 'Seabed Mining Advisory Opinion') (2011) 50 ILM 458, para 117.

[128] Neil McDonald, 'The Role of Due Diligence in International Law' (2019) 68(4) ICLQ 1041–54 arguing that legal requirement to exercise due diligence may be a component part of a primary rule of international law, but this can only be determined by referring back to the primary rule in question.

[129] See UNGPs (n 114). See also Seabed Mining Advisory Opinion (n 127) para 117, which noted that '[due diligence obligations] may also change in relation to the risks involved in the activity'.

[130] The Due Diligence Rule (n 106) 44.

[131] ibid.

[132] UNGP Guiding Principle 17(b) states that due diligence 'will vary in complexity with ... the risk of severe human rights impacts'; UNGPs (n 114).

[133] Stephens and French (n 119).

[134] Due Diligence Obligations in International Law (n 112) 101.

[135] See also Monnheimer, 'Due Diligence in International Human Rights Law' (n 106).

Drawing on Principle 15 of the UNGPs,[136] one could characterize it as an assessment process derived from an obligation of conduct, aimed at identifying and accounting for how development policy and projects might affect states' international law obligations or their ability to fulfil such obligations. It would go beyond standard E&S due diligence undertaken pursuant to development E&S policies of IOs or IFIs, and would involve comprehensive and systematic legal due diligence on states' international legal obligations relevant to their development activities, either as donors or partners, based on recognition of the idea that 'the law of treaties may prove key to addressing international law's fragmentation as its fields deepen, mature and increasingly interact'.[137] The assessment could also cover relevant and applicable rules of customary international law.

In terms of timing, the international law due diligence would be undertaken at different stages: first, it should be carried out prior to development actors' elaboration of policies and procedures. It would also be conducted during the concept and design phase of projects and programmes—in the way E&S due diligence is currently undertaken by IFIs and their clients—in order to identify, prevent, and mitigate any potential negative impacts of development policy and projects on states' international law obligations (or on their ability to fulfil these). In this respect it is based on the proposition that development activities should not undermine relevant international rules or norms or interfere with the ability of partner states to fulfil the obligations they generate.

Crucially, it would have to be undertaken *ex ante*—in drafting or consultation phase of policy development, at the scoping and planning phase of a policy dialogue or at the concept stage of an investment lending project, policy dialogue, technical assistance, or budget support operation. However, it might also have a role through the life cycle of a project or programme during implementation, monitoring, and evaluation.

In essence, this international law due diligence could generate requirements to take preventative measures and uphold a principle of 'do no harm'—to avoid harm to particular rights or to particular rights-holders.[138] It could result in a requirement to mitigate risks of undermining specific international law obligations and might result in a pause on the preparation or implementation of project, or in the application of a policy, if there were evidence of a potential breach of an

---

[136] UNGPs (n 114).

[137] Oxford Guide to Treaties (n 15) 8 (citing ILC Study Group Report (n 38) 11–12).

[138] See e.g. Principle 16 of the UNGPs ('In order to meet their responsibility to respect human rights, business enterprises should have in place policies and processes appropriate to their size and circumstances, including:
- (a) A policy commitment to meet their responsibility to respect human rights;
- (b) A human rights due diligence process to identify, prevent, mitigate and account for how they address their impacts on human rights;
- (c) Processes to enable the remediation of any adverse human rights impacts they cause or to which they contribute') UNGPs (n 114).

international law norm or obligation. It might identify an obligation to act, or to remedy any harm resulting from such a breach; this might involve compensation or restitution, or the establishment and maintenance of an administrative and judicial apparatus capable of investigating and sanctioning the breach of the international rule in question.[139] It might also involve more positive, prospective actions based on an analysis of how development policies and activities can help states fulfil their international law obligations in the future, such as diagnostic work to ascertain where additional support may be necessary, capacity building, technical assistance, and training in development institutions. This could relate to the ratification of new treaties, the transposition of international obligations into national law, or the implementation of existing obligations.

d. Addressees

The requirement to undertake due diligence would be primarily incumbent upon states, as the primary duty bearers in international law. Relying on the tripartite definition of the ILA Study Group, it would be potentially applicable to all states vis-à-vis any other state(s). In the development context, it would apply to states in all their actions, whether they act as donors or partners/borrowers in development institutions and IFIs.[140] However, it could have implications for development actors at large, including IFIs themselves, of which states are members, and possibly for other participants in the international legal system.[141]

e. Sphere of application

Once the initial scoping stage of the international law due diligence exercise has established that a rule or norm of international law is relevant or applicable, the operational implications and sphere of application might relate to treaty interpretation, policy elaboration, interpretation, or application.

(i) Treaty interpretation

Assuming that states may have conflicting legal obligations, the issue is how to respond to those actual or potential conflicts. The proposal for international law due diligence would impose upon the states in question (either directly or through their participation on IO or IFI boards)[142] an obligation to interpret international

---

[139] Monnheimer, 'Due Diligence in International Human Rights Law' (n 106) 86.
[140] UNGPs (n 114) Principle 10.
[141] See Robert McCorquodale chapter in this volume.
[142] As Dapo Akande has noted 'IOs will necessarily and routinely have to interpret the treaty setting up the international organization. In *Certain Expenses* (Advisory Opinion), the IJC accepted that

treaties in the development sphere (including constitutive instruments of IOs or IFIs) harmoniously with a state's other treaty obligations, relying on articles 31 and 32 of the Vienna Convention on the Law of Treaties, which establish the rules of treaty interpretation as well as recourse to supplementary materials.[143] For instance, interpretations by IOs and IFIs of their constituent instruments, a financing or guarantee agreement (concluded between an IO and a Member State), would need to take into account other relevant and applicable treaty obligations of the state in question (identified through the international law due diligence screening).[144]

A key preliminary element would be to acknowledge the concurrent application of both the IFI financing agreement or constitutive instrument, and any other relevant or applicable international treaty, and afford due regard to the latter in interpreting the former. Former Senior Vice President and General Counsel Ibrahim Shihata acknowledged that breaches of international obligations relevant to the Bank should be taken into account. Opining in the context of the interpretation of the World Bank Articles' 'political prohibitions', Shihata wrote

> an extensive violation of political rights which takes pervasive proportions could impose itself as an issue in the Bank's decisions. This would be the case if the violation had significant economic effects, or it led to the breach of international obligations relevant to the Bank, such as those created under binding decisions of the UN Security Council.[145]

Another important element would be to resist assumptions of inevitable conflicts between international obligations, such between obligations under IFI charters and other international treaties or agreements. Such an interpretative approach would be driven by the objective of ensuring policy coherence[146] and reconciling potentially conflicting norms of international law for states' parties to more than one treaty.[147] In doctrinal terms, the interpretative approach could rely

---

'each organ [of the UN] must, in the first place at least, determine its own jurisdiction'. Dapo Akande, 'International Organizations', in Malcolm Evans (ed), *International Law* (OUP 2010) 261.

[143] Vienna Convention on the Law of Treaties (n 27). Article 31 establishes the general rule of interpretation while Article 32 addresses the use of supplementary means in the process of treaty interpretation and with the relationship of that use to the general rule. It confirms the circumstances under which such means may be invoked in treaty interpretation, what weight is to be given to them and how they relate to the other rules of interpretation.

[144] An example of where this might occur arises in the context of human rights treaties and the political prohibitions that are contained in the constative instruments of most IFIs.

[145] Ibrahim Shihata, *Political Activity Prohibited in World Bank Legal Papers* (Brill 2000) 235. The chapter reproduced a Legal Opinion of the General Counsel, dated 11 July 1995 (Sec M95-707, 12 July 1995).

[146] It would also be necessary because of absence of conflict avoidance clauses in development law.

[147] See Dinah Shelton, 'International Law and "Relative Normativity"', in Malcolm Evans (ed), *International Law* (OUP 2003) 148–49.

on the presumption against normative conflict in international law and the principle of systemic integration,[148] viewed by some as 'the most influential principle in terms of reception of international law'.[149] It is derived from Article 31(3)(c) of the Vienna Convention on the Law of Treaties, which provides that, in addition to the treaty's context, there shall be taken into account 'any relevant rules of international law applicable in relations between parties'.[150] In essence, the principle

> prescribes that a treaty be interpreted by reference to its 'normative environment' which includes all sources of international law. That means that when several norms bear on a single issue, they should, to the greatest extent possible, be interpreted so as to give rise to a single set of compatible obligations.[151]

(ii) Policy content

Under the proposal presented here, international law due diligence would be integral to the elaboration of development law and policies, and inform their substantive and procedural requirements. It would also guide the appraisal, design, and implementation of particular development projects, dialogues, technical assistance, or other activities in specific sectors. It would require that international law rules identified in the international law due diligence screening as relevant or applicable would be systematically integrated in the policy, project, or activity being elaborated.

This might result in the development policies of bilateral and multilateral actors making general provision for relevant and applicable rules of international law, in the way Environmental and Social Standard 1 (ESS1) of the World Bank Environmental and Social Framework (ESF) does. Paragraph 26 of ESS1 provides:

> The Borrower will ensure that the environmental and social assessment takes into account in an appropriate manner all issues relevant to the project, including: (a) the country's applicable policy framework, national laws and regulations, and institutional capabilities (including implementation) relating to environment and social issues; variations in country conditions and project context; country

---

[148] See Campbell McLachlan, 'The Principle of Systemic Integration and Article 31(3)(c) of the Vienna Convention' (2005) 54 Int'l & Compar LQ 279 (proposing that article 31(3)(c) of the VCLT expresses systemic integration as a general principle of treaty interpretation); see also Vassilis Tzevelekos, 'The Use of Article 31 (3) (c) in the VCLT in the Case Law of the ECtHR: An Effective Anti-Fragmentation Tool or a Selective Loophole for the Reinforcement of Human Rights Teleology?' (2010) 31(3) Mich J Int'l L 621.

[149] Magdalena Forowicz, *The Reception of International Law in the European Court of Human Rights* (OUP 2010) 13.

[150] See VCLT (n 27).

[151] Jean D'Aspremont, 'The Systemic Integration of International Law by Domestic Courts: Domestic Judges as Architects of the Consistency of the International Legal Order', in Ole Kristian Fauchald and André Nollkaemper (eds), *The Practice of International and National Courts and the (De-)Fragmentation of International Law* (Hart Publishing 2012) 148.

environmental or social studies; national environmental or social action plans; *and obligations of the country directly applicable to the project under relevant international treaties and agreements.*[152]

It would be driven by the goal of ensuring greater international policy coherence in the elaboration, content, and operation of development policies. The UNGPs call upon states to ensure policy coherence. A similar principle could be adopted with respect to IOs and IFIs, such that states should ensure that governmental departments, agencies, and other state-based institutions responsible for development policy and practice are aware of and observe the state's international law obligations when fulfilling their respective mandates and elaborating and approving policies, procedures, and internal rules.[153]

(iii) Policy interpretation and application

A related application of international due diligence involves the interpretation and application of development policies to projects and activities. The results of the due diligence assessment or screening undertaken would help guide the interpretation and application of policies, particularly where those policies: (i) make general provision for the consideration of international treaties and agreements; (ii) include specific international law rules; or (iii) contain analogous norms or principles.[154] The fact that the bodies interpreting such policies have a limited jurisdiction does not imply a limitation on the scope of the law applicable in the interpretation and application of such policies.[155] Examples include human rights principles such as participation, non-discrimination, free prior and informed consent, or the precautionary principle.

Development policies would therefore need to reflect and uphold explicit provisions on relevant and applicable international law rules (e.g. Para 26 in ESS1 of the World Bank ESF),[156] or ensure in some other way that such rules are taken into account and afforded precedence in the case of a conflict with a policy requirement.[157] The principal justification for such precedence would be the qualitative difference in the normative weight of international law obligations as binding international law. This qualitative difference goes beyond formal attributes. To quote Brunnée and Stephen Toope again, 'what distinguishes law from other types

---

[152] World Bank, 2016 *Environmental and Social Framework*, ESS1, para 26 (emphasis added).
[153] UNGPs (n 114) Principle 8.
[154] One such example was the 2005 World Bank Indigenous Peoples Policy provision on 'free prior and informed consultation' in lieu of 'free prior informed consent'; the latter was enshrined in the 2007 UN Declaration on the Rights of Indigenous Peoples <https://www.un.org/development/desa/indigenouspeoples/wp-content/uploads/sites/19/2018/11/UNDRIP_E_web.pdf> accessed 20 May 2023.
[155] Stephens and French (n 119) 11–12, para 45.
[156] Discussed in section 2.
[157] This precedence would be justified on the grounds that development policy is not a formal source of international law and that under an informal hierarchy, general international law occupies a superior position.

of social ordering is not form, but adhere to specific criteria of legality: generality, promulgation, non-retroactivity, clarity, non-contradiction, not asking the impossible, constancy, and congruence between rules and official action'.[158]

This international due diligence will also mean that where a rule of international law has been deemed relevant or applicable (through the international due diligence assessment or screening), the decisions, opinions, and rulings related to that rule promulgated by international bodies, such as courts, tribunals, and treaty monitoring bodies—as the authoritative bodies legally mandated with the monitoring, interpretation, and application of international law norms—could be taken into account in the interpretation and application of development policies. The proposal for international due diligence would, however, not involve any formal monitoring or enforcement role for development actors, IOs, or IFIs, although development actors and the governments of partner and donor countries would each have a role the process of undertaking such due diligence. International court, tribunals, and monitoring bodies would also have a role in assessing whether development actors had interpreted the rules and norms under their jurisdiction correctly or taken relevant rulings thereon into account in an appropriate matter.

In line with the goal of international policy coherence, this would rely on effective partnerships and coordination between international law actors and development actors. Like Georges Abi-Saab's proposal for coordination and harmonization in the context of tribunals, it would involve 'correlation into a kind of constellation, however loose it may be'.[159] In this respect it would respect the distinct and complementary roles of different international actors and the natural division of labour between special regimes and their institutions. More broadly, however, it might also imply that greater efforts be made to harmonize the development of soft law and political commitments with existing treaty obligations. For example, the human rights framework and the sustainable development agenda could be further aligned which would require, *inter alia*, 'recognition of the human rights framework as a normative basis for certain global obligations for sustainable development, the objects of which coincide with the objects of internationally recognized human rights'.[160]

7. Conclusion

This chapter has argued that development policy and practice could be strengthened by promoting greater international policy coherence and by upholding

---

[158] Jutta Brunnée and Stephen J Toope, 'The Sovereignty of International Law?' (2017) 67(4) Univ Tor Law J 496–511; see also Jutta Brunnée and Stephen Toope, *Legitimacy and Legality in International Law: An Interactional Account* (CUP 2010) 6.
[159] Abi- Saab (n 88) 926.
[160] Global Obligations for Sustainable Development (n 57).

international legal accountability. Relying in part on the principle of systemic integration, it has put forward a proposal for international law due diligence to ensure that relevant and applicable international law rules are acknowledged in development law and that they are interpreted by reference to the relevant and applicable sources of international law. In this way, it has contended that development policy, programming, and dialogues should be subject to the legal constraints of international law.[161] The proposal is offered not in the spirit of seeking triumph of one set of rules over another but rather, to paraphrase McLachlan, to work out in detail how important values of international society are articulated and harmonized.[162] There have been, in recent years, clear signs of more 'joined-up thinking' in development frameworks and declarations. The SDGs and the content of *Transforming our World: The 2030 Agenda for Sustainable Development* are obvious examples.[163] The GA Resolution provides:

> The new Agenda is guided by the purposes and principles of the Charter of the United Nations, including full respect for international law. It is grounded in the Universal Declaration of Human Rights, international human rights treaties, the Millennium Declaration and the 2005 World Summit Outcome. It is informed by other instruments such as the Declaration on the Right to Development.[164]

In addition, in the Resolution Member States commit to:

> implement the Agenda for the full benefit of all, for today's generation and for future generations. In doing so, we reaffirm our commitment to international law and emphasize that the Agenda is to be implemented in a manner that is consistent with the rights and obligations of States under international law. … and reaffirm the importance of the Universal Declaration of Human Rights, as well as other international instruments relating to human rights and international law.[165]

Elsewhere in the Resolution, Member States resolve to take action in conformity with international law[166] and the Resolution encourages states to refrain from engaging in economic and other actions that are not in accordance with international law; some of the targets themselves reference international law.[167]

---

[161] Ginther, Denters, and de Weert (104) 10 (discussing whether development policy dialogues are subject to any legal constraints and whether such dialogues have the capacity to reconstitute the international legal order to better meet the exigencies of sustainable development).

[162] Campbell McLachlan, 'After Baghdad: Conflict or Coherence in International Law' (2003) 1 NZJPIL 25, 48.

[163] UN General Assembly, *Transforming our World: the 2030 Agenda for Sustainable Development* (A/Res/70/1, 2015).

[164] ibid para 10.

[165] ibid paras 18, 19.

[166] ibid paras 23, 35.

[167] Target 14.5 and 14.c.

As other chapters in this book illustrate, international law is relevant to every aspect of sustainable development. This chapter has argued that a more systematic and holistic approach to assessing that relevance and the applicability would further strengthen accountability in development law, policy, and practice to the benefit of both international law and SDGs.

Acknowledgement

Thanks to Robert McCorquodale, Nate Lankford, and Talya Lockman-Fine for invaluable comments on an earlier draft of this chapter. Thanks also to Christian Jimenez and Wendy Melis for research assistance and to Wolfgang Albrecht for editorial support. Responsibility for errors or omissions remains with the author.

3
The Role of International Law in Development Practice

Arnold N Pronto[*]

1. Introduction

Why law? Why are the lawyers here? This is a refrain sometimes heard in the corridors and meeting rooms in which 'big-picture' policy discussions on matters of global concern, such as sustainable development, are held. Such a question may seem somewhat trite, especially to readers of this book (which is dedicated precisely to a recapitulation of the variety of ways in which law, particularly international law, contributes to the goal of sustainable development).

This chapter has been inspired by the experience of being confronted with such questions (and variations thereof) on a number of occasions during my work at the United Nations (UN); to the extent that a significant amount of energy (more than one might expect) was expended on first explaining what contribution the law might make, even before delving into the content of the law. While usually motivated by genuine curiosity, such questions do on occasion reveal a thinly-veiled opposition (sometimes even bordering on animosity) to the very idea that law should play a role when confronting the issues at hand. As a lawyer interacting with practitioners in other fields, it was not uncommon to be provided with reasons why 'going legal' was a bad idea. Doing so would significantly complicate the intricate balance of interests, introduce unnecessary rigidity into a rapidly changing landscape, and so on. The practice of law is also, on occasion, about confronting 'baggage' in the form of preconceived ideas that others hold as to the role (and utility) of law.

To be clear, the recognition of the existence of a legal dimension to development is by no means novel.[1] Courses on environmental law and the law of development have been taught in various forms and manifestations at universities and elsewhere

---

[*] Principal Legal Officer, United Nations Office of Legal Affairs, member of the Secretariat of the International Law Commission. The views expressed herein do not necessarily reflect the position of the United Nations.

[1] Priscilla Schwarz, 'Sustainable Development in International Law' (2005) 5 Non-State Actors & IL 127; M Comino, 'Sustainable Development: The Role of Law' (1991) 16 LSB 57.

for decades. The UN's Sustainable Development Goals (SDGs)[2] cover a number of legal aspects (both directly and indirectly). One only has to peruse the following chapters in this book to find substantiation of such assertion.

We lawyers all share in the conviction that law does play a role, on occasion even a central one. However, the basic assertion made herein is that what goes without saying for most if not all lawyers is not necessarily (or even at all) obvious for other epistemological communities dealing with similar (or the same) subject matter. It is a fact that in recent times the ambition of contemporary international law (its scope *ratione materiae*), and of international lawyers alike, has expanded significantly into areas of human activity not traditionally regulated by international law. This has been driven in large measure by a perceived need to contribute to the overall improvement of the human condition.[3] However, many such areas of work are not 'new' at all. Some have been the subject of extensive study, scrutiny, and activity for decades and are well stocked with various groups of experts and other professionals toiling in a number of adjacent fields of expertise. As such, we international lawyers should, at the very minimum, be aware that we may be perceived as traversing (the less charitable might say trespassing) into fields where we are no longer the sole occupants, and in fact, where we might be but one of several communities, and where, viewed from the macro level, law and legal concerns are at times relatively marginal considerations in a broader sea of policy imperatives.

Hence, while it is certainly important to be familiar with all the existing rules, and the latest thinking on the applicable legal theory and practice, it is also advisable to be prepared to offer non-lawyers plausible reasons and explanations as to why they should care. In the experience of the present writer, it is a mistake to assume that the relevance of the law is self-evident. We should be ready to explain how the law applies and what it offers (and to defend it from superficial understandings or even the occasional opposition). In fact, there is value in taking the time to ponder the answers, if not only to find ways of obtaining greater 'buy-in' among non-lawyers then also by way of gaining a deeper understanding of why it is that we do what we do.

Law, including international law, does not exist for its own sake. We have moved beyond the traditional *raison d'être* of international law, as designed primarily with the settlement of international disputes between states in mind. Instead, contemporary international law increasingly also involves the marshalling of legal arguments and tools in the cause of confronting the challenges of our time (not least those arising from the imperative to ensure sustainable development).[4]

---

[2] UN General Assembly Res 70/1 (25 September 2015).
[3] See Theodore Meron, *The Humanization of International Law* (Martinus Nijhoff 2006).
[4] For a critique of this phenomenon and the tensions underlying it, see, generally, Martti Koskenniemi, *The Politics of International Law* (Hart Publishing 2011).

2. What Role for International Law?

So, what is the role of law, particularly international law, in the pursuit of sustainable development? In keeping with the practical orientation of this book, no attempt will be made at yet another reprise of the philosophical or jurisprudential arguments for the relevance of law. Nor are we concerned here with what the law is or says on particular aspects of sustainable development. Instead, the question being addressed in the context of sustainable development concerns the promise of the law. As a practical matter, what added value does it offer?[5] What is its claim to relevance?

There are likely many answers to these questions. In the present writer's view, one such possible explanation is that law plays a central role in connection with the need to manage complexity.[6] Modern societies are driven by complex, overlapping, and at times contradictory policy imperatives (usually in response to daunting contemporary challenges). To see this, one only has to look at the breath-taking scope and complexity of the issues covered by the SDGs. Yet, this is precisely the aspiration of the law.[7] This is so for a number of reasons. Law provides both the framework and discourse narrative for managing complexity, typically by constraining the actions of states and other actors to a series of predictable outcomes. It can be both rear-facing and future-oriented.

It looks backwards in the sense that it is in the law (including international law) that previously hard-fought (and won) gains are locked in. The proof of social and political progress in contemporary international society is also to be found memorialized in international law, particularly but not exclusively in treaties. There are many examples of systematic progress having been made through the consecutive negotiation and adoption of international conventions in areas such as international human rights and the protection of the environment. While much can be said about this phenomenon (most of which would be beyond the scope of the present chapter), a few points are worth highlighting.

First, the act of concretizing societal gains in law-making is a goal in itself. It goes without saying that achieving sustainable development requires not only efforts at

---

[5] See Joel P Trachtman, *The Future of International Law: Global Government* (CUP 2013), 22–40.
[6] Barbara A Cosens and others, 'The Role of Law in Adaptive Governance' (2017) 22 Ecol Soc 30; Barbara A Cosens and others, 'Designing Law to Enable Adaptive Governance of Modern Wicked Problems' (2020) 73 Vand L Rev 1687; Barbara A Cosens and others, 'Governing Complexity: Integrating Science, Governance, and Law to Manage Accelerating Change in the Globalized Commons' (2021) 118 Proc Natl Acad Sci e2102798118 <https://doi.org/10.1073/pnas.2102798118> accessed 20 May 2023.
[7] Olivia O Green and others, 'Barriers and Bridges to the Integration of Social–Ecological Resilience and Law' (2015) 13 Front Ecol Environ 332; Daniel A DeCaro and others, 'Legal and Institutional Foundations of Adaptive Environmental Governance' (2017) 22(1) Ecol Soc 32 <https://www.ecologyandsociety.org/vol22/iss1/art32/> accessed 20 May 2023; Jan McDonald and Phillipa C McCormack, 'Rethinking the Role of Law in Adapting to Climate Change' (2021) 12(5) WIREs Climate Change e726 <https://doi.org/10.1002/wcc.726> accessed 21 May 2023; Joseph Wenta, Jan McDonald, and Jeffrey S McGee, 'Enhancing Resilience and Justice in Climate Adaptation Laws' (2018) 8 TEL 89.

the national level, but also global action involving states and other entities, such as relevant international organizations (and civil society) acting in concert, within their respective mandates. International law provides both the tool and the method for operationalizing such concerted action at the international level. International law in the post-war era has shifted from the law of peaceful coexistence, to that of cooperation[8] and now, increasingly, to the law of coordination. This shift has occurred on the basis of the *acquis* painstakingly negotiated by our predecessors and concretized in the law. Once incorporated into law, it becomes very difficult to revert back to the prior position since it would require the abrogation of existing law (which is by design a difficult thing to do).

Such outcome of the process just described is not always fully appreciated, especially by those who claim that incorporating societal gains into law serves to retard further progress. Law, particularly international law, has a built-in tension between stability and change. While the focus is usually on the change part (some things will be said below about it), the primary reason for international law is stability. By incorporating gains in treaties, states are in essence leveraging the promise of stability. As such, stability is actually a feature, not a bug.

However, the law is not timeless. Just as society is constantly in flux, so too the law can change and does change. Depending on one's perspective, it is in fact constantly changing. Indeed, providing a predictable and stable process for change is exactly one of the functions of law (including, very much so, international law). For current purposes, the key point to appreciate is that once progress is incorporated into law, it then becomes the minimum threshold for future gains. It is the only game in town and as such becomes the springboard for future efforts. What emerges then is a cyclical process where progress is precisely achieved through sequential incorporation into law. Progress thus becomes measured by reference to the law.[9]

Second, contemporary international law exists in many forms. It is true that it is still a system predominantly anchored by international treaties (now numbering in the tens of thousands and growing). However, it is also accompanied by a robust body of customary international law. The proliferation of states in the international community has led to a veritable explosion in the sheer amount of state practice (some of which accompanied by the required *opinio juris*).[10] The revival of customary international law is also a consequence, in no small measure, of a similar proliferation of courts and tribunals (resulting in much exploration of evidence of the existence of customary obligations, in the absence of applicable treaty rules).

---

[8] See Wolfgang Friedmann, *The Changing Structure of International Law* (Stevens & Sons 1964).
[9] See Thomas Skouteris, *The Notion of Progress in International Law Discourse* (T M C Asser Press 2010).
[10] See Michael Scharf, *Customary International Law in Times of Fundamental Change: Recognizing Grotian Moments* (CUP 2013).

While these have certainly been important developments, the most significant (including for present purposes) has been the emergence of a penumbra of non-binding norms (soft law). Despite being a relatively recent phenomenon, the contemporary body of soft law already dwarves that of its hard-law counterpart. There are several reasons for this development, some of which are pertinent for present purposes. As a practical matter, treaties are complicated (and expensive) to negotiate and customary international law takes time to form and its existence is notoriously difficult to prove conclusively. There are also political reasons for why the transaction costs involved in the treaty route can be high (sometimes prohibitively so). Some states might prefer not to undertake their interactions at the international level through binding rules that may trigger further legal consequences as a result of non-performance.

In addition, negotiating a treaty is a complex political undertaking, not only from the external perspective of reaching a common understanding with another state or group of states. It also has an internal dimension: most modern states subject treaties to complex and lengthy national ratification processes, which involve a balancing of competing interests and views within the state itself. Such factors contribute to drawn-out treaty negotiations and are also at the root of why some such treaty outcomes prove underwhelming. While not necessarily completely absent, such constraints are less prominent when coming to the production of soft law, which can occur at a much quicker pace and subject to less national oversight. Also, and no less important, different from treaties which are notoriously difficult to modify, soft law can be changed, abrogated, or superseded relatively easily.

Furthermore, treaty-making is largely the province of states, in the sense that only states (and sometimes international organizations) have the authority, under international law, to enter into binding agreements (treaties). Non-state entities (other than international organizations) are not considered subjects of international law and as such do not, as a rule, possess treaty-making authority. No such limitation exists as regards soft law. Indeed, while states certainly are themselves generators of soft rules, a large proportion of such rules arise from the actions of non-state actors.[11] It is thus not that they actively choose the soft law mode, but rather that it is the only path open to them. Viewed from such perspective, the effect of the soft law mode is to democratize law-making, by including a much larger range of actors, over and above states.

The implications do not end there. The interaction between customary international law and soft law—relatively unexplored terrain—is arguably also very important. Soft law texts may actually reflect customary international law in an expository manner, or include components that enjoy such status (which is a

---

[11] Anne-Marie Slaughter, 'The Role of NGOs in International Law-Making' (2000) 285 Recueil des Cours 96.

phenomenon more common than usually admitted).[12] Importantly, soft law and the practice surrounding its implementation might also actually contribute to the formation of customary international law. While such processes may seem somewhat arcane and theoretical to those less familiar with international law, it is submitted that they should not be overlooked for the simple reason that customary international law is generally binding on all states, without any need for additional internal acceptance. In plain terms, it offers another (possibly easier) path to reaching the same goal as treaty-making. In fact, we can go even further by observing that law-making by treaty typically involves some component of codification of customary international law rules into treaty form.

Hence, viewed from such perspective, soft law that informs the formation of customary international law might also be part of a larger feedback loop that results in the consolidation of certain practices and understandings in the form of rules subsequently encapsulated in a treaty. While the SDGs were not necessarily drafted with the law in mind, they are already buttressed by a number of treaties dealing with specific aspects of what is more broadly considered to be sustainable development, such as in the area of the exploitation of the resources of the sea and the protection of the environment. What is more is that the SDGs can serve as a catalyst for the development of further, more specific, rules in the future.

On the other hand, sometimes norms are reflected in soft law instruments precisely because they (the norms) are not suitable for transformation into binding rules (whether on the basis of custom or treaty). There exists a vast plethora of standards and norms, typically of a more technical nature, which by their nature, need not be included in a treaty (perhaps because doing so would be overkill or because they are of a more ephemeral nature). Given the inherently imprecise delimitation of the concept, such norms would be considered as applicable 'soft law', regardless of whether the authors had had any understanding or expectation that theirs was also a legal undertaking. The precise specification of the nature of such rules is almost beside the point. Instead, what matters is the valuable role they play in providing context and content for 'hard' rules.

In point of fact, while all such options are provided by international law to be pursued individually, the real power lies in their combined use. Indeed, this is already happening. There exist today areas of common interest to the international community as a whole regulated by a network of interlocking treaties (sometimes anchored in international organizations and serviced by international Secretariats), buttressed by a body of customary law rules, and filled out by a penumbra of soft rules in the form of accompanying guidance and policies for interpretation and

---

[12] The views of the present writer on this point are presented in more detail in: Arnold N Pronto, 'Understanding the Hard/Soft Distinction in International Law' (2015) 48 Vand J Transnat'l L 941. For a critique of soft law, see Jean D'Aspremont, 'Softness in International Law: A Self-Serving Quest for New Legal Materials' (2008) 19 EJIL 1075.

implementation (and which may straddle the divide with customary international law). What emerges is a complex picture of the nuanced interplay between 'hard' and 'soft' rules, providing at the same time both rigidity (structure) and flexibility.

It is in such arrangements that one then finds the 'forward-looking' role of international law, referred to earlier. Law, not least international law, is very much also about aspiration. At a minimum, hortatory components abound in hard and soft rules alike. But, even binding rules reflect a certain vision of a reality reflected in a circumscribed range of permissible or required conduct of states. Such understandings and preferences are incorporated into international law precisely in order to ensure a desired outcome (or range of possible outcomes) in the future. As indicated earlier, progress is baked into the law-making process, which takes the form of a cyclical process of promotion of ideas followed by consolidation of gains on the basis of which further progress is attempted, and so on.

This also means that compliance and implementation of the law can provide a litmus test of sorts for measuring progress in achieving societal goals. There is much to be said about compliance and implementation (some of which will appear below) but doing so would require a detour beyond the intended scope of the present chapter. Suffice it to point out that there is a general perception that international law has a weak system of implementation, in the sense of a relatively underdeveloped system of compulsion. This misses the basic point that such an arrangement actually arises more by design than by defect. International law is, generally speaking, a horizontal system of law. States take part in it voluntarily because it is in their interest to coordinate their actions with other states. While the possibility of the settlement of disputes through the judicial or arbitral process has expanded in recent years, the jurisdiction of existing courts and tribunals is limited (it being itself a voluntarist undertaking). Instead, the system of implementation in international law is more diffuse (than that under national law) and also includes among its options modes of enforcement in the political realm. In fact, the problem might not be as extensive as made out by standard critiques of international law.

Overall, most international law is implemented most of the time, precisely because states want (or see it in their interest) to do so. This is not to deny that there exist challenges when coming to ensuring implementation. Rather, it is important to maintain a sense of overall perspective on these matters.

In fact, sometimes implementation is not strictly speaking the goal. Law can also play a regulatory function. Its mere existence serves to constrain actions. How do we know what actions are permissible or recommended, or for that matter, impermissible or inadvisable? This is typically done by reference to a legal rule. It is not a question then of implementation but rather of regulation. This is best illustrated through the example of proscription. The best way of determining what actions are impermissible or even unlawful is by reference to law. It is a principle of law, including international law, that if there is no rule prohibiting an action, then generally speaking that action is, by definition, lawful.[13] We can only speak of unlawfulness in the context of an existing explicit legal prohibition.

The corollary of this seemingly straightforward rule is that if the goal is to constrain the actions of states, then there needs to be a legal rule in place (binding on those states) prohibiting other actions. If no such rule is in place, then states retain their freedom of action. In other words, not only might law be desirable, in some contexts, it might actually be required in order to achieve certain outcomes.

At the same time, and notwithstanding the above, it is important to remain sanguine about the law's limitations. Reference has already been made to the problem of implementation. The reality is that while the law might play a role in guiding the proverbial horse to the water, in many cases it will not guarantee that the thirst will be quenched. Therefore, a true appreciation of the role of law also implies a modicum of humility and acceptance of the fact that in some circumstances, law (including international law) will necessarily be limited to playing a secondary (even if still necessary) role.

3. The Challenge for International Law

A key challenge facing international law is how to sustain its relevance. The role of international law in sustainable development is also about its potential for affecting the lives of hundreds of millions (if not more) of people. The success of the law then is to be measured in relation to its qualitative impact in furthering the cause of sustainable development (as seen by the extent to which the SDGs are met by the end of the present decade). As already stated, this is relatively uncharted territory for international law, and its success will also be important for its ability to be harnessed in confronting other large-scale challenges facing humanity (such as those posed by climate change). As such, it is important to avoid pursuing law for the sake of the law.

Rather, the key to unlocking the law's potential lies in its effectiveness: it has to resonate with its intended audience. What is more is that it not only has to be effective, but it has to be seen as such (both in terms of fostering accountability and in actually contributing to making a difference 'on the ground'). When coming to designing new law, or formulating a response based on existing law, it is therefore really important to think about its perceived overall effectiveness.[14]

Implementation is central to effectiveness. Much time and effort are already spent by legal thinkers and practitioners alike on how best to ensure implementation. Quantifying and establishing criteria for measuring the success of potential

---

[13] *The Case of the SS 'Lotus'* [1927] Series A No 10 (PCIJ).
[14] See, generally, Jean d'Aspremont, *Epistemic Forces in International Law* (Edward Elgar 2016) 167–74.

outcomes envisaged in the law has increasingly become a feature of legal discourse. No attempt will be made herein at a recapitulation of all those efforts. Rather, this section is dedicated to the simple assertion that ensuring effectiveness is also a function of the ability to leverage relationships with other communities engaged in the same process.

In the previous section, we explored the role and function of the law, particularly international law. International lawyers are almost by definition protagonists for a basic idea (or even worldview), namely the rule of law. Yet, in many of the thematic areas of activity falling within the broad umbrella of sustainable development, such idea is at times but one organizing concept among several (sometimes many) others. As suggested above, this means that when interacting with other professional communities, international lawyers may need to confront the threshold question of (or even doubts as to) what contribution the law can realistically make?

However, this works in the opposite direction as well. As lawyers engaged in these matters, we also need to be receptive to ideas and concepts originating from outside of the law.[15] It is really important to step down from our ivory towers and engage on the playing field with other professional and epistemic communities. To be fair, this is already happening in some quarters. Scientific information is already routinely influencing the law, both in how it is crafted and interpreted. The argument made herein is that this needs to be broadened to include other communities as well and deepened so as to also be reflected at the theoretical level.

Sustainable development is also the province of a number of other professional communities and implicates questions of economics, environmental science, politics, development policy, demographics, and so on. Many of these communities have been hard at work on the problem for decades and have well-established theoretical and empirical models. International law should aspire to benefit from such knowledge. In short, this is a plea for a greater multi-disciplinary approach, with all the complexity and challenges (and obligatory buzzwords) that come with it. There is strength in diversity of thought and experience. In order to make a meaningful contribution, international law (and international lawyers) should embrace the multidisciplinary approach and engage with others already occupying the space. This might also mean on occasion letting go of traditional guardrails and adapting the legal technique with a view to finding novel solutions to novel problems.

Such an approach requires an appreciation for the interconnectedness of our work with that of others. International lawyers should actively seek out opportunities to interface and leverage synergies with such communities and stakeholders. It also requires a recognition both of the impact of the law on the work of others, as well as the contribution that they can make to the law. What this implies is a greater orientation towards systems thinking, with the legal dimension being but

---

[15] See Philip Alston, 'The Myopia of the Handmaidens: International Lawyers and Globalization' (1997) 3 EJIL 435.

one piece of a larger puzzle. This may require giving other communities a stake in the success of the law, by allowing them a say in its creation and implementation.

It may also mean greater openness to being flexible and creative in how lawyers approach the legal dimensions of the problems at hand. Traditional legal solutions might not always provide the best course of action. Indeed, we need to admit that on occasion the promise of the law has been constrained by its traditional contours. New understandings of existing rules and procedures might need to be pursued. Emphasis might have to be placed more on ensuring greater inter-disciplinary policy coherence, and less on legal orthodoxy. In some cases, entirely new approaches to the law that take into account cross-cutting concerns and considerations might have to be developed. The point being made here is that we might best do this by leveraging the knowledge (and solutions) developed by others.

Why do this? The answer lies in the opening thought of this section: that the relevance of the law is tied to its effectiveness. The question then is how do we enhance the effectiveness of the law? The submission herein is that we do this in various ways, including by incorporating, to the extent possible, the value-added of other epistemic communities engaged in the same endeavour. Their efforts can provide context and content to the law, and contribute to the measurement of its success.[16] Of these three, the latter is particularly important. Seeking the input of such other communities might also provide a reality check, as to what actions are appropriate (regardless of their 'legality') or even feasible.

Let's take one example by way of illustration of these ideas: international efforts at promoting sustainable development rest on several assumptions, one of which is the significance of international cooperation. That is why states pursue the matter at the international level, including both at and through international organizations. International cooperation is at the heart of much of the work of the UN and other international organizations as well. What is the role of law in international cooperation? Can one say that there exists a legal obligation to cooperate? The quick positivist answer is likely 'yes'. There exist examples of treaty provisions envisaging cooperation in the sharing of information and scientific know-how, in the coordination of activities, in providing early warning and in coming to the aid of other states in times of crisis, to name but a few. But, does it makes sense to analyse such obligations through the traditional Hohfeldian rights-obligations construction, such that the presence of the obligation, framed in legal terms, implies the existence of a corresponding right under international law to receive such cooperation? The traditional conception of international law compels an answer in the affirmative.

However, the consequence of such a conclusion is that non-performance of the obligation would amount to an internationally wrongful act and potentially trigger

---

[16] See Malgosia Fitzmaurice, 'The Contribution of Environmental Law to the Development of Modern International Law' in Jerzy Makarczyk (ed), *Theory of International Law at the Threshold of the 21st Century: Essays in honour of Krzysztof Skubiszewski* (Kluwer 1996) 909–25.

the international responsibility of the non-performing state. Such a situation could then, still theoretically, fall to be adjudicated by an international court. However, how realistic is such an outcome? Many, if not most, involved in the non-legal aspects of the work on sustainable development will likely confirm that it is not realistic at all; that the idea of adjudicating the legal interests involved in the pursuit of sustainable development through international courts is simply a non-starter. Cooperation is a voluntarist action par excellence. The idea that states could be compelled to do so goes against the grain and could actually have a chilling effect by discouraging future commitments to cooperate for fear of being sued in an international court.

Such insight is valuable both in its own right, but also because it should then trigger a conversation as to where the disconnect between the law and reality actually lies? Perhaps, we need a different conception of what is meant by a legal obligation to cooperate. In fact, the law already does some of the work on this through the mechanism of the distinction (drawn entirely from the creative imagination of lawyers) between obligations of conduct and those of result. Once repackaged as an obligation of conduct (the scope of which is a function of the resources available to the state to cooperate), and not necessarily one to ensure a particular result, then a different, more nuanced, outcome emerges.

Two points of relevance for present purposes arise out of this. First, testing the efficacy of the solutions provided by the law by reference to the understanding of others introduces an element of realism that can only strengthen the effectiveness of the law. Second, it is quite conceivable that the knowledge and collective expertise of such other groups could be mined to provide further such creative solutions, which could in turn be enlisted in the service of enhancing the relevance of the law.

4. Conclusion

This chapter started with a question: why law? Perhaps it could have been better framed as: why not law? The expansion of international law into areas beyond its traditional remit has brought it (and by extension, international lawyers) into contact with other professions (and professional communities). This is also very much the case when confronting the various facets of sustainable development, the contemporary understanding of which has likewise grown to include areas traditionally regulated by international law, such that there is an increasing overlap with international law.

The argument made herein is that there is value in embracing such interaction. While it brings with it certain responsibilities (to promote an understanding of the role and function of the law), there are also potential benefits for enhancing the effectiveness of international law and thereby its overall relevance.

PART II
THE ROLE OF HUMAN RIGHTS LAW

4
The Triangle of Human Rights, International Law, and Sustainable Development

Jan Wouters and Michiel Hoornick

1. Introduction

This chapter explores the triangular relationship between human rights obligations of states and international organizations, international law, and (sustainable) development. It first considers how international human rights obligations of states and of international organizations affect these actors' policies and practices in the field of development and the implementation of the United Nations' (UN's) Sustainable Development Goals (SDGs), and how such obligations are being implemented and/or integrated in these policies and practices.

Second, we explore the relationship between international law and the SDGs: how is this relationship unfolding in the run-up to 2030? Are the SDGs themselves (as well as their targets and indicators) gradually becoming part of public international law? Finally, we consider how a 'human rights-based approach' (HRBA) to (sustainable) development has been conceived and operationalized in practice and to what extent such approach is explicitly grounded in international (human rights) law.

2. Impact of International Human Rights Obligations on Development Policies and Practices, including the Implementation of the SDGs

In terms of thematic areas covered, the UN 2030 Agenda for Sustainable Development (2030 Agenda) constitutes the most ambitious and elaborate bid for sustainable development to date. The SDGs are also the most recent step in an international normative process that has been ongoing for at least four decades. The concept of sustainable development can be traced back to the 1987 World Commission on Environment and Development (the Brundtland Commission), which defined it as 'development that meets the needs of the present without compromising the ability of future generations to meet their own needs'.[1]

This intergenerational element, complemented by an increased realization of the finity of the planet and the interconnectedness of economic, social, and environmental issues, lies at the foundations of 2030 Agenda.[2] Moreover, whereas the focus of the SDGs' predecessor, the UN Millennium Development Goals (MDGs), was on a limited number of developmental problems, the SDGs adopt a more expansive definition of sustainable development[3] which goes further than economic growth, but also includes a broad range of social and environmental concerns.

Human rights and sustainable development share a number of the same philosophical propositions and aim to protect humanity from a wide range of dangers, including 'the depletion of natural resources, increase of poverty and exploitation of human beings, especially the most vulnerable'.[4] Together, they constitute two of the three interconnected pillars of the UN—next to the maintenance of peace and security.[5] Writing on the MDGs in 2005, former UN Special Rapporteur on extreme poverty and human rights, Phillip Alston, noted that the human rights and development agendas resemble 'ships passing one another in the night, each with little awareness that the other is there, and with little if any sustained engagement with one another'.[6] Yet, international human rights obligations of states and of international organizations affect these actors' policies and practices in the field of development and—since 2015—the implementation of the SDGs.

The MDGs made an explicit distinction between responsibilities of the Global North and South. By contrast the SDGs stipulate that both developing and developed states are responsible for their own sustainable development,[7] although each

---

[1] Brundtland Commission, *Report of the World Commission on Environment and Development (Brundtland Report)* (A/42/1987 11, 1987); Chris Sneddon, Richard B Howarth, and Richard B Norgaard, 'Sustainable Development in a Post-Brundtland World' (2006) 57 Ecol Econ 253.

[2] Yong-Shik Lee, 'Sustainable Development and the SDGs: A Note on Current Development' (SSRN Scholarly Paper 3367957, Social Science Research Network, 2019) <https://papers.ssrn.com/abstract=3367957> accessed 22 May 2023.

[3] Joyeeta Gupta and Courtney Vegelin, 'Sustainable Development Goals and Inclusive Development' (2016) 16 Int Environ Agreem-P 433, 434. The eight MDGs focused on extreme poverty and hunger; universal primary education; gender equality and women empowerment; child mortality; maternal health; the fights against HIV/AIDS, malaria, and other diseases; environmental sustainability; and global partnership.

[4] Béatrice Delzangles, 'Les Objectifs de Développement Durable des Nations Unies: Une Approche Renouvelée des Droits Humains?' (2019) 104 Communications 119, 121 (hereafter 'Les Objectifs de Développement Durable des Nations Unies').

[5] UN General Assembly, World Summit Outcome, A/RES/60/1, 16 September 2005, para 9; Emmanuelle Jouannet-Tourme, *Le Droit International* (2nd edn, PUF 2016) 84–121.

[6] Philip Alston, 'Ships Passing in the Night: The Current State of the Human Rights and Development Debate Seen through the Lens of the Millennium Development Goals' (2005) 27 Hum Rights Q 755.

[7] Philippe Hugon, 'Du Bilan Mitigé des Objectifs du Millénaire pour le Développement aux Difficultés de Mise en Œuvre des Objectifs de Développement Durable' (2016) 174 Mondes en Développement 15, 23; Les Objectifs de Développement Durable des Nations Unies (n 4) 122. In parallel, there was a similar development in climate agreements. The 1992 UNFCCC and its 1997 Kyoto Protocol made a distinction between so-called Annex I (developed) and Annex II (developing) countries, where the developed countries carried most of the responsibilities. The 2015 Paris Agreement

state still has its own challenges, depending on its context. The flexible thematic nature of the SDGs enables governments to focus on their own respective difficulties. Thus, while poverty alleviation and economic growth remain on the top of the agenda for least developed countries (LDCs), climate action, or gender equality may be a priority for states in the Global North. One particular target stands out in this regard. Goal 17.2 calls for developed countries to dedicate 0.7 per cent of their gross national incomes to official development assistance (ODA) to developing countries.[8]

While their respective agendas may operate separately from each other, the fulfilment of human rights and the achievement of sustainable development are integrally connected. As acknowledged by the UN, without human rights, (sustainable) development has no chance.[9] When a child cannot go to school, when a migrant worker does not enjoy safe labour standards, or when minorities cannot enjoy their civil and political rights, development will be hampered. 2030 Agenda itself notes that 'the achievement of full human potential and of sustainable development is not possible if one half of humanity continues to be denied its full human rights and opportunities'.[10]

This has been recognized in a number of the key human rights treaties. For instance, the preamble of the UN Convention on the Elimination of All Forms of Discrimination against Women (CEDAW) notes that its States Parties are 'convinced that the full and complete development of a country, the welfare of the world and the cause of peace require the maximum participation of women on equal terms with men in all fields'.[11]

International law provides an elaborate toolbox to enforce or implement the broad range of human rights obligations set out in international or regional legal instruments. Human rights conventions are typically multilateral treaties, which often have legal effect in and of themselves, especially in 'monist' states, where

---

sets out its objective for the world as a collective ambition and although it still refers to the differentiated responsibilities, it sets out that all countries have a responsibility in mitigating climate change. See also David Freestone, 'The United Nations Framework Convention on Climate Change—The Basis for the Climate Change Regime' in Kevin R Gray, Richard Tarasofsky, and Cinnamon Carlarne (eds), *The Oxford Handbook of International Climate Change Law* (vol 1, OUP 2016) 97–119; *Adoption of the Paris Agreement* (FCCC/CP/2015/L9/Rev/1, 12 December 2015).

[8] UN General Assembly, *Transforming Our World: The 2030 Agenda for Sustainable Development* (A/RES/70/1, Goal 17.2, 2015) (hereafter '2030 Agenda'). Here too, there is a parallel with the climate change regime. The 2015 Paris Agreement and 2021 Glasgow Climate Pact both reaffirm that developed countries deliver on their commitment to mobilize US$100 billion a year to support developing countries on climate change mitigation, as first made in the 2011 Copenhagen Accord (COP17).

[9] See, inter alia, UNGA, *World Summit Outcome* (A/RES/60/1, 16 September 2005) para 9, recognizing that 'development, peace and security and human rights are interlinked and mutually reinforcing'. See also paras 72 and 135.

[10] 2030 Agenda (n 8) para 20.

[11] *Convention on the Elimination of All Forms of Discrimination Against Women* (1249 UNTS 13, 18 December 1979) (opened for signature 18 December 1979, entered into force 3 September 1981).

provisions of international treaties are in many cases directly applicable before the national courts.[12] This makes that international human rights law simultaneously has horizontal as well as vertical relationships. On the one hand, it is a subset of international law, where states enter into horizontal commitments vis-à-vis other states. Certain provisions included in human rights treaties outlawing the most serious human rights violations may have an *erga omnes* character:[13] by their very nature, they are the concern of all states and generate obligations to the international community as a whole (eg prohibition of genocide, protection against slavery, prohibition of racial discrimination). Among others, the International Court of Justice (ICJ) has applied the International Convention on the Elimination of Racial Discrimination (ICERD) and the Convention against Torture (CAT) in this manner.[14] At the same time, human rights treaties also set out vertical obligations for a State vis à vis its citizens and other persons under its jurisdiction. These commitments in turn lead to the promise of accountability and possible venues of enforcement that the development sphere does not have.

Moreover, the nine UN human rights treaties—including the International Covenant on Civil Political Rights (ICCPR) and the International Covenant on Economic, Social and Cultural Rights (ICESCR)—may have a broader effect by generating soft law (in addition to the binding hard law they contain). This may occur through the operation of their respective UN Treaty Bodies (UNTBs): each of these conventions is supervised by a supervising body mandated by their respective treaties to monitor their implementation through periodic reviews and/ or individual—and inter-state complaints.[15] In addition, regional instruments

---

[12] Jan Wouters, Cedric Ryngaert, Tom Ruys, and Geert De Baere, *International Law: A European Perspective* (Hart Publishing 2018) 179–80; Karen J Alter, *The New Terrain of International Law: Courts, Politics, Rights* (Princeton University Press 2014).

[13] International Law Commission, 'Draft Articles on Responsibility of States for Internationally Wrongful Acts' (2001) art 48(1)(b).

[14] ICJ, Questions relating to the Obligation to Prosecute or Extradite (*Belgium v Senegal*) (2012); ICJ, Application of the International Convention on the Elimination of All Forms of Racial Discrimination (*Qatar v United Arab Emirates*) (2018); ICJ, Application of the International Convention for the Suppression of the Financing of Terrorism and of the International Convention on the Elimination of All Forms of Racial Discrimination (*Ukraine v Russian Federation*) (2021). See, for the ICJ's jurisdiction, *International Convention on the Elimination of All Forms of Racial Discrimination* (660 UNTS 195, opened for signature 7 March 1966, entered into force 4 January 1969) art 22. See also the CEDAW art 29; *International Convention on the Protection of the Rights of All Migrant Workers and Members of Their Families* (2220 UNTS 3, opened for signature 18 December 1990, entered into force 1 July 2003) art 92; *Convention Against Torture and Other Cruel, Inhuman or Degrading Treatment or Punishment* (1465 UNTS 85, opened for signature 10 December 1984, entered into force 26 June 1987) art 30; *International Convention for the Protection of All Persons from Enforced Disappearance* (2716 UNTS 3, opened for signature 20 December 2006, entered into force 23 December 2010) art 42.

[15] Walter Kälin and Jörg Künzli, *The Law of International Human Rights Protection* (2nd edn, OUP 2019) 204; Jane Connors, 'United Nations' in Daniel Moeckli and others (eds), *International Human Rights Law* (3rd edn, OUP 2018) 369–410. Until recently, such state-to-state complaints were not used. In 2018, the CERD received three complaints and accepted their admissibility. For an update on *State of Qatar v Kingdom of Saudi Arabia*; *State of Qatar v United Arab Emirates*; *State of Palestine v Israel*, see UNHCR, 'Inter-state Communications Committee on the Elimination of Racial Discrimination' <https://www.ohchr.org/EN/HRBodies/CERD/Pages/InterstateCommunications.aspx> accessed 22 May 2023.

such as the Charter of Fundamental Rights of the European Union, the European Convention on Human Rights (ECHR), the African Charter on Human and Peoples' Rights (ACHPR or 'Banjul Charter'), and the Inter-American Convention on Human Rights (ACHR) have their own courts and enforcement procedures.[16]

Beyond their standard application to states, international organizations (IOs) are not free from international human rights obligations either. As indicated above, international human rights law has long been built on the special relationship between the individual and the state as respective right-holder and duty-bearer.[17] However, as IOs operate increasingly autonomously from states they have their proper rights and duties under international law. Their separate international legal personality has been recognized by the ICJ in its influential 1949 Advisory Opinion on Reparation for Injuries Suffered in the Service of the United Nations.[18] Furthermore, in Interpretation of the Agreement of 25 March 1951 between the WHO and Egypt (1980), the ICJ held that ' [i]nternational organizations are subjects of international law and, as such, are bound by any obligations incumbent upon them under general rules of international law, under their constitutions or under international agreements to which they are parties'.[19]

More recently, in 2011, the International Law Commission (ILC) produced Articles on the Responsibility of International Organizations (ARIO), which elaborate on internationally wrongful acts in connection with the conduct of an IO.[20] Moreover, it has been increasingly accepted that non-state actors including IOs have a vital role in the development and implementation of international (human rights) norms.[21] As most IOs are not a party to human rights conventions—the

---

[16] Christian Tomuschat, *Human Rights: Between Idealism and Realism* (3rd edn, OUP 2014) 216–19 (hereafter 'Human Rights').

[17] Andrew Clapham, 'Looking at Rights' in Andrew Clapham, *Human Rights: A Very Short Introduction* (2nd edn, OUP 2015); Paola Gaeta, Jorge E Viñuales, and Salvatore Zappalà, *Cassese's International Law* (3rd edn, OUP 2020) 404 (hereafter 'Cassese's International Law').

[18] *Reparation for Injuries Suffered in the Service of the Nations, Advisory Opinion* (1949) ICJ Rep 174 (ICGJ) 232 (ICJ 1949).

[19] *Interpretation of the Agreement of 25 March 1951 between the WHO and Egypt* (ICJ Rep 73, 1980) para 37.

[20] ILC, 'Draft Articles on the Responsibility of International Organizations' (2011) art 1 <https://legal.un.org/ilc/texts/instruments/english/draft_articles/9_11_2011.pdf> accessed 22 May 2023 (hereafter 'Draft Articles').

[21] International organizations may have a role in international law-making through decisions, declarations, recommendations, or codes of practice, and as such may either confirm existing norms, challenge existing customary law, or even create new law. For instance, the World Meteorological Organization (WMO) and the United Nations Environment Programme (UNEP) established the International Panel on Climate Change (IPCC) in 1988, whose reports formed the factual basis of the 1992 UNFCCC and consequent climate change conventions. Similarly, the UNHCR annually convenes its Executive Committee in order to discuss and improve its budget and policies, as well as to adopt the so-called Concluding Observations which have an important role in the development of the legal framework on refugees. See Nigel D White, 'Lawmaking' in Jacob Katz Cogan, Ian Hurd, and Ian Johnstone (eds), *The Oxford Handbook of International Organizations* (OUP 2016) 559–80; Cassese's International Law (n 17) 197; Navraj Singh Ghaleigh, 'Science and Climate Change Law—The Role of the IPCC in International Decision-Making' in Cinnamon Piñon Carlarne, Kevin R Gray, and Richard Tarasofsky (eds), *The Oxford Handbook of International Climate Change Law* (OUP 2016) 55–71, 58;

exception is the European Union's (EU's) participation in the UN Convention on the Rights of Persons with Disabilities[22]—the human rights obligations of IOs are mainly based on customary international law, *jus cogens,* general principles and engagements in their founding treaties or practice.[23]

In addition to the legal mechanisms available, both states and IOs have non-legal incentives to respect human rights that include upholding, protecting, or building a reputation,[24] socialization with like-minded states or organizations,[25] or—in the case of breaches of international law—retaliation.[26]

Human rights obligations under international or regional legal frameworks continue to apply and are not replaced by obligations in the field of (sustainable) development. Development does not occur in, nor create, a legal vacuum. Law continues to bind states when they engage in development activities, whether as donors or partners. In numerous instances, 2030 Agenda refers to the obligations of states set out in international human rights treaties.[27] They are not mutually exclusive, but rather two sides of the same coin. While the history of international thinking on (sustainable) development has been amply documented,[28] it is useful to recall the way in which international human rights law has engaged with development since the 1960s, especially through the configuration of the right to development.[29]

Marion Fresia, 'Building Consensus within UNHCR's Executive Committee: Global Refugee Norms in the Making' (2014) 27 J Refug Stud 514.

[22] Convention on the Rights of Persons with Disabilities (2515 UNTS 3, opened for signature 13 December 2006, entered into force 3 May 2008).

[23] See, inter alia, Matteo Tondini, 'The "Italian Job": How to Make International Organisations Compliant with Human Rights and Accountable for Their Violation by Targeting Member States' in Jan Wouters and others (eds), *Accountability for Human Rights Violations by International Organisations* (Intersentia 2010) 169–212, 169, 177. On the question whether IOs are bound by the human rights treaties concluded by their Member States see, Frederik Naert, 'Binding International Organisations to Member State Treaties or Responsibility of Member States for Their Own Actions in the Framework of International Organisations' in Jan Wouters and others (eds), *Accountability for Human Rights Violations by International Organisations* (Intersentia 2010) 129–68, 130–55.

[24] Emilie M Hafner-Burton and Christina J Schneider, 'The Company You Keep: International Organizations and the Reputational Effects of Membership' (2019) 113 AJIL Unbound 242; Kristina Daugirdas, 'Reputation as a Disciplinarian of International Organizations' (2019) 113 Am J Int'l L 221; Rachel Brewster, 'Unpacking the State's Reputation' (2009) 50 Harv Int'l L J 231.

[25] Ryan Goodman and Derek Jinks, *Socializing States: Promoting Human Rights through International Law* (OUP 2013).

[26] Denis Alland, 'Countermeasures of General Interest' (2002) 13 EJIL 1221; Michel Virally, 'Le Principe de Réciprocité dans le Droit International Contemporain' (*Collected Courses of the Hague Academy of International Law*, 1967) <https://referenceworks.brillonline.com:443/entries/the-hague-academy-collected-courses/le-principe-de-reciprocite-dans-le-droit-international-contemporain-volume-122-A9789028615922_01> accessed 22 May 2023.

[27] It has been estimated that 'over 90% of SDG targets are embedded in human rights treaties': Permanent Missions of Denmark and Chile to the UN in Geneva, 'Human Rights and the SDGs. Pursuing Synergies' (2017) 4.

[28] United Nations Development Programme (UNDP), 'Human Development Report 2000: Human Rights and Human Development' (2000) <https://hdr.undp.org/content/human-development-report-2000> accessed 22 May 2023; Martha C Nussbaum and Amartya Sen (eds), *The Quality of Life* (Clarendon Press 1993).

[29] Already in 1968, the Proclamation of Tehran at the twentieth anniversary of the UDHR proclaimed that: 'the widening gap between the economically developed and developing countries impedes

Beyond the first and second generation of rights commonly distinguished (civil and political versus economic, social, and cultural rights), a third generation of rights has emerged in more recent decades. Where the first two generations took the individual as the starting point, a fundamental characteristic of this third generation is its collective nature and the possibility of groups or communities as rights-holders. The right to development was first elaborated by the Senegalese lawyer Kéba Mbaye in 1972[30] and later proclaimed by the UN General Assembly as an 'inalienable' human right in 1986.[31] While the right to development has yet to be included in a binding treaty on the international level, article 22(2) of the ACHPR does recognize the right to development, as well (in article 24) the right to a 'general satisfactory environment'. More recently, the UN Human Rights Council and the UN General Assembly (UNGA) also adopted resolutions recognizing that a clean, healthy, and sustainable environment is a human right.[32]

In addition, while 2030 Agenda, proclaimed in an UNGA resolution, is not in itself legally binding, and consists of voluntary commitments for a better planet, many of its individual provisions are covered by international human rights treaties.[33] According to a 2016 report by the UN Secretary-General (UNSG), 'more than half of the targets of the SDGs […] are already being monitored […] by the [UN] human rights mechanisms', primarily on economic, social, and

---

the realization of human rights in the international community' and that 'the achievement of lasting progress in the implementation of human rights is dependent upon sound and effective national and international policies of economic and social development'. Similarly, the 1972 Stockholm Declaration states that 'both aspects of man's environment, the natural and the man-made, are essential to his well-being and to the enjoyment of basic human rights—even the right to life itself'. Proclamation of Teheran, Final Act of the International Conference on Human Rights (13 May 1968) paras 12 and 13; *Stockholm Declaration and Action Plan for the Human Environment* (UN Doc A/CONF 48/14/Rev1, 16 June 1972).

[30] Kéba Mbaye, 'Le Droit au Développement comme un Droit de l'Homme' [1972] Revue des Droits de l'Homme 503. As noted by Uvin, this should be linked to the debates on the New International Economic Order (NIEO), where countries in the Global South—not in the least the members of the Organisation of the Petroleum Exporting Countries (OPEC)—sought to redefine international relations. Peter Uvin, 'From the Right to Development to the Rights-Based Approach: How "Human Rights" Entered Development' (2007) 17(4–5) Dev Pract 597–606 (hereafter 'From the Right to Development').

[31] *Declaration of the Right to Development* (A/RES/41/128, 4 December 1986).

[32] *The Human Right to a Clean, Healthy and Sustainable Environment* (A/HRC/RES/48/13, 8 October 2021); *The Human Right to a Clean, Healthy and Sustainable Environment* (A/RES/76/300, 28 July 2022). In addition, the UN Human Rights Council established the mandates of a number of special mandate holders (SMHs) to further develop the implementation of these respective rights, including the Intergovernmental Open-ended Working Group on the Right to Development (1998), Special Rapporteur on Human Rights and the Environment (2012), Special Rapporteur on the Right to Development (2016), and Expert Mechanism on the Right to Development (2019). For an updated list of SMHs, see UNHCR, 'Special Mandate Holders Thematic Mandates' <https://spinternet.ohchr.org/ViewAllCountryMandates.aspx?Type=TM&lang=en> accessed 23 May 2023.

[33] The Danish Institute for Human Rights (DIHR) established a tool that links the seventeen SDGs and their targets to the applicable conventions and declarations on human rights, labour rights, and the environment. DIHR, 'The Human Rights Guide to the Sustainable Development Goals' (2019) <https://sdg.humanrights.dk/en> accessed 23 May 2023 (hereafter 'The Human Rights Guide').

cultural rights.[34] This allows the existing compliance mechanisms to also take into account the commitments under 2030 Agenda. This applies particularly for the UNTBs. Among others the CEDAW, the Committee on the Elimination of Racial Discrimination (CERD) and the Committee on the Rights of the Child (CRC) regularly refer to the SDGs while monitoring the implementation of their respective treaties.[35] This can include extending recommendations to 'take into account' particular Goals and targets or to 'take fully into account its obligations under the Covenant in the implementation of the 2030 Agenda for Sustainable Development at the national level'.[36] In another example, CAT recommended Uzbekistan to 'take appropriate measures to fulfil Goal 16, target 10.1'.[37]

Yet, these interactions have their limits. For instance, the UNTBs do not cover all seventeen Goals, and 2030 Agenda and human rights treaties are qualitatively different. The SDGs have been adopted as an UNGA resolution (see also section 3.a in this chapter), while human rights treaties have legally binding force. Not all human rights mechanisms use the SDGs to their advantage. For instance, the SDGs are rarely referred to in the Universal Periodic Review (UPR) of the UN Human Rights Council.[38] Moreover, as only a limited group of countries has the facilities and resources to keep up with the high amount of reporting, the resulting 'reporting fatigue' may also affect cross-references to the SDGs.[39]

---

[34] *Question of the Realization in all Countries of Economic, Social and Cultural Rights* (A/HRC/34/25, 2016) para 41.

[35] Concluding Observations on Austria 2020 CRC/C/AUT/CO/5, paras 5, 13, 23, 34, 36–37; *General Recommendation No 38 on Trafficking in Women and Girls in the Context of Global Migration* (CEDAW/C/GC/38, 2020) para 21; *General Recommendation No 36 on Preventing and Combating Racial Profiling by Law Enforcement Officials* (CERD/C/GC/36, 2020) para 9; Michiel Hoornick, 'Conference Paper: Achieving the Sustainable Development Goals through Human Rights' (Academic Council on the United Nations System 2021).

[36] Concluding Observations on Greece (2019) CRPD/C/GRC/CO/1, para 8; *Concluding Observations on Latvia* (E/C12/LVA/CO/2, 2021) para 51.

[37] *Concluding Observations on Uzbekistan* (CAT/C/UZB/CO/5, 2020) para 68.

[38] Some countries do refer to the SDGs in their recommendations. Paraguay recommended Rwanda in November 2020 to '[e]stablish a permanent national mechanism for the implementation, reporting and monitoring of human rights recommendations, considering the possibility of receiving cooperation for this purpose, within the framework of Sustainable Development Goals 16 and 17' and Switzerland recommended Malawi to 'continue to fight against human trafficking and its root causes, as well as against the sexual exploitation of women and girls, in accordance with targets 5.2 and 8.7 of the Sustainable Development Goals, by setting up programmes to increase skills and women's income'. See UPR-Info, 'UPR Info's Database of UPR Recommendations and Voluntary Pledges' <https://upr-info-database.uwazi.io/> accessed 23 May 2023.

[39] Cosette D Creamer and Beth A Simmons, 'The Proof Is in the Process: Self-Reporting Under International Human Rights Treaties' (2020) 114 Am J Int'l L 1, 45.

3. Relationship between International Law and the SDGs

a. References to international law in 2030 Agenda

The 2030 Agenda does not set out a legally binding set of rules. It was adopted by consensus as Resolution 70/1 of the UNGA and thus, formally, is a legally non-binding instrument.[40] It would be hard to imagine a state facing countermeasures or sanctions for not living up to its commitments on sustainable development. Rather than being based on a division between duty-bearers and right-holders or reliant on legal accountability, the SDGs are organized as a common effort with a focus on collaboration. The annual High-level Panel Forum on Sustainable Development (HLPF) is the prime venue for countries to share their experiences and has 'the central role in overseeing follow-up and review at the global level'. In so-called 'Voluntary National Reviews' (VNRs), states set out their efforts to work towards 2030.[41] States are expected to submit a VNR every few years in order to track the process made.[42] The focus of these reports lies on the contributions made rather than the performance achieved, with little secondary opinions by civil society.[43] Yet, it does push states to provide transparency on their efforts, and to review their progress.

Still, the SDGs are not disconnected from international law. 2030 Agenda itself makes references to international legal instruments throughout the text, and some of the language used in the SDGs is covered by—or overlaps with—international law.

First, 2030 Agenda reaffirms the 'commitment' and 'respect' for international law on multiple occasions and makes specific references to binding legal documents, including the UN Framework Convention on Climate Change (UNFCCC) and the UN Convention on the Law of the Sea (UNCLOS).[44] It also reaffirms other (soft law) instruments on human rights and development, including the Universal Declaration on Human Rights (UDHR) and the 1992 Rio Declaration on Environment and Development (the Rio Declaration).[45] The Danish Institute for

---

[40] Following Chapter IV of the UN Charter, the UNGA may 'initiate studies and make recommendations to promote international political cooperation, the development and codification of international law, the realization of human rights and fundamental freedoms, and international collaboration in the economic, social, humanitarian, cultural, educational and health fields' (art 13). However, in terms of 'binding' decisions, the UNGA has the mandate to 'consider and approve' the UN budget (art 17) as well as to elect members of the UN Security Council, the UN Economic and Social Council, and the UN Trusteeship Council (art 18). *UN Charter* (1 UNTS XVI, 26 June 1945) (opened for signature 26 June 1945, entered into force 24 October 1945).

[41] 2030 Agenda (n 8) para 47.

[42] UNDESA, 'Voluntary National Reviews: Sustainable Development Knowledge Platform' <https://sustainabledevelopment.un.org/vnrs/> accessed 23 May 2023.

[43] Kate Donald and Sally-Anne Way, 'Accountability for the Sustainable Development Goals: A Lost Opportunity?' (2016) 30 Ethics Int Aff 201, 206 (hereafter 'Accountability for the Sustainable Development Goals').

[44] 2030 Agenda (n 8) paras 10, 18, 31, Goals 13(a) and 14(c).

[45] ibid 10–11.

Human Rights has identified a wide overlap between the seventeen Goals on the one hand, and international and regional human rights instruments, international labour standards, and key environmental instruments on the other hand.[46] To what extent the Goals already reflect international law varies by subject. This may not be the same for Goal 11 on sustainable cities as it might be for Goals 3 and 5 related to health or gender equality.[47]

Second, language used in 2030 Agenda may also feature in documents that are 'harder' in nature. For instance, as Béatrice Delzangles notes, sustainable development as a notion is already included in over 320 treaties and trade agreements.[48] In this way, the SDGs play a wider role in the development of particular norms. This applies particularly to Goal 13 on climate change, which refers to 'the commitment of all States to work for an ambitious and universal climate agreement' at the then upcoming climate conference in Paris, which would take place in December 2015 and resulted in the Paris Agreement.[49] As a treaty and binding legal instrument, the Paris Agreement has been referred to in recent court cases before the Court of Appeal of The Hague and the Administrative Court of Paris, which found that the respective Dutch and French government's inadequate action on climate change violated a duty of care to its citizens under the ECHR.[50]

b. 2030 Agenda as a Policy and Legal Instrument

The 2030 Agenda fits into a wider development of international law and global governance where 'goal-setting' is increasingly practiced as an alternative to rule-making.[51] From a legal perspective, this may raise issues of accountability, and authors have identified the lack of formal compliance monitoring for the SDGs as a missing piece.[52] As Philippe Hugon stated, the SDGs cannot be limited to a 'checklist of juxtaposed objectives'.[53] Similarly, Inga Winkler and Carmel Williams noted that, 'if the SDGs are to be more than lofty global goals, it is necessary to have transparent and binding accountability processes and mechanisms in place'.[54]

---

[46] The Human Rights Guide (n 33).

[47] SDG 3 on 'good health and well-being' and SDG 5 on 'gender equality' are well covered by the UDHR 1948, arts 2 and 25.1; International Covenant on Economic, Social and Cultural Rights 1966, arts 2.2, 3, and 12.1; CEDAW, particularly art 12.1.

[48] Les Objectifs de Développement Durable des Nations Unies (n 4) 120.

[49] 2030 Agenda (n 8) para 32; Paris Agreement 2015.

[50] In both cases, the domestic courts used articles 2 (the right to life) and 8 (the right to respect for private and family life): *Urgenda Foundation v Government of the Netherlands* [2018] ECLI:NL:GHDHA:2018:2610; *Association Oxfam Francais et al v République Française* [2021] No 1904967 [3 February 2021].

[51] Frank Biermann, Norichika Kanie, and Rakhyun Kim, 'Global Governance by Goal Setting: Novel Approach of the UN Sustainable Development Goals' (2017) 26–27 Curr Opin Environ Sustain 26.

[52] Accountability for the Sustainable Development Goals (n 43) 202.

[53] Hugon (n 7) 17.

[54] Inga T Winkler and Carmel Williams, 'The Sustainable Development Goals and Human Rights: A Critical Early Review' (2017) 21 Int J Hum Rights 1023, 1025.

The SDGs are not—technically speaking—legally binding, yet they are clearly not devoid of political commitment.[55] As stated in Resolution 70/1, 'each country has primary responsibility for its economic and social development'.[56] The repeatedly stated pledges to sustainable development and to 'leave no-one behind' raise the expectation that all countries strive towards the progressive implementation of the 2030 Agenda.[57] While countries may not comply in absolute terms, what matters is the extent to which they make progress towards achieving the Goals.[58] The focus on conduct rather than result is similar to the focus on progressive realisation in the context of economic, social, and cultural rights. For instance, article 2(1) of the ICESCR provides that:

[e]ach State Party to the present Covenant undertakes to take steps, individually and through international assistance and cooperation, especially economic and technical, to the maximum of its available resources, with a view to achieving progressively the full realization of the rights recognized in the present Covenant by all appropriate means, including particularly the adoption of legislative measures.

In this context, one should also highlight the focus on indicators as a means to track progress towards 2030 Agenda. The seventeen Goals and 169 targets that encompass 2030 Agenda are monitored through 231 unique indicators. Different international organizations are mandated with providing comprehensive data on the progress made and, in addition, states are expected to submit their own data in their VNRs.[59] During the yearly HLPF, states base their discussions on these indicators. Indicators provide clarity in an increasingly complex world, enable comparisons between countries, and help bureaucracies to draft better policy based on systematic measurement and data collection.[60]

However, the use of indicators is not the magic want as sometimes promised to be. The lack of data can be one obstacle, while oversimplification of numbers may not always reflect real-world realities. For instance, indicator 8.1.1 measures an annual growth rate of real GDP per capita, but it does not include the informal economy or voluntary work, nor the level of inequality within a particular area or sustainability of an economy. Similarly, renewable energy as measured in indicator 7.2.1 includes biofuels: a renewable source of energy that derives from biomass

---

[55] Graham Long, 'Underpinning Commitments of the Sustainable Development Goals: Indivisibility, Universality, Leaving No One Behind' in Duncan French and Louis J Kotzé (eds), *Sustainable Development Goals: Law, Theory and Implementation* (Edward Elgar 2018) 91–116, 92.
[56] 2030 Agenda (n 8) para 41.
[57] ibid preamble and paras 4, 26, 48, 72, 74(e).
[58] Xinyuan Dai, 'Why Comply? The Domestic Constituency Mechanism' (2005) 59 Int'l Org.
[59] 2030 Agenda (n 8) 47. The VNR's are available via Sustainable Development Knowledge Platform, 'Voluntary National Reviews' <https://sustainabledevelopment.un.org/vnrs/#VNRDatabase> accessed 23 May 2023.
[60] Kevin E Davis, Benedict Kingsbury, and Sally Engle Merry, 'Indicators as a Technology of Global Governance' (2012) 46 L & Soc'y Rev 71.

such as agricultural waste, woods, or crops such as corn and sugarcane. However, while they count as green energy, the environmental harm they cause is not taken into account.

c. 2030 Agenda and the Wider Development of International Law

The SDGs may also trickle down through other routes in international law and in the process take on a more legal character. A number of UN organizations have a special role in 'mainstreaming' the SDGs.[61] As is widely known, international organizations may have a role in international law-making through the confirmation of existing norms or even through (nudging) the generation of new rules, thereby possibly strengthening the legal status of the SDGs.[62]

The 2030 Agenda also pays particular attention to the regional and national levels.[63] At national level, accountability mechanisms could include National Action Plans on Business and Human Rights, ombudspersons, and National Human Rights Institutions (NHRI).[64] EU law has also been highlighted as a way in which the SDGs could gain in legal status.[65] This is particularly true for the fight against climate change. The European Green Deal and its ambitions are at the centre of EU policy, among others aiming to cut greenhouse gas emissions by at least 55 per cent by 2030. The 2021 European Climate Law gives further legal significance to some of these aims.[66]

Finally, 2030 Agenda may also have an impact on customary international law.[67] As indicated above, one of the great advantages of 2030 Agenda is its universal scope, as well as the continuous support it enjoys from the international community. In its founding UNGA resolution, 2030 Agenda is described as 'a charter for people and planet in the twenty-first century' and 'a decision of historical significance'.[68] The key notion of the SDGs to 'leave no-one behind' has been at the centre of global governance since 2015.[69] Both 2030 Agenda and its many follow-up

---

[61] *Mainstreaming of the Three Dimensions of Sustainable Development throughout the United Nations System* (A/74/72, 2019) paras 3, 11–20.
[62] See further Draft Articles (n 20).
[63] 2030 Agenda (n 8) paras 78–81.
[64] Accountability for the Sustainable Development Goals (n 43) 207–08.
[65] Maryna Rabinovych, 'The Legal Status and Effects of the Agenda 2030 within the EU Legal Order' (2020) 16 J Contemp Eur Res 182, 190 (hereafter 'The Legal Status and Effects').
[66] Regulation (EU) 2021/1119 of the European Parliament and of the Council of 30 June 2021 establishing the framework for achieving climate neutrality and amending Regulations (EC) No 401/2009 and (EU) 2018/1999 (European Climate Law) OJ 2021, L243/1. In recitals 4, 9, and 32 of the Preamble reference is made to the SDGs and 2030 Agenda.
[67] The Legal Status and Effects (n 65) 190.
[68] 2030 Agenda (n 8) 49–50.
[69] The Legal Status and Effects (n 65) 190.

dynamics and reports, including at regional and national levels, constitute practice (and possibly evidence of *opinio juris*) for the purposes of customary international law. Indeed, according to the ILC, 'diplomatic acts and correspondence; conduct in connection with resolutions adopted by an international organization or at an intergovernmental conference; conduct in connection with treaties; executive conduct, including operational conduct "on the ground"; legislative and administrative acts; and decisions of national courts', offer evidence of these.[70]

4. Human Rights-Based Approaches and (Sustainable) Development

In the run-up to 2030 Agenda, former High Commissioner for Human Rights Navanethem Pillay emphasized the importance of a Post-2015 Agenda that is 'built on a human rights-based approach, both in process and substance'.[71] The final UNGA Resolution 70/1 does integrate pro-human rights language and 'seeks to realize the human rights of all', resolves 'to protect human rights', and 'envisages a world of universal respect for human rights and human dignity'.[72] However, these references are limited to the preamble and introductory paragraphs. Only one of the Goals itself makes a weak reference to human rights.[73] Similarly, while the 2030 Agenda is 'grounded in the Universal Declaration of Human Rights, international human rights treaties, the Millennium Declaration and the 2005 World Summit Outcome',[74] none of the actual Goals makes reference to the relevant human rights treaties. Despite their significant subject matter overlaps, Goal 5 on gender equality does not refer to CEDAW. Goal 4 on education similarly does not mention the CRC.

Putting aside for a moment the added benefits of an HRBA to sustainable development, it would be good to recall what Jeffrey Dunoff referred to as the 'compliance trilemma', where drafters of international agreements have to balance between

---

[70] UNGA, *Report of the International Law Commission on the Work of its Seventieth Session* (RES/73/556, 2018) 17.

[71] 'Open Letter from the High Commissioner on Human Rights: Human Rights in the Post-2015 Agenda' (6 June 2013) 3 <https://www.ohchr.org/sites/default/files/Documents/Issues/MDGs/OpenLetterMS_Post2015.pdf> accessed 23 May 2023.

[72] 2030 Agenda (n 8) preamble and paras 3 and 8.

[73] Goal 4.7:

By 2030, ensure that all learners acquire the knowledge and skills needed to promote sustainable development, including, among others, through education for sustainable development and sustainable lifestyles, human rights, gender equality, promotion of a culture of peace and non-violence, global citizenship and appreciation of cultural diversity and of culture's contribution to sustainable development.

[74] 2030 Agenda (n 8) para 10.

widespread participation, ambitious legal norms, and high rates of compliance.[75] The SDGs are ambitious and have been universally accepted, but only after a long and complex negotiation process. In particular the G77 + China group rejected terminology on accountability and monitoring and asserted that this wording 'has no place and mandate in this debate'.[76] As Kate Donald and Sally-Anne Way note, many countries opposed this terminology, not because of a rejection of accountability from the state to its citizens, but rather to prevent 'finger pointing' by the Global North.[77] In this light, it would be unlikely that the 2030 Agenda would have been universally accepted with the same ambitions had it included references to binding human rights instruments and other legal accountability mechanisms.

Human rights entered the development world in more prominent terms in the 1990s, before which rights—or law more generally—played a relatively minor role.[78] As Peter Uvin observed, the new interest was attributable to the end of the Cold War and a renewed 'missionary zeal', in part because of a lack of government accountability and in part because of a search for a definition of development that extended beyond purely economic growth.[79] Normatively, an HRBA helps 'setting out a vision of what ought to be' and providing a normative framework for development.[80] Moreover, it grounds (sustainable) development in human rights law and accompanying obligations. Coming back to the SDG indicators on economic growth (8.1.1) and renewable energy (7.2.1) as referred to above, an HRBA provides for a more holistic understanding of what should be included in our understanding of these indicators.

It has sometimes been said that a human-rights based approach amounts to 'rhetorical repackaging'.[81] However, an HRBA could better be described as a method of implementing human rights in a development context.[82] Rather than a single rights-based approach, there are multiple rights-based approaches.[83] Under

---

[75] Jeffrey L Dunoff, 'Is Compliance an Indicator for the State of International Law?' in Heike Krieger, Georg Nolte, and Andreas Zimmermann (eds), *The International Rule of Law: Rise or Decline?* (OUP 2019) 183–203.

[76] Thembela Ngculu, 'Statement of South Africa, on Behalf of the Group of 77 and China, on the Occasion of the Debate on "Follow-up and Review for the Post-2015 Development Agenda"' (2015) <https://www.g77.org/statement/getstatement.php?id=150520> accessed 23 May 2023. Where such propositions were not included, the 2030 Agenda finally notes that 'governments have the primary responsibility for follow-up and review' (2030 Agenda, 47–48).

[77] Accountability for the Sustainable Development Goals (n 43) 202.

[78] Though, as we have seen, notions of development were already included in, inter alia, the 1968 Tehran Proclamation and the 1972 Stockholm Declaration. See (n 29).

[79] From the Right to Development (n 30) 163.

[80] Andrea Cornwall and Celestine Nyamu-Musembi, 'Putting the "Rights-Based Approach" to Development into Perspective' (2004) 25 Third World Q 1415, 1416; Morten Broberg and Hans-Otto Sano, 'Strengths and Weaknesses in a Human Rights-Based Approach to International Development—an Analysis of a Rights-Based Approach to Development Assistance Based on Practical Experiences' (2018) 22 Int J Hum Rights 664, 673 (hereafter 'Strengths and Weaknesses').

[81] From the Right to Development (n 30) 167.

[82] Strengths and Weaknesses (n 80) 664.

[83] Celestine Nyamu-Musembi and Andrea Cornwall, *What is the Rights-based Approach All about?: Perspectives from International Development Agencies* (IDS 2004) 1415 (hereafter 'What is the Rights-based Approach?').

an HRBA, development actors—including states, IOs, non-governmental organizations (NGOs), and donors—adopt a way of thinking in their policies guided by legal human rights standards set out in the broad set of international and regional human rights conventions and their structural and operational principles. Morten Broberg and Hans-Otto Sano identify six characteristics of an HRBA:

1. The employment of the concept of rights;
2. A corresponding obligation;
3. Donor focus on enabling the duty-bearer to respond to claims from the ultimate recipients of the development assistance and to ensure the fulfilled of fundamental rights;
4. Recognition of discrimination and inequality as important causes of poverty;
5. Activism and advocacy as tools of implementation; and
6. Recognition that far from all forms of development can be directly cast as secured rights.[84]

How this materializes in practice differs according to actor and context; for instance, an NGO might place more emphasis on human rights advocacy.[85] A coalition of UN Agencies in 2003 adopted a document to set out a common understanding of an HRBA to development cooperation.[86] It set forth, inter alia, that:

1. All programmes of development co-operation, policies and technical assistance should further the realisation of human rights as laid down in the Universal Declaration of Human Rights and other international human rights instruments.
2. Human rights standards contained in, and principles derived from, the Universal Declaration of Human Rights and other international human rights instruments guide all development cooperation and programming in all sectors and in all phases of the programming process.
3. Development cooperation contributes to the development of the capacities of 'duty-bearers' to meet their obligations and/or of 'rights-holders' to claim their rights.[87]

In the operationalization of this 'common understanding', there was a dedicated role for accountability and the rule of law, for participation and inclusion, and for equality and non-discrimination.[88]

---

[84] ibid 667–669.
[85] ibid 665.
[86] UN Development Group, 'The Human Rights Based Approach to Development Cooperation Towards a Common Understanding Among UN Agencies' <https://unsdg.un.org/resources/human-rights-based-approach-development-cooperation-towards-common-understanding-among-un> accessed 23 May 2023.
[87] ibid 1.
[88] Strengths and Weaknesses (n 80) 667.

It is important to recognize that an HRBA does not exclude the importance of other approaches, such as those based on the principle of good governance as developed by the World Bank, the International Monetary Fund, the African Development Bank, and others.[89] Similarly, the UN Development Programme (UNDP) has since 2001 adopted the 'human security' approach, including military security but also economic, health, and environmental security, among others.[90]

In terms of current developments, the height of scholarly attention for the human rights-based approach lied in the mid-2000s and mid-2010s, after which the nexus between rights and development would still be researched extensively.[91] In practice, the different interpretations of an HRBA have given way to a wider variety of operations. For instance, OHCHR and UNDP published a good practice guide on 'how the Universal Periodic Review process supports sustainable development', showcasing how UPR follow-up, public participation, and capacity building has an effect on the implementation of the SDGs.[92]

Also, a number of trade-related mechanisms actively link human rights obligations with sustainable development. The EU's General Scheme of Preferences (GSP) includes a special incentive arrangement for sustainable development and good governance (the so-called GSP+ scheme), where eligible countries have to implement a set of twenty-seven international conventions related to human and labour rights, the environment, and good governance, in return for partial or full cuts in import duties.[93] Trade has been signalled out as a key element in the SDGs as well. Goal 17 includes three targets specifically on this and recognizes international trade as 'an engine for inclusive economic growth and poverty reduction, and contribut[ing] to the promotion of sustainable development'.[94]

---

[89] Human Rights (n 16) 62; Aaron Fellmeth and Siobhán McInerney-Lankford, 'International Human Rights Law and the Concept of Good Governance' (2022) 44 Hum Rights Q 1.

[90] Human Rights (n 16) 62.

[91] Hannah Miller and Robin Redhead, 'Beyond "Rights-Based Approaches"? Employing a Process and Outcomes Framework' (2019) 23 Int J Hum Rights 699, 702.

[92] OHCHR and others, 'UN Good Practices—How the Universal Periodic Review Process Supports Sustainable Development' (2022) <https://www.ohchr.org/sites/default/files/2022-02/UPR_good_practices_2022.pdf> accessed 23 May 2023.

[93] Regulation (EU) No 978/2012 of the European Parliament and of the Council of 25 October 2012 applying a scheme of generalized tariff preferences and repealing Council Regulation (EC) No 732/2008. As of 13 August 2022, there are seven beneficiary countries under the GSP+: Bolivia, Cape Verde, Kyrgyzstan, Mongolia, Pakistan, the Philippines, and Sri Lanka. See 'Generalised Scheme of Preferences Plus (GSP+)' (Access2Markets) <https://trade.ec.europa.eu/access-to-markets/en/content/generalised-scheme-preferences-plus-gsp> accessed 23 May 2023.

[94] 2030 Agenda (n 8) para 68.

a. The added value of an HRBA

Neither human rights nor sustainable development should be neglected under the guise of achieving the other.[95] As noted by the OHCHR, 'rights imply duties, and duties demand accountability'.[96]

The Working Group on the Right to Development, in its most recent draft convention on said right, builds on the HRBA: 'development is a human right and should be realized as such and, in a manner, consistent with and based on all other human rights'.[97] In practice, an HRBA can take many different shapes and forms. For instance, it can make its mark on programming, budgeting and the choice of what indicators to use.[98]

A number of elements of added value are inherent in an HRBA. An HRBA has potential to live up better to the promise of the SDGs to 'leave no-one behind' and advance the fight against discrimination and marginalization through development policies.[99] The importance of non-discrimination in development is already explicitly referenced in a number of UN human rights treaties. The UN Convention on the Rights of Persons with Disabilities, for instance, refers to development in a number of occasions, including its article 32(1) (a) on measures to 'ensur[e] that international cooperation, including international development programmes, is inclusive of and accessible to persons with disabilities'.[100] The UN Convention on the Elimination of All Forms of Racial Discrimination similarly sets out that:

> States Parties shall, when the circumstances so warrant, take, in the social, economic, cultural and other fields, special and concrete measures to ensure the

---

[95] A similar debate occurred in 2018, when China proposed a resolution in the UN Human Rights Council entitled 'Promoting the international human rights cause through win-win cooperation', eventually adopted with a changed title as 'Promoting mutually-beneficial cooperation in the field of human rights'. As Human Rights Watch noted, the use of language surrounding 'win-win' 'gut[s] procedures to hold countries accountable for human rights violations, suggesting "dialogue" instead'. Such language fails to specify any course of action when rights violators refuse to cooperate with UN experts, retaliate against human rights defenders, or actively reject human rights principles. *Promoting Mutually Beneficial Cooperation in the Field of Human Rights* (A/HRC/RES/37/23, 6 April 2018); 'Is China Winning Its Fight against Rights at the UN?' (*Human Rights Watch*, 12 December 2018) <https://www.hrw.org/news/2018/12/12/china-winning-its-fight-against-rights-un> accessed 13 August 2022.

[96] OHCHR, 'Principles and Guidelines for a Human Rights Approach to Poverty Reduction Strategies' (2002) para 24 <https://www.ohchr.org/sites/default/files/Documents/Publications/PovertyStrategiesen.pdf> accessed 23 May 2023. What is the Rights-based Approach? (n 83) 1417.

[97] Working Group on the Right to Development, 'Draft Convention on the Right to Development, with Commentaries (A/HRC/WG2/21/2/Add1)' <https://undocs.org/A/HRC/WG.2/21/2/ADD.1> accessed 23 May 2023.

[98] Axel Marx and others, 'Human Rights and Service Delivery: A Review of Current Policies, Practices and Challenges' in Jan Wouters and others (eds), *The World Bank Legal Review Volume 6 Improving Delivery in Development: The Role of Voice, Social Contract, and Accountability*, 37–57 (The World Bank 2015) <http://elibrary.worldbank.org/doi/book/10.1596/978-1-4648-0378-9> accessed 23 May 2023.

[99] Strengths and Weaknesses (n 80) 672.

[100] *Convention on the Rights of Persons with Disabilities* (2515 UNTS 3, opened for signature 13 December 2006, entered into force 3 May 2008) art 32 (1)(a).

adequate development and protection of certain racial groups or individuals belonging to them, for the purpose of guaranteeing them the full and equal enjoyment of human rights and fundamental freedoms.[101]

Likewise, through its grounding in legal rights and obligations, an HRBA underscores legal accountability and helps to strengthen the channels through which individuals can assert their position and claims as right-holders.[102] This is particularly pertinent for the reliance on human rights before local and national courts as well as before the regional and international mechanisms and tribunals described above.[103]

b. Examples of the need for an HRBA: The right to housing and the right to a nationality

Although (sustainable) development and human rights often find themselves on the same side of the battlefield, they may occasionally be at odds with each other. One increasingly relevant example is the right to housing in light of land speculation, commodification, and wider economic development.[104] Development projects, often under the rationale of economic development, may lead to wider economic growth but displace communities previously living on the land.[105] For instance, a hydro-electric dam across China's Yangtze River might on the one hand displace or impact local communities yet at the same time bring affordable power to millions and protect cities from regular floodings and other disasters—as is the case for the Three Gorges Dam.[106] An HRBA in this case would not need to prevent any effect or relocation; but it would introduce valuable concepts such as 'full and prior informed consent' regarding relocation, as well as accountability, compensation, and other criteria in case of resettlement.[107]

---

[101] ICERD (n 14) art 2(2); Patrick Thornberry, *The International Convention on the Elimination of All Forms of Racial Discrimination: A Commentary* (OUP 2016) 231.

[102] Strengths and Weaknesses (n 80) 673.

[103] ibid.

[104] Miloon Kothari, 'The Global Crisis of Displacement and Evictions: A Housing and Land Rights Response' (*Rosa Luxembourg Foundation*, 2015) <https://www.rosalux.de/en/publication/id/8609/the-global-crisis-of-displacement-and-evictions> accessed 23 May 2023.

[105] Usha Ramanathan, 'A Word on Eminent Domain' in Lyla Mehta (ed), *Displaced by Development—Confronting Marginalisation and Gender Injustice*, 133 (SAGE 2009) <https://www.ielrc.org/content/a0902.pdf> accessed 23 May 2023.

[106] Sean-Shong Hwang, Yue Cao, and Juan Xi, 'The Short-Term Social, Economic, and Health Impact of China's Three Gorges Dam Project: A Prospective Study' (2011) 101 Soc Indic Res 73–92.

[107] UN Basic Principles and Guidelines on Development-based Evictions and Displacement, as introduced in annex to the *Report of the UN Special Rapporteur on Adequate Housing as a Component of the Right to an Adequate Standard of Living* (E/HRC/4/18, 5 February 2007) <http://www.undocs.org/A/HRC/4/18> accessed 23 May 2023, para 56(e).

A second example. SDG 16.9 sets out to achieve legal identity for all, including birth registration. Digital solutions, including through Identification for Development (ID4D) initiatives, are offered to fight poverty and enable communities to access services in education, health care or employment. While newly set up digital identification systems may offer development opportunities, they also bring risks for communities that are often already marginalised minorities or poor groups unable to access these systems. Moreover, there are an estimated ten million stateless persons identified by the UNHCR.[108] An approximate 75 per cent of these individuals belong to a minority group.[109] Full achievement of SDG 16.9 can only work if they live up to their promise to 'leave no-one behind'.[110]

c. The limitations of an HRBA to sustainable development

In terms of limitations, not all contexts of (sustainable) development are suitable for am HRBA. First, with an HRBA, the focus tends to be more on ensuring the fulfilment of minimum standards of rights, and less on general capacity building.[111] An HRBA might not have an ideal effect in some specific circumstances. For instance, as Dan Banik describes, human rights accountability mechanisms may not be accessible such as in rural areas where the right-holders may be illiterate.[112]

Similarly, there are institutions with mandates subject to political prohibitions that make adopting an HRBA more difficult. The obligations that come with human rights limit the discretion normally given to donors.

Moreover, while the SDGs aim to 'involve Governments as well as parliaments, the United Nations system and other international institutions, local authorities, indigenous peoples, civil society, business and the private sector, the scientific and academic community – and all people',[113] an HRBA focuses primarily on the legal accountability of governments. Furthermore, instead of cooperating towards a common future, the involvement of courts or other legal accountability

---

[108] A stateless person is, following article 1(1) of the 1954 Convention Relating to the Status of Stateless Persons, 'not considered as a national by any state under the operation of its law'. The right to a nationality is moreover protected under various UN human rights conventions, including: the *International Covenant on Civil and Political Rights* (999 UNTS 171, opened for signature 16 December 1966, entered into force 23 March 1976) art 24 (3); the *Convention on the Rights of the Child* (opened for signature 20 November 1989, entered into force 2 September 1990) art 7; ICERD art 5 (d) (iii); and CEDAW art 9. Carol Batchelor, 'Stateless Persons: Some Gaps in International Protection' (1995) 7 (2) IJRL 232, 235.

[109] UNHCR, 'This is Our Home—Stateless Minorities and their Search for Citizenship' (2017) 1.

[110] Institute on Statelessness and Inclusion, 'Making SDG16.9 Work for the Wider Sustainable Development Agenda: Lessons from the Citizenship, Stateless and Legal Identity Community' (2019) <https://files.institutesi.org/legal_identity_policy_brief.pdf> accessed 23 May 2023.

[111] Strengths and Weaknesses (n 80) 673.

[112] Dan Banik, 'Support for Human Rights-Based Development: Reflections on the Malawian Experience' (2010) 14 Int J Hum Rights 34.

[113] 2030 Agenda (n 8) para 52.

mechanisms may place these groups in opposition of each other. Thus, an HRBA has the risk of politicising previously non-political issues and, through the clear distinction between duty-bearers and rights holders, of polarizing different groups of society.[114]

As indicated above, sustainable development rests on three pillars. While human rights align strongly with its social and economic goals, the environment is only a newly incipient element of human rights. Although some jurisdictions acknowledge natural elements such as rivers (such as the Whanganui River in Aotearoa New Zealand) or nature at large (such as Ecuador in its constitution) as right-holders,[115] the environment comes into the human rights sphere predominantly as a resource or condition for human life and flourishing. Thus, Goals related to 'life below water' (SDG 14) or 'life on land' (SDG 15) have a weaker foundation in international human rights law than, for instance, those on 'health' (SDG 3), quality education (SDG 4), or gender equality (SDG 5).[116]

5. Conclusion

With 2030 Agenda the current 193 UN Member States have set out on an elaborate and ambitious mission to achieve seventeen SDGs by 2030. At the same time, the equally elaborate human rights framework and its various regional and international mechanisms provides for legal obligations for states to respect, protect, and fulfil human rights. This chapter has explored the triangular relationship between human rights obligations of states and IOs, international law, and (sustainable) development. It also tackled specific questions, such as whether and to what extent the SDGs themselves (as well as their targets and indicators) are gradually becoming part of public international law. Finally, we paid attention to the human rights-based approach to development, which has received much attention since the 1990s.

We found that, in spite of sometimes justified criticism and scepticism, an HRBA is particularly important for the protection and empowerment of poor, discriminated, or otherwise marginalized groups, as it provides a lens that focuses on vulnerable groups. However, not all contexts of (sustainable) development are suited to

---

[114] Samuel Hickey and Diana Mitlin (eds), *Rights-Based Approaches to Development: Exploring the Potential and Pitfalls* (Kumarian Press 2009) 225.

[115] Anna Leah, Tabios Hillebrecht, and María Valeria Berros, 'Can Nature Have Rights? Legal and Political Insights' (RCC Perspectives: Transformations in Environment and Society 2017) 6 <Can Nature Have Rights? Legal and Political Insights | Environment & Society Portal (environmentandsociety. org)> accessed 23 May 2023.

[116] Also within individual Goals, the value of the HRBA may differ per target. For instance, within the Goal on 'decent work and economic growth' (SDG 8), target 8.5 to 'achieve full and productive employment and decent work for all women and men' has a strong foundation in the right to work (e.g. UDHR art 23.1, ICESCR art 6.1, and the relevant ILO Conventions), while target 8.9 on sustainable tourism has a weaker legal foundation.

the application of a human rights-based approach. With a HRBA, the focus tends to be more on ensuring the fulfilment of minimum standards of rights, and less on capacity building in general. Moreover, an HRBA carries the risk of politicizing previously non-political issues and, through legal accountability, contestation, and the clear distinction between duty-bearers and right-holders, of polarizing different groups of society.

5
United Nations Human Rights Treaty Bodies' Approaches

Anganile Willie Mwenifumbo, Harumi Fuentes Furuya, and Marie-Joseph Ayissi

1. Introduction

The United Nations (UN) 2030 Agenda for Sustainable Development (2030 Agenda) adopted in 2015 is an embodiment of the international community's commitment to pursue lofty goals to address some of the world's most intractable development challenges.[1] The 2030 Agenda represents a paradigm shift from the Millennium Development Goals (MDGs) that embraces a plan of action grounded in human rights standards. The integration of human rights reflects efforts during the negotiations to craft an action plan for 'people, planet and prosperity' that pursues dignity and human rights for all.[2] A number of UN treaty bodies (TBs) played a fundamental role in these negotiations to ensure that human rights standards guided the process of the elaboration of the agenda.[3] This was based on the understanding that human rights and sustainable development are interdependent and mutually reinforcing—constituting converging commitments and obligations that should be realized in an integrated manner.[4]

Since the adoption of the 2030 Agenda, TBs have played a key role in monitoring the implementation of Sustainable Development Goals (SDGs)-related human

---

[1] UN General Assembly, *Transforming our World: the 2030 Agenda for Sustainable Development* (A/Res/70/1, 2015) <https://sdgs.un.org/2030agenda> accessed 24 May 2023 (hereafter '2030 Agenda').
[2] ibid.
[3] Since the adoption of the Universal Declaration of Human Rights (UDHR) in 1948, ten core UN human rights treaties have been included: the International Covenant on Civil and Political Rights 1966 (ICCPR); International Covenant on Economic, Social and Cultural Rights 1966 (ICESCR); International Convention on the Elimination of All Forms of Racial Discrimination 1965 (ICERD); Convention on the Elimination of All Forms of Discrimination against Women 1979 (CEDAW Convention); Convention against Torture and Other Cruel, Inhuman or Degrading Treatment or Punishment 1984 (CAT); Convention on the Rights of the Child 1989 (UNCRC); International Convention on the Protection of the Rights of All Migrant Workers and Members of their Families 1990 (ICMW); Convention on the Rights of Persons with Disabilities 2006 (ICRPD); and International Convention for the Protection of All Persons from Enforced Disappearance 2006 (ICPED).
[4] 2030 Agenda (n 1).

rights obligations under their respective treaties.[5] In light of the anchoring of the 2030 Agenda in human rights standards, TBs have been implicated in the role of monitoring implementation, placing them in a privileged position to track progress as they fulfil their procedural and substantive mandates. TBs have principally sought to track progress on SDG implementation under the state party reporting procedure where they have supported states to implement SDG-related recommendations; and through reporting to the UN High Level Political Forum (HLFP) on key trends and best practices.[6]

This chapter analyses the different approaches and perspectives of TBs towards the 2030 Agenda in the discharge of their functions. It has two substantive parts excluding this introduction. The first part outlines the normative framework by highlighting the linkages between TBs and the 2030 Agenda, particularly their role in the negotiation process. It then engages into a discussion of their varying approaches and perspectives in dealing with the 2030 Agenda, focusing on understanding how TBs utilize both their procedural and substantive mandates. The last part concludes the discussion.

2. Normative Framework: Treaty Bodies and the Sustainable Development Agenda

The core UN human rights treaties establish TBs (also known as committees),[7] whose primary function is to monitor the implementation of treaty obligations by state parties. There are currently ten TBs composed of independent experts of recognized competence in human rights.[8] The procedures and working methods that they employ include the review of state party reports, the consideration of individual complaints,[9] the conduct of enquiries, the issuance of General Comments/ Recommendations and statements.[10] The state party reporting procedure remains

---

[5] United Nations, 'Committee's Contribution to the High Level Political Forum on Sustainable Development' <https://www.ohchr.org/en/treaty-bodies/cedaw/committees-contribution-high-level-political-forum-sustainable-development-hlpf> accessed 24 May 2023.
[6] ibid.
[7] United Nations, 'Fact Sheet No 30(Rev 1): The United Nations Human Rights Treaty System' (*OHCHR*, 1 August 2012) <https://www.ohchr.org/en/publications/fact-sheets/fact-sheet-no-30-rev-1-united-nations-human-rights-treaty-system> accessed 24 May 2023 (hereafter 'UN Factsheet').
[8] The ten treaty bodies include, the Human Rights Committee (HRC); Committee on Economic, Social and Cultural Rights (CESCR); Committee on the Elimination of Racial Discrimination (CERD); Committee on the Elimination of Discrimination against Women (CEDAW); Committee against Torture and Other Cruel, Inhuman, or Degrading Treatment or Punishment (CAT); Subcommittee on Prevention of Torture (SPT); Committee on the Rights of the Child (CRC); Committee on the Protection of the Rights of All Migrant Workers and Members of Their Families (CMW); Committee on the Rights of Persons with Disabilities (CRPD); Committee on Enforced Disappearances (CED). ibid.
[9] Currently, eight treaty bodies have the mandate to consider individual communications; ibid.
[10] ibid.

their primary function that culminates in the adoption of country-specific recommendations known as concluding observations.[11]

a. Role and contributions of UN treaty bodies in shaping the UN 2030 Agenda

In the discharge of their supervisory functions, TBs have gained venerated legitimacy, not only in issuing country-tailored recommendations for states, but also in shaping international policy towards the realization of human rights for all.[12] As such, in the lead up to the adoption of the 2030 Agenda, TBs played a critical role in the crafting of this post-2015 development agenda. Very early into the consultations, TBs recognized the importance of the international community to design an agenda that was based on human rights. They, therefore, collectively and individually set out to ensure that the agenda sat on a solid plinth of human rights standards accompanied by a robust accountability framework.

Led by the chairpersons of the ten TBs, they collectively issued two joint statements. In May 2013, the chairpersons argued for the grounding of the new development agenda in human rights, justice, and the rule of law.[13] In addition, they argued for the use of human rights indicators to measure progress towards the realization of the SDGs.[14] They also called for the strengthening of accountability by linking development goals to legal obligations under human rights treaties and by engaging human rights mechanisms, including TBs, both as monitoring mechanisms and as sources of information.[15] In January 2015, the chairpersons issued yet another statement that commented on the content of the draft 2030 Agenda.[16] While welcoming the integration of human rights, particularly the inclusion of equality and non-discrimination, the chairpersons emphasized the need for the creation of a strong accountability framework accompanied by a systematic and institutionalized flow of information from and to existing monitoring mechanisms, including TBs.[17] This, they argued, would help ensure synergies between existing mechanisms and the monitoring and review framework to be constructed for the 2030 Agenda.[18]

---

[11] ibid.
[12] Helen Keller and Geir Ulfstein, *Human Rights Treaty Bodies: Law and Legitimacy* (CUP 2012).
[13] United Nations, 'Joint Statement of the Chairpersons of the UN Human Rights Treaty Bodies on the Post-2015 Development Agenda' (May 2013) <https://www.ohchr.org/Documents/HRBodies/TB/AnnualMeeting/JointStatementChairsMeetingMay2013.doc> accessed 24 May 2023.
[14] ibid.
[15] ibid.
[16] United Nations, 'Joint Statement of the Chairpersons of the UN Human Rights Treaty Bodies on the Post-2015 Development Agenda' (18 January 2015) <https://www.ohchr.org/en/statements/2015/01/joint-statement-chairpersons-united-nations-human-rights-treaty-bodies-post-2015?LangID=E&NewsID=15505> accessed 24 May 2023.
[17] ibid.
[18] ibid.

THE ROLES OF INTERNATIONAL LAW IN DEVELOPMENT   83

Individually, the Committee on Economic Social and Cultural Rights (CESCR), the Committee on the Elimination of Discrimination against Women (CEDAW), and the Committee on the Rights of Persons with Disabilities (CRPD) engaged either directly or indirectly with the negotiation process to underscore the need to include human rights. The manner of engagement was not uniform, with CESCR preferring to engage state parties to the International Covenant on Economic, Social and Cultural Rights (ICESCR), while CEDAW and CRPD directly engaged with the negotiators.

In a letter of November 2012, the CESCR chairperson urged all state parties to the ICESCR, to explicitly align the post-2015 development goals with human rights principles, including non-discrimination, equality between men and women, participation and inclusion, and transparency and accountability.[19]

In February 2014, the CEDAW chairperson directly engaged with the UN General Assembly Working Group on the SDGs and issued a statement, which underscored the importance for all goals, targets and indicators to be aligned with human rights standards.[20] This is based on the premise that human rights standards are intrinsically linked to development, such as those related to food, education, health, housing, non-discrimination, political participation and freedoms of expression and assembly.[21] It, therefore, behoved the international community to ensure that the SDGs fostered the implementation of these human rights as matter of obligation and not as policy choice.[22] In addition, the statement also argued that building the new agenda on equality and non-discrimination would ensure that no one is left behind.[23] Specifically, CEDAW called for the inclusion of a stand-alone goal on gender equality and for mainstreaming gender in all goals, including through disaggregating all indicators by sex.[24] Moreover, CEDAW argued that it should play a critical role in ensuring accountability for gender equality.[25]

CRPD issued two statements in May 2013 and in January 2014, which called for the inclusion of the rights of persons with disabilities, the participation of persons with disabilities, and the definition of disability-rights indicators, including the

---

[19] United Nations, 'Letter on the Post-2015 Development Agenda sent by the Chairperson of the CESCR to State Parties to the ICESCR' (30 November 2012) <https://www.cesr.org/sites/default/files/downloads/CESCR_ChairLetterSPto_ICESCR_30.11.12.pdf> accessed 18 August 2023.
[20] United Nations, 'Statement of the Chairperson of the Committee on the Elimination of Discrimination against Women to the Eighth Session of the General Assembly Open Working Group on the Sustainable Development Goals: Promoting Equality, including Social Equity, Gender Equality and Women's Empowerment' (5 February 2014) <https://www.ohchr.org/sites/default/files/Documents/HRBodies/CEDAW/StatementsChair/Statement_CEDAWchair_OWG_SDGs_05.02.14.pdf> accessed 24 May 2023.
[21] ibid.
[22] ibid.
[23] ibid.
[24] ibid.
[25] CEDAW, 'Statement of the Committee on the Post-2015 Development Agenda and the Elimination of Discrimination Against Women' (26 February 2014) <https://www.ohchr.org/sites/default/files/Documents/HRBodies/CEDAW/Statements/CEDAW201526Feb2014.pdf> accessed 24 May 2023.

collection of disaggregated data.[26] It also called for the establishment of a strong accountability mechanism to monitor progress, including through existing international human rights mechanisms.[27]

It is arguable that the request by TBs to align the 2030 Agenda around human rights principles as opposed to obligations is due to the fact that these principles run through all core UN human rights treaties such that an alignment around obligations could not have elicited unanimity among TBs since treaties address multiple and differing obligations. This arguably explains the lack of push from any TB to include a stand-alone human right in the SDGs as this could have easily triggered questions about which human rights needed prioritization and the rationale behind such prioritization.

Nevertheless, following the issuance of the draft 2030 Agenda, there was still an opportunity for TBs to suggest changes to the formulation of specific SDGs to adopt treaty-obligation language. For instance, this could have entailed revising the goal on achieving gender equality to follow the formulation of article 2 of the Convention on the Elimination of All Forms of Discrimination against Women (CEDAW Convention) to 'eliminate discrimination against women [and girls]' in all its forms and manifestations.[28] At the very least, TBs could have called for a twin-track approach to human rights—meaning a stand-alone goal on human rights and explicit human rights language/commitments throughout the framework that could have required all Member States of the UN to respect, protect, and promote human rights for all.

b. Linkages between the SDGs and human rights standards

The human rights standards and norms enunciated by the core UN human rights treaties indirectly suffuse the 2030 Agenda by design.[29] The international community consciously set out to craft a development framework for cooperation to address inequality and achieve human rights for all.[30] While this political

---

[26] United Nations, 'Statement of the Committee on the Rights of Persons with Disabilities on Including the Rights of Persons with Disabilities in the Post 2015 Agenda on Disability and Development' (May 2013) <https://www.ohchr.org/Documents/HRBodies/CRPD/StatementInclusionPost2015.doc> accessed 25 May 2023; CRPD, 'Statement on Sustainable Development Goals, addressed to the Eighth Session of the Open Working Group on Sustainable Development Goals by the Committee on the Rights of Persons with Disabilities' (31 January 2014) <https://www.ohchr.org/en/statements/2014/02/statement-sustainable-development-goals-addressed-eighth-session-open-working> accessed 25 May 2023.
[27] ibid.
[28] United Nations, 'Article 2 of the Convention on the Elimination of All Forms of Discrimination against Women' (18 December 1979) <https://www.ohchr.org/en/instruments-mechanisms/instruments/convention-elimination-all-forms-discrimination-against-women> accessed 25 May 2023.
[29] UNGA, 'Resolution A/RES/70/1' (21 October 2015) <https://www.un.org/en/development/desa/population/migration/generalassembly/docs/globalcompact/A_RES_70_1_E.pdf> accessed 3 March 2022 (hereafter GA Resolution A/RES/70/1).
[30] ibid.

commitment should be understood in the context of the shortfalls of the MDGs and the UN Charter requirement enjoining UN Member States to cooperate to realize human rights and find solutions to international economic, social, and health problems,[31] the SDGs contain neither explicit human rights language nor a stand-alone goal on human rights.

It has been argued that this omission is 'indicative of a global climate where more and more states are assertively pushing back against universal human-rights standards'.[32] Nevertheless, the implicit infusion of human rights standards into the SDGs is inescapable and it might point to an understanding by TBs to include principles of general application common to all treaties in lieu of specific human rights obligations due to their multifarious nature and the impossibility to agree on any priority areas.

Along with the 'leave no one behind' (LNOB) principle, the SDGs located the political commitment in the principles of equality and non-discrimination, which are foundational for the mandates of TBs.[33] Some TBs focus on specific groups of people who are often left behind, including women, children, persons with disabilities, indigenous peoples, national, ethnic and racial minorities, persons in detention, migrant workers, and people suffering enforced disappearance.[34] The manifold interrelationships of human rights, however, have compelled all TBs to dedicate considerable attention to these groups and other cross-cutting issues in the context of addressing inequality and discrimination.[35]

In addressing the overarching principles of equality and non-discrimination, which find expression in the LNOB principle, TBs derive relevance in using the SDGs to assess implementation of their respective treaty obligations and vice versa. For instance, in addressing a question and recommendation to Senegal to eliminate gender based violence in the public and private spheres of life, CEDAW implicated SDG 5 and target 5.1 in addition to employing its articles 1, 2, and 5 of the CEDAW Convention.[36] In its list of issues to Senegal, CEDAW recalled Senegal's obligations under articles 1 and 2 of the CEDAW Convention, target 5.1 and indicator 5.1.1 of the SDGs when requesting for information on measures taken to end all forms of discrimination against all women and girls everywhere, and the state party's timeline for the completion of the process of harmonizing legislation and policies on equality and non-discrimination on the basis of sex in all areas

---

[31] Article 55 of the Charter of the United Nations, <https://www.un.org/en/about-us/un-charter> accessed 3 March 2022.
[32] Human Rights First, 'The SDGs' Missed Opportunity on Human Rights' <https://www.humanrightsfirst.org/blog/sdgs-missed-opportunity-human-rights> accessed 15 July 2022.
[33] All the core human rights treaties reflect this general principle; UN Factsheet (n 7).
[34] ibid.
[35] The particular groups and cross-cutting issues include, inter alia, children, women and issues of equality and non-discrimination. See, for instance, International Covenant on Civil and Political Rights (ICCPR) (1966) arts 3, 6, 8, 17, 24 and 26; International Covenant on Economic, Social and Cultural Rights (1966) arts 3, 10, 12(2)(a) and 13(2); ICERD arts 5 and 7.
[36] CEDAW, *Concluding Observations on Senegal* (CEDAW/C/SEN/CO/8) para 23.

covered by the CEDAW Convention.[37] Similarly, the HLPF utilizes the information provided by CEDAW based on its review of country situations to assess levels of implementation by states of SDG-related treaty obligations.[38] This provides a rare opportunity for the mutual enforcement of the SDGs and treaty obligations under the two institutional frameworks.

Beyond the principles of equality and non-discrimination that permeate the SDGs, it is notable that the SDGs themselves are an indirect expression of various human rights standards and norms in many respects. This emanates in part from explicit references to the Universal Declaration of Human Rights (UDHR) and UN human rights treaties throughout the text of the resolution.[39] A close analysis of the SDGs reveals that the seventeen SDGs directly or indirectly implicate human rights standards and the majority of 169 targets are linked to the standards of the core UN human rights treaties and labour instruments.[40] For instance, Goal 1 to 'end poverty in all its forms everywhere' is a reflection of various human rights standards on the right to an adequate standard of living,[41] right to social security,[42] and equal rights of women in social economic life.[43] Goal 2 on ending hunger implicates the right to food[44] and international cooperation to ensure equitable distribution of food supplies.[45] Corollary, various human rights enshrined in a number of core UN human rights treaties find expression in the SDGs. These include, among others, the rights to life and health (SDG 3),[46] education (SDG 4),[47] gender equality and elimination of all forms of discrimination against women (SDG 5),[48]

---

[37] CEDAW, List of Issues and Questions in Relation to the Eighth Periodic Report of Senegal' (CEDAW/C/SEN/Q/8) para 1 <https://tbinternet.ohchr.org/_layouts/15/treatybodyexternal/Download.aspx?symbolnc=CEDAW%2FC%2FSEN%2FQ%2F8&Lang=en> accessed 19 July 2022.

[38] United Nations, '2021 Voluntary National Reviews Synthesis Report' <https://sustainabledevelopment.un.org/content/documents/294382021_VNR_Synthesis_Report.pdf> accessed 15 July 2022.

[39] Paragraph 10 of GA Resolution A/RES/70/1 (n 29).

[40] Danish Institute for Human Rights (DIHR), 'The Human Rights Guide to the SDGs' <http://sdg.humanrights.dk/> accessed 3 March 2022.

[41] Universal Declaration of Human Rights (UDHR), art 25; International Covenant on Economic, Social and Cultural Rights (ICESCR), art 11; Convention on the Rights of the Child (Child Rights Conveniton) art 27.

[42] UDHR art 22; ICESCR art 9; Convention on the Rights of Persons with Disabilities (ICRPD) art 28; CRC art 26.

[43] Convention on the Elimination of All Forms of Discrimination against Women (CEDAW Convention) arts 11, 13, 14(2)(g), 15(2), 16(1).

[44] UDHR art 25; ICESCR art 11; UNCRC, art 24(2)(c).

[45] UDHR art 28; ICESCR arts 2(1), 11 (1), 11(2).

[46] For instance, the right to life (UDHR art 3; International Covenant on Civil and Political Rights, art 6), particularly of women (CEDAW Convention, art 12) and children (UNCRC, art 6); the right to health (UDHR, art 25; ICESCR, art 12), particularly of women (CEDAW Convention, art 12); and children (UNCRC, art24); the special protection for mothers and children (ICESCR, art10).

[47] Also the right to education (UDHR, art 26; ICESCR, art 13), particularly in relation to children (CRC, arts 28, 29); persons with disabilities (CRC, art 23(3), CRPD, art 24); and indigenous peoples (United Nations Declaration on the Rights of Indigenous Peoples, art 14).

[48] Also the elimination of all forms of discrimination against women (CEDAW Convention, arts1 to 5) and girls (UNCRC, art 2), particularly in legislation, political and public life (art 7), economic and social life (arts 11, 13), and family relations (art 16).

the right to safe drinking water (SDG 6),[49] adequate standard of living (SDG 7),[50] and the right to work (SDG 8).[51]

It bears mentioning that while the 2030 Agenda is grounded in human rights standards, there is no express inclusion of human rights in the SDGs. Practically, this would have entailed framing the SDGs using the language of human rights treaties. For instance, Goals 1 and 3 on ending poverty and good health could have taken the form of the rights to an adequate standard of living and the right to highest attainable standard of physical and mental health protected under articles 11(1) and 12 of ICESCR, respectively. Arguably, the international community was cognizant of the fact that not all Members States have ratified the UN core human rights treaties. Therefore, consensus on the 2030 Agenda could have not been reached because some states would not have accepted formulations that directly subjected them to obligations provided in human rights treaties that they have deliberately decided to exempt themselves from through non-ratification.

Nevertheless, the affirmation in the General Assembly Resolution, proclaiming that the SDGs seek to realize human rights for all, places human rights obligations and TBs at the centre of global efforts to implement the SDGs. The realization of the critical role that TBs can play to reinforce and complement efforts to realize the SDGs led to calls to ensure that TBs are part and parcel of these efforts. As early as 2013, the then High Commissioner for Human Rights, Navi Pillay, called for a strong accountability framework linked to human rights mechanisms, including TBs.[52] Subsequently, the UN Human Rights Council adopted a series of resolutions that recognized that the protection of human rights and the implementation of the 2030 Agenda were 'interrelated and mutually reinforcing' and acknowledged the role of TBs in promoting implementation.[53]

Furthermore, the realization of the weaknesses of the HLPF, as an accountability platform of the SDGs, arguably led to specific calls for TBs to play a complementary role. Unlike TBs, participation in the HLPF is on a voluntary basis that does not lead to the rigorous adoption of country-specific recommendations beyond

---

[49] Also the right to safe drinking water and sanitation (ICESCR art 11); right to health (UDHR, art 25; ICESCR, art 12).

[50] Also the right to an adequate standard of living (UDHR, art 25; ICESCR, art 11); the right to enjoy the benefits of scientific progress and its application (UDHR, art 27; ICESCR, art 15(1)(b)).

[51] Also the right to work and to just and favourable conditions of work (UDHR, art 23; ICESCR, arts 6, 7, 10; CRPD, art 27; ILO Declaration on Fundamental Principles and Rights at Work).

[52] Navanethem Pillay, 'Letter sent to all UN Member States by the UN High Commissioner for Human Rights' (6 June 2013) <https://www.ohchr.org/sites/default/files/Documents/Issues/MDGs/HCOpenLetterPost2015.pdf> accessed 12 March 2022.

[53] For example, UN Human Rights Council, *Promotion and protection of human rights and the implementation of the 2030 Agenda for Sustainable Development* (A/HRC/RES/37/24) https://documents-dds-ny.un.org/doc/UNDOC/GEN/G18/103/41/PDF/G1810341.pdf?OpenElement; UN Human Rights Council Resolution, *The need for an integrated approach to the implementation of the 2030 Agenda for Sustainable Development for the full realization of human rights, focusing holistically on the means of implementation* (A/HRC/RES/37/25) <https://digitallibrary.un.org/record/1485564?ln=en> accessed 17 August 2023.

the theme of the review.[54] The current Voluntary National Review (VNR) processes impose a time limitation for governments' presentations and questions from Member States and civil society, preventing meaningful engagement.[55] On the other hand, TBs promote meaningful dialogue and elaborate engagement with states and civil society that is followed by the issuance of concrete recommendations that follow up on their previous recommendations and other emerging issues. This seeks to define pathways for states to address specific domestic challenges relating to the fulfilment of their human rights obligations. These qualitative gaps of the HLPF have partly legitimized the criticality of TBs' contributions to the HLPF and the need to promote a synergized two-way interaction that has been the subject of calls by TBs and others over the years.[56]

It is clear from the foregoing that the decision to ground the SDGs in human rights standards highlighted the relevance of binding international human rights obligations to the pursuit of the SDGs. This implicated TBs at two important levels. First, TBs directly or indirectly supervised the implementation of the SDGs as they performed their mandated function of monitoring states implementation of treaty obligations. Second, TBs such as CEDAW, CERD, CESCR, and CRPD are inclined to engage with the HLPF in light of the considerable information that they process and generate that is relevant to tracking progress on implementation by the HLFP. These processes reinforce the implementation of the SDGs and treaty obligations by both TBs and the HLPF in the execution of their respective mandates.

3. Approaches and Perspectives of Treaty Bodies towards the Sustainable Development Agenda

a. Concluding observations

Under the State party reporting procedure, which leads to the issuance of concluding observations, treaties bodies have established a practice of referring to their own precedents, including general comments/recommendations and other sources of soft or hard law. The reference by TBs to the SDGs should be understood within this context, taking into account the different nature of treaty obligations and the SDGs.

The SDGs are a pragmatic facet in the implementation of some human rights standards because the targets that they promote are intrinsically linked to human

---

[54] Women's Major Group, 'Position Paper on HLPF Review' <https://www.womensmajorgroup.org/wp-content/uploads/2021/01/HLPF-Review-FINAL-1.pdf> accessed 5 July 2022.
[55] ibid.
[56] CERD, 'Contribution to the 2017 HLPF Meeting' <https://sustainabledevelopment.un.org/content/documents/14579OHCHR_Comm_on_the_Elimination_of_Racial_Discrimination.pdf> accessed 4 March 2022 (hereafter 'CERD's 2017 HLFP Contribution').

rights.[57] Thus, the realization of the SDGs serves as a vehicle for the implementation of human rights obligations by States. For instance, the attainment of the goal to end hunger is itself a realization of the right to be free from hunger, which is the standard below which States parties to ICESCR are not allowed to fall below in their progressive realization of the maximalist standard that finds expression in the right to adequate food.[58] In that regard, for TBs, referring to the SDGs in their work mostly serves to promote the implementation of the obligations enshrined in treaties. In other words, it could be understood that, although goals are of a policy nature, their realization could help promote the enjoyment of the corresponding rights enshrined in human rights treaties by rights-holders.

This is also relevant from the view that concluding observations contain policy recommendations formulated to States to achieve the exigencies of treaty obligations, which as such, pursue the policy objectives of the SDGs. From that angle, a purposive complementarity of enforcement exists between the SDGs and TBs through, inter alia, their concluding observations. Furthermore, SDGs may help to orientate policy recommendations formulated in concluding observations and vice versa, although the spirit emanates from a differing basis in terms of their binding nature with SDGs assuming a soft law status and treaty obligations a peremptory one. Likewise, it is arguable that the effective implementation of treaty obligations through concluding observations is a tool to help observe the SDGs domestically.

It is notable that the SDGs' poverty eradication paradigm has led TBs to observe approaches that differ from one another. It is trite that they refer to the SDGs in the context of economic, social and cultural rights more frequently than to civil and political rights. Although a number of the SDGs reflect some rights protected under human rights instruments, such as the right to health or to education, only a limited number of TBs have explicitly embodied them in their outputs. In most cases, this has been done in concluding observations and general comments/recommendations by CESCR, CEDAW, CRC, CRPD and CMW. The following section explores such approaches in detail.

i. CESCR, CEDAW, and CRC: A holistic approach

CESCR and CEDAW have adopted a more inclusive approach to the SDGs in their work that arguably illustrates the importance that these TBs attach to the UN 2030 Agenda, or how central they view the 2030 Agenda to the fulfilment of the rights enshrined in these instruments. Following the adoption of the 2030 Agenda by the General Assembly, CESCR and CEDAW's concluding observations include a standalone standard paragraph inviting States parties to implement the SDGs together with their respective treaty obligations. So far, they remain the only two TBs

---

[57] UN GA Resolution A/RES/70/1 (n 29) para 55.
[58] ICESCR, art 11(2).

that took the procedural step to draft and issue guidance to States on how to report on the SDGs as part of their reporting obligations.[59]

CESCR invites States parties not only to take into account their obligations under ICESCR but also to ensure the full enjoyment of rights thereunder 'in their implementation of the 2030 Agenda for Sustainable Development at the national level.'[60] CESCR has adopted a human –rights based approach towards the realization of the SDGs as it requires States parties to consider all beneficiaries of public programmes implementing the SDGs as rights holders. Arguably, this injects the idea of State accountability in delivering on the promise 2030 Agenda through the use of economic, social and cultural rights as surrogates.[61]

CEDAW's approach is similar as it reflects the SDGs in a standard paragraph that seeks to augment the implementation of the gender equality Goal 5 noting that gender equality can be achieved through the process of implementing the UN 2030 Agenda. The approach also underlines the particular importance of Goal 5 and of mainstreaming the principles of non-discrimination and equality in all SDGs. Additionally, CEDAW recognizes that the SDGs should facilitate and operate as an implementation tool for gender equality in line with the objectives of the CEDAW Convention, hence the reference of the SDGs in all recommendations related to all rights under the CEDAW Convention.[62]

CRC does not appear to grant a deferential status to the SDGs. Notably, the invocation of the SDGs appears in the form of 'recalling' the importance of SDGs as they may serve as a tool to facilitate the implementation of treaty obligations.[63] Nonetheless, CRC has also adopted a standard paragraph, which relates not only to linkages between the main treaty and SDGs but also encompasses the two substantive optional protocols. In this standard paragraph, CRC calls on States to ensure the realization of children's rights in accordance with these three instruments and also urges State to integrate all SDG targets in national frameworks.[64]

ii. CMW, CRPD, and CRC: A case-by-case approach

The terminology repeatedly used by these TBs in their concluding observations points to a recognition of the role of the SDGs in the context of the realization of

---

[59] CEDAW, 'Guidance note for States parties for the preparation of reports under article 18 of the Convention on the Elimination of All Forms of Discrimination against Women in the context of the Sustainable Development Goals' <https://tbinternet.ohchr.org/_layouts/15/treatybodyexternal/Download.aspx?symbolno=CEDAW/C/74/3&Lang=en> accessed 12 March 2022 (hereafter 'CEDAW SDG Guidance Note'); and CESCR Statement, 'The Pledge to "Leave No One Behind": The International Covenant on Economic, Social and Cultural Rights and the 2030 Agenda for Sustainable Development'<https://www.ohchr.org/Documents/HRBodies/CESCR/E_C_12_2019_1.docx> accessed 12 March 2022.
[60] CESCR, 'Concluding observations on Latvia' (E/C12/LVA/CO/2) para 51.
[61] ibid.
[62] CEDAW SDG Guidance Note (n 59).
[63] ibid.
[64] CRC, Concluding observations on Tunisia, CRC/C/TUN/CO/4-6, para 5.

respective treaty provisions. Not all TBs adopted a specific standalone paragraph on the SDGs (as is the practice for CESCR and CEDAW) but many refer to specific targets when formulating their recommendations. This is arguably aimed at contextualizing issues by encouraging the States parties concerned to achieve practical results in the implementation of specific treaty obligations.

Unsurprisingly, the language used by these TBs is less peremptory urging States parties to act 'in accordance' or 'in line' with or to 'bear in mind' the SDGs or a specific goal's target. They also 'recall', 'take into account', and 'take into consideration' the SDGs or a specific target before formulating recommendations.[65] Arguably, this language diminishes down the weight ascribed to the SDGs. However, it aligns with TBs' established practice of referring to soft law to guide States parties in the implementation of treaty provisions. It is clear that the 2030 Agenda does not create supplementary legal obligations in the context of treaty reporting but constitutes a critical political framework that is in consonance with treaty obligations and reinforces TB outputs.

CRPD recognizes the utility of the SDGs as a tool to help implement the Convention on the Rights of Persons with Disabilities (ICPRD) and thus takes into account the linkages that exist between some of its provisions and corresponding SDG targets when formulating its recommendations to States parties. CMW, which does not include a specific standard paragraph on SDGs in its recommendations, mainstreams SDGs in relation to the specific rights set in the International Convention on the Protection of the Rights of All Migrant Workers and Members of Their Families (ICMW).[66] Although TBs have adopted different approaches towards SDG targets, including by using different terminological formulations, references to the SDGs purport to help implement treaty obligations undertaken by States parties.

b. Substantive human rights treaty provisions and the SDGs: Civil and political rights

Treaty bodies have referred to the principles of equality and non-discrimination as cornerstones for the realization of all human rights. The reference of these principles in the SDGs provides a basis for cross-referencing. However, a very limited number of civil and political rights have been mentioned in relation to the SDGs unlike economic, social and cultural rights with linkages to the rights of specific groups, such as women, children, migrants and persons with disabilities.

---

[65] CRC, 'Concluding observations on Belarus' (CRC/C/BEL/CO/5-6) paras 16, 23, and 26.
[66] See, for example, CMW, 'Concluding observations on Rwanda' (CMW/C/RWA/CO/2) para 38 (hereafter 'CMW Rwanda'); CMW, 'Concluding observations on Colombia' (CMW/C/COL/CO/3) para 33 (hereafter 'CMW Colombia'); CMW, 'Concluding observations on Guatemala' (CMW/C/GTM/CO/2) para 35.

i. Participation in political, economic, and public life

The right to participate in political and public life embodied in some human rights treaties is reflected in Goal 5 and is closely related to the achievement of gender equality and the empowerment of women and girls. To some extent, Targets 16.6 and 16.7 also reflect this right. Although it is included in some treaty provisions, in the SDGs, participation in political, economic and public life is focused on women as a group in order to promote equal opportunities for them at leadership levels, thus upholding gender equality. In some human rights treaty provisions, participation in political life is limited to the public sphere and does not explicitly cover the economic dimension. Arguably, the SDGs go beyond treaty provisions. However, this right in the SDGs is not promoted universally, i.e. beyond women as group, which is another difference compared to human rights treaty provisions such as article 25 of the International Covenant on civil and Political Rights (ICCPR) and article 5 (c) of the International Convention of all forms of Racial discrimination (ICERD).

Goal 5 is reflected in numerous recommendations of various treaties bodies although not always directly. Explicit linkages of the SDGs to this right have been made largely by CEDAW, which has addressed it from the perspective of unequal treatment of women, and called for the adoption of temporary special measures, including statutory quotas, to enhance the representation of women in decision-making positions, including the civil service, the foreign service, security and armed forces.[67] CEDAW has also called on States parties to provide incentives for political parties to nominate an equal number of female and male candidates for elections, including focusing on women belonging to disadvantaged groups and access to adequate campaign financing for women candidates.[68]

Additional efforts to realize this goal relate to the need to guarantee in law specific quotas for women within political parties and to raise awareness among political leaders and the public to ensure the full, equal and democratic participation of women on an equal basis with men in political and public affairs.[69]

ii. Other civil rights and fundamental freedoms

Target 16.9 is to 'provide universal legal identity' and is relevant to addressing the barriers and obstacles to the right to birth registration and nationality in health facilities or in the civil registration system, which prevent children, particularly, from being registered and obtaining identity documents, including citizenship[70]

---

[67] CEDAW, 'Concluding observations on Moldova' (CEDAW/C/MDA/CO/6/) para 27 (hereafter 'CEDAW Moldova').
[68] ibid.
[69] CEDAW, Concluding observations on Bosnia Herzegovina' (CEDAW/C/BIH/CO/6) para 30 (hereafter 'CEDAW Bosnia Herzegovina').
[70] CRC, 'Concluding observations on Swaziland' (CRC/C/SWZ/CO/2-4) para 33 (hereafter 'CRC Swaziland'); and CMW Rwanda (n 66) para 38.

or being at risk of statelessness.[71] As a result, TBs urge States to raise awareness of the importance of birth registration, mainly among marginalized communities.[72]

Treaty bodies have also linked the SDGs to the right to the security and the protection of the person, such as protection from labour exploitation, abuse and violence, trafficking in persons, and other forms of ill-treatment. In that vein, CRC addresses the protection of children against violence and abuses in relation to Target 16.2, under which it has stressed that this should include the implementation of policies and strategies to end such violence, including the investigation of violent acts and the protection of child victims.[73] With regard to the protection of children against forced marriage, CRC has used Target 5.3 to underscore the need to both criminalize such a practice and to raise awareness about its harmful effects.[74]

In its interpretation of article 16 of ICPRD, the CRPD has drawn linkages between Targets 5.1, 5.2, and 5.5 of the SDGs, and the right to protection from violence and abuse in mental health facilities and the prevention and the protection of women and girls with disabilities against gender-based violence.[75] To that end, the CRPD observes that comprehensive strategies to prevent and combat all forms of violence and exploitation against persons with disabilities are necessary to curb this vice, including disability-related stigma and stereotypes. Moreover, States parties should ensure that persons with disabilities have access to information about complaint mechanisms and redress available to them.[76]

CMW has cited Targets 8.7, 8.8, and 16.2 of the SDGs in the context of addressing trafficking in persons, and linked these to various aspects of substantive and procedural rights necessary to combat this phenomenon, in particular the identification, prosecution, and punishment of offences of trafficking in persons and also access to legal representation for victims.[77] Realizing these targets and treaty obligations simultaneously also requires efforts to increase labour inspections and taking action against persons or groups that exploit and abuse migrant workers.[78] In fact, labour inspections and other actions including investigations

---

[71] ibid (CRC Swaziland) para 35; CMW, 'Concluding observations on Mongolia' (CMW/C/MDG/CO/1) para 40 (hereafter 'CMW Mongolia').

[72] CMW, 'Concluding Observations on Bosnian Herzegovina' (CMW/C/BIH/CO/3) para 46; CMW, 'Concluding observations on Mozambique' (CMW/C/MOZ/CO/1) para 46 (hereafter 'CMW Mozambique'); CMW, 'Concluding observations on Guyana' (CMW/C/GUY/CO/1) para 43 (hereafter 'CMW Guyana').

[73] CRC Swaziland (n 71) para 39; and CRC, 'Concluding Observations on Switzerland' (CRC/C/CHE/5-6) para 28.

[74] CRC, 'Concluding observations on Czechia' (CRC/C/CZE/CO/5-6) para 28 (hereafter 'CRC Czechia').

[75] CRPD, 'Concluding Observations on France' (CRPD/C/FRA/CO/1) para 35 (CRPD France).

[76] CRPD, 'Concluding observations on Estonia' (CRPD/C/EST/CO/1) para 33 (hereafter 'CRPD Estonia').

[77] CMW Colombia (n 66) para 33.

[78] CMW, 'Concluding Observations Guatemala' (CMW/C/GTM/CO/2) para 35; CMW Mozambique (n 72) para 32; and CMW Guyana (n 72) para 33.

and prosecutions against abusers, if effective, should contribute towards the reinforcement of the implementation of treaty obligations that protect against trafficking in persons. In the same vein, other similar policy measures aimed at observing relevant treaty obligations could support the realization of the corresponding above-mentioned targets.

CMW recognizes that providing assistance, protection, and rehabilitation to victims of sexual and labour exploitation, especially migrant women and children, is a critical measure to effectively fight against trafficking in persons and various forms of exploitation, which are closely linked to the SDGs.[79]

c. Substantive human rights treaty provisions and the SDGs: Economic, social, and cultural rights

Since the SDGs are largely overlapping with the promotion of economic, social and cultural rights and addressing inequality and discrimination among specific groups, it is unsurprising that it is primarily TBs responsible for monitoring economic, social and cultural rights that have had the most recourse to them. As such, CESCR, CMW, CRPD, and CRC are the only TBs that have persistently linked their respective treaty provisions to the SDGs, primarily relating to poverty reduction (Goal 1), health (Goal 3), education (Goal 4), social security/protection (Goal 5), work and employment, including conditions of work and remuneration (Goal 8).

i. Poverty reduction (Goal 1)
Treaty bodies have addressed poverty reduction more frequently in regard to the protection of persons in the most vulnerable situations such as women, children living in rural areas and persons with disabilities.[80] TBs' recommendations on measures to achieve Goal 1 have included a set of initiatives of financial and protective nature such as the adoption of human rights-based poverty reduction strategies, the economic empowerment of disadvantaged women, including through the provision of credit loans, and access to education, health, water and sanitation, and employment.[81] This has also included the need to establish a social protection floor to provide basic income,[82] to increase allowances for persons with disabilities to contribute towards improving their standard of living;[83] and the provision of

---

[79] CMW on Mongolia (n 71) para 34; CMW, 'Concluding observations on Algeria' (CMW/C/DZA/CO/2) para 34.

[80] CESCR, 'Concluding observations on Guinea' (E/C12/GIN/CO/1) para 38 (hereafter 'CESCR Guinea'); CEDAW, 'Concluding observations on Eritrea' (CEDAW/C/ERI/CO/6) para 44 (hereafter 'CEDAW Eritrea'); CRPD Estonia (n 76) para 55.

[81] ibid (CESCR Guinea) (n 76) para 38.

[82] CESCR, 'Concluding observations on Benin' (E/C12/BEN/CO/3) para 32 (hereafter 'CESCR Benin').

[83] CRPD, 'Concluding observations on Ecuador' (CRPD/C/ECU/CO/2-3) para 50 (CRPD Ecuador).

other appropriate services such as housing, in particular for women and migrants with disabilities.[84]

ii. Health (Goal 3)

Regarding the right to health, TBs have focused on Target 3.7 (Goal 3). The most cited relates to ensuring universal access to sexual and reproductive health services, the prevention of early pregnancy and sexually transmitted infections; and the inclusion of sexual and reproductive education in school curricula.[85] This has also included the provision of affordable modern contraceptives to all women and girls, including those belonging to disadvantaged groups.[86] It has been noted that realizing Target 3.7 hinges on promoting efforts to address maternal mortality, malnutrition and communicable diseases through, inter alia, hygiene improvement and access to water and sanitation for women and girls.[87]

Efforts to realize the right to health have also involved references to Targets 1.3, 3.1, 3.4, 3.3, 3.5, 3.7, 3.8, and 5.6. CRC has consistently associated the realization of the right to health with access to social protection. Under Target 1.3, CRC has called for the development of a social assistance and protection strategy to reduce poverty for the most vulnerable households.[88] CRC has also called upon States parties to provide an adequate social housing system and social benefits to support families in the most need to improve the living conditions necessary for children's development in accordance with articles 26(2) and 27(3) of the Convention on the Rights of the Child (UNCRC).[89] The reduction of infant and child mortality through access to quality primary health services, particularly in rural areas, by allocating sufficient human and financial resources for health infrastructure and availability and access to medicines under Goal 3, is also linked to efforts to realize the right to health under the UNCRC.[90] Under Target 3.4, CRC has interpreted that the right to health encompasses the prevention of suicide among children, adequate responses to the mental health of children,[91] and the need to effectively address the causes of child malnutrition and obesity.

CRPD has addressed the right to health of persons with disabilities under Targets 3.7 and 3.8 in line with article 25 of ICPRD. It has mainly focused on accessibility, including regarding health services to achieve the relevant Targets of Goal 3.[92] Equally, the development and promotion of universal design of medical

---

[84] CRPD Estonia (n 76) para 55.
[85] CEDAW, 'Concluding observations on Bulgaria' (CEDAW/C/BGR/CO/8) para 34 (hereafter 'CEDAW Bulgari'a); CEDAW, CEDAW Eritrea (n 80) para 40; CEDAW Bosnia Herzegovina (n 69) para 38.
[86] ibid (CEDAW Bulgaria) para 34.
[87] CRC Swaziland (n 70) para 55; and CRC Czechia (n 74) para 38.
[88] CRC Swaziland (n 70) para 61.
[89] CRC Czechia (n 74) para 41.
[90] CRC Swaziland (n 70) para 53.
[91] CRC Czechia (n 74) para 37.
[92] CRPD, 'Concluding observations on Greece' (CRPD/C/GRC/CO/1) para 37 (hereafter 'CRPD Greece'); CRPD, 'Concluding observations on India' (CRPD/C/IND/CO/1) para 53.

devices and equipment is necessary.[93] Achieving the right to health under Goal 3 also requires that States parties consult with relevant organisations of women with disabilities and to promote training for health staff, and ensure access to health care services for women and girls.[94]

iii. Education (Goal 4)
Treaty bodies have addressed the right to education, particularly regarding the promotion of inclusive education for all children relevant to Targets 4.1, 4.2 and 4.5, 4.7 of Goal 4. TBs recognize that this requires that States parties ensure that girls and boys have access to quality inclusive education and measures to improve enrolment, in particular for girls belonging to the most marginalized groups such as minority groups, refugee, migrant, asylum seekers, girls with disabilities, and those who are victims of violence and abuses.[95] In addition, TBs have called on States parties to allocate sufficient funds for developing early childhood education and creating an adequate number of childcare educational facilities.[96]

The implementation of inclusive education also calls for the elimination of gender disparities and guaranteeing equal access to education at all levels including vocational training for specific groups such as persons with disabilities, and providing the necessary support for ensuring access to education taking into account their particular requirements.[97] This also includes reducing school dropouts, especially in rural areas; ensuring that pregnant girls and adolescent mothers remain in school; addressing obstacles such as repetition rates, early pregnancy; and reducing physical distance from homes to secondary schools and improving the quality of school infrastructure.[98] Furthermore, in reference to Targets 4a and 4c, States parties are called to eliminate the hidden costs of schooling, in particular top-up tuition fees and costs for uniforms and transportation to school.[99]

iv. Social security and protection/economic and social benefits (Goal 5)
The right to social security and assistance is enshrined in Goal 5 of the SDGs but TBs have also addressed it in their references to Goals 1 and 10. This approach, consisting of linking social security/protection to poverty reduction, is particularly evident in the work of CESCR. In addressing this right, CESCR has argued that a national minimum income standard should be provided to prevent persons from falling below national poverty lines.[100] It has, therefore, called on States parties to

---

[93] CRPD on France (n 75) para 53.
[94] ibid; and CRPD on Estonia (n 76) para 49.
[95] CEDAW Bosnia Herzegovina (n 69) para 34.
[96] CRC Czechia (n 74) para 42.
[97] CRPD France (n 75) para 51; CRPD Estonia (n 76) para 47.
[98] CRC Swaziland (n 70) para 63.
[99] ibid.
[100] CESCR, 'Concluding Observations on Mali' (E/C/MLI/CO/1) para 31; CESCR Benin (n 82) para 32.

develop universal health coverage and to establish a social protection system or to create a social protection floor by providing basic income security for the population.[101] This should focus, in particular, on the most disadvantaged and marginalized groups in order to guarantee decent living conditions.[102]

In a similar approach, referring to Target 1.3 of the SDGs (Goal 1) in the context of the application of article 28 of ICPRD, CRPD has stressed that guaranteeing social protection to persons with disabilities requires that State parties consistently review the amount of allocation provided to adults with disabilities.[103] CRPD has also linked the right to an adequate standard of living and social protection to Target 10.2 (Goal 10), inviting States parties to establish a national social security for persons with disabilities, which would help improve their living standard, in particular for marginalized groups.[104]

According to CEDAW, referring to Target 5a (Goal 5), the right to social security for women must be guaranteed through strengthened funding for social protection schemes targeting women belonging to disadvantaged groups.[105] As an additional measure to enhance social protection under Target 5a, the promotion of social security/protection could also be driven by allowing more access by women to land and property on an equal basis with men and to enhance their access to financial credits and loans.[106]

v. Work and employment (Goal 8)

Under articles 6 and 7 of ICESCR, CESCR has addressed mainly the protection of rights at work and employment in the informal economy. It has recommended that States parties adopt measures to guarantee just and favourable work conditions, including undertaking labour inspections and providing social insurance coverage to workers in informal sectors of the economy.[107]

Relying on Target 8.5 of the SDGs (Goal 8), the CEDAW has focused on several issues emanating from the rights at work and in employment. It has stressed that States parties need to improve the employment rates of women in the formal economy, to establish a social security system for women in vulnerable situations, to guarantee the principle of equal pay for work of equal value, and to protect women from sexual harassment in the workplace.[108] To do so, States parties should

---

[101] CESCR Benin (n 82) para 32; CESCR, 'Concluding observations on South Africa' (E/C12/ ZAF/CO/1) para 49; CESCR, 'Concluding observations on Kazakhstan' (E/C12/KAZ/CO/2) para 35.
[102] CESCR, 'Concluding observations on Mali' (E/C12/MLI/CO/1) para 31; CESCR, 'Concluding observations on Mali' (E/C12/NER/CO/1) para 43.
[103] CRPD France (n 75) para 57.
[104] CRPD Ecuador (n 83) para 50.
[105] CEDAW Moldova (n 67) para 37.
[106] CEDAW Bosnia Herzegovina (n 69) para 40.
[107] CESCR on Guinea (n 80) para 28.
[108] CEDAW Moldova (n 67) para 33.

adopt and enforce legislation to combat sexual harassment, and ensure access by victims to independent, confidential complaint procedures.[109]

In compliance with article 27 of ICRPD, CRPD has approached the right to work and employment through the lens of Target 8.5 (Goal 8). It has focused on addressing the obstacles that bar persons with disabilities from accessing the open labour market and has called for their meaningful inclusion in both the private and public sectors, regardless of the type of impairment or level of support required.[110] CRPD also stressed that States parties should guarantee that there is no pay gap for work of equal value for persons with disabilities, in particular that their remuneration is not below the minimum wage.[111] Other measures require that States parties ensure that persons with disabilities have access to general technical and vocational guidance programmes and trainings; that their right to seek individualized support through the provision of reasonable accommodation in the workplace is recognized by employers; and that employees with disabilities are informed about how to request reasonable accommodation.[112]

Finally, CMW has addressed the working conditions of migrant workers under Targets 8.8 of the Goal 8. It has dealt with the protection of labour rights and the promotion of safe and secure working environments for all workers, including migrant workers and, in particular women migrants, and those in precarious employment. CMW has also underlined that the protection of their rights implies that States parties ensure that migrant domestic workers benefit from substantive and procedural rights to protect them from abuses and guarantee them adequate working conditions, including access to complaint mechanisms.[113] Additionally, the preservation of workers' rights also demands that migrant workers are not subjected to remuneration discrimination vis-à-vis nationals.[114]

In conclusion, although TBs have adopted different approaches to referencing the SDGs in their work, particularly in their concluding observations, all of them have integrated the holistic poverty eradication focus of the SDGs through the lens of economic, social and cultural rights. On the other hand, the SDGs' LNOB principle pervades their jurisprudence on civil and political rights. In this way, the references to the SDGs have tended to reflect the material scope of treaty provisions. It is clear that the TBs referring to the SDGs reflects an expectation that the realization of the SDGs might facilitate or further the implementation of treaty obligations.

---

[109] ibid.
[110] CRPD France (n 75) para 55; CRPD Estonia (n 76) para 53; CRPD Greece (n 92) para 39.
[111] CRPD France (n 75) para 55(b); CRPD Estonia (n 76) para 53(b).
[112] CRPD France (n 75) para 55; CRPD Estonia (n 76) para 53; CRPD Greece (n 92) para 39; CRPD Ecuador (n 83) para 48.
[113] CMW, 'Concluding observations on Argentina' (CMW/C/ARG/CO/2) para 39.
[114] CMW Mozambique (n 72) para 40; CMW Guyana (n 72) para 41; CMW, 'Concluding observations on Saint Vincent and the Grenadines' (CMW/C/VCT/CO/1) para 37.

d. General Comments/General Recommendations

General Comments/General Recommendations are one of the tools at the disposal of TBs to provide authoritative guidance to States parties and other actors on the measures that are necessary to ensure compliance with treaty provisions. During the period following the adoption of the 2030 Agenda in September 2015 until March 2022, eight TBs adopted a total of 26 General Comments.[115] However, only half of the General Comments refer specifically to the UN 2030 Agenda, the SDGs or its principles.

Treaty bodies have included the 2030 Agenda in their General Comments to varying degrees, with CEDAW, CERD, and CRPD demonstrating some consistency. References to the 2030 Agenda in General Comments adopted by CESCR, CRC, CRPD, and, in some cases, CEDAW, are generally broad and cursory, without an explicit mention of specific goals. In other words, TBs' General Comments have tended to refer to the SDGs as a framework for development without expounding on the specific goals.

For instance, CEDAW's General Recommendation on rural women contains numerous references to the SDGs as a framework without linking specific goals to the subject matter.[116] CEDAW notes that many of the SDGs called for specific attention to and addressed the situation of rural women and are an important opportunity to advance both process and outcome indicators.[117] CEDAW further calls for data collection and disaggregation on the situation of rural women, including for relevant indicators, and underlined the need for gender mainstreaming in all agricultural and rural development policies in line with the SDGs.[118]

In its General Comment on the right to sexual and reproductive health, CESCR recalls that the 2030 Agenda also included relevant goals and targets to be achieved.[119] CRC's General Comment on public budgeting for the realization of children's rights simply acknowledges that the 2030 Agenda addressed financial management that had an impact on children.[120]

CRPD's General Comment on women and girls with disabilities only has one reference to the 2030 Agenda. It calls on states parties to ensure that all international cooperation be disability and gender sensitive, and inclusive; and that data on women with disabilities be included in the implementation of the 2030

---

[115] United Nations Treaty Body Database <https://tbinternet.ohchr.org/_layouts/15/TreatyBodyExternal/TBSearch.aspx> accessed 11 February 2022 (hereafter 'UN TB Database').
[116] CEDAW, 'General recommendation No 34 (2016) on the rights of rural women' (CEDAW/C/GC/34) para 3
[117] ibid para 2.
[118] ibid paras 36(a) and 94.
[119] CESCR, 'General comment No 22 (2016) on the Right to sexual and reproductive health (article 12 of the International Covenant on Economic, Social and Cultural Rights)' (E/C12/GC/22) para 1.
[120] CRC, 'General comment No 19 (2016) on Public Budgeting for the Realization of children's rights (art 4)' (CRC/C/GC/19) para 10.

Agenda, goals, targets, and indicators.[121] In its General Comment on the participation of persons with disabilities, including children and their representative organizations, CRPD highlights the relevance of the 2030 Agenda and the participation of persons with disabilities at the international level 'for instance at the high-level political forum on sustainable development' and in implementation and monitoring of the SDGs.[122]

In other instances, TBs have made specific references to specific SDGs. Goal 4, that seeks to ensure inclusive and equitable quality education and promote lifelong learning opportunities for all, has been widely referred to in General Comments adopted by CEDAW, CRC, and CRPD.[123] Nevertheless, it is surprising that the TBs did not cross-reference Goal 4 with others, such as Goals 1–6 despite their interrelation with education attainment.

In its General Comment on the right to inclusive education, CRPD generally notes that, just like ICRPD, Goal 4 also 'affirms the value of inclusive, quality and equitable education'.[124] In relation to monitoring inclusive education, CRPD calls for the development of disability-inclusive indicators to be used consistent with the 2030 Agenda.[125] Similarly, CEDAW's General Recommendation on the right to education fails to cross-reference education with other SDGs. While CEDAW refers to the importance of Goal 4 and the inextricable link between gender equality and achieving education for all, it does not explicitly address Goal 5.[126] However, CEDAW reminds states parties of the fact that while the 2030 Agenda and other political commitments and global strategies are non-binding, they serve to 'reiterate the responsibilities of Governments in recognizing education as a catalyst for accelerating national development and social transformation'.[127]

In its General Comment on the implementation of the rights of the child during adolescence, CRC refers to Goal 4 and highlights that states should introduce comprehensive and proactive measures to address all factors that contribute to the high levels of early school leaving of adolescents.[128] This statement clearly brings into the discourse factors that drive school drop-outs, such as sexual and gender-based

---

[121] CRPD, 'General comment No 3 (2016) on Women and Girls with Disabilities' (CRPD/C/GC/3) para 63 (e).
[122] CRPD, 'General comment No 7 (2018) on the Participation of Persons with Disabilities, including Children with Disabilities, through their Representative Organizations' (CRPD/C/GC/7) paras 9, 32, and 94 (r).
[123] CRPD, 'General comment No 4 (2016) on the right to inclusive education', CRPD/C/GC/4 (hereafter 'CRPD/C/GC/4'); CEDAW, 'General recommendation No 36 (2017) on the right of girls and women to education', CEDAW/C/GC/36 (hereafter 'CEDAW/C/GC/36') and CRC, 'General comment No 20 (2016) on the implementation of the rights of the child during adolescence' (CRC/C/GC/20) (hereafter 'CRC/C/GC/20').
[124] CRPD/C/GC/4 (n 123) para 2.
[125] ibid para 12 (i).
[126] CEDAW/C/GC/36 (n 123) para 3.
[127] ibid para 12.
[128] CRC/C/GC/20 (n 123) paras 4 and 71.

violence, child labour, and hunger, that implicate Goals 1, 2, and 5. However, like other TBs, CRC failed to provide a fuller analysis of these implications.

Goal 10 on reduced inequalities is another goal that has been recalled by numerous TBs and has been specifically referred to in General Comments by CEDAW, CERD, and CRPD.[129] CERD, in its General Recommendation on preventing and combatting racial profiling by law enforcement officials, noted that the 2030 Agenda, particularly Goals 10 and 16, constitute the framework of the general recommendation, and serve as entry points for its work.[130] In its General Comment on equality and non-discrimination, CRPD recalled states parties' obligations to develop monitoring frameworks with human rights indicators, and specific benchmarks and targets for each indicator, consistent with Goal 10. It also underlined that all data collection and development of indicators, as well as international cooperation must aim to advance non-discrimination policies in line with ICRPD and the 2030 Agenda.[131]

CRPD, in its General Comment on the right to independent living, noted the special importance of Goal 10, target 10.2, empowerment and promotion of social, economic, and political inclusion for all, and target 11.1, ensuring access to adequate, safe, and affordable housing, and affordable services for all.[132] Besides drawing attention to the achievement of Goal 10, CEDAW has comprehensively integrated the 2030 Agenda and interlinkages among SDGs.

In its General Recommendation on gender-based violence against women, updating general recommendation No 19, CEDAW called on states parties to prioritize the implementation of the relevant SDGs, in particular Goals 5, to achieve gender equality and empowerment of all women and girls.[133] This also includes Goal 16, to promote peaceful and inclusive societies for sustainable development, provide access to justice and build effective, accountable and inclusive institutions at all levels; and to support national plans to implement all Goals in a gender-responsive and participatory manner.[134]

In its General Recommendation on trafficking in women and girls in the context of global migration, CEDAW highlighted that states need to address the factors that heighten the risks of trafficking and promote gender equality, including the civil, political, economic, social, and cultural rights of women and girls in line with

---

[129] CEDAW, 'General Recommendation No 35 (2017) on Gender-based Violence against Women, Updating General Recommendation No 19' (CEDAW/C/GC/35) (hereafter 'CEDAW/C/GC/35'); CRPD 'General Comment No 6 (2018) on Equality and Non-discrimination' (CRPD/C/GC/6) (hereafter 'CRPD/C/GC/6'); and CERD, 'General Recommendation No 36 (2020) on Preventing and Combating Racial Profiling by Law Enforcement Officials' (CERD/C/GC/36) (hereafter 'CERD/C/GC/36').
[130] ibid (CERD/C/GC/36) para 9.
[131] CRPD/C/GC/6 (n 129) paras 71 and 72.
[132] CRPD, 'General Comment No 5 (2017) on Living Independently and Being included in the Community' (CRPD/C/GC/5) para 14.
[133] CEDAW/C/GC/35 (n 129) para 35.
[134] ibid.

Goals 1, 3, 4–5, 8, 10–11, 13, and 16.[135] If permitted by national law, CEDAW also called for disaggregated data collection relevant to victims and perpetrators of trafficking in line with indicator 16.2.2.[136]

In its General Recommendation on the gender-related dimensions of disaster-risk reduction in the context of climate change, CEDAW underlined that gender equality was a precondition for the realization of the SDGs.[137] It noted that the SDGs contained important targets on gender equality, including those in Goals 3–6 and 10, and on climate change and disaster-risk reduction, in Goals 11 and 13.[138] CEDAW, like CRPD, also noted that monitoring mechanisms need to be developed with indicators, including gender-responsive indicators, to establish baselines and measure progress;[139] and called on states parties to build the capacity of national statistical offices.[140] CEDAW acknowledged that the 2030 Agenda and the SDGs had been a concerted effort at policy coherence on disaster-risk reduction, climate change, and sustainable development, but noted a discord at the national, regional, and international levels to align programmes of action, budgets, and strategies.[141]

Finally, it bears mentioning that CESCR is in the process of developing a General Comment on Sustainable Development and the ICESCR to guide states parties' efforts in discharging their Covenant obligations in relation to sustainable development.[142]

e. Treaty body statements and 2030 Agenda

The issuance of statements enables TBs to adopt positions swiftly and respond to global and national human rights situations and developments of concern in order to advocate for specific positions. Between September 2015 and February 2022, TBs had adopted thirty-three statements, including joint statements.[143] Of these, less than half (fourteen) contain a specific reference to the 2030 Agenda and the SDGs. The statements also reveal that TBs have taken different approaches in their efforts to include the 2030 Agenda. Similar to General Comments, these range from very general references to systematic inclusion and reference to specific goals.

---

[135] ibid paras 21 and 47.
[136] ibid para 110.
[137] CEDAW, 'General recommendation No 37 (2018) on the gender-related dimensions of disaster risk reduction in the context of climate change' (CEDAW/C/GC/37) para 7.
[138] ibid para 22.
[139] ibid para 40 (b).
[140] ibid para 40 (c).
[141] ibid para 41.
[142] CESCR, 'General Comment on Sustainable Development and the International Covenant on Economic, Social and Cultural Rights' <https://www.ohchr.org/EN/HRBodies/CESCR/Pages/CESCR-GC-Sustainable-Development.aspx> accessed 15 February 2022.
[143] UN TB Database (n 115).

The first category includes those statements that have broad references to the 2030 Agenda and underscore the importance of implementing human rights treaties to achieve the 2030 Agenda. The joint Human Rights Committee—CESCR statement, for instance, recalls that implementation of the two covenants on civil and political rights and on economic, social, and cultural rights is 'indispensable for the achievement of the [SDGs] and the implementation of the 2030 Agenda'.[144] Equally, the joint UN Women-CEDAW-CRPD statement on ending sexual harassment against women and girls with disabilities recalled that legal obligations under the treaties echoed the 2030 Agenda to 'eliminate all forms of violence against all women and girls in the public and private spheres'.[145] It underscored that meaningful consultation and involvement of women with disabilities is crucial in order to change societies where women with disabilities are often being left behind.[146]

In its statement on women's activism in political processes, CEDAW recalled the crucial importance of a free, democratic, participatory, and inclusive election process that fully respects women's rights that is free from flaws or coercion.[147] It highlighted that equal participation of women and men in political and public life and decision-making are human rights at the centre of the commitments of all UN Member States enshrined in the SDGs.[148]

In its statement on the protection of children from sale, sexual exploitation, and recruitment and use in hostilities, the chairperson of CRC underlined the need for the international community to redouble efforts to end violence against children by 2030.[149] The statement recalled the need to transform the commitments made in the Optional Protocol to the UNCRC on the Involvement of Children in Armed Conflict into reality, especially for children trapped in armed conflict.[150] Furthermore, in its statement on Universal Children's Day, CRC highlighted that the principles and provisions of the UNCRC constituted a crucial reference for the implementation of the Agenda 2030.[151] It thus recalled that children deprived of

---

[144] CESCR and Human Rights Committee, 'Joint Statement The International Covenants on Human Rights: 50 years on' para 8 <https://digitallibrary.un.org/record/862148?ln=en> accessed 7 March 2022.
[145] UN Women, CEDAW and CRPD, 'Joint statement on ending sexual harassment against women and girls with disabilities' (22 October 2020) <https://www.unwomen.org/en/news/stories/2020/10/statement-joint-un-women-cedaw-and-crpd>; (hereafter 'Joint UN Women-CEDAW-CRPD Statement') accessed 10 March 2022; and CEDAW, 'Women's activism in political processes' (3 September 2020) <https://tbinternet.ohchr.org/_layouts/15/treatybodyexternal/Download.aspx?symbolno=INT/CEDAW/STA/9245&Lang=en> accessed 10 March 2022 (hereafter 'CEDAW Statement on Women's Activism in Political Processes').
[146] Joint UN Women-CEDAW-CRPD Statement (n 145).
[147] CEDAW Statement on Women's Activism in Political Processes (n 145).
[148] ibid.
[149] United Nations, 'UN experts on child rights' statement on protecting children from sale, sexual exploitation and recruitment and use in hostilities, 20 May 2020' <https://violenceagainstchildren.un.org/news/un-experts-urge-states-protect-children-sale-sexual-exploitation-and-recruitment-and-use> accessed 20 March 2022.
[150] ibid.
[151] United Nations, 'Statement of UN Child Rights Experts on Universal Children's Day – marking the 27th anniversary of the Convention on the Rights of the Child, 20 November 2016' <https://tbinter

their liberty had been left behind and called for the safeguarding of children's rights in the face of the many pressing concerns.[152]

In its statement on rural women CEDAW noted that there needed to be effective implementation of the SDGs, many of which reflect on the situation of rural women and girls. It underlined that addressing the situation of rural women would contribute to the development of societies, the strengthening of norms and standards of human rights, and the realization of the SDGs.[153] In a joint statement for International Migrants Day, the chairs of CMW and CEDAW recalled that the UN Global Compact for Safe, Orderly and Regular Migration should also contribute to achieving commitments and targets set for migrant women and girls in the 2030 Agenda.[154]

The second category of statements reveals an effort by TBs to explore specific SDGs and the interrelationship between SDGs and human rights. A notable and singular case is CESCR's statement on the pledge to leave no one behind.[155] In addition to outlining the rights-based methodology applicable to all rights, which should guide states parties actions in all policy areas, CESCR expounded on the link between rights under ICESCR and the SDGs as follows:[156]

> The rights protected in the Covenant underpin the SDGs. These include the equal enjoyment of all Covenant rights between men and women (Goal 5 and gender mainstreaming into all other SDGs); the right to work and just and favourable conditions of work (Goal 8); the right to social security (Goals 1–3, 5, 10); protection and assistance to the family (Goals 3, 5); the right of everyone to an adequate standard of living, including adequate food, clothing, housing and water (Goals 1, 2, 6, 7, 11–16); the right to the highest attainable standard of physical and mental health (Goals 3, 6); the right to education (Goal 4); the right of everyone to take part in cultural life (Goal 16), and the right of everyone to enjoy the benefits of scientific progress and its applications (Goals 9–10). SDG 10 commits States to 'reduce inequality within and among countries'.

---

net.ohchr.org/_layouts/15/treatybodyexternal/Download.aspx?symbolno=INT%2fCRC%2fSTA%2f8 117&Lang=en> accessed 4 March 2022.

[152] ibid.
[153] CEDAW, 'Statement on the rights of rural women, 4 March 2016' <https://tbinternet.ohchr.org/Treaties/CEDAW/Shared%20Documents/1_Global/INT_CEDAW_STA_7934_E.pdf> accessed 4 March 2022.
[154] United Nations, 'Joint statement for International Migrants Day by the Chairpersons of CMW and CEDAW' (18 December) <https://tbinternet.ohchr.org/_layouts/15/treatybodyexternal/Download.aspx?symbolno=INT%2fCMW%2fSTA%2f8618&Lang=en> accessed 4 March 2022.
[155] CESCR, 'The Pledge to "Leave No One Behind": The International Covenant on Economic, Social and Cultural Rights and the 2030 Agenda for Sustainable Development'<https://tbinternet.ohchr.org/_layouts/15/treatybodyexternal/Download.aspx?symbolno=E%2FC.12%2F2019%2F1&Lang=en> accessed 7 March 2022.
[156] ibid para 5.

It should be noted that the COVID-19 pandemic spurred the issuance of multiple statements that refer to the 2030 Agenda, specifically urging states to be guided by the principle of LNOB in all COVID-19 response efforts.[157] CEDAW noted the opportunity offered by the pandemic to implement change guided by the principle of LNOB, with women at the centre of response and recovery strategies.[158] It thus called for joint action and collaboration among national human rights institutions, the UN system, and the UN human rights TBs and special procedures to design the way forward for both states and civil society actors.

A joint statement of the chair of CRPD and the Special Envoy of the United Nations Secretary-General on Disability and Accessibility reiterated that ICRPD is the legally binding framework for the achievement of the SDGs and all related targets, including those that did not explicitly refer to persons with disabilities, in order to protect their lives and rights during the COVID-19 pandemic.[159] CRPD clarified that by implementing their obligations under ICRPD and achieving the targets in the 2030 Agenda, states would safeguard the rights and lives of persons with disabilities.[160] The joint statement also recalled the diversity among persons with disabilities, the need for age and gender consideration in responses to the pandemic, and the specific situation of those left behind, namely, persons with disabilities facing deprivation and hardship.[161]

CESCR's statement on universal affordable vaccination against the coronavirus disease draws linkages between the SDGs. In expressing concerns about vaccine inequity, CESCR highlighted that the insufficient production of vaccines and the unequal global distribution, particularly affecting many least developed and developing countries is an issue of discrimination, impacting negatively on progress to achieve Goals 3, 10, and 17.[162]

In their joint statement on protecting and empowering girls and demanding equality, CEDAW and CRC recognized the interrelatedness of the SDGs and the need for a holistic approach towards implementation. While the statement highlights specifically Goal 5, it underscores that achieving gender equality is not a stand-alone goal and that gender equality is at the centre of the Member States' commitments enshrined in the 2030 Agenda. Importantly, the statement

---

[157] CESCR, 'Statement on the Coronavirus Disease (COVID-19) Pandemic and Economic, Social and Cultural Rights' (E/C12/2020/1) (6 April 2020); CEDAW, 'Raising Women's Voices and leadership in COVID-19 policies' (22 April 2020) and CRPD, Statement on COVID-19 and the human rights of persons with disabilities (9 June 2020); See United Nations Compilation of statements by human rights treaty bodies in the context of COVID-19 <https://www.ohchr.org/Documents/HRBodies/TB/COVID19/External_TB_statements_COVID19.pdf> accessed 7 March 2022.
[158] ibid 39.
[159] ibid 26, para 1.
[160] ibid para 4.
[161] ibid.
[162] CESCR, 'Statement on universal affordable vaccination against coronavirus disease (COVID-19), international cooperation and intellectual property' (E/C12/2021/1) (23 April 2021) para 1.

recognized that Goal 5 cuts across the entire SDG framework as a principle recognizing that girls' equality and participation are preconditions to achieving all the SDGs.[163]

Furthermore, the joint CEDAW-CRC statement on the occasion of the International Day of the Girl Child highlighted that the disruptions suffered in education systems due to the COVID-19 pandemic risked reversing the progress made in the area of girls' education and hence negatively impacting on the achievement of the SDGs, particularly those related to poverty reduction, health and well-being, quality education, and gender equality.[164]

4. Participation of the Treaty Bodies in the High-Level Political Forum on Sustainable Development

Every year TBs can provide input to the thematic review of the HLPF, which serves as the main platform for follow-up and review of the 2030 Agenda. While more than half of the TBs have made submissions to the HLPF since its establishment, their levels of engagement has varied.[165] By December 2021, CRPD had contributed four times. CED, CESCR CMW, and CRC had all contributed twice, and CERD, once. The Committee against Torture, the Human Rights Committee, or the Sub-Committee on the Prevention of Torture had not engaged in the HLPF process. CEDAW remains the only TB that has consistently contributed inputs annually from 2016 to 2021.[166]

In its submissions, CEDAW often recalls that it has fully integrated the SDGs in its work. In its 2021 submission, it highlighted that it had issued a guidance note in 2019 for state parties on how to prepare periodic reports in the context of the SDGs, which encourages them to include updated information on the progress made in achieving the SDGs under the state reporting procedure.[167] Its 2021 submission underscores that states parties' economic recovery strategies should focus on gender equality as a driving force of sustainable development, in line with Goal 5 of the SDGs.[168]

---

[163] CEDAW and CRC, 'Joint statement on protecting and empowering girls and demanding equality' (11 October 2019) <https://tbinternet.ohchr.org/_layouts/15/treatybodyexternal/Download.aspx?symbolno=INT%2fCEDAW%2fSTA%2f8980&Lang=en> accessed 1 March 2022.
[164] CEDAW and CRC, 'Joint statement on the occasion of the International Day of the Girl Child' (11 October 2021) <https://previous.ohchr.org/Documents/HRBodies/CRC/Statements/Joint-Statement-International-Day-Girl-Child.pdf> accessed 25 March 2022.
[165] United Nations High Level Political Forum, <https://sustainabledevelopment.un.org/inputs/> accessed 1 March 2022.
[166] ibid.
[167] CEDAW, '2021 submission to HLFP' <https://sustainabledevelopment.un.org/content/documents/27294CEDAW_Contribution_to_2021_HLPF.PDF>accessed 7 March 2022.
[168] ibid.

In its 2022 submission, CRPD recalled the integrated, indivisible, and interlinked nature of rights and SDGs; and urged states to address the disability specific impacts of the COVID-19 pandemic in all the SDGs. It also identified a number of action points and policy recommendations in areas that were greatly affected during the pandemic, such as access to information, disability- and gender-based violence, education, and health.[169] Previous submissions focused on the concern that persons with disabilities were left out of the COVID-19 pandemic response and recovery efforts, which demonstrates that the ICRPD has not been effectively implemented.[170]

CESCR submitted its statement on the pledge to leave no one behind underlining how the protection and promotion of economic, social, and cultural rights had a central in the fulfilment of the 2030 Agenda, and highlighting how a rights-based approach may contribute to the pledge.[171] While acknowledging the significant interlinkages between the SDGs and their respective treaties, CED and CMW have highlighted the need for states to increase ratifications; and to take into account a gender perspective in their policies and measures relating to their treaties.[172]

The Chairs of TBs made two submissions in 2016 and 2021.[173] These submissions are significant as they express the commitment of the UN TB system to consolidate a two-way interaction with the HLPF on the 2030 Agenda and to ensure complementarity between the treaties and the SDGs. The submissions provide a comprehensive overview of the work of the TBs and their contribution to the 2030 Agenda. In the 2016 submission, relating to 'Ensuring that No One is left Behind', the chairs of the TBs noted how the human rights treaties were of particular relevance, given their emphasis on equality and non-discrimination or the rights of persons who are often left behind.[174]

The two-way TB–HLFP interaction is a hallmark of engagement of the UN human rights TBs in relation to the 2030 Agenda that somehow promotes policy coherence in terms of implementation. On one hand, the reporting of states

---

[169] CRPD, '2022 submission to HLPF' <https://sustainabledevelopment.un.org/content/documents/29591CRPD_2022.pdf> accessed 7 March 2022.

[170] CRPD, '2021 submission to HLPF' <https://sustainabledevelopment.un.org/content/documents/27279CRPD_input_to_2021_HLPF.pdf> accessed 7 March 2022.

[171] CESCR, '2020 submission to HLPF' <https://sustainabledevelopment.un.org/content/documents/25896Letter_to_ECOSOC_Chair_HLPF_2020.pdf> accessed 7 March 2022.

[172] CRPD, '2018 submission to HLPF' <https://sustainabledevelopment.un.org/content/documents/18285Comments_by_CMW_on_the_SDGs_HLPF_2018.pdf> and CED, '2019 submission to HLPF' <https://sustainabledevelopment.un.org/content/documents/21755CED_HLPF_2019.pdf> accessed 1 March 2022.

[173] United Nations, 'Chairs of Treaty bodies' 2016 submission to HLPF' <https://sustainabledevelopment.un.org/content/documents/10323Human Rights Treaty Bodies contribution 2016-May-26.pdf> (hereafter 'UN Chairs' 2016 HLFP Submission') and United Nations, 'Chairs of Treaty bodies' 2021 submission to HLPF <https://sustainabledevelopment.un.org/index.php?page=view&type=30022&nr=2873&menu=3170> accessed 1 March 2022 (hereafter 'UN Chairs' 2021 HLFP Submission').

[174] UN Chairs' 2016 HLFP Submission.

regarding their implementation of treaty obligations generates information that is closely related to the implementation of the SDGs. In this regard, it 'provides a readymade source of data to help track progress on SDG implementation'.[175] On the other hand, the information relating to national implementation of the SDGs provided to the HLFP is also related to treaty implementation and of relevance to the work of TBs.[176] The chairs' submission recalled that many TBs were already engaging with the 2030 Agenda, including by referring to relevant SDGs and targets in their constructive dialogues with states and making recommendations in the concluding observations that link implementation of particular treaty provisions with SDGs and targets.[177] The submission underscored that 'the aim is not only to have rights-based SDGs implementation but also to help use treaty reporting as a means of tracking SDG and national development plan achievements'.[178]

The political declarations that emanate from HLPF meetings have traditionally included a few references to human rights and efforts by states to ensure people's enjoyment of human rights. Only the 2018 and 2021 declarations were adopted by consensus. It is noteworthy that the 2021 declaration explicitly reiterates the recognition that the 2030 Agenda is 'grounded in the Universal Declaration of human rights and international human rights treaties'.[179] It contains an unprecedented number of explicit human rights references, especially with regard to the commitment of leaving no one behind, the recovery from the COVID-19 pandemic and some of the issues that the chairs recommended in their 2021 submission.[180]

Albeit largely ad hoc, the voluntary national reviews (VNRs) provide an additional platform for TB engagement on the 2030 Agenda. VNRs aim to facilitate the sharing of experiences at the national level to accelerate the implementation of the 2030 Agenda through reporting and the creation of partnerships.[181] TBs use voluntary national reports, HLPF submissions and outcome documents in the drafting of lists of issues and the preparation for state party reviews. Notably, some states are taking deliberate measures to link reporting to TBs with the 2030 Agenda. TBs, as one of the multiple stakeholders engaging with the HLPF also contribute to national reviews. CERD, for instance, has provided information to the HLPF regarding countries that are party to ICERD having undergone a state party review and scheduled for a voluntary review at the HLPF.[182]

[175] Ibid.
[176] ibid.
[177] ibid.
[178] ibid.
[179] United Nations, 'Ministerial declaration of the high-level segment of the 2021 HLPF' para 33 <https://sustainabledevelopment.un.org/content/documents/28872MD_9_July_2021_FINAL.pdf> accessed 7 March 2022.
[180] UN Chairs' 2021 HLFP Submission.
[181] UN sustainable development knowledge platform <https://sustainabledevelopment.un.org/vnrs/> accessed 12 March 2022.
[182] CERD, '2017 submission to HLPF' <https://sustainabledevelopment.un.org/content/documents/14579OHCHR_Comm_on_the_Elimination_of_Racial_Discrimination.pdf> accessed 10 March 2022.

5. Conclusion

The 2030 Agenda adopts a pragmatic approach to the implementation of the norms and standards embodied in the various core UN human rights instruments. Since TBs are at the core of the international edifice designed to monitor human rights obligations, the 2030 Agenda places them at the heart of efforts to support states in ensuring that their actions towards the implementation of the SDGs adhere to those obligations. Most TBs have actively assumed the role of tracking and reporting on states' implementation of the SDGs through the systematic employment of a gamut of procedural and substantive tools. The approaches, albeit varying, have entailed the use of the reporting procedure, the issuance of general comments/recommendations, the promulgation of guidance and statements, and reporting to the HLFP.

The inclusion of the LNOB principle (reflective of the principle of equality and non-discrimination) and human rights, particularly economic, social, and cultural rights, in the SDGs, albeit implicit, has provided TBs with a strong basis to reinforce their jurisprudential efforts in supervising the implementation of states' treaty obligations whilst tracking their implementation of the SDGs. As a result, TBs continue to perform the twin function of generating crucial data on SDGs and issuing important recommendations that guide states' efforts towards the realization of the SDGs. This has enabled them to authoritatively play an important role in the advancement of the 2030 Agenda at both global and local levels.

Consequently, TBs have not only become troves of crucial data on the SDGs that other players such as the HLPF can utilize to assess and track progress, but they also contribute towards shaping the states' efforts in their implementation of the SDGs by integrating SDG-tracking within their supervisory mandates under the respective treaties. The relationship cultivated between UN TBs and the HLPF has also helped foster policy coherence in the enforcement of the SDGs and UN core human rights treaties as complimentary frameworks for sustainable development.

On the one hand, the HLFP's invitation to TBs to make submissions on key SDG trends observed in their work, including the continuous references of UN treaties in VNR processes, reinforces the use of hard law to complement the enforcement of the SDGs, which are soft law. On the other hand, the use by TBs of the SDGs, which have been universally adopted by UN Member States, in assessing the level of implementation of human rights treaties by states underscores their relational importance to development and hence the need to implement them with speed. Importantly, since the 2030 Agenda is time-bound, acceleration of the realization of the SDGs concomitantly speeds states implementation of treaty obligations.

6
The ILO's Dialogical Standards-Based Approach to International Labour Law

Katerina Tsotroudi and Jordi Agustí Panareda[*]

1. Introduction

The International Labour Organization (ILO) is an international organization created in 1919,[1] with the constitutional mandate to promote social justice, notably by setting international labour standards and supervising their application. Its founders recognized the importance of social justice in securing peace, against the background of workers' exploitation in the industrializing nations of that time and an increasing understanding of the world's economic interdependence and the need to obtain similarity of working conditions in countries competing for markets.

Reflecting these ideas, the Preamble of the ILO Constitution states:

> Whereas universal and lasting peace can be established only if it is based upon social justice;
>
> And whereas conditions of labour exist involving such injustice, hardship and privation to large numbers of people as to produce unrest so great that the peace and harmony of the world are imperilled; and an improvement of those conditions is urgently required;
>
> Whereas also the failure of any nation to adopt humane conditions of labour is an obstacle in the way of other nations which desire to improve the conditions in their own countries.

The areas of improvement listed in the Preamble remain relevant today, ranging from fundamental civil liberties, notably freedom of association and

---

[*] Respectively, Global Programming and Collaboration Coordinator and Head of Unit and Coordinator for Freedom of Association, at the ILO International Labour Standards Department (NORMES). The authors would like to thank the editors and ILO colleagues Corinne Vargha, Carlien Van Empel, Colin Fenwick Coen Kompier, Ritash Sarna, Dora Sari, Justine Tillier, and Peter Wichmand, for their thoughtful review and comments. The views expressed herein are the authors and do not necessarily represent those of the ILO.

[1] The ILO was created in the wake of World War I in 1919 by Part XIII of the Treaty of Peace of Versailles.

Katerina Tsotroudi and Jordi Agustí Panareda, *The ILO's Dialogical Standards-Based Approach to International Labour Law* In: *The Roles of International Law in Development*. Edited by: Siobhán McInerney-Lankford and Robert McCorquodale, Oxford University Press. © Katerina Tsotroudi and Jordi Agustí Panareda 2023.
DOI: 10.1093/oso/9730192872906.003.0006

non-discrimination, to the regulation of working time and labour supply, the prevention of unemployment and the provision of an adequate living wage and social protection for workers, children, and young persons.

In 1945, the ILO adopted the Declaration of Philadelphia, which later became part of its constitution and proclaims that 'labour is not a commodity', that 'all human beings, irrespective of race, creed or sex, have the right to pursue both their material well-being and their spiritual development in conditions of freedom and dignity, of economic security and equal opportunity' and that it is the responsibility of the ILO to examine and consider all international economic and financial policies and measures in the light of these fundamental objectives. The Declaration still constitutes the charter of aims and objectives of the ILO.[2]

The ILO became the first specialized agency of the United Nations (UN) in 1946 and is today an integral part of the UN system.[3] As mentioned above, its central mandate is to adopt legally-binding international treaties that can be ratified by Member States, known as Conventions (or Protocols), along with non-binding guidelines, known as Recommendations.[4] These are known as International Labour Standards (ILS) and serve to set out the basic rights, obligations, and institutions governing the world of work with the aspiration of setting a global level playing field that leaves no one behind.

The ILS adoption process involves the three main constitutionally established organs of the ILO: the International Labour Conference (ILC) which is the annual assembly of 187 Member States currently, the governing body (GB) which meets three times a year and adopts all decisions pertaining to the organization's governance and the International Labour Office which is the secretariat of the ILC and GB. The ILO is a tripartite organization: the ILC and GB are composed of representatives of governments and employers' and workers' organizations (the three ILO constituents). The Office is composed essentially of international civil servants. After a lengthy preparatory, drafting and negotiation process which can take several years, ILS are discussed and adopted by tripartite vote at the ILC.

Once adopted, ILS set international rules on the rights and obligations that should be applicable in the world of work, but they are not immediately binding

---

[2] The Declaration drew upon principles that were already included in the original 1919 ILO Constitution—art 41 (427 of the Treaty of Versailles), referring, inter alia, to equal remuneration for work of equal value, freedom of association, abolition of child labour, and the nature of work as not being a commodity.

[3] In addition to its constitution, the organization's status is grounded on the agreement signed with the UN in 1945 and the 1947 Convention on the Privileges and Immunities of the Specialized Agencies. As an international organization, the ILO is a subject of international law, thus also bound by general and other sources of international law.

[4] Oftentimes conventions lay down the basic principles and related recommendations that supplement them by providing more detailed guidance, though recommendations can also be autonomous. See ILO ILS website <https://www.ilo.org/dyn/normlex/en/f?p=NORMLEXPUB:1:0::NO:::> accessed 3 August 2023; ILO, 'Manual for drafting ILO instruments' (2006) <https://www.ilo.org/wcmsp5/groups/public/---dgreports/---jur/documents/publication/wcms_426015.pdf> accessed 3 August 2023.

at national level. Conventions become binding only after having been ratified. The ILO supervisory bodies monitor, in turn, the implementation of ratified conventions in law and in practice through an elaborate supervisory mechanism involving reports-based and complaints-based procedures. To date the ILO has adopted 190 conventions, six protocols, and 206 recommendations. The ILO through the GB regularly monitors the status of these instruments to make sure that they are up to date and periodically undertakes the revision, withdrawal, or abrogation of older instruments parallel to the adoption and promotion of up-to-date instruments in various technical areas.[5] For the purposes of this article, therefore, 'international labour law' denotes the exercise of the ILO's centenary old mandate to set, promote, supervise, and review ILS.[6]

As noted by the ILO Committee of Experts on the Application of Conventions and Recommendations (CEACR) recently,[7] ILS are an integral part of the international human rights norms and standards and give expression to human rights both in the civil and political as well as in the economic, social, and cultural sphere. In the civil and political sphere, ILS give expression to the right to freedom of association;[8] the right of peaceful assembly;[9] the right to freedom of expression and freedom of thought, conscience, and religion;[10] the right to equal and effective protection against discrimination;[11] the right to freedom from slavery, servitude, and forced or compulsory labour;[12] and most recently, the right to be free from violence and harassment[13] at work; as well as the rights of the child[14] and those

---

[5] Mechanisms to review the status of ILS have been established three times in the ILO's history. Most recently, a Standards Review Mechanism (SRM) was established in 2011 for the review of ILS through a Tripartite Working Group (TWG) meeting annually since 2016. For more information on the work of the SRM, see ILO, 'Standard Review Mechanism Tripatrtite Working Group' <https://www.ilo.org/global/standards/WCMS_449687/lang--en/index.htm> accessed 21 May 2023.

[6] For an overview of ILS and the ILO's supervisory system, see ILO, 'Rules of the Game: An Introduction to the Standards-related Work of the International Labour Organization (Centenary Edition 2019)' (2019) <https://www.ilo.org/global/standards/information-resources-and-publications/publications/WCMS_672549/lang--en/index.htm> accessed 21 May 2023.

[7] 'Report of the Committee of Experts on the Application of Conventions and Recommendations (CEACR)' Report III (Part A) International Labour Conference 110th Session (2022) paras 129–37. See also 'Joint Statement between the CEACR and Eight Human Rights Treaty Monitoring Bodies, Addendum to the CEACR Report' Report III(A)/Addendum International Labour Conference, 111th Session (2023).

[8] Freedom of Association and Protection of the Right to Organise Convention (1948) (No 87); Right to Organise and Collective Bargaining Convention (1949) (No 98).

[9] Compilation of Decisions of the Committee on Freedom of Association, ILO, Geneva (2018) paras 77 and 202–32 (hereafter 'Compilation').

[10] Compilation, paras 233–69; Abolition of Forced Labour Convention (1957) (No 105); Discrimination (Employment and Occupation) Convention (1958) (No 111) (hereafter 'Discrimination').

[11] Compilation (n 10) paras 1072–79; ibid (Discrimination).

[12] Forced Labour Convention (1930) (No 29); Abolition of Forced Labour Convention (1957) (No 105).

[13] Violence and Harassment Convention (2019) (No 190).

[14] Minimum Age Convention (1973) (No 138); Worst Forms of Child Labour Convention (1999) (No 182).

of indigenous peoples.[15] In the economic, social, and cultural sphere, ILS substantiate within the world of work human rights such as the right to work;[16] the right to social security;[17] the right to safe and healthy working conditions;[18] the right to fair wages[19] and to equal remuneration for work of equal value without distinction of any kind;[20] the right to rest, leisure, and reasonable limitation of working hours and periodic holidays with pay;[21] or the right to maternity protection.[22]

In addition, ILS complement international human rights law by adding key dimensions that facilitate the duty of states to respect, protect, and fulfil the human rights at work of individuals within their territory and/or jurisdiction, notably:

— by promoting social dialogue at all levels (including labour dispute settlement mechanisms) as an essential means of realizing human rights at work, complementing laws or regulations;
— by establishing labour market institutions that make the protection or promotion of human rights at work a daily practice (examples of institutions include labour inspection services promoting compliance with measures taken to realize the right to safe and healthy working conditions; or public employment services pursuing the best possible organization of the labour market with a view to realizing the right to work without discrimination and 'leaving no one behind'); and
— by benchmarking or operationalizing human rights at work as declared in UN instruments (examples include providing a system of minimum age for admission to work in order to support the children's right to be protected from economic exploitation and from performing hazardous or harmful work;[23] or stipulating measures to prevent forced labour and trafficking of persons for forced labour).

Respecting human rights and relevant international standards is also a corporate responsibility. The ILO has developed a close collaboration with the UN Working

---

[15] Indigenous and Tribal Peoples Convention (1989) (No 169).
[16] For example, Employment Policy Convention (1964) (No 122); among other ILS.
[17] Social Security (Minimum Standards) Convention (1952) (No 102); among other ILS.
[18] Occupational Safety and Health Convention (1981) (No 155); Promotional Framework for Occupational Safety and Health Convention (2006) (No 187); among other ILS.
[19] Protection of Wages Convention (1949) (No 95); Minimum Wage Fixing Convention (1970) (No 131); among others.
[20] Equal Remuneration Convention (1951) (No 100).
[21] Hours of Work (Industry) Convention (1919) (No 1); Hours of Work (Commerce and Offices) Convention (1930) (No 30); Weekly Rest (Industry) Convention (1921) (No 14); Forty-Hour Week Convention (1935) (No 47); Weekly Rest (Commerce and Offices) Convention (1957) (No 106); Reduction of Hours of Work Recommendation (1962) (No 116); Holidays with Pay Convention (Revised) (1970) (No 132); among others.
[22] Maternity Protection Convention (2000) (No 183).
[23] Minimum Age Convention (1973) (No 138); Worst Forms of Child Labour Convention (1999) (No 182).

Group on Business and Human Rights (UNWG) established by the UN Human Rights Council in 2011 to 'promote the effective and comprehensive dissemination and implementation of the Guiding Principles on Business and Human Rights' (known as the Ruggie principles). This collaboration is based on the provisions of the ILO Tripartite Declaration of Principles concerning Multinational Enterprises and Social Policy which draws on relevant ILS and follows up on ILO supervisory body comments on the application of ILS in an implicit albeit important way.[24]

By promoting democracy, human rights, and the rule of law in the world of work, ILS are an integral part of the 2030 Agenda and the Sustainable Development Goals (SDG). The ILO is custodian agency for fourteen SDG indicators,[25] all of which are linked to relevant ILS. Certain SDG indicators, such as SDG 8.7, draw on the language of ILO Conventions for their formulation while others such as SDGs 8.8.2 and 16.10.1 draw on the texts of the ILO supervisory bodies in order to evaluate the levels of respect for freedom of association and collective bargaining principles and rights.

In addition to its normative mandate, the ILO has had from the outset an operational mandate to deliver country level assistance, notably in order to draft national laws and regulations giving effect to international labour law.[26] The ILO Constitution espouses a coherent and synergistic approach between the ILO's normative and operational mandates—the international law codified into ILS thus provides a fundamental blueprint for all ILO operations. In 2014, the ILO proposed to replace the notion of 'technical cooperation' (TC) with the term 'development cooperation' (DC) broadly understood to encompass 'inter alia, elements of rights, dialogue, good governance, social justice, equality and capacity development' and stemming 'from the realization that development is a complex, universal and long-term process which can succeed only if grounded on comprehensive, mutual and accountable partnerships'.[27]

This chapter explores the journey toward increased synergy between the ILO's normative and operational mandates, including as to how the organization's internal policies and procedures allude to incorporate ILS (section 3), and the distance that remains to be travelled in terms of effective ILS mainstreaming in the organization's DC activities (section 4), all in light of ILO's specificities (section 2).

---

[24] 'Briefing Note: The Linkages between International Labour Standards The United Nations Guiding Principles on Business and Human Rights and National Action Plans on Business and Human Rights, ILO and UN Working Group on Business and Human Rights, Geneva' (2021) <https://www.ilo.org/empent/areas/mne-declaration/WCMS_800261/lang--en/index.htm> accessed 23 August 2023.
[25] See Annex at the end of the chapter.
[26] The ILO Constitution mandates the International Labour Office (the ILO secretariat, hereafter 'the Office') to 'accord to governments at their request all appropriate assistance within its power in connection with the framing of laws and regulations on the basis of the decisions of the Conference and the improvement of administrative practices and systems of inspection'.
[27] 'ILO's Technical Cooperation Strategy (2015–17)' (2014) Document GB322/POL/6.

2. The ILO's Integrated Standards-Setting and Operational Mandate

A brief presentation of certain ILO traits is essential to understanding the ILO approach to promotion of ILS through DC. Two interrelated elements account for ILO's idiosyncrasies:

a. ILS embody considerable flexibility

ILS allows for choice of means and methods of application as well as progressive engagement. Certain standards allow for possible exclusions from their scope or modulations of the level of protection to facilitate ratification.[28] Others allow ratifying states to select the sections in Conventions by which they will be bound to the exclusion of others, undertake obligations progressively,[29] or provide for the possibility of substantial equivalence.[30] Moreover, ILS can evolve with time, some having undergone successive revisions and others containing in-built mechanisms to this effect.[31]

b. Tripartism and social dialogue play a central role throughout the ILS 'lifecycle'

Social dialogue is a key element of the institutional makeup of the ILO. All ILO governance bodies are tripartite, made up of representatives from governments as well as workers' and employers' organizations. The tripartite constituents are

---

[28] ILO conventions often possess a certain flexibility, which does not need to compromise the aim of providing concrete guidance, given the interplay of conventions (binding treaties) and recommendations. See Nicolas Valticos, 'Conventions de l'Organisation Internationale du Travail à la Croisée des Anniversaires' (1996) Revue Générale de Droit International Public 5–43, 36; ILO Document GB244/SC/3/3, or George Politakis, 'Deconstructing Flexibility in International Labour Conventions', in ILO, *Les Normes Internationales du Travail* (ILO 2004).

[29] An example of this approach is the Social Security (Minimum Standards) Convention (1952) (No 102).

[30] That is the case of the Maritime Labour Convention (2006) (MLC).

[31] On the evolution of the ILO regulatory approach to private employment agencies, see the ILO 2019 SRM TWG Technical Note. Even fundamental conventions may be subject to revision and updating—the latest example being the adoption of the Protocol of 2014 to the Forced Labour Convention of 1930. In recent years the ILO has developed more sophisticated revising mechanisms which facilitate regular updating—a paramount example being provided by the MLC and the review and revision mechanisms provided, in particular through a Special Tripartite Committee. See Desirée LeClerq, 'Sea Change: New Rulemaking Procedures at the ILO' (2015) 22 ILSA JICL 1. Another mechanism at the disposal of the ILO to ensure standards are up to date is the Constitutional amendment of 1997, which entered into force on 8 October 2015 and allows the ILC to abrogate a convention in force if it appears that it has lost its purpose or that it no longer makes a useful contribution to attaining the objectives of the organization.

not only at the origin of ILS, having participated in all stages of their preparation, discussion, and final adoption at the ILC, but also partake in discussions on their eventual review, withdrawal, or abrogation.[32] The fact that ILS are set up through active tripartite involvement at the international level means that they constitute the concrete expression of a global tripartite consensus on a specific technical subject—a 'package deal' of sorts, which therefore does not allow for reservations at the time of ratification.[33]

At national level, the ILO's tripartite constituents participate in transforming the ILS provisions into concrete laws and frameworks through social dialogue. The oftentimes general nature of ILS guidance as well as the flexibility mechanisms embedded in them leave sufficient policy space for tripartite concertation taking place chiefly through consultations in the framework of tripartite committees set up in line with the Tripartite Consultation (ILS) Convention, 1976 (No 144). ILS serve in this framework as guideposts in the search for concrete solutions to national challenges identified through social dialogue instead of readymade, one-size-fits-all solutions. Tripartite consultations serve to examine not only how to exercise flexibility and adopt concrete implementation measures, but also how to report thereon to the ILO supervisory bodies.[34]

Finally, the tripartite constituents actively participate in the supervision of standards not only by triggering various supervisory mechanisms, eg through complaints, but also in their capacity as members of tripartite supervisory bodies which function alongside independent, expert, and non-partisan elements.[35]

The 'dialogical' approach described above creates policy space for tripartite deliberations and promotes tripartite ownership of ILS both at global and national levels.[36] It is only natural in this context, that the ILO takes special care to promote stakeholder ownership of DC projects and partnerships. The organization's dialogical approach results in tripartite involvement in the elaboration, implementation, monitoring, and evaluation of mid-term planning frameworks known as

---

[32] ILO (n 6).
[33] See the ILO 1951 Memorandum to the International Court of Justice.
[34] Clauses requiring governments to consult employers' and workers' organizations on the implementation of their provisions are very common in ILS. ILO, 'Manual for drafting ILO instruments' (2006) s 2.2.2.
[35] Tripartite delegates to the ILC compose one of the ILO's central supervisory bodies, the Committee on the Application of Standards (CAS) which is a standing ILC committee meeting every year in order to examine the application of ratified conventions in selected cases. The tripartite constituents also trigger and participate in the 'representations' and 'complaints' procedures set out respectively in articles 24–25 and 26 of the ILO Constitution. The constituent, hence partisan, involvement in the ILO supervisory system (and in the preparation, adoption, and revision of ILS) is balanced by the existence of expert independent mechanisms—in particular the CEACR (whose observations are used by the CAS to discuss cases). Commissions of Inquiry established on the basis of article 26 complaints constitute the pinnacle of the supervisory system, which has been resorted to only on thirteen occasions in the history of the organization.
[36] For an analysis of the ILO's approach compared to approaches in the financial field, see Katerina Tsotroudi, 'International Labour Standards as a Model for the Future: The Case of Financial Regulation' in ILO, *Les Normes Internationales du Travail* (ILO 2004) 615–42.

Decent Work Country Programmes (DWCPs)[37] and DC partnerships and projects for their realization.

3. International Labour Standards and Technical Cooperation: The Journey to Synergy

The path towards synergy between DC operations and the guidance provided through standards and supervisory bodies monitoring their application, has been long. During the ILO's first quarter century, and until the aftermath of the Second World War, assistance to ILO members, which at the time were dominantly western industrialized states, was essentially focused on the drafting of labour laws. The ILO's main activity was the adoption and supervision of ILS embodied in international instruments, including seminal Conventions setting down fundamental rights at work in the areas of freedom of association, equality and non-discrimination, and forced labour, often preparing the ground for the subsequent adoption of UN human rights treaties. In the 1950s and 1960s, decolonization and the growing influence of the newly independent countries in the ILO's governing organs led the ILO to gradually engage in country-level operations to promote mainly employment and other development objectives.[38] Acknowledging this development, the supervisory bodies began referring to technical assistance in their comments in the 1950s.[39]

For a long time, DC was not seen as complementary to the ILO's traditional normative role, but rather as an alternative approach to realizing the ILO's mandate. Former director general Francis Blanchard went as far as referring to a 'psychodrama that may have led to fearing a schism' in the organization. He observed how, with the growth of the 'practical' or 'operational' activities staff focusing on such activities paid little attention to the ILS adopted by their own organization.[40]

Gradual steps were taken as of the mid-80s to mainstream ILS in DC more systematically.[41] In 1994, the ILO director general's report noted: 'It cannot be denied

---

[37] DWCPs represent a medium-term planning framework that guides the work of the ILO in a country in accordance with priorities and objectives agreed upon with governments, trade unions, and employers. They constitute the central programming framework for delivery of ILO support to member countries.
[38] See eg Guy Fiti Sinclair 'A Bridge and a Pivot: The ILO and International Organizations Law in Times of Crisis' in ILO, *ILO:100. Law for Social Justice* (ILO 2019) 125.
[39] The CAS mentioned technical assistance for the first time in 1953: ILC 36th session (1953), Provisional Records, Annex VI, and Governing Body 114th Session (March 1951), Minutes, p 390. The CEACR started to refer to technical assistance at the end of the 1950s.
[40] See Francis Blanchard, *L'Organisation Internationale du Travail: De la Guerre Froide à un Nouvel Ordre Mondial* (Seuil 2004) 69.
[41] Circular No 163 Series 2, 29.05.1987 on 'Links between International Labour Standards and ILO Technical Cooperation Activities'; André Aboughanem, *A Study of the Relationship between International Labour Standards and Technical Cooperation* (ILO 1985); Corinne Vargha, *Premier Bilan des Études de Cas sur les Normes Internationales du Travail et la Coopération Technique: Les Différentes*

that over the years, and for reasons deriving from both the political context and from the mechanisms by which technical cooperation was carried out, the two lines of ILO action [ILS and TC] moved separately and in parallel. It is time they converged'.[42] A more synergistic relationship between the promotion of economic development and the protection of rights at work gradually emerged and was consolidated in the late 1990s with the adoption of the Decent Work agenda.[43]

Decent Work aimed at overcoming the dilemma of rights versus economic development through an integrated approach based on four interdependent, interrelated, and mutually reinforcing pillars—ie fundamental principles and rights at work, employment, social protection, and social dialogue. This integrated approach opened the way towards improved ILS mainstreaming in DC. As of 2005, the ILO GB held regular discussions on standards policy including an integrated approach to promoting ILS through technical cooperation and assistance.[44] The Office started to systematically follow up on supervisory body recommendations offering technical assistance to Member States facing particular difficulties and developed tools to enhance the impact of ILS through TC.[45]

Decent Work gradually found its way in the Millennium Development Goals, from which it had been initially absent, and became a central tenet of the 2030 Agenda, explicitly targeted in the framework of SDG.8, which is placed under joint ILO-World Bank custodianship.

Factors which helped to bring about this result include:

(i) a set of political declarations emerging from the need for a social floor to mitigate the externalities caused by globalized trade, investment, and finance as well as, more recently, environmental disasters including the COVID-19 pandemic;

Facettes de la Complémentarité entre les Activités Normatives et Celles de Coopération Technique (BIT Département des Normes 1993).

[42] ILC, 'Defending Values Promoting Change' Report of the Director General to the International Labour Conference (ILC) 81st Session (1994) 87.
[43] 'Decent Work' Report of the Director General to the ILC, 86th Session (1999).
[44] See 'Improvements in the Standards-related Activities of the ILO: Outlines of a Future Strategic Orientation for Standards and for Implementing Standards-related Policies and Procedures', Document GB294/LILS/4, 17–20. Standards' policy, including ILS promotion through 'technical cooperation and assistance' was discussed in the ILO GB from March 2005 until March 2012. Since then, ILS promotion through DC was taken up in other contexts, eg the 107th session of the ILS (2018) which held a general discussion on 'Effective Development Cooperation in Support of the SDGs' Provisional Record 7A, ILC 107th Session (May–June 2018). As a follow up to that discussion, the GB adopted the 'ILO Development Cooperation Strategy 2020–2025' and its Implementation Plan, which include several references to ILO's normative action and envisage, inter alia, 'Multi-stakeholder partnerships, alliances and networks convened by the ILO, or with ILO and its constituents' participation, [which] integrate the value of, and respect for, international labour standards, tripartism and social dialogue in support of decent work.' Document GB341/POL/4, 7.
[45] ILO, 'Improving the Impact of International Labour Standards through Technical Cooperation— A Practice Guide' (2008).

(ii) Emergence of DC projects and partnerships linking standards and their supervision with economic development, trade, and investment;
(iii) Landmark cases where the ILO supervisory mechanism was combined with assistance on the ground;
(iv) The adoption of the 2030 Agenda for Sustainable Development and the repositioning of the UN development system.

a. A set of tripartite political declarations

The 1995 UN Social Summit and 1996 WTO Ministerial Conference in Singapore took place in a context of intense debates over the unintended effects of global trade and the need for a universal social floor to govern the global economy. Taking advantage of the political momentum and building on the ILO Director General's 1994 report,[46] the ILC adopted in 1998 the Declaration on Fundamental Principles and Rights at Work (FPRW).[47] The Declaration laid down the principles and rights that all ILO Member States are to respect by virtue of their membership of the ILO, regardless of ratification of the relevant fundamental Conventions in the areas of freedom of association[48] and collective bargaining,[49] equality and non-discrimination,[50] forced labour,[51] and child labour. In 2022, the Declaration was amended to include a safe and healthy working environment in the list of FPRW. Two ILO Conventions on Occupational Safety and Health were consequently added in the list of fundamental instruments.[52]

The 1998 Declaration is accompanied by a monitoring mechanism. Initially this was supposed to offer an easier way than ratification for countries to express their commitment, as they could, importantly, signal the kind of technical cooperation they needed in their annual reports on efforts to realize the principles of the Conventions. This positive encouragement was eventually replicated in the regular supervisory mechanism, leading a large number of countries to ratify the fundamental Conventions, bringing rates of the fundamental Conventions to nearly

---

[46] See n 42.
[47] ILO, 'ILO Declaration on Fundamental Principles and Rights at Work and its Follow-up', International Labour Conference 86th Session, Geneva (18 June 1998; revised 15 June 2010 and 10 June 2022). Kari Tapiola, 'What Happened to International Labour Standards and Human Rights at Work?' (ILO 2021), 56–58 (hereafter 'Tapiola, What Happened').
[48] Freedom of Association and Protection of the Right to Organise Convention (1948) (No 87); Right to Organise and Collective Bargaining Convention (1949) (No 98).
[49] Equal Remuneration Convention (1951) (No 100); Discrimination (Employment and Occupation) Convention (1958) (No 111).
[50] Forced Labour Convention (1930) (No 29); Protocol of 2014 as well as Abolition of Forced Labour Convention (1957) (No 105).
[51] Minimum Age Convention (1973) (No 138); Worst Forms of Child Labour Convention (1999) (No 182).
[52] Occupational Safety and Health Convention (1981) (No 155); Promotional Framework for Occupational Safety and Health Convention (2006) (No 187).

universal levels. As Kari Tapiola observes, 'such a change in the attitude to ratifications would not have been possible without increased linkage to technical cooperation.'[53] Building a synergetic relationship between ILS and DC through the 1998 Declaration gave the fundamental principles the status of a global acquis— eg generating a worldwide consensus on the need to take action against child labour and human trafficking, which is nowadays pursued in the framework of SDG Alliance 8.7, as well as the need to promote gender equality at work, nowadays pursued in the framework of the Equal Pay International Coalition (EPIC).[54]

Finally, the Declaration provided explicitly that FPRW should not be used for trade protectionist purposes, something which helped to appease the fears of developing countries at the time. Despite some apprehension that the Declaration would lead to a two-tier system of standards, this seminal instrument marked the beginning of a series of ILO Declarations reaffirming the central role that standards play for sustainable development.[55]

In 2008, the Social Justice Declaration for a Fair Globalisation endorsed the Decent Work Agenda and provided a roadmap towards its realization with a view to furthering social justice and enabling everyone to draw a fair share from the benefits of globalization. The 2008 Declaration added to the list of standards calling for immediate promotion four Conventions termed 'most significant from the viewpoint of governance' in the areas of employment promotion,[56] labour inspection,[57] and social dialogue.[58] It underlined the need to promote the role of standards as a useful means of achieving the constitutional objectives of the organization and answered key questions on how standards link to DC, notably by subordinating the provision of ILO assistance within the framework of bilateral or multilateral agreements to the latter's compatibility with ILO obligations.[59] Importantly, it expanded

---

[53] Tapiola, What Happened (n 47) 58.

[54] This having been said, the results have not been of the same magnitude when it comes to promoting partnerships in the area of freedom of association and collective bargaining, despite notable examples of DC partnerships that promote social dialogue parallel to economic development. For example, the 'Strengthening Labour Relations and its Institutions in Egypt' (SLARIE) project focuses, inter alia, on the registration of independent trade union committees and establishment of national social dialogue institutions in Egypt. Another example is the 'Advancing the Decent Work Agenda in North Africa' (ADWA) project which embraces different pillars of the Decent Work Agenda in an integrated approach, including employment, social dialogue, and ILS ratification and application.

[55] Gerry Rodgers, Lee Swepston, Eddy Lee, and Jasmien van Daele, *The International Labour Organization and the Quest for Social Justice, 1919-2009* (ILO 2009) (hereafter Rodgers and others, *The ILO and the Quest for Social Justice*)291-20.

[56] Employment Policy Convention (1964) (No 122).

[57] Labour Inspection Convention (1947) (No 81); Labour Inspection (Agriculture) Convention (1969) (No 129).

[58] Tripartite Consultation (International Labour Standards) Convention (1976) (No 144).

[59] The 2008 ILO Social Justice Declaration thus states that 'How Members achieve the strategic objectives [of the Decent Work Agenda] is a question that must be determined by each Member subject to its existing international obligations and the fundamental principles and rights at work with due regard, among others, to: (i) the national conditions and circumstances, and needs as well as priorities expressed by representative organizations of employers and workers; (ii) the interdependence, solidarity and cooperation among all Members of the ILO that are more pertinent than ever in the context of a global economy; and (iii) the principles and provisions of international labour standards' (section IC).

on the 1998 Declaration by providing that 'the violation of fundamental principles and rights at work cannot be invoked or otherwise used as a legitimate comparative advantage' while reiterating that 'labour standards should not be used for protectionist trade purposes' (section I.A.iv).

The 2008 Declaration also had another, less obvious, but equally important, implication for the promotion of ILS through DC. In endorsing the integrated approach of the Decent Work agenda with its four interdependent, interrelated, and mutually reinforcing pillars, it consolidated results-based management and the rights-based approach which had been introduced since 2002 with the integration of the ratification and application of standards into the ILO's strategic policy framework and Programme and Budget (P&B). Gradually, standards were mainstreamed across the operational outcomes of the ILO's P&B—a positive example of institutional design that structures outcomes around Policy Outcomes (POs), Country Programme Outcomes (CPOs) and DWCPs rather than internal structures. This serves to reinforce the message that work on ILS is not 'owned' by any single department but calls for everybody's engagement at global, regional and country level in order to achieve results for the ILO Member States as ultimate beneficiaries.

The year 2019 marked one hundred years since the ILO's founding. In this context, the Centenary Declaration on the Future of Work focused on the transformative changes of the world of work, driven by technological innovations, demographic shifts, climate change, and globalization, reaffirming the 'fundamental importance' of standards for a human-centred approach to the future of work. It called on the ILO to: 'assist its Members in the ratification and effective application of standards' (section A); deliver development cooperation services consistent with its mandate (section D); and take an important role in the multilateral system, by inter alia developing institutional arrangements with other organizations to promote policy coherence, recognizing the strong, complex, and crucial links between social, trade, financial, economic, and environmental policies (section F). In so doing, the Centenary Declaration built on the Philadelphia Declaration which sets the organization's fundamental aims and purposes and calls upon the ILO to assess all international economic and financial policies and measures in light of its mandate.[60]

The adoption of the Centenary Declaration was preceded by national and regional tripartite dialogues, as well as the work of the Global Commission for the Future of Work which recommended a 'universal labour guarantee' to the effect that 'All workers, regardless of their contractual arrangement or employment

---

[60] Improving the Impact of International Labour Standards through Technical Cooperation—A Practice Guide, ILO Geneva, 2008, 6–11. Independent Evaluation of ILO's Strategy to Support Member States to Improve the Impact of International Labour Standards, No 857, ILO Geneva, 2008. Accessible at the i-eval Discovery database: https://www.ilo.org/ievaldiscovery/#asnauk5.

status, should enjoy fundamental workers' rights, an 'adequate living wage' (ILO Constitution), maximum limits on working hours, and safety and health at work'. This proposal opened the way for occupational safety and health to be recognized as a fundamental principle and right at work by the International Labour Conference in June 2022, through an amendment to the 1998 Declaration on Fundamental Principles and Rights at Work.[61] Thus will no doubt give further impetus to DC projects focusing on the promotion of the human right to health and to a healthy environment in the course of work.[62]

The impetus to develop a universal labour guarantee continues; in the midst of the COVID-19 crisis, the 109th session of the ILC (2021) adopted the Global Call to Action for a human-centred recovery from the COVID-19 crisis. The ILO aims through the Global Call to Action to meet the compelling need for leadership so that COVID-19 response strategies can address the worrying setbacks on fundamental freedoms and escalating inequalities that emerged during the pandemic and threaten the achievement of the 2030 Agenda.

While reasserting the main message of the Centenary Declaration, the Global Call to Action alludes to the universal labour guarantee by calling on the ILO to:

> provide all workers with adequate protection, reinforcing respect for international labour standards, and promoting their ratification, implementation and supervision, with particular attention to areas where serious gaps have been revealed by the crisis. This includes respect for fundamental principles and rights at work; an adequate minimum wage, either statutory or negotiated; maximum limits on working time; and safety and health at work with particular attention to the ongoing challenges presented by the COVID-19 pandemic.

In the framework of the follow up to the Global Call to Action decided by the ILO GB, as well as the UN SG's report Our Common Agenda, increasing attention is also drawn to the fact that social security is another area of key importance for poverty alleviation especially in the current context of multiple and protracted crises and transitions.[63]

Thus, over the last three decades and against the backdrop of economic, social, and environmental challenges to globalization, the ILO, through successive tripartite political declarations, has placed special emphasis on civil, political, social, and economic rights as a necessary foundation for DC. This resulted in placing a spotlight on a set of ILS which serve to give the constitutive elements a level playing

---

[61] Documents GB343/INS/6 and GB343/INS/PV para 217.
[62] Zahra Yusifli and Colin Fenwick, Workers' Rights and Human Rights: Toward a New Fundamental Principle?, in Kimberly Ann Elliot (ed), *Handbook on Globalisation and Labour Standards* (EE Publishing 2022), 108–26.
[63] See, for example, CEACR 2022 Report (n 7), para 20.

field and introduce a measure of predictability, fairness, and social justice in the global arena.

b. Emergence of DC programmes and partnerships linking standards and their supervision with sustainable development, trade, and investment

Since the 1990s, the ILO has increasingly relied on the provisions of ILS in various DC interventions as a means to build actions in the relevant technical area which promote a fairer distribution of the benefits of a globalized economy and build national institutions necessary for sustainable progress beyond the conclusion of a DC project.[64] This approach, which emerged modestly in the early 1990s, gained impetus after the adoption of the 2030 Agenda for sustainable development. As indicated at the outset, ILS, as an integral part of the Decent Work Agenda, are well integrated throughout the SDGs.[65] Today, all five of the ILO flagship DC programmes are linked to relevant SDGs and draw upon ILS as their essential foundation. This development constitutes in and of itself a paradigm change in terms of ILO's approach to ILS mainstreaming in DC, stemming from an increasing recognition of the ILO's normative mandate as one of its main comparative advantages in the framework of partnerships for development.[66]

The first major DC programme linking standards to development has been the International Programme on the Elimination of Child Labour (IPEC). Launched in 1992, IPEC has been the precursor of SDG Alliance 8.7 to end child labour, forced labour, modern slavery, and human trafficking, and the International Programme on the Elimination of Child Labour and Forced Labour (IPEC+). Today, IPEC+ supports global efforts to eradicate all forms of child labour by 2025 and all forms of contemporary slavery and human trafficking by 2030 in sixty-six countries. At the basis of the Alliance's target to end child labour, forced labour, and human trafficking lie the ILO fundamental conventions on child labour and forced labour, the universal ratification and application of which constitutes one of the programme's targets leading, in 2019, to the universal ratification of Convention No 182 by all 187 ILO Member States. IPEC has also been the first programme that collaborated with the ILO supervisory bodies, through consistent data and information sharing on the progressive elimination of child labour at country level, enabling

---

[64] Bruce Jenks, 'Global Norms: Building an Inclusive Multilateralism', Dag Hammarskjöld Foundation Development Dialogue Paper No 21 (February 2017).
[65] See Annex (Table 6.1) to this chapter.
[66] A recent donor assessment identifies the ILO's standard-setting role and mandate, its tripartite constituency and its technical expertise as its key comparative advantages: Multilateral Organisation Performance Assessment Network (MOPAN), MOPAN Assessment Report: ILO 2020 Assessment Cycle, Paris (2021).

the supervisory bodies to systematically track the project's impact on the application of ratified conventions.

The other four flagship programmes also rely on ILS and draw on them:

— the Global Programme on Building Social Protection Floors for All, launched in early 2016, is guided by ILO's social security standards such as the Social Protection Floors Recommendation, 2012 (No 202) and the Social Security (Minimum Standards) Convention, 1952 (No 102). Working across fifty priority countries, it aims to change the lives of millions of people by 2025 and provide evidence on ILO's contribution to SDGs 1.3, 3.8, and 8.b;
— The ILO Safety + Health for All Flagship Programme is rooted in conventions on occupational safety and health[67] and plays a lead role to advance SDG target 8.8 and indicator 8.8.1;
— The Jobs for Peace and Resilience programme draws on the guidance of the Employment and Decent Work for Peace and Resilience Recommendation, 2017 (No 205) in order to build ILO interventions in humanitarian contexts and along the peace-development nexus. The scope of Recommendation No 205 includes environmental disasters, including the COVID-19 pandemic in response to which the ILO has taken a lead role;[68] and
— The Better Work programme which started in 2001 as an ILO—International Finance Corporation (IFC) collaboration aimed at certifying factories in Cambodia, evolved into the Better Work programme which is now active in 1,700 factories employing more than 2.4 million workers in nine countries, with a view to improving working conditions and respect of labour rights for workers while boosting the competitiveness of apparel businesses. The programme draws on a wide range of standards covering not only the fundamental conventions, but also areas with an important impact on working conditions, such as occupational safety and health, wages, working time, etc.[69]

This account of the progressive integration of standards in DC would not be complete without reference to trade partners' interest in linking ILS supervision and DC.[70] ILS, as seen through the prism of the 1998 Declaration, found their way into

---

[67] Particularly the Occupational Safety and Health Convention (1981) (No 155); Occupational Health Services Convention (1985) (No 161); Promotional Framework for Occupational Safety and Health Convention (2006) (No 187).

[68] Global call to action for a human-centred recovery from the COVID-19 crisis that is inclusive, sustainable, and resilient, ILC 109th session (June 2021).

[69] Adrianna Rossi, 'Better Work: Lessons learned and the way forward for decent work in the global garment industry', in Guillaume Delautre, Elizabeth Echeverría Manrique, and Colin Fenwick, *Decent Work in a Globalized Economy: Lessons from Public and Private Initiatives* (ILO 2021), 243–56.

[70] In 2018, the ILC acknowledged this development by calling on the ILO to deliver assistance for the implementation of the comments of the ILO supervisory bodies, upon request, in the context of its General Discussion on Effective Development Cooperation in Support of the SDGs. 'Resolution on Effective Development Cooperation in Support of the Sustainable Development Goals' (2018) para

trade preferences accorded to countries which desire to respect fundamental labour standards[71] through a mechanism known as the 'generalized system of preferences' (GSP) of the United States and the European Union (EU). In this context, DC programmes delivering ILS-related support often have as their counterpart social clauses in bilateral and regional trade agreements which serve to open up access to industrial country markets for developing country products on certain conditions, including improved labour protection. The credibility of this mechanism is seen to be guaranteed by the ILO supervisory bodies, as an acknowledged source of authoritative and independent assessments of beneficiary countries' compliance with commitments to respect and promote ILS.[72]

Respect for standards and principles on freedom of association and collective bargaining is one of the most important areas promoted in the framework of trade agreements. In this framework, the ILO supervisory bodies play a key role in preventing serious violations of trade unionists' civil liberties and their work in this area feeds into SDG 8.8 and 16.10.1. The supervisory bodies include, notably, the Committee on Freedom of Association (CFA) which is mandated to examine complaints of violations of freedom of association rights and principles, regardless of ratification of the relevant conventions by the countries concerned.[73]

The scope of the CFA's mandate serves to compensate, at least in part, for the fact that the two fundamental conventions on freedom of association and collective bargaining have received to date, less ratifications than the other fundamental conventions.

Free trade agreements often extend beyond the eight ILO fundamental conventions which lie at their core, in order to embrace labour inspection, social dialogue, occupational safety and health, and other subjects.[74] Looking ahead, multiple avenues exist for ILS to serve as a basis for partnerships in favour of policy coherence. Examples include ILO collaboration with the UN Working Group on Business and Human Rights[75] and with Multilateral Development Banks (MDBs) for the

9(1)(g)). See also 'Towards 2030: Effective Development Cooperation in Support of the Sustainable Development Goals', ILC 107th Session, Report IV (2018) paras 151–52, 195.

[71] Jordi Agustí-Panareda, Desirée LeClercq, and Franz Ebert, 'ILO Labor Standards and Trade Agreements: A Case for Consistency' (2015) 36 Comp Lab L & Pol'y J 347. Also, Tapiola, What Happened (n 47) 59.
[72] In this context, the Trade for Decent Work Project exemplifies since 2013 'the EU strong support to the ILO work regarding the application of the Fundamental Conventions'. See the ILS website for more information. Karen Curtis and Elizabeth Echeverría Manrique explore the limits of this approach when it comes to addressing decent work deficits in supply chains and possible options for linking more closely international trade rules with labour standards. Trade arrangements and labour standards in a supply chain world: current issues and future considerations, in Rossi (n 69) 109.
[73] Compilation (n 9) para 6.
[74] An inventory of trade agreements can be found in the 'ILO Labour Provisions in Trade Agreements Hub'. <https://www.ilo.org/LPhub/> accessed September 2023.
[75] Briefing note: The linkages between international labour standards, the United Nations Guiding Principles on Business and Human Rights, and National Action Plans on Business and Human Rights, ILO (June 2021).

development and monitoring of Environmental and Social Safeguards (ESS) systems.[76]

These examples of programmes and partnerships where standards and their supervision have been linked to the ILO's operational mandate over the last few decades have resulted in strategically positioning the ILO at the crossroads of economic and social sustainability in favour of promoting democratic, inclusive, and resilient societies in the framework of the 2030 Agenda.

c. Landmark cases

An elaborate supervisory mechanism for labour rights exists at the international level, monitoring the extent to which ILS are translated into tangible realities on the ground. As noted in the previous section, this monitoring function is especially synergetic and complementary to DC operations. This can be further illustrated in a number of examples from ILO's history. Over the years, certain landmark cases demonstrated the impact that the combination of standards supervision with DC can have in making a difference in the lives of women and men on the ground as well as the crucial role that ILO's tripartite structure can play in this context.

The first historical example is ILO's action against South Africa's apartheid regime between 1961 and 1994. The ILO supervisory bodies' calls to address human rights violations laid the ground for ILO's action as of the early 1960s and culminated in a Fact-Finding and Conciliation Commission, one of the most elaborate supervisory procedures, established in 1991 to examine violations of freedom of association in collaboration with the UN Economic and Social Council (ECOSOC), as South Africa was no longer an ILO member since 1966.

The social partners played a key role in mobilizing public opinion and building constant political pressure while technical and material support was provided to the national liberation movements and trade unions fighting apartheid, through funding and capacity building. This technical and material support was a precursor

---

[76] Over the last two decades, ILO work with MDBs on ESS has involved the World Bank (International Bank for Reconstruction and Development (IBRD)), the IFC, the European Bank for Reconstruction and Development (EBRD), and the Inter-American Development Bank (IADB). To the extent that these social standards and safeguards draw on ILS, the ILO may be, and indeed has been, called upon to provide technical support and assistance to the governments which are accountable for their implementation. The ILO's Programme and Budget for 2024–2025 illustrates this development by indicating for example, that

> [w]ithin the broader framework of ILO initiatives to strengthen policy coherence, development cooperation will respond to the growing demand from constituents in the public and the private sector to apply international labour standards in their environmental, social and governance initiatives, including labour provisions in trade and investment arrangements and in supply chains.

'The Director General's Programme and Budget proposals for 2024–25', Document GB347/PFA/1, para 67.

of today's DC-type of engagement and demonstrated the role the social partners can play in providing alternative entry points for interventions in areas that would otherwise be inaccessible to purely intergovernmental organizations.[77] This strategy was crowned with success in 1994, when South Africa re-joined the ILO after having held its first free elections.

A more recent example is the case of Uzbekistan: following a series of CAS discussions in 2010, 2011, and 2013 on the use of child labour in the cotton harvest and an agreement with the Uzbek government and employers' and workers' organizations, the ILO began monitoring the cotton harvest for child labour in 2013 and expanded monitoring to forced labour as of 2015 as part of an agreement with the World Bank. A comprehensive DWCP agreed with the tripartite constituents in 2015 targeted the root causes of child labour by strengthening, inter alia, employment policies, labour inspection, and social dialogue. As a result, an ILO report released in March 2022 concluded that systemic forced labour and child labour has come to an end in Uzbek cotton (although some local vestiges remain).[78]

The above examples illustrate how the ILO combines ILS, tripartism, and country-level interventions to generate impact in these and other cases, including, more recently, Bangladesh,[79] Colombia, Greece,[80] Guatemala,[81] Myanmar,[82] and

---

[77] See eg Rodgers and others, *The ILO and the Quest for Social Justice* (n 55) 91:

overall, the ILO has demonstrated that continued attention to a situation, based on its supervisory work, can put it in a position to lend practical assistance [through DC] once the national situation has evolved. The tripartite nature of the ILO has allowed it to go where a purely intergovernmental organization often fears to tread. Its concern with freedom of association, apartheid, Myanmar, migrant workers and indigenous and tribal peoples, inter alia, bears witness to this.

[78] ILO, '2021 ILO Third-Party Monitoring Report of the Cotton Harvest in Uzbekistan' (March 2022).

[79] See Report by the Government of Bangladesh on progress made with the timely implementation of the road map taken to address all outstanding issues mentioned in the complaint concerning alleged non-observance of the Labour Inspection Convention, 1947 (No 81), the Freedom of Association and Protection of the Right to Organise Convention, 1948 (No 87), and the Right to Organise and Collective Bargaining Convention, 1949 (No 98) (GB343/INS/10(Rev.2)) and Minutes of the Institutional Section (INS) GB343/INS/PV.

[80] On the work of the ILO supervisory mechanism evaluating the impact of the support package introduced by the troika of creditors in Greece on the application of eleven ratified conventions during the financial crisis of 2010, see ILO, 'Report on the High Level Mission to Greece, 19–23 September 2011' (December 2011); Eric Gravel, Tomi Kohiyama, and Katerina Tsotroudi, 'A Legal Perspective on the Role of International Labour Standards in Rebalancing Globalization' (2014) 49 Revue Interventions Économiques 1–16.

[81] On Guatemala, see Annual report on the implementation of the ILO technical cooperation programme 'Strengthening of the National Tripartite Committee on Labour Relations and Freedom of Association in Guatemala for the effective application of international labour standards' GB343/INS/7 and Minutes of the Institutional Section (INS) GB343/INS/PV.

[82] The case of Myanmar is the most longstanding one in which all the ILO supervisory procedures have been used, including Article 33 of the ILO Constitution which provides that, if a government does not implement the recommendations of a Commission of Inquiry, 'the Governing Body may recommend to the Conference such action as it may deem wise and expedient to secure compliance therewith'. Measures, including action under Article 33 of the Constitution of the International Labour Organization, to secure compliance by the Government of Myanmar with the recommendations of the Commission of Inquiry established to examine the observance of the Forced Labour Convention, 1930 (No 29), Document GB277/6, Geneva, March 2000.

Qatar.[83] While each case has its own particularities, some common elements can be identified:

- Findings of serious violations of rights at work by the ILO supervisory bodies;
- A request by the government concerned, often in association with the social partners, for ILO support, usually in order to implement a tripartite negotiated plan of action giving effect to ILO supervisory body guidance;
- The design and delivery of a time-bound DC project under close monitoring by the ILO supervisory bodies and/or the GB; and
- ILO presence on the ground through, eg a senior liaison officer in Myanmar, special representatives of the ILO director-general in Colombia and Guatemala, a liaison officer in Greece, and ILO offices in charge of delivering DC in Bangladesh and Qatar.

In terms of effectiveness, this approach has produced historical outcomes in certain cases illustrated above, and mitigated results in others—eg in Myanmar.[84] In the case of Qatar, a recent Independent Evaluation of the ILO's Technical Cooperation Programme in that country confirmed that the ILO's supervisory function is an effective and relevant driver for legislative reform, when adequately leveraged. According to the evaluation 'Workers interviewed used statements such as "we feel heard;" "domestic workers in Qatar now feel and see a different Qatar" [etc.]'.[85] While these highly publicized cases have shed a spotlight on the impact of DC on the ratification and application of ILS, it would be an exaggeration to say that they have led to generalized ILS mainstreaming in DC seems to depend on a number of factors that merit deeper analysis given a lack of metadata and recent research on this subject.

d. 2030 Agenda and repositioned UN development system

The ILO Constitution—especially the Declaration of Philadelphia—and the Decent Work Agenda are concrete policy manifestations of the concept of socially sustainable development while the integrated approach that they espouse, bringing together rights and socioeconomic development through normative

---

[83] This is an instance where an ILO DC programme has been self-funded by the government concerned. See, inter alia, project website The ILO in Qatar (Arab States) <https://www.ilo.org/beirut/countries/qatar/lang--en/index.htm> and Progress report on the technical cooperation programme agreed between the Government of Qatar and the ILO (GB 340/INS/11).

[84] Follow-up to the resolutions concerning Myanmar adopted by the International Labour Conference at its 102nd (2013) and 109th (2021) Sessions, Document GB343/INS/8 and Minutes of the Institutional Section (INS) (GB343/INS/PV).

[85] Final Independent Evaluation of the Technical Cooperation Programme in Qatar (2018–2021) (June 2022), 4–5.

and operational action, constitute precursors of the 2030 Agenda and the SDGs. Moreover, as indicated by the CEACR in its latest report, labour rights are human rights at work[86] giving concrete substance to a wide range of civil and political as well as economic, social and cultural rights entrenched in UN human rights instruments. Along with the ILO supervisory system that monitors their application, ILS constitute the ILO's niche in the UN development system[87] which was elevated by General Assembly resolution 72/279 to the most important instrument for planning and implementation of the UN development activities at country level in support of the implementation of the 2030 Agenda. Drawing on ILS and its centenary mandate for the promotion of social justice, the ILO is well positioned in this context to exert a convening power for the creation of multilateral policy dialogues, multi-stakeholder partnerships and alliances.

As already mentioned above, examples of alliances and partnerships which are firmly grounded on the ILO fundamental Conventions include Alliance 8.7 and EPIC. In this framework, as custodian of SDG.8 on Decent Work and Economic Growth, together with the World Bank, the ILO has developed methodology for the measurement of labour rights (indicator 8.8.2), child labour and youth employment (indicator 8.b.1), as well as guidelines for the measurement of forced labour, drawing on the text of the relevant Conventions and ILO supervisory body comments on their application.[88] Indeed, SDG indicator 8.8.2, of which the ILO is custodian, is a unique SDG indicator as it draws directly on the ILO supervisory bodies' comments (textual sources) in order to assess progress in respecting freedom of association principles and the ILO fundamental Conventions on freedom of association.[89]

The ILO and its standards are relevant to other SDGs, such as SDG.1 to end poverty, notably through employment promotion and social protection floors; SDG.3 on healthy lives and wellbeing for all as they link to social security; and SDG.16 on peaceful and inclusive societies. SDG 16.10.1 in particular, links directly to the extensive work of the ILO supervisory bodies for the defence of trade unionists' civil liberties and their protection from grave human rights violations such as extrajudicial killings and disappearances.[90]

Furthermore, as a member of the UN family, the ILO follows the current repositioning of the UN Development System which aims at achieving the effective

---

[86] See 'Report of the Committee of Experts on the Application of Conventions and Recommendations (CEACR)' (n 7) para 131; also, 'Introduction: Labour Rights, Human Rights' (1998) 137 International Labour Review 2; George Politakis (ed), *Protecting Labour Rights as Human Rights: Present and Future of International Supervision* (ILO 2007); Philip Alston, 'Labour Rights as Human Rights: The Not So Happy State of the Art' in Philip Alston (ed), *Labour Rights as Human Rights* (OUP 2005).
[87] See UN, 'United Nations Sustainable Development Cooperation Framework Guidance' (2019).
[88] Report III: 'Report of the Conference, 20th International Conference of Labour Statisticians' (10–19 October 2018) Document ICLS/20/2018/3.
[89] David Kucera and Dora Sari, 'New Labour Rights Indicators' (2019) 158 ILR 3, 419–46.
[90] Compilation (n 9) paras 67–314.

implementation of the 2030 Agenda and engages closely with the UN notably through the Secretary-General's Call to Action for Human Rights (C2A) and Our Common Agenda, adopted in 2021 to accelerate the achievement of the SDGs. As the Common Agenda priorities, eg to leave no one behind and promote a renewed social contract anchored in human rights, a new era for universal social protection and decent work, are closely related to the ILO's mandate and ILS, the ILO is actively involved in the realization of these priorities. It notably leads the SG's initiative to launch a Global Accelerator on Jobs and Social Protection for Just Transitions, while also co-leading the implementation of the recommendations related to social protection, the informal economy, gender equality/care economy, youth employment, and the coalition of ministers to accelerate investments in the green and digital economies. Most recently, in the context of the lead up to three seminal conferences, namely, the SDG Conference (September 2023), the Conference of the Future (September 2024), and the World Social Summit which will take place in September 2025, the ILO Director General has undertaken to forge a global coalition for social justice, mobilizing political, technical, and financial support for ILO's social justice mandate as a central tenet of Our Common Agenda.[91]

4. Mainstreaming the Normative-Operational Integration: Lessons Learned, Challenges and Opportunities Ahead

At the time of preparing this chapter, the ILO had a DC budget of US$666.93 million, involving 877 projects across the world.[92] While ILS are, in principle, actively promoted under certain of these DC projects, with an estimated take up rate of 60 per cent, at present there is no comprehensive data or systematic monitoring of ILS mainstreaming in DC.[93] An independent evaluation[94] carried out in 2008 identified a number of challenges. Progress made and remaining challenges were noted in more recent studies which partially covered ILS.[95]

---

[91] 'Update on the Global Coalition for Social Justice', Document GB347/INS/4.
[92] Updated information may be accessed through ILO, 'Development Cooperation Dashboard' <https://www.ilo.org/DevelopmentCooperationDashboard> accessed 21 May 2023.
[93] See MOPAN assessment (n 66) 99, s 2.3-E3.
[94] ILO, 'Independent Evaluation of the ILO's Strategy to Support Member States to Improve the Impact of International Labour Standards' (2008) (hereafter '2008 Evaluation') accessible online. <https://www.ilo.org/ievaldiscovery/#b8pbato>.
[95] ILO Evaluation Office, 'Decent Work Results and Effectiveness of ILO Operations: Ex-post Meta-analysis of Development Cooperation Evaluations, 2020 and 2021 (partial)' (September 2021), 19, 21, and 28. ILO, 'Independent High-Level Evaluation on ILO's Strategies and Action on Fundamental Principles and Rights at Work' (2023).

Overall, while gradual progress is being made in terms of mainstreaming ILS in DC projects, comprehensive data is absent and more systematic monitoring and evaluation (M&E) is needed at all levels of the ILO results framework.[96] ILS mainstreaming in programming documents,[97] unit workplans and performance management frameworks can greatly help to advance a culture change and make work on the basis of ILS the business of every ILO official, and not just legal specialists. The introduction of results-based programming in the ILO since the early 2000s has favoured this cultural change, but more needs to be done to change behaviour patterns.

Effective ILS mainstreaming into DC is often impeded by the tendency towards technical over-specialization of staff, which may lead to narrowly perceived mandates preventing ILS mainstreaming across functions. As noted above, quoting former ILO director-generals, an old danger lies in perceiving ILS as one technical field of ILO activity among others[98]—or in considering that ILS fall within the reserved domain of certain specializations to the exclusion of all others. Both approaches tend to prevent effective standards mainstreaming in operations and partnerships. In short, tackling the challenges of standards mainstreaming requires overcoming expertise turfs and silo dynamics.[99]

Even where tools such as checklists exist to promote ILS mainstreaming, their effectiveness can be hindered by a tendency to pay lip service to standards, eg by ticking the 'normative' box or including superficial references without specific focus and 'depth' in project proposals. Factors that favour this dynamic include insufficient knowledge and ownership of ILS by those designing and implementing the projects. The integration of standards may thus sometimes be relegated to an afterthought rather than serving as a project's driver. Capacity building is the means to address this.

---

[96] ILO, 'Independent High-level Evaluation of ILO's Technical Cooperation Strategy' (2015) 12–21; ILO, 'High-level Independent Evaluation of the ILO's Decent Work Programme in the Andean Countries of the Plurinational State of Bolivia, Colombia, Ecuador, Peru and the Bolivarian Republic of Venezuela, 2016–19' (2020); ILO, 'High-level Independent Evaluation of the ILO's Decent Work Programme in Bangladesh, Nepal, Sri Lanka and Pakistan, 2018–21' (2021).

[97] For example, according to the 'ILO Development Cooperation Internal Governance Manual 2017', all activity proposals need to go through a verification of conformity with ILS, while additional tools to improve the impact of ILS through TC, such as a 2008 Practice Guide, aim to provide guidance to ILO staff on how to identify strategic entry points for promoting and further strengthening the impact of ILS.

[98] For example, the 2017 Development Cooperation Internal Governance Manual can be read as conveying at times such problematic understanding—eg when referring to 'the promotion of ILO's objectives, such as gender equality, international labour standards (ILS), social dialogue and tripartism'—mistaking ILS as one strategic objective among others, when, as set out in the 2008 Social Justice Declaration, ILS are to be understood as a means to achieve all strategic objectives (see last sentence in Preamble of the Declaration).

[99] On organizational silos, see eg Fabio Bento, Marco Tagliabue, and Flora Lorenzo, 'Organizational Silos: A Scoping Review Informed by a Behavioral Perspective on Systems and Networks' (2020) 10 Societies 56.

A recent Guidance Note on adapting evaluations to the ILO's normative mandate shares practitioners' insights as a means to address this challenge. The note explains how presenting the motivation to integrate ILS in project design should go beyond mere conformity with a set of rules, and be seen as a driver of change and part of a transformative strategy reflected in a project's Theory of Change.[100] To make this possible, capacity building on ILS should be extended across the ILO, including its constituents and the Office as a whole, in order to ensure that ILS are not only well-known, but also fully owned at all levels and stages of the DC cycle, gradually becoming a central tenet of all facets of ILO's work, both technical and operational.

Appropriately reflecting ILS in project design is necessary to enable systematic data collection and analysis, throughout the project M&E cycle, of the extent to which ILS are addressed and ultimately have an impact on the project beneficiaries. A good practice in this regard would be to include by default in the evaluation of all ILO DC projects an assessment of their impact on promoting ILS ratification and application. Systematic evaluations of the normative results of DC projects could open up communication and cross-fertilization channels between DC and ILS, including the ILO supervisory bodies.[101] The ILO's database on evaluations could play a central role in highlighting ILS-related aspects of DC operations, enabling the ILO supervisory bodies to carry out dynamic analyses of realities on the ground based on first-hand data[102] and facilitating thematic analyses known as General Surveys. Furthermore, this data could serve as upward feedback to ILS discussions, including the Standards Review Mechanism examinations of the extent to which certain standards adequately address members' needs on the ground.

DC includes partnerships, not only for funding, but also for policy coherence across the UN. In fact, since the adoption of the 2030 Agenda and the repositioning of the UN development system, human rights and ILS concern the work of all UN entities and not just the ILO. The influence of ILS in sustainable development depends to an extent on the degree to which the ILO and development agencies promote international policy coherence, since the same Member States participate in various UN entities including the ILO and the International Financial Institutions, for example.

It is, therefore, necessary to work on effectively mainstreaming ILS in human rights policies and operations, not only as part of United Nations Country Team level work, but also through multilateral policy dialogues, multi-stakeholder

---

[100] ILO, 'Guidance Note 3.2: Adapting Evaluation Methods to the ILO's Normative and Tripartite Mandate' (June 2020).
[101] ibid.
[102] This is the *i*-eval Discovery database <https://www.ilo.org/ievaldiscovery/#b8pbato> accessed 23 August 2023. A systematic practice in this regard had developed in the past in the framework of the IPEC project which maintained a small legal unit, but was not subsequently followed up. 2008 Evaluation (n 94) 33.

partnerships, and policy alliances. However, even though much progress has been made in recent years, ILS uptake across the UN system still faces challenges due to misconceptions on the nature of ILS and differences in operating procedures between UN entities focused on country-level operations and agencies with normative mandates such as the ILO.[103]

Sometimes, ILS mainstreaming in the work of other UN entities is not without its risks, as different entities may perceive different aspects of ILS and their application in their own ways. An example outside of the UN context, is the development of Environmental and Social Safeguards (ESS) by MDBs and the extent to which they reflect the ILO fundamental principles and rights at work and related conventions. As recent internal study[104] indicates, for example, that in the area of discrimination, there are few references in the ESS to prohibiting discrimination on all the grounds covered by ILO Convention No 111, with national origin and political opinion often missing from these requirements.[105]

As concerns freedom of association and collective bargaining, several of the MDBs commit themselves to following national law on freedom of association and collective bargaining and not the more stringent requirements of ILO Conventions Nos 87 and 98. There is also a large gap in the treatment of freedom of association and the rights to organize by all the ESS, in that they fail to take any account of the rights and roles of employers' organizations. As concerns forced and child labour, all the MDBs prohibit their use. However, the identification of and correction of child labour and forced labour can be highly technical problems and compliance of national law can be difficult to assess. The problem of trafficking is sometimes mentioned briefly,[106] which is important because it is likely to arise on large-scale

---

[103] See 2008 Evaluation, ibid, 48. A UN Interagency Network for Human Rights, Leave No One Behind, and Sustainable Development which supports the UN S-G's C2A first thematic priority on sustainable development, have recently taken two important steps to address this gap. First, it elaborated in 2022 a review on the levels of integration of human rights, LNOB, and gender in forty-four CCAs and forty Cooperation Frameworks (CFs) developed between 2019 and mid-2021. The study found that there is an urgent need to step up ambition and operationalization of human rights integration into UN development analysis and programming work at country level. Second, the network elaborated two self-evaluation Checklists drawing on existing guidance on integrating human rights, LNOB, and gender equality and women's empowerment in CCAs and CFs to facilitate human rights mainstreaming in a practical, hands-on way. The study and the checklists integrate ILS and the ILO supervisory body comments among other human rights norms and standards, thereby providing comprehensive assistance and guidance.

[104] ILO, 'The ILO and Safeguards Systems of International Financial Institutions' (unpublished) 11–12.

[105] As an example, the 'World Bank Environmental and Social Framework Guidance Note for Borrowers no 2 on Labour and Working Conditions' (ESS2) provides in relation to non-discrimination that decisions are to be made 'without regard to personal characteristics that are unrelated to the inherent work requirements' (GN13.2). Such distinctions 'can arise with respect to inappropriate treatment or harassment of project workers related, for example, to gender, age, disability, ethnicity, or religion' (GN13.4). This omits any reference to political opinion, which is also prohibited by Convention No 111 (ibid).

[106] See eg 'World Bank Environmental and Social Framework Guidance Note for Borrowers ESS 2: Labor and Working Conditions', para 20, 1st edn, June 2018.

infrastructure projects, but little information is available on how trafficking is detected or dealt with, except by prohibiting the hiring of trafficked workers.

Finally, it might often be the case that national law is well below the international standards, especially in the way in which it is applied in practice, leading the MDB to approve a loan on the assumption that it complies with the ESS, without the country, or the client, necessarily complying with the requirements of ILO standards. In order to address this, there is need for effective partnerships with other international organizations, including the IFIs and MDBs, based on continuous dialogue, capacity building and respect for each entity's distinct and complementary roles, so as to safeguard policy coherence.[107]

A further challenge to ILS promotion through DC is political. History shows that the ILO effectively promotes rights at work through DC when the three ILO constituents act cohesively. This has not always been the case in an institutional landscape comprising three constituencies, multiple geographical regions, different socio-economic and legal systems, as well as different levels of economic development. To the extent that all Members agree on the benefits to be drawn from promoting ILS through DC, consensus can be maintained over the ILO's positive trajectory in this respect. The ILO's independent and non-partisan secretariat plays a pivotal role in ensuring that all constituents can make their voices heard when it comes to priority setting and proposing ways forward to discharge the organization's mandate that garner tripartite consensus.

Setting the organization's DC priorities so that ILS remain high on the priority list in a context of limited resources is also very important. Special accounts of unearmarked funds are particularly helpful, for instance, in delivering support to countries beyond the immediate priorities of donors and beneficiaries with regard to ILS.[108] In a context of resource limitations and drawbacks to the realization of the 2030 Agenda, the ILO is also seeking diversification of funding modalities in order to allocate funding more flexibly whilst creating greater efficiencies of scale, in line with the UN Funding Compact.[109] However, this implies strengthening capacities within the Office to implement innovative partnerships and funding modalities.

---

[107] The CEACR acknowledges this fact and 'encourages further engagement with multilateral development banks in developing their social safeguards and advising them on standards-related issues that arise in the application of these safeguards in the interest of coherence between national policies that derive from standards-related commitments and resources drawn from development financing' (CEACR 2022 report (n 7) para 29).

[108] See ILO, 'The ILO's Regular Budget Supplementary Account: Update for the Governing Body 313th Session, March 2012' (March 2012) <https://www.ilo.org/wcmsp5/groups/public/---dgreports/---exrel/documents/genericdocument/wcms_176092.pdf> accessed 23 August 2023.

[109] For instance, light earmarked funding and the pilot of structured funding dialogues, where the ILO presents its offer and 'ask'.

An additional challenge lies in the fact that while a repositioned UN development system bodes well for the promotion of ILS through DC, the same is not necessarily the case for tripartism and the ILO's dialogical approach. Other UN entities may not be as advanced as the ILO in terms of integration of non-government actors in governance and operational procedures. UN Cooperation Frameworks and DC partnerships with other UN entities are not automatically open to tripartite engagement like the ILO programming and DC processes are. Overcoming this challenge will necessitate awareness raising, capacity building and inter-entity dialogue to enhance an understanding of the ILO's idiosyncrasies within the UN system.

Dialogue does not take place in an institutional void and requires specific structures and skill sets. Drawing on its longstanding experience in this field, a central calling for the ILO within the UN system is to serve as a point of reference providing expertise, assistance, and training on prerequisites, safeguards, and best practices and processes in support of a dialogical approach. A virtuous articulation between operational activities and the application of international axiologies could thus be embraced across UN entities, building on both domains synergistically, in the light of each entity's mandate and specificities.

In conclusion, this chapter described the path travelled over the organization's centenary existence in terms of generating and promoting international labour law across its 187 Member States through DC.

The mandate entrusted to the ILO in the beginning of the twentieth century is today just as relevant. It has been fully integrated in the 2030 Agenda and the SDGs against the background of unprecedented challenges, such as ensuring a just transition to a zero-carbon economy, recovering from the global COVID-19 pandemic, managing the digital evolution, and addressing the geostrategic risks of an increasingly polarized world. In this rapidly changing environment, the ILO will continue to draw on the 'tried-and-trusted' foundation of ILS and its dialogical approach based on social dialogue, in order to carry forward its centenary-old mandate and contribute to sustainable development.

Annex

Table 6.1 ILO Custodianship of SDG Indicators and Links to International Labour Standards

SDG of which ILO is custodian	Indicator	Relevant ILS (non-exhaustive)	Other information including coalitions/ partnerships under ILO (co-)lead
Goal 1: Reduce poverty	1.3.1: Population covered by social protection floors	Social Security (Minimum Standards) Convention (1952) (No 102) Social Protection Floors Recommendation (2012) (No 202)	Global Accelerator for Jobs and Social Protection for just transition launched by the UN Secretary General in September 2021 to accelerate the delivery of the 2030 agenda through economic and social rights in the context of recovery from the COVID-19 pandemic.
Goal 5: Gender equality and women's empowerment	5.5.2: Women in managerial positions	Equal Remuneration Convention (1951) (No 100) Discrimination (Employment and Occupation) Convention (1958) (No 111)	EPIC
Goal 8: Economic growth and Decent Work	8.2.1, 8.3.1: GDP growth by employed person and informal economy (joint custodianship with the World Bank).	Employment Policy Convention (1964) (No 122); Transition from the Informal to the Formal Economy Recommendation (2015) (No 204)	
	8.5.1: Average hourly earnings of female and male employees	Equal Remuneration Convention (1951) (No 100); Protection of Wages Convention (1949) (No 95); Minimum Wage Fixing Convention (1970) (No 131); Minimum Age Convention (1973) (No 138);	
	8.5.2, 8.6.1, and 8.b.1: Unemployment and youth employment	Employment Policy Convention (1964) (No 122); Employment Service Convention (1948) (No 88); Private Employment Agencies Convention (1997) (No 181);	

Table 6.1 Continued

SDG of which ILO is custodian	Indicator	Relevant ILS (non-exhaustive)	Other information including coalitions/ partnerships under ILO (co-)lead
	8.7.1: Child labour (joint custodianship with UNICEF) 8.8.1: Fatal and non-fatal occupational injuries	Employment Promotion and Protection against Unemployment Convention (1988) (No 168); Human Resources Development Convention (1975) (No 142);	Alliance 8.7 to end child labour, forced labour, modern slavery, and human trafficking.
	8.8.2: National compliance of labour rights (freedom of association and collective bargaining) based on ILO textual sources	Worst Forms of Child Labour Convention (1999) (No 182); Minimum Age Convention (1973) (No 138); Forced Labour Convention (1930) (No 29); Abolition of Forced Labour Convention (1957) (No 105); Occupational Safety and Health Convention (1981) (No 155) and its Protocol; Labour Inspection Convention (1947) (No 81); Labour Inspection (Agriculture) Convention (1969) (No 129); Freedom of Association and Protection of the Right to Organise Convention (1948) (No 87); Right to Organise and Collective Bargaining Convention (1949) (No 98);	This is the only SDG indicator drawing on the reports of bodies monitoring the application of these conventions in both ratifying and non-ratifying Member States.
Goal 10: Reduce inequality	10.4.1: Labour share of GDP 10.7.1: Recruitment cost borne by migrant workers	Equality of Treatment (Social Security) Convention (1962) (No 118); Maintenance of Social Security Rights Convention (1982) (No 157);	

(*continued*)

Table 6.1 Continued

SDG of which ILO is custodian	Indicator	Relevant ILS (non-exhaustive)	Other information including coalitions/ partnerships under ILO (co-)lead
		Social Security (Minimum Standards) Convention (1952) (No 102); Right to Organise and Collective Bargaining Convention (1949) (No 98); Minimum Wage Fixing Convention (1970) (No 131); Migration for Employment Convention (Revised) (1949)	
		(No 97); Migrant Workers (Supplementary Provisions) Convention (1975) (No 143); Private Employment Agencies Convention (1997) (No 181)	
Goal 14: Sustainable oceans	14.c.1: Respect for ocean-related instruments that implement international law (joint custodianship with UN-DOALOS, FAO, UNEP, other UN oceans agencies);	Maritime Labour Convention (2006)	

Note: The International Labour Organization (ILO) is also involved in four indicators under Goal 1 (end poverty), Goal 4 (education), and Goal 16 (peaceful and inclusive societies). In relation to the latter, indicator 16.10.1 on 'the number of verified cases of killing, kidnapping, enforced disappearance, arbitrary detention and torture of journalists […] trade unionists and human rights advocates' draws, inter alia, on the work of the ILO Committee on Freedom of Association which examines related cases on a regular basis.

EPIC = Equal Pay International Coalition

FAO = Food and Agriculture Organization of the United Nations

GDP = gross domestic product

MLC = Maritime Labour Convention

SDG = Sustainable Development Goals

UNEP = United Nations Environment Programme

UNICEF = United Nations International Children's Emergency Fund

7
Achieving Gender Equality

Sandra Fredman

1. Introduction

The ambition of Sustainable Development Goal (SDG) 5 to achieve gender equality and empower all women and girls appears further away than ever. The COVID-19 pandemic, the climate emergency, and ongoing war and conflicts have exacerbated inequalities, reversing what progress has been made and magnifying the challenges going forward. Yet there are many ways in which the SDGs still represent an important opportunity for advancing gender equality. In a particularly important breakthrough, SDG 5 promises to recognize and value unpaid care and domestic work, including through the provision of public services and infrastructure, social protection policies, and the promotion of shared responsibility within the household. It promises to eliminate all forms of violence against women and girls; to ensure women's full participation in political, economic, and public life, and to ensure universal access to sexual and reproductive health and reproductive rights. This comes together with several other related goals. SDG 3 commits the world to reducing maternal mortality and providing reproductive health rights. SDG 4 promises universal quality primary and secondary education for both girls and boys. SDG 8 aims to achieve decent work and equal pay for work of equal value, while SDG 6 undertakes to provide clean water and sanitation, which should reduce the drudgery of domestic work for so many women.

This chapter will examine the ways in which these promises interact with legally binding international human rights law, especially the Convention on the Elimination of all forms of Discrimination against Women (CEDAW); the International Convention on Economic, Social and Cultural Rights (ICESCR), and International Labour Organization (ILO) Conventions. The SDGs contrast with international human rights law in several important ways.[1] Most importantly, human rights are legally-binding obligations, with corresponding apparatus, both internationally and at domestic level, to achieve compliance. States that have ratified international human rights instruments are required to provide periodic reports to the relevant treaty monitoring body, and this has more recently been

---

[1] See Sandra Fredman, *Working Together: Human Rights, the Sustainable Development Goals and Gender Equality* (British Academy 2018) (hereafter 'Working Together').

complemented by the opportunity for individuals to complain to these bodies about breach of their rights. This international framework for monitoring states' compliance and holding them accountable is underpinned by the obligation of individual states to give effect to human rights and to provide effective remedies at domestic level for human rights breaches.[2]

By contrast, development goals are political commitments, which can wax and wane depending on political priorities. Indeed, much of the development agenda has traditionally been seen as concerning transfers of aid and other assistance from developed to developing countries. It was hoped by advocates of a human rights-based approach to development goals that some of these weaknesses would be addressed by an express reference to human rights in the SDGs.[3] However, the United Nations' (UN's) document 'Transforming our World: The 2030 Agenda on Sustainable Development' (hereafter 'the 2030 Agenda') makes it clear that follow-up and review processes are voluntary and state-led.[4] States are encouraged to conduct regular reviews of progress at the national level 'which are country-led and country-driven'.[5] At global level, the task of oversight of follow-up and review processes is given to the United Nations High Level Political Forum on Sustainable Development (HLPF), a mechanism which was mandated in 2012 and met for the first time in September 2013. Regular reviews by the HLPF are voluntary and state-led and are expected to be based on the national reviews, which are themselves voluntary. Follow up and review at the HLPF is informed by an annual SDG report to be prepared by the UN Secretary General.[6]

This does not in itself preclude human rights treaty bodies from taking some responsibility, in their own right, for monitoring SDGs. In particular, there is scope for international treaty bodies, without going beyond their mandate, to insist that states report on how implementation of the SDGs is being used to further states' responsibilities under the relevant treaty. The committee responsible for monitoring CEDAW in its Concluding Observations (COs) regularly includes a call for 'the realisation of substantive gender equality, in accordance with the provisions of the Convention, throughout the process of implementation of the 2030 Agenda for Sustainable Development'.[7] However, thus far, the Committee's insertions of SDGs into its own COs are somewhat formulaic. The call for the realization

---

[2] ICCPR, art 2.
[3] OHCHR, 'Human Rights in the Post-2015 Development Agenda' (first open letter from the High Commissioner for Human Rights) (6 June 2013) <http://www.ohchr.org/Documents/Issues/MDGs/Post2015/HCOpenLetterHRPost2015Agenda.pdf> accessed 25 May 2023.
[4] UN General Assembly, *Transforming our World: the 2030 Agenda for Sustainable Development* (A/Res/70/1, 2015) (agreed on 25–27 September 2015) para 74a <https://sustainabledevelopment.un.org/post2015/transformingourworld> accessed 25 May 2023.
[5] ibid para 79.
[6] ibid para 83.
[7] For example, CEDAW Concluding Observations Chile (CEDAW/C/CHL/CO/7, 2018) para 53; CEDAW Concluding Observations Korea (2018) para 49; CEDAW Concluding Observations Fiji (2018) para 65; CEDAW Concluding Observations Malaysia (2018) para 57.

of substantive gender equality in the implementation of the SDGs is identically worded in a series of COs, coming immediately after a similar formula in relation to the Beijing Declaration and Platform of Action.[8] The Committee on Economic, Social and Cultural Rights (CESCR) also regularly mentions the SDGs, usually by recommending that when the state party implements the 2030 Agenda, it should fully take its obligations under the ICESCR into account.[9]

Nevertheless, it should not be assumed that human rights have answers to these challenges which always advance substantive gender equality. Reproductive health and even gender-based violence have only recently been recognized as binding human rights. Poverty is only tangentially recognized. Moreover, there are also potential conflicts of rights. Human rights recognize a right to gender equality, health, and security of the person, but also protect a right to freedom of religious belief and thought. The vocabulary of human rights has been used forcefully to prevent reproductive rights and abortion.[10] In addition, the international human rights accountability mechanisms, while stronger than that of the SDGs, remain heavily dependent on the credibility and persuasiveness of the various monitoring bodies. The enforcing committees can only make recommendations, leaving it up to states to follow in good faith. This is true too for the individual communications procedures, which now allow individuals to bring complaints against states. It is at national level that the main potential for enforcement lies; and this depends on the openness of domestic courts and legislatures to absorbing international norms.[11]

The SDGs, with their many interlocking goals touching on gender equality, represent great promise. However, their focus on aggregate outcomes pays too little attention to the qualitative dimensions of substantive gender equality, while the inadequacy of the accountability mechanisms leaves the attainment of the SDGs vulnerable to political will. The human rights framework, for its part, adds a greater level of accountability and more attention to the individual, as well as aiming to put in place ways to achieve the ultimate goals, and checking that these in turn are human rights compliant. However, the substance of human rights, through the prism of gender equality, is still contested, particularly in relation to women in poverty. Moreover, the accountability structures, while in principle legally binding, are only as strong as the political will of signatory states to implement them. Thus,

---

[8] For example, CEDAW Concluding Observations Korea (2018) para 48; CEDAW Concluding Observations Fiji (2018) para 64; CEDAW Concluding Observations Malaysia (2018) para 56

[9] CESCR Concluding Observations Colombia (2017) para 71; CESCR Concluding Observations Russian Federation (2017) para 62; CESCR Concluding Observations Sri Lanka (2017) para 74; CESCR Concluding Observations Uruguay (2017) para 61; CESCR Concluding Observations Pakistan (2017) para 91; CESCR Concluding Observations Australia (2017) para 61.

[10] Marta Rodriguez de Assis Machado, 'Conservative Mobilization in Latin America and its Impacts on Women's and Adolescents' Human Rights' (9 February 2018) <http://ohrh.law.ox.ac.uk/conservative-mobilization-in-latin-america-and-its-impacts-on-womens-and-adolescents-human-rights/> accessed 25 May 2023.

[11] For a leading example, see *María de los Ángeles González Carreño v Ministry of Justice,* Judgment No 1263/2018 Spanish Supreme Court (17 July 2018) particularly 23–28.

it is vital for the two structures to work together in a synergistic manner to achieve transformative gender equality and to ensure that the ambitious promises of the SDGs are not simply fleeting hopes.[12]

Crucially, both the human rights mechanisms and the SDGs should be seen as important focus points for collective organization through non-governmental organizations (NGOs) and grassroots movements at local, national, and international level. Through shadow reporting to the human rights monitoring groups, as well as publicity and political pressure in their home countries, collective organization can leverage binding human rights commitments to put pressure on governments to comply. The SDGs are capable of performing a similar function. All of these should be fed into domestic political activity and domestic human rights frameworks, which are more likely to be binding, although also may be challenging so far as remedies are concerned. It is therefore of great importance to find appropriate synergies between the SDGs and human rights, so that each is capable of giving added weight to the other.

Section 2 will examine the substantive vision of gender equality in the SDGs, including its measurement framework, with a specific focus on care-giving and reproductive rights. Section 3 asks whether and how far international human rights law can underpin the SDGs in relation to substantive gender equality, considering how these two different institutional aspirations towards gender equality could complement each other. Section 4 briefly examines how resources for the SDGs should be focused consistently with gender equality, with a closer look at the risks posed in the current climate for gender equality in relation to reproductive rights and care-giving. The chapter will pay particular attention to intersectional concerns, especially in the light of the COVID-19 pandemic and the climate emergency.

2. Substantive Gender Equality in the Development Goals

a. Substantive gender equality: A four-dimensional approach

The concept of discrimination is widespread in international law, but its meaning is still contested. There is now a greater acceptance that simply requiring equal treatment regardless of gender can entrench and perpetuate inequality where there is already pre-existing disadvantage. But the meaning of the right to substantive equality remains contested. I have argued that this concept resists reduction into a single principle, such as dignity, but instead should be viewed as including four, mutually supportive dimensions in relation to outgroups: (i) redressing disadvantage;

---

[12] Working Together (n 1).

(ii) addressing stigma, stereotyping, prejudice, and violence; (iii) facilitating voice and participation; and (iv) accommodating difference and achieving structural change. These need to be achieved simultaneously, so far as possible. This section briefly elaborates on this concept.[13]

The first dimension is the need to redress disadvantage. This recognizes that it is not so much the classification, such as race or gender, which is the problem, but the disadvantage attached to it. The right to substantive equality is not an egalitarian ideal which is fulfilled whether everyone is treated equally badly or everyone is treated equally well. Instead, it focuses on levelling up, or extending benefits accorded to advantaged groups to outgroups. Crucially, it is also an asymmetric concept. Where unequal treatment is necessary to redress disadvantage, substantive equality is furthered. This means that affirmative action is not a breach of the right to equality, but a means to achieve equality.

But disadvantage is not sufficient. It needs to be recognized that it is often stigma and stereotyping that fuel disadvantage. This is the second dimension. In particular, the stereotyping of women as primarily responsible for child-care and domestic work has made it difficult to enter the labour market on equal terms as men. Paying attention to the interaction between stereotyping and disadvantage reveals that it is no coincidence that women predominate among precarious workers, low-paid workers, and workers in the informal sector and that they continue to do more hours of unpaid work than men. Stereotyping of caring work as 'women's work' which can be done unpaid in the home also means that when caring and domestic work is done in the paid labour market, the work is undervalued on the assumption that it can be done unpaid at home. Given the undervaluation of this kind of work, it is not surprising that there is a very wide gender pay gap almost everywhere in the world.

This has become particularly salient during the COVID-19 pandemic, when in many countries, schools, nurseries, and other child-caring supports were closed, and unpaid caring work multiplied. At the same time, the Covid-19 pandemic exposed how reliant society is on care workers, domestic workers, and similar workers. No matter how low paid and tenuous their work is, they often had to continue to go to work, despite major risks to themselves and their families. This dimension further requires attention to be paid to gender-based violence. Racist violence, sexual violence, homophobic violence, and other violence against protected groups are not simply constituted by individual acts of violence against other individuals, which are in any case prohibited by criminal law. Such violence is fuelled and perpetuated by deep-seated stereotypes and stigmatic 'othering'.[14]

---

[13] This section is based on Sandra Fredman, 'Beyond the Dichotomy of Formal and Substantive Equality: Towards a New Definition of Equal Rights' in Ineke Boerefijn and others (eds), *Temporary Special Measures* (Intersentia 2003); Sandra Fredman, 'Substantive Equality Revisited' (2016) 14 ICON 712; Sandra Fredman, *Discrimination Law* (3rd edn, OUP 2022), ch 1.

[14] Fredman, *Discrimination Law* (n 13) ch 1.

The third dimension of the right to substantive equality requires the facilitation of participation by those who are excluded and marginalized, both by the political process and socially. Participation is a key aspect of the right to equality. As Iris Marion Young argues, the focus of theories of justice should be on structures which exclude people from participating in determining their actions.[15] For her, therefore, social equality refers both to the distribution of social goods, and to the full participation and inclusion of everyone in major social institutions.[16] This is endorsed by Nancy Fraser who sees parity of participation as the normative core of her conception of justice, encompassing both redistribution and recognition without reducing either one to the other.[17] When past discrimination has blocked the avenues for political and social participation, equality laws are needed both to compensate for this absence of political voice and to open up the channels for greater participation in the future.

The US Supreme Court has declared that judicial intervention under the equality guarantee is particularly necessary because of the way in which 'prejudice against discrete and insular minorities ... tends seriously to curtail the operation of those political processes ordinarily to be relied upon to protect minorities'.[18] Crucially, the first dimension (redressing disadvantage) combined with the participative dimension requires close attention to be paid to intersectionality. It is not sufficient simply to amplify the voice of elite women. Women who are particularly disadvantaged and marginalized and who are able to speak to the needs of the counterparts must be included.

The fourth dimension recognizes that inequality is more than the sum of many individual acts of prejudice, but inheres in the structures of society, fuelled by imbalances of power.[19] In particular, structures which require conformity to the male norm will continue to perpetuate inequality. To achieve the right to substantive equality therefore requires accommodation of difference and structural change. The fourth dimension of substantive equality therefore addresses the need for structural change. Crucially, it recognizes that conformity should not be a prerequisite for the right to equality. Existing social structures must be changed to accommodate difference, rather than requiring members of out-groups to conform to the dominant norm.

Substantive equality is therefore potentially transformative. For example, working hours have always been patterned on the assumption that childcare takes place outside the labour market. Women who wish to participate in the paid labour market must conform to this paradigm, either by foregoing having children, or leaving their children with family members or child-carers, who are most likely to

---

[15] Iris M Young, *Justice and the Politics of Difference* (Princeton Paperbacks 1990) 31–32.
[16] ibid 173.
[17] Nancy Fraser and Axel Honneth, *Redistribution or Recognition* (Verso 2003) 36–37.
[18] *United States v Carolene Products Company* [1938] 304 US 144 152 (per Stone J) n 4.
[19] Young (n 15) 31–32.

be low-paid women. Substantive equality aims to change such institutions so that participative parenting is compatible with participation of all parents in the paid labour market. Similarly, the built environment must be adapted to accommodate the needs of persons with disabilities, and dress codes and holidays must accommodate ethnic and religious minorities.

Behind all of these is the overriding need to redress inequalities in power. Disadvantage is most easily understood in the context of redistribution of resources and benefits, addressing under-representation in jobs, underpayment for work of equal value, or limitations on access to credit, property, or similar resources. However, disadvantage should encompass more than maldistribution of resources. It needs also to take on board the constraints which power structures impose on individuals because of their status.[20] As Young argues, the focus should be on domination, or structures which exclude people from participating in determining their actions.[21] For example, women's disadvantage cannot be characterized solely in terms of income poverty, but is centrally related to imbalances of power within and outside the family.[22] The same is true for power structures which create and perpetuate discrimination against Black people, people with disabilities, poor people, and other disadvantaged groups. It is for this reason that the first dimension, the need to redress disadvantage both materially and of power, must interact closely with the other dimensions: the need to enhance voice and participation and to bring about structural change.

b. Applying substantive gender equality in the context of the SDGs

Looked at in the light of this four-dimensional understanding of substantive equality, there are many ways in which the SDGs present a huge opportunity for advancing gender equality. This is reflected in the ambition of SDG 5 on gender equality which states expressly that the world promises to achieve gender equality and the empowerment of all women and girls by 2030. This is particularly evident in relation to two key themes: care-giving and reproductive rights.

The need for recognition of unpaid care and domestic work was one of the central demands in the negotiations over the SDGs.[23] This campaign yielded some important successes. In a particularly important breakthrough, SDG 5 commits

---

[20] ibid 16.
[21] ibid.
[22] Sylvia Chant, 'The "Feminisation of Poverty" and the "Feminisation" of Anti-Poverty Programmes: Room for Revision?' (2008) 43 J Dev Stud 165–97.
[23] For an important intervention, see UNGA, *Report of the Special Rapporteur on Extreme Poverty and Human Rights: Unpaid Care Work and Women's Human Rights* (UN Doc A/68/293, 2013) <https://ssrn.com/abstract=2437791> accessed 25 May 2023.

the world to recognize and value unpaid care and domestic work. Target 5.4 calls on states to 'recognise and value unpaid care and domestic work through the provision of public services, infrastructure and social protection policies and the promotion of shared responsibility within the household and the family as nationally appropriate'. This is a crucial step towards addressing both the second dimension, redressing stereotyping, and the first dimension, redressing disadvantage. SDG 5 also addresses the need for structural change. It emphasizes the provision of public services and infrastructure, social protection policies and the promotion of shared responsibility within the household as the explicit means to recognize and value unpaid care and domestic work.

On its own the emphasis on unpaid care and domestic work in SDG 5 is insufficient. It leaves out of account the crucial interaction between unpaid and paid work, whether through the undervaluation of caring work or through the difficulty in reconciling unpaid care and domestic work with full participation of women in the paid workforce. This gap is filled to some extent by SDG 8 which contains several targets specifically referring to decent work.[24] These are helpful in advancing substantive gender equality, particularly by addressing disadvantage in the labour market, emphasizing intersectionality and addressing stigma and stereotyping through undervaluation of women's work.

Target 8.5 aims to achieve full and productive employment and decent work for all women and men, and equal pay for work of equal value. This is complemented by Target 8.8, which aims to protect labour rights and promote safe and secure working environments for all workers. It makes specific reference to migrant workers, in particularly women migrants, and those in precarious employment. Some aspects of structural change are included: Target 8.3 aims to promote development-oriented policies that support, inter alia, decent job creation and the formalisation and growth of micro-, small-, and medium-sized enterprises. Given the very high prevalence of women in informal and precarious employment as well as among migrants, especially in Sub-Saharan Africa, these two targets are potentially of great importance for women. Finally, Target 8.7 aims to eradicate forced labour, end modern slavery, and human trafficking and secure the prohibition and elimination of the worst forms of child labour.

Similarly, the SDGs make a significant contribution to substantive gender equality in the field of reproductive rights,[25] situating the prevention of maternal

---

[24] Shirin Rai, Benjamin Brown, and Kanchana Ruwanpura, 'SDG 8: Decent Work and Economic Growth—a Gendered Analysis' (2019) 113 World Dev 368.

[25] See Alicia Yamin, 'Power, Politics and Knowledge Claims: Sexual and Reproductive Health and Rights in the SDG Era' (2019) 10 Glob Policy 52; Alanna Galati, 'Onward to 2030: Sexual and Reproductive Health and Rights in the Context of the Sustainable Development Goals' (2015) 18(4) GPR <https://www.guttmacher.org/gpr/2015/10/onward-2030-sexual-and-reproductive-health-and-rights-context-sustainable-development> accessed 25 May 2023; Ann Starrs, 'How SRHR has Become Central to Achieving the SDGs' (*Devex*, 30 November 2015) <https://www.devex.com/news/how-srhr-has-become-central-to-achieving-the-sdgs-87337> accessed 25 May 2023.

mortality and reproductive rights as part of a more general commitment to gender equality and the empowerment of women and girls. SDG 3, which promises to ensure healthy lives and promote well-being for all, has two targets relating to reproductive rights. Target 3.1 commits the world to reducing maternal mortality to fewer than 70 per 100,000 live births by 2030 on maternal mortality. The shockingly high statistics on maternal mortality, reaching as many as 152 deaths per 100,000 live births in 2020,[26] reflect one of the major assaults on all dimensions of gender equality.

Given that it is highly preventable, maternal mortality represents the ultimate negation of women's value as people, deepening their disadvantage because of stereotyping, prejudice, and violence, extinguishing their voice and reinforcing structural power imbalances. However, preventing death in childbirth is clearly not sufficient to address these issues. Access to contraception, proper health-care services, and comprehensive sexuality education are crucial to address these structural inequalities. Target 3.7 deals with some of these issues. It pledges to ensure 'universal access to sexual and reproductive health-care services, including for family planning, information and education, and the integration of reproductive health into national strategies and programmes', again, by 2030. This is complemented by further targets in SDG 5. A result of sustained and well-developed campaigning by women's groups,[27] SDG 5 includes the commitment to ensure universal access to sexual and reproductive health and reproductive rights (Target 5.6). Also crucial is Target 3.8 which commits the world to achieve universal health coverage, including access to quality essential health-care services. To support these changes, Target 3.c undertakes to substantially increase health financing and the recruitment, training, and development of the health workforce in developing countries.

c. Measuring substantive gender equality in the SDGs

On the face of it, therefore, the SDGs tick the boxes for all four dimensions of substantive equality. However, when we look at the measurement framework, we see a very different picture, draining the ideals of some of their energy. Thus, the radical potential inherent in the promise to recognize and value unpaid care work is undermined by the fact that progress is measured only by collecting data on the

---

For the process leading up to the SDGs, see Kate Donald and Sally-Ann Way, 'Accountability for the Sustainable Development Goals: A Lost Opportunity' (2016) 30 Ethics Int Aff 201; Malcolm Langford, 'Lost in Transformation? The Politics of the Sustainable Development Goals' (2016) 30 Ethics Int Aff 167.

[26] Bill and Melinda Gates Foundation, 'Maternal Mortality: Global Progress and Projections for Maternal Mortality' (*Goalkeeper*) <https://www.gatesfoundation.org/goalkeepers/report/2021-report/progress-indicators/maternal-mortality/> accessed 25 May 2023.
[27] Yamin (n 25).

time spent by men and women on unpaid work by sex, age, and location. Given that time-use surveys are not available in many countries,[28] this will yield at best a partial picture. More seriously, there is no attempt to ensure the structural changes required to redistribute unpaid caring work. In particular, there is there no measurement indicator for the provision of public services and infrastructure and social protection policies, and the promotion of shared responsibility within the household and the family as promised by SDG 5.

The framework for assessing progress towards targets on paid work is just as inadequate as that for unpaid caring work. The indicator for Target 8.3 on decent job creation simply counts the proportion of informal employment in non-agricultural employment, disaggregated by sex. The omission of agricultural employment is particularly glaring. Women comprise over 37 per cent of the global rural agricultural workforce, rising to 48 per cent for low-income countries.[29] According to the UN Food and Agricultural Organization (FAO), these percentages are very likely to underestimate women's full contribution to agriculture, since their work, which is frequently unpaid, is not always sufficiently reflected in official statistics. Moreover, women are severely limited in their capacity to benefit from their work due to gender-based constraints. In particular, rural women are more likely than men to be employed as low-wage, part-time, and seasonal workers. As such they are without legal or social protection and are paid less than men even if they are more qualified.[30] Substantive gender equality would demand greater attention to these disadvantages and the stereotypes and structural barriers faced by women in agriculture which cause them. As the UN FAO puts it: 'The root cause of these discriminations lies in social norms, attitudes and beliefs, which shape how women and men are expected to behave, the opportunities that are offered to them and the aspirations they can pursue.'[31]

For Target 8.5 on full employment and decent work, there are only two indicators. The first measures the unemployment rate by sex, age, and persons with disabilities. The second measures average hourly earnings of female and male employees by occupation, age, and persons with disabilities. Although average hourly earnings are an important measure, this indicator will not on its own capture the different ingredients of hourly earnings discrepancies, which include job segregation, lack of seniority, undervaluation of work, and lack of access to lucrative overtime and bonus opportunities. This makes it difficult to create effective pathways to change. Moreover, by focusing on employees, it entirely leaves out of account

---

[28] UN Women, 'Spotlight on Sustainable Development Goal 5: Achieve Gender Equality and Empower all Women and Girls' (5 July 2017) <http://www.unwomen.org/en/digital-library/multimedia/2017/7/infographic-spotlight-on-sdg-5> accessed 25 May 2023.
[29] Food and Agricultural Organization of the United Nations, 'FAO Policy on Gender Equality 2020–2030' (2020) <FAO Policy on Gender Equality 2020–2030> accessed 25 May 2023.
[30] ibid 4.
[31] ibid 3.

workers who fall outside of the formal sector and are precarious. Particularly glaring is the absence of any other criteria for decent work, such as maximum hours, holiday leave, parental leave, and sickness leave. The need for paid sickness leave has become a crucial issue in the wake of the Covid-19 pandemic. When workers cannot afford to stay at home despite being potentially infected with the virus, it becomes obvious that paid sickness leave is a community issue.

A substantive gender equality approach would focus attention, not just on average earnings, but on the stereotypes, lack of voice, and structural barriers to decent work faced by women. Data should measure the extent to which care work can enhance the quality of life and feasible options available to carers, for example, through quality public child-care and decent pay and conditions. Qualitative measurement should include the extent to which care work is properly valued, free of gender stereotypes, and shared between men and women and others in society. The structural dimension requires data to measure the role of the state in providing public services and ensuring decent pay, countering the neo-liberal ideology of privatization and insisting on transparency and an absence of cronyism in the use of public funds.

A similar pattern is evident in relation to reproductive rights. Under the lens of substantive gender equality, the question arises as to whether the prescribed indicators can truly address disadvantage, stigma and stereotyping, lack of participation and structural obstacles, and the interactions between them.[32] Particularly disappointing are the indicators for maternal mortality, where the two main indicators are the maternal mortality ratio (Indicator 3.1.1), and the proportion of births attended by skilled health personnel (Indicator 3.1.2). These simply replicate the indicators in the Millennium Development Goals, which preceded the SDGs and which were criticized for obscuring inequalities and rights violations.[33]

There are at least three ways in which these do not fulfil the requirements of substantive equality. Firstly, they do not fully address women's disadvantage, the first dimension. Emergency obstetric care, seen as key to decreasing women's mortality and morbidity in childbirth, is not mentioned. Particularly stark is the absence of any mention of abortion, which is a key contributor to maternal death in childbirth. Secondly, no attention is paid to stigma, stereotyping, prejudice, and violence. In particular, there is no mention of the need to decrease obstetric violence, an increasingly recognized experience of women who face abuse and assault during childbirth.[34] Thirdly, and most saliently, the SDG indicators focus on

---

[32] Sandra Fredman and Beth Goldblatt 'Gender Equality and Human Rights Discussion Paper' (2015) Discussion Paper No 4 for Progress of the World's Women 2015–2016 <https://www.unwomen.org/-/media/headquarters/attachments/sections/library/publications/2015/goldblatt-fin.pdf?la=en&vs=1627> accessed 25 May 2023.

[33] Audrey Chapman, 'Evaluating the Health-related Targets in the Sustainable Development Goals from a Human Rights Perspective' (2017) 21 IJHR 1098.

[34] Camilla Pickles, 'Leaving Women Behind: The Application of Evidence-based Guidelines, Law, and Obstetric Violence by Omission' in Camilla Pickles and Jonathan Herring (eds), *Childbirth, Vulnerability and the Law* (Routledge 2019) 140–60.

outcomes rather than the means to achieve those outcomes and do not grapple with some of the deep-seated obstacles to full reproductive rights for women. This means that structural change, required by the fourth dimension, is unlikely to be achieved.

Substantive gender equality is better reflected in relation to universal access to sexual and reproductive health care services, including family planning and education. The crucial new contribution of SDG 5.6 is that it includes targets which emphasize the centrality of women's voice in relation to their reproductive rights (the third dimension). Thus Indicator 5.6.1 measures the proportion of women aged fifteen to forty-nine years who make their own informed decisions regarding sexual relations, contraceptive use, and reproductive health care. The United Nations Population Fund (UNFPA), which is the custodian for SDG Indicator 5.6.1,[35] emphasizes that women can only be considered to have autonomy in reproductive health decision-making if they assert that the make their own decisions in three key areas: reproductive health care, contraceptive use, and sexual relations. Indicator 5.6.1 therefore asks who makes the decisions on these three issues and as of early 2020, there were fifty-seven countries with data on all three questions.

However, the survey is limited in two key respects. Firstly, until 2020, data only covered women and adolescent girls who were using any kind of contraception. The next round of data will helpfully be extended to respondents whether they are using contraception or not, but data thus far must be read with the background assumption that many women and girls who have not been using contraception are likely to have had limited autonomy in this respect. The second major limitation, which has not been corrected, is that unmarried women and girls are not included. The stigma and stereotyping in many communities of girls and women who have sexual relations without being married is therefore entirely ignored in the representation of progress towards greater empowerment of women. In this light, the figure of only 55 per cent of married or in-union women already using contraception who making their own decisions about sexual and reproductive health rights should be regarded as giving a partial picture at best.[36] UNFPA itself acknowledges that too often women are not able to exercise the voice in decision-making on these issues due to harmful and discriminatory social norms and practices.[37]

Secondly, the main indicator for SDG 5.6 measures the extent to which laws and regulations guarantee full and equal access to women and men aged fifteen years and older to sexual and reproductive health care, information, and education (SDG Indicator 5.6.2). In an important acknowledgement of the synergy between the

---

[35] United Nations Population Fund, 'Ensure Universal Access to Sexual and Reproductive Health and Reproductive Rights: Measuring SDG Target 5.6' (29 February 2020) <https://www.unfpa.org/sdg-5-6> accessed 26 May 2023.
[36] UNFPA, 'Tracking Women's Decision-making for Sexual and Reproductive Health and Reproductive Rights' (February 2020) <https://www.unfpa.org/node/24015> accessed 26 May 2023.
[37] ibid 4–5.

SDGs and human rights, UNFPA, which also the custodian of Indicator 5.6.2, uses a measurement framework which is guided by the CESCR in its General Comment on Health. This states that states must repeal and eliminate laws, practices, and politics that criminalize, obstruct, or undermine an individual or a group's access to health facilities, services, goods, and information.[38] The framework notably includes the legal status of abortion and post abortion care, as well as the legal and regulatory framework on comprehensive sexual education and information, and contraception and family planning.[39] At one level, this might be regarded as going some way towards addressing the structural barriers faced by women (the fourth dimension).[40] However, as UNFPA found, the existence of an enabling legal system is far from sufficient. Instead, there is a significant gulf between the legal measures in place and women's actual experience.[41]

In addition, the SDG's use of aggregate numbers to demonstrate progress means that they are heavily dependent on the collection of reliable data by different countries. UNFPA points out that more than one hundred countries do not have available data on either of women's decision-making or on the relevant laws.[42] Calls for urgent action to collect the data might actually divert resources from meeting the needs of women, while at the same time, allowing states to attribute delays in taking measures to lack of data. On the other hand, the SDGs do not put in place specific obligations or steps which states must take to achieve these goals. The closest it gets is Indicator 3.8.1, which measures the average coverage of essential health services, including reproductive and maternal health. However, progress on this target is not auspicious. According to the 2019 SDG report, based on available data from 2013 to 2018, more than 55 per cent of countries had fewer than forty nursing and midwifery personnel per 10,000 people. The picture was particularly bleak in least developed countries, all of which had fewer than ten medical doctors per 10,000 people, and almost all (98 per cent) had fewer than forty nursing and midwifery personnel per 10,000 people.[43]

---

[38] CESCR, *General Comment No 22 (2016) on the Right to Sexual and Reproductive Health (Article 12 of the International Covenant on Economic, Social and Cultural Rights)* (UN Doc E/C12/GC/22, 2016) <https://tbinternet.ohchr.org/_layouts/15/treatybodyexternal/Download.aspx?symbolno=E/C.12/GC/22&Lang=en> accessed 26 May 2023. See <https://unstats.un.org/sdgs/metadata/> accessed 26 May 2023.

[39] UNFPA, 'Legal Commitments for Sexual and Reproductive Health and Reproductive Rights for All: Achieving Sustainable Development Goal Indicator 5.6.2' <https://www.unfpa.org/sites/default/files/resource-pdf/UNFPA-SDG562-A4-Brochure-v4.15.pdf> accessed 26 May 2023.

[40] UNFPA (n 35).

[41] UNFPA, 'Staggering Numbers of Women unable to Exercise Decision-making over their own Bodies, New UNFPA Report Shows' (1 April 2020) <https://www.unfpa.org/news/staggering-numbers-women-unable-exercise-decision-making-over-their-own-bodies-new-unfpa-report> accessed 26 May 2023.

[42] ibid.

[43] UN Economic and Social Council, 'Special Edition: Progress towards the Sustainable Development Goals Report of the Secretary-General' (8 May 2019) UN Doc E/2019/68, para 24 <https://undocs.org/E/2019/68> accessed 26 May 2023.

3. Filling the Gaps: International Human Rights Law

The quest for substantive gender equality in the SDGs, while opening up many possibilities, still remains elusive. As we saw in the introductory section, the SDGs are not legally binding, but are purely a matter of political commitment and good will. This raises the question of whether the international human rights framework is able to complement the development goals in ways which strengthen their ability to achieve substantive gender equality.

The preamble of the founding document of the SDGs, the 2030 Agenda, declares that the SDG agenda is grounded in the Universal Declaration of Human Rights and international human rights treaties. Furthermore, it resolves to protect human rights and promote gender equality and the empowerment of women and girls.[44] However, as Yamin argues, 'inserting the language of rights into the declaration of the Agenda 2030 or the SDG targets did not guarantee either the laws, social practices or institutional structures to promote, interpret and enforce them'.[45] Most governments, global institutions, and private sector actors were quite content with a weak accountability structure. The proliferation of indicators became a conveniently technical edifice to obscure these normative commitments.[46]

The CESCR has attempted to redress this deficit by pointing out that national actions plans for the implementation of the SDGs should take full account of the recommendations it issues to states parties in the context of the periodic reporting process.[47] In its statement on the ICESCR and the SDGs in 2019, the CESCR sets out what it calls a 'rights-based methodology' for states in implementing their obligations under the covenant. According to the statement, the covenant requires outcomes to be realized in ways that are consistent with the principles of participation, transparency, accountability, non-discrimination, empowerment of beneficiaries, and respect for the rule of law. This normative framework, the statement declares, can be applied to the implementation of all SDGs.[48] While these are all laudable, they tend to be process-oriented rather than providing a substantive content. This is especially true of the principles of participation, transparency, accountability, and respect for the rule of law.

Instead, it is to the substance of the legally binding obligations in CEDAW, ICESCR, and the ILO that we need to turn to determine if the gaps can be filled. To achieve substantive gender equality, these would need to simultaneously optimize the four dimensions of redressing gendered disadvantage, addressing stigma

---

[44] United Nations Department of Economic and Social Affairs Sustainable Development, 'Transforming our world: the 2030 Agenda for Sustainable Development' (25 Sept 2015) UN Doc A/RES/70/1, Preamble and paras 3 and 8 <https://sdgs.un.org/2030agenda> accessed 2 August 2023.
[45] Yamin (n 25) 55.
[46] ibid.
[47] CESCR, 'The Pledge to "Leave No One Behind": The ICESCR and the 2030 Agenda for Sustainable Development' (8 March 2019) para 19.
[48] ibid paras 11–12.

and stereotyping, amplifying women's voice, and achieving structural change. Importantly, gender equality is a right which must be fulfilled for each individual. Progress cannot be measured wholly in aggregate outcomes. Moreover, the human rights framework should be oriented towards the duties undertaken by states to further the fulfilment of the right to gender equality. This too entails an emphasis on the steps to be taken to achieve the right, rather than on collecting outcome data which have no normative implication in themselves.

Several of these principles can be discerned in these instruments. Under article 12 of CEDAW, states parties undertake to ensure appropriate services to women in connection with pregnancy, confinement, and the post-natal period. This goes beyond the SDGs in the requirement to take positive steps to achieve this outcome, including granting free services where necessary, as well as adequate nutrition during pregnancy and breast-feeding.[49] This means that it is not sufficient to report solely on outcome data. In addition, states must report on how they supply free services where necessary to ensure safe pregnancy, childbirth, and post-partum periods for women. In a gesture towards intersectionality, this right extends specifically to rural women.[50] This is an important contribution to addressing gendered disadvantage in relation to pregnancy and safe childbirth.

Similarly, the CESCR's General Comment 22 on reproductive rights (GC22)[51] states that at the very least sexual and reproductive health services should be affordable for all. Essential goods and services in relation to sexual and reproductive health should be provided at no cost or ensure that people without sufficient means are given the support to cover the costs. Moreover, essential goods and services relating to the underlying determinants of sexual and reproductive health are covered too.[52] All of this must be of good quality, evidence-based, and up to date.[53] Particularly striking is the inclusion of the right to emergency obstetric services, which, as we have seen, was not included in the SDG measurement framework. CEDAW's General Recommendation 24 emphasizes that the duty of states parties to ensure women's right to safe motherhood includes the right to emergency obstetric services.[54] The CESCR General Comment goes even further. Far from simply ignoring the importance of emergency obstetric services, as the SDGs do, it declares that lack of emergency obstetric care services constitutes a violation of the right to life and can amount to cruel, inhuman, or degrading treatment.[55]

---

[49] *Convention on the Elimination of All Forms of Discrimination Against Women* (CEDAW) (UN Doc A/RES/34/180, adopted 18 December 1979, entered into force 3 September 1981) art 12(1).
[50] ibid art 14(2)(g).
[51] CESCR, *General Comment No 22 (2016)* (n 38).
[52] ibid para 17.
[53] ibid para 21.
[54] CEDAW *General Recommendation No 24: Article 12 of the Convention (Women and Health)* (UN Doc A/54/38/Rev. 1, 1999) para 27.
[55] CESCR, *General Comment No 22 (2016)* (n 38) para 10.

CEDAW also recognizes that the commitment to gender equality must be underpinned by measures to address the stereotyping of women as primarily responsible for child-care, the second dimension. Article 5 requires states parties to take all appropriate measures 'to modify the social and cultural patterns of conduct of men and women, with a view to achieving the elimination of prejudices and customary and all other practices which are based on the idea of the inferiority or the superiority of either of the sexes or on stereotyped roles for men and women'. Particularly important, in this context, is article 5's requirement that states parties ensure that family education includes a 'proper understanding of maternity as a social function and the recognition of the common responsibility of men and women in the upbringing and development of their children'.

To this extent, these two covenants take seriously the need for structural change to properly address gendered disadvantage in relation to reproductive justice. However, without paying attention to caring work, both paid and unpaid, these deeply entrenched barriers to substantive gender equality will remain in place. In fact, there is little direct attention to this issue in either CEDAW or ICESCR. Indeed, there are many respects in which the SDGs are ahead of the human rights framework in their explicit acknowledgement of care and domestic work, and the need both to value care for its own sake, while also reducing the drudgery associated with domestic work and redistributing care between men and women and society more generally.

Nevertheless, the human rights framework underpins the SDGs along many dimensions of substantive equality, and most particularly in its emphasis on individual rights rather than purely aggregate outcomes. The first dimension is found in several provisions of CEDAW which aim to redress women's disadvantage in the workforce due to their role in child-care. Article 11 CEDAW requires states parties to prohibit dismissal on grounds of pregnancy or maternity leave and introduce maternity leave with pay without loss of former employment, seniority, or social allowances. The interaction between stereotyping of women's work and women's disadvantage is further recognized by article 11's requirement of the right to equal treatment in respect of work of equal value. CEDAW also goes some way towards structural change in its requirement, in article 11, that states should encourage parents to combine family obligations with work responsibilities and participation in public life, especially through promoting the establishment of a network of child-care facilities.

The ILO has paid much more direct attention to care work, producing a series of reports to underline its commitment to achieving decent work for women by reducing, revaluing, and redistributing care work. However, in many ways, this commitment reaches beyond legally binding ILO standards. The ILO was a pioneer in maternity protection, with the Maternity Protection Convention (No 3) adopted in 1919, representing the first international treaty on gender equality. Nevertheless, the ILO itself acknowledges that, over a hundred years later, the modernized Maternity Protection Convention 2000 (No 183) is 'still overwhelmingly out of reach for the large majority of women round the world'.[56] By 2021, this convention had only been ratified by forty countries in 2021, with 147 still to ratify. Moreover, the ILO has found that regardless of ratification, eighty-two countries do not meet at least one ILO standard on maternity leave, leaving an estimated 649 million women with inadequate protection.[57] In any event, this convention's focus on maternity, while crucial for women, risks reinforcing the stereotyping of women as primarily responsible for children, and thus perpetuating structural forces maintaining gender inequality.

The Workers with Family Responsibilities Convention (No 156) (1981) goes some way to recognizing the role of men as well as the broader society in relation to the balance of unpaid care work with paid work. However, although the ILO regards the convention as paving the way for parental leave and the right to childcare, its provisions are relatively weak. Under the convention, Members are simply required to make it an aim of national policy to enable persons with family responsibilities to work without being subject to discrimination. Members also undertake to take measures to account for the needs of such workers in employment, including enabling them to re-enter the labour force after an absence due to family responsibilities. At most, Members undertake to develop services such as child-care and family services. Even so, by 2021, only forty-five countries had ratified Convention 156, with only four new ratifications in the previous decade. This means that as many as 142 countries have still yet to ratify.

The ILO has therefore robustly aligned itself behind SDG 5.4 and its call to recognize and value unpaid care and domestic work.[58] In its 2019 Centenary Declaration for the Future of Work, the ILO emphasized the importance of the care economy for a transformative gender equality agenda, calling for more investment, and a ramping up of ratifications and implementation of maternity protection standards.[59]

Clearly, it is only by working together that the promises in both the SDGs and international human rights law stand any chance of success. However, as 2030 grows ever closer, the challenges appear only to magnify. The promise of progress apparent in 2015 is quickly receding from view, as the world struggles to shake free of the COVID-19 pandemic, while war and conflict drain resources away from achieving gender equality, and the climate emergency is ignored. A key issue going forward will be the form and framework for financing both development goals and human rights after the immense shock of the pandemic. The next section very briefly emphasizes the importance of mustering resources, and assesses, from the

---

[56] Laura Addati, Umberto Cattaneo, and Emanuela Pozzan, *Care at Work: Investing in Care Leave and Services for a More Gender Equal World of Work* (ILO 2022) (hereafter 'Care at Work') 42.
[57] ibid 25.
[58] ibid 43.
[59] ibid 45.

perspective of substantive gender equality, how they should be directed in the remaining years before 2030.

4. Resourcing Gender Equality: What are the Demands of Substantive Equality?

In his preface to the 'Financing for Sustainable Development Report 2021' (hereafter 'Financing for Development Report'), UN General Secretary Antonio Guterres warns of the risk of a lost decade unless the yawning gap between political ambition and development financing can be closed.[60] The report demonstrates many instances in which women have been particularly badly affected by the pandemic, both in relation to job losses and extra burdens of care.

It is clear that the pandemic exposed and deepened existing schisms. The unprecedented disruption of the labour market disproportionately damaged labour-intensive services employing low-skilled workers, where women are clustered. This was particularly true of employment in sectors such as accommodation and food service, which are contact intensive. Lockdowns leading to closures of schools and child-care amplified the cost to women, both by affecting their employment and by shifting the responsibility for children and their schooling back into the home.[61] At the same time, because women predominate among precarious workers, they are less likely than men to be covered by social protection measures.[62] As the report points out, the pandemic has exposed the large gaps in social protection coverage, especially for workers in the informal economy and migrant workers.[63]

This raises the question of how to close the gap between the ambition of the SDGs and the reality in relation to women. There are several different sets of proposals from both the development and the human rights perspectives. A prominent theme is to point to investment in the SDGs as itself a source of protection against future pandemics as well as a key to future recovery. The Financing for Development Report states that the economic and social costs of the pandemic could have been significantly diminished with a relatively small investment in prevention and preparedness. Insufficient progress on the SDGs was itself a cause of vulnerability, particularly in relation to women.[64] Indeed, it argues, investment in the SDGs will reduce risk and can constitute a major force for resilience.[65]

---

[60] Inter-agency Task Force on Financing for Development, 'Financing for Sustainable Development Report 2021' (2021) 1 <https://developmentfinance.un.org/fsdr2021> accessed 26 May 2023 (hereafter 'Financing for Development Report').
[61] ibid 2.
[62] ibid 16.
[63] ibid Box II.6.
[64] ibid 16.
[65] ibid 17.

Focusing more on the issues of care and reproductive justice points us to the ILO, which makes a robust case for the benefits of specific investment in universally accessible care policy packages. UN Women further highlights key measures needed to make the most of the opportunity to "'build back better" through sustained investments in gender-responsive social protection and care systems'.[66]

What then does substantive gender equality demand from the various proposals for financing the SDGs promises on gender equality, and specifically on reproductive justice and caring work? One key emphasis has been on social protection systems in the short and medium term as a means of countering precarity in the workforce, unemployment, and poor health. Notably, the Financing for Development Report draws on the human rights framework to set the standards to be achieved.[67] This takes the form of the ILO Social Protection Floors Recommendation,[68] which sets out four basic social security protection guarantees which should constitute the main planks in all national social protection floors. The first is access to essential health care, including maternity care, which meet the criteria of availability, accessibility, acceptability, and quality. The second is basic income security for children, providing access to nutrition, education, care, and other necessary goods and services. The third is basic income security for persons of active age who are unable to earn sufficient income, in particular due to sickness, unemployment, maternity, and disability; and the fourth is basic income security for older persons.[69] ILO Member States are encouraged to monitor progress, especially through national consultations, and to collect data, disaggregated by gender.

Social protection certainly has a role to play in furthering substantive gender equality. In particular, it has the potential to redress women's disadvantage in relation to unpaid caring work, for example through enhancing income security for children, including access to education and care. The Social Protection Floor also includes some very basic protections for maternity, such as access to essential maternity care, and basic income security for the inability to work due to maternity. However, on its own, the ability of the Social Protection Floor to truly address the ways in which stereotyping, lack of voice, and structural forces continue to sustain gendered inequality, is limited. A particular challenge arises from the fact that an estimated two-thirds of working people in developing countries earn their living in the informal economy.[70]

---

[66] UN Women, 'Covid and the Care Economy' (Policy Brief No 16).
[67] Financing for Development Report (n 60) 55.
[68] ILO, 'R202—Social Protection Floors Recommendation (No 202)' (2012) <https://www.ilo.org/dyn/normlex/en/f?p=NORMLEXPUB:12100:0::NO::P12100_INSTRUMENT_ID:3065524> accessed 26 May 2023.
[69] ibid para 5.
[70] Franziska Ohnsorge and Shu Yu (eds) *The Long Shadow of Informality: Challenges and Policies* (World Bank Group 2022) <https://www.worldbank.org/en/research/publication/informal-economy> accessed 2 August 2023, 3–4.

Yet the paradigm worker envisaged by the social protection model works full time and continuously in the formal economy, gradually accumulating benefits through employment taxes and pension deductions. It is not surprising that women predominate among those excluded by this paradigm. UN Women found that a mere 11 per cent of social protection and labour market measures identified by their COVID-19 Gender Response Tracker addressed unpaid care and strengthened care services for children, older persons, or persons with disabilities. This was in any event through allowances, wage subsidies, or unemployment benefits for workers with family responsibilities rather than through the provision of public services envisaged by the SDGs.[71] At most such measures might address gendered disadvantage. They do not deal with stereotypes or structural obstacles.

The ILO itself is more ambitious, proposing sustained public investment in childcare and long-term care services as a means of both boosting the economy and achieving a high level of decent work opportunities for women. It estimates that such investment could generate up to 299 million jobs globally by 2035.[72] Of these new jobs, 78 per cent will be held by women and 84 per cent will be in formal employment. The annual investment required to achieve these goals by 2035 would amount to US$5.4 trillion or 4.2 per cent of total gross domestic product (GDP) before taxes. Since tax revenue from increased earnings and employment would rise too, the funding requirement would be reduced to net 3.2 per cent of GDP (after taxes) in 2035. As well as importantly addressing gendered disadvantage and triggering structural change through revaluing care work, the ILO makes an effort to ensure the participation of women, proposing that those who receive and provide care should also be part of charting this pathway.[73]

This approach is supported by UN Women, who likewise demonstrate that prioritizing investment in robust, gender-responsive care systems is crucial for future recovery. UN Women show how important it is to ensure that this is understood in the light of substantive gender equality. Otherwise, the extent to which women's unpaid care and domestic work subsidizes formal health and care systems is obscured.[74] This means that more is needed than investment in childcare and long-term care services. There is also a need to invest in basic infrastructure such as water, sanitation, and electricity; as well as time-saving domestic technology such as fuel-efficient cookstoves, to decrease women's drudgery and time.[75]

A focus on financing, however, reveals the limited traction both the SDGs and the human rights framework have on advancing substantive gender equality. This is particularly evident in respect of reproductive rights. A case in point is

---

[71] UN Women, 'Covid-19 and Fiscal Policy: Applying Gender-Responsive Budgeting in Support and Recovery Measures' (Policy Brief No 21) 2.
[72] Care at Work 36.
[73] ibid.
[74] UN Women, 'Covid-19 and Fiscal Policy' (n 71) 6.
[75] ibid.

the notorious 'Global Gag Rule', which requires any foreign non-governmental organization to agree not to provide abortion-related services or to advocate for abortion rights as a condition as a condition of receiving US funding.[76] This applies even if they use other sources of funding for this aspect of their work. Although Democratic presidents have revoked the rule while in office, it has regularly been reinstated by Republican presidents, most recently by President Donald Trump in 2017. The Trump administration massively expanded the rule to apply to all US global health assistance, affecting about US$12 billion in estimated planned funding, even when unrelated to family planning, including projects on HIV/AIDS, nutrition, malaria, water and sanitation, and infectious diseases. Moreover, in 2019, it was extended to organizations associated with 'gagged' organizations, even if they did no work supported by the US government.

The Guttmacher Institute has charted the immense damage done by this strangulation of funding, at every level, from people seeking care, to health-care providers and implementing partners, and public health systems.[77] Although the Global Gag Rule was fortunately rescinded by President Joe Biden in 2021,[78] US foreign aid is still substantially limited by the Helms Amendment, enacted in 1973, which prohibits foreign assistance funds from paying for abortion or motivating the practice of abortions. This applies even in countries where abortion is lawful.[79] More broadly, the failure by the US to ratify the key international human rights instruments as well as the relevant ILO Conventions[80] means that the leading economy in the world remains outside of their sphere of influence, both domestically and internationally.

The human rights framework makes a gesture towards the obligation to fund progress towards achieving relevant rights. Under ICESCR, states parties must take steps to implement recognized rights to the maximum of their available resources, and where needed, through international assistance and cooperation.[81] The nature of the duty of international assistance is, however, still disputed.[82] The CESCR has

---

[76] Secretary of Health and Human Services and Administrator of the United States Agency for International Development, Executive Office of the President, 'Presidential Documents: The Mexico City Policy' (Memorandum for the Secretary of State) (23 January 2017) 82(15) Federal Register 8495 <https://www.gpo.gov/fdsys/pkg/FR-2017-01-25/pdf/2017-01843.pdf> accessed 26 May 2023.
[77] Zara Ahmed, 'The Unprecedented Expansion of the Global Gag Rule: Trampling Rights, Health and Free Speech' (28 April 2020) <https://www.guttmacher.org/gpr/2020/04/unprecedented-expansion-global-gag-rule-trampling-rights-health-and-free-speech> accessed 26 May 2023.
[78] The White House, 'Memorandum on Protecting Women's Health at Home and Abroad' (28 January 2021) <https://www.whitehouse.gov/briefing-room/presidential-actions/2021/01/28/memorandum-on-protecting-womens-health-at-home-and-abroad/> accessed 26 May 2023.
[79] Elizabeth A Sully and Zara Ahmed, 'The Case for Ending the "Global Gag Rule" and the Helms Amendment' (22 February 2021) <https://www.guttmacher.org/article/2021/02/case-ending-global-gag-rule-and-helms-amendment> accessed 26 May 2023.
[80] The US has signed but not ratified CEDAW and ICESCR. It has only ratified fourteen out of 190 conventions, the most important being the Abolition of Forced Labour Convention (1957) (C105) and the Worst Forms of Child Labour Convention (1999) (C182).
[81] ICESCR, art 2(1).
[82] Takhimina Karimova, 'The Nation and Meaning of "International Assistance and Cooperation" under the International Covenant on Economic, Social and Cultural Rights' in Eibe. Riedel, Giles Giacca,

consistently declared that it is 'particularly incumbent on states parties and other actors in a position to assist, to provide international assistance and cooperation, especially economic and technical assistance, which enable developing countries to fulfil their core obligations.'[83] However, Magdalena Sepúlveda concludes[84] that this cannot be said to include a general obligation to devote 0.7 per cent of gross national product to international development assistance, a long-standing commitment set in place under the auspices of the UN in 1970, and reiterated in 2002.[85] Some countries, such as the UK, deliberately cut their aid programmes, citing the pandemic as their excuse.

The SDGs themselves envisaged a major reliance on the private sector for financing and implementation. However, market-based solutions have not had a good record in furthering gender equality. The development agenda, both in relation to domestic budgeting and overseas aid, must ultimately be regarded as a state responsibility, as the pandemic has painfully revealed. At best, governments may be convinced by the argument that investing in care and reproductive justice in ways that further substantive gender equality is 'smart economics', as UN Women and other feminist economists have done. However, instrumental solutions might always be caught out by empirical studies disproving their positive effects. Ultimately the responsibility to further equality must be regarded as a matter of binding human rights, with resources channelled to their fulfilment rather than human rights being a fortunate by-product of utilitarian aims. Moreover, human rights must be infused with gender-based substantive equality if they are genuinely advance the promises under SDG 5.

5. Conclusion: Creating Synergies

Furthering substantive gender equality requires a concerted effort on many fronts. The SDGs, with their many interlocking goals touching on gender equality, represent great promise. However, their focus on aggregate outcomes pays too little attention to the qualitative dimensions of substantive gender equality, while the inadequacy of the accountability mechanism leaves the attainment of the SDGs vulnerable to political will. The human rights framework, for its part, adds a greater level of accountability and more attention to the individual, as well as aiming to

---

and Christophe Golay (eds), *Economic, Social, and Cultural Rights in International Law: Contemporary Issues and Challenges* (OUP 2014) 163–92..

[83] (CESCR GC No 14) para 45; (GC No 15) para 37–38; (GC No18) paras 29–30; see also (CESCR GC No 3) para 13.
[84] Magdalena Sepúlveda, 'Obligations of "International Assistance and Cooperation" in an Optional Protocol to the International Covenant on Economic, Social and Cultural Rights' (2006) 24 NQHR 271.
[85] (UN Doc A/CONF198/11) para 42.

put in place ways to achieve the ultimate goals, and checking that these in turn are human rights compliant. However, the substance of human rights, through the prism of gender equality, is still contested, particularly in relation to women in poverty. Moreover, the accountability structures, while in principle legally binding, are only as strong as the political will of signatory states to implement them.

It is crucial therefore for the two structures to work together in a synergistic manner to achieve substantive gender equality and to ensure that the ambitious promises of the SDGs are not simply fleeting hopes. Sustained civil society action plays a key role in holding governments to account both for their promises under the SDGs and under the human rights structure, mobilizing all relevant forums both internationally and domestically. As Inga Winkler and Carmel Williams put it: 'Because the world adopted the SDGs, they offer one of our best, contemporary global opportunities to oppose social injustices that human rights advocates can use as a tool.'[86] To do so, however, requires both the SDGs and human rights to be deliberately imbued with the perspective of substantive gender equality.

---

[86] Inga Winkler and Carmel Williams, 'The Sustainable Development Goals and Human Rights: A Critical Early Review' (2017) 21(8) Int J Hum Rights 1024.

8
Race and Discrimination

Harum Mukhayer[*]

1. Introduction

[T]he term 'racial discrimination' shall mean any distinction, exclusion, restriction or preference based on race, colour, descent, or national or ethnic origin which has the purpose or effect of nullifying or impairing the recognition, enjoyment or exercise, on an equal footing, of human rights and fundamental freedoms in the political, economic, social, cultural or any other field of public life.[1]

'Without distinction as to race, colour, sex, language, religion':[2] this legal imperative carries the doctrinal weight of the principles of equality and non-discrimination in international human rights law. It is a provision familiar to domestic and international lawyers of both the common and civil law traditions as it is enshrined in the International Bill of Rights and constitutions across several jurisdictions.[3] The principles of non-discrimination and equality are fundamental to the protection of human rights under international law and the domestic laws of many jurisdictions.[4]

It is established and uncontroversial under international law that discrimination on grounds of race is prohibited and that protection from racial discrimination constitutes an obligation *erga omnes*.[5] Originally dealt with in the Minority

---

[*] All the views expressed in this chapter are the author's own and do not reflect or represent those of the World Bank, its Board, or Member countries.

[1] Article 1(1) of the International Convention on the Elimination of All Forms of Racial Discrimination (ICERD) (opened for signature 21 December 1965, entered into force 4 January 1969) 660 UNTS 195.

[2] This imperative finds various expressions across international human rights law (IHRL); UNHCR, General Comment 18 (Non-Discrimination) (10 November 1989).

[3] Philip Alston and others, *Non-Discrimination in International Law: A Handbook for Practitioners* (Interights 2011).

[4] Para 1, UNHCR, 'General Comment 18 (Non-Discrimination) (10 November 1989)'.

[5] Mentioned in the *dicta* of the Barcelona Traction case, the *erga omnes* character of non-discrimination is generally accepted as part of customary international law: *Case Concerning The Barcelona Traction, Light and Power Company, Limited (Belgium v Spain) (Judgment)* [1970] ICJ Rep 3 [34]; Erika de Wet, 'Jus Cogens and Obligations Erga Omnes' in Dinah Shelton (ed), *The Oxford Handbook of International Human Rights Law* (OUP 2013) 1–23.

Treaties,[6] the principles of equality and non-discrimination are enshrined in the United Nations (UN) Charter 1945, Article 1(3), and more explicitly reaffirmed in Article 2 of the Universal Declaration of Human Rights (UDHR) 1948.

The principle of non-discrimination is frequently read together with the principle of equality and equal protection before the law, which is reflected in Article 7 of the UDHR, and other international and regional instruments. The two principles are posited as 'two sides of the same coin',[7] and are often substantively and procedurally intertwined. Even though the principles find expression in separate articles under most human rights instruments,[8] equality before the law and non-discrimination were considered by the eminent jurist and legal scholar Hersh Lauterpacht as 'the starting point of all other liberties'.[9]

A year after the International Convention on the Elimination of Racial Discrimination (ICERD) was adopted on 21 December 1965, the International Covenant on Civil and Political Rights (ICCPR), and International Covenant on Economic, Social and Cultural Rights (ICESCR) were adopted in December 1966. Together with the UDHR, the ICESCR,[10] and the ICCPR (and its two Optional Protocols)[11] make up the International Bill of Human Rights (IBHR). Within the framework of international human rights, Article 1(4) of the ICERD advances special measures, or affirmative action, to ensure equal enjoyment of human rights.

As a corollary to the principles of equality and non-discrimination enshrined in the UN Charter, the IBHR, as well as the ICERD, the UN General Assembly (UNGA) Resolution 41/128 Declaration on the Right to Development brings together two key obligations on states: the imperative on states to undertake all necessary measures to ensure development, and the imperative to do so without discrimination. In placing the obligation for non-discrimination within the development context, the Human Rights Council (HRC) at its forty-eighth session on 8

---

[6] Carole Fink, 'The League of Nations and the Minorities Question' (1995) 157 Wld Aff 197 (hereafter 'The League of Nations').

[7] Johannes Morsink, *The Universal Declaration of Human Rights: Origins, Drafting, and Intent* (University of Pennsylvania Press 2000) 45.

[8] Under the UDHR, art 2 (non-discrimination) and art 7 (equality) are stated separately; ICESR sets out art 2(2) (non-discrimination) and art (3) (equality); ICCPR, art 2(1) (non-discrimination) and art 3 (equal rights of men and women); *Universal Declaration of Human Rights* (UNGA Res 217 A(III) (UDHR), adopted 10 December 1948) art 14 (equality before the law) and art 26 (equality and non-discrimination); *International Covenant on Civil and Political Rights* (999 UNTS 171 (ICCPR), opened for signature 16 December 1966, entered into force 23 March 1976); *International Covenant on Economic, Social and Cultural Rights* (993 UNTS 3 (ICESCR), opened for signature 16 December 1966, entered into force 3 January 1976).

[9] In his seminal proposal for an International Bill of the Rights of Man, Lauterpacht's Article 7 on Equality Before the Law enshrined the principle of non-discrimination 'on account of religion, race, colour, language, or political creed': Hersch Lauterpacht, 'Human Rights, the Charter of the United Nations and the International Bill of the Rights of Man' (UNHRC 1948) 115 (hereafter 'Human Rights, the Charter').

[10] International Covenant on Economic, Social and Cultural Rights (opened for signature 16 December 1966, entered into force 3 January 1976) 993 UNTS 3 (ICESCR).

[11] International Covenant on Civil and Political Rights (opened for signature 16 December 1966, entered into force 23 March 1976) 999 UNTS 171 (ICCPR).

October 2021 adopted two resolutions: Resolution 48/7 on negative impact of the legacies of colonialism on the enjoyment of human rights; and Resolution 48/10 on the right to development.[12]

The timing of the HRC Resolutions is not coincidental. Both HRC Resolutions reiterate the importance of the principles of equality and non-discrimination. Resolution 48/7 is cognizant of the fact 'that colonialism has led to racism, racial discrimination, xenophobia'[13] against minorities of African and Asian descent and Indigenous Peoples; and Resolution 48/10 emphasizes the urgency of the right to development by reference to the importance of human rights in shaping the response to the coronavirus disease of 2019 (COVID-19) through international cooperation.[14]

Although the 1986 Declaration on the Right to Development and the 2021 HRC Resolutions are not legally binding, the principles they enshrine have been given legal effect through regional instruments. The African Charter on Human and Peoples' Rights (also known as the Banjul Charter) enshrines the principle of non-discrimination (Article 2), and the right to development (Article 20). The Arab Charter on Human Rights affirms the principles of non-discrimination (Article 3) and equality (Article 11), and the right to development as a fundamental human right (Article 37).

Signed on 4 November 1950, the Convention for the Protection of Human Rights and Fundamental Freedoms (European Convention on Human Rights (ECHR))[15] establishes a firm commitment to the principles of equality and non-discrimination. This is reflected in Article 14 of the Convention and is read together with Protocol 12 (Article 1). The European Union and its Member States, despite their commitment to inclusive and non-discriminatory development, are expressly 'not in favour of the elaboration of an international legal standard [on a right to development] of a binding nature'.[16]

While the Right to Development may be subject to divergent views,[17] the principles of equality and non-discrimination are universally accepted principles of international law and form the principled basis on which this chapter is based. The principle of non-discrimination is the legal prism through which questions of race, discrimination, and development are contextualized. The intersection between

---

[12] UN Human Rights Council Resolution 48/10, *Right to Development* (UN Doc A/HRC/RES/48/10, 8 October 2021).

[13] UN Human Rights Council Resolution 48/7, *Negative Impact of the Legacies of Colonialism on the Enjoyment of Human Rights* (UN Doc A/HRC/RES/48/7, 8 October 2021).

[14] Right to Development HRC Resolution 48/10.

[15] Convention for the Protection of Human Rights and Fundamental Freedoms (European Convention on Human Rights, as amended (ECHR) (1950)) 34.

[16] European External Action Service (EEAS), 'EU General Statement' (HRC 22nd Session of the Working Group on the Right to Development, 22 November 2021).

[17] Surya Subedi, 'Declaration on the Right to Development' (United Nations Audiovisual Library of International Law 2021); Nico Schrijver, 'A New Convention on the Human Right to Development: Putting the Cart before the Horse?' (2020) 38 NQHR 84.

race, discrimination, and development is, as this chapter highlights, a complex process that is still in continuous evolution. It is closely intertwined with the history of the League of Nations, the introduction of international human rights, and the decolonization process. The complexity of the process is enhanced by divergent lived experiences and the intersectionality inherent in the human experience.

The primary aim of the next section is to reflect the legal nuance concerning the delicate balance between race, racial discrimination, and development within the wider framework of human rights. The third section of this chapter highlights the conceptual context. The fourth section explores the legal framework on non-discrimination; the extent to which it informs anti-racism in development policy, and inspects more closely whether aspirations for non-discrimination translate into reality, given the challenges of institutional racism. The fifth section considers racial discrimination in both development policy and practice through the example of the global response to COVID-19. The final section provides some concluding remarks.

2. Definitions of Race, Racial Discrimination, and Racism

This chapter takes as its starting point the ICERD definition of racial discrimination.[18] It does so for two reasons: first, the ICERD encapsulates anti-racism and affirms the illegality of discrimination through the principles of equality and non-discrimination under international law; second, the ICERD definition circumvents the ever-present racism blind spot which confronts the practice of discrimination law, even in the most practiced of jurisdictions.[19] This blind spot[20] is attributed to the often narrow interpretations of race in the case law on racial discrimination.

The narrowly construed legal definitions of race, and its proxies, is notoriously fraught with structural racism, whether this is in the interpretation of racial discrimination laws or their applications vis-à-vis racial groups. By way of example, in 2000, the US Supreme Court decided one of the most important Hawaiian cases: *Rice v. Cayetano*. On certiorari from the United States Court of Appeals for the Ninth Circuit, the US Supreme Court held that the electoral rights reserved to native Hawaiians by the Office of Hawaiian Affairs (OHA) violated the Fifteenth

---

[18] Article 1(1) of the ICERD: '[T]he term "racial discrimination" shall mean any distinction, exclusion, restriction or preference based on race, colour, descent, or national or ethnic origin which has the purpose or effect of nullifying or impairing the recognition, enjoyment or exercise, on an equal footing, of human rights and fundamental freedoms in the political, economic, social, cultural or any other field of public life.'

[19] Shreya Atrey, 'Structural Racism and Race Discrimination' (2021) 74 CLP 1.

[20] In her paper, 'Human Rights Racism', Anna Spain Bradley exposes this blind spot and demonstrates how international law has not explicitly defined nor prohibited racism. She further advances the claim that racism should be recognized as a human rights violation; see Anna Spain Bradley, 'Human Rights Racism' (2019) 32 Harv Hum Rts J 1.

Amendment. Passed by Congress in 1969, the Fifteenth Amendment to the US Constitution extended the right to vote to all citizens of the United States and held that 'vote shall not be denied or abridged by the United States or by any state on account of race, color, or previous condition of servitude'.[21]

The *Rice v. Cayetano* case, which concerned electoral rights, was interpreted as a racial discrimination case, based on the Court's interpretation of the legal meaning of the term 'ancestry' as defined by the OHA's electoral bylaws. Based on their interpretation of ancestry as a proxy for race, the US Supreme Court held that in denying Rice, a non-native Hawaiian citizen, his right to vote in trustee elections OHA had discriminated against him because he lacked the required ancestral descent that would qualify him as a native Hawaiian. The fact that the OHA took affirmative action to limit the right to vote to persons of a defined ancestry, was, according to the US Supreme Court, considered racial discrimination.

The *Rice* case hinged on a very black-and-white interpretation of the law in which ancestry was used 'as a proxy for race'.[22] The judgment in *Rice* lies contrary to the affirmative action international legal reasoning in *Lovelace v Canada* in which the Human Rights Committee (HRCt) 'recognize[d] the need to define the category of persons […] for such purposes as […] protection of […] the identity of its people'.[23] In 2019, the HRC relied on this legal reasoning in its Communications concerning Sami political rights in Finland.[24] In the Sami decisions of 2019, the HRCt held that the definition, or criteria for defining, who a Sami peoples are (or are not) is for the Sami themselves to define, and not for Finland to determine.

These precedents demonstrate that ancestry may serve as a proxy for race, but it must do so with many caveats.[25] The advantage of adhering to the safe definitional parameters of the ICERD is that race, ethnicity, or caste, for good reasons, do not have a prescribed legal definition in international law. This reasoning resonates with the observation of the Trial Chamber in the trial of Goran Jelisic, in which the Trial Chamber cautioned that 'to attempt to define a national, ethnical or racial group today using objective and scientifically irreproachable criteria would be a perilous exercise […]'.[26]

---

[21] *United States of America: Constitution* (National Authorities 1787) <https://www.refworld.org/docid/3ae6b54d1c.html> accessed 22 August 2023.

[22] *Rice v Cayetano* [2000] 528 US 495 (US Supreme Court) 496.

[23] *Sandra Lovelace v Canada* [1981] HRC Communication No 24/1977, UN Doc CCPR/C/OP/1 [15].

[24] *Tiina Sanila-Aikio v Finland* [2018] HRC Communication No 2668/2015, UN Doc CCPR/C/124/D; *Klemetti Käkkäläjärvi et al v Finland* [2018] HRC Communication No 2950/2017, CCPR/C/124/D.

[25] For a discussion on the ancestry, racial purity, and the racist ideologies underpinning race laws in the US, see Madison Grant, 'The Racial Transformation of America' (1924) 219 North Am Rev 343; Judy Scales-Trent, 'Racial Purity Laws in the United States and Nazi Germany: The Targeting Process' (2001) 23 HRQ 259; Jordan J Paust, 'Race-Based Affirmative Action and International Law' (1997) 18 MJIL 20.

[26] *Prosecutor v Goran Jelisic (Trial Judgement)* [1999] ICTY IT-95-10-T [70].

Despite the limitations of defining racial groups, a more prescriptive approach is adopted in the UK Equality Act 2010. For the purposes of the Act, section 9 states that the protected category of Race 'includes—(a) colour, (b) nationality, (c) ethnic or national origins'.[27] Sections 9(2)(a) and (b) apply both to individuals[28] as well as persons of a particular racial group. In the jurisprudence on discrimination in the courts of England and Wales, discrimination on grounds of race was also found to extend to discrimination on religious grounds. This is based on the precedent set in the Court of Appeals case *E v The Governing Body of JFS*, under the Race Relations Act 1976.

In *JFS*, the UK Supreme Court affirmed that discrimination on the basis of ethnic (or religious) grounds constituted direct racial discrimination under section 1 of the Race Relations Act 1976.[29] The Court's determination was in response to whether the requirement of matrilineal Jewish descent as a criterion for admissions constituted discrimination on grounds of race, or whether it was justified on the basis of religious belief. In the dicta of the *JFS* judgment, the Court engaged in a doctrinal determination of whether there exists an objective 'but for' test in determining what constitutes discrimination on grounds of race.[30]

The legal reasoning behind this objective test is that there is a subjective element underlying discrimination, one that is founded on belief and motive which can be dispelled by resort to the facts. The distinction the Court makes between fact and belief is an important one. Sedley J offers the example of the religious belief held by the Dutch Reform Church of South Africa that 'God had made black people inferior and had destined them to live separately from whites'.[31] He argues that if the theological grounds for discrimination were a viable justification for discrimination on the basis of race, then they 'would be able to discriminate openly without breaking the law'.[32] The grounds of any such discrimination is that 'the victim was black; its religious motive would be immaterial'.[33]

In toeing a slightly dangerous line between racism and legal rigor, Lord Clarke openly agrees with Sedley J, however, he does so without the anti-racist nuance. He quotes Sedley to support the view that discrimination on grounds of race is not overtly *racist*, but overtly *racial*.[34] A confusing

---

[27] UK Equality Act 2010.
[28] *Sandeep & Reena Mander v Royal Borough of Windsor & Maidenhead* [2019] EWFC C01RG184, B64.
[29] *R (on the application of E) v Governing Body of JFS and the Admissions Appeal Panel of JFS and others* [2009] UKSC 15 (Supreme Court) (hereafter '*JFS UKSC Appeal* [2009]').
[30] ibid [16].
[31] *R (on the application of E) v The Governing Body of JFS* [2009] 626 EWCA Civ 6 (Court of Appeal (Civil Division)) [30] (hereafter '*JFS Case* [2009]'); ibid [150].
[32] *JFS Case* [2009] [30].
[33] ibid; *JFS UKSC Appeal* [2009] (n 29) [21].
[34] In determining what they mean by 'racial' the Court elaborates on the mental process of the discriminator, they rely on the simple example of a 'fat black man' who is refused service by a shopkeeper. They posit that if the fat black man was refused service because he is fat then it is not racial, but if it is

distinction[35] that was critiqued in legal scholarship.[36] Compelled by some degree of decorum and politeness, Lord Philips, Lord Hope, and Lady Hale collectively joined Lord Clarke in asserting the view that '[a]ny suggestion or implication that they are "racist" in the popular sense of that term can be dismissed'.[37]

While the Justices of the UK Supreme Court may be bound by the customary etiquette of His Majesty's Court, the argument unfortunately fails to be antiracist. Admittedly, anti-racism is not a legal term defined under any jurisdiction. Therefore, in the absence of a black-letter definitions of anti-racism, the general definition of racial discrimination under Article 1 of the ICERD shall suffice as the definitional basis for this chapter.

3. Conceptual Context

a. General

To capture the formative significance of the principles of equality and non-discrimination to international human rights, and their influence on international development, this chapter starts with a brief overview of the historical context. The history of race and non-discrimination far exceeds the scope of this chapter, but the brief overview of the period following World War I (WW I) towards the end of World War II (WW II) demonstrates the evolutionary character of international law as it relates to racial discrimination and issues of race.

During this initial period 'race' was not drawn along colour lines that segregate and separate white from black, but rather reflected ethnic divisions as between 'Anglo-Saxon, Teuton, and the English-speaking Races',[38] many of whom were all Caucasian. This section briefly engages with notions of what race is, and the indeterminacy of race as a construct, and the legal use of the term race prior to the introduction of human rights law and the coupling of race with colour.

In this historical context international organizations played a pivotal role. Enshrined in Article 22 of the Covenant of the League of Nations was a sacred-trust

---

because he is black, then it is racial. Admittedly, a problematic example that leaves many questions unanswered; *JFS UKSC Appeal* [2009] (n 29) [21].

[35] The UK Supreme Court's emphasis on 'racial' is attributed to the wording of sections 1 and 3 of the Race Relations Act 1976 which prohibits discrimination on 'racial grounds'. The Race Relations Act was repealed by the Equality Act 2010. *JFS UKSC Appeal* [2009] (n 29) [21]; Race Relations Act (Repealed) 1976 c 74 1976.

[36] Atrey (n 19); Karon Monaghan, 'Case Comment: R € v Governing Body of JFS & Ors [2009] UKSC 15' (*UKSCBlog*, 21 December 2009).

[37] *JFS UKSC Appeal* [2009] (n 29) [54].

[38] For a more detailed analysis on the definition of race, see Arjun Narayan Sharath, 'The Anglo-American Relationship: Race and the Perception of German Threat 1890–1910' (University of Cambridge 2019) 29 (hereafter 'The Anglo-American Relationship').

based on the principle of well-being and development of those 'peoples not yet able to stand by themselves under the strenuous conditions of the modern world'.[39] Conceived as a commitment to peace-keeping after WW I, the League of Nations,[40] with its autonomous bodies[41] and intellectual cooperation,[42] attempted to piece together a war-ravaged world in the pursuit of international peace and security. The League's commitment to development was part of the mandate of the constituent organs of the League of Nations. As such, the technical assistance provided by its specialized agencies, such as the Economic and Financial Organisation (EFO), was to aid in the economic development international monetary policy during the Great Depression of the 1930s until the dissolution of the League of Nations in 1946.

Development during that time did not take the same form, nor did it serve the same function, as development at the present moment. Neither did notions of race and non-discrimination carry the same meanings as they do now. This historical context serves to complicate rather than simplify the complexity of the legal framework at the time. History, in hindsight, complicates the narrative on race inadvertently because the words we use now had fundamentally different meanings then.

It is in this historically and linguistically complex context that the chapter cites the contributions of international jurists, intellectuals, and expert scholars. The voices of individual legal and juridical experts enable the chapter to advance the view that human experiences matter to the changes witnessed between the end of WW I, and the beginnings of international human rights law that followed the end of WW II. The lived experiences of the actors in international organizations colour the blank canvas of international administrative law at a formative stage. Their lived experiences like a splattering of spectral colours after the sun clears away the rain, illuminating a rainbow of words and their meanings. In part enabling our understanding of race, and how the concept of race and non-discrimination may be (mis)understood or (mis)interpreted depending on the perspective from which it is viewed.

b. History matters: Race not colour

In 1920, the Council of the League of Nations entrusted the International Committee of Jurists with the task of preparing an Advisory Opinion on the Legal Aspects of the Åland Islands Question. The question entrusted to the three International Jurists (namely Ferdinand Larnaude, Antoon A M Struycken, and

---

[39] The Covenant of the League of Nations (adopted 28 April 1919 as amended).
[40] William E Rappard, 'The Evolution of the League of Nations' (1927) 21 Am Polit Sci Rev 792.
[41] Namely, the Permanent International Court of Justice (1920–1946) and the ILO (1919–to date).
[42] UN Archives, 'League of Nations: Intellectual Cooperation: International Institute of Intellectual Cooperation' (*UN Library Resources*, 11 May 2022).

Max Huber) included whether the autonomy of the Åland Islands should be left to the jurisdiction of Finland and its domestic laws, or whether it should be subject to international law.[43]

The Jurists found that the Åland Islanders aspirations for self-determination was a matter of international law and not for Finland to determine based on its own domestic laws. They asserted that self-determination played 'an important part in modern political thought'[44] however, that it did not constitute a positive rule of the League of Nations at the time. They concluded that the Åland Islanders have no right to determine whether they remain as part of Finland or secede to join Sweden. In so doing they established one of the leading precedents on the right to self-determination.

What is noteworthy about the Åland Islands Opinion, is that the Jurists placed an emphasis on the fact that the population of the Åland Island is united by 'ties of race, language and traditions to the Swedish race'.[45] To accommodate for the racial proximity between the Islanders and the Swedish *race*, the Jurists cite the special legal regime of protection of racial and religious minorities introduced in the Treaty of Versailles and guaranteed through the League of Nations.

The Treaty of Versailles and the Covenant of the League of Nations provide only a limited guidance on the topic of race, and the guidance provided is limited to the rights of minorities in Europe.[46] Despite the Japanese delegations explicit proposals for anti-racist language,[47] the Treaty of Versailles and the League of Nations Covenant notably lack express provisions on non-discrimination on racial or religious grounds.[48]

During the League of Nations Covenant Drafting Committee's tenth meeting on 13 February 1919, Baron Nobuaki Makino proposed an anti-discrimination clause to be added to draft Article 21 on religious freedom. The proposal read as follows:

> The equality of nations being a basic principle of the League of Nations, the High Contracting Parties agree to accord, as soon as possible, to all alien nationals of States members of the League, equal and just treatment in every respect, making no distinction, either in law or fact, on account of their race or nationality.[49]

---

[43] 'Report of the International Committee of Jurists Entrusted by the Council of the League of Nations with the Task of Giving an Advisory Opinion upon the Legal Aspects of the Aaland Islands Question Report' (1920) 3(Special Supplement) LNOJ vi.

[44] ibid.

[45] ibid.

[46] The League of Nations (n 6).

[47] Paul Gordon Lauren, 'Human Rights in History: Diplomacy and Racial Equality At the Paris Peace Conference' (1978) 2 Dipl Hist 257.

[48] It should be noted that the Treaty of Versailles art 86 (Czecho-Slovak State) and art 93 (Poland) include references to race; art 49–50 (Saar Basin) annex I, ch II includes religious liberties, language, and voting without discrimination of sex. Treaty of Peace with Germany signed at Versailles 28 June 1919 (entered into force 10 January 1920) (Treaty of Versailles 1919).

[49] David Hunter Miller, *The Drafting of the Covenant* (GP Putnam's Sons 1928) 324.

The entirety of draft Article 21 was struck out. The general consensus of the Committee members (including the jurist Larnaude who was one of the three jurists entrusted with the Aaland Islands Question) was that 'questions of race and religion would certainly be dealt with in the future by the League of Nations, but that it would be better for the moment not to allude to them'.[50] Evident from the history that ensues, and the horrors of WW II which prompted considerations of racial discrimination, questions of race were neither alluded to nor dealt with by the League of Nations.

The centrality of non-discrimination in international human rights law, particularly non-discrimination on racial grounds, can be traced to the atrocities witnessed by the end of WW II. Until that time, race had not taken on a discrete legal definition, much less a conceptual one. Perhaps attributed to the Eurocentric character of international law-making at the time,[51] notions of race were only vaguely delimited such that racist ideologies associated with racial superiority did not necessarily apply along colour lines delimiting 'whites' from 'non-whites'.[52] In fact, notions of race primarily referred to European races, as observed by William E B Du Bois in 1901.[53] Du Bois describes the racial milieu in Europe by reference to three significant realities: 'the Jew and Socialist in France, the Expansion of Germany and Russia, and the race troubles of Austria'.[54] He comes to the obvious conclusion that: 'None of these bring us directly upon the question of colour; and yet nearly all touch it indirectly.'[55]

The era of the League of Nations was one in which states were the primary international actors. Although the principle of state sovereignty reigned supreme, the failure of the League of Nations and the atrocities of WW II demonstrated the need for international cooperation in the interest of maintaining peace and security.[56] The period following the end of WW II marked a critical era in the evolution of international law as it relates to non-discrimination, and to some extent race. By the end of the 1940s, the international legal stage for the diversification of the

---

[50] ibid 323–25.
[51] Antony Anghie, *Imperialism, Sovereignty and the Making of International Law* (CUP 2005) (hereafter 'The Making of International Law'); James Thuo Gathii, 'Foreword: Alternative and Critical: The Contribution of Research and Scholarship on Developing Countries to International Legal Theory' (2000) 41(Symposium issue) Harv Int'l L J 263; Mohsen A L Attar, 'Must International Legal Pedagogy Remain Eurocentric?' (2021) 11 Asian JIL 176.
[52] The term 'color line' was coined by the prolific race scholar Du Bois. For further details, see William E B Du Bois, *The Problem of the Color Line at the Turn of the Twentieth Century: The Essential Early Essays* (Fordham University Press 2015).
[53] ibid.
[54] William EB Du Bois, 'The Present Outlook for the Dark Races of Mankind (1900)' in William Edward Burghardt Du Bois and Nahum Dimitri (eds), *The Problem of the Color Line at the Turn of the Twentieth Century: The Essential Early Essays* (Fordham University Press 2014) 111–138, 118 (hereafter 'The Present Outlook for the Dark Races') <https://doi.org/10.1515/9780823254576-007>.
[55] For a more detailed account of race and racial politics between 1890 and 1910, see ibid (The Present Outlook for the Dark Races) 118 and The Anglo-American Relationship (n 38), respectively.
[56] James Crawford, *Chance, Order, Change: The Course of International Law, General Course on Public International Law* (Brill 2014).

subjects of international law was beginning to be set[57]—moving beyond the territorial state, affirming the non-territorial international organization, enveloping the universality of rights vested in the human person, and finally, the gradual wave of decolonization (of colonized peoples[58] and decolonization of international law more generally).[59]

Except for anti-slavery conventions and agreements,[60] before WW II the legal framework of international law included only limited provisions against discrimination on racial grounds. Following WW II, the heinous crimes witnessed during the Holocaust, the racism that characterized the period of racial segregation in the US, the apartheid regime in South-West Africa, and the progress made towards minority rights provided enough experience of unspeakable cruelty and unimaginable human suffering to warrant concrete legal action against racial discrimination.[61]

c. Lived experiences matter

The International Labour Organization (ILO) was established in 1919 as a specialized agency of the League of Nations. After the end of WW II, among the various amendments to the original text of the ILO Constitution, the 1944 amendment is particularly notable.[62] Adopted on 10 May 1944, during the ILO's General Conference at its Twenty-sixth Session in Philadelphia, the 1944 Declaration renews the ILO's pledge to international peace and security. The non-discrimination clause 'all human beings, irrespective of race, creed or sex'[63] was introduced in this amendment and acts as a poignant reminder that non-discrimination must be the subject of an explicit undertaking.

Contrary to the attitude prevalent during the negotiations of the Covenant of the League of Nations in 1919, the ILO's constitutional amendment asserts that it does not suffice for non-discrimination to be merely alluded to in the *travaux préparatoires* of negotiations, to be dealt with at a later point but rather must be explicitly stated as a mandated commitment. The ILO's declaration in 1944 reflects

---

[57] For a more detailed account of the subject, see Jan Klabbers, 'The Subjects of International Law', in Jan Klabbers, *International Law*, 67–90 (CUP 2013).

[58] James R Crawford, *The Creation of States in International Law* (2nd edn, OUP 2007) 604.

[59] Sundhya Pahuja, *Decolonising International Law: Development, Economic Growth and the Politics of Universality* (CUP 2011) (hereafter 'Decolonising International Law').

[60] Kevin Bales and Peter T Robbins, '"No One Shall Be Held in Slavery or Servitude": A Critical Analysis of International Slavery Agreements and Concepts of Slavery' (2001) 2 Hum Rights Rev 18.

[61] Kevin Boyle and Anneliese Baldaccini, 'A Critical Evaluation of International Human Rights Approaches to Racism', in Sandra Fredman (ed), *Discrimination and Human Rights: The Case of Racism*, 135–92 (OUP 2001) 141.

[62] Constitution of the International Labour Organisation (ILO) (adopted 1 April 1919, as amended 10 May 1944).

[63] ILO Constitution.

the beginning of change in the attitude towards non-discrimination. In 1945, Hersh Lauterpacht published an ambitious model for an International Bill of Rights. Lauterpacht's Bill of Rights provided inspiration for the UDHR in 1948.[64] Two years after the non-binding UDHR, the ECHR was adopted in 1950 introducing a legally binding affirmation that lived experience of human suffering matter, and must be backed with legal obligations to prevent the kind of racial policies adopted in Nazi Germany.

The language of non-discrimination as reflected in Article 2 of the UDHR captures all forms of discrimination through the statement 'without distinction of any kind, such as race, colour, sex, language, religion, political or other opinion, national or social origin, property, birth or other status'.[65] It specifically refers to both: distinctions based on race as well as colour. This stands as a marked contrast to notions of race prevalent during the early days of the League on Nations. This may suggest that, as observed by Du Boise, the use of the term 'race' had previously not included notions of colour until after WW II. To place this reasoning within its historical context, it is necessary to revisit the tragic events leading up to WW II. What follows is a brief and inadequate overview of state-sponsored persecution and anti-semitism, which nevertheless warrants a trigger warning.

On 30 January 1933, Adolf Hitler was appointed Chancellor of Germany and thereby the Nazi Party was in power. The Nazi Party's ideology of 'racial purity' marked the beginning of an abhorrent campaign of antisemitism. By September 1939, all ambitions of delivering mankind from the menace of war were discarded as WW II erupted with the German invasion of Poland. The optimism that accompanied the League of Nations and the promise of international peace and security had dissipated. The Nazi's ideology of racial hatred based on the notion that there existed a 'master race' resulted in the mass murder and systematic extermination of European Jews,[66] a crime that became known as genocide,[67] and deemed an international crime against humanity.[68]

In the field of international law, the origins of genocide and international crimes against humanity are credited to two international lawyers and eminent scholars: Hersch Lauterpacht (1897–1960) and Raphael Lemkin (1900–1959). Like countless others, both Lauterpacht and Raphael Lemkin suffered grave personal losses because of the Holocaust; Lauterpacht's entire family perished by mid-1940

---

[64] Human Rights, the Charter (n 9) vii.
[65] Universal Declaration of Human Rights (adopted 10 December 1948 UNGA Res 217 A(III)) (UDHR).
[66] Raphael Lemkin, *Axis Rule in Occupied Europe: Laws of Occupation, Analysis of Government, Proposals for Redress* (Carnegie Endowment for International Peace, Division of International Law 1944).
[67] Raphael Lemkin, 'Genocide as a Crime under International Law' (1947) 41 AJIL 145.
[68] Philippe Sands, *East West Street: On the Origins of 'Genocide' and 'Crimes against Humanity'* (Knopf 2016).

and Lemkin's parents and forty-nine members of his extended family were tortured and brutally murdered by the Nazis.[69]

The story of Lauterpacht and Lemkin is eloquently told in Philippe Sands' book, *East West Street*.[70] Sands infuses the legal developments that lead to the conceptualized crime of genocide and crimes against humanity with the intertwined lived experiences of the two men. In his seminal book, *The Function of Law in the International Community*, Lauterpacht discusses at great length the safeguards against judicial partiality and conscious bias. Asserting that conscious bias is a dereliction of judicial duty, however, Lauterpacht acknowledges with normative feeling that '[T]he subconscious factor cannot be entirely eliminated, it is to a large extent a function of the human will.'[71]

While biases and experiences impress on the mind of the international lawyer,[72] the subconscious factors may enable the legal practitioner to see things with feeling. This section has highlighted that at the very core of the complex web of rights and obligations, it is the individual lawyers, jurists, bureaucrats, technical experts, and administrators that inform the process of international administrative law and the norms that underpin it.[73] Each an actor with their own lived experience and notions of how things should be. This is not to say that the religious, cultural, or racial backgrounds of the individuals involved in the process of international norm-making is *the* determining factor. But rather this section aims to advance the notion that race is a construct with its meanings in constant flux, rather than an immutable or objective concept. Even if legal reasoning is 'devoid of a particularly cultural coloration',[74] the outcomes cannot be claimed to be racially neutral. The lived experience of legal practitioners' and those around them matter,[75] even if the colour of their skin does not.

d. Black Lives Matter

Although general international human rights law did not exist until the end of WW II, it has now been over seventy years since the 1948 UDHR, and almost five decades since the ICERD became effective in 1969. The illegality of racial discrimination notwithstanding, heinous acts of racism and discrimination continue

---

[69] Ana Filipa Vrdoljak, 'Human Rights and Genocide: The Work of Lauterpacht and Lemkin in Modern International Law' (2009) 20 EJIL 1163.
[70] Sands (n 68).
[71] Hersch Lauterpacht, *The Function of Law in the International Community* (OUP 2011) 224.
[72] ibid 171.
[73] Eyal Benvenisti, 'The Interplay between Actors as a Determinant of the Evolution of Administrative Law in International Institutions' (2005) 68 LCP 319.
[74] Werner Levi, 'International Law in a Multicultural World' (1974) 18 Int Stud Q 417.
[75] For a discussion on the interplay and biases involved in the process of international norm making, see Eyal Benvenisti, 'Exit and Voice in the Age of Globalization' (1999) 98 Mich L Rev 167.

throughout the world—affecting the lives of racial minorities in all corners of the world.

In the context of this present century, the world was appalled by the brutal murder of George Floyd on 25 May 2020 at the hands of the Minneapolis police in the United States (US). Starting with anti-racism protests in the US, global outrage was sparked because of police violence against African Americans. Anti-racism protests against police brutality and institutional racism which started spread from the US to different parts of the United Kingdom (UK), across Europe (in France, Germany, Italy, Denmark, and Poland),[76] in Latin America (Mexico, Brazil), Australasia (Australia, New Zealand),[77] and Asia (Indonesia,[78] Japan,[79] South Korea).[80] The fact that the universality of human rights requires that all lives matter, the principles of equality and non-discrimination support the resounding message of the global protests that: Black Lives Matter (BLM).

The series of BLM-inspired protests shed light on all forms of discrimination beyond the white/black binary and across various colour lines. The ripple effect resonated in countries across the colour spectrum, inviting cultural relativity and nuance in demands for anti-racism, anti-castism,[81] Indigenous Peoples rights,[82] and non-discrimination writ large.

The outrage and protests which started in the US in response to police brutality against unarmed Black individuals, inspired a critical moment in the field of international development and international law. The global support for BLM triggered an emotive discourse within the field of legal theory and practice. One in which lawyers have engaged, both intellectually[83] and introspectively[84] with issues of race, key among these were commitments to anti-racism by multilateral institutions.

---

[76] Noa Milman and others, *Black Lives Matter in Europe: Transnational Diffusion, Local Translation and Resonance of Anti-Racist Protest in Germany, Italy, Denmark and Poland* (The German Institute of Integration and Migration 2021) 45.

[77] Sergei Klebnikov, 'Floyd Protests Go Global—From Mexico, London, Germany And France—And Sometimes Violent' *Forbes* (6 June 2020).

[78] Amy Gunia, 'Will Indonesia's 'Papuan Lives Matter' Translate to Support for Independence?' (*Time*).

[79] Ryusei Takahashi, 'Black Lives Matter Spreads to Tokyo as 3,500 People March to Protest Racism' *The Japan Times* (14 June 2020).

[80] Jason Strother, 'America's BLM Protests Find Solidarity in South Korea' *The World from PRX* (8 June 2020).

[81] Human Rights Watch, 'Caste Discrimination: A Global Concern' (Human Rights Watch 2001); Charanya Krishnaswami and Guha Krishnamurthi, 'Title VII and Caste Discrimination' (2021) 134 Harv L Rev 456; Murali Shanmugavelan, 'Caste Discrimination is Blocking Progress on the SDGs' *Global Policy Journal* (26 March 2019).

[82] Amna Nawaz and Maea Lenei Buhre, 'Indigenous Peoples Echo Black Lives Matter's Call for Justice' (*PBS NewsHour*, 12 October 2020).

[83] Catherine Powell, 'Introduction: Interlocking Pandemics' (2020) 114 Proceedings of the ASIL Annual Meeting 371(hereafter 'Interlocking Pandemics'); Lawrence Hill-Cawthorne, 'Racism Will Not Pass' (*EJIL: Talk!*, 20 July 2020).

[84] Abigail Harris, 'Sandie Okoro, SVP and GC for the World Bank Group, on Practical Strategies to Drive Diversity and Inclusion' (*Global Leaders in Law*, 1 October 2020); Lana Barnett, 'A Killing in Broad Daylight' (*Harvard Law Today*, 23 July 2020); David Malpass, 'June 18, 2020: Ending Racism' (*World Bank Blogs*, 18 July 2020); Daisy Serem and Gregory Felder, 'What Will It Take to End Racial

The outcomes of BLM have been resounding in the field of international law and international development. As the next section highlights, the response to BLM from international organizations (IOs), international financial institutions (IFIs) (such as the World Bank Group (WBG)), and intergovernmental organisations (such as the European Commission (EC) and the European Union (EU)) resulted in affirmations for the principles of equality and non-discrimination.

4. Racial Discrimination in Development Policy (and Practice)

This section engages with the concept of race and the principle of non-discrimination under international law in the context of international development. It acknowledges the colonial origins of international law[85] and the disconnect between the development undertaken under the sacred trust of civilizations[86] after WW I, and the development and reconstruction of post-war Europe after WW II. This section also recognizes the challenge of confronting and situating race and racism in international development. The challenge is two-fold: it relates to the structural racism inherent in the system of international development, as well as the challenge of ending institutional racism.

The first challenge of structural racism has been the topic of study elsewhere.[87] It is a challenge that runs parallel to the challenges of decolonization.[88] The second challenge relates to the character of international development as it is implemented by IOs. Their international character means that ideas of race and racism are not uniformly determined. Besides being bound by principles of international law, IOs do not have a universal commitment to anti-racism, the practices of inclusivity and diversity in hiring and promotion may differ from one country office to another, and from one institution to another.

Discrimination?' (*IFC Insights*, 28 July 2020); DLA Piper, 'Sustainability Report 2020/2021' (*DLA Piper*, April 2021) 33.

[85] The Making of International Law (n 51) 13–31.
[86] Art 22, The Covenant of the League of Nations (adopted 28 April 1919 as amended).
[87] Decolonising International Law (n 59); Arturo Escobar, *Encountering Development: The Making and Unmaking of the Third World* (Princeton University Press 2011) (hereafter 'Encountering Development'); Daron Acemoglu and others, 'The Colonial Origins of Comparative Development: An Empirical Investigation' (2001) 91 Am Ec Rev 1369 (hereafter 'The Colonial Origins'); Kathryn Nwajiaku-Dahou and Carmen Leon-Himmelstine, 'How to Confront Race and Racism in International Development' (*ODI: Think Change*) (hereafter 'How to Confront Race and Racism'); Balakrishnan Rajagopal, 'Laying the Groundwork: The Mandate System', in Balakrishnan Rajagopal (ed), *International Law from Below: Development, Social Movements and Third World Resistance* (CUP 2003); Anna Spain Bradley, 'International Law's Racism Problem' (*Opinio Juris*, 4 September 2019).
[88] On the overlap between the colonial and developmentalist regimes after World War II, see Escobar (n 87). For a more recent post-BLM account, see How to Confront Race and Racism (n 87).

IFIs support development efforts and are accountable to their state membership. In doing so, they are constrained by their constitutions and mandates, and bound only to their articles of agreement. Thus, IOs and IFIs are confronted with a dilemma.[89]

Described by Samuel A Bleicher as the 'dilemma of functionalism',[90] this dilemma is essentially one in which IOs are expected to respond to the demands of international cooperation, while at the same time operating within the narrow confines of the functions for which they are mandated.

Such demands for international cooperation may teeter on the precipice of political neutrality. As the former General Counsel of the World Bank, Ibrahim Shihata, cautions: not all IOs are created with equal mandatory provisions.[91] The World Bank's mandate, for example, contains an explicit provision prohibiting it from interfering in the political affairs of its members, whereas the European Bank for Reconstruction and Development (EBRD) does not have such a mandatory restriction. In Shihata's view, human rights fall within the functionally dilemmatic scope of political interference. He argues that while the World Bank's mandate does not contain an express function to take positive human rights action, its goal of poverty alleviation accommodates human rights, for without 'freedom from poverty [...] no other human right could be fully enjoyed'.[92]

Despite this dilemma, IOs and IFIs are presented with an opportunity to be agents of change in the field of international development.[93] This has especially been the case following the murder of George Floyd and the commitments to anti-racism by IOs. Aided by the established legal framework on non-discrimination and the illegality of racism under international law, IOs and IFIs as subjects of international law made commitments to ending racism. These commitments include the World Bank's Anti-Racism Charter and the EU's Anti-Racism Action Plan discussed in this section.

For the purposes of this section, development policy is defined broadly as the policies adopted by multilateral organizations involved in delivering or financing international development activities. It includes prohibitions against racial discrimination that are relevant to them as actors under international law, as well as non-discrimination as an inherent part of their legal due diligence. The term refers to the collection of requirements and procedures embodied in an IO's development policy, and not necessarily a clearly stipulated 'policy' as such.

---

[89] Eric Toussaint and Patrick Bond, 'South Africa: The Support of the World Bank and the IMF to the Apartheid Regime' (*CADTM*, 11 July 2022); Samuel A Bleicher, 'UN v IBRD: A Dilemma of Functionalism' (1970) 24 Int'l Org 31 (hereafter 'UN v IBRD').
[90] ibid (UN v IBRD).
[91] Ibrahim F I Shihata, 'Democracy and Development' (1997) 46 ICLQ 635.
[92] Shihata (n 91).
[93] Günther Handl, 'The Legal Mandate of Multilateral Development Banks as Agents for Change Toward Sustainable Development' (1998) 92 AJIL 642.

a. The Law and IO's response to apartheid in South West Africa/Namibia

The 'sacred trust of civilization' referred to in Article 22 of the Covenant has as its purpose the development of certain specified peoples to 'stand by themselves under the strenuous conditions of the modern world'. The 'modern world' under whose 'strenuous conditions' the peoples of the Mandate were 'not yet [in 1920] able to stand by themselves', is a multi-racial world. [...] Obviously 'the modern world' is not a static concept and could not have been so considered by the framers of the Covenant of the League.[94]

Policies of differentiation such as, e.g., separate schools, separate residential areas, reserves for the different ethnic groups, influx control, etc., were applied by the Germans, and were being applied by the Respondent in the Territory at the time the Mandate came into existence. The vast differences between the different groups made this both natural and inevitable.[95]

The heinous acts of torture and discrimination described in the memorials and proceedings of the *South West Africa Cases* warrant a trigger warning as they entail potentially disturbing content. Similarly, any review of the *South West Africa Cases* must be placed in the context of the law prevailing at the time, in line with the principle of intertemporal law.[96] This is necessary because any reflection of the dispute as it stood at the time will fail to capture the extent of suffering experienced by the inhabitants of South West Africa under the apartheid regime.

On 4 November 1960, Liberia and Ethiopia submitted a claim to the International Court of Justice (ICJ) concerning the mandate over South West Africa (present-day Namibia). The basic premise of the claim brought by Liberia and Ethiopia concerned the racist regime of apartheid over South West Africa. The applicants submitted that the Mandatory's system of apartheid goes against the spirit of Article 22 of the Covenant, and violates Articles 2(2) and 6 of the Mandate Agreement.[97]

To widespread chagrin,[98] the long-awaited judgment was finally delivered on 18 July 1966. Despite the fact that the ICERD was adopted while the *South West Africa*

---

[94] *South West Africa Cases (Dissenting Opinion of Judge Jessup), First Phase, Judgment*, ICJ Reports [1962] 440.
[95] *South West Africa Cases (Separate Opinion Van Wyk), Second Phase, Judgment*, ICJ Reports [1966].
[96] For a more detailed discussion of the principle of intertemporal law, see a general discussion by Elias and the original reference to the principle in the Island of Palmas Case: TO Elias, 'The Doctrine of Intertemporal Law' (1980) 74 AJIL 285; *Island of Palmas Case (or Miangas), United States v Netherlands, Award*, [1928] II RIAA 829, ICGJ 392 (PCA 1928) [4 April 1928].
[97] Mandate Agreement Regarding German South West Africa of 17 December 1920.
[98] Rosalyn Higgins, 'The International Court and South West Africa: The Implications of the Judgment' (1966) 42 Int'l Aff 573 (hereafter 'The International Court and South West Africa'); Richard A Falk, 'The South West Africa Cases: An Appraisal' (1967) 21 Int'l Org 1; Shiv R S Bedi, *The Development of Human Rights Law by the Judges of the International Court of Justice* (Bloomsbury Publishing 2007) 146.

Cases proceedings were ongoing, there was no mention of racial discrimination and its illegality under international law. As argued by Tenaka J in his dissenting opinion, non-discrimination or non-separation on the basis of race had at that time become a rule of customary international law, creating binding obligations on the Republic of South Africa as the Mandatory administratively responsible for South West Africa.[99] The ICJ dismissed the claims against the apartheid government in South West Africa on procedural technicality and made no substantive determination on the merits. The reasoning was that the claims against the apartheid government in South Africa were '[p]olitical, moral and humanitarian considerations not in themselves generative of legal rights and obligations'.[100]

The legal controversy generated by the ICJ Judgment[101] stood at odds with the legal-political momentum for decolonization and the explicit resolutions by the UNGA and UN Security Council (UNSC) at the time. Namely, the GA [Decolonization] Resolution 1514 (XV) of 14 December 1960[102] (and GA Resolution 1654 (XVI) of 27 November 1961 which was tasked with the implementation of GA 1514);[103] GA Resolution 2131 (XX) of 21 December 1965[104] (which marked the acceleration of the decolonization process);[105] GA Resolution 2054 (XX) on the South African policies of apartheid,[106] recalls SC Resolutions 134 (1960) on the killing of unarmed protesters;[107] SC Resolution 181 (1963)[108] calls for an arms embargo; SC Resolution 191 (1964)[109] on persons imprisoned, interned, or sentenced to death for their opposition to the policy of apartheid.

From a development standpoint, the legal ambiguity generated by the ICJ Judgment on the illegality of the apartheid regime may have undermined a more concerted effort against the racist regime in South West Africa.[110] In particular, it hindered an anti-racist response from the specialized agencies of the UN, despite

---

[99] *South West Africa Cases (Dissenting Opinion of Judge Tenaka), Second Phase, Judgment*, ICJ Reports [1966] 285.

[100] South West Africa, Second Phase, Judgment, ICJ Reports [1966] 6.

[101] John Dugard, *The South West Africa/Namibia Dispute: Documents and Scholarly Writings on the Controversy between South Africa and the United Nations* (University of California Press 1973) 239.

[102] *Declaration on the Granting of Independence to Colonial Countries and Peoples* (UNGA Res 1514 XV, 14 December 1960) (adopted by eighty-nine votes to none; nine abstentions).

[103] UNGA Res 1654 (XVI) (27 November 1961); the situation with regard to the implementation of the Declaration on the granting of independence to colonial countries and peoples.

[104] *Declaration on the Inadmissibility of Intervention in the Domestic Affairs of States and the Protection of Their Independence and Sovereignty* (UNGA Res 2131 XX, 21 December 1965).

[105] Edward McWhinney, 'Declaration on the Inadmissibility of Intervention in the Domestic Affairs of States and the Protection of Their Independence and Sovereignty' (1966) 60 AJIL 662.

[106] UNGA Res 2054 XX (15 December 1965); the policies of apartheid of the Government of the Republic of South Africa.

[107] SC Resolution 134 of 1 April 1960.

[108] SC Resolution 181 of 7 August 1963.

[109] SC Resolution 191 of 18 June 1964.

[110] For a pessimistic account of the challenges faced in mobilizing the community of IOs for action on the UNGA Resolutions on apartheid, see Seymour M Finger, 'A New Approach to Colonial Problems at the United Nations' (1972) 26 Int'l Org 143.

the various UNGA resolutions.[111] The UNGA received decidedly non-committal responses from International Telecommunications Union (ITU), Universal Postal Union (UPU), and the World Bank.[112] In a letter dated June 1966, the Food and Agricultural Organization (FAO) responded to the UNGA Resolutions by stating that it 'does not contemplate taking any action on this matter pending a decision by the UNDP authorities'.[113]

In letters between the UN and the World Bank on the binding nature of UNGA Resolutions, Bleicher describes the UN's invitation to the Bank to provide information about its financing to the government of South Africa.[114] The Bank, bound by its mandate on political neutrality asserted its Articles of Agreement, and committed to 'take account of the situation as it developed'.[115] According to Bleicher, the argument advanced by the World Bank is that there is no imperative requirement on the Bank to comply with UNGA Resolutions, but that it 'takes note' of its members' Charter obligations.[116]

While the role of the General Assembly and the non-binding legal effect of UNGA Resolutions is well established, UNSC Resolutions adopted in accordance with Chapter VII of the Charter, have binding force as per Article 25 of the Charter.[117] Prior to the ICERD effectiveness, the legal landscape in 1960s generated an ambivalence suggesting that the response of IOs was clearly a product of its time. By October 1966, when the Mandate over South West Africa was terminated by the UNGA Resolution 2146 (XXI),[118] the World Bank had already long ended its financing to South Africa.[119] With the ICJ's hesitation to rule on the merits of the illegality of South Africa's continued presence in Namibia, the apartheid regime continued, and so too did the UN's efforts towards racial equality.[120]

Despite its complex histories and hierarchies, as its most fundamental basis, international law deems any form of racist regime abhorrent.[121] As a matter of

---

[111] Rosalyn Higgins and Trevor Parfitt, 'South Africa's Standing in International Organizations' (1963) 19 The World Today 507.

[112] Richard E Bissell, *Apartheid and International Organizations* (Routledge 1977) 20.

[113] UN Archives, *Response of International Organizations to the UN Resolutions on Portugal and South Africa* (UN Document A/AC 109/194, 19 August 1966) 46.

[114] For a spirited critique of the WB's financing during that era, see Toussaint and Bond (n 89); Eric Toussaint and others, *The World Bank: A Critical Primer* (Pluto Press 2008).

[115] Ibrahim FI Shihata, 'The World Bank and Human Rights: An Analysis of the Legal Issues and the Record of Achievements' (1988) 17 Denv J Int'l L & Pol'y 39.

[116] It should be noted that according to the UN Relationship Agreement between the IBRD and the UN, Article VI requires the IBRD to 'have due regard for decisions of the Security Council under Articles 41 and 42 of the United Nations Charter' Agreement between the UN and IBRD 1947; Bleicher (n 89).

[117] Erika de Wet, *The Chapter VII Powers of the United Nations Security Council* (vol 3, Hart 2004).

[118] UNGA 2145 (XXI) (27 October 1966) Question of South Africa; UNGA Res 2145 (XXI) (27 October 1966) (1967) 649.

[119] World Bank, 'Nelson Mandela, South Africa and the World Bank Group' (*World Bank*, 17 July 2022).

[120] UN Archives, 'Measures Taken by Member States and Intergovernmental Organizations in the Light of United Nations Resolutions on Apartheid'.

[121] The International Court and South West Africa (n 98).

international human rights law as well as customary and general international law, the principle of non-discrimination prohibits the discrimination against ethnic and racial minorities.[122] Finally, both international and regional law assert the illegality of discrimination on racial grounds as discussed earlier. The following section provides a more recent account of the anti-racism commitments and efforts by IOs.

b. Multilateral commitments to anti-racism

Following the murder of George Floyd, a number of multilateral institutions expressed their solidarity with the global response to BLM, and reaffirmed commitments to anti-racism. As an affirmation to Article 14 (Prohibition of discrimination) of the ECHR[123] and Article 21 (Non-discrimination) of the EU Charter on Fundamental Rights,[124] on 17 June 2020 the European Commission (EC) President Ursula von der Leyen addressed the European Parliament about the need to talk about race[125] and equality.[126] Shortly after the parliamentary session, a resolution was passed by the European Parliament,[127] and by the end of the year the EC had launched its Anti-Racism Action Plan.[128] The European Union's (EU's) anti-discrimination laws, and the Race Equality Directive[129] in particular, prohibits discrimination on grounds of race and ethnic origin and gives legal effect to the principle on non-discrimination in EU law.

Enacted in 2000, the Race Equality Directive established one of the most stringent equality and non-discrimination legal frameworks. Under EU law, the aims

---

[122] *Barcelona Traction, Light and Power Company Limited (New Application, 1962), Belgium v Spain, Judgment, Merits, Second Phase*, ICJ GL No 50, [1970] ICJ Rep 3, (1970) [33–34].

[123] Council of Europe, *Convention for the Protection of Human Rights and Fundamental Freedoms*, as amended by Protocols No. 11 and 14, 4 November 1950, ETS 5 <https://www.eods.eu/library/CoE_European%20Convention%20for%20the%20Protection%20of%20Human%20Rights%20and%20Fundamental%20Freedoms_1950_EN.pdf> accessed 22 August 2023.

[124] 'Charter of Fundamental Rights of the European Union' (2012) OJEU 1 <https://eur-lex.europa.eu/legal-content/EN/TXT/PDF/?uri=CELEX:C2012/326/02> accessed 31 May 2023.

[125] Maia de la Baume and David Herszenhorn, 'President von Der Leyen "We Need to Talk about Racism"' (*European Commission*, 17 June 2020) (hereafter ' "We Need to Talk About Racism" ').

[126] Equality and non-discrimination are fundamental principles enshrined in the founding treaties of the EU: see Treaty on European Union [1992] (OJ C191/112) <https://eur-lex.europa.eu/EN/legal-content/summary/treaty-of-maastricht-on-european-union.html> accessed 22 August 2023; Treaty on the Functioning of the European Union [2016] (OJ C202/313) <https://eur-lex.europa.eu/EN/legal-content/summary/treaty-on-the-functioning-of-the-european-union.html> accessed 22 August 2023.

[127] European Parliament Resolution of 19 June 2020 on the anti-racism protests following the death of George Floyd 2020 <https://www.europarl.europa.eu/doceo/document/TA-9-2020-0173_EN.html> accessed 22 August 2023.

[128] EU Commission, 'A Union of Equality: EU Anti-racism Action Plan 2020–2025' (*European Website on Integration*, 18 September 2020) <https://ec.europa.eu/migrant-integration/library-document/union-equality-eu-anti-racism-action-plan-2020-2025_en> accessed 19 September 2023.

[129] Council Directive 2000/43/EC of 29 June 2000 Implementing the Principle of Equal Treatment between Persons Irrespective of Racial or Ethnic Origin 2000.

set out in the treaties and conventions are translated into legal obligations in the form of legally binding regulations, directives which must be incorporated into national law of EU Member States, and decisions which are binding upon certain Member States. The Race Equality Directive prohibits discrimination on grounds of race and ethnic origin and was adopted unanimously by EU Member States. The concept of discrimination in the Directive includes direct and indirect discrimination, and harassment.[130]

The significance of von der Leyen's statements and the commitment to anti-racism goes beyond what is mandated in EU Law and reflects on the challenge of racial diversity within the organization itself. In her statement, the Commission's President remarks that '[t]he diversity of our [European] society is not represented' in the institutions of the EU.[131] During the same parliamentary session, a number of the Members of the European Parliament (MEPs) demanded that the EC does more. Pierrette Herzberger-Fofana, a German-Malian, and Germany's only Black MEP,[132] described her own traumatic encounter with the Brussels Police.[133] The Commission President pointed out that this is a lived experience which the privileged many 'in this room just do not know about'.[134]

Similarly, on 18 June 2020, the World Bank President David Malpass reflected on the 'deeply emotional and thoughtful dialogue taking place within the World Bank Group' and shared his thoughts on the horrific murder of George Floyd.[135] To substantiate the WBG's commitment to ending racism, Malpass launched an Anti-Racism Task Force chaired by Sandie Okoro, WBG Senior Vice President and General Counsel.[136]

The Anti-Racism Task Force has two phases: Phase One's recommendations focus on the workplace, and Phase Two's have a more external focus. The Task Force commissioned the WBG's first-ever survey on race, conducted by a third-party firm. The results of that survey helped inform the development of recommendations by the Task Force for consideration and eventual implementation by the WBG's Senior Management. In 2021, the Office of the General Counsel launched one of the first substantive deliverables from the recommendations of the Anti-Racism Task Force: the WBG Anti-Racism Charter.[137]

---

[130] ibid arts 2(2)(a), 2(2)(b), and 2(3).
[131] "We Need to Talk About Racism" (n 125).
[132] Rajnish Singh, 'Pierrette Herzberger-Fofana: Standing up for Justice' (*The Parliament Magazine*, 13 November 2020).
[133] Jennifer Rankin, 'The German MEP Leading the Fight against Racism in Brussels' (*The Guardian*, 19 June 2020).
[134] 'We Need to Talk About Racism' (n 125).
[135] David Malpass, 18 June 2020: Ending racism, <https://blogs.worldbank.org/voices/june-18-2020-ending-racism>.
[136] World Bank, 'Addressing Racism and Racial Discrimination' (*Factsheet*, 11 November 2021) (hereafter 'Addressing Racism and Racial Discrimination').
[137] World Bank, 'World Bank Group Anti-Racism Charter' (*The World Bank*, September 2021).

Guided by the Bank's mandate and the overarching twin goals of ending extreme poverty and boosting shared prosperity in a liveable planet, the WBG Anti-Racism Charter embodies six Principles. Each Principle is directed at the future, but also cognizant of the past,[138] acknowledging that from the present moment the WBG commits to zero-tolerance of racism and racial discrimination.[139] Principles 1–3 are inward looking and reflect a commitment to anti-racism within the organization, including recruitment and talent management. Principles 4–5 are outward looking and assert the Bank's commitment to anti-racism in its financing and engagement with communities. Principle 6 asserts the long overdue conviction that the WBG 'recognizes that racism and racial discrimination are morally condemnable, contrary to our Core Values, and illegal under both international law and the laws of most of its member countries'.[140]

The anti-racism challenges confronting the EU, the EC, and the WBG are not unique to these institutions. In fact, racial discrimination continues to be a challenge even in IOs that have been leading the world's fight against discrimination, like the United Nations Educational, Scientific and Cultural Organization (UNESCO)[141] and the ILO.[142] The UN has a track record of commitments aimed at tackling racial discrimination since 1997 and continues to confront contemporary challenges.[143] The challenges faced by these IOs are as intersectional and multifaceted as the workforces that carry out their mandates. Most IOs have country offices of varying sizes in different parts of the world where perceptions of race and racism[144] may differ within the country, as well as across sub-country offices.

During a UN Townhall on June 4, 2020, the UN Secretary General, António Guterres acknowledged the UN's stellar policies on discrimination, harassment, and abuse of authority.[145] These policies notwithstanding, he added that the Organization has not paid enough attention to 'racist bias and racist

---

[138] For a relevant analysis of the World Bank's safeguard policies in a changing global order, see Philipp Dann and Michael Riegner, 'The World Bank's Environmental and Social Safeguards and the Evolution of Global Order' (2019) 32 LJIL 537.
[139] Addressing Racism and Racial Discrimination (n 136).
[140] ibid principle 6.
[141] UNESCO, 'Leading the World's Fight against Racism for 70 Years' (*UNESCO*, 5 February 2015); UNESCO, 'Master Class Series against Racism and Discriminations' (*UNESCO Events*, 23 March 2022); 'UNESCO Calls for Strong Action against Racism and Discrimination' (*UNESCO*, 26 March 2021) <https://www.unesco.org/en/articles/fightracism-fulfillthedream-unesco-calls-strong-action-against-racism-and-discrimination> accessed 31 May 2023.
[142] ILO Constitution, 'ILO Calls for Papers to Help Stop Racial Discrimination at Work' (18 March 2022); Percy K Yiadom, 'Interrogating Child Labour from an Anti-Racism Prism' in Joanna Newton and Arezou Soltani (eds), *New Framings on Anti-Racism and Resistance: Resistance and the New Futurity* (vol 2, Sense Publishers 2017) 129–137.
[143] Rosana Garciandia and Philippa Webb, 'The UN's Work on Racial Discrimination: Achievements and Challenges' (2022) 25 UNYB 216.
[144] Theo Van Boven, 'Discrimination and Human Rights Law: Combating Racism' in Sandra Fredman (ed), *Discrimination and Human Rights: The Case of Racism* (Oxford Scholarship Online 2001) 111–34.
[145] UN Secretary-General's Bulletin Prohibition of Discrimination, Harassment, including Sexual Harassment, and Abuse of Authority (2008) (ST/SGB/2008/5).

discrimination'.[146] But the challenges of having anti-racist dialogue in a multilateral organization with many specialized agencies includes finding a common vocabulary for words that have different meanings in different contexts. In addition to the intersectionality inherent in identity,[147] the nuances on anti-racist dialogue are many and must account for 'different duty stations, different structures, different teams, different grade levels and different contract types'.[148] This potentially creates discrepancy between local and international staff in different country offices.

To take two examples, both the UNESCO and ILO enshrine non-discrimination in their constituent documents as it applies to their operations and programmes. However, for most agencies the internal commitments to anti-racism in day-to-day workplace interactions are distinct from the overarching mandate. For example, in a similar effort as the Anti-Racism Taskforce at the WBG, the UN Offices in Geneva launched a ten-person Working Group on Addressing Racism in the Workplace.[149] Whether non-discrimination is enshrined in the constitution or articles of agreement of an IO, or as an organic commitment to anti-racism, how these institutions deal with and navigate the intersectional challenges to eliminating race discrimination will be unique to the lived experiences of anti-racism they create in the corridors of their virtual and in-person workplaces, in their day-to-day operations, and the boardrooms where the most important institutional decisions are made. This requires a multifaceted and principled response.

These commitments to non-discrimination are commendable. However, it cannot be determined with certainty whether multilateral organizations can singlehandedly end multidimensional forms of racism in the global world in which they operate. What is becoming more evident, as the next section will discuss, is that anti-racism in practice is much more challenging than anti-racism in policy.

c. Racial discrimination and development practice

> Structural discrimination happens when the legal regime and institutional structures seem to afford equal enjoyment of rights to all citizens but, in effect, deny the enjoyment of their rights to one or more sectors of society.
>
> (Mirjana Najcevska, former Acting Chair,
> Working Group of Experts on People of African Descent (2010))

---

[146] UN Secretary-General, 'Note to Correspondents: Secretary-General's Letter to Staff on the Plague of Racism and Secretary-General's Remarks at Town Hall' (9 June 2020).

[147] Kimberle Crenshaw, 'Mapping the Margins: Intersectionality, Identity Politics, and Violence against Women of Color' (1991) 43 Stan L Rev 1241; Neha Kagal and Lia Latchford, 'Towards an Intersectional Praxis in International Development: What Can the Sector Learn from Black Feminists Located in the Global North?' (2020) 28 Gend Dev 11.

[148] Laura Johnson, 'Unbelievably Yes—There's Racism at the UN' (*UN Today*, 1 April 2022).

[149] Matthew Wilson, 'Where There Is a Will There Is a Way' (*UN Today*, 21 January 2022).

The principle of non-discrimination takes on legally binding force as an obligation *erga omnes*,[150] and is posited to constitute a *jus cogens* norm from which derogation is not permissible.[151] In the context of development, the prohibition of racial discrimination binds IOs in their programmes as well as their policies. Through Draft Article 14 of the Draft Articles on the Responsibility of International Organizations, an IO 'which aids or assists' a state or another IO in the commission of an internationally wrongful act is held internationally responsible. Where an IO's due diligence 'neglects structural or historical discrimination'[152] in the delivery of development assistance, this may not represent a violation of international law. However, it potentially poses reputational, as opposed to legal, risks.

The obligation incumbent on IOs is therefore to ensure non-discrimination in the development assistance they provide. This hinges on the alignment of their internal policies with the prevailing international rules and standards, and the rigour with which they conduct their own due diligence. Such an obligation is reflected in the environmental and social safeguards IFIs and multilateral development banks (MDBs), such as the World Bank's Environmental and Social Framework (ESF),[153] the International Finance Corporation's (IFC) Performance Standards,[154] the Asian Development Bank's (ADB) safeguard policies,[155] the Asian Infrastructure Investment Bank's (AIIB) ESF,[156] the African Development Bank's (AfDB) Integrated Safeguards System,[157] the Green Climate Fund's (GCF) Environmental and Social Policy,[158] to name a few.

---

[150] Maurizio Ragazzi, *The Concept of International Obligations Erga Omnes* (OUP 2000) 118–31; Theodor Meron, 'The Meaning and Reach of the International Convention on the Elimination of All Forms of Racial Discrimination' (1985) 79 AJIL 283.

[151] Cathryn Costello and Michelle Foster, 'Race Discrimination Effaced at the International Court of Justice' (2021) 115 AJIL 339; Dinah Shelton, 'Are There Differentiations among Human Rights? Jus Cogens, Core Human Rights, Obligations Erga Omnes, and Non-Derogability' (CDL-UD (2005) 020 11European Commission for Democracy Through Law, Venice Commission 2005).

[152] Siobhán McInerney-Lankford, 'Human Rights and Development: A Comment on Challenges and Opportunities from a Legal Perspective' (2009) 1 J Hum Rights Prac 51.

[153] World Bank, 'The World Bank Environmental and Social Framework (ESF)' (2017) <https://thedocs.worldbank.org/en/doc/837721522762050108-0290022018/original/ESFFramework.pdf> accessed 22 August 2023.

[154] IFC, 'Performance Standards on Environmental and Social Sustainability' (1 January 2012) <https://www.ifc.org/content/dam/ifc/doc/mgrt/ifc-performance-standards.pdf> accessed 22 August 2023.

[155] Asian Development Bank (ADB), 'Safeguard Policy Statement' (June 2009) <https://www.adb.org/sites/default/files/institutional-document/32056/safeguard-policy-statement-june2009.pdf> accessed 22 August 2023.

[156] Asian Infrastructure Investment Bank (AIIB), 'Environmental and Social Framework' (November 2022) <https://www.aiib.org/en/policies-strategies/_download/environment-framework/AIIB-Environmental-and-Social-Framework_ESF-November-2022-final.pdf> accessed 22 August 2023.

[157] Maman-Sani Issa and others, 'African Development Bank's Integrated Safeguards System Update' (*African Development Bank*, 12 April 2023) <https://www.afdb.org/en/documents/integrated-safeguards-system-april-2023#:~:text=In%202013%2C%20the%20African%20Development,policies%2C%20as%20well%20as%20cross%2D> accessed 22 April 2023.

[158] Green Climate Fund, 'Environmental and Social Policy' (*Green Climate Fund*, 13 September 2021) <https://www.greenclimate.fund/sites/default/files/document/revised-environmental-and-social-policy.pdf> accessed 22 August 2023.

While non-discrimination laws may be introduced and IO or MDB development policies may be adjusted with anti-racism in mind, the underlying problems may remain unaddressed.[159] As part of the Special Procedures of the HRC, and during a visit to the UK, the Special Rapporteur on contemporary form of racism Tendayi Achiume reported on such underlying issues in the context of financing for non-discrimination in the domestic context.

In her report, Achiume acknowledges the firm basis in the UK's legal framework for tackling structural and institutional forms of racism, but expresses grave concern for the lack of budgetary allocations to finance equality impact assessments. Stating that '[t]he non-mandatory nature of these [equality impact] assessments in the UK undermines pursuit of racial equality in too many sectors of British life'.[160] On the face of it, there is nothing inherently discriminatory with a national government's decision to limit public funds and adopt austerity measures. However, how financing is allocated, and the specific measures adopted when administering public funds, has been shown to disproportionately affect racial or ethnic minorities.

Similarly, at a sub-national level, the financing decisions by municipal governments may not present litigable violations of the right to be free from discrimination. Public funds are notoriously constrained, and governments are pressed to justify expenditure on grounds of the most pressing public needs. This may result in a situation where the needs of the majority dominate the needs of the minority.

In such cases, an individual or a group may be better able to substantiate a legal claim for discrimination by adjoining it with an administrative right to participation, consultation, or self-government. In a socio-legal study, Angel Cabrera describes the judicial actions undertaken by the indigenous Pichátaro community towards budgetary autonomy. Located in the Purhépecha plateau, the Pichátaro fall within the jurisdiction of a predominantly non-indigenous municipality in the Mexican State of Michoacán. The town administration in which the Pichátaro were located managed the municipal budget such that public funds were allocated to larger towns rather smaller indigenous villages.

Rather than claiming discrimination on racial grounds, the Pichátaro community mobilized through judicial action to claim their right to budgetary autonomy under Article 4 of the United Nations Declaration on the Rights of Indigenous

---

[159] Cabrera Silva Angel, 'At the Margins of the Indigenous Rights Ecosystem: Underrepresented Struggles for Self-Determination' (2022) 35 Harv Hum Rts J.
[160] UNHRC, 'UN Doc A/HRC/41/54/Add: Visit to the United Kingdom of Great Britain and Northern Ireland—Report of the Special Rapporteur on Contemporary Forms of Racism, Racial Discrimination, Xenophobia and Related Intolerance' (*OHCHR Country Reports*, 27 May 2019).

Peoples (UNDRIP). While this example refers to financing through government transfers, it can easily extend to development financing.

In the context of development financing and the response to COVID-19, Malpass stated that '[p]art of the inequality problem is global finance itself and the unequal structure of the stimulus'.[161] Highlighting the influence of the World Bank and the International Monetary Fund (IMF), as well as the Organization for Economic Cooperation and Development (OECD), Achiume points to the role of IOs in racial justice and sustainable development. In the report, Achiume relayed the historical failures of both the World Bank and the IMF[162] to operationalize international human rights principles.[163] While asserting that a 'fundamental overhaul of economic and financial theories'[164] is required, Achiume commended the WBG's commitment to countering 'racial discrimination at institutional, systemic and structural levels, highlighting [the WBG's] use of environmental and social frameworks'.[165]

In lieu of an immediate and fundamental overhaul of world order, the concrete commitments to anti-racism by IOs and especially IFIs and MDBs may prove a more effective short-term remedy. It goes without saying that IFI, MDBs, and IO policies, even with the aid of principles like those reflected in the WBG Anti-Racism Charter, are unlikely to 'address all deep-rooted sources of racial discrimination'.[166] Such non-binding principles adopted at the institutional level may present concrete ways in which development practitioners may 'assess structural, institutional or economic factors that enable such discrimination to persist' and propose 'measures to address any resulting adverse risks and impacts'.[167]

---

[161] Andrea Shalal, 'Global Finance System Partly to Blame for Inequality—World Bank's Malpass' *Reuters* (6 December 2021).

[162] For an empirical investigation of the extent to which ethno-linguistic and cultural fractionalization impact the implementation of IMF programmes and conditions, see Krishna Chaitanya Vadlamannati and Samuel Rueckert Brazys, 'Does Cultural Diversity Hinder the Implementation of IMF-Supported Programs? An Empirical Investigation' (2 May 2022) <https://ssrn.com/abstract=4099004> accessed 22 August 2023.

[163] UNHRC, 'UN Doc A/HRC/50/60: Report of the Special Rapporteur Tendayi Achiume on Contemporary Forms of Racism, Racial Discrimination, Xenophobia and Related Intolerance' (*OHCHR Thematic Reports*, 17 June 2022).

[164] UNHRC, 'UN Doc A/HRC/50/60: Report of the Special Rapporteur Tendayi Achiume on Contemporary Forms of Racism, Racial Discrimination, Xenophobia and Related Intolerance' (*OHCHR*, 17 June 2022).

[165] The WBG's Environmental and Social Framework (ESF) will be discussed in Section 5(a) and (b) detail in the following sections. ibid.

[166] World Bank, 'Technical Note on Addressing Racial Discrimination through the Environmental and Social Framework (ESF)' (19 March 2021) <https://docslib.org/doc/12054808/technical-note-on-addressing-racial-discrimination-through-the-environmental-and-social-framework-esf-march-19-2021> accessed 22 August 2023.

[167] ibid.

5. Inequality and Racial Discrimination: Lessons from the COVID-19 Pandemic

In the preceding section, examples of anti-racism in development policy were highlighted, and the challenges of non-discrimination in policy and practice where juxtaposed. These challenges were made all the more clear during the Launch of the January 2022 Global Economic Prospects (GEP) Report. In his opening remarks, the president Malpass situates the GEP forecasts in light of the devastating effects of COVID-19, indicating that '[d]eveloping countries are facing severe long-term problems related to lower vaccination rates, global macro policies and the debt burden'.[168] The inequality Malpass describes relates to the inequality between countries in their development trajectories, resulting in a situation whereby 'people in the developing world [are] left behind and poverty rates rising'.[169] In addition to global inequalities, COVID-19 has exposed and exacerbated structural inequalities between racial groups,[170] as well as nation states,[171] leading some medical practitioners to call for 'decolonizing COVID-19',[172] and more closely interrogate the structural inequalities of public health systems.[173]

Described as 'vaccine discrimination'[174] and 'vaccine apartheid',[175] the differentiated response to COVID-19 raised a fundamental concern as to discrimination against low-income countries in the Global South.[176] The devastating disparity in the effects of COVID-19 on racial and ethnic minorities and the low rate of vaccinations among countries in the Global South prompted the Committee on the Elimination of Racial Discrimination (CERD) to issue a statement in April 2022. The CERD's statement came as a result of the shockingly wide vaccine equity gap of 16 per cent in lower-income countries compared to 80 per cent in the higher-income countries. The CERD's statements attributes the unequal distribution of COVID-19 vaccines to the legacies of 'slavery and

---

[168] World Bank, 'Opening Remarks by World Bank Group President David Malpass during the Launch of the January 2022 Global Economic Prospects Report' (*World Bank*, 11 January 2022).
[169] ibid.
[170] Kamaldeep Bhui, 'Ethnic Inequalities in Health: The Interplay of Racism and COVID-19 in Syndemics' (*eClinicalMedicine*, 2021).
[171] UNHCR, 'UN Expert Urges States to End "Vaccine Apartheid"' (*OHCHR*, 14 June 2022) (hereafter 'Vaccine Apartheid').
[172] The Lancet Global Health, 'Decolonising COVID-19' (*The Lancet Global Health*, 2020) e612.
[173] Gabriel R Sanchez and others, 'Discrimination in the Healthcare System is Leading to Vaccination Hesitancy' (*Brookings*, 20 October 2021); 'Africa's Experience with Covid-19 with Dr Stephanie Salyer' (*Ralph Bunche Institute*, 17 May 2021).
[174] Tommy Wilkes, '"Extreme" Vaccine Discrimination Risks Leaving Africa behind—Report' (*Reuters*, 6 December 2021); Mo Ibrahim Foundation, 'COVID-19 in Africa: A Challenging Road to Recovery' (2021) <https://mo.ibrahim.foundation/sites/default/files/2021-12/en_2021_interim-report_pr.pdf> accessed 22 August 2023.
[175] Vaccine Apartheid (n 171).
[176] ibid.

colonial-era racial hierarchies […] which further deepen[s] structural inequalities affecting vulnerable groups protected under the Convention'.[177]

International law has been at the centre of the global response to COVID-19:[178] through international trade law, patent law, and intellectual property rights,[179] and the resort to soft law guidance to control the spread of COVID-19 across hard borders without discrimination.[180] However, unequal access to COVID-19 prevention, containment, and treatment has been attributed to legal obstacles within the framework of international law. On 13 June 2022, Achiume urged the World Trade Organization (WTO) to adopt a comprehensive COVID-19 waiver of the Agreement on Trade-Related Aspects of Intellectual Property Rights (TRIPS).[181] Co-sponsored by fifty-six members of the WTO, South Africa and India originally submitted a proposal for a temporary COVID-19 waiver in October 2020.[182]

The WTO, by virtue of paragraph 6 of the 2001 Doha Declaration on the TRIPS Agreement and public health,[183] institutes an interim waiver. The Doha Declaration frames the health policy context of the intellectual property system and recognizes the urgency of responding to public health problems facing low-income countries. The Doha Declaration provides a temporary flexibility in terms of licensing and export of pharmaceutical products to countries that are unable to manufacture them. On 17 June 2022, at its twelfth session, the WTO Ministerial Conference adopted a Draft Ministerial Decision on the TRIPS Agreement which removes certain legal obstacles with the aim of easing access to COVID-19 pharmaceutical products.

This section sets out the COVID-19 response with specific reference to equality and the role of IOs and IFIs in ensuring the delivery of COVID-19 vaccines without discrimination as to race or national origin. This section highlights the important role these institutions play; through the commitment of anti-racism by those who work within them; by adhering to their mandates; and promoting inclusivity and non-discrimination through their due diligence and safeguards policies.

---

[177] CERD Statement 2 Statement on the Lack of Equitable and Non-discriminatory Access to COVID-19 Vaccines (2022).
[178] Armin von Bogdandy and Pedro Villarreal, 'The Role of International Law in Vaccinating Against COVID-19: Appraising the COVAX Initiative' (2021) 81 HJIL 89–116.
[179] Mitja Kovac and Lana Rakovec, 'The COVID-19 Pandemic and Long-Term Incentives for Developing Vaccines: Patent Law under Stress' (2022) 25 J World Intellect Prop 292–316; 'Reforming Patent Law: The Case of Covid-19' (*Cato Institute*, 14 October 2021); Brink Lindsey, 'Why Intellectual Property and Pandemics Don't Mix' (*Brookings*, 3 June 2021).
[180] WHO, 'Interim Guidance: Controlling the Spread of COVID-19 at Ground Crossings: Interim Guidance' (World Health Organization 2020) WHO/2019-nCoV/Ground_crossings/2020.1.
[181] Tendayi Achiume, 'Open Letter from the Special Rapporteur on Contemporary Forms of Racism, Racial Discrimination, Xenophobia and Related Intolerance to the World Trade Organization's Twelfth Ministerial Conference' (13 June 2022).
[182] Katie Gallogly-Swan and others, 'Waiving Intellectual Property Rules on COVID-19 Products' (2021) GEGI Policy Brief 11.
[183] Declaration on the TRIPS Agreement and Public Health (adopted on 14 November 2001).

a. Early days of the pandemic

Less than two months before the murder of George Floyd, Jean-Paul Mira and Camille Locht appeared on French television on 2 April 2020 to discuss potential solutions to the vaccine challenge. In a shocking turn to the conversation, the doctors discussed the possibility of vaccine trials in Africa to determine whether tuberculosis vaccines would be effective against coronavirus. Mira posited a deeply problematic proposal:

> If I can be provocative, shouldn't we be doing this study in Africa, where there are no masks, no treatments, no resuscitation? ... A bit like as it is done elsewhere for some studies on AIDS. In prostitutes, we try things because we know that they are highly exposed and that they do not protect themselves.[184]

Mira's proposition was met with predictable and justified outrage on social media.[185] During a COVID-19 virtual press conference on 6 April 2020 Tedros Ghebreyesus, the elected Head of the World Health Organisation (WHO) issued a statement in response to the remarks. Ghebreyesus said '[T]hese kind of racist remarks actually would not help, it goes against the solidarity. Africa cannot and will not be a testing ground for any vaccine.... The hangover from a colonial mentality has to stop—and WHO will not allow this to happen.'[186]

Mira, through his employer French National Institute of Health and Medical Research, Inserm, issued an apology for his racist remarks.[187] However, the mere idea of drug testing in the African continent had already revived memories of the grim history of medical experimentation on people of African descent.[188] Thus by the summer of 2020[189] a motion of interlocking pandemics—poverty, COVID-19,[190] and discrimination (discrimination against racial and ethnic minorities, as well as an entire continent regardless of race)—was set in motion.

---

[184] Rebecca Rosman, 'Racism Row as French Doctors Suggest Virus Vaccine Test in Africa' (*Al Jazeera*, 4 April 2020).

[185] BBC, 'Coronavirus: France Racism Row over Doctors' Africa Testing Comments' (*BBC News*, 3 April 2020); Didier Drogba, 'Africa Isn't a Testing Lab.' (*Twitter*, 2 April 2020).

[186] WHO, 'COVID-19 Virtual Press Conference—6 April 2020' (*World Health Organization* 2020).

[187] Wilson Wong, 'French Doctor Apologizes for Comments on Testing a COVID-19 Vaccine in Africa That Prompted Outrage on Social Media' (*NBC News*, 7 April 2020).

[188] 'COVID-19 Revives Grim History of Medical Experimentation in Africa' (*Global Voices*, 11 April 2020); Debbie Elliott, 'In Tuskegee, Painful History Shadows Efforts To Vaccinate African Americans' (*NPR*, 16 February 2021).

[189] Vaccine Apartheid (n 171).

[190] Interlocking Pandemics (n 83).

b. COVAX, AVAT, and the global response

Through the COVID-19 Vaccines Global Access (COVAX) Facility, the Coalition for Epidemic Preparedness Innovations (CEPI), GAVI (known as Gavi, the Vaccine Alliance), the WHO, and United Nations International Children's Emergency Fund (UNICEF) spearheaded an expedient response to the COVID-19 pandemic. Recognizing the urgent need for country access to COVID-19 vaccines, the World Bank approved the first phase of a Global COVID-19 Response Program[191] on 2 April 2020. By August 2020, the inequality in vaccine distribution efforts by COVAX made it clear that a more targeted effort towards vaccinations in Africa was necessary. The African Vaccine Acquisition Task Team (AVATT) was established in August 2020, and by November 2020 the African Vaccine Acquisition Trust (AVAT) was formed.

By 30 June 2022, the World Bank had approved US$10.1 billion towards vaccine rollout in seventy-eight countries and provided COVID-19 preparedness support in over one hundred countries.[192] Through an innovative partnership[193] between the African Export-Import Bank (Afreximbank), and the AVATT, the WBG supported expedited deployment of 400 million vaccines in Africa.[194]

The COVAX Facility, AVAT, WHO, and UNICEF, the World Bank's Global COVID-19 Response Program (also called the COVID-19 Strategic Preparedness and Response Program (SPRP)) generated a monumental effort. This effort was executed through the individuals working tirelessly within these institutions and ensuring seamless collaboration across them. The WHO, World Bank, and UNICEF each provided technical expertise within their mandated areas of expertise. For example, to help countries assess their vaccine readiness the WHO and the World Bank integrated their vaccine assessment and readiness tools into one comprehensive framework;[195] and in collaboration with UNICEF provided real-time technical assistance and capacity building to enable efficient deployment of vaccines.[196]

---

[191] World Bank, 'COVID-19 Strategic Preparedness and Response Program (SPRP) Using the Multiphase Programmatic Approach (MPA) Additional Financing' (2020).
[192] World Bank, 'World Bank Support for Country Access to COVID-19 Vaccines' (*The World Bank*).
[193] World Bank, 'World Bank and African Union Team Up to Support Rapid Vaccination for Up to 400 Million People in Africa' (*The World Bank*, 21 June 2021).
[194] World Bank, 'Africa Announces the Rollout of 400m Vaccine Doses to the African Union Member States and the Caribbean' (*The World Bank*, 5 August 2021).
[195] The joint framework is called VIRAT-VRAF 2.0, and includes WHO's Vaccine Introduction Readiness Assessment Tool (VIRAT) and the World Bank's Vaccination Readiness Assessment Framework (VRAF); WBG Development Committee, 'COVID-19: World Bank Group Support for Fair and Affordable Access to Vaccines by Developing Countries' (2021) DC2021-0003 para 32.
[196] World Bank, 'The World Bank, UNICEF Support COVID-19 Vaccine Deployment and Lifesaving Health Services for Children and Women in South Sudan' (*The World Bank*).

Each of the COVID-19 projects proposed for World Bank financing was prepared consistent with the Bank's operational policies and in compliance with its ESF.[197] The ESF sets out the Bank's vision for sustainable development and consists of both Bank and Borrower responsibilities throughout the project's life cycle for investment lending. The Bank's review and due diligence responsibilities are governed by the Environmental and Social Policy, the Environmental and Social Directive, and the Directive on Disadvantaged and Vulnerable Individuals or Groups.[198] The commitments set out in the Bank's environmental and social safeguards reflect obligations, under domestic and international law, to ensure non-discrimination in Bank financing. After the events of 2020 and in response to the urgency of ending racism, the ESF Directive on Disadvantaged and Vulnerable Individuals or Groups was revised to add an explicit reference to race.

Within the ESF, the Borrower's obligations include the assessment, implementation, and compliance with ten environmental and social standards (ESSs); Environmental, Health, and Safety Guidelines (EHSG); and, wherever relevant, specific Guidance Notes.[199] Once a project is prepared, the Bank and Borrower responsibilities are reflected in a number of environmental and social instruments, and the commitments enshrined in a legally binding Environmental and Social Commitment Plan (ESCP).

In both Bank financed projects, as well as projects co-financed with other IFIs,[200] '[a]ll investment projects are assessed for consistency with the ESF objectives of non-discrimination and social inclusion'.[201] Such safeguards account for all forms of discrimination against poor, vulnerable, and other marginalized groups. This was especially necessary in countries where non-citizens were excluded from accessing vaccines. For example, the Lebanon Health Resilience Project (P163476),[202] extended vaccination coverage to 70 per cent of the population, circumventing discriminatory laws introduced by the Lebanese government, which explicitly excluded refugees.[203]

By leveraging their resources and delivering on their mandates, these IOs have extended vaccines to many millions of people around the world. As the pandemic lingers, these organizations, as well as those who work within them, continue to learn from this collective lived experience. The current trifecta of pandemics[204]—poverty, COVID-19, and racial discrimination—is one in which a concerted

---

[197] Note the ESF applies to projects processed under Investment Project Financing (IPF) World Bank (2017).
[198] World Bank (n 153); World Bank (n 166).
[199] World Bank (n 153).
[200] For an example of a project co-financed by AIIB, see World Bank, 'World Bank Approves $500 Million in Additional Financing for Turkey's COVID-19 Pandemic Response' (*The World Bank*).
[201] WBG Development Committee (n 195) 18.
[202] World Bank, 'Lebanon Health Resilience Project (P163476)' (*The World Bank*).
[203] HRW, 'Lebanon: Refugees at Risk in Covid-19 Response' (*Human Rights Watch*, 2 April 2020).
[204] University of Chicago, 'The Trifecta: When a Pandemic Meets an Economic Recession and Racial Conflict' (*Civic Engagement*, 15 July 2020).

effort is needed, and the recognition that no human is an island entirely unto themselves.[205]

6. Conclusion

This chapter concludes with a number of caveats concerning the fact that any conclusion on the topic of race, discrimination, and development under international law made at this present moment would be grossly premature. The prematurity of any conclusions on the topic are attributed to the fact that this is an area of law that is so closely intertwined with non-legal narratives that cannot be easily captured. Following Russia's invasion of Ukraine, Black and Brown refugees have been subjected to unacceptable forms of racism at border crossings.[206] The UN High Commissioner for Refugees (UNHCR) has condemned the 'discrimination, violence and racism' targeting people of colour attempting to flee Ukraine.[207]

Both international law and domestic law are yet to rise to the challenge of ending racism expressly or reflect the nuance of lived experiences of racism everywhere. The principles of equality and non-discrimination provide an effective doctrinal footing, but the path to eliminating racism is not one that can be based on principles alone.

It suffices to conclude that non-discrimination is a structural feature of international human rights law and a principle that carries the weight of an obligation *erga omnes*. While the boundaries of international law as it relates to race and discrimination are in constant flux, so are the personalities and lived experiences of those who operate within the sphere of international law. The individuals carrying out the mandates of IOs, and the institutional commitments to anti-racism are part of the colourful canvas of international law and international development, and mark steps towards the continuous project of decolonization. If anything, questions of race have been a running narrative throughout the history of international law and continue to be so, as evidenced by the global response to anti-racism after the brutal murder and suffocation of George Floyd at the hands of the Minneapolis Police.

Thus, another caveat is that the explicit references to non-discrimination and equality in the constituent documents of IOs, in their due diligence and safeguarding policies, and internal procedures, are part of the journey rather than the desired destination. In Section 3, the history of colonization and the process

---

[205] John Donne, *No Man Is an Island* (Souvenir Press 1988).
[206] Jude Mary Cénat and others, 'War in Ukraine and Racism: The Physical and Mental Health of Refugees of Color Matters' (2022) 67 Int J Public Health 1604990; Rashawn Ray, 'The Russian Invasion of Ukraine Shows Racism Has No Boundaries' (*Brookings*, 3 March 2022).
[207] Chris Melzer and Chris Wolf, 'UNHCR Chief Condemns "Discrimination, Violence and Racism" against Some Fleeing Ukraine' (UN News, 21 March 2022).

of decolonization was positioned in the context of development. The sacred trust underpinning the Mandate Systems, which was superseded by the Trustee System, marked a moment of collective consciousness in which Ios slowly caught up to the wave of decolonization, some slower than others.

With the not-so-distant history of colonization in mind, the BLM Movement provided multilateral institutions an opportunity to lead the charge in anti-racism. If followed up with concrete and concerted actions, the groundbreaking commitments by the EC, EU, and the WBG present an opportunity for meaningful change towards promoting non-discrimination and equality in both development policy and practice. While such efforts by IOs are unlikely to overhaul the global system of inequality—between rich and poor, low-income countries and high-income countries—they present measurable results against which IOs can be held accountable.

In section 4, the global, and racialized, effects of the COVID-19 pandemic demonstrated that there is a colour line dividing the Global North from the Global South. A line that IOs may help blur through development financing and environmental and social safeguards.

The BLM and the COVID-19 pandemic triggered a snowball effect that has brought to the forefront a global conversation on racial inequality in the field of development. A conversation that has long been documented in legal history, continues to plague justice systems around the world, and yet occupies such a limited space in legal scholarship. In contributing to the unique gap this edited volume occupies in the legal scholarship, this chapter makes two final concluding caveats: The first is on the legal definitions of race and the second is on the dichotomies that trap international legal thinking in self-perpetuating binaries.

International law is a law of dichotomies: it is founded on the notion that there exists a national law from which international law is distinct; a sovereign state from which the non-state is distinguished; an external-self that is determined, within which the internal-self resides. It is a legal framework that is fraught with restrictive binaries. Among these restrictive binaries is imperialism: potentially the most restrictive of all dichotomies in international law is the dichotomy between colonizer and colonized. The period, which Anghie refers to as the colonial confrontation, is attributed as the moment of 'birth of international institutions'.[208]

Institutions under international law are many and varied, they represent a multifaceted range of international and regional organizations, each with its own distinct mandate and personality. While it is established in the field of development economics that institutions matter,[209] and that the colonial origins of institutions have an enduring effect on the comparative development of decolonized states,[210] the practical impacts of international institutions are more

---

[208] The Making of International Law (n 51) 115.
[209] Douglass C North, *Institutions, Institutional Change and Economic Performance / Douglass C. North*. (CUP 1994); Douglass North, 'Institutions Matter' (1994) *Economic History*.
[210] The Colonial Origins (n 87).

challenging to quantify. Nevertheless, given the impact of international rules and norms on domestic actors,[211] it is widely accepted that *international* institutions matter.[212]

International institutions, as the term is broadly used in this edited volume, includes multilateral institutions involved in international development. The chapter has consciously engaged with the challenges inherent in the oversimplification of deeply complex questions of race and rejected black and white formulas and binaries of race as a legal or conceptual construct. In section 3, the conceptual context of the term 'race' as it was used in 1919 was juxtaposed with the principle of non-discrimination on the bases of 'race' and 'colour'. The legal framework within which non-discrimination as a principle evolved cannot be taken outside its historical context, and without acknowledgement of the racial biases that characterized development under the sacred trust as reflected in the Covenant of the League of Nations in 1919, and development as it later emerged in response to the Great Depression ten years later in the 1930s.

The dangers of international law's oversimplification of dichotomies results in categories like the subnational, the transboundary, and the non-binary falling between the cracks.[213] This is a challenge in both international legal theory and practice, often attributed to the 'marked absence of gender and race' in international legal history.[214] Although a great deal is written about diversity in international law, it remains to be a field of scholarship in which there is scope for further diversity and inclusion.[215]

---

[211] Andrew P Cortell and James W Davis, 'How Do International Institutions Matter? The Domestic Impact of International Rules and Norms' (1996) 40 Int'l Stud Q 451.

[212] Ronald B Mitchell, 'Of Course International Institutions Matter: But When and How?' in Heiko Breit and others (eds), *How Institutions Change: Perspectives on Social Learning in Global and Local Environmental Contexts* (VS Verlag für Sozialwissenschaften 2003) 35–52.

[213] Harum Mukhayer, 'Transboundary Rights and Indigenous Peoples between Two or More States' in Dwight Newman (ed), *Research Handbook on the International Law of Indigenous Rights* (Edward Elgar Publishing 2022) 413–37, 413.

[214] Janne E Nijman, 'Marked Absences: Locating Gender and Race in International Legal History' (2020) 31 EJIL 1025.

[215] Maiko Meguro, 'Appraisal of Diversity in International Law: A Note on Self-Serving Biases and Interdisciplinarity' (*Elgar Online*, 8 December 2022) <https://www.elgaronline.com/edcollchap/book/9781800373006/book-part-9781800373006-16.xml> accessed 22 August 2023.

9
The Right to Water

Laurence Boisson de Chazournes, Mara Tignino, and Haoua Savadogo[*]

1. Introduction

Water is essential for life, human dignity, and the health of people and planet.[1] The human right to safe drinking water is, therefore, foundational to the realization and enjoyment of all other human rights.[2] For instance, unclean water often leads to diarrhoea, which remains the second-largest cause of mortality in children under five, therefore access to safe water is necessary for the realization of the right to health.[3] Further, the right to education cannot be guaranteed where water is not available at school and access to water is essential for agriculture in order to realize the right to adequate food.[4] This essential nature of water led all Member States of the United Nations (UN) in September 2015 to commit to ensuring access to safe drinking water and sanitation for all through Sustainable Development Goal 6 (SDG 6) of the 2030 Agenda for Sustainable Development.[5] They further explicitly reaffirmed their commitment to the human rights to water and sanitation in the Agenda's declaration.[6] This proclamation is just one in a long history of recognition of the human rights to water and sanitation by states and UN bodies and institutions. In the present contribution, the focus will be placed on the right to water.

---

[*] Laurence Boisson de Chazournes is Professor at the Faculty of Law of the University of Geneva and Member of the Global High-Level Panel on Water and Peace; Mara Tignino is a Reader at the Faculty of Law and the Institute for Environmental Sciences of the University of Geneva and Lead Legal Specialist of the Platform for International Freshwater Law at the Geneva Water Hub; Haoua Savadogo is a PhD Candidate and Teaching and Research Assistant at the Faculty of Law of the University of Geneva.

[1] This chapter is part of a research project entitled 'Corporate Social Responsibility in Water Management: The Path towards Action for Protecting Human Needs and Biodiversity', conducted under the aegis of the Centre for Philanthropy of the University of Geneva and the Platform for international water law of the Geneva Water Hub.

[2] United Nations General Assembly (UNGA), *The Human Right to Water and Sanitation* (A/RES/64/292, 28 July 2010) s 1; 'SDG 6 and the Human Right to Water and Sanitation' (*Sustainable Development Goals Knowledge Platform*, 11 July 2016) <https://sustainabledevelopment.un.org/index.php?page=view&type=20000&nr=423&menu=2993> accessed 2 June 2023.

[3] UN Human Rights Council, 'Realising the Human Right to Water and Sanitation: A Handbook by the UN Special Rapporteur Catarina de Albuquerque' (UNHRC 2014) 37.

[4] ibid 38.

[5] UN General Assembly, *Transforming our World: The 2030 Agenda for Sustainable Development* (A/Res/70/1, 2015), 18 (hereafter '2030 Agenda').

[6] ibid 3.

The human right to water is defined as 'the right of everyone to sufficient, safe, acceptable and physically accessible and affordable water for personal and domestic uses'.[7] For the realization of the human right to water, three factors are applicable in all circumstances.[8]

The first one is *availability*, which means that the water supply for each person must be sufficient and continuous for personal and domestic uses.[9] These uses ordinarily include drinking, personal sanitation, washing of clothes, food preparation, and personal and household hygiene.[10] According to the World Health Organization (WHO), between fifty and one hundred litres of water per person per day are needed to meet the most basic needs.[11] The second factor pertains to the *quality* of water. This means that the water required for each personal or domestic use must be safe, free from micro-organisms, chemical substances, and radiological hazards that constitute a threat to a person's health.[12] The third key factor relates to the *accessibility* of water facilities. Physical accessibility means that everyone has the right to a water service that is physically accessible within, or in the immediate vicinity of the household, school, workplace, or health institution.[13] According to the WHO, the water source has to be within 1,000 metres of the home and collection time should not exceed thirty minutes.[14] Economic accessibility requires that water and water facilities and services be affordable for all.[15] The United Nations Development Programme (UNDP) suggests that water costs should not exceed 3 per cent of household income.[16] Accessibility also includes non-discrimination, which means that water, and water facilities and services, must be accessible to all, including the most vulnerable or marginalized segments of the population, in law and in fact without discrimination on any of the prohibited grounds.[17] Accessibility further includes the right to seek, receive, and impart information concerning water issues.[18]

---

[7] UN Committee on Economic, Social and Cultural Rights (UNCESCR), *General Comment No 15: The Right to Water (Arts 11 and 12 of the Covenant)* (E/C12/2002/11, 20 January 2003) s 2 (hereafter 'General Comment No 15'); Human Rights Council, *The Human Rights to Safe Drinking Water and Sanitation* (A/HRC/39/L11, 21 September 2018) s 1.

[8] ibid (General Comment No 15) (n 7).

[9] ibid.

[10] ibid.

[11] World Health Organization (WHO), *The Right to Water* (Health and Human Rights Publication Series No 3, 2003) 13 (hereafter 'The Right to Water'); United Nations, 'Global Issues: Water' <https://www.un.org/en/global-issues/water> accessed 4 August 2023; World Bank, 'Atlas of Sustainable Development Goals 2023' <https://datatopics.worldbank.org/sdgatlas/goal-6-clean-water-and-sanitation/> accessed 4 August 2023.

[12] CESCR, General Comment No 15 (n 7); UN Water, 'International Decade for Action 'Water for Life' 2005–2015' (2014).

[13] General Comment No 15 (n 7).

[14] The Right to Water (n 11).

[15] General Comment No 15 (n 7).

[16] Office of the High Commissioner for Human Rights (OHCHR), 'Fact Sheet No 35, The Right to Water' (2010) 11.

[17] General Comment No 15 (n 7).

[18] ibid.

In the present contribution, we will highlight the steps taken towards the recognition and consolidation of the human right to water (section 2) and its importance for sustainable development (section 3) before delving into its interfaces with SDG 6 (section 4). We will further address the role of SDG 6 for ensuring non-discrimination (section 5) and the accountability of the private sector (section 6) in the implementation of the human right to water.

2. The Path towards the Recognition of the Human Right to Water

The recognition of the human right to water can be traced back to the early 1970s.[19] Since then, a number of resolutions and declarations were adopted, and conferences and forums were held in order to address the seriousness of the problems facing the water resources sector, including the issue of the right to water. Four conferences have played a key role in the emergence of the human right to water.

First, the 1972 United Nations Conference on the Human Environment, held in Stockholm, identified water as one of the natural resources that needed to be safeguarded for the benefit of the present and future generations through careful planning or management.[20] This conference reflected a growing interest in issues related to water resources conservation worldwide and laid the foundation for a global governance approach by emphasizing the necessity for humanity to safeguard water resources.

Second, the United Nations Mar del Plata Water Conference was held in Argentina in 1977.[21] Devoted exclusively to discussing the emerging water resources problems, the Mar del Plata Water Conference issued the Mar del Plata Action Plan, which included a number of recommendations and resolutions dealing with various issues such as an assessment of water resources, water use, and water efficiency.[22] More importantly, the Mar del Plata Water Conference agreed, as part of the Action Plan, to proclaim the period 1981 to 1990 as the 'International Drinking Water Supply and Sanitation Decade' during which governments would assume a commitment to provide all people with water of safe quality in adequate quantity.[23] The Mar del Plata Water Conference is considered today as the starting point for the recognition of the right to water.[24] Indeed, Resolution II of the Action

---

[19] Salman M A Salman and Siobhán McInerney-Lankford, *The Human Right to Water: Legal and Policy Dimensions* (World Bank 2004) 7 (hereafter 'The Human Right to Water').

[20] Declaration of the United Nations Conference on the Human Environment (UN Doc A/CONF48/14/Rev1, 16 June 1972) principles 2, 4.

[21] Report of the United Nations Water Conference (Mar del Plata, 14–25 March 1977).

[22] ibid 7.

[23] ibid 14; Edward O'Rourke, 'The International Drinking Water Supply and Sanitation Decade: Dogmatic means to a debatable end' (1992) 26(7–8) Wat Sci Tech 1929.

[24] The Human Right to Water (n 19).

Plan on 'Community Water Supply' was pioneering and declared that '[a]ll peoples, whatever their stage of development and their social and economic conditions, have the right to have access to drinking water in quantities and of a quality equal to their basic needs.'[25]

Third, in January 1992, an international Conference on Water and the Environment was held in Dublin. The Dublin Statement on Water and Sustainable Development was issued.[26] The conference participants called for fundamental new approaches to the assessment, development, and management of freshwater resources, which can only be brought about through political commitment and involvement from governments and communities.[27] They also urged all governments to adopt specific measures and means of implementation of the recommendations and to translate them into urgent action programmes for water and sustainable development.[28] Furthermore, while indicating that 'water has an economic value in all its competing uses and should be recognized as an economic good', the Dublin Statement clarified that 'it is vital to recognize first the basic right of all human beings to have access to clean water ... at an affordable price.'[29] This is considered to be a confirmation of the right to water at an affordable price.[30]

Fourth, in June 1992, the United Nations Conference on Environment and Development (UNCED) was held in Rio de Janeiro (the Rio Summit). A comprehensive plan of action for sustainable development (Agenda 21) was adopted.[31] With respect to fresh water resources, Agenda 21 aims at 'satisfy[ing] the freshwater needs of all countries for their sustainable development'.[32] As regards the right to water, the Agenda indicates that 'water resources have to be protected, ... in order to satisfy and reconcile needs for water in human activities. In developing and using water resources, priority has to be given to the satisfaction of basic needs and the safeguarding of ecosystems.'[33]

These conferences have prompted the adoption of a number of resolutions and other instruments leading to the recognition of the human right to water. Several instruments ought to be mentioned. The first one is the United Nations General Assembly's (UNGA's) resolution on 'The Right to Development' adopted

---

[25] United Nations Water Conference, *Mar del Plata Action Plan* (Mar del Plata, Argentina, 14–25 March 1977) 63.
[26] 'The Dublin Statement on Water and Sustainable Development' (*Return to Water Resources*) <https://www.gdrc.org/uem/water/dublin-statement.html> accessed 3 June 2023.
[27] ibid s 4.
[28] ibid s 5.
[29] ibid principle 4.
[30] The Human Right to Water (n 19).
[31] United Nations Conference on Environment & Development (UNCED) (Rio de Janeiro), 'Agenda 21' (*Sustainable Development Goals Knowledge Platform*, 3–14 June 1992) <https://sustainabledevelopment.un.org/outcomedocuments/agenda21> accessed 3 June 2023.
[32] ibid s 18(2).
[33] ibid s 18(8).

in 2000.[34] There the UNGA reaffirmed that, 'in the realization of the right to development, ... the rights to food and clean water are fundamental human rights and their promotion constitutes a moral imperative both for national Governments and for the international community.'[35] This constitutes a very strong and unambiguous statement in declaring a human right to water, and linking the latter to the issue of development.

This resolution was followed by the United Nations Millennium Declaration, adopted unanimously by the UNGA in September 2000.[36] The Declaration addresses eight Millennium Development Goals to be achieved by 2015. Among those goals, Target 7C of the Millennium Development Goal 7 aims at reducing by half the proportion of people without sustainable access to safe drinking water.[37] This target of halving the proportion of people without access to improved sources of water was achieved five years ahead of schedule. Between 1990 and 2015, 2.6 billion people gained access to improved drinking water sources.[38]

In November 2002, the Committee on Economic, Social and Cultural Rights (CESCR), established under the International Covenant on Economic, Social and Cultural Rights (ICESCR), issued General Comment 15 on the right to water. The General Comment underscores the fact that water is a limited natural resource and a public good fundamental for life and health.[39] It also emphasizes that water is a prerequisite for the realization of other human rights.[40] Moreover, the General Comment notes that '[a]n adequate amount of safe water is necessary to prevent death from dehydration, to reduce the risk of water-related diseases and to provide for consumption, cooking, personal and domestic hygienic requirements.'[41] It further calls on the states parties to 'adopt effective measures to realize, without discrimination, the right to water as set out in this General Comment'.[42]

In July 2010, the UNGA adopted a landmark instrument exclusively dedicated to the right to safe and clean drinking water as a human right that is essential to the realization of all human rights.[43] The Resolution calls upon states and international organizations to provide financial resources; help capacity-building and

---

[34] UNGA, *Declaration on the Right to Development: Resolution/adopted by the General Assembly* (A/RES/41/128, 4 December 1986).
[35] ibid 4.
[36] UNGA, *United Nations Millennium Declaration, Resolution Adopted by the General Assembly* (A/RES/55/2, 18 September 2000).
[37] ibid 5.
[38] Cecilia Tortajada and Asit K Biswas, Achieving Universal Access to Clean Water and Sanitation in an Era of Water Scarcity: Strengthening Contributions from Academia' (2018) 34 Curr Opin Environ Sustain 21.
[39] General Comment No 15 (n 7) s 1.
[40] ibid.
[41] ibid s 2.
[42] ibid s 1.
[43] UNGA, *The Human Right to Water and Sanitation: Resolution/adopted by the General Assembly* (A/RES/64/292, 3 August 2010).

technology transfer to help states, in particular developing countries; and to provide safe, clean, accessible, and affordable drinking water for all.[44]

Another resolution was adopted in September 2010 by the Human Rights Council. When affirming the human right to safe drinking water, the UN organ considered, in line with the CESCR, that the right to water derives from the right to an adequate standard of living and the right to health.[45]

Lastly, the 2030 Agenda for Sustainable Development (the 2030 Agenda)[46], which was unanimously adopted by the Member States of the UNGA,[47] confirmed the human right to water by reaffirming the commitments of all states regarding universal access to safe drinking water for all.[48] The 2030 Agenda enshrines seventeen Sustainable Development Goals (SDGs) and 169 targets encompassing the economic, social, and environmental dimensions of sustainable development.[49] To achieve sustainable development by 2030, water has a significant role to play.[50] That is why the UN Member States committed themselves to ensuring access to safe drinking water in Sustainable Development Goal 6 (SDG 6) by 2030.[51] SDG 6 aims at guiding the policy decisions of the UN Member States and also of other actors, including international organizations and the private sector, towards universal access to water.

Recognition of the right to water is also enshrined in treaties. The Convention on the Rights of the Child requires states parties to take appropriate measures to combat disease and malnutrition through, inter alia, the provision of clean drinking water.[52] The Convention on the Elimination of All Forms of Discrimination against Women provides that states parties shall take all appropriate measures to eliminate discrimination against women in rural areas in order to ensure that they enjoy adequate living conditions, particularly in relation to sanitation and water supply.[53] Similarly, the Convention on the Rights of Persons with Disabilities requires state parties to ensure equal access by persons with disabilities to clean water services.[54]

---

[44] ibid 3.
[45] UN Human Rights Council (UNHRC), *Human Rights and Access to Safe Drinking Water and Sanitation: Resolution/adopted by the Human Rights Council* (A/HRC/RES/15/9, 6 October 2010) s 3.
[46] 2030 Agenda (n 5) 18.
[47] United Nations Population Fund, 'Historic New Global Goals Unanimously adopted by United Nations' (*United Nations Population Fund*, 25 September 2015) <https://www.unfpa.org/news/historic-new-global-goals-unanimously-adopted-united-nations> accessed 3 June 2023.
[48] 2030 Agenda (n 5) Declaration s 7.
[49] ibid preamble, s 3.
[50] Water Europe and UNESCO, 'Water in the 2030 Agenda for Sustainable Development: How can Europe Act? (*UNESDOC Digital Library*, 2019) 7 <https://unesdoc.unesco.org/ark:/48223/pf0000372496> accessed 3 June 2023.
[51] 2030 Agenda (n 5) 22.
[52] *Convention on the Rights of the Child* (1577 UNTS 3, opened for signature 20 November 1989, entered into force 2 September 1990) art 24(2)(c)(e).
[53] *Convention on the Elimination of All Forms of Discrimination against Women* (1249 UNTS 13, opened for signature 18 December 1979, entered into force 3 September 1981) art 14(2)(h).
[54] *United Nations Convention on the Rights of Persons with Disabilities* (2515 UNTS 3, opened for signature 30 March 2007, entered into force on 3 May 2008) art 28(2)(a).

Furthermore, access to safe drinking water and sanitation is implicitly included in the ICESCR.[55] As previously mentioned, for the CESCR, the right to water clearly falls within the category of guarantees essential for securing an adequate standard of living protected by article 11 of the CESCR.[56] The CESCR also stated that the core obligations in relation to the right to water require states parties to take measures to prevent, treat, and control diseases linked to water.[57]

3. The Importance of the Right to Water for Sustainable Development

Water is a crucial natural resource for sustainable development and plays a central role in socio-economic development, the maintenance of a healthy planet, and human survival. Good management of water resources can therefore boost countries' economic prosperity and contribute to poverty reduction.[58]

Sustainable development is defined as 'development that meets the needs of the present without compromising the ability of future generations to meet their own needs'.[59] It requires meeting the essential needs of people, which include good health, food, and peaceful and prosperous societies.[60] Water is critical in satisfying these needs.

Access to safe and affordable drinking water is essential for improving global public health, as a poor quantity and quality of water causes millions of people to die from preventable diseases each year.[61] Inadequate management of urban, industrial, and agricultural waste water leads to drinking-water contamination or pollution.[62] Contaminated water is linked to transmission of diseases such as cholera, diarrhoea, dysentery, hepatitis A, typhoid, and polio.[63] For instance, more than 829,000 people die each year from diarrhoea as a result of unsafe drinking

---

[55] *International Covenant on Economic, Social and Cultural Rights* (993 UNTS 3, opened for signature 19 December 1966, entered into force 3 January 1976) art 11(1) (hereafter 'ICESCR'); General Comment No 15 (n 7) s 3.

[56] General Comment No 15 (n 7) s 3.

[57] ibid s 37.

[58] World Health Organization (WHO), 'Fact Sheet: Drinking-water' (*World Health Organization*, 2022) <https://www.who.int/news-room/fact-sheets/detail/drinking-water> accessed 12 May 2022 (hereafter 'Drinking-water'); World Bank, 'Water, Sanitation & Hygiene at a Glance' (*Open Knowledge Repository*, 2003) <http://hdl.handle.net/10986/9715> accessed 3 June 2023.

[59] *Report of the World Commission on Environment and Development: Our Common Future* (1987) 41 (hereafter 'The Brundtland Report', as it is otherwise known).

[60] ibid 42.

[61] UN Water, *Sustainable Development Goal 6: Synthesis Report on Water and Sanitation* (2018) 18 (hereafter 'Synthesis Report').

[62] Drinking-water (n 58); Centers for Disease Control and Prevention, 'Water Contamination and Diseases' (*Drinking-water*, 2022) <https://www.cdc.gov/healthywater/drinking/contamination.html?CDC_AA_refVal=https%3A%2F%2Fwww.cdc.gov%2Fhealthywater%2Fdrinking%2Fpublic%2Fwater_diseases.html#print> accessed 4 August 2023.

[63] Synthesis Report (n 61) 132; Drinking-water (n 58).

water.[64] It is also worth mentioning that the COVID-19 pandemic shed light on the inequalities, hardships, and global health risks that result from the collective failure to uphold the human right to water. In many communities around the world, the lack of water supply deprived people of their most basic protections against the spread of the virus.[65] Guaranteeing a reliable supply of drinking water will therefore help people to remain in good health, thus reducing medical costs.

Water is also key to food security and nutrition. It is crucial to ecosystems, including forests, lakes, and wetlands, which provide food security and nutrition to millions of people.[66] In particular, an appropriate quality and quantity of water is not only essential for drinking, but also for food production (fisheries, crops, and livestock) and food processing, transformation, and preparation.[67]

Water can equally be a powerful vehicle for peace and cooperation among communities and countries.[68] Access to water and water allocation and use can cause tensions, which may potentially spill over into conflict, within or between states.[69] Tensions between countries that share a river basin may hinder sustainable development, thus indirectly driving poverty, migration, and social instability.[70] It is therefore important for states to set up joint management and protection plans over shared water resources, allowing for participation of local communities and cooperation in various areas including forestry, land use, and fisheries.[71] Institutional arrangements are also key to ensure sustainable utilization of water resources.[72] An emblematic example is the Senegal River Development Organisation, established in 1972, which oversees the operation and maintenance of common works and the sharing of benefits (including energy production, land irrigation, potable water, and navigation) between its four Member States.[73] In 2002, the riparian countries

---

[64] Drinking-water (n 58).
[65] UN Water, 'COVID-19 Pandemic and the Human Rights to Water and Sanitation' (*UN Water*, 2020) <https://www.unwater.org/covid-19-pandemic-and-the-human-rights-to-water-and-sanitation/> accessed 3 June 2023.
[66] High Level Panel of Experts (HLPE), *Report on Food Security and Nutrition* (2015) 11 (hereafter 'Report on Food Security').
[67] ibid; Institute for Human Rights and Business (IHRB), *The Right to Food and Water: Dependencies and Dilemmas* (2010) 15 (hereafter 'The Right to Food and Water').
[68] Geneva Water Hub, 'A Matter of Survival-Report of the Global High-level Panel on Water and Peace' (*Geneva Water Hub*, 2017) <https://www.genevawaterhub.org/resource/matter-survival> accessed 3 June 2023.
[69] OECD, *Water and Violent Conflict, Issues Brief* (2005) 1.
[70] ibid.
[71] See, for example, *The Protocol for Sustainable Development of Lake Victoria Basin* (*East African Community*, 2003) art 3, which details the areas of cooperation related to sustainable development <https://www.internationalwaterlaw.org/documents/regionaldocs/Lake_Victoria_Basin_2003.pdf> accessed 3 June 2023.
[72] Komlan Sangbana, *African Basin Management Organizations: Contribution to Pollution Prevention of Transboundary Water Resources* (Brill Research Perspectives in International Water Law, Brill 2020).
[73] Mara Tignino, 'Joint Infrastructure and the Sharing of Benefits in the Senegal and Niger Watersheds' (2016) 41(6) Water Int 835, 835–50; Kabine Komara, 'Setting the Example for Cooperative Management of Transboundary Water Resources in West Africa' (*World Bank Blogs* 2014) <https://blogs.worldbank.org/nasikiliza/setting-example-cooperative-management-transboundary-water-resources-west-africa> accessed 3 June 2023.

of this basin were also the first to recognize explicitly the human right to water as a guiding principle for the sharing of an international watercourse in the spirit of sustainable development.[74]

In September 2015, UN Member States explicitly reaffirmed their commitment to the human right to water and dedicated SDG 6 to access to water for all through the 2030 Agenda.

4. Interfaces between the Human Right to Water and SDG 6: Moving Boundaries

SDG 6 comprises eight global targets.[75] They cover the entire water cycle, including: provision of drinking water (Target 6.1) and sanitation and hygiene services (Target 6.2); treatment and reuse of wastewater and ambient water quality (Target 6.3); water-use efficiency and scarcity (Target 6.4); integrated water resources management (IWRM) including through transboundary cooperation (Target 6.5); protecting and restoring water-related ecosystems (Target 6.6); international cooperation and capacity-building (Target 6.a); and participation in water and sanitation management (Target 6.b).[76]

In this chapter, we will focus on SDG Target 6.1 through which the UN Member States pledged to achieve universal and equitable access to safe and affordable drinking water for all by 2030. In doing so, we will show that the scope of SDG Target 6.1 is pushing the boundaries of the right to water in enlarging its scope, contributing therefore to reaching the most vulnerable people and achieving other SDGs. The SDG's objective of 'leaving no one behind' is central to the realization of the human right to water, which is in danger of being missed given that still, in 2020, two billion people remain without safe, managed drinking water.[77]

Indeed, the practice of international organizations suggests that the SDG Target 6.1, while strengthening the recognition and implementation of the right to water, covers various additional dimensions. First, SDG 6 Target 6.1 enshrines the human right to water as a core commitment of Agenda 2030.[78] The UN Member States,

---

[74] Organisation pour la mise en valeur du fleuve sénégal (OMVS), 'Charte des Eaux du Fleuve Sénégal' (2002) <https://rim-rural.org/2021/02/16/charte-des-eaux-du-fleuve-senegal/> accessed 4 August 2023.
[75] General Comment No 15 (n 7) s 3.
[76] 2030 Agenda (n 5) 18–19.
[77] See 'SDG6: Ensure Availability and Sustainable Management of Water and Sanitation for All' (*UN Department of Economic and Social Affairs, Sustainable Development*) <https://sdgs.un.org/goals/goal6> accessed 3 June 2023.
[78] Nada Al- Nashif, UN Deputy High Commissioner for Human Rights, '2020 High-level Political Forum, UN-WATER Official Launch of the SDG 6 Global Acceleration Framework' (*OHCHR*, 9 July 2020) <https://www.ohchr.org/EN/HRBodies/HRC/Pages/NewsDetail.aspx?NewsID=26062&LangID=E> accessed 3 June 2023; UN Water, *Sustainable Development Goal Synthesis Report on Water and Sanitation* (2018) 35 (hereafter 'Sustainable Development Goal Synthesis'); Programme Solidarité-Eau,

while committing themselves to ensuring access to safe drinking water in SDG Target 6.1, explicitly reaffirmed their commitment to the human right to water in the Agenda's Declaration.[79] Moreover, UN Water, an inter-agency mechanism which coordinates the efforts of United Nations entities and international organizations working on water and sanitation issues, stated that the human right to water is captured in SDG Target 6.1, as the latter seeks to secure water for drinking and hygiene purposes within households for all.[80]

Second, SDG Target 6.1 goes further than the human right to water when it comes to physical accessibility of water. The CESCR stated in 2002 that, under the human right to water, 'sufficient, safe and acceptable water must be accessible within, or in the immediate vicinity, of each household, educational institution and workplace.'[81] However, for the WHO/ United Nations International Children's Emergency Fund (UNICEF) Joint Monitoring Programme (JMP), the custodian of global data on Water Supply, Sanitation and Hygiene (WASH), the word 'universal' in SDG Target 6.1 implies that all settings, not only households, but also schools, healthcare facilities, workplaces, and other public spaces, are included.[82]

Furthermore, for the JMP, in order to meet the new global standard for safely managed drinking water services set out in the monitoring Indicator 6.1.1, a household must use an improved water source that is accessible on the premises (i.e. located within the dwelling, yard or plot).[83] This goes beyond the scope of the human right to water. As a comparison, the CESCR had stated that, under this right, adequate water facilities and services must be within safe physical reach for all sections of the population,[84] without being specific about when water services are considered to be within safe physical reach for all.

Third, just as with the human right to water,[85] SDG Target 6.1 calls for the elimination of inequalities in drinking water services. The link between SDG Target 6.1 and the principle of non-discrimination stems from two aspects. A first dimension is the commitment to 'leave no one behind' included in the 2030 Agenda for Sustainable Development, which 'aims to allow all people in all countries to benefit

Sustainable Development Goals for Water and Sanitation: Interpreting the Targets and Indicators (March 2018) 7.

[79] 2030 Agenda (n 5) 3.
[80] UN Water, 'Indicator 6.1.1 "Proportion of population using safely managed drinking water services"' <https://www.sdg6monitoring.org/indicators/target-61/> accessed 4 August 2023.
[81] General Comment No 15 (n 7) s 12.
[82] WHO and UNICEF, *Progress on Drinking Water, Sanitation and Hygiene: 2017 Update and SDG Baselines* (WHO 2017), 44 (hereafter 'Progress on Drinking Water'); HLPF, *Review of SDG Implementation: SDG 6-Ensure Availability and Sustainable Management of Water and Sanitation for All* (2018) 2 (hereafter 'Review of SDG Implementation'); UN Water, 'Sustainable Development Goal 6 Synthesis Report on Water and Sanitation' (*UN*, 2018) 11 <https://www.unwater.org/publications/sdg-6-synthesis-report-2018-on-water-and-sanitation/> accessed 3 June 2023.
[83] ibid (Progress on Drinking Water) 24.
[84] General Comment No 15 (n 7) s 12.
[85] ibid.

from socio-economic development and to achieve the full realization of human rights, without discrimination on the basis of gender, age, race, language, religion, political ... opinions, national or social origin, property, disability, residency status ... or any other social, economic or political status'.[86] For UN Water, such commitment requires an 'increased attention on disadvantaged groups and efforts to monitor elimination of inequalities in drinking water services'.[87]

A second dimension is that SDG Target 6.1, by calling for universal and equitable access to water for all, 'implies eliminating inequalities in service levels'.[88] The High-level Political Forum on Sustainable Development, the main United Nations platform entrusted with the task of following-up and reviewing the 2030 Agenda, has underscored the need to eliminate inequalities in access to water. For the UN platform, 'inequalities exist in every country where marginalized communities and disadvantaged groups such as women, children, the poor, indigenous peoples, rural communities and those living in fragile States do not have equal access to water ... '.[89] As we will see in the next section, SDG Target 6.1 has allowed for the putting in place of various means for eliminating discrimination.

It is also worth mentioning that the 2030 Agenda can assist in the realization of the human right to water through the variety of stakeholders that are called upon to implement the seventeen SDGs and their targets. One of the defining features of the 2030 Agenda is its universal nature.[90] It commits all UN Member States to contribute towards a comprehensive effort aiming at achieving the Agenda and its seventeen SDGs.[91] This implies, among others, working in synergy with other development partners to mobilize financial and technical assistance to strengthen their scientific, technological, and innovative capacities to achieve SDGs.[92] Therefore, all states, even those that are not parties to the International Covenant on Economic, Social and Cultural Rights (ICESCR) are called upon to implement SDG 6 by achieving universal access to water by 2030.

Moreover, the sustainable development landscape is expanding, encompassing an increasing number of new actors. Parliaments, regional and local authorities, research institutions, philanthropic organizations, international organizations and financial institutions, cooperatives, the private sector, and civil society have become instrumental partners in reaching the most vulnerable and marginalized

---

[86] World Water Assessment Programme (WWAP), 'The United Nations World Water Development Report: Leaving No One Behind' (*UNESCO*, 2019) 36 <https://en.unesco.org/themes/water-security/wwap/wwdr/2019#download> accessed 3 June 2023.
[87] Sustainable Development Goal Synthesis (n 78) 11.
[88] Progress on Drinking Water (n 82) 7.
[89] Review of SDG Implementation (n 82) 6.
[90] *Universality and the 2030 Agenda for Sustainable Development: From a UNDG Lens. Discussion Note* (2016) 1.
[91] 2030 Agenda (n 5) preamble, s 2.
[92] ibid Declaration ss 28 and 39; UNGA, *Addis Ababa Action Agenda of the Third International Conference on Financing for Development (Addis Ababa Action Agenda)* (A/RES/69/313, 17 August 2015) ss 35–36 (hereafter 'Addis Ababa Action Agenda').

people and achieving the SDGs.[93] Multi-stakeholder partnerships and the resources, knowledge, and expertise of these actors complement the efforts of governments in achieving the SDGs.[94]

Achieving SDG 6 therefore means acting both nationally and internationally. The participation of a wide range of actors is required. In this context, it is interesting to note that the CESCR has recommended 'that the State[s] part[ies] take fully into account their obligations under the Covenant and ensure the full enjoyment of the [human right to water] enshrined therein in the implementation of the 2030 Agenda for Sustainable Development at the national level, with international assistance and cooperation'.[95] The 2030 Agenda is thus acknowledged as an important driver for achieving the right to water, while also a means for developing its content further still.

5. The Human Right to Water, SDG 6, and the Fight against Discrimination

The fight against discrimination plays a crucial role for universal access to water for all. Since 1990, the JMP has been drawing attention to inequalities in access to safe drinking water. It does so by highlighting inequalities between rural and urban areas, between rich and poor, and between other groups and the general population.[96]

As opposed to the MDG target, which aimed to halve the proportion of the population without access to drinking water and sanitation services by focusing on aggregate coverage[97] that concealed disparities affecting the poorest

---

[93] 2030 Agenda (n 5) Declaration s 52; Petrică Nițoaial and Gabriel Camară, 'Roles of Actors in Promoting Sustainable Development' (2018) 12(1) De Gruyter Open 170; Jens Martens, 'The Role of Public and Private Actors and Means in Implementing the SDGs: Reclaiming the Public Policy Space for Sustainable Development and Human Rights' in Markus Kaltenborn, Markus Krajewski, and Heike Kuhn (eds), *Sustainable Development Goals and Human Rights* (Interdisciplinary Studies in Human Rights, vol 5, Springer 2020) 208 (hereafter 'The Role of Public and Private Actors').

[94] Addis Ababa Action Agenda (n 92) s 10; ibid (The Role of Public and Private Actors) 209.

[95] CESCR, *Concluding Observations on the Seventh Periodic Report of Ukraine* (E/C12/UKR/CO/7, 2 April 2020) s 50.

[96] WHO and UNICEF, *Safely Managed Drinking Water—Thematic Report on Drinking Water* (WHO 2017) 34.

[97] Aggregation is a way of transforming a multidimensional picture into a single value. In the context of the MDGs, aggregation appears in two dimensions: vertical and horizontal. Vertical aggregation in the MDGs follows a two-step process. In the first stage, indicators of a specific country are aggregated (averaged) into a single MDG target. In the second stage, the targets are aggregated (averaged) to obtain the average rate of progress for each goal. Horizontal aggregation refers to combining information on a single goal (or target or indicator) across various states, with the aim of representing a single value for regions. Aggregation conceals inequalities within states. Inequalities can occur along many dimensions: male/female, urban/rural, across regions, wealth quintiles, or different ethnic and racial groups. Discrimination on grounds of disability is also a critical factor fuelling inequality, though frequently overlooked in the context of the MDGs. The common use of averages and aggregate data in both global and country-level in MDG reporting has tended to make such inequalities invisible. For further details, see Degol Hailu and Raquel Tsukada, 'Achieving the Millennium Development Goals: A Measure of

groups,[98] the SDGs have a much stronger focus on inequalities, with Goal 10 dedicated to 'reducing inequalities between and within countries'.[99] SDG 10 calls for reducing inequalities in income as well as those based on age, sex, disability, race, ethnicity, origin, religion, economic, or other status within a state.[100] That Goal also addresses inequalities among states, including those related to representation, migration, and development assistance.[101]

The 2030 Agenda further commits UN Member States to 'leave no one behind'[102] and provides that SDG indicators should be disaggregated, where relevant, by income, sex, age, race, ethnicity, migratory status, disability and geographic location.[103] 'Leave no one behind' seeks to redress the failure of the MDGs to tackle inequalities by making progress for the poorest groups central to the realization of the SDGs.[104]

The principle of non-discrimination is a well-entrenched principle in human rights law.[105] Discrimination is defined as 'any distinction, exclusion, or restriction which has the purpose or the effect of impairing or nullifying the recognition, enjoyment or exercise, on an equal basis with others, of human rights and fundamental freedoms in the political, economic, social, cultural, civil or any other field.'[106]

Some obligations deriving from the human right to water are subject to progressive realization.[107] This means that states are required to take steps, individually and through international assistance and cooperation, to the maximum of their available resources, towards fulfilling progressively the human right to water.[108]

Progress' (Working Paper No 78, 2011) 9; CESCR, 'The MDGs, A Decade On: Keeping the Promise, Fulfilling Rights' (2010) <https://www.cesr.org/mdgs-decade-keeping-promise-fulfilling-rights/> accessed 3 June 2023.

[98] Emma Samman and others, '"Leave No One Behind"—Five Years into Agenda 2030: Guidelines for Turning the Concept into Action' (*ODI*, 2021) 14 (hereafter 'Leave No One Behind').
[99] 2030 Agenda (n 5) 21.
[100] ibid SDG Targets 10.1 and 10.2.
[101] ibid SDG Targets 10.6, 10.7, and 10.b.
[102] ibid Declaration s 4.
[103] ibid Declaration s 7 (g).
[104] Leave No One Behind (n 98).
[105] For an analysis of the right to water and the principle of non-discrimination, see Priscila Neves-Silva and Léo Heller, 'The Right to Water and Sanitation as a Tool for Health Promotion of Vulnerable Groups' (2016) 21(6) Ciência & Saude Coletiva 1861–70.
[106] UN Water, 'Eliminating Discrimination and Inequalities in Access to Water and Sanitation' (Policy and Analytic Briefs, UN Water Publications 2015) 8 <https://www.unwater.org/publications/eliminating-discrimination-inequalities-access-water-sanitation/> accessed 3 June 2023 (hereafter 'Eliminating Discrimination'); other instruments dedicated to the fight against discrimination include, inter alia, ILO's *Convention No 111 Convention concerning Discrimination in Respect of Employment and Occupation* (entered into force on 15 June 1960) art 1(1); *International Convention on the Elimination of All Forms of Racial Discrimination* (660 UNTS 195, entered into force on 4 January 1969) art 1(1); *Convention on the Elimination of All Forms of Discrimination against Women* (1249 UNTS 13, opened for signature 18 December 1979, entered into force 3 September 1981) art 1.
[107] ICESCR (n 54), art 2(1).
[108] ibid; Léo Heller, 'The Obligation of Progressive Realization in the Context of Human Rights to Water and Sanitation' (Report A/HRC/45/10, 2020) 1.

By contrast, the obligation of non-discrimination is of immediate effect.[109] This means that the state must immediately outlaw discrimination in laws, policies, and programmes.[110] To comply with their obligation of non-discrimination in the realization of the human right to water, states must eliminate both formal and substantive discrimination.[111] While eliminating formal discrimination requires ensuring that 'a State's constitution, laws, and policy documents do not discriminate on prohibited grounds', eliminating substantive discrimination requires 'paying sufficient attention to groups of individuals which suffer historical or persistent prejudice instead of merely comparing the formal treatment of individuals in similar situations'.[112]

States parties must therefore immediately adopt the necessary measures to prevent, diminish, and eliminate the conditions and attitudes which cause or perpetuate substantive or *de facto* discrimination. For example, ensuring that all individuals have equal access to water will help to overcome discrimination against persons living in informal settlements and rural areas.[113]

Building on this crucial principle, various organizations are working towards the elimination of inequalities and discriminatory practices. With respect to access to water, the WHO/UNICEF JMP has made clear that there are not only significant inequalities in water services between regions and between states, but also within individual states and between urban and rural areas.[114] For the High-level Political Forum on Sustainable Development, inequalities exist in states where marginalized communities and disadvantaged groups, such as women, children, the poor, indigenous peoples, rural communities, and those living in fragile states, do not have equal access to water and are more susceptible to the impacts of pollution and water-related disasters.[115]

Groups and individuals particularly disadvantaged in access to water include, first and foremost, women and girls. For instance, studies indicate that in sub-Saharan Africa, 71 per cent of the burden of collecting water falls on women and girls.[116] In its General Recommendation No 34, the Committee on the Elimination of Discrimination against Women emphasized the gendered effects of water

---

[109] UNECE and World Health Organization Regional Office for Europe, *The Human Rights to Water and Sanitation in Practice: Findings and Lessons Learned from the Work on Equitable Access to Water and Sanitation under the Protocol on Water and Health in the Pan-European Region* (United Nations Publication 2019) ch 2, 11; Eliminating Discrimination (n 106) 10.
[110] Eliminating discrimination (n 106) 10.
[111] CESCR, *General Comment No 20: Non-Discrimination in Economic, Social and Cultural Rights (art 2, para 2, of the International Covenant on Economic, Social and Cultural Rights)* (E/C12/GC/20, July 2009) 3.
[112] ibid.
[113] ibid.
[114] Progress on Drinking Water (n 82) 34.
[115] Sustainable Development Goal Synthesis (n 78) 6.
[116] Eliminating Discrimination (n 106) 11; Anne Hellum, 'Engendering the Right to Water and Sanitation: Integrating the Experiences of Women and Girls' in Malcolm Langford and Anna F. S. Russell (eds), *The Human Right to Water: Theory, Practice and Prospects* (CUP 2017) 276–99.

scarcity. It noted that rural women and girls are among those who are the most affected by water scarcity, as they are frequently obliged to walk long distances to fetch it, sometimes exposing them to a heightened risk of sexual violence and attack.[117]

Race, ethnicity, religion, and nationality are also grounds of discrimination in access to water. In some states, indigenous peoples, pastoralists, and/or nomadic communities lack access to safe water in disproportionate numbers.[118] Migrant workers or asylum seekers often face difficulties in accessing water, as host states do not make such facilities available to them.[119]

Disability, age, and health status are sometimes grounds of discrimination with respect to access to water.[120] In some states, people with disabilities are disproportionately represented among those that do not enjoy their right to water, as public water facilities are often not designed to meet their needs.[121] Accessibility problems also apply to children, those who are (chronically) ill and older people, as facilities may not be within easy and safe reach.[122]

Residence and economic and social status may also be grounds for discrimination when it comes to access to water.[123] Global monitoring shows a stark discrepancy between persons living in rural and urban areas. For instance, in 2012, 3.6 per cent of the urban population lacked access to an improved water source compared to 18.8 per cent of the rural population.[124]

This data shows why improving data disaggregation is fundamental for the full implementation of the 2030 Agenda. In this regard, the UN Statistical Commission has requested the Inter-Agency and Expert Group on SDG Indicators (IAEG-SDGs) to make efforts to develop the necessary statistical standards and tools, and build capacity on disaggregated data to measure progress for those who are vulnerable or in vulnerable situations.[125] In response to this request, the IAEG-SDGs has developed and compiled a series of tools and resources for states including: (i) a compilation of categories and dimensions of data disaggregation currently in place and planned by custodian agencies for the global SDG indicators; (ii) the development of a minimum disaggregation set; (iii) a comprehensive summary of disaggregation standards that currently exist for all SDG indicators; and (iv) a compilation

---

[117] CEDW, *General Recommendation No 34 on the Rights of Rural Women* CEDAW/C/GC/34 (2016) s 82.
[118] Eliminating Discrimination (n 106) 13.
[119] ibid.
[120] ibid.
[121] ibid.
[122] ibid.
[123] ibid 14.
[124] ibid.
[125] IAEG-SDGs and United Nations Statistics Division (UNSD), 'IAEG-SDGs, Data Disaggregation for the SDG Indicators' (*UN Sustainable Development Goals*) <https://unstats.un.org/sdgs/iaeg-sdgs/disaggregation/> accessed 4 June 2023.

of policy priorities concerning the most vulnerable population groups.[126] These tools help assess progress in a manner that had not been pursued earlier.

The global indicators for SDG Target 6.1 play a key role in the elimination of discrimination and inequalities in access to water by revealing and tracking inequalities through the use of data disaggregated by income, sex, age, race, ethnicity, migration status, disability, geographic location, and other characteristics relevant in national contexts. However, disaggregated data alone does not automatically result in reduction of inequalities. Governments and other stakeholders need to take measures to tackle the inequalities that are revealed.[127]

6. Corporate Accountability, the Human Right to Water, and SDG 6

The private sector is one of the key players for achieving SDG 6 by providing resources, expertise, and knowledge to complement governments' related efforts.[128] Indeed, while sustainable service delivery for water relies primarily on domestic public resources and international development aid, private investments are critical to achieving universal access to safe and affordable drinking water by 2030, as public resources do not suffice.[129]

The president of the 72nd Session of the UNGA underscored the importance of private investments for achieving SDG 6 on universal access to water in 2017. It stated that '[t]raditional financial sources, including official development assistance, are not sufficient, even though critical for many developing countries. We must rely on all sources available, national and international, public and private, ...'[130] He further mentioned that the private sector must be involved in developing

---

[126] IAEG-SDGs and UNSD, *Compilation of Tools/guidance of Existing Materials for Data Disaggregation* (2021) 3.

[127] Eliminating Discrimination (n 106) 31–32.

[128] 2030 Agenda (n 5) 29; Addis Ababa Action Agenda (n 92) 6; Dina Hestad, 'The Evolution of Private Sector Action in Sustainable Development' Brief 12 (International Institute for Sustainable Development 2021); Lesley Pories, Catarina Fonseca, and Victoria Delmon, 'Mobilising Finance for WASH: Getting the Foundation Right' (2019) 10 Water 2425.

[129] 2030 Agenda (n 5) 11; Addis Ababa Action Agenda (n 92) 8 and 18; Laurence Boisson de Chazournes, 'The Sustainable Development Goals (SDGs) and The Rule of Law: A Propos SDG 6 on Access to Water and Sanitation' in American Society of International Law (ed), *Proceedings of the ASIL Annual Meeting: The Promise of International Law, Sustainable Development and International Law* (CUP 2021) 146 (hereafter 'The Sustainable Development Goals').

[130] Miroslav Lajčák, 'Achieving Universal Access to Water and Sanitation' (2018) LV(1) The Quest for Water <Achieving Universal Access to Water and Sanitation | United Nations> accessed 4 June 2023; see also the opening remarks by Angel Gurría, OECD Secretary-General during the OECD's Private Finance for Sustainable Development (PF4SD) Conference: Angel Gurría, 'Private Finance for Sustainable Development (PF4SD) Conference' (*OECD* 2020) <https://www.oecd.org/development/private-finance-for-sustainable-development-conference-paris-january-2020.htm> accessed 4 June 2023; Islamic Development Bank, 'Financing the Sustainable Development Goals: The Contributions of the Multilateral Development Banks, Report' (2020) v.

plans and policies aiming at achieving universal access to safe and affordable drinking water for all by 2030.[131] The UNGA itself did not hesitate in 2015 to call upon the private sector in its multiple forms, ranging from micro-enterprises to co-operatives to multinationals, to apply its creativity and innovation to implementing the 2030 Agenda, including the SDGs.[132]

While corporations do not have the legal obligation of states to protect and fulfil the human right to water,[133] the baseline for all business enterprises under international law is that they have the responsibility to respect the human right of individuals and communities to water while carrying out their activities.[134] This means they should avoid infringing the human right to water of others and should address adverse impacts on access to water with which they are involved.[135] Discharging the responsibility to respect the human right to water requires due diligence whereby companies become aware of, prevent, and mitigate adverse impacts on access to water of their activities and relationships.[136] Moreover, to deliver on SDG 6, corporations are encouraged to support government and other stakeholder efforts to provide universal access to clean water. They can do so by undertaking commitments or activities to support and promote access to water.[137]

The UN Global Compact, a voluntary initiative based on corporations' commitments to implement universal sustainability principles, has developed two initiatives related to private companies and water governance. The first one is the CEO Water Mandate, a public-private initiative launched in 2007 that mobilizes

---

[131] ibid (Lajčák).
[132] 2030 Agenda (n 5) Declaration ss 41 and 67.
[133] United Nations, 'Protect, Respect and Remedy' Framework for Business and Human Rights (2010) 2; OHCHR, Frequently Asked Questions about the Guiding Principles on Business and Human Rights (2014) 28 (hereafter 'OHCHR, Frequently Asked Questions'); John Gerard Ruggie, 'Entreprises et Droits de l'homme: Nouvelles Mesures pour la Mise en Œuvre du Cadre de Référence "Protéger, Respecter et Réparer"' (A/HRC/14/27, 2010) s 55; John Gerard Ruggie, 'The Corporate Responsibility to Respect Human Rights' (Harvard Law School Forum on Corporate Governance 2010) <https://corpgov.law.harvard.edu/2010/05/15/the-corporate-responsibility-to-respect-human-rights/> accessed 4 June 2023; Carlos López, The Ruggie Process: From Legal Obligations to Corporate Social Responsibility? (CUP 2013) 65; Robert McCorquodale, 'Corporate Social Responsibility, and International Human Rights Law' (2009) 87 J Bus Ethics 391.
[134] UN, Guiding Principles on Business and Human Rights: Implementing the United Nations 'Protect, Respect and Remedy' Framework (2011) 13 (hereafter 'UN Guiding Principles'); OECD, OECD Guidelines for Multinational Enterprises (OECD Publishing 2011) 31 (hereafter 'OECD Guiding Principles'); ILO, Tripartite Declaration of Principles concerning Multinational Enterprises and Social Policy (2017) 4; IHRB, 'Business, Human Rights and the Right to Water: Challenges, Dilemmas and Opportunities, Roundtable Consultative Report' (Business & Human Rights Resource Centre, 2009) 4 <[PDF] Draft - Business, Human Rights and the Right to Water: Challenges, Dilemmas and Opportunities, Roundtable Consultative Report - Business & Human Rights Resource Centre (business-humanrights.org)> accessed 4 June 2023.
[135] ibid (UN Guiding Principles) (OECD Guiding Principles).
[136] ibid; John Gerard Ruggie, 'Protect, Respect and Remedy: A United Nations Policy Framework for Business and Human Rights', in American Society of International Law (ed), Proceedings of the Annual Meeting: International Law as Law (CUP 2009) 285.
[137] UN Guiding Principles (n 134), 13; OHCHR Frequently Asked Questions (n 133) 10.

business leaders on water, sanitation, and the SDGs.[138] In particular, as a commitment platform, the Mandate gathers a number of business leaders to address global water challenges through Corporate Water Stewardship,[139] an emerging paradigm for private-sector participation in water resources management. In this context, some private actors including multinationals that have endorsed the CEO Water Mandate, have undertaken water-saving measures and initiatives to increase local access to drinking water and enhance sustainable management of water resources through Corporate Water Stewardship.[140]

For the Alliance for Water Stewardship (AWS), a global membership collaboration comprising businesses, non-governmental organizations, and the public sector and promoting sustainable management of water resources, Water Stewardship refers to 'the use of water that is socially and culturally equitable, environmentally sustainable and economically beneficial, achieved through a stakeholder-inclusive process that includes both site- and catchment- based actions.'[141] Water Stewardship goes beyond short-term-oriented corporate social responsibility/philanthropic activities, to include companies recognizing that water is a strategic issue of their business and crucial for long-term growth opportunities, rather than just an issue leading to reputational gains.[142] In fact, Corporate Water Stewardship is rooted in the premise that effective public water governance is critical to the long-term business viability of water-intensive industries and that companies can play a role in achieving this end.[143]

Corporate Water Stewardship allows companies to identify and manage water-related business risks, understand and mitigate their adverse impacts on ecosystems and communities, and contribute to more sustainable management of shared freshwater resources.[144] This concept has the potential to increase water security by promoting access to water and enforcing sustainable water management through companies' operations and supply chains.[145] For instance, through Corporate Water Stewardship Programs, some business enterprises have been able

---

[138] CEO Water Mandate, 'What is the Mandate?' (*UN Global Compact*) <https://ceowatermandate.org/about/what-is-the-mandate> accessed 4 June 2023.
[139] ibid.
[140] Examples include: Unilever, 'Water Stewardship' (*Unilever*) <https://www.unilever.com/planet-and-society/protect-and-regenerate-nature/water-stewardship/> accessed 4 June 2023; PepsiCo, 'Water' (*PepsiCo*) <https://www.pepsico.com/esg-topics-a-z/water> accessed 4 June 2023; Coca Cola, 'Water Stewardship' <https://www.coca-colacompany.com/sustainability/water-stewardship> accessed 7 August 2023.
[141] Alliance for Water Stewardship (AWS), 'About the Alliance for water Stewardship' (*Alliance for Water Stewardship*) <https://a4ws.org/about/> accessed 4 June 2023.
[142] Jasmin Guggisberg and others, '(Corporate) Water Stewardship: A Study on the Critical Success Factors and Financing Mechanisms for Water Stewardship Projects at the Field Level' University of St Gallen (2017) 10 (hereafter '(Corporate) Water Stewardship').
[143] Pacific Institute, 'Corporate Water Stewardship' (*Pacific Institute*) <https://pacinst.org/corporate-water-stewardship/> accessed 4 June 2023.
[144] (Corporate) Water Stewardship (n 142) 8.
[145] Jessica Williams, 'Water Flows towards Money: The Private Sector and Water Governance' Global Water Forum (2015) 2.

to provide local communities with safe drinking water and contribute to water conservation.[146]

The second initiative developed by the CEO Water Mandate to foster private actors' commitments for sustainable management of water resources is the 'Guide to Responsible Business Engagement with Water Policy', which was published in 2010.[147] The goal of this guide is to make a compelling case for responsible water policy engagement and to support it with insights, strategies, and tactics needed to do so effectively.[148] Corporate engagement with water policy is defined broadly as

> initiatives that involve interaction with government entities, local communities, and/or civil society organizations with the goal of advancing two objectives: 1) responsible internal management of water resources within direct operations and supply chains in line with policy imperatives ... and 2) the sustainable and equitable management of the catchment in which companies and their suppliers operate.[149]

The guide identifies five aspirational principles that underpin responsible water policy engagement. First, responsible corporate engagement in water policy must be motivated by a genuine interest in furthering efficient, equitable, and ecologically sustainable water management.[150] Second, responsible corporate engagement in water policy entails ensuring that activities do not infringe upon, but rather support, the government's mandate and responsibilities to develop and implement water policy.[151] Third, responsible engagement in water policy promotes inclusiveness and meaningful partnerships across a wide range of interests.[152] Fourth, responsible engagement in water policy proceeds in a coherent manner that recognizes the interconnectedness between water and many other policy arenas.[153] Fifth, companies engaged in responsible water policy are fully transparent and accountable for their role in a way that ensures alignment with sustainable water management and promotes trust among stakeholders.[154]

While these initiatives are based on commitments voluntarily undertaken by corporations, a question remains as to the effects deriving from these

---

[146] Examples include the Nestlé's Water, Sanitation and Hygiene promotion (WASH) program which helped over 465,000 people in Nestlé's cocoa farming communities in Ghana and in Côte d'Ivoire to have access to safe drinking water. See Christian Vousvouras, 'WASH in Africa' (2021) <https://www.nestle.com/stories/nestle-ifrc-partnership-africa> accessed 4 June 2023.

[147] CEO Water Mandate, 'Guide to Responsible Business Engagement with Water Policy' (The Global Compact 2010) 112.

[148] ibid 12.
[149] ibid 13.
[150] ibid 36.
[151] ibid 37.
[152] ibid.
[153] ibid 38.
[154] ibid.

commitments.[155] Building on commitments through programmes and activities is a way to take private operators at their word, to assess their impacts, and to build effectiveness.[156] This allows for dialogues to be engaged and accountability to play a role.[157] Accountability is indeed crucial for building trust with all stakeholders and concerned actors.

The activities of private companies can adversely affect the availability and sustainable management of water resources. For instance, mining-related water usage and investment activities in farmlands can have a significant impact on the quality, quantity, and availability of water in countries around the world.[158] In this context, issues concerning access to safe drinking water and damage to water resources have been brought before international arbitral tribunals in disputes concerning tariff regimes and their effect on the affordability of water,[159] failures to establish a contractually agreed number of water connections,[160] and threats of pollution of drinking water resources.[161]

Interestingly, in the case concerning *Urbaser v Argentina*, which dealt with a dispute over privatized water supply services, the tribunal referred to the notion of corporate social responsibility. The claimant in the *Urbaser* case was a shareholder in a corporate concessionaire that supplied water and sewerage services in Buenos Aires.[162] Following Argentina's financial crisis in 2001–02, the latter Argentina adopted emergency measures that exacerbated the concession's financial difficulties.[163] After the concessionaire had become insolvent, the claimant commenced arbitral proceedings against Argentina for violations of the Spain-Argentina bilateral investment treaty.[164] Argentina raised counterclaims, based on the concessionaire's failure to provide the necessary level of investment in the concession, which it claimed, led to violations of the human right to water.[165] The tribunal started its analysis by opposing the assertion that 'guaranteeing the human right to water is a duty that may be born solely by the State'.[166] It further rejected

---

[155] The Sustainable Development Goals (n 129) 147.
[156] ibid.
[157] ibid.
[158] Richard Frimpong Oppong, 'SDG 6: Clean Water and Sanitation' in Ralf Michaels, Verónica Ruiz Abou-Nigm, and Hans van Loon (eds), *The Private Side of Transforming our World—UN Sustainable Development Goals 2030 and the Role of Private International Law* (Intersentia Online 2021) 2 <https://www.intersentiaonline.com/publication/the-private-side-of-transforming-our-world-un-sustainable-development-goals-2030-and-the-role-of-p/8> accessed 7 August 2023.
[159] See, for example, *Compañiá de Aguas del Aconquija SA and Vivendi Universal SA v Argentine Republic* [2007] ICSID Case No ARB/97/3 Award [20 August 2007].
[160] See, for example, *Impregilo SpA v Argentine Republic* [2011] ICSID Case No ARB/07/17 Award [21 June 2011] s 262.
[161] See, for example, *Azurix Corp v The Argentine Republic* [2006] ICSID Case No ARB/01/12 Award [14 July 2006].
[162] *Urbaser SA and Consorcio de Aguas Bilbao Bizkaia, Bilbao Biskaia Ur Partzuergoa v The Argentine Republic* [2016] ICSID Case No ARB/07/26, Award [8 December 2016] s 34.
[163] ibid.
[164] ibid s 35.
[165] ibid ss 36–37.
[166] ibid s 1193.

the view that corporations are not subjects of international law by stating that such a principle 'has lost its impact and relevance'.[167] While relying on various types of instruments[168], the tribunal explained that corporate social responsibility requires corporations to conduct their operations in a manner that complies with human rights.[169]

For the tribunal, both public and private actors are bound by human rights obligations.[170] While the tribunal was not specific about the content of the human rights obligations incumbent upon businesses, the language used suggests that these are 'do-not-harm'-type obligations.[171] For the tribunal, to ensure that companies are subject to appropriate obligations 'the focus must be, therefore, on contextualizing a corporation's specific activities as they relate to the human right at issue in order to determine whether any international law obligations attach to the non-State individual'.[172]

This sheds light on the issue of corporate human rights obligations in international law. As previously mentioned, private sector actors are not bound directly by international treaties ratified by states which deal with access to water.[173] States have the obligation to protect their people against human rights abuses within their territory and/or jurisdiction by third parties, including business enterprises.[174] However, the UN Guiding Principles on Business and Human Rights clarify that business enterprises have the responsibility to respect human rights including the human right to water.[175]

The corporate responsibility to respect human rights means that corporations should act with due diligence to avoid infringing on the human rights of others, and to identify, prevent, and address any harms that do occur.[176] This entails a need to assess human rights impacts, integrate respect for human rights across the corporation internally, and track, as well as communicate on how to address, human rights impacts.[177]

The responsibility of business enterprises to respect the human right to water is distinct from issues of legal liability, which remain largely defined by national

---

[167] ibid s 1194.
[168] ibid ss 1196–98.
[169] ibid s 1195.
[170] Laurence Boisson de Chazournes, 'Changes in the Balance of Rights and Obligations: Towards Investor Responsabilization', in *La Protection des Investissements Étrangers* (Pédone 2018) 92.
[171] ibid.
[172] *Urbaser SA and Consorcio de Aguas Bilbao Bizkaia, Bilbao Biskaia Ur Partzuergoa v The Argentine Republic* [2016] ICSID Case No ARB/07/26 Award [8 December 2016] s 1195.
[173] Mara Tignino, 'Private Investments and the Human Right to Water' in Yannick Radi (ed), *Research Handbook on Human Rights and Investments* (Edward Elgar 2018) 482 <https://archive-ouverte.unige.ch/unige:101268> accessed 7 August 2023.
[174] ibid; UN Guiding Principles (n 134) 13.
[175] ibid (UN Guiding Principles); see also OECD Guiding Principles (n 134) 31; ILO, *Tripartite Declaration of Principles concerning Multinational Enterprises and Social Policy* (2017) 4, s 10, let. a.
[176] UN Guiding Principles (n 134).
[177] ibid.

law provisions in relevant jurisdictions.[178] It is a global standard of expected conduct for all business enterprises wherever they operate and exists independently of states' abilities and/or willingness to fulfil their own human rights obligations.[179]

As said, at the national level, individuals may bring actions before courts and tribunals alleging adverse impact on water resources arising from business activities and they can be successful in their endeavours. For instance, in *Vedanta v Lungowe*, residents of the Zambian city of Chingola brought proceedings in the English courts in 2015 against Vedanta Resources Plc (Vedanta), a UK incorporated parent company, and Konkola Copper Mines Plc (KCM), its Zambian subsidiary, claiming that waste discharged from the Nchanga copper mine, owned and operated by KCM, had polluted the local waterways that provide their only source of water for drinking and irrigation for their crops.[180] Both Vedanta and KCM challenged jurisdiction. In 2016, the High Court of London held that the claimants could bring their case in England, despite the fact that the alleged tort and harm occurred in Zambia, where both the claimants and KCM are domiciled.[181] This decision was upheld on appeal by the Court of Appeal in October 2017.[182] In April 2019, the Supreme Court unanimously dismissed the companies' appeal, upholding the Court of Appeal's ruling.[183]

While framed as a domestic tort law case, the decision of the Supreme Court is significant for international efforts aimed at holding businesses accountable for their adverse impacts on human rights, including the human right to water. It suggests that 'parent companies that hold themselves out in public disclosures as overseeing the human rights, environmental, social, or labor standards employed by their subsidiaries assume a duty of care to those harmed by the subsidiary.'[184]

Subsequently, the Supreme Court of Canada said in 2020 that 'it is not 'plain and obvious' that corporations today enjoy a blanket exclusion under customary international law from direct liability for violations of 'obligatory, definable, and universal norms of international law'.[185] In the aforementioned case, the judicial organ mentioned that the breaches of customary international law relied on by the plaintiffs may well apply to the company.[186] In doing so, the Supreme Court opened the door to common law civil liability for extraterritorial corporate human rights abuses.

---

[178] Nicolas Bueno and Claire Bright, Implementing Human Rights due Diligence through Corporate Civil Liability (2020) 69 Int Comp Law Q 793.
[179] UN Guiding Principles (n 134).
[180] *Vedanta Resources Plc and Konkola Copper Mines Plc v Lungowe and Ors* [2019] UKSC 20, s 1.
[181] ibid s 5.
[182] ibid.
[183] ibid.
[184] Tara Van Ho, 'Vedanta Resources Plc and Another v Lungowe and Others in American' (2020) 114(1) AJIL 110.
[185] *Nevsun Resources Ltd v Araya* [2020] SCC 5, s 113.
[186] ibid s 114.

7. Conclusion

Access to safe drinking water is an internationally recognized human right. In September 2015, the UN Member States brought a new dimension to the human right to water by committing themselves to ensuring universal and equitable access to safe drinking water in SDG 6 of the 2030 Agenda. In doing so, they contributed to enlarging the scope of the right to water, while putting in place the means for preventing discrimination. This reinforces the crucial role of the right to water in achieving the SDGs.

The UN Member States also emphasized that achieving universal access to safe drinking water for all by 2030 requires a whole-of-society approach. Governments, citizens, civil society organizations, academia, and the private sector all have roles to play in contributing to the sustainable management of water resources. Indeed, while service delivery for water relies primarily on domestic public resources and international development aid, private investments are an important part of achieving universal access to safe and affordable drinking water by 2030, as public resources will not suffice. As a way of encouraging private actors to assist with securing universal access to safe drinking water, certain initiatives have been developed to incentivize the positive impact that business activities can have on water resources. This is a welcome step forward and it is hoped further steps are made in this direction in the near future.

PART III
THE ROLE OF ENVIRONMENTAL, HUMANITARIAN, AND REFUGEE LAW

10
Environmental Law and Climate Change: A Perspective from Africa

Bakary Kanté

1. Introduction

The United Nations (UN) has described climate change as the 'long-term shifts in temperatures and weather patterns'. The global temperature has been increasing steadily since 1900. More specifically, there has been an increase of 1°C. These long-term shifts in temperatures and weather patterns are real. The globe is getting warmer and we are experiencing extreme weather patterns, such as intense floods and severe droughts as a result of this environmental challenge.[1]

The causes of global warming, climate change, and the consequences are primarily anthropogenic. The causes are multiple and they include the burning of fossil fuels, unsustainable land-use practices, such as the massive deforestation and agriculture, and industrial processes. The anthropogenic causes responsible for climate change are primarily greenhouse gases (GHGs), such as carbon dioxide (CO_2) (65 per cent), methane (CH) (16 per cent), nitrous oxide (NOx) (6 per cent), and chlorofluorocarbons (CFCs) (2 per cent).[2] The increase in global temperatures is likely to continue if immediate and concrete actions are not taken to curb the root causes.

These changes are already undermining the life-supporting systems, society, the economy, overall development, and human well-being. The impacts are already being felt more by the poorer and vulnerable population of society. Africa is one region where its poor and vulnerable communities are feeling the pinch of the threats posed by climate change.[3] This is partly due to the inadequate capacity possessed

---

[1] UN Climate Action, 'What is Climate Change?' (*Climate Action*) <https://www.un.org/en/climatechange/what-is-climate-change> accessed 4 June 2023.

[2] Lal Kurukulasuriya, 'MEAS Dealing With Climate Change: UNFCC, Kyoto Protocol And Paris Agreement' (International Network for Environmental Compliance and Enforcement (INECE) Presentation, January 2021).

[3] United Nations Framework Convention on Climate Change (UNFCCC), 'Climate Change is an Increasing Threat to Africa' (*United Nations Climate Change*, 27 October 2020) https://unfccc.int/news/climate-change-is-an-increasing-threat-to-africa accessed 4 June 2023 (hereafter 'Climate Change').

by the region to adapt to climate change and its impacts. This is compounded by the deficiency in know-how and other solutions to address the crisis.[4]

A number of strategies exist to control and manage the root causes of climate change and the adverse effects. One important strategy among the numerous interventions is the law. This chapter will discuss the role of law in addressing climate change. It will first highlight some of the impacts of climate change on the three dimensions of sustainable development, namely the environment, society, and the economy with a perspective from Africa. It will discuss some of the avenues existing within the scope of law that may be instrumental in reversing or slowing down the climate change challenge by elaborating on the basic rights relating to the environment; relevant concepts and principles of law, both within international and domestic laws relevant to the environment; the environmental rule of law; and the evolving climate litigation. Finally, it will offer some thoughts on the way forward regarding the climate challenge and its impact, and the role of law in furtherance of sustainable development.

2. Impacts of Climate Change on Sustainable Development

Climate change and sustainable development are intertwined. Climate change and its impacts can undermine sustainable development. The range of consequences of climate change can include degradation and loss of biodiversity, natural disasters, immigration and conflict, poverty, and economic losses among others, as will be shown.

a. Impacts on the environment

The impacts of climate change on the environment are already visible. Due to the long-term increase in temperatures, oceans are becoming warmer and acidic, and the glaciers or ice caps are melting and filling the ocean. Due to that, the sea level within the last one hundred years has risen between 10 and 25 cm. It is predicted that the figures may double to approximately 50 cm in the next century or it may worsen to approximately 95 cm if a business-as-usual situation persists. The rise in sea level poses a significant threat to coastal ecosystems. The warmer temperatures are also causing coral bleaching in some parts of the world. In addition, the change in the climate can affect ecosystems generally. The change can disrupt the functioning of ecosystems that may increase the risk of harm or extinction of some species. Ecosystems provide food, however, the change may disrupt the constant

---

[4] UN Development Programme (UNDP), *Climate Change Adaptation in Africa UNDP Synthesis of Experiences and Recommendations* (2018).

supply of food. Furthermore, many parts of the world have experienced changes in rainfall, resulting in more floods, droughts, or intense rain, and more frequent and severe heat waves. The frequency of wildfires has increased in recent years. The United States (US) alone has recorded an average of 70,000 wildfires per year since 1983.[5]

Climate change is already having an impact on Africa's poor and vulnerable communities. Stress on water resources, devastating floods, drought caused by La Niña, and invasion of locusts are visible signs witnessed in the continent. In addition, sea level rise is said to reach 5 mm per year in some areas whereas in other areas it has exceeded 5 mm per year, especially in the south-western Indian Ocean from Madagascar toward Mauritius. This increase is higher than the average global sea level rise, which is 3–4 mm per year. This is causing degradation and erosion of the coastlines of the continent, especially in West Africa. It is estimated that 56 per cent of the coastlines of Benin, Côte d'Ivoire, Senegal, and Togo are eroding and the situation is expected to worsen in the future. Furthermore, Southern Africa suffered extensive drought in 2019. On the other hand, the normally drier areas, especially the Greater Horn of Africa witnessed a shift from very dry conditions in 2018 and most part of 2019 to floods and landslides due to heavy rainfall in late 2019. Flooding was also witnessed in the Sahel and the surrounding areas from May to October 2019.[6]

b. Impacts on society

Climate-induced sea level rise threatens coastal communities. As the ocean swells, people's land and homes get buried under water and it displaces them. At times they end up becoming climate refugees. Wherever they relocate to, they face new social problems including discrimination and land tenure conflicts. In addition, salt water intrusion contaminates potable water and destroys their food gardens.[7]

Prolonged droughts also threaten crop productivity and food security. In drought prone areas of Africa, the primary risks to agriculture, especially crop productivity, are linked with heat and increased pest damage, disease damage, and flood impacts on food system infrastructure that results in serious adverse effects

---

[5] US Environmental Protection Agency (EPA), 'Climate Change Indicators: Ecosystems' (*US Environmental Protection Agency*, 12 May 2021) <https://www.epa.gov/climate-indicators/ecosystems> accessed 4 June 2023; Alan Buis, 'The Climate Connection of a Record Fire Year in the US West' (*NASA Global Climate Change*, 22 February 2021) <https://climate.nasa.gov/ask-nasa-climate/3066/the-climate-connections-of-a-record-fire-year-in-the-us-west/> accessed 4 June 2023.

[6] Hope Mafaranga, 'Sea Level Rise may Erode Development in Africa' (*Eos*, 13 November 2020) <https://doi.org/10.1029/2020EO151568> accessed at 4 June 2023.

[7] Integrated Regional Information Networks, 'Papua New Guinea: The World's First Climate 'Refugee'' (*Worldpress.org*, 11 June 2008) <https://www.worldpress.org/Asia/3171.cfm> accessed 4 June 2023 (hereafter 'Papua New Guinea').

on food security and livelihoods. It is predicted that by the middle of this century, cereal crops in Africa will be negatively affected. UN Framework Convention on Climate Change (UNFCCC) predicts that 'under the worst case climate change scenario, a reduction in mean yield of 13 per cent is projected in West and Central Africa, 11 per cent in North Africa, and 8 per cent in East and Southern Africa'.[8]

Increases in temperature and the changing patterns in rainfall is predicted to have health ramifications for the African region. Warmer temperatures and higher rainfall can increase habitat suitability for insects that transmit diseases, such as dengue fever, malaria, and yellow fever. It has been witnessed recently that new diseases are emerging in areas where they never existed before. For instance, it is estimated that in 2017, 93 per cent of global malaria deaths occurred in Africa. Malaria epidemic occurs after heavy rainfall. Furthermore, malaria carrying mosquitoes now tend to survive on higher altitudes of East Africa due to the warming of the highlands.[9]

c. Economic impacts

Climate change certainly has some economic ramifications. The World Bank has predicted that the climate crisis will increase the costs of development in the poorest countries by between 25 and 30 per cent. This is of particular impact on Africa because many of the poor live in Sub-Saharan Africa. The climate crisis and its impacts on the various sectors, including health, environment and natural resources, agriculture, crop production, and food security, all come at a social and/ or economic cost. Take for instance the agriculture and natural resource sectors. Yields in some countries are predicted to reduce by 50 per cent and net revenues will be reduced by 90 per cent by 2100. In Namibia, it is predicted that the impacts of climate change on agriculture and livestock can reduce gross domestic product (GDP) by 1–6 per cent over twenty years. In the energy sector it is predicted that cooling demand and energy costs will increase with a possible 30 per cent increase. In addition, data in East Africa reveals that the cost of major flood and drought in East Africa is equivalent to 10 per cent or more of GDP, and represents a long-term liability that will affect long-term economic growth. The loss of ecosystem services and biodiversity, especially coral bleaching, in Kenya contributed to the losses in the tourism sector for the country. These are only a few illustrations of economic losses tied to climate change and its impacts.[10]

---

[8] Climate Change (n 3).
[9] ibid.
[10] Paul Watkiss, 'Economics of Climate Change: Key Messages' (Financing for Development, Conference on Climate Change, 2009).

3. Legal Responses to Climate Change and its Impacts

The law has been instrumental in shaping numerous positive outcomes. In particular, as will be demonstrated, the law's deterring power has regulated negative behaviour and prevented the recurrence of wrongdoing. Likewise, it has a significant role to play in rectifying behaviour that causes climate change and its adverse impacts. It is high time the law must be applied strictly to regulate behaviour and punish those are responsible for contributing to the root causes of climate change and its consequences. This summary statement can be made primarily because of the fact that climate change and its adverse effects have reached a critical stage now where, if immediate actions are not taken to halt or reverse the trend, then there is a point of no return where the life supporting systems will crumble and humanity will face its own extinction.

a. Environmental rule of law

The environmental rule of law has been adopted from the general definition of rule of law for application in the environmental context, including climate change and its impacts. The general description of rule of law has its origin from the 2004 Report of the Secretary General of the United Nations. It provides:

> [The rule of law] refers to a principle of governance in which all persons, institutions and entities, public and private, including the State itself are accountable to laws that are publicly promulgated, equally enforced and independently adjudicated, and which are consistent with international human rights, norms and standards. It requires as well, measures to ensure adherence to the principles of supremacy of law, equality before the law, accountability to the law, separation of powers, participation in decision-making, legal certainty, avoidance of arbitrariness and procedural and legal transparency.[11]

Historically, the environmental rule of law first evolved during the 2013 meeting of the United Nations Environment Programme (UNEP) Governing Council. It was adopted by the Governing Council under Decision 27/9 entitled: 'Advancing Justice, Governance and Rule of Law for Environmental Sustainability'. Under that decision, the UNEP Executive Director was requested by the Member States:

> [to assist with the] development and implementation of environmental rule of law with attention at all levels to mutually supporting governance features,

---

[11] UN, *The Rule of Law and Transitional Justice in Conflict and Post-conflict Societies* (Report of Secretary General Kofi Annan, 23 August 2004).

including information disclosure, public participation, implementable and enforceable laws, and implementation and accountability mechanisms including coordination of roles as well as environmental auditing and criminal, civil and administrative enforcement with timely, impartial and independent dispute resolution.[12]

The concept evolved to deal with the constant non-compliance or violations of environmental laws. The underlying perception for the adoption of the environmental rule of law emanates from the view that non-compliance or violation of environmental law has the potential to undermine the achievement of sustainable development. Moreover, the concept emerged to hold wrongdoers, both individuals and corporations, accountable for breaching environmental laws as well as to pave the way for stringent enforcement with tougher penalties for lawbreakers. As can be imagined, stringent enforcement or tougher penalties can deter violations of the law.[13]

Furthermore, emphasis regarding the strengthening of the environmental rule of law took place in 2014 during the first United Nations Environment Assembly (UNEA). The Member States adopted resolution 1/13, which requested countries 'to work for the strengthening of Environmental Rule of Law at the international, regional and national levels'.[14]

In addition, during the First World Environmental Law Congress in 2016, which was jointly sponsored by International Union for Conservation of Nature- (IUCN-)The World Conservation Union and UNEP, the IUCN World Declaration on the Environmental Rule of Law, was adopted.[15] The Declaration states that: 'environmental rule of law should thus serve as the legal foundation for promoting environmental ethics and achieving environmental justice, global ecological integrity, and a sustainable future for all, including for future generations, at local, national, subnational, regional, and international levels.' The Declaration encompasses thirteen principles that serve as the foundation for the development and implementation of solutions for ecologically sustainable development. These principles are important for all environmental challenges including climate change and its impacts. The thirteen principles are set out in full below due to their importance to the issues analysed:

---

[12] UNEP, *Decisions adopted by the Governing Council/Global Ministerial Environment Forum at its First Universal Session* (16–22 February 2013).
[13] UNEP, *Environmental Rule of Law First Global Report* (2019) (hereafter 'Environmental Rule of Law Report').
[14] UNEP, *Resolutions and Decisions Adopted by the United Nations Environment Assembly of the United Nations Environment Programme at its First Session on 27 June 2014* (2014).
[15] IUCN World Commission on Environmental Law, *World Declaration on the Environmental Rule of Law* (2016).

Principle 1 Obligation to protect nature
Each state, public or private entity, and individual has the obligation to care for and promote the well-being of nature, regardless of its worth to humans, and to place limits on its use and exploitation.

Principle 2 Right to nature and rights of nature
Each human and other living being has a right to the conservation, protection, and restoration of the health and integrity of ecosystems. Nature has the inherent right to exist, thrive, and evolve.

Principle 3 Right to environment. Each human, present and future, has the right to a safe, clean, healthy, and sustainable environment.

Principle 4 Ecological sustainability and resilience
Legal and other measures shall be taken to protect and restore ecosystem integrity and to sustain and enhance the resilience of social-ecological systems. In the drafting of policies and legislation, and in decision-making, the maintenance of a healthy biosphere for nature and humanity should be a primary consideration.

Principle 5 *In dubio pro natura*
In cases of doubt, all matters before courts, administrative agencies, and other decision-makers shall be resolved in a way most likely to favour the protection and conservation of the environment, with preference to be given to alternatives that are least harmful to the environment. Actions shall not be undertaken when their potential adverse impacts on the environment are disproportionate or excessive in relation to the benefits derived therefrom.

Principle 6 Ecological functions of property
Any natural or legal person or group of people, in possession or control of land, water, or other resources, has the duty to maintain the essential ecological functions associated with those resources and refrain from activities that would impair such functions. Legal obligations to restore ecological conditions of land, water, or other resources are binding on all owners, occupiers, and users of a site, and liability is not terminated by the transfer of use or title to others.

Principle 7 Intragenerational equity
There shall be a fair and equitable sharing of the benefits of nature, including appropriate access to ecosystem services. There shall be a fair and equitable sharing of efforts and burdens. Natural resources shall be used and managed in an ecologically sustainable manner.

Principle 8 Intergenerational equity
The present generation must ensure that the health, diversity, ecological functions, and beauty of the environment are maintained or restored to provide equitable access to the benefits of the environment by each successive generation.

Principle 9 Gender equality
Gender equality shall be incorporated into all policies, decisions, and practices in recognition of the often-disproportionate impacts of environmental degradation on women and girls, and their key role in achieving sustainability.

Principle 10 Participation of minority and vulnerable groups
The inclusion of minority and vulnerable groups and perspectives across generations shall be actively addressed with regard to effective access to information, open and inclusive participation in decision-making, and equal access to justice.

Principle 11 Indigenous and tribal peoples
Indigenous and tribal peoples' rights over, and relationships with, their traditional and/or customary lands and territories shall be respected, with their free, prior, and informed consent to any activities on or affecting their land or resources being a key objective.

Principle 12 Non-regression
States, sub-national entities, and regional integration organizations shall not allow or pursue actions that have the net effect of diminishing the legal protection of the environment or of access to environmental justice.

Principle 13 Progression
In order to achieve the progressive development and enforcement of the environmental rule of law, States, sub-national entities, and regional integration organizations shall regularly revise and enhance laws and policies in order to protect, conserve, restore, and ameliorate the environment, based on the most recent scientific knowledge and policy developments.

These thirteen principles of the environmental rule of law in one way or another have some relevance to control and manage climate change and its impacts. For example, Principles 1 and 2, which are related to the rights of nature and the obligation to preserve nature are relevant as, as shown above, we know that nature or biodiversity and species are being impacted to the point of degradation and loss due to climate change. These two principles should remind us that nature also has the right to exist and we have a duty to uphold this. Nature should be conserved for its intrinsic value and not because of its value based on human needs.[16] Furthermore, humans have an ethical and moral obligation to conserve nature by preventing drivers of change such as climate change from driving it toward premature extinction. In conserving nature, we can be assured that it will be passed on to future generations (Principle 8).

Moreover, Christopher Stone's influential work regarding the need to confer rights upon nature has set precedence for some countries in recent years who took bold steps in conferring nature legal rights in both statutory law and enforcing them in courts.[17] For instance, in 2008, Ecuador became the first country in the world to adopt the rights of nature by including it in its new Constitution (article 71

---

[16] Ronald Sandler, *Intrinsic Value, Ecology, and Conservation* (2012) 3(10) Nature Education Knowledge 4.

[17] Christopher D Stone, 'Should Trees Have Standing?—Towards Legal Rights for Natural Objects' (1972) 45 S Cal L Rev 450–501.

under chapter 7). Thus, article 71 states: 'Nature, or Pacha Mama, where life is reproduced and occurs, has the right to integral respect for its existence and for the maintenance and regeneration of its life cycles, structure, functions and evolutionary processes.'

The conferring of legal personhood to nature means that nature has the right to defend itself in court against harm caused by climate change, development projects, and pollution.

In addition, the judicial enforcement of the rights of nature have been witnessed in countries including New Zealand and Colombia. In 2014, New Zealand granted the Whanganui River the legal personhood meaning that the river holds rights and responsibilities that are equivalent to that of a person.[18] Also, in 2016, Colombia granted similar right of personhood to Atrao River recognizing the river as a rights-holding subject and deserves protection, conservation, maintenance, and restoration.[19] In a latter case it further ruled in recognition of the Colombian Amazon as 'subject of rights' similar to the recognition of the Atrao River by the Constitutional Court, and as such the Colombian Amazon was entitled to protection, conservation, maintenance, and restoration.[20]

Finally, there are numerous significant elements within environmental rule of law that are relevant to climate change and the broader environmental challenge. The UNEP Governing Council identified seven core elements of the environmental rule of law. These seven elements are sound laws, access rights, institutional integrity, clear mandates, dispute resolution, human rights nexus, and clear interpretive criteria.[21]

b. Concepts and principles

A number of significant concepts and principles are engrained in the body of environmental law, and they can be useful to deal with climate change and its adverse effects. Some of these concepts and principles include prevention of transboundary pollution and environmental harm, the precautionary principle, intergenerational equity, and common but differentiated responsibility.

---

[18] Waitangi Tribunal, 'The Whanganui River Report' (GP Publications, 1999).
[19] *Center for Social Justice Studies et al v Presidency of the Republic et al* [2016] Constitutional Court of Columbia Judgement T-622/16.
[20] *Future Generations v Ministry of the Environment and Others (Demanda Generaciones Futuras v Minambiente)* [2018] Constitutional Court of Columbia.
[21] UDEP, 'Advancing Justice, Governance and Law for Environmental Sustainability: Rio+20 and the World Congress of Chief Justices, Attorneys General and Auditors General' (30 November 2012) <https://wedocs.unep.org/bitstream/handle/20.500.11822/9969/advancing_justice_governance_law.pdf?sequence=1&amp%3BisAllowed=> accessed 20 September 2023.

i. Prevention of transboundary pollution and environmental harm

The duty to prevent transboundary pollution and environmental harm is engrained in both soft and hard law, customary international law, and judicial precedent. The principle of prevention exists to direct individuals and companies to avoid unforeseeable risks and harm. In fact, it allows one to take preventive measures to safeguard environmental harm before it occurs. Avoiding environmental harm from occurring can save one costs rather than attempting to rectify damage when it has already been done which can be costly.[22]

One soft law instrument that embodies the principle of prevention of environmental harm is the Stockholm Declaration. The prevention of environmental harm is embodied in Principle 6, which provides that:

> The discharge of toxic substances or of other substances and the release of heat, in such quantities or concentrations as to exceed the capacity of the environment to render them harmless, must be halted in order to ensure that serious or irreversible damage is not inflicted upon ecosystems. The just struggle of the peoples of all countries against pollution should be supported.

It must be noted that the emission of GHGs into the atmosphere constitutes a transboundary pollution that has caused irreparable harm to the ozone layer and the consequences of global warming and other adverse effects being faced by the world today.[23] Although GHGs may be released by one or a few countries, it affects several or all of the countries. It is in this context that the United Nations Convention on the Law of the Sea (UNCLOS) has codified the 'no harm' rule within its scope. Article 194(2) of UNCLOS states:

> States shall take all measures necessary to ensure that activities under their jurisdiction or control are so conducted as not to cause damage by pollution to other States and their environment, and that pollution arising from incidents or activities under their jurisdiction or control does not spread beyond the areas where they exercise sovereign rights in accordance with this Convention.

UNCLOS is progressive in that it went beyond the prevention of environmental harm caused only to neighbouring countries to include the protection of areas beyond national jurisdiction (ABNJ). The atmosphere and the ozone layer is one such common area that exists beyond a state's national jurisdiction that can be

---

[22] Encyclopedia Britannica, 'Principles of Environmental Law' (*Britannica*, 2022) <Environmental law - Precautionary Principle, Polluter Pays Principle, and Environmental Impact Assessment | Britannica> accessed 4 June 2023.

[23] Guus Velders, 'Effect of Greenhouse Gas Emissions on Stratospheric Ozone Depletion', RIVM Report No 722201011 (1997).

guaranteed protection under this rule. UNCLOS imposes a duty on states to prevent environmental harm from occurring.[24]

Various actors, including individuals, companies, and states, are duty bound to prevent transboundary pollution and environmental harm from occurring.[25] The principle of 'no harm' has been established in the *Trail Smelter* arbitration that involved the US and Canada. This case involved a factory on the Canadian side of the border to cause transboundary air pollution and damage to the nearby environment and beyond its own jurisdiction extending into the US territory as well as causing distress to people. The tribunal held that 'no state has the right to use or permit the use of its territory in such a manner as to cause injury by fumes in or to the territory of another'.[26] The tribunal went further to award not only damages to the US, but also imposed a regime on how to prevent future emissions from Canada. This decision strengthened the duty of a state to prevent, reduce, and control environmental harm.[27] The rule of 'no harm' established under the *Trial Smelter* arbitration eventually entered both soft and hard law and it is codified and can be applied to transboundary pollution including climate change and its impact.[28]

ii. Precautionary principle

The precautionary principle or approach is similar to the prevention of the no harm principle, as the precautionary principle requires action to be taken prior to conducting any activity that has the potential of causing environmental harm including scientific uncertainty. The lack of scientific evidence should not be reason for engaging in potentially harmful activity that may cause change to the environment or impact human health.

The precautionary principle first appeared in 1984 during a series of intergovernmental conferences that were held to protect the marine environment of the North Sea.[29] The principle later made its way into numerous regional and multilateral environmental agreements (MEAs) as well as domestic environmental laws.

---

[24] Specific reference is made under article 194 of UNCLOS imposing an obligation upon parties to take measures to prevent reduce and control pollution of the marine environment.

[25] Alistair Rieu-Clarke, 'The Duty to take Appropriate Measures to Prevent Significant Transboundary Harm and Private Companies: Insights from Transboundary Hydropower Projects' (2020) 20 Int Environ Agreements 667–82 <https://link.springer.com/article/10.1007/s10784-020-09504-5> accessed 4 June 2023.

[26] Casebriefs LLC, 'Trail Smelter Arbitration (United States v Canada)' (*Casebriefs*, 2022) <https://www.casebriefs.com/blog/law/international-law/international-law-keyed-to-damrosche/chapter-18/trail-smelter-arbitration-united-states-v-canada/> accessed 4 June 2023.

[27] Patricia Birnie and Allan Boyle, *International Law and the Environment* (OUP 1993).

[28] UN, 'UN Reports of International Arbitral Awards: *Trail Smelter Case (United States v Canada)*' (vol III, 16 April 1938 and 11 March 1941) 1905–82 (hereafter 'Trail Smelter Case').

[29] Ellen Hey, 'The Precautionary Approach: Implications of the Revision of the Oslo and Paris Conventions' (2022) 15(4) Mar Policy 244–54 <https://www.sciencedirect.com/science/article/abs/pii/0308597X9190002S> accessed 4 June 2023.

For instance, the UNFCCC has included the precautionary principle in article 3(3) of the Convention, which includes these words:

> parties should take precautionary measures to anticipate, prevent or minimize the cause of climate change and mitigate its adverse effects. Where there are threats of serious or irreversible damage, lack of full scientific certainty should not be used as a reason for postponing such measures, taking into account that policies and measures to deal with climate change should be cost-effective so as to ensure global benefits at the lowest possible cost.

iii. Polluter pays principle

The polluter pays principle (PPP) evolved to respond to polluters or free riders[30] who externalize the cost of environmental pollution and harm arising from their activities. For instance, a facility emitting fumes or gases into the atmosphere as a by-product from its activities, placed the burden of bearing the costs of pollution on the public or community rather than internalizing its costs. The PPP ensures that the polluter is obligated to pay the real costs of its own pollution arising from its activities. One fact that must be noted is that the PPP is not a liability or legal principle, but rather an economic principle to allocate the cost of pollution prevention.[31]

Since PPP first emerged in 1972 through the Organization for Economic Cooperation and Development's (OECD's) work entitled 'Guiding Principles Concerning International Economic Aspects of Environmental Policies', it has since entered both hard- and soft law instruments.[32] For instance, Principle 16 of the Rio Declaration adopted the PPP in 1992 during the United Nations Conference on Environment and Development (UNCED) in Rio de Janeiro states:

> National authorities should endeavor to promote the internalization of environmental costs and the use of economic instruments, taking into account the approach that the polluter should, in principle, bear the cost of pollution, with due regard to the public interest and without distorting international trade and investment.[33]

---

[30] The free rider problem in the environmental context arises when the environment, which is a common good, is being used by an individual or entity, for instance, a company, for its private gains while placing the costs on the public to bear. An example would be a manufacturing plant that operates for profits simultaneously pollutes the air and expects the public to bear the cost of cleaning it while the owner enjoys the free ride. Ideally, the manufacturing plant must bear the cost of cleaning the polluted air before emitting it into the atmosphere through various measures, such as through the installation of equipment or clean technology within the plant so as to purify the polluted air.

[31] Sanford E Gaines, 'Taking Responsibility for Transboundary Environmental Effects' (1991) 14 Hastings Int'l & Comp L Rev 781 <https://repository.uchastings.edu/hastings_international_comparative_law_review/vol14/iss4/3> accessed 4 June 2023.

[32] OECD, *The Polluter Pays Principle OECD Analysis and Recommendations* (1992).

[33] UN, *Report of the United Nations Conference on Environment and Development* (1992).

The PPP has been adopted into regional, as well as domestic, laws. An example at the regional level is the Single European Act.[34] The PPP was included in the Single European Act in 1986 under article 130r(2): 'Action by the Community relating to the environment shall be based on the principles that preventive action should be taken, that environmental damage should as a priority be rectified at source, and that the polluter should pay'.

The PPP can influence polluters to produce cleaner products or use cleaner technologies in their production or manufacturing processes with a view to internalize the costs of pollution and environmental degradation. This can be extremely useful for climate change.

iv. Intergenerational equity

The principle of intergeneration equity is about fairness between the present and future generations. Climate change has a clear link with intergenerational equity. We already know that the present generation is responsible for the emissions of GHGs that contributes to the climate crisis. This transforms the environment which will be unfit to pass it on to the next generation. This trend works contrary to the duty that all generations have an obligation to maintain the environment in a state that is fit for use by the next generation before they pass it on. In fact, all generations are partners. There is a moral and ethical obligation the present generation owes the future generations to preserve the environment and pass it on to the next in the manner that was received from the previous generation.[35]

v. Common but differentiated responsibilities

The principle of common but differentiated responsibilities has two components. First, it recognizes that the protection of the global environment and climate change, and its negative impacts in particular, is a common concern for all, and it is the responsibility of everyone, regardless of whether one is privileged or underprivileged to address it. This component of the principle is captured clearly in the preambular text of the UNFCCC. It states that the 'change in the Earth's climate and its adverse effects are a common concern of humankind'.[36]

The second component of this principle, the differentiated responsibility, is tied to fairness. It stems from the fact that not all states are equally responsible for the anthropogenic emission of GHGs and climate change. Historically, developed countries contributed most of the GHGs responsible for climate change now. Also, the varying development paths of countries, the capabilities and resources does not

---

[34] Single European Act (opened for signature in February 1986 in Luxembourg and The Hague and entered into force on 1 July 1987).
[35] Edith Brown Weiss, *In Fairness to Future Generations: International Law, Common Patrimony, and Intergenerational Equity* (UNU Press and Transnational Publishers 1989).
[36] UN Framework Convention on Climate Change (UNFCCC) (opened for signature in 1992 and entered into force on 21 March 1994) (hereafter 'UNFCCC').

place countries on an equal footing. As such the responsibility to address climate change must be different where developed countries should take a bigger role in solving the crisis. Differentiated responsibilities should mean that there must be different targets for different countries, which can then attract a wider participation by all countries in efforts to address climate change and its impacts.[37]

4. International Environmental Law on Climate Change

The three primary MEAs, being agreements between many countries, which have been concluded so far to address the climate crisis at the global level, are the UNFCCC, the Kyoto Protocol, and the Paris Agreement. These MEAs, which are summarized below, lay out both general and specific frameworks that are needed at the global level to combat the threats posed by the climate crisis. In other words, these MEAs provide platforms for concerted efforts by the international community. Various important principles, including the precautionary principle and the common but differentiated responsibilities were codified under these legally binding instruments. In addition, specific targets were set for the states parties to achieve within given timeframes. Also, various mechanisms were created, including the joint implementation (JI), the clean development mechanism (CDM) and the nationally determined contributions (NDC).

a. UNFCCC

When UNCED met in Rio de Janeiro in 1992, the UNFCCC was adopted. The objective of the UNFCCC was to stabilize GHGs at a level that would prevent harmful anthropogenic activities from further disrupting the climate system. It was noted that timeframes were to be set to ensure ecosystems adapt naturally to climate change, sustain food production, and economic development.[38] The UNFCCC covers both adaptation and mitigation measures. Premised on the principle of common but differentiated responsibilities, the Convention requires the industrialized developed countries—known as the 'Annex I countries'—to lead in the adaptation and mitigation efforts of cutting back on GHG emissions. Furthermore, the Convention upholds the precautionary principle or approach. Regardless of the absence of sufficient scientific evidence the Convention placed emphasis on the taking of a precautionary approach to prevent harm to the global environment.

---

[37] Malek Romdhane, 'What is the Common But Differentiated Responsibilities and Respective Capabilities (CBDR-RC) Principle?' (*ClimaTalk*, 2022) < https://climatalk.org/2021/07/12/what-is-the-cbdr-rc-principle/> accessed 4 June 2023 (hereafter 'What is the Common').

[38] UNFCCC (n 36).

b. Kyoto Protocol

Five years after the UNFCCC, the Kyoto Protocol[39] was adopted, primarily to operationalize the UNFCCC. The Protocol placed emphasis again on the principle of common but differentiated responsibilities by committing and placing heavier burdens on the industrial developed countries and on countries with economies in transition (EIT), especially those countries listed under Annex B, to limit and reduce GHGs emissions in accordance with agreed individual targets. This did not leave the developing countries out.

The developing countries are equally held accountable under the first component of the principle of common but differentiated responsibilities. As the climate crisis is a common concern for humanity it is everyone's responsibility, including the developing countries, to do their part by taking measures to combat climate change. As such, the developing countries are also required under the Protocol to develop national adaptation plans to deal with the climate crisis. In addition to the requirement for countries to meet their targets through national measures, they are also presented with a number of other opportunities to meet their targets. These options include market-based mechanisms, such as international emissions trading, the CDM and the JI.[40]

An additional significant requirement under the Protocol is the establishment of a monitoring, review and verification mechanism for actual emissions by the countries. The Protocol also established a compliance mechanism to ensure transparency as well as to ensure countries comply with their obligations under the Protocol.[41]

c. Paris Agreement

The most recent climate related MEA is the Paris Agreement of 2015.[42] It was adopted to strengthen the global response to the threat of climate change with a view to promote sustainable development and eradicate poverty. One specific

---

[39] *Kyoto Protocol to the United Nations Framework Convention on Climate Change* (adopted for signature on 11 December 1997 and entered into force on 16 February 2005); United Nations Treaty Collection, 'Kyoto Protocol to the United Nations Framework Convention on Climate Change' (*United Nations Treaty Collection*, 11 December 1997) <https://treaties.un.org/Pages/ViewDetails.aspx?src=TREATY&mtdsg_no=XXVII-7-a&chapter=27&clang=_en> accessed 4 June 2023.

[40] What is the Common (n 37).

[41] United Nations Climate Change, 'What is the Kyoto Protocol?' (*United Nations Climate Change*, 2022) <https://unfccc.int/kyoto_protocol> accessed 4 June 2023.

[42] United Nations Treaty Collection, *Paris Agreement* (adopted on 12 December 2015 and entered into force on 4 November 2016); United Nations Treaty Collection, 'Paris Agreement' (*United Nations Treaty Collection*, 12 December 2015) <https://treaties.un.org/Pages/ViewDetails.aspx?src=IND&mtdsg_no=XXVII-7-d&chapter=27&clang=_en> accessed 4 June 2023.

requirement under the Agreement is to maintain the global average temperatures below 2°C above pre-industrial levels and take measures to limit the temperature increase to 1.5°C above pre-industrial levels as stipulated under Article 2 (a) of the Agreement

These concrete targets are intended to reduce significantly the impacts of climate change and the threats it poses, as well as to enable the planet and its life-supporting systems to adapt to the adverse effects of climate change and foster climate resilience. Furthermore, the Agreement established under Article 4 paragraph 2. The nationally determined contributions (NDCs), where the state parties are required to prepare, communicate every five years and pursue mitigation measures to meet the objectives of the NDCs.

In fact, the African region has made great strides since the adoption of the Paris Agreement. Over 90 per cent of the African countries have ratified the Paris Agreement. Following their ratification, 52 of the African countries have submitted their first NDCs followed by the submission of the revised NDCs in 2020. Many of them have committed to transitioning to green energy.[43] An additional requirement under the Agreement is for the Parties to take steps to conserve sinks and reservoirs of GHGs such as forests as stipulated under Article 5 of the Agreement. Finally, the Agreement has established a compliance mechanism to facilitate the implementation of requirements and obligations of the Parties which is covered under Article 15 paragraph 1 and 2.

5. Constitutional Law

The constitution of a country is usually broad and covers all aspects of society and prescribes how a country should govern its affairs. Many modern constitutions now include in their provisions general statements related to environmental protection. This usually provides the basis for the enactment of more elaborate legislations on the environment including specific legislations on climate change. The constitutions also outline fundamental rights, both substantive and procedural, as well as obligations. Some of them go to the extent of including provisions on a constitutional right to a clean and healthy environment.

---

[43] African Development Bank Group, 'African Nations Join Front-Runners in Ratifying Paris Agreement on Climate Change' (*African Development Bank Group*, 3 October 2016) <https://www.afdb.org/en/news-and-events/african-nations-join-front-runners-in-ratifying-paris-agreement-on-climate-change-16184> accessed 4 June 2023.

a. Substantive rights

Numerous substantive rights in many constitutions relate directly or indirectly to the environment and, in particular, the climate crisis. Some of these substantive rights include the right to life, the right to a clean and healthy environment, the right to water and food and the right to domicile. It is a fact that approximately 70 per cent of the countries in Africa have included environmental provisions in their constitutions.[44] On a regional scale, the African Charter on Human and People's Rights in article 24 recognizes the right to a satisfactory environment for development as a fundamental human right. Furthermore, at the national level, section 24 of the Constitution of South Africa is dedicated to the environment, and it reads:

> Everyone has the right (a) to an environment that is not harmful to their health or well-being; (b) to have the environment protected, for the benefit of present and future generations, through reasonable legislative and other measures that (i) prevent pollution and ecological degradation; (ii) promote conservation; and (iii) secure ecologically sustainable development and use of natural resources while promoting justifiable economic and social development.

Ethiopia's Constitution has established 'Environmental Objectives', where it provides that the '[g]overnment shall endeavor to ensure that all Ethiopians live in a clean and healthy environment', and state that '[t]he design and implementation of programmes and projects of development shall not damage or destroy the environment'. Numerous other countries in Africa provide similar provisions in their constitutions.[45]

We do know now that climate change and its impacts can be life threatening, degrade the environment to point where it will not be conducive to live in and enjoy, deprive humans of water and food and force people out from their homes. Some of these incidents are already happening.

The impacts of climate change, especially heavy rainfalls and floods or extremely high temperatures and prolonged dry periods, are life threatening. Lives get lost in these climate induced weather conditions thus jeopardizing the right to life. Prior to the recognition of the constitutional right to a clean and healthy environment, the fundamental right to life was expanded by some courts around the world and applied to environmental degradation and loss. The courts that did so perceived the fundamental right to life as having an expansive and wide meaning where they interpreted it to include life as not mere existence, but the amenities that contribute

---

[44] Environmental Law Institute (ELI) and United Nations Environment Programme (UNEP), *Constitutional Environmental Law: Giving Force to Fundamental Principles in Africa* (2nd edn, ELI and UNEP 2007) (hereafter 'Constitutional Environmental Law').
[45] ibid 42.

to life or existence, such as a healthy and safe environment. This expansive interpretation of the fundamental right to life includes the quality of life and human dignity.

Some examples from around the world exist. In India, the fundamental right to life enshrined in its Constitution has been expanded to include numerous other rights. One such right is the right to live in a proper and healthy environment, the maintenance of health, proper sanitation systems, and the preservation of the environment. In expanding and enforcing this right, the Supreme Court of India in *Vellore Citizens Welfare Forum vs Union of India*[46] held that industry plays a significant role in development, and in the process causes pollution, however, they must also take into consideration the principle of sustainable development, which includes the environmental dimension, as a balancing concept. Also, in the US in *Munn v Illinois*,[47] the Court made reference to the term 'life' as something more than a mere animal existence. Thus, life is perceived to embrace within its ambit not only the physical existence, but also the quality of life that enriches it, including a safe and healthy environment.

Many countries around the world including, approximately 70 per cent of African countries have now included the right to a clean and healthy environment in their Constitutions.[48] UNEP has reported in its first global report on the environmental rule of law in 2019 that 'since the 1970s, 88 countries have adopted a constitutional right to a healthy environment, with an additional 62 countries enshrining environmental protection in their constitutions in some form—a total of 150 countries from all over the globe with constitutional rights and/or provisions on the environment.'[49] This now provides a foundation for those that have their rights violated by the impacts of climate change to enforce their constitutional rights in the courts.

In addition to the impacts of climate change on the right to life, we do know that climate change also violates the right to food and water, and the right to domicile. Food, water, and homes are fundamental elements that enrich life itself. The prolonged high temperatures or droughts, heavy rainfalls, and floods destroy agricultural lands and food production. Potable water is contaminated by salt water intrusion and food gardens are also destroyed by salt-water intrusion due to sea level rise. Heavy rains, floods, and sea level rise also destroy homes thus displacing various communities including coastal communities. Those that have lost their homes and land have become climate refugees.[50]

---

[46] *Vellore Citizens Welfare Forum v Union of India & Ors* [1996].
[47] *Munn v Illinois* [1876] 94 US 113 [1876].
[48] Constitutional Environmental Law (n 44).
[49] Environmental Rule of Law Report (n 13).
[50] Papua New Guinea (n 7).

b. Procedural rights

In addition to substantive rights, procedural or democratic rights are defined within the Constitutions, and they can be useful to the environment. The bundle of procedural or democratic rights including access to information, public participation, and access to justice. They have also been expanded to include matters relating to the environment. The public has the right of access to information regarding the environment, the right to participate in environmental decision making, and the right of access to justice regarding environmental matters.[51]

Under these procedural rights, where they occur, the public has a right to seek, receive, and impart information regarding the environment. This procedural right is also enshrined in international law instruments including the Universal Declaration of Human Rights (UDHR) (art 19) and the International Covenant on Civil and Political Rights (ICCPR) (art 19). It forms part of the right to freedom of expression under these two international instruments. Likewise, everyone has the right to participate in environmental decision-making. This right is also embedded in the UDHR (art 21) and the ICCPR (art 25). In addition, everyone has the right of access to justice or the courts to resolve violation of fundamental rights guaranteed under the constitution or any other law. This right is also recognized under the UDHR (art 8) and the ICCPR (art 2(3)).

6. Statutory Law

Statutes have been enacted based on the general provisions on environmental protection provided under the constitution. UNEP observed again in its first global report on the environmental rule of law that a majority of countries around the world, including African countries, possess some form of legal framework to protect, conserve, and use the environment in a sustainable manner. The report further observed that over 176 countries have laws on the environment.[52] In addition to the general laws on the environment, some countries have enacted climate specific legislations to deal with the issues surrounding the impacts of climate change.

Others are in the process of developing climate related legislation while others are yet to develop such laws. This is no exception for African countries. For instance, South Africa has recently published its Climate Change Bill.[53] Nigeria has developed a comprehensive stand-alone legislation on climate change in 2021. It is perceived that the Climate Change Act, 2021 will serve as a foundation for

---

[51] Environmental Rule of Law Report (n 13).
[52] African Development Bank Group (n 43); Constitutional Environmental Law (n 44).
[53] Businesstech, 'New Climate Change Laws Planned for South Africa' (*Businesstech*, 20 April 2022) <https://businesstech.co.za/news/energy/579000/new-climate-change-laws-planned-for-south-africa/> accessed on 5 June 2023.

advocacy and climate litigation in the future.[54] Kenya has passed its Climate Change Act in 2016. This law aims at providing a framework for promoting climate resilient low carbon economic development.

7. Climate Litigation

Climate related litigation is in its infancy in the African region. However, the number of cases worldwide is multiplying in recent years. It is estimated that since 2015, approximately 1,000 cases have been filed globally. The cases have been brought against companies for violation of human rights or against governments for not doing enough to reverse or stop climate change and its adverse effects.[55] Among them are some successful ones. Two most notable cases are the *Millieudiffensie et al v Royal Dutch Shell*[56] [2019] case and the *Neubauer et al v Germany* case[57] [2020].

First, *Millieudiffensie et al v Royal Dutch Shell* [2019] is a landmark case. This case was presented before The Hague District Court. The issue at hand for the court to decide was whether a private company, in this case Royal Dutch Shell, violated a duty of care and its human rights obligations to take adequate measures to reduce its contributions to climate change. The specific laws used to file the case were article 6(162) of the Dutch Civil Code (duty of care) and articles 2 and 8 of the European Convention on Human Rights (ECHR).

The plaintiffs served the defendant (Royal Dutch Shell (Shell)), a summons alleging that Shell's contribution to climate change violated the duty of care and human rights obligations under the respective provisions of the laws just mentioned above and the Paris Agreement. In this case the plaintiffs were seeking a ruling from the Court to request Shell to reduce its CO2 emissions by 45 per cent by 2030 compared to 2010 levels and to zero by 2050, in accordance with the Paris Agreement. After hearing presentations of facts and evidence from the defendant and plaintiff, the Court ruled in May 2021 in favour of the plaintiffs. The Court ordered Shell to reduce its emissions by net 45 per cent at the end of 2030, relative to 2019, across all activities including both its own emissions and end-use emissions.

Second, in *Neubauer et al vs Germany* [2020], the plaintiffs brought the case before the German Federal Constitutional Court. The issue was for the Court to determine whether Germany's GHG reduction goals violated human rights.

---

[54] London School of Economics (LSE) Grantham Research Institute on Climate Change and the Environment, 'Climate Change Laws of the World' (*LSE*, 2022) <https://climate-laws.org/geographies/kenya/laws/climate-change-act-2016> accessed on 5 June 2023.
[55] UNEP, *Global Climate Litigation Report 2020 Status Review* (2020).
[56] *Milieudefensie et al v Royal Dutch Shell* [2021] ECLI:NL:RBDHA:2021:5337 (hereafter *Milieudefensie et al v Royal Dutch Shell*).
[57] *Neubauer et al v Germany* [2021].

Numerous provisions under the German Basic Law (its constitution) were applied to the case, especially article 1 (the principle of human dignity), article 2 (protection of the right to life and physical integrity), and article 20a (protection of the natural foundations of life in responsibility for future generations).

The plaintiffs alleged that Germany's Federal Climate Protection Act (KSG) that set the target of GHGs reduction at 55 per cent by 2030 from 1990 levels was insufficient and, as such, constituted a violation of human rights. The plaintiffs further alleged that the KSG 2030 target did not take into consideration Germany's, and the EU's, obligations under the Paris Agreement to maintain global temperature increase to below 2°C or, if possible, 1.5°C. The plaintiffs argued that the 2030 target of 55 per cent reduction of GHGs adopted by the KSG was insufficient to keep global temperatures well below 2°C . It would require a GHGs reduction of 77 per cent to be able to maintain the global temperature below 2°C. After hearing arguments from the plaintiff and defendant the court ruled in favour of the plaintiff in April 2021.[58]

The Court ordered that by 2022, the German legislature should set clear provisions on reduction targets from 2031 onward. It further ruled that the provisions of the KSG were incompatible with fundamental rights and, as such, it had to be revised. The German government subsequently announced the day after the decision that adjustments would be made to the KSG to reflect the Court's decision.

8. Conclusion

Climate change, as we have discussed above, is real and the need to address it is urgent. Its impacts on sustainable development, and especially its three dimensions, namely, the environment, society, and the economy are particularly harsh for the African region, especially the poor and vulnerable communities. These impacts are violating the fundamental rights of people and nature alike including the right to life, the right to a clean and healthy environment, the right to water and food, and the right to domicile. Moreover, the negative impacts of climate change are seen to hinder development and human well-being.

In response to the negative impacts of climate change on development and human well-being, the African continent as a whole has been proactive in recent times regarding climate action with 90 per cent of African countries having ratified the Paris Agreement and fifty-two of them have developed their NDCs. However, there are gaps and more is yet to be done, especially in the area of climate litigation in Africa, if one were to see tangible outcomes to reverse climate change and

---

[58] Columbia Law School Sabina Center for Climate Change Law, 'Climate Change Litigation Database' (2022) <http://climatecasechart.com/> accessed on 5 June 2023.

its impacts and allow for development to flourish. Stricter penalties are needed to hold violators accountable and correct their behaviours.

In fact, the basic tools needed to pursue climate related litigation are present. The constitutions define the various substantive and procedural rights: the right to life, the right to a clean and healthy environment, and the right of access to justice. Both general and climate specific international and domestic environmental legal frameworks exist. In addition, various significant principles including the precautionary principle, the prevention of environmental harm, the polluter pays principle, and the intergenerational equity exist and have been codified in both soft and hard law at the international and national levels. In addition, the environmental rule of law and its principles exist to be applied. Those contributing to climate change should be held legally accountable to play their part in mitigating climate change.

In order for climate litigation to succeed and hold violators responsible, support structures are needed in addition to the basic tools mentioned in this chapter. There are three support structures that we see as significant to succeed in any climate litigation. The support structures include good lawyers, proactive judges, and funds to support litigation. Good lawyers are needed to argue the case successfully by telling a convincing story to the judge in court. Proactive judges are a necessity to decide the case in favour of the plaintiff. Finally, money is needed to fund the cost of litigation. In many cases a genuine plaintiff willing to fight to reverse climate change and allow development to thrive may not have the money to pursue the case. As a result, the plaintiff may end up dropping the case or not pursuing the case at all. These three support structures are need to win a case. Innovative ways must be thought out to ensure that the three support structures are present before pursuing climate litigation for the sake of development and well-being.

11
Forced Displacement, International Law, and the World Bank

Duygu Çiçek, Paige Casaly, and Vikram Raghavan[*]

1. Introduction

At the end of 2021, over eighty-nine million people had fled their homes owing to conflict, persecution, and violence across the world.[1] Barely six months later, this number had surged past 100 million, with the total reaching 108 million by the end of 2022.[2] This dramatic spike reflects a ten-year trend in rising numbers of forcibly displaced persons annually. Presently, more persons are displaced than at any point since the end of World War II (WW II).[3] These numbers are, of course, inadequate proxies for the underlying and inestimable human toll. Millions of displaced persons have endured enormous suffering in myriad ways: bodily injury and mental trauma, livelihoods lost, future prospects disrupted, and property left behind or looted.

Yet, these numbers remind us that forced displacement remains a persistent challenge to global development and growth. This is particularly because a majority of the world's displaced persons are currently located in low- and middle-income countries.[4] Reflecting this reality, the United Nations General Assembly

---

[*] The authors work in the World Bank's Legal Department. This article reflects their personal opinions and experience. Its content does not necessarily reflect the World Bank's policies, practice, or views on the subject. The authors would like to thank Guy S Goodwin-Gill, Daniel D Bradlow, Benedict Kingsbury, Siobhán McInerney-Lankford, Aristeidis Panou, Jonathan Lindsay, Jorge Luis Alva-Luperdi, Jessica Buchler, Alreem Kamal, Carson Poling, and Sophia Dilworth for their valuable insights and feedback on this chapter.

[1] This number includes 53.2 million internally displaced persons (IDPs), 27.1 million refugees, 4.6 million asylum seekers, and 4.4 million Venezuelans displaced abroad. United Nations High Commissioner for Refugees (UNHCR), *Global Trends: Forced Displacement in 2021* (June 2022) 2 (hereafter 'UNHCR Global Trends 2021').

[2] This number includes 62.5 million internally displaced persons (IDPs), 35.3 million refugees, 5.4 million asylum seekers, and 5.2 million others in need of international protection: United Nations High Commissioner for Refugees (UNHCR), 'Global Trends: Forced Displacement in 2022' (June 2023) 2 <https://www.unhcr.org/global-trends-report-2022> accessed 24 August 2023 (hereafter 'UNHCR Global Trends 2022').

[3] ibid.

[4] See UNHCR Global Trends 2021 (n 1) 2; Internal Displacement Monitoring Centre, 'Global Report on Internal Displacement: 2022' (Norwegian Refugee Council, May 2022). Countries are categorized according to the Bank's country income groups. See World Bank Group, 'Data: World Bank Country

---

Duygu Çiçek, Paige Casaly, and Vikram Raghavan, *Forced Displacement, International Law, and the World Bank* In: *The Roles of International Law in Development*. Edited by: Siobhán McInerney-Lankford and Robert McCorquodale, Oxford University Press. © Duygu Çiçek, Paige Casaly, and Vikram Raghavan 2023.
DOI: 10.1093/oso/9780192872906.003.0011

(UNGA) included forcibly displaced persons in its 2030 Agenda for Sustainable Development (2030 Agenda) by pledging to 'leave no one behind' in pursuit of the Sustainable Development Goals (SDGs).[5] It also led the World Bank (the Bank) and other development institutions to deepen analytical work, step up operational engagements, and mobilize financing to help countries address the challenge of forced displacement.[6]

In this chapter, we examine the dynamic interplay between the Bank's forced displacement engagements and international law and institutions.[7] Specifically, we explore how the Bank's policies, projects, and practice strengthen existing and emerging principles of public international law. The chapter opens by discussing the evolution of the Bank's development approach to forced displacement. The chapter then summarizes relevant international legal norms and principles on forced displacement. These norms and principles are primarily derived from international refugee law, but they also emerge from international human rights, humanitarian law, and other sources. Next, the chapter analyses how these norms and principles are referenced in or influence the Bank's development strategies, policies, and operations relating to forced displacement. This includes a brief discussion of the Bank's institutional relationship with the United Nations High Commissioner for Refugees (UNHCR).

We argue that the Bank's forced displacement policies, practice, projects, and partnerships could contribute to greater global policy coherence and better development outcomes while also contributing to and strengthening the existing and emerging international norms and standards relating to forced displacement. We also consider the extent to which this grounding of Bank activities in international refugee law could be adapted to other norms and contexts in pursuit of sustainable development.

---

and Lending Groups' (*Data Help Desk*, updated 1 July 2022) <https://datahelpdesk.worldbank.org/knowledgebase/articles/906519-world-bank-country-and-lending-groups> accessed 23 August 2023. For further explanation, see UNHCR, 'Refugee Data Finder: Classifying Refugee Host Countries by Income Level' <https://www.unhcr.org/refugee-statistics/> accessed on 5 June 2023.

[5] UN General Assembly (UNGA), *Transforming Our World: the 2030 Agenda for Sustainable Development* (UN Doc A/RES/70/1, 25 September 2015); UNGA Res 71/313 (UN Doc A/RES/71/313, 6 July 2017) (hereafter 'UNGA Res 71/313'); UN Statistical Commission, *Report on the Fifty-first Session* (E/2020/24-E/CN3/2020/37, 3–6 March 2020).

[6] The 'World Bank' or 'Bank' comprises the International Bank for Reconstruction and Development (IBRD) and the International Development Association (IDA). These institutions, together with the International Finance Corporation (IFC), the Multilateral Investment Guarantee Agency (MIGA), and the International Centre for Settlement of Investment Disputes (ICSID) comprise the 'World Bank Group'.

[7] This chapter only addresses the intersection between the Bank's forced displacement engagements and public international law in situations of armed conflict, generalized violence, and natural or man-made disasters. Involuntary resettlement that occurs in the context of a Bank-financed project goes beyond the scope of this chapter. For a brief analysis on this topic, see the section below on the World Bank Environmental and Social Framework and ESS5 (Land Acquisition, Restrictions on Land Use and Involuntary Resettlement).

2. Evolution of Bank Activities on Forced Displacement

a. Early approach to forced displacement

The Bank's legal charter is its Articles of Agreement (the Articles). The Articles were drafted and adopted at the United Nations Monetary and Financial Conference, which took place in July 1944 at Bretton Woods in New Hampshire.[8] Delegations from forty-four countries participated in the conference even as WW II actively raged in many parts of the world. Some delegates at the conference were themselves refugees. They represented occupied countries' governments in exile. Others had children or relatives fighting on the North Atlantic beaches and elsewhere. It was impossible for delegates to overlook the sheer magnitude of deaths, destruction, devastation, and displacement continuing to unfold particularly in Europe. This fact greatly influenced the conference's debates and deliberations and indelibly shaped the Bank's institutional design. Thus, the Articles assign a prominent role to the Bank in the post-war reconstruction and recovery of its members.[9]

This is evident from the charter's opening provision, article I(i), which declares that the Bank's purposes are, among other things:

> To assist in the reconstruction and development of territories of members by facilitating the investment of capital for productive purposes, including the restoration of economies destroyed or disrupted by war, the reconversion of productive facilities to peacetime needs and the encouragement of the development of productive facilities and resources in less developed countries.[10]

The Articles do not explicitly refer to forced displacement. This is largely because the United Nations Relief and Rehabilitation Administration (UNRRA) was to handle refugee issues. In fact, UNRRA was established, even before the Bretton Woods conference in 1943. Its primary purpose was to provide relief to war victims and support their return home.[11] Yet, the Bank could not completely overlook

---

[8] United States Department of State (ed), *United Nations Monetary and Financial Conference, Bretton Woods, New Hampshire, July 1 to July 22, 1944: Final Act and Related Documents* (United States Government Printing Office 1944) (hereafter 'Final Act and Related Documents').

[9] See ibid 3–6. Also see, generally, Kurt Schuler and Andrew Rosenberg, *The Bretton Woods Transcripts* (The Center for Financial Stability 2012).

[10] International Bank for Reconstruction and Development Articles of Agreement (entered into force 27 December 1945) 2 UNTS 134, art I. In the same vein, article I of the Articles of Agreement of the International Development Association highlights IDA's purposes as to promote economic development, increase productivity, and raise standards of living in less developed areas within the association's membership. *International Development Association Articles of Agreement* (entered into force 24 September 1960) 439 UNTS 249.

[11] UNRRA was established in 1943 by the same group of forty-four countries that attended the Bretton Woods conference the following year. It became part of the United Nations (UN) when the latter was established in 1945. Later, UNRRA's forced displacement related functions were transferred to a UN temporary specialized agency called the International Refugee Organization (IRO), which was superseded by the Office of the UN High Commissioner for Refugees (UNHCR) in 1952. See Guy

refugee issues as it began an ambitious programme of European reconstruction. For example, in applying for a Bank loan in 1947, Denmark referred to significant expenditures for German refugees.[12]

The Bank continued to sporadically encounter forced displacement issues even after its early reconstruction phase ended in the 1950s. In the 1970s, for instance, the Bank served as the secretariat for a donor group called the India Consortium.[13] Among other things, the Consortium sought to mobilize funds to deal with East Pakistan refugees in India.[14] To do so, the Bank produced a remarkably detailed report on the direct economic costs to India from the refugee influx. But the Bank itself, did not provide any financial support for refugee programmes.[15] Implicit in the Bank's decision was the assumption that any such support would be perceived as humanitarian relief rather than development assistance.[16]

b. Partnerships with UNHCR on forced displacement issues

In 1984, the Bank entered into an interesting partnership with UNHCR to help Afghan refugees in Pakistan.[17] The Bank's involvement was based on a strong economic development rationale. Under the partnership arrangement, the Bank would design, appraise, and execute projects to assist the economic integration of Afghan refugees by generating jobs for both the refugees and local population.[18]

S Goodwin-Gill, 'International Refugee Law in the Early Years' in Cathryn Costello, Michelle Foster, and Jane McAdam (eds), *The Oxford Handbook of International Refugee Law* (OUP 2021) 40–41; Emily Haslam, 'United Nations Relief and Rehabilitation Administration (UNRRA)' in *Max Planck Encyclopedia of Public International Law* (OUP 2006) <https://opil.ouplaw.com/home/mpil> accessed 14 August 2022.

[12] The Secretary of the IBRD, *Danish Loan Application* (Sec-743, 11 June 1947) 13.
[13] The India Consortium consisted of a group of donors coordinating long-term financing to India's development plan. The Bank functioned as the Consortium's secretariat, with Bank staff providing economic analysis and reports for discussion at Consortium meetings, supplying financial data, monitoring the progress of development, and providing secretariat support and meeting documentation. World Bank Archives, 'Exhibit: The World Bank Group's Role in the India Consortium' (*World Bank Archives, Explore History*) <The World Bank Group's Role in the India Consortium> accessed on 5 June 2023.
[14] World Bank, *Office Memorandum: India—Meeting with Delegation: Contacts with Member Countries: India—Correspondence 04* (Folder ID 1771076, ISAD(G, Reference Code WB IBRD/IDA 03 EXC-10-4549S, World Bank Group Archives, 27 October 1971) 48.
[15] World Bank, 'Cost of Refugee Relief in India' in International Bank for Reconstruction and Development/International Development Association, *Cost of Refugee Relief in India* (Folder ID 448171, ISAD(G, Reference Code WB IBRD/IDA SAR, World Bank Group Archives, 5 October 1971).
[16] See Sydney H Schanberg, 'World Bank says Refugee Cost may Stunt Indian Development' *The New York Times* (New Delhi, 16 September 1971).
[17] Shahid Javed Burki, 'Statement of Mr Shahid Javed Burki, Director, International Relations Department, The World Bank, at the International Conference on African Refugee Assistance held in Geneva' (English) (World Bank Group July 1984) 2. See also Stefano Petrucci, 'Generating Income for Afghan Refugees in Pakistan (English)' (OED Précis, No 129, World Bank Group November 1996).
[18] Pakistan Income Generating Project for Refugee Areas (IGPRA), Operations Evaluation Department, *Pakistan Impact Evaluation Report: Income Generating Project for Refugee Areas; Second*

The projects would, in turn, contribute to Pakistan's economic development. The first project was well rated in an evaluation and paved the way for a second and a third project.[19] Tellingly, the Bank did not actually provide any of its own funds for these operations. Rather, the projects were financed by donor grants, mostly through a Bank-administered trust fund.[20] Even so, this was an important inflection point in the Bank's position on forced displacement.

In the years that followed, the Bank increased its outreach to UNHCR and other agencies on forced displacement issues in the context of its development operations. In 1993, for instance, Bank representatives joined UNHCR staff in visiting three refugee camps in Mauritania. The mission's objective was to understand the refugee situation in Mauritania, Mali, and the broader Sahel region. These visits engendered an internal debate about whether the Bank could get more deeply involved in refugee issues.[21]

In the early 1990s, the Bank participated in a coordinated international aid initiative for Mozambique. Among other things, the country was grappling with severe forced displacement problems. While the Bank focused primarily on economic and finance reforms, its support complemented UNHCR's humanitarian aid and refugee resettlement efforts at the community level.[22] These early engagements bore modest fruit. However, it was increasingly clear that greater institutional coordination was required between the Bank and UNHCR if their partnership was to be effective and produce credible development outcomes.[23]

These experiences emboldened the Bank in the early 2000s to allocate a modest amount from its Post Conflict Fund, a Bank-administered trust fund, for refugee-related activities. In 2001, the Bank provided grants to international non-governmental organizations (NGOs) working with Afghan refugees in Peshawar, Pakistan.[24] Three years later, the Bank approved a significant financing for the HIV/AIDS response in Africa's Great Lakes region. The grant's beneficiaries included refugees, migrants, and transport workers who frequently cross borders in that region.[25] UNHCR remained an active partner with the Bank throughout these efforts.

Income Generating Project for Refugee Areas; Third Income Generating Project for Refugee Areas (Report No 15862-PAK, World Bank 28 June 1996) (hereafter 'Pakistan Impact Evaluation Report').

[19] Second Income Generating Project for Refugee Areas (IGPRA II) and Third Income Generating Project for Refugee Areas (IGPRA III). See ibid.
[20] Pakistan Impact Evaluation Report (n 18).
[21] Katherine Marshall, 'The Bank and Mauritania' in David L Delmonte and others, *Bank's World* (vol 12, no 9, World Bank Group September 1993).
[22] Katherine Marshall, 'From War and Resettlement to Peace Development: Some Lessons from Mozambique and UNHCR and World Bank Collaboration' (Paper 633, Harvard Institute for International Development 1998).
[23] ibid 9.
[24] World Bank, *Afghanistan—World Bank Approach Paper (English)* (Working Paper, World Bank Group November 2001).
[25] World Bank, *Africa Region—Great Lakes Initiative on HIV/AIDS (GLIA) Support Project (English)* (Project Information Document, World Bank Group 2004).

c. Gradual engagements with internal displacement

In the 1990s, the Bank took a more active role in dealing with internally displaced persons (IDPs) in the context of its development projects. Thus, a 1995 Bank-financed rehabilitation programme for Azerbaijan included support for IDP health and education issues.[26] The Bank also began providing support for IDPs returning to their homes after a conflict. This support covered agricultural activities, basic social and economic infrastructure, delivery of services, housing, and social protection.[27] And in 2007, the Bank approved a project for IDP housing in Sri Lanka. The project endeavoured to provide IDP beneficiaries with permanent housing and regularized land titles.[28] The Bank's experience with this project is notable. It revealed the complexities and challenges of addressing forced displacement issues which require a more careful approach beyond the provision of funding. As originally designed, the project relied on a 2006 UNHCR baseline survey to determine beneficiary eligibility. However, the Sri Lankan government subsequently opposed the use of that survey. The project had to be restructured to accommodate the government's insistence and ease growing tensions between the host communities and IDP communities.[29]

For many years, the Bank's IDP interventions were largely ad hoc. Like its fledgling engagements with refugees, the Bank's IDP activities were implemented without an overarching operational strategy or policy framework. In recent years, the Bank's work on internal displacement aims to provide more balanced direct support for IDPs, returnees, and their host communities. Yet, at present, the Bank's IDP engagements are predominantly through indirect support without targeting displaced persons directly.[30] Instead, the Bank aims to ensure through its environmental and social safeguards framework that IDPs, as a vulnerable group, benefit from operations where they are located.

---

[26] World Bank, *Report and Recommendation of the President of the International Development Association to the Executive Directors on a Proposed Rehabilitation Credit of SDR 41.6 Million to the Azerbaijan Republic* (Report No P-6655-AZ, World Bank 26 July 1995).

[27] Independent Evaluation Group (IEG), *World Bank Group Support in Situations Involving Conflict-Induced Displacement: An Independent Evaluation* (2019) <World Bank Group Support in Situations Involving Conflict-Induced Displacement: An Independent Evaluation> accessed 5 June 2023 (hereafter 'IEG Report').

[28] World Bank, *Sri Lanka: World Bank to Help Rebuild Lives of Internally Displaced People in Puttalam (English)* (Announcement, 20 February 2007).

[29] World Bank, *Proposal to Restructure the Puttalam Housing Project—IDA Credit 4261-CE (PI00390)—for Social Democratic Republic of Sri Lanka (English)* (Project Paper, World Bank Group 10 September 2009).

[30] IEG Report (n 27) 13 (Box 2.1).

d. Global Program on Forced Displacement

In 2009, the Bank established the Global Program on Forced Displacement (GPFD). The programme was designed to raise awareness about conflict-induced displacement and enhance a 'global development response' through economically and socially sustainable solutions.[31] Among other things, the GPFD commissioned new research on the development dimensions of forced displacement with a focus on refugees and host communities.

This nascent approach to displacement came just as conflict erupted in Syria and refugees began pouring out of the country. In response, the Bank made several grants from its State and Peacebuilding Fund to assist Lebanon and Jordan, which were grappling with refugee flows.[32] In 2011, the Bank provided substantial financing from IDA's Crisis Response Window (CRW) to tackle drought in the Horn of Africa. This financing covered nutrition, health, and sanitation activities in Somali refugee settlements in Kenya and Ethiopia.[33] In 2015, the Bank approved an innovative operation to provide cash grants for displaced persons in Pakistan's Federally Administered Tribal Areas.[34] Significantly, the government undertook to ensure that the project would be implemented consistently with the UN's 'Guiding Principles on Internal Displacement'.[35]

3. The 'Development Approach' to Forced Displacement

The Bank's early engagements coincided with an evolution of international responses to humanitarian crises. Until this time, forced displacement was seen primarily as a humanitarian issue. However, this approach was not sustainable because the increasing scale and protracted nature of conflict was putting pressure on the existing system for crisis response.[36] A turning point was reached in 2015,

---

[31] IEG Report (n 27).
[32] The State and Peacebuilding Fund is a World Bank-administered multi-donor trust fund that provides financing to help prevent conflict, support rapid crisis response, and build long-term resilience in situations of fragility, conflict, and violence. World Bank, 'About SPF' available at <https://www.worldbank.org/en/programs/state-and-peace-building-fund/overview> accessed 14 August 2022.
[33] The grant, which was administered by UNHCR, was the first CRW grant issued directly to a UN agency. World Bank, *World Bank, UNHCR Join Efforts in an Emergency Response to Malnutrition and Disease in Horn of Africa Refugee Camps (English)* (Press Release, World Bank Group 15 September 2011).
[34] World Bank, 'Pakistan—FATA Temporarily Displaced Persons Emergency Recovery Project (P154278)' (*The World Bank*, 26 August 2015, updated 20 January 2023) <https://projects.worldbank.org/en/projects-operations/project-detail/P154278> accessed 5 June 2023.
[35] UN Commission on Human Rights, *Guiding Principles on Internal Displacement* (UN Doc E/CN4/1998/53/Add2, 11 February 1998) (hereafter 'Guiding Principles on Internal Displacement'). World Bank, *Pakistan—FATA Temporarily Displaced Persons Emergency Recovery Project (English)* (Project Appraisal Document, World Bank Group 12 August 2015) 26, 75 (hereafter 'Pakistan FATA PAD').
[36] Roger Zetter, 'Theorizing the Refugee Humanitarian-Development Nexus: A Political-Economy Analysis' (2021) 34(2) JRS 1766, 1770.

when the conflict in Syria intensified and led to a refugee crisis in Europe. This led to efforts by the international community to strengthen the coordination and complementarity between humanitarian and development efforts to address the multifaceted dimensions of forced displacement.[37]

a. Forced displacement and development

In this context, the Bank published a lengthy report in March 2016 entitled 'Forced Displacement and Development'.[38] Drawing on the Bank's emerging operational experience and analytical work in this area, the report announced the World Bank Group's intention to adopt a 'development approach' to forced displacement and increase assistance for this purpose to low- and middle-income refugee-hosting countries. This announcement was a major paradigm shift in the Bank's evolving attitudes to forced displacement. Six months later, the development approach was elaborated and expanded upon in a flagship report 'Forcibly Displaced', produced in close partnership with UNHCR.[39]

Briefly stated, under the development approach, the Bank would utilize its comparative advantage to focus on the medium- to long-term socioeconomic dimensions of forced displacement. The Bank would help address specific vulnerabilities of refugees and IDPs. It would support sustainable development in host communities. And it would work with governments to strengthen their institutions, policies, and capacity to handle forced displacement. The approach called for the Bank's forced-displacement-related activities to be implemented in partnership with humanitarian, political, diplomatic, and security institutions and agencies.

b. Coordination with other organizations

The Bank's development approach to forced displacement was not a unilateral initiative. It was underpinned by close coordination with other multilateral development banks (MDBs), notably the African Development Bank, the Asian Development Bank, the European Bank for Reconstruction and Development, the European Investment Bank, the Inter-American Development Bank, and the

---

[37] As Zetter (ibid) points out, this effort to strengthen the 'humanitarian-development nexus' has resulted in a variety of coordinated institutional initiatives. This includes the 2015 'Grand Bargain'; the 2016 World Humanitarian Summit; the 2016 United Nations High-level Meeting on Addressing Large Movements of Refugees and Migrants; and the 2018 Global Compacts on Refugees and Migration.

[38] World Bank Group, *Forced Displacement and Development* DC2016-0002 (Report prepared for the 16 April 2016 Development Committee Meeting, 25 March 2016) (hereafter '2016 Development Committee Report'). Also see IEG Report (n 27).

[39] World Bank, *Forcibly Displaced: Toward a Development Approach Supporting Refugees, the Internally Displaced, and Their Hosts* (2017) (hereafter 'Forcibly Displaced Report').

Islamic Development Bank. This collaborative approach to forced displacement is emphasized in a 2016 paper jointly prepared by the World Bank Group and other MDBs, which endorses the development approach and articulates a shared commitment to its implementation.[40]

In April 2018, the development banks launched an MDB Coordination Platform on Economic Migration and Forced Displacement to enhance collaboration among themselves. At the 2019 Global Refugee Forum, the MDB platform specifically committed to support countries dealing with forced displacement through enhanced coordination, key stakeholder engagements, and rapid assistance, including through dedicated financing instruments.[41]

4. Relevant Legal Norms and Principles

The above-described Bank's development approach embraces international forced displacement norms and principles in several ways. These norms and principles are derived from several international legal frameworks and sources. They are summarized below.

a. International refugee law

i. International instruments

Following the horrors of WW II and the Holocaust, the United Nations Convention relating to the Status of Refugees (1951 Convention) was adopted at a diplomatic conference in Geneva in 1951. The 1951 Convention defines refugees as persons outside their countries of nationality or habitual residence, who are unable or unwilling to avail themselves of those countries' protection, due to a 'well-founded fear of being persecuted' based on race, religion, nationality, membership of a particular social group, or political opinion.[42] The 1951 Convention initially applied only to refugees displaced by events occurring in Europe before 1 January 1951, but this temporal and a further optional geographic limitation were removed by

---

[40] African Development Bank, Asian Development Bank, European Bank for Reconstruction and Development, European Investment Bank, Inter-American Development Bank, Islamic Development Bank, and World Bank Group, *The Forced Displacement Crisis: A Joint Paper by Multilateral Development Banks* (Open Knowledge Repository, 2017) <The Forced Displacement Crisis: A Ioint Paper by Multilateral Development Banks (worldbank.org)> accessed 5 June 2023.

[41] UNHCR, *UNHCR Stocktaking Report on Multilateral Development Banks' Engagement in Situations of Forced Displacement: Assessing Progress made since the 2019 Global Refugee Forum* (Global Compact on Refugees, 2021) (hereafter 'UNHCR Stocktaking Paper') <UNHCR stocktaking report on multilateral development banks' engagement in situations of forced displacement | The Global Compact on Refugees | UNHCR (globalcompactrefugees.org)> accessed on 5 June 2023.

[42] *Convention relating to the Status of Refugees* (189 UNTS 150, opened for signature 28 July 1951, entered into force 22 April 1954) art 1(A).

the 1967 Protocol relating to the Status of Refugees (1967 Protocol), which expanded the 1951 Convention's scope and application.[43]

The 1951 Convention and its 1967 Protocol constitute the bedrock of international refugee law. These instruments establish legally binding obligations for state parties relating to the treatment and protection of asylum seekers and refugees. They grant refugees a distinct legal status and confer specific rights and protections upon them.[44] In practice, states parties to these instruments give effect to these rights and protections through national laws, policies, and strategies.

Article 33 of the 1951 Convention enshrines the *non-refoulement* principle. Simply put, *non-refoulement* prohibits the return of refugees to a country where they face serious threats to their life or freedom. This principle is now widely considered to be a part of customary international law, i.e. it applies to states that are not parties to the 1951 Convention and the 1967 Protocol.[45]

ii. Regional instruments

Refugee protection under the 1951 Convention and its 1967 Protocol is complemented by specific regional instruments. Two important examples are the 1969 Organization of African Unity Convention (the OAU Convention)[46] and the 1984 Cartagena Declaration of Refugees (the Cartagena Declaration). The OAU Convention expands the 1951 Convention's refugee definition to include people displaced due to 'external aggression, occupation, foreign domination or *events seriously disturbing public order*'.[47] The OAU Convention does not define or describe events that may seriously disturb public order. Relying on this formulation, however, UNHCR has argued that persons displaced by the adverse effects of climate change and natural disasters may have valid claims for refugee status under the OAU Convention in certain circumstances.[48]

---

[43] *Protocol Relating to the Status of Refugees* (606 UNTS 267, entered into force 4 October 1967). For further detail on the optional geographic limitation, which was not widely adopted, see Guy Goodwin-Gill and Jane McAdam, *The Refugee in International Law* (4th edn, OUP 2021) 572–73 n 7 (hereafter 'The Refugee in International Law').

[44] These rights include, inter alia, non-discrimination (art 3), freedom of religion (art 4), personal status and associated rights (art 12), moveable and immoveable property (art 13), work (arts 17–18), housing (art 21), public education (art 22), social security (art 24), freedom of movement (art 26), and identity papers (art 27) and travel documents (art 28).

[45] UNHCR, *Advisory Opinion on the Extraterritorial Application of* Non-Refoulement *Obligations under the 1951 Convention relating to the Status of Refugees and its 1967 Protocol* (26 January 2007). See also Hélène Lambert, 'Customary Refugee Law' in Cathryn Costello, Michelle Foster, and Jane McAdam (eds), *The Oxford Handbook of International Refugee Law* (OUP 2021) 240–57.

[46] Organization of African Unity (OAU) *Convention Governing the Specific Aspects of Refugee Problems in Africa* (1001 UNTS 45, opened for signature 10 September 1969, entered into force 20 June 1974).

[47] ibid art 1 (emphasis added).

[48] UNHCR, *Legal Considerations regarding Claims for International Protection made in the Context of the Adverse Effects of Climate Change and Disasters* (*refworld*, 1 October 2020) <https://www.refworld.org/docid/5f75f2734.html> accessed on 5 June 2023.

The Cartagena Declaration is a non-binding instrument that has influenced or contributed to the adoption of displacement-related laws and policies in Latin America. Among other things, the declaration expands the 1951 Convention's refugee definition. Under Cartagena, refugees include persons who flee based on a claim that their lives, safety, or freedom are threatened by generalized violence, foreign aggression, internal conflicts, massive violation of human rights, or other circumstances which seriously disturbed public order.[49]

b. International law on IDPs

There is no codified international instrument for IDPs like the 1951 Convention and the 1967 Protocol for refugees. However, there is a framework of legal principles and standards on IDP protection.[50] These principles and standards are primarily derived from the 1998 UN Guiding Principles on Internal Displacement (Guiding Principles).[51]

The Guiding Principles comprise IDP-related norms and principles drawn from a variety of legal frameworks. Among other things, the Guiding Principles define IDPs as persons who flee or leave their homes or habitual residence without crossing internationally recognized borders to escape armed conflict, generalized violence, human rights violations, or natural or human-made disasters.[52] Under the Guiding Principles, states are primarily responsible for ensuring that IDP rights are enforced in a non-discriminatory manner. Furthermore, the norms and principles set out in the Guiding Principles protect IDPs not only when these persons are displaced from their homes but also through their return, resettlement, and reintegration.

Principles and standards on internal displacement may also be derived from certain regional frameworks. A notable example is the legally binding 2009 African Union Convention for the Protection and Assistance of Internally Displaced

---

[49] Colloquium on the International Protection of Refugees in Central America, Mexico and Panama, *Cartagena Declaration on Refugees* (22 November 1984) (emphasis added).

[50] Although normative and operational challenges pertaining to their implementation remain. For further details, see Jane McAdam, 'The Guiding Principles on Internal Displacement: 20 Years on' (2018) 30 IJRL 187. See also, Walter Kälin, 'Consolidating the Normative Framework for IDPs' (2018) 30 IJRL 314.

[51] Guiding Principles on Internal Displacement (n 35). These various frameworks include, as applicable, core international human rights instruments, including the International Covenant on Civil and Political Rights (ICCPR); International Covenant on Economic, Social and Cultural Rights (ICESCR); the Convention on the Rights of the Child (CRC); the Convention on the Elimination of all Forms of Discrimination Against Women (CEDAW); International Convention on the Elimination of All Forms of Racial Discrimination (ICERD); and the Convention on the Rights of Persons with Disabilities (CRPD), as well as international humanitarian law (particularly the four Geneva Conventions of 1949 and two Additional Protocols of 1977). The Guiding Principles also draw on relevant elements of international refugee law by analogy.

[52] Guiding Principles on Internal Displacement (n 35) para. 2.

Persons in Africa (Kampala Convention).[53] This regional convention draws on and expands the Guiding Principles to provide a comprehensive framework for IDP protection. It has accordingly shaped national laws and policies in several African countries.

c. International human rights law

International norms and principles relating to forced displacement may also be derived from sources beyond international refugee and IDP law. These interconnected and complementary sources include, most notably, international human rights law as well as international humanitarian law, and international criminal law.[54]

Among other things, international human rights law emphasizes states' obligations to respect, protect, and fulfil the human rights of individuals within their territory or jurisdiction, subject to the particularities of the right in question. It is particularly noteworthy that the 1951 Convention and 1967 Protocol are influenced by the Universal Declaration of Human Rights (UDHR).[55] Article 14 of the UDHR recognizes the human right to seek and enjoy asylum.[56] International human rights law is also salient in protecting IDPs who generally remain citizens or habitual residents of their states. Under this framework, each state, as the primary duty-bearer, has the responsibility to protect and assist displaced persons as long as they remain in the state's jurisdiction.

Human rights principles are also relevant to protecting persons who are displaced by climate change impacts and environmental crises and who cross international borders to seek protection. These displaced persons do not readily enjoy the international protection framework afforded to refugees who flee on account of 'a well-founded fear of being persecuted'. However, they may avail of so-called 'complementary' protection from removal under human rights-based *non-refoulement*.

---

[53] *African Union Convention for the Protection and Assistance of Internally Displaced Persons in Africa* (Kampala Convention) 3014 UNTS 447 (adopted 23 October 2009, entered into force 6 December 2012). Other examples include *Council of Europe Recommendation 6 of the Committee of Ministers to Member States* (2006); *Organization of American States Resolution 2850 on IDPs* (2014); *League of Arab States Resolution 761* (2016), among others.

[54] UNHCR, *Expert Meeting on Complementarities between International Refugee Law, International Criminal Law and International Human Rights Law, Arusha, Tanzania, 11–13 April 2011: Summary Conclusions* (July 2011).

[55] UNHCR, *A Guide to International Refugee Protection and Building State Asylum Systems: Handbook for Parliamentarians No 27* (Inter-Parliamentary Union and UNHCR 2017). See also UNHCR Executive Committee of the High Commissioner's Programme Conclusion No 85 (XLIX) 'Conclusion on International Protection' (9 October 1998).

[56] UDHR, UNGA Res 217 A (III) (10 December 1948) art 14. Note, however, that neither the 1951 Convention nor the 1967 Protocol explicitly recognize a right to seek asylum.

This principle prevents states from removing individuals to another country where they would be at risk of death or torture.[57]

d. International humanitarian law

International humanitarian law also provides protection to refugees and IDPs located in states or areas in which an armed conflict is occurring. Among other things, humanitarian law prohibits parties to an armed conflict from compelling civilians to leave their homes and protects those who are displaced during armed conflicts (including both IDPs and refugees) and offers special protection for refugees.[58]

5. Other Recent Developments on Sustainable Development and Forced Displacement

These legal frameworks were not traditionally associated with the development sector. However, a growing body of 'soft law' instruments and norms has been recently developed that help anchor forced displacement solutions within a broader framework of sustainable development.

a. Agenda 2030 and the SDGs

In September 2015, the UNGA adopted the 2030 Agenda, which lays out seventeen SDGs.[59] The SDGs constitute the common aspirational blueprint for sustainable development shared by all UN Member States. These goals highlight the shared commitment to 'leave no one behind'. They are aimed at furthering peace and prosperity, protecting the climate, reducing poverty and inequalities, promoting economic growth, ending hunger and food insecurity, securing health care and education, improving health and education, and providing employment and decent work.[60]

---

[57] Jane McAdam, *Complementary Protection in International Refugee Law* (Oxford Monographs in International Law, OUP 2007).

[58] See e.g. Fourth Geneva Convention, art 44 and Additional Protocol I, art 73. *Geneva Convention Relative to the Protection of Civilian Persons in Time of War* (Fourth Geneva Convention) (75 UNTS 287, entered into force 21 October 1950); *Protocol Additional to the Geneva Conventions of 12 August 1949, and relating to the Protection of Victims of International Armed Conflicts (Protocol I)* (1125 UNTS 3, entered into force 7 December 1979).

[59] UNGA Res 70/1 (n 5). More information is available at UN, 'Transforming our World: The 2030 Agenda for Sustainable Development' (*United Nations*) <https://sdgs.un.org/2030agenda> accessed on 5 June 2023.

[60] In this context, it is important to remember that although the SDGs are not legally binding commitments, they are grounded in international law. There has been substantial literature on the

Forced displacement is not directly mentioned in any SDG, nor was it initially included in the comprehensive indicator framework to measure progress in achieving specific goals.[61] Although a refugee-specific target was later added to this monitoring framework, it arguably does not adequately address the global development challenge of forced displacement.[62] Indeed, given their objective of leaving no one behind, most SDGs are relevant to the protection and welfare of displaced persons.[63] And yet, displaced persons rank among the most neglected social groups with respect to achieving SDG outcomes.[64]

b. Global compacts on refugees and migration

In 2016, the General Assembly adopted the New York Declaration for Refugees and Migrants.[65] This declaration began two parallel processes that resulted in the finalization of two non-binding global compacts: one on migration and one on refugees. The Global Compact for Safe, Orderly and Regular Migration (Migration Compact) was negotiated and agreed in an intergovernmental process by UN Member States. It was adopted by a majority of Member States and formally endorsed by the General Assembly in December 2018.[66] UNHCR held the labouring

relationship between human rights and development. See e.g. Siobhán McInerney-Lankford, 'ESIL-International Human Rights Law Symposium: Human Rights and Development Regimes—Reflections on Convergence and Influence' (*EJIL: Talk!*, 10 February 2016) <ESIL-International Human Rights Law Symposium: Human Rights and Development Regimes – Reflections on Convergence and Influence – EJIL: Talk! (ejiltalk.org)> accessed 5 June 2023. See also, World Bank and Organisation for Economic Co-operation and Development (OECD), *Integrating Human Rights into Development: Donor Approaches, Experiences, and Challenges* (3rd edn, The World Bank and OECD 2016). This was originally published in 2006, updated in 2012 and 2016, and through its fourth edition.

[61] The framework included a single Target that dealt broadly with migration and mobility. It refers to facilitating orderly, safe, regular, and responsible migration and mobility, including through the implementation of planned and well-managed migration policies (Target 10.7). UNGA Res 71/313 (n 5). For further information on the SDG Indicator framework, see UN, 'SDG Indicators: Global Indicator Framework for the Sustainable Development Goals and Targets of the 2030 Agenda for Sustainable Development' (*UN Sustainable Development Goals*) <https://unstats.un.org/sdgs/indicators/indicators-list/> accessed on 5 June 2023.
[62] Chiara Denaro and Mariagiulia Giuffré, 'UN Sustainable Development Goals and the "Refugee Gap": Leaving Refugees Behind?' (28 December 2021) 41(1) Refug Surv Q 79, 105.
[63] International Peace Institute, 'Reaching Internally Displaced Persons to Achieve the 2030 Agenda for Sustainable Development' (*International Peace Institute*, 17 July 2018) <https://www.ipinst.org/2018/07/internally-displaced-persons-2030-agenda-sustainable-development#2> accessed on 5 June 2023.
[64] See e.g. International Rescue Committee, 'Missing Persons: Refugees Left Out and Left Behind in the SDGs' (23 September 2019) <http://rescue.org> accessed 28 June 2023. See also Petra Nahmias and Natalia Krynsky Baal, 'Including Forced Displacement in the SDGs: A New Refugee Indicator' (*UNHCR Blogs*, 2019) <www.unhcr.org/blogs/including-forced-displacement-in-the-sdgs-a-new-refugee-indicator/> accessed on 5 June 2023.
[65] *New York Declaration for Refugees and Migrants* (UN Doc A/RES/71/1, 19 September 2016) (adopted unanimously).
[66] The text of the 'Global Compact for Safe, Orderly and Regular Migration' was informally agreed on 13 July 2018 in the culmination of an inter-governmental negotiations process at UN Headquarters. The

oar for the Global Compact on Refugees (Refugees Compact). This compact was formulated in close consultation with Member States and other stakeholders. This compact was affirmed and endorsed by the General Assembly in December 2018.[67]

The Refugees Compact explicitly links forced displacement with the SDGs and emphasizes that refugees must be included in all efforts towards achieving those goals.[68] The compact encourages states and other development actors to step up their support for refugees and host communities.[69] It also promotes complementarity between humanitarian interventions and development actors, while respecting country leadership and ownership consistent with national development strategies, and alignment with the 2030 Agenda. The Refugees Compact also creates a periodic Global Refugee Forum for states and other actors to make pledges towards these ends.[70]

Both compacts facilitated consensus building among states and stakeholders. They contributed to the emergence of certain normative principles on forced displacement whose codification through a binding instrument would have been unlikely.[71] Despite its non-binding character, the Refugees Compact represents the international community's political will for strengthened cooperation and solidarity with refugees and affected host countries.[72] The compact exhorts states to avoid protection gaps in implementation and calls upon them to ensure that all who need international protection receive it.[73] Yet, commentators have suggested it misses an opportunity to address the relationship between internal displacement, refugees, and others displaced across borders by factors such as disasters and climate change.[74]

Like the Refugees Compact, the Migration Compact explicitly references the SDGs, but is silent about internal displacement.[75] However, unlike the former, the latter directly applies to cross-border displacement due to climate change

---

Compact was then formally adopted by 164 UN Member States on 11 December 2018 at an intergovernmental conference, after which it was formally endorsed by the UNGA via UNGA Res 73/195 (UN Doc A/RES/73/195, 19 December 2018) (adopted by 152 votes for, to five against; twelve abstentions) (hereafter 'Global Compact for Migration').

[67] UNGA, *Report of the United Nations High Commissioner for Refugees, Part II: Global Compact on Refugees* (UN GAOR 73rd Session Supp No 12 UN Doc A/73/12 (Part II, 2 August 2018) (hereafter 'Global Compact on Refugees'). The Compact was affirmed by the UNGA via UNGA Res 73/151 (UN Doc A/RES/73/151, 17 December 2018) para 23.
[68] ibid para 9.
[69] ibid para 32.
[70] ibid para 65.
[71] Tim Hoflinger, 'Non-binding and Therefore Irrelevant? The Global Compact for Migration' (2020) 75(4) Int'l J 662.
[72] Global Compact on Refugees (n 67) para 4.
[73] ibid para 61.
[74] For a general assessment on the gaps pertaining to the Global Compact on Refugees, see Alexander Aleinikof, 'The Unfinished Work of the Global Compact on Refugees' (2018) 30(4) IJRL 611. See Global Compact on Refugees (n 67) paras 12 and 89.
[75] Global Compact for Migration (n 66) paras 18(a)–(b) and 35(a).

and other factors. Objective 2 of the Migration Compact calls for addressing the root causes and structural factors that compel people to leave their countries of origin. The compact offers a suite of potential actions to achieve this goal. These actions include joint analysis and information sharing on movements due to natural disasters, climate change, and environmental degradation.[76] Objective 5 focuses on enhancing the availability and flexibility of pathways for regular migration. To this end, the compact calls on states to cooperate in identifying and improving solutions for migrants fleeing disasters, climate change, and environmental degradation for whom, *in situ*, adaptation or return is not possible.[77]

6. International Law Dimensions of the Bank's Development Approach to Forced Displacement

As discussed previously, using a development approach, the Bank has broadened and deepened its financing and analytical activities relating to forced displacement. In operationalizing the development approach, the Bank clearly acknowledged that its forced displacement engagements must be designed, implemented, and monitored consistently with relevant legal norms and principles. These norms and principles are derived from international and regional instruments like the 1951 Convention, the 1967 Protocol, the OAU Convention, and the Kampala Convention, as well as other sources such as the Guiding Principles on Internal Displacement, Agenda 2030, the Migration Compact, and the Refugees Compact.

a. Dedicated financing mechanisms

To implement the development approach to forced displacement, the Bank has formulated specific financing mechanisms to assist countries hosting refugees and host communities.[78] These mechanisms include the Global Concessional Financing Facility (GCFF or the Facility) and IDA Window for Host Communities and Refugees (WHR or the Window). As discussed below, the Facility provides concessional financing to middle-income host countries while the Window does so with respect to low-income countries. Relevant international refugee protection norms are incorporated in both mechanisms.

---

[76] ibid para 18(h).
[77] ibid para 21(h).
[78] This is in part due to differing member state considerations and incentives associated with internal displacement as opposed to refugee situations. For example, WHR financing is meant to incentivize IDA countries to provide support to refugees—who are not their citizens—without detracting from the country's regular IDA resource allocations. The Window does not support IDP programming. IDA, 'Special Theme: Fragility, Conflict & Violence' (Discussion Paper, 24 May 2019) n 98.

i. Global concessional financing facility

The GCFF is a financial intermediary fund for which the Bank serves as trustee. It was established in 2016 by the Bank, the United Nations, and the Islamic Development Bank.[79] The Facility provides concessional financing for middle-income host countries whose borrowings are typically at market rates. The Facility's resources comprise donor contributions from Bank members as well as loans from MDBs. The Facility blends these resources to provide concessional assistance to eligible middle-income countries. As of this writing, the GCFF had approved US$551 million in funding to support projects in four middle-income countries: Lebanon, Jordan, Colombia, and Ecuador.[80]

To be eligible for GCFF financing, a country must host more than 25,000 refugees which must represent more than 0.1 per cent of its population. It must also commit to principles that contribute to long-term solutions, benefitting both refugees and host communities.[81] This commitment is measured by the country's adherence to international refugee norms and principles. However, a beneficiary host country need not be party to the 1951 Convention, the 1967 Protocol, or any regional refugee instrument, as long as its national policies and practices are consistent with these instruments' refugee protection principles.

ii. IDA Window for Host Communities and Refugees

The WHR is a financing facility of IDA—the World Bank Group's concessional-assistance institution. IDA has a AAA rating and borrows from commercial markets. However, the Association continues to rely on donor contributions to sustain its concessional assistance model. IDA donors make contributions in three-year cycles or replenishments. These resources are made available for projects and programmes in IDA members that qualify for concessional assistance.[82] Each member, which qualifies for IDA's assistance, is assigned a country allocation based on a complex formula.[83] Beyond its country allocation, an IDA member may qualify for

---

[79] The GCFF began as the Concessional Financing Facility for Jordan and Lebanon, which was launched in April 2016 to meet the needs of those two middle-income countries which were hosting large numbers of Syrian refugees. In September 2016, it was renamed the Global Concessional Financing Facility and its scope was broadened from only Jordan and Lebanon to any middle-income country meeting the established eligibility criteria.

[80] Global Concessional Financing Facility, 'Supported Projects' (*GCFF*, 2022) <https://globalcff.org/supported-projects/> accessed on 6 June 2023.

[81] GCFF, *GCFF Operations Manual* (approved 28 July 2016, amended 7 September 2016 and 20 April 2017) <https://globalcff.org/wp-content/uploads/2017/10/CFF-Operations-Manual-as-amended-on-4-20-17.pdf> accessed on 6 June 2023.

[82] A member's eligibility for IDA's resources is determined primarily by its relative poverty. Relative poverty is defined as gross national income per capita below a specific annually updated threshold. The eligibility threshold is US$1,315 for fiscal year 2024. IDA, 'Management's Discussion & Analysis and Financial Statements' (30 June 2023) 8 <https://thedocs.worldbank.org/en/doc/b38629a142167d3f5b6dcf39646379c5-0040012023/original/IDA-Financial-Statements-June-2023.pdf> accessed 24 August 2023.

[83] Country allocations are calculated annually using a formula reflecting changes in the country's performance, eligibility for IDA financing, availability of resources, and country needs. IDA, *Building*

additional resources from the association's windows that focus on specific development themes.

The Window is one such additional source of IDA assistance. It was first established by donors through the association's eighteenth replenishment (IDA18) in January 2017.[84] Donors agreed to continue setting aside resources for the Window in IDA's nineteenth and twentieth replenishments in 2020 and 2022, respectively.[85] As of this writing, the Window has approved fifty-six operations focusing on refugees and host communities in sixteen refugee-hosting IDA countries.[86] The WHR under IDA20 offers a total of US$2.4 billion in dedicated funding for IDA countries hosting refugees if they meet certain criteria.

There are two basic eligibility criteria for an IDA recipient country to access the Window. First, the country must host UNHCR-registered refugees that number at least 25,000 or that comprise 0.1 per cent of the country's population. Second, the country must adhere to an adequate framework for the protection of refugees. It must also have an acceptable strategy or plan with concrete actions, including policy reforms, to provide long-term solutions for host communities and refugees.[87] This second eligibility criterion under the Window explicitly links financing to an IDA member's adherence to international or regional instruments or, in the case of non-signatories, its policies and practice that reflect international refugee protection standards.

An eligibility assessment under this criterion inexorably examines whether the host country's strategies, policies, and practice reflect international principles and standards on refugee protection. In determining whether a country satisfies this criterion, the Bank requests and obtains an assessment from UNHCR. Implicit in the Bank's reliance on UNHCR is its recognition that the Bank has limited technical expertise on protection issues. It is also a recognition of UNHCR's specialized mandate, competence, and significant operational experience in dealing with refugee protection issues.[88]

Back Better from the Crisis: Toward a Green, Resilient and Inclusive Future (World Bank Group 17 February 2022) 130 (hereafter 'IDA20 Replenishment Report').

[84] IDA, *Towards 2030: Investing in Growth, Resilience and Opportunity* (World Bank Group 12 January 2017, modified 31 January 2017) 115.

[85] IDA20 Replenishment Report (n 83); IDA, *Ten Years to 2030: Growth, People, Resilience* (World Bank Group 11 February 2020) 122 (hereafter 'IDA19 Replenishment Report').

[86] These countries are Bangladesh, Burkina Faso, Burundi, Cameroon, Chad, Democratic Republic of the Congo, Djibouti, Ethiopia, Kenya, Mauritania, Niger, Pakistan, Republic of the Congo, Rwanda, South Sudan, and Uganda.

[87] IDA20 Replenishment Report (n 83) (emphasis added).

[88] UNHCR is a subsidiary organ of the General Assembly with the mandate to provide international protection and seek permanent solutions for refugees, including by promoting the conclusion of international conventions for the protection of refugees and supervising their application. *Statute of the Office of the UN High Commissioner for Refugees* (UNGA Res 428 (V) of 14 December 1950 (Annex)) paras 1–2, 8(a). See also The Refugee in International Law (n 43) 487–89.

Yet an IDA recipient's threshold eligibility for financing resources from the Window does not put it over the finish line. The country must continue to satisfy the Window's eligibility criteria to access the resources at any point in time. IDA rules require a recipient country to continue satisfying the eligibility criteria throughout a Window-financed project's life cycle, ranging from appraisal to approval and implementation.[89] In addition, the financing agreements between the association and an eligible IDA recipient for Window-financed projects expressly codify the protection adequacy criterion. By their terms, these agreements only become effective if the association is satisfied that the recipient country has an adequate refugee protection framework. What is more is that the agreements provide that IDA may suspend disbursements under a Window-financed project if the recipient fails to satisfy the first eligibility criterion because its refugee protection framework is no longer adequate. This remedy is available irrespective of whether the change in that country's protection adequacy impacts the actual WHR-financed operation. At this writing, this remedy has not been invoked in any case. In practice, the Bank works closely with UNHCR and the recipient's authorities to address doubts and concerns about the country's protection framework.

The Bank's adoption of the WHR framework is a significant milestone in its history and evolution as a development institution. Indeed, some would argue that the codification of the protection adequacy requirement for host countries in the Bank's legal agreements has far-reaching implications for the theory and practice of development as well as for international refugee law.

Besides providing financing for projects and programmes, the WHR framework encourages host countries to consider policy reforms to promote long-term solutions for refugees and host communities. These reforms may promote refugees' welfare and inclusion in the host country's socio-economic structures. Besides social and economic aspects, these reforms may include legal solutions with respect to refugees' freedom of movement, participation in the workforce, identification documents and residency permits, and access to quality services, including education.[90] In fact, as discussed below, the Bank has developed a Refugee Policy Review Framework (RPRF) to gauge progress in countries eligible for the Window toward these policy reforms in an effort to identify further opportunities for IDA support.[91]

---

[89] IDA20 Replenishment Report (n 83) 130.
[90] ibid.
[91] World Bank, 'Refugee Policy Review Framework: Technical Note' (*World Bank*, 2021) <https://documents.worldbank.org/en/publication/documents-reports/documentdetail/159851621920940734/refugee-policy-review-framework-technical-note> accessed on 6 June 2023 (hereafter 'RPRF Technical Note').

b. Bank Policies and Procedures

i. 'Fragility, conflict, and violence' policy

In August 2021, the Bank updated its policy framework for engaging in situations of fragility, conflict, and violence (FCV).[92] The updated FCV policy includes a dedicated section on the Bank and forced displacement. Recognizing the evolution of the institution's forced displacement activities, the policy emphasizes that the Bank's focus is on medium- to long-term development challenges arising from forced displacement. According to the policy, the Bank does so by addressing the specific vulnerabilities of refugees and IDPs and supporting sustainable economic and social development in refugee and host communities. The policy also recognizes that the Bank may work with governments to strengthen relevant institutions and policies and build capacity, while account of social, economic, and political sensitivities in host countries.

Outlining modalities for support, the policy states that the Bank supports refugee-hosting member countries in: (i) mitigating the shocks caused by refugee inflows and creating social and economic development opportunities for refugee and host communities; (ii) facilitating sustainable solutions to protracted refugee situations, including through the sustainable socio-economic inclusion of refugees in the host country and/or their return to the country of origin; and (iii) strengthening country preparedness and resilience for increased or potential new refugee flows. The policy also declares that the Bank may assist countries of origin in addressing root causes of displacement and preparing for sustainable repatriation, as appropriate.

A noteworthy feature of the FCV policy is its reference to the Window's eligibility criterion on the adequacy of a country's protection framework. The policy, however, stops short of imposing this requirement for all Bank operations. Rather, it states that the Bank 'considers' the adequacy of member countries' refugee protection frameworks and operates in coordination with relevant international specialized agencies, including UNHCR.[93] This formulation permits the Bank to consider a country's protection framework in determining whether to provide financing from sources other than the IDA Window or GCFF. So far, there is insufficient practice to comment on whether the adequacy requirement has been applied more generally to operations financed from other sources.

With respect to internal displacement or the return of forcibly displaced populations, the policy declares that the Bank follows the overall development approach described above within the broader context of supporting countries and

---

[92] World Bank, *Updated Bank Policy: Development Cooperation and Fragility, Conflict, and Violence* (World Bank Group 2021) (hereafter 'Updated FCV Policy').
[93] ibid para. 11.

populations. The role of international standards and principles in this area may be developed further through Bank practice.

ii. Environmental and Social Framework

Besides the FCV Policy, the Bank's Environmental and Social Framework (ESF) is also an important source of policy rules and principles that impact Bank engagements in forced displacement.[94] Applicable to investment projects only, the ESF comprises several elements: an aspirational vision statement, a set of standards called the Environmental and Social Standards (ESSs), a policy document called the Environmental and Social Policy (E&S Policy), its accompanying 'directive' on E&S requirements for investment operations (E&S Directive),[95] as well as a Directive on Addressing Risks and Impacts on Disadvantaged or Vulnerable Individuals or Groups (the Directive on Disadvantaged or Vulnerable Individuals or Groups).[96] The ESSs outline certain basic requirements for Bank borrowers in managing environmental and social risks and impacts associated with projects. The Bank's responsibilities on this subject are set out in the E&S Policy, the E&S Directive, and the Directive on Disadvantaged or Vulnerable Individuals or Groups.

The ESF, as a whole, does not specifically target refugees or IDPs. However, several ESF principles and criteria are relevant to the Bank's engagements in forced displacement situations and could be applied to refugees or displaced persons including IDPs. For instance, the E&S Policy imposes specific inclusion, security, and consultation requirements that are relevant and applicable to Bank operations involving forced displacement.[97] Similarly, the Directive on Disadvantaged or Vulnerable Individuals or Groups prescribes due diligence obligations on the Bank to identify and mitigate risks and impacts on such individuals or groups. These may apply—and have been applied—to refugees and IDPs.[98]

Moreover, ESS1 (Assessment and Management of Environmental and Social Risks and Impacts) requires a borrower to ensure that a Bank-financed project's

---

[94] World Bank, 'Environmental and Social Framework' (2016) <https://www.worldbank.org/en/projects-operations/environmental-and-social-framework> accessed on 6 June 2023 (hereafter 'ESF'). The World Bank's ESF became effective on 1 October 2018 and applies to all investment policy financing (IPF) projects initiated after this date. As such, the ESF replaced older 'Safeguard Policies'.

[95] World Bank, *Environmental and Social Policy for Investment Project Financing* (became effective on 1 October 2018) (hereafter 'E&S Policy'); World Bank, *Bank Directive: Environmental and Social Directive for Investment Project Financing* (issued on 28 November 2021, became effective on 19 November 2021).

[96] World Bank, *Directive on Addressing Risks and Impacts on Disadvantaged or Vulnerable Individuals or Groups* (issued and became effective on 27 March 2021) (hereafter 'Directive on Disadvantaged or Vulnerable Individuals or Groups').

[97] See E&S Policy (n 95).

[98] The Bank's 'OP 8.00 on Rapid Response to Crises and Emergencies' also explicitly includes IDPs as an example of a 'vulnerable group' whose economic reintegration may be an objective of the Bank's rapid response efforts. See World Bank, *OP/BP 8:00—Rapid Response to Crises and Emergencies* (revised on 1 July 2014).

environmental and social assessment appropriately takes into account the country's applicable policy framework, national laws, and regulations relating to the project as well as that country's obligations under relevant international treaties and agreements directly applicable to the project.[99] In appropriate and relevant cases, these international obligations, laws, and regulations may also include norms and principles applicable to forced displacement.

According to ESS1, social risks and impacts in any Bank-financed project may include threats to human security as well as discrimination in accessing project benefits particularly for disadvantaged or vulnerable individuals or groups.[100] Accordingly, if the project's environmental and social assessment identifies specific disadvantaged and vulnerable individuals or groups, the borrower must take 'differentiated measures' to ensure that adverse impacts do not disproportionately affect these individuals or groups. These individuals and groups should not be disadvantaged in terms of development benefits and opportunities resulting from the project.[101] Furthermore, the Directive on Disadvantaged or Vulnerable Individuals or Groups lays out due diligence requirements for Bank teams with respect to these groups.[102]

ESS2 (Labor and Working Conditions) is also relevant to forced displacement. The standard aims at protecting project workers, including 'vulnerable workers' such as migrant workers. ESS2 provides that such workers should not be discriminated against, and it requires the borrower to provide protection and assistance to address vulnerabilities of project workers[103] and to prevent the use of forced labour or trafficking of persons in connection with the project.[104] Another relevant standard is ESS10 (Stakeholder Engagement and Information Disclosure). It calls for meaningful consultation and participation with stakeholders and communities, which may include refugees and IDPs, in identifying and mitigating environmental and social risks and impacts and in designing protection mechanisms to address them.

A special mention must be made of ESS5 (Land Acquisition, Restrictions on Land Use and Involuntary Resettlement). This standard makes a threshold distinction between project-induced displacement and displacement due to other reasons including natural disasters, conflict, crime, or violence unrelated to a project. This distinction is necessary to clarify that ESS5 applies only to project-related displacement, i.e. displacement that is a direct consequence of land acquisition or land-use restrictions for projects. The standard does not apply to other forms or

---

[99] ESF (n 94) ESS1, para 26.
[100] ibid ESS1, para 28(b).
[101] ibid ESS1, para 29.
[102] Directive on Disadvantaged or Vulnerable Individuals or Groups (n 96) paras 2–10.
[103] ESF (n 94) ESS2, paras 13–15.
[104] ibid ESS2, para 20 and fn 15.

causes of forced displacement.[105] At the same time, ESS5 does apply to refugees or IDPs who are further displaced as a result of Bank-financed project activities.[106] The guidance note on ESS5 reinforces this point further. It states that an affected person, who is originally a refugee, is not precluded from receiving assistance like any other project-affected person.[107] The application of ESS5 in such situations requires 'a case-by-case assessment, taking into account, as appropriate, advice from agencies such as the [UNHCR]'.[108]

Although the technical scope of ESS5 generally excludes refugees and IDPs who are not displaced due to a Bank-financed project,[109] the Bank may draw upon its rich operational experience in dealing with complex issues involving involuntary resettlement of project-affected persons in designing projects that focus on forced displacement, refugees, and IDPs.[110]

c. Refugee policy reform and dialogue with Member States

A key tenet of the Bank's development approach is its recognition that financing is no silver bullet in confronting forced displacement challenges. Equally or more important are the host country's institutions and policies focusing on refugees and host communities. Indeed, there are several refugee-related institutional actions and policy reforms, which countries may adopt, that evidence shows can be truly transformational and maximize development outcomes.[111] It is this fact which underpins the Bank's policy dialogue with governments on forced-displacement issues.[112]

i. Analytics and diagnostic tools

Over the past two decades, the Bank has undertaken considerable technical assistance as well as analytical and advisory work on forced displacement. Besides influencing the Bank's financing interventions, such assistance, analytical, and advisory activities are particularly useful in shaping the institution's outreach to, and discussions with, governments on forced displacement matters.[113] These discussions may cover a broad array of topics. They include potential reforms to laws, policies, and strategies to align national refugee protection frameworks with

---

[105] ibid ESS5, para 5. See also, World Bank, *Guidance Note (GN)—ESS5: Land Acquisition, Restrictions on Land Use and Involuntary Resettlement* (1st edn, June 2018) GN9.1.
[106] ibid GN9.2.
[107] ibid.
[108] ibid.
[109] ibid.
[110] Michael M Cernea, 'Bridging the Research Divide: Studying Refugees and Development Oustees' REP481 (Working Paper, 1996) 293–317.
[111] 2016 Development Committee Report (n 38) 6; Forcibly Displaced Report (n 39) 8.
[112] See IDA19 Replenishment Report (n 85) para 116.
[113] 2016 Development Committee Report (n 38) 6.

international norms and standards. Indeed, in many countries, legal and policy actions taken by governments, in the broader context of a Bank-supported operation, are often derived from or based on applicable international norms and standards.

It is also apparent that the Bank's analytical and advisory activities as well as its diagnostic tools on forced displacement are significantly influenced by accepted or emerging international legal norms and standards. One such tool is the RPRF. The framework, which was devised in consultation with UNHCR and other stakeholders, provides a basic methodology to systematically review a Window-eligible IDA recipient country's refugee policy and institutional environments. An RPRF exercise is intended to gauge progress, identify reform opportunities, and inform further IDA support for refugee hosting countries.[114]

Among other things, the RPRF methodology calls for a comprehensive consideration of whether a country's refugee policy framework is consistent with international norms and standards irrespective of whether the country is a signatory to relevant international instruments.[115] Since at this writing the RPRF is a relatively new diagnostic tool concerning a country's policy and institutional environment on forced displacement, it is difficult to accurately state whether, or in what manner, the exercise can meaningfully measure or influence national institutions and policies on forced displacement to ensure their consistency with international standards.

The Bank has also undertaken a fair degree of analytical work and some policy dialogue on internal displacement. Overall, the Bank's reliance on international principles and standards when dealing with IDP issues is somewhat muted when compared to its refugee engagements. There are, however, some notable exceptions. For example, in 2018 the Bank published an important study on land and conflict.[116] This report refers prominently to the Guiding Principles and the Kampala Convention and recommends that the Guiding Principles be applied in designing relocation projects for displaced persons.

ii. Bank-financed operations

As discussed earlier, utilizing resources from the IDA Window and GCFF, the Bank has financed a considerable number of operations focusing on refugees and host communities. These projects and programmes support improving refugee access to basic health and education services, social protection, and jobs.[117] In most cases, these operations' development objectives do not include advancing refugee protection or rights. Even so, the underlying documents in many projects

---

[114] RPRF Technical Note (n 91); IDA19 Replenishment Report (n 85).
[115] ibid (RPRF Technical Note) 11.
[116] Barbara McCallin and Eleonore Mai, *Land and Conflict: Thematic Guidance Note 01: Restitution Compensation and Durable Solutions to Displacement and Dispossession* (World Bank Group 2018) 10.
[117] See Development Finance, Corporate IDA, and IBRD (DFCII), *IDA19 Mid-Term Refugee Policy Review (English)* (World Bank Group 2021) Annex 3.

and programmes include numerous references to applicable international refugee principles and standards. For example, the Project Appraisal Document for one operation notes that 'there has been a positive evolution in the international and domestic policy framework for refugee inclusion.' It also acknowledges the recipient country's endorsement of the Refugees Compact.[118] Similarly, the appraisal document for another operation points to the country's 'efforts to safeguard refugees and maintain protection standards that align with international norms and practices'.[119]

The design and content of these operations are increasingly informed by the Bank's analytical work and policy dialogue. In investment projects typically, a country's specific policy commitments are not directly reflected through financing conditionality beyond the general eligibility criteria under the Window or GCFF. In a small number of cases, however, the Bank has provided direct budget support for a government's programme of policy and institutional reforms regarding refugees. One such example is the 2019 Colombia Second Fiscal Sustainability, Competitiveness, and Migration Development Policy Financing Project.[120] This project was financed from GCFF resources and supported the Colombian government's policies to facilitate the integration and inclusion of refugees and migrants from Venezuela. The Bank-supported programme, in this case, included specific policy actions to regularize the legal status of irregular Venezuelan migrants and refugees to facilitate their access to the labour market and basic services such as education and health.[121]

A similar approach was taken in the 2016 Economic Opportunities for Jordanians and Syrian Refugees Program for Results Project,[122] which was also financed by the GCFF. This operation sought to improve economic opportunities for Syrian refugees in Jordan through labour market reform in line with the government's action plan.[123] One of the supported outcomes included granting

---

[118] World Bank, 'Ethiopia—Second Phase Development Response to Displacement Impacts Project in the Horn of Africa Project (English)' (Project Appraisal Document, *World Bank*, 26 May 2022) para 24 <https://projects.worldbank.org/en/projects-operations/project-detail/P178047> accessed on 6 June 2023.

[119] World Bank, *Pakistan—Balochistan Livelihoods and Entrepreneurship Project (English)* (Project Appraisal Document, *World Bank*, 5 February 2020) <https://projects.worldbank.org/en/projects-operations/project-detail/P159292> accessed on 6 June 2023.

[120] World Bank, 'Colombia Second Fiscal Sustainability, Competitiveness, and Migration DPF' (*World Bank*) <https://projects.worldbank.org/en/projects-operations/project-detail/P162858> accessed on 6 June 2023.

[121] World Bank, *Colombia—Second Fiscal Sustainability, Competitiveness, and Migration Development Policy Financing Project (English)* (Program Document, World Bank Group 23 April 2019) 36–38. This is available on the Colombia DPF project website (n 113).

[122] World Bank, 'Economic Opportunities for Jordanians and Syrian Refugees PforR' <https://projects.worldbank.org/en/projects-operations/project-detail/P159522> accessed on 6 June 2023 (hereafter 'Jordan PforR Project Website').

[123] World Bank, *Jordan—Economic Opportunities for Jordanians and Syrian Refugees Program for Results Project (English)* (Project Appraisal Document, World Bank Group 2 September 2016) para 24, table 1 (hereafter 'Jordan PAD'). This is available on the Jordan PforR project website (n 122).

Syrian refugees access to the labour market in line with international standards.[124] This action was taken pursuant to the Jordan Compact, which included financing commitments for the Jordanian government's policy incentives for refugees.[125] Under its legal agreement with Jordan, the Bank would disburse funds based on the actual numbers of work permits issued to Syrian refugees.[126]

The World Bank's IDP operations differ, in some respects, from its refugee financing. The Bank adopts what a recent paper calls an 'IDP lens' across its entire portfolio. This approach seeks to ensure that IDPs are recognized as vulnerable or marginalized groups across the Bank's broad spectrum of operations and treated accordingly in terms of access to project entitlements and benefits.[127] At present, the Bank does not envision a dedicated funding window for IDPs like the WHR.[128] However, like the Bank's refugee operations, documents for Bank operations that encounter or deal with IDPs include multiple references to international principles and standards. For example, the appraisal document for the 2015 Pakistan project discussed above specifies that returns of internally displaced persons will be voluntary, safe, and dignified in conformity with the 'internationally recognized' Guiding Principles and the government's Return Policy Framework.[129]

7. Conclusion: Interplay between International Law Norms and Bank Policies and Practice concerning Forced Displacement

The Bank's recognition of the development dimensions of forced displacement and its commitment to addressing them marks a watershed moment in its own institutional evolution as an international financial institution. To make this commitment, the Bank had to overcome significant internal and external scepticism about its own role and mandate in humanitarian crises. Yet, in so doing, the Bank contributed to a paradigm shift in the theory, policy, and practice of sustainable development.

---

[124] ibid (Jordan PAD) 2.
[125] The Jordan Compact was agreed at the Supporting Syria and the Region Conference in London, United Kingdom on 4 February 2016. See Government of Jordan, 'The Jordan Compact: A New Holistic Approach between the Hashemite Kingdom of Jordan and the International Community to deal with the Syrian Refugee Crisis' (2016) <https://reliefweb.int/report/jordan/jordan-compact-new-holistic-approach-between-hashemite-kingdom-jordan-and> accessed 23 August 2023. See also Cindy Huang and Kate Gough, 'The Jordan Compact: Three Years on, Where Do We Stand?' (*Center for Global Development*, 11 March 2019) <https://www.cgdev.org/blog/jordan-compact-three-years-on> accessed 14 August on 5 June 2023.
[126] Jordan PAD (n 123) table 5.
[127] World Bank, *A Development Approach to Conflict-Induced Internal Displacement* (World Bank, 2021) 7 <A Development Approach to Conflict-Induced Internal Displacement (worldbank.org)> accessed on 6 June 2023 (hereafter 'IDP Approach Paper').
[128] ibid.
[129] Pakistan FATA PAD (n 35) 26 (Annex 2).

Promoting international norms and principles relating to forced displacement was not an explicit objective of the Bank's development approach. However, in designing operations and producing analytical work on forced displacement, the Bank drew upon international norms and principles to ensure the sustainability, effectiveness, and credibility of its interventions, particularly in the refugee context. From a normative perspective, this approach is noteworthy for several reasons.

First, by explicitly and implicitly referring to applicable international legal principles and standards in its operations, policy dialogue, and analytical and advisory services, the Bank has contributed to spreading awareness about these principles and standards. In so doing, the Bank helps reinforce their normative character. This is particularly evident in the Bank's emphasis on the adequacy of national refugee protection frameworks for financing eligibility under the Window and GCFF. It could be argued that this incentivizes the implementation of international refugee protection standards by recipient host countries.[130] This is buttressed by the inclusion of the protection adequacy requirement in the Bank's legal agreements with WHR recipient countries irrespective of whether they are signatories to the relevant international instruments. As discussed earlier, the Bank's FCV Policy also recognizes the adequacy of a national refugee protection framework as an important consideration for future Bank engagement on forced displacement. With all applicable caveats, these facts could constitute evidence of emerging state practice that could eventually contribute to the generation of customary law on minimum standards for refugee protection.[131] This will depend on how widespread the protection adequacy requirement becomes and how consistently and in what manner the Bank, other MDBs, humanitarian agencies, or NGOs emphasize it in their outreach, dialogue, and activities.

The Bank's contribution to the progressive development of specific international norms is documented in other contexts.[132] For example, it seems clear that the Guiding Principles themselves may have been influenced by the Bank's policies and practice on involuntary resettlement in the context of development projects.

---

[130] Of the sixteen WHR benefitting countries, Bangladesh and Pakistan are not parties to the 1951 Convention or its 1967 Protocol. Of the four GCFF benefitting countries, Jordan and Lebanon are not parties to these instruments.

[131] For discussion of the formation of customary international law, see generally 'Final Report of the Committee: Statement of Principles Applicable to the Formation of General Customary International Law' in Antonio Parra and others (eds), *The World Bank in a Changing World: Selected Essays and Lectures* (Brill 2000); Andrew T Guzman, 'Saving Customary International Law' (2005) 27 Mich J Intl L 115; Jörg Kammerhofer, 'Uncertainty in the Formal Sources of International Law: Customary International Law and Some of Its Problems' (June 2004) 15(3) EJIL 523; Anthea Elizabeth Roberts, 'Traditional and Modern Approaches to Customary International Law: A Reconciliation' (2001) 95(4) AJIL 757.

[132] Guiding Principles on Internal Displacement (n 35) principle 7. For similar arguments concerning the Bank's role in the development of international environmental law, see Ibrahim Shihata, 'The World Bank's Contribution to The Progressive Development of International Environmental Law' in Antonio Parra and others (eds), *The World Bank in a Changing World* (Brill 2000) 487–516.

Indeed, the annotated commentary[133] on the Guiding Principles repeatedly cites the Bank's policies and directives on involuntary resettlement.[134]

Second, the Bank's emphasis on refugee norms and standards in its financing and country dialogue also contributes to policy coherence at the international level, overcoming the traditional separations between the humanitarian and development paradigms. As discussed earlier, the Bank's development approach to forced displacement was conceived and is shared by several MDBs. However, to date, only the Bank has dedicated financial instruments for refugee-hosting countries conditioned on their adherence to international refugee protection principles and standards.[135] These instruments underscore the linkages between sustainable development and forced displacement as articulated in the Refugees Compact.[136] More widespread engagement by other MDBs and international financial institutions on the normative and policy dimensions may further contribute to even greater policy coherence in international refugee law and sustainable development.

Third, to facilitate its engagement with refugee issues, the Bank has forged a close institutional and operational relationship with UNHCR. This partnership recognizes each institution's distinct mandates and core competence while leveraging their respective expertise and experience in formulating effective solutions to forced displacement.[137] Besides close operational collaboration, the Bank's partnership with UNHCR also enables reciprocal access to relevant information and expertise. This is exemplified by the establishment of the UNHCR-World Bank Joint Data Center on Forced Displacement in 2018. The centre includes staff, resources, and capacities from both organizations to improve the evidence base for policy and operations related to forced displacement.[138] The World Bank and UNHCR also signed a global Framework Data Sharing Agreement in June of 2023. This Agreement was designed to facilitate timely access to data related to the socio-economic condition of refugees, internally displaced and stateless populations.

The Bank's partnership with UNHCR has been particularly important in ensuring the smooth implementation of the GCFF and WHR financing mechanisms. While the Bank has a long-standing record in development financing, its adoption

---

[133] Walter Kälin, 'Guiding Principles on Internal Displacement: Annotations' (The American Society of International Law, Studies in Transnational Legal Policy No 38, 2008).

[134] The Annotated Commentary makes references to World Bank Operational Policy 4.12 of 2001 and its former Directive 4.30 throughout. The ESF replaced older 'Safeguard Policies', including OP/BP 4.12 (see ESS5 on Land Acquisition, Restrictions on Land Use, and Involuntary Resettlement).

[135] UNHCR Stocktaking Paper (n 41) 3.

[136] Global Compact on Refugees (n 67) paras 64–65.

[137] See Updated FCV Policy (n 92) paras 1, 7, 11, and 17–18.

[138] See UNHCR-World Bank Group Joint Data Center on Forced Displacement, 'Who We Are' (July 2021) <https://www.icvanetwork.org/uploads/2021/07/JDC-Advisory-Council-4-September-2019_CLEAN.pdf> accessed 24 August 2023; *World Bank-UNHCR Joint Data Center on Forced Displacement: Terms of Reference for the Strategic Advisory Council* (4 September 2019) <https://www.unhcr.org/news/press-releases/world-bank-unhcr-data-sharing-agreement-improve-assistance-forcibly-displaced> accessed 24 August 2023.

of the development approach to forced displacement called for extensive technical competence and expertise on forced displacement and refugee protection issues. The Bank plainly lacked such competence and expertise. Its operational partnership with UNHCR—particularly on refugee protection issues—was, therefore, vital to the success of its operational and policy engagements in forced displacement.

The Bank's collaboration with UNHCR on such issues was ad hoc at first. Over time, the modalities and procedures for such collaboration were set down in nonbinding internal staff guidance on determining the adequacy of a member's refugee protection framework for WHR eligibility. The involvement of UNHCR provides legitimacy and technical rigour to the process by ensuring that such determinations are based on accurate, up-to-date information and expertise in identifying serious and systematic refugee protection issues. More importantly, this partnership promotes greater institutional coordination on refugee financing and protection which leads to better policy dialogue and sustainable development outcomes.

Finally, this approach has shed light on how the nature of the international refugee framework has facilitated its integration into the Bank's development activities. In establishing the WHR and supporting operations for refugees and host communities, the Bank explicitly referred to refugee protection norms because they are codified in widely accepted international instruments. It is also evident that these norms have influenced specific programming and operational decisions, including eligibility determinations.

The Bank's focus on international refugee norms and standards also reflects the dichotomy of the international regime applicable to those who move across international borders. From an international law perspective, such individuals are generally characterized as either refugees, who are subject to the specific, widely adopted international refugee law regime, or voluntary migrants, who are subject to a more fragmented and diffuse international regime.[139] The former are entitled to legal protection and extensive rights, while the latter are covered by a patchwork of international norms whose application can vary from country to country. This duality is arguably further exacerbated by the adoption of separate global compacts for refugees and migration, which have been criticized for reinforcing unhelpful binaries between voluntary and forced migration.[140] Although it is indeed recognized that distinguishing between refugees and voluntary migrants is extremely

---

[139] International law applicable to 'voluntary' international migrants draws norms and standards from a variety of fields, including labour law, consular and diplomatic protection, and human rights law, and instruments, such as bilateral or regional labour, movement, or trade agreements. Some scholars conceptually include the international refugee law framework as part of a nascent 'global migration law' or 'international migration law' regime. See 'Framing Global Migration Law' (2017) 111(Special Issue) AJIL Unbound; Vincent Chetail, *International Migration Law* (OUP 2019).

[140] Mixed Migration Centre, *Final Statement on the Global Compact for Safe, Orderly and Regular Migration in Advance of the 6th and Final Round of Negotiations* (2018). For a detailed assessment, see Jane McAdam and Tamara Wood, 'The Concept of "International Protection" in the Global Compacts on Refugees and Migration' (2021) 12 UNSWLRS 2.

difficult in practice, it could be argued that this legal bifurcation facilitated the Bank's reliance on international refugee norms and standards by providing a self-contained regime with clear conceptual boundaries and defined circumstances for application.

The Bank's focus on international refugee law also contrasts with its relatively limited dealings with the norms and principles related to internal displacement. This may be related to the diffuse nature of relevant IDP obligations and the lack of a centralized, binding instrument at the international level. However, it is more clearly explained by varying incentives arising from institutional practicalities, including the Bank's country-based engagement model. As the IDP Approach Paper notes, the WHR was established because it seemed clear that refugee-hosting member countries were unwilling to use finite budget or development aid resources on refugees because they were non-citizens who in theory were only residing in the country temporarily.[141] However, the paper points out that this objection does not readily apply to a member country's internally displaced citizens or residents, who remain in the member country. For this reason, through its 'IDP lens' the Bank seeks to ensure that the internally displaced are identified as a vulnerable group in the context of Bank-funded operations. In so doing, the Bank could build on its development approach by drawing on relevant norms and principles, such as those embodied in the Guiding Principles, when dealing with internal displacement or IDPs in the course of its projects.

Like other themes explored in this volume, international forced displacement law intersects with and influences the theory and practice of sustainable development. This fact is evident from the Bank's relevant policies, projects, and analysis—particularly regarding refugees—which refer to or rely on international legal principles and standards. This dynamic is still developing and is likely to be further explored in the Bank's 2023 World Development Report on cross-border mobility.[142] Yet, it is undeniable that the development approach illuminates and emphasizes the somewhat overlooked socio-economic dimensions of international refugee protection. In so doing, the approach has facilitated an unprecedented global partnership and common understanding among development agencies, humanitarian actors, and governments on this topic. Finally, the approach has strengthened the moral, normative, and legal case for protecting refugees and supporting host communities to facilitate their integration.

---

[141] IDP Approach Paper (n 127) 39; see also 2016 Development Committee Report (n 38) 8.
[142] See 2023 World Development Report: World Bank Group, 'Migrants, Refugees, and Societies' (*World Bank*, 2023) <https://www.worldbank.org/en/publication/wdr2023> accessed on 6 June 2023.

12
Problematizing the Role of the World Bank in Latin America Mining Reforms

Ximena Sierra-Camargo

1. Introduction

In the late nineties, the World Bank (the Bank) adopted strategies in favour of policies aimed at strengthening foreign investment in the mining sector in the Global South states. A core element of the mining reforms promoted by the Bank was the modification of the role of the state in the mining sector. Adjusting the legal and institutional frameworks in the domestic sphere, the Bank sought the state to stop being an 'operator' and become a 'regulatory' state. This transition implied a new mining model in which foreign mining companies had the priority directly to carry out exploration and exploitation activities, under the supervision of the states, but without excessive controls or obstacles to obtain permits and licences.

The 'economic openness' environment that emerged with the neo-liberal turn, facilitated the implementation of various privatization programmes in the mining sector. These processes were favourable for strengthening private investors and mining corporations, which, in turn, were part of extensive mergers and acquisitions to become more attractive to investors in the financial market. After several meetings such as the one that took place in Washington DC in 1994, on 'Development, Environment and Mining', in which some international organizations discussed the importance of redefining the roles of both the state and private actors in the mining sector, the Bank issued in 1996 the document 'The Mining Strategy for Latin America and the Caribbean'[1] which had been preceded by 'The African Mining Strategy' issued in 1992.[2]

---

[1] World Bank and the International Bank for Reconstruction and Development (IBRD), *A Mining Strategy for Latin America and the Caribbean* (World Bank Technical Paper No 345, Industry and Mining Division, Industry and Energy Department, 1996) <https://documents1.worldbank.org/curated/en/650841468087551845/pdf/multi0page.pdf> accessed 7 June 2023 (hereafter 'A Mining Strategy').

[2] World Bank and IBRD, *Strategy for African Mining* (World Bank Technical Paper No 181 Mining Unit, Africa Technical Department Series, Industry and Energy Division, 1992) <https://documents1.worldbank.org/curated/en/722101468204567891/pdf/multi-page.pdf> accessed 7 June 2023 (hereafter 'Strategy for African Mining').

In the 1996 document, the Bank established the guidelines for the Latin American states regarding their constitutional and law reforms in the mining sector. As will be discussed, these guidelines were aimed at guaranteeing the legal certainty of foreign investors in the mining sector, granting them non-discriminatory treatment in relation to public sector companies regarding access to natural resources, and offering them favourable conditions for the development of their activities, including measures such as fiscal and commercial benefits. These measures aimed to create an attractive and predictable environment for the private actors with a minimal state intervention in their mining operations.

The Bank, pursuant to its mandate to fight poverty and improve the living conditions of people in developing countries, highlighted the importance of its own role[3] in interceding between investors and the Global South states, so that these latter could attract foreign investment in the mining sector, as long as the states facilitated the conditions for extracting natural resources through the adaptation of their legal and institutional frameworks. Unlike what happened in the 1960s and 1970s, during the 'decolonization' period,[4] the policies in the mining sector promoted by international organizations such as the Bank since the end of the twentieth century were no longer aimed at the state recovering control over its natural resources, but rather at guaranteeing to private actors, through the states' apparatus, the necessary conditions directly to exploit natural resources.

In Colombia for instance, the Bank noted that although the government had made significant efforts to promote some mining reforms, the mining policy established in the Colombian 1988 mining code was fragmented.[5] This policy was considered insufficient for foreign investors to carry out efficiently their large-scale mining projects. According to the classification made by the Bank, Colombia was in the third group of states along with Brazil and Venezuela. These states had a mining industry and had begun to make efforts to adjust their mining regime, however, they still needed to incorporate a series of much more ambitious reforms to adapt their internal legal systems to the World Bank guidelines.

In order to implement the new mining model in the Latin American states, the Bank noted the importance of adjusting the constitutions of these states, since by modifying the constituent pacts, greater guarantees of legal certainty and long-term predictability could be achieved for foreign investors in the mining sector. Yet the Bank also stated that it was necessary to modify the existing mining legislation and issue new mining codes and other regulations to unify the mining policies in the Latin America region according to the new guidelines.

---

[3] A Mining Strategy (n 1) viii, xiii–xiv.
[4] See Antony Anghie, *Imperialism, Sovereignty and the Making of International Law* (1st edn, CUP 2005).
[5] A Mining Strategy (n 1) 7–8.

Moreover, appealing to a new ostensibly environmentally-friendly discourse, the Bank highlighted the need to incorporate the element of 'sustainability'[6] in the new mining legislation to achieve 'sustainable mining'.[7] In this sense, the Bank pointed out that the idea of development incorporated in the new mining reforms and policies should respond to the notion of 'sustainable development',[8] with the purpose of promoting 'development' in the regions where mining operations would take place, while mitigating environmental impacts.

However, with the inclusion of the notion of 'sustainable development' in the policies promoted by the Bank in the mining sector, the possibility of rethinking the 'extractivist paradigm'[9] by slowing down the processes of accumulation and extraction of resources, was not considered. The incorporation of some environmental concerns in mining policies resulted in thinking about how an economic model based on the intensive and endless extraction of natural resources could be sustained, while mitigating the impacts on the environment. Under the new categories such as 'sustainability' or 'sustainable mining' some key elements like the scale at which mining activities are carried out or the endless nature of extractive activities were not questioned. Similarly, the participation of local communities in the decisions of this type of process was raised mainly as the contribution of unskilled labour by these communities in mining projects, but without questioning the particular development view embedded in the mining projects supported by the Bank and by the foreign investors.

In this vein, the main objective of this chapter is to examine, from a critical developmental perspective, the guidelines and policies in the mining sector

---

[6] ibid xviii, 36, 46.
[7] ibid xii–xiv, 79.
[8] See s 3.1 in this chapter.
[9] The extractivist paradigm implies the development of intense large-scale extractive activities mainly by private foreign investors in the global south. The necessity of this policy is justified by the necessity of currency of the Global South states and by the rationality of capital accumulation and endless resources extraction according to an economic hegemonic model. This paradigm has been reupdated under the notion of (neo)extractivism or new extractivism which emphasizes on the role of global actors and the emergence of local social and environmental conflicts. This notion is in turn connected to the phenomenon known as the 'mining boom', which began at the end of the twentieth century and continues to this day. This notion of (neo)extractivism was coined firstly by Anthony Bebbington who referred to the direct relationship between the increase of investment in extractive activities and the emergence of social and environmental conflicts in Latin America, regardless of the political ideologies behind each government. Secondly, other authors such as Eduardo Gudynas, Henry Veltemeyer, and James Petras have referred to such notion emphasizing the extractive economies leaded by the governments of the so-called 'new Latin American left', which attracted foreign investment in the mining sector arguing that the resources derived from such activities should be redistributed among the population through social programmes. Finally, when referring to the notion of new extractivism, Dougherty emphasized the mining industry and not the political regimes, arguing that the effects produced by such industry are equally negative regardless of the political ideology of each government. See Michael Dougherty, 'From the Global Peripheries to the Earth's Core: The New Extraction in Latin America' in Kalowatie Deonandan and Michael Dougherty (eds), *Mining in Latin America. Critical Approaches to the New Extraction* (1st edn, Routledge 2016) 5–6.

promoted by the Bank in Latin America since the 1990s, which reveal the 'extractivist paradigm' that guided such reforms and that were promoted in a context of 'global coloniality' which led to updating colonial hierarchies and legacies between the Global South and the Global North.[10] Indeed, the policies promoted by key international actors to mobilize global capital, such as the World Bank, have deeply influenced the configuration of the Global South states as 'mining states', which have had to adapt their constitutions and legislation with the purpose that foreign investors, mostly from Global North states, can carry out large-scale mining activities.

In this transnational law-making process, international law and in particular, international economic law, has played a key role. The adaptation of domestic legal systems to the demands of international financial organizations that mobilize global capital has also been reinforced by international investment agreements which tend to include broad clauses that protect the rights and expectations of the foreign investors. These clauses have in turn caused the restriction of the autonomy and regulatory capacity of the states to design and modify their policies in the domestic sphere, making the 'extractivist paradigm' practically immoveable. It has made it possible to strengthen the private actors in the mining sector and the intensive extraction and accumulation of resources processes. Under this scheme, the profits received by the state derived from mining activities are minimal and are restricted to incomes derived from royalties.

Using a genealogy on the new mining model created at the transnational level after 1990s, this chapter discusses whether the incorporation of categories such as 'sustainable development' in the mining reforms promoted by the Bank, are addressed mainly to sustain an hegemonic economic model, but not the 'environment' itself, and how, ultimately, it has ended up sustaining mainly capital gains in the mining sector. Moreover, this chapter questions how the process of commodification of nature under the 'sustainable development' notion is mediated by the state itself, which, in turn, acts as an interface between nature and capital, and between the global order and the local order. Despite the great difficulties in carrying out 'sustainable' large-scale mining projects, the discourse of 'sustainable development' vis-à-vis 'responsible mining' has ended up legitimizing itself, precisely because what is at stake is an economic model which is based on a sustained growth and an endless capital accumulation.

---

[10] See Ramón Grosfoguel, 'Developmentalism, Modernity and Dependency Theory in Latin America' in Mabel Moraña, Enrique Dussel, and Carlos A Jáuregui (eds), *Coloniality at Large: Latin America and the Postcolonial Debate* (1st edn, Duke University Press 2008) 307–33.

2. World Bank and Mining Reform in the Global South

The World Bank is one of the main institutions promoting a neoliberal reform agenda,[11] primarily since the so-called Washington Consensus.[12] This institution, created at the end of World War II as part of the Bretton Woods agreement, and whose main function is to assist technically and financially the so-called developing countries. By the end of the twentieth century, on the advice of the Swedish economist, Assar Lindbeck, the Bank attributed the responsibility for the crisis in which they found themselves to the mismanagement of resources by the indebted states.[13]

According to the Bank, these states had not managed the market properly and had made a series of mistakes, such as the imposition of subsidies on basic products and assistance to the agricultural sector through loans and other mechanisms. To counteract these errors, the Bank imposed a series of measures aimed mainly at removing subsidies, eliminating all kinds of barriers in capital transactions and independent central banks with the aim of protecting the value of money and the security of investors.[14] Moreover, during the 1990s, the World Bank began to issue a series of recommendations to developing countries on the way in which they should carry out activities in the mining sector. These recommendations were mainly guided by the idea of new technologies for extracting resources while they were framed in a friendly environment for foreign investors.[15]

The report 'Mineral Sector Technologies: Policy Implications for Developing Countries' was published by the World Bank at the beginning of the 1990s. It explains that the duty of international agencies was to continue stimulating developing countries to promote policies and mechanisms under the idea of free trade, to prevent governments from intervening directly in the mining sector, arguing

---

[11] Ngaire Woods, *The Globalizers. The IMF, the World Bank and Their Borrowers* (1st edn, Cornell University Press 2007); Rodrigo Uprimny and César Rodríguez Garavito, 'Justicia para todos o Seguridad para el Mercado? in El Neoliberalismo y la Reforma Judicial en Colombia y en América Latina' in Darío Restrepo Botero (ed), *La Falacia Neoliberal. Críticas y Alternativas* (Universidad Nacional de Colombia 2003) 415–52; Harvey David, *A Brief History of Neoliberalism* (1st edn, OUP 2005); Germán Burgos Silva, *Estado de Derecho y Globalización. El Papel del Banco Mundial y las Reformas Institucionales en América Latina* (1st edn, ILSA 2009).

[12] John Williamson, 'The Washington Consensus as Policy Prescription for Development', Lecture for the Series 'Practitioners of Development', The World Bank Washington, DC (*Peterson Institute for International Economics*, 13 January 2004) <The Washington Consensus as Policy Prescription for Development | PIIE> accessed 7 June 2023.

[13] See World Bank, Office of the Vice President, Economics and Research Staff, *Report on the World Bank Research Program Part II* (Report No 5325, 1984).

[14] Kari Polanyi Levitt, *From the Great Transformation to the Great Financialization. On Karl Polanyi and Other Essays.* (1st edn, Zed Books 2013) 12–13.

[15] A Mining Strategy (n 1) viii, xiii–xvii; World Bank and International Finance Corporation (IFC), 'Mining Reform and the World Bank: Providing a Policy Framework for Development' (Global Mining Series, The World Bank Group's Oil, Gas, Mining and Chemicals Department, 2003) <https://documents1.worldbank.org/curated/en/511531468782172927/pdf/313750mining0reform0and0the0wb.pdf> accessed 7 June 2023 (hereafter 'Mining Reform and the World Bank').

that excessive controls and cumbersome procedures to obtain mining titles could represent an obstacle to foreign investment and for the insertion of new technologies.[16]

Invoking its mandate to fight poverty and help improve the living conditions of people in developing countries, the Bank pointed out that since one of the main sources of income for these states was foreign investment in the mining sector, it was up to the Bank to serve as a bridge between governments, private investors, and civil society to ensure the issuance and implementation of mining reforms, aimed at effective risk mitigation management and to achieve an 'evolution towards a acceptable and environmentally sustainable development'.[17]

The Bank stated that considering that the poorest population is the one that is generally most exposed to the risks derived from mining operations, its mission should be to provide support to governments in the creation of regulatory frameworks and institutions that could contribute to sustainable development. This institution also argued that, through its financial arm, the International Finance Corporation (IFC), it had a responsibility to promote 'responsible private investment' in mining projects in developing countries.[18]

In 1994, the same year in which the General Agreement on Tariffs and Trade (GATT) became the World Trade Organization (WTO), and in which the North American Free Trade Agreement (NAFTA) was signed, various organizations, including the Bank, United Nations Conference on Trade and Development (UNCTAD), the United Nations Environment Program (UNEP), and the International Council on Metals and the Environment (ICME), held an International Conference on Development, Environment and Mining in Washington DC. In this conference, a series of guidelines were issued regarding the role of the public and private sectors in the mining industry, so that governments could follow them.

According to the new guidelines, governments should create and maintain a favourable environment that allowed private companies in the mining sector to be competitive in the international market. The Bank pointed out that, although the public mining companies or the state-owned mining enterprises (SOEs) had been established in the 1960s under the notion that foreign private investors did not act in the public interest, private companies had managed to prove for three decades that they were much more efficient and competitive than SOEs, and more effective in raising capital.[19]

---

[16] Craig B Andrews, 'Mineral Sector Technologies: Policy Implications for Developing Countries' (1992) 16(3) Nat Resour For 212–20 <https://onlinelibrary.wiley.com/doi/epdf/10.1111/j.1477-8947.1992.tb00571.x> accessed 7 June 2023.

[17] World Bank and IFC, 'An Asset for Competitiveness: Sound Environmental Management in Mining Countries' (Global Mining Series, World Bank Group's Oil, Gas, Mining and Chemicals Department, 2002) 14–15 <https://dokumen.tips/documents/mining-and-development-world-and-development-mining-anddevelopment-an-asset-for.html?page=4> accessed 7 June 2023.

[18] ibid.

[19] Mining Reform and the World Bank (n 15) 18.

The Bank pointed out that private sector investors can be encouraged and regulated to act responsibly and to reflect national interests through appropriate mining policies and efficient administrative and legal procedures. For this reason, the Bank explained that SOEs are rare in successful mining jurisdictions, and that cases such as Codelco in Chile was considered as an exception.[20] The Bank stated that the presence of SOEs should not be contemplated in any mining reform initiative. On the contrary, the Bank's assistance in this matter, in those states with a significant presence of SOEs, should be concentrated fundamentally on the processes of closure and privatization of their operations.[21]

An example of the processes considered successful by the Bank for this type of reform is the case of the Bolivian company COMIBOL. Between 1989 and 1997, this company closed more than 80 per cent of its operations with the assistance of the Bank and within the framework of 'The Mining Sector Rehabilitation Project'.[22] Another example took place in Africa where the Bank promoted a technical assistance project to restructure the company Zambia Consolidated Cooper Mines (ZCCM). This project aimed to close those operations that were considered 'unviable' and privatize those that were considered viable by the Bank.[23]

The emphasis on the 'regulatory' role of the states in the mining reform processes promoted by the Bank, led it to formulate a new series of guidelines that should guide the actions of the governments. Thus, the Bank stated that governments should firstly establish an efficient, consistent, and fair legal framework; second, promote a solid technical structure both at the national and departmental levels; third, develop government agencies at both levels that are responsive to the needs of mining companies; fourth, assist development policies and eliminate inefficient practices; fifth, encourage diversification in order to remove government subsidies; sixth, encourage foreign investment and allow the entry of new technologies and practices; seventh, work hand in hand with local financial institutions to improve access for foreign mining companies through loans; and lastly, to ensure that investors did not receive 'discriminatory' treatment in access to the nation's mineral resources.[24]

The pressure exerted by the World Bank on the governments of the developing countries led to reforms in their mining codes being promoted in most

---

[20] ibid.
[21] ibid.
[22] World Bank, *Republic of Bolivia Mining Sector Rehabilitation Project* (Report No 7630-BO, Industry, Trade and Finance Operations Division, Country Department III Latin America and the Caribbean Region, 17 April 1989).
[23] World Bank, *Implementation Completion Report Republic of Zambia, Mining Sector Technical Assistance Project (CREI)IT 2269-ZA)* (Report No 18094, Mining and Industry Unit Energy, Mining and Telecommunications Department Private Sector Finance, Africa Regional Office, 25 June 1998).
[24] World Bank, *Enhancing the Contribution of the Mineral Industry to Sustainable Development* (Post Conference Summary, Development, Environment and Mining, 1-3 June 1994) <http://www-wds.worldbank.org/external/default/WDSContentServer/WDSP/IB/1999/09/10/000009265_3980429111207/Rendered/PDF/multi_page.pdf> accessed 7 June 2023.

Latin American states since the end of the twentieth century. Reforms in the Latin American region particularly followed the Chilean model, as Chile was the first state in the Latin American region to modify its mining legislation.[25] In Chile during the 1970s, it issued the Decree 600 of 1974, through which the new Foreign Investment Statute was established. In 1981, Law 18.097 of 1981, better known as the Organic Constitutional Law on Mining Concessions, was issued. The reform of the Water Code was also promoted, and in 1983 the reform of the Mining Code was approved. These reforms were considered as examples of successful legal frameworks and were presented as 'models' in other Latin American states, in order to create favourable opening conditions for transnational mining companies throughout the region.[26]

These initiatives and legislative reforms were aimed: first, to guarantee the legal certainty of the rights over mining concessions, granting foreign investors the necessary guarantees for this; second, to promote enormous fiscal and commercial benefits through measures such as the suppression and reduction of rates and taxes on foreign investors, and the extension of said benefits for periods of up to twenty-five and thirty years; and, third, to establish very soft controls, especially in relation to environmental liabilities due to mining and with environmental inspection and control bodies.[27] In this sense, the World Bank considered that the regulatory reforms that were promoted in Chile in the mining sector were successful insofar as they established a non-discriminatory treatment for foreign investors and a minimum intervention of the governments in the mining activities carried out by transnational companies. Likewise, with said reforms, investors were given stability in legal and fiscal terms.[28]

The subsequent reforms that were promoted in various Latin American states, starting in the 1990s, gave rise to a considerable increase in investments in mining in the region, moving from US$200 million in 1990 to US$1,300 million in 1998. Investments in the mining sector grew by a percentage equivalent to 400 per cent in Latin America, in contrast to the increase that occurred in the rest of the world, being equivalent to 90 per cent.[29] This was also due to the large increase in world demand for metals during the 1990s, which, according to the United Nations Economic Commission for Latin America and the Caribbean (ECLAC),[30] was

---

[25] Mining Reform and the World Bank (n 15) 1–2.
[26] ibid 1, 24.
[27] Horacio Machado Aráoz, 'El Auge de la Minería Transnacional en América Latina. De la Ecología Política del Neoliberalismo a la Anatomía Política del Colonialismo' in Héctor Alimonda (ed), *La Naturaleza Colonizada. Ecología Política y Minería en América Latina* (Clacso 2011) 159–60.
[28] Mining Reform and the World Bank (n 15) 24.
[29] ibid 5.
[30] The Economic Commission for Latin America and the Caribbean (ECLAC) (also known as CEPAL for its acronym in Spanish) was established by the Economic and Social Council Resolution 106(VI) of 25 February 1948, to contribute to the economic development of Latin America and strengthen economic ties among countries in the region and with other nations of the world. See ECLAC, 'About' (*UN ECLAC*) <https://www.cepal.org/en/about> accessed 7 June 2023.

reflected in the policy of opening up to foreign investment in the mining sector, and at the same time contributed to the concentration of business ownership.[31] In this regard, ECLAC explains that in the second half of the 1990s, a process of mergers and acquisitions occurred with greater intensity in the mining industry worldwide. According to ECLAC, between 1995 and 2001 this process reached a total of US$151,900 million in 569 operations. Morever, 2001 was the year in which the highest amount was reached, equivalent to US$40,000 million. Similarly, between 1990 and 1999, US$28.3 billion dollars were spent on 146 gold projects.[32]

Some of the reasons invoked to explain this process were 'the need to strengthen companies to increase their profitability through adequate synergies, improve their ability to attract investment funds in the stock markets and boost this productive sector that has lost participation relative to world trade.'[33] The foreign capital that was invested in the mining sector during those years in the Latin American region corresponded to 30 per cent of the investments in the world. For this reason, Latin America was considered the main beneficiary of mining capital during that period and the main supplier of a large part of the mining resources for world demand. For example, in terms of gold, production in the region went from 5 per cent in 1980, to 10 per cent in 1990, and to 14.9 per cent in 2004.[34]

In the report 'Mining and International Competitiveness in Latin America', ECLAC stated that, for the period 2000–04, Latin America became the primary producer of gold in the world, exporting 391.2 tons, compared to the period 1990–99 in which it exported 276.9 tons, and to the period between 1986 and 1989, when it was equivalent to 214.6 tons. According to the Bank, in the 1990s, and specifically in the period between 1990 and 1997, not only a large number of mining reforms were promoted, but there was also a considerable increase in the prices of metals considered commodities. This situation caused a massive flow of mining companies to the Global South, especially those companies known as 'risk-taking junior'.[35] From the early 1990s to 1997, these companies expanded their activities

[31] Humberto Campodónico and Georgina Ortiz, 'Características de la Inversión y del Mercado Mundial de la Minería a Principios de La Década de 2000' (Serie Recursos Naturales e Infraestructura No 49, Division on Natural Resources and Infraestructure, ECLAC, 2000) <https://repositorio.cepal.org/bitstream/handle/11362/6409/S0210819_es.pdf?sequence=1> accessed 7 June 2023 (hereafter 'Características de la Inversión').

[32] ibid 27–28.

[33] ibid 6.

[34] Fernando Sánchez-Albavera and Jeannette Lardé, *Minería y Competitividad Internacional en América Latina* (Serie Recursos Naturales e Infraestructura No 109, ECLAC 2006) 124.

[35] Although risk-taking junior companies are considered small entities, the risks associated with these companies are high because these use to be new in the market and have no necessarily proven their asset base. According to the Bank, in the mining sector these companies became important players by the end of the 1990s by utilizing some of the world's best exploration talent. In this regard, the Bank states that these entities

> led the gold exploration of the late 1980s and early 1990s, bringing in the major international houses as partners when significant prospects were found. As the price of gold flattened in the early 1990s, the juniors diversified and took advantage of the high prices of base metals and diamonds until 1997. As many unexplored developing countries with high geological potential

to other metals. The Bank pointed out that the share of foreign investment, particularly in exploration activities in the mining sector in several developing countries in Africa, Asia, and Latin America, went from 35 per cent in 1989 to 63 per cent in 1997. In 2001, although there was a fall in the high prices of commodity metals, it only fell to 58 per cent.[36]

Despite the fall in the price of these metals at the end of the 1990s, Latin America was the only region that kept intact the percentage reached by foreign investment in mining exploration activities. This percentage that had risen from 13 per cent to 29 per cent between 1990 and 1997.[37] According to the Bank, this phenomenon is related to the fact that between 1994 and 1995 the Latin American region was the main region in the world with the highest mining prospecting, due to the fact that investment in Latin America in that activity, increased by 130 per cent in the 1990s, from US$300 million to US$700 million.[38]

According to the Bank, the considerable increase in these activities was also due to the appearance of capital markets willing to invest in the mining sector and particularly in prospecting and extraction projects, such as the Toronto and Vancouver stock exchanges.[39] Moreover, according to ECLAC, most states in the Latin American region are considered states specialized in the export of raw materials. In this regard, it has pointed out that, since the end of the twentieth century, there was an increase in relation to exports and foreign direct investment in natural resources. This was reflected in the increase in foreign direct investment for metal mining, which in 2010 amounted to 22 per cent in Brazil, 41 per cent in Chile, 34 per cent in Bolivia, and 30 per cent in Colombia.[40]

3. Mining Reforms at the End of the Twentieth Century in Latin America

Before the mining reforms that were introduced in the 1990s, the actions promoted by the World Bank group in the mining sector in Latin America came through two of its main institutions: The International Bank for Reconstruction and Development (IBRD) and The International Development Association (IDA). These were mainly oriented towards the construction of infrastructure and the

> opened their mining sectors to foreign investment and the risk-taking juniors achieved some spectacular finds in the newly accessible areas, the entire industry realized that it had little choice but to review its development strategies.
>
> Mining Reform and the World Bank (n 15) 4–5.

[36] ibid.
[37] ibid.
[38] A Mining Strategy (n 1) xiii.
[39] ibid xiv.
[40] ECLAC, *Foreign Direct Investment in Latin America and the Caribbean 2010* (UN 2011).

financing of both fuel and non-fuel resource extraction projects. These projects could be carried out both by companies affiliated with the private sector and by SOEs.[41]

However, based on the view that SOEs had not had the same performance in the mining projects as private sector companies, at the end of the 1980s the Bank began to review its guidelines in relation to the policy of resource extraction. As a consequence of this, this institution presented two main policies, one aimed at the African continent, 'The Strategy for African Mining' (1992)[42] and another one for Latin America, 'The Mining Strategy for Latin America and the Caribbean' (1996).[43]

In the strategy for the African continent, the Bank highlighted the importance of tax revenues and foreign exchange derived from mining activities. Likewise, it stressed that African states had not been effective in mobilizing risk capital and investment funds necessary for adequate development of the mining sector. Regarding the strategy designed for the Latin American region, the Bank focused mainly on adapting mining legislation to make it easier for private companies to operate exploration and exploitation activities, restructuring public institutions in the mining sector, formalization of artisanal and small-scale mining, and management of social and environmental issues.

The Bank's priority in relation to the mining of non-fuel resources was to provide technical and financial support to developing countries, in such a way that they could evaluate, adjust, and promote the necessary reforms in their mining policies, following the guidelines from the Bank. These reforms should be aimed at stimulating the participation of the private sector, at privatizing the assets of state companies or SOEs, and at establishing the conditions for the development of 'sustainable' mining.[44]

These reforms promoted in Latin America emphasized the role of the private sector as 'operator' and 'investor', while at the same time exalting the role of the state as 'regulator'. According to the Bank, the reform processes in the mining sector should be tied to the establishment of a good macroeconomic and commercial environment, open to foreign investment and free trade.[45] Unlike what happened in the years following the decolonization process in the second half of the twentieth century, under the Bank reforms promoted in the 1990s, the role of the state no longer consisted of trying to gain control over its resources, but mainly in attracting foreign capital for its extraction, and in providing companies from the private sector with the necessary guarantees so that they could directly operate mining activities in safe conditions.[46]

---

[41] Mining Reform and the World Bank (n 15) 6–8.
[42] Strategy for African Mining (n 2).
[43] A Mining Strategy (n 1).
[44] Mining Reform and the World Bank (n 15) 6–7.
[45] ibid 11.
[46] ibid 2–4, 7–8; A Mining Strategy (n 1) 11–13.

According to the Bank, the states had to create an adequate legal framework that would ensure the rights of private investors over the resources to be extracted. To do this, areas that could be previously reserved for the state for exploration had to be released to investors. It would allow granting rights to investors through standardized agreements, and permitting the assignment and transfer of the state's rights over the mines to be able to carry out unrestricted exploration activities and exploitation.[47] The Bank pointed out that the reforms to be promoted should include a stable and consistent apparatus of laws and regulations, as well as institutions in charge of applying both norms and codes of conduct in a transparent manner, and taking into account in particular the social impacts and environmental issues derived from mining activities.

a. Shaping the constitutions in the mining reform processes

Arguing the neccesity of modernizing the legislation in the mining sector in Latin America, the Bank highlighted the importance of mainly promoting reforms at the constitutional level in order to ensure further the rights of foreign investors. In this regard, the Bank explained that, since constitutions are more difficult to modify compared to other types of norms such as laws or decrees, elevating certain guarantees on mining titles acquired by foreign investors to the constitutional level could create a situation of greater legal certainty for these actors.

According to the Bank, most Latin American states in the mid-1990s had constitutions that established an inalienable domain of the state over mineral resources.[48] This feature was reflected primarily in the recognition of the sovereignty and the exclusive power of the state to regulate all matters related to mining, including the terms and conditions under which mining rights could be acquired and maintained, and the actors who could access those rights. However, among the different constitutions of the Latin American region, there were key differences regarding the degree of protection of the mining rights of foreign companies and their access to mining titles.

As it was mentioned above, the Bank highlighted the Chilean mining model, including the Constitution of 1980, as an example to follow for the rest of the states in the region. According to the Bank, this constitution explicitly established a high degree of protection over mining titles acquired by foreign companies. The Bank also highlighted the Peruvian Constitution of 1993 for reinforcing the protection of mining concessions against the so-called 'unjust expropriations' understood as expropriations without compensation.[49]

---

[47] ibid 12–14.
[48] A Mining Strategy (n 1) 10–11.
[49] ibid 11; see *Political Constitucion of Peru* (1993) art 70 <https://pdba.georgetown.edu/Parties/Peru/Leyes/constitucion.pdf> accessed 7 June 2023.

On another hand, the Bank drew attention to states, such as Bolivia, Mexico, and Brazil, for containing provisions in their constitutions that restricted access and transfer of mining titles to individuals and that hindered foreign investment in the mining sector. For instance, in the case of Bolivia, the Bank noted that the Bolivian Constitution's prohibition on transferring nationalized mining properties to private individuals had complicated and delayed measures to privatize COMIBOL's mines, which belonged to the state and are managed by it.[50]

The Bank classified the constitutional provisions of Latin American states depending on whether they protected or hindered the foreign investment in mining. The purpose of this classification was to promote reforms aimed at shaping the sovereignty of states over their mineral resources in a manner to protect the rights of private actors over mining resources. The Bank pointed out that the constitutional provisions established in the Latin American states were of two types. First, the Bank highlighted the constitutional provisions addressed to protect foreign investement such as: (i) declarations of sovereignty and ownership of mineral resources, and of the authority to grant mining rights to the private sector; (ii) the guarantees of non-discriminatory treatment of the private sector and foreign interests by law; and (iii) the guarantees against the expropriation of private property through the payment of the fair value of the property in convertible currency.[51]

Second, the Bank highlighted a series of constitutional provisions that, according to it, established obstacles to foreign investment. Among these provisions, the Bank highlighted: (i) the prohibitions on transferring state properties to the private sector or to foreigners; (ii) the prohibitions for foreign companies to acquire mining rights or ownership of other assets in border areas; (iii) the authority at the head of the executive branch to prohibit access for extraction to certain places by creating reserves; (iv) discriminatory provisions against the private sector or foreign investors in the eligibility criteria for mining rights; and (v) the so-called 'outdated or restrictive definitions' of mining or minerals that could frustrate the use of modern extraction techniques.[52]

b. Guidelines to reform mining legislations and to attract foreign investment

Starting from the idea that, in order to carry out mining reforms effectively in Latin American states, they should promote reforms in their constitutions as a priority, the new legal frameworks recommended by the Bank implied the redefinition of

---

[50] A Mining Strategy (n 1) 12.
[51] ibid 13–19.
[52] ibid.

the state in such a way that investors could count on sufficient guarantees to be able to freely operate and trade their resources.[53] The Bank emphasized the need to strengthen certain aspects for the required reforms. The first aspect, which was considered a priority in order to attract foreign investment, was the 'security of tenure'.[54] The strengthening of this aspect, would allow to guarantee that private companies had the certainty of obtaining a secure property title to the mine, and of having sufficient time to be able to carry out both exploration and exploitation activities in the mines on which they had acquired their titles and rights.

The Bank pointed out that it was necessary to establish an 'automatic' exploitation right for the benefit of the company that had discovered the mine, as a consequence of the previous exploration activities. According to it, it was not attractive for a mining company that, after a considerable investment in exploration and prospecting activities and after having incurred a high risk for it, its right to exploit the mine was not guaranteed.

Related to this first aspect, investors should have the possibility of transferring their rights to other companies, anticipating those cases in which, after a long period of exploration, they found deposits with few amounts of resources that did not report the expected profits. In this sense, the policy promoted by the Bank highlighted the importance of companies having the power to mortgage their titles to obtain financial sources.

The second aspect related to 'private sector access to mineral resources'.[55] The Bank considered that it was essential that the states establish the necessary regulatory provisions to release those mining areas that were reserved exclusively for the state and to prevent it from reserving new areas for its exclusive use. The Bank pointed out that, in order to guarantee the effective access of private companies to mineral resources, the states should also suppress and modify those provisions that were 'discriminatory' with foreign investors and that could discourage their participation in the mining sector, such as those that granted preferential treatment to state entities to access mining titles.

Third, the Bank highlighted the importance of creating a 'formal system for granting mining titles',[56] which would guarantee foreign companies access to mining property titles under secure conditions and reduce the margin of discretion in awarding them. The Bank issued a series of recommendations to redefine the formal system for granting titles in each of the states of the Latin-American region, depending on whether it was an administrative, adjudication, or contractual system, but with a warning that the most adequate system was the administrative one. According to the Bank, this system had less discretionary criteria for awarding

[53] ibid 10–19.
[54] ibid.
[55] ibid 19–21.
[56] ibid 10–19.

titles, offered greater security conditions to investors and was more responsive to policy changes.

The Bank also explained that, in an administrative system for granting titles, the entity in charge of granting mining titles had to be independent from the state mining entities, and that this in turn had to be differentiated particularly from those entities within the state that carried out the operation of mining activities. This was intended to guarantee transparency in the award of titles, to provide a 'non-discriminatory' treatment to foreign companies and to hold state authorities accountable for their actions.

Fourth, the Bank stated the need to create and maintain an 'open registry of mining titles'[57] that could be accessed publicly. It was intended that investors in the mining sector could quickly determine which areas were available to start exploration or exploitation activities. In this sense, the Bank insisted on the need to modernize the cadastral registry[58] in Latin American states and to update it according to universally accepted identification standards for mining areas.

Fifth, the Bank emphasized the need to create a regulation aimed at carrying out a type of socially and environmentally responsible mining.[59] According to the Bank, the 'environment' in the mining sector had become a determining factor in attracting foreign investment. For this reason, this institution pointed out that, in order to carry out activities in the mining sector, an environmental impact assessment (EIA) should be carried out. An EIA is understood as a legal instrument 'for introducing environmental planning and control into company management at the feasibility stage of mining ventures'.[60] The main objective of this instrument is to prevent, mitigate and restore damage to the environment as well as to regulate the activities to avoid or reduce their negative effects on the environment. This requirement had to be approved by the competent state institutions before the granting of the mining titles or before starting operations in the area to extract. Likewise, when examining the environmental impacts, not only the effects that could be caused on the environment of should be considered, but also the so-called 'social impacts' understood as the impacts on the communities' lives in cultural terms, on their living conditions and on their ways of life.

Sixth, the Bank highlighted the need to promote a series of reforms in Latin American states aimed at establishing and improving a 'stable and competitive fiscal regime',[61] which allowed investors to obtain the maximum possible benefits

---

[57] ibid 20.
[58] The cadastral registry is understood as an instrument to facilitate concession boundary identification and to avoid overlapping concessions. This instrument also allows to minimize conflicts and disputes and to integrate the existing concession rights. This is because the cadastral registry works as a census of real estate, which has the purpose of locating, describing, and recording the physical characteristics of each real estate in order to detect its intrinsic particularities that define it materially and that identify its legal and technical information through a cadastral code. ibid 18.
[59] ibid 69–92.
[60] ibid 68.
[61] ibid 25–28.

from extractive activities and that guaranteed that the taxes that the mining companies had to pay did not change drastically. The Bank argued that it could be more favourable for mining companies to establish taxes on the profits and benefits obtained by the company or the so-called 'profit-related taxes', such as corporate income taxes, withholding of dividends or taxes on additional benefits. Likewise, for governments, other types of taxes could be more attractive, such as royalties or taxes on transactions and withholdings, as well as import duties and payments for labour and salary taxes.

Because of the special interest of transnational actors in strengthening foreign private actors through legal reforms to liberalize the mining sector, the Bank stated that governments should create a stable and equitable tax regime, giving priority to taxes based on companies' income. For this reason, it emphasized that royalties, as well as taxes on the import of mining equipment, should be minimal; and that a series of provisions should also be established to offset taxes on assets and compulsory participation in profits. Lastly, the World Bank pointed out that it should be created a mechanism to obtain reimbursement of value-added tax paid on inputs.[62]

The Bank expressed its willingness to provide technical assistance to the teams formed in each state to prepare the drafts of the new mining codes. According to the Bank, this support would vary in each case according to the capacity of each state to carry out autonomously the process of reforming its mining legislation. In this sense, the states that, according to the Bank, had a greater institutional capacity, would only require simple opinions on the general objectives and key instruments established in the law.[63] On another hand, in states considered to have less capacity and autonomy to carry out mining reforms under the terms established by the Bank, it would play a very active role in assisting national authorities in the preparation of laws.[64] In this way, in order to carry out the reforms in the terms required by the Bank, it promoted various measures and instruments such as sectoral and structural adjustment loans, which included public policy reform programs; technical assistance programmes that had loans and credits to finance studies and advisory services; and loans from funds created by the IBRD by other Member States and by other international organizations.[65]

As part of the structural adjustment strategy, the technical assistance projects that were promoted were part of the so-called multisectoral programmes financed by the Bank through the so-called programmatic structural adjustment loans (PSALs) and the programmatic structural adjustment credits (PSACs). Moreover, the IFC continued to finance large-scale mining projects for non-fuel resources.[66]

---

[62] ibid xvi.
[63] Mining Reform and the World Bank (n 15) 13.
[64] ibid.
[65] ibid 7.
[66] ibid.

Finally, it should be noted that one of the aspects to which the Bank particularly drew attention was the strategy concerning assistance to artisanal and small-scale mining. In the Mining Strategy for Latin America and the Caribbean, it stated the necessity for restricting the national mining industry to small-scale mining activities, arguing that the large international mining companies are usually only willing to invest in large-scale deposits.[67] In this regard, the Bank explained that the large companies were not interested in small deposits, which were often found as a result of explorations in search of large deposits. For this reason, the Bank highlighted the importance of promoting the national mining industry, but only in relation to small-scale mining.[68]

4. New Strategies to Strengthen the Mining Sector

These new strategies adopted by the Bank were promoted in part because of the fall in mineral and metal prices at the end of the twentieth century.[69] New actions were introduced to strengthen the mining sector. These were aimed at earning the 'social licence'[70] of the communities and to promote 'environmental protection'.

Moreover, as a consequence of the process of mergers and acquisitions in the mining industry that began in the 1990s, at the beginning of the twenty-first century, particularly between 2000 and 2001, large acquisitions of mining companies took place. The promotion of this type of transaction between large companies in the mining sector occurred in part as a result of the perception of an unfavourable environment for the mining industry due to the drop in metal prices. According to ECLAC, the strategy of increasing the size of companies through mergers and acquisitions was promoted with the purpose of trying to obtain financing at a competitive cost in the stock markets of industrialized states.[71]

Given that acquisitions could take place through this type of transactions between private companies or through the purchase of state-owned public companies, the privatizations of that took place during the 1990s in various parts of the world, including the Latin American region, was also part of the wide spectrum of reforms with an openness and neo-liberal content, which characterized the policies of many developing countries.[72] In this sense, the interest of the mining industry to strengthen its companies and increase their size to make the sector more attractive for investors, not only involved the process of merger and acquisition of companies in the private sector, but also a whole policy of privatization mainly supported by

---

[67] A Mining Strategy (n 1) xvii.
[68] Mining Reform and the World Bank (n 15) 8–9.
[69] Características de la Inversión (n 31) 20–42.
[70] See s 3.1 in this chapter.
[71] Características de la Inversión (n 31) 20–42.
[72] ibid 33.

the Bank. According to ECLAC, Latin America was the region with the greatest participation in mining privatization processes. This Commission stated that

> from 1990 to 1999, total privatizations carried out by developing countries and countries in transition amounted to US$315,712 million, corresponding to the mining companies the sum of US$9,000 million (3%). This figure, however, is only a small percentage of the total spent on mergers and acquisitions in the decade (US$150,000 million).[73]

The process of mergers and acquisitions in the mining industry also led to an increase in the level of concentration of metals and minerals around the world in the hands of a few companies. In 2001, the level of concentration increased by 11 per cent and reached 27 per cent. Two British companies were able to get the largest share of non-energy mining production in the world: Anglo American and Rio Tinto.[74] The strategy of acquiring and merging large mining companies to overcome the crisis of low metal prices led to Latin America positioning itself as 'the most important destination for investments in mining exploration in the world'.[75] According to ECLAC, for the year 2001, investments in the Latin American continent amounted to US$575.8 million, equivalent to 28.8 per cent of investments in mining exploration worldwide.[76]

a. Social licence of local communities

According to the Bank, as a consequence of the reforms promoted in several Latin American states since the end of the twentieth century and during the 2000s, it was possible to implement in almost the entire Latin American region 'modern mining codes and stable and equitable fiscal regulations, clear and non-discriminatory, as well as non-negotiable processes and adequate environmental regulations'.[77] Moreover, due to the legal reforms that were implemented in different Latin American states, large companies were able to obtain the mining titles and permits necessary to carry out long-term mining exploration and exploitation activities.

Despite the fact that the governments in Latin America, through the modification of their constitutions and their legislations, facilitated the conditions so that the transnational mining companies could carry out their activities without major

---

[73] ibid 33.
[74] ibid 34.
[75] ibid 42.
[76] ibid.
[77] Fernando Sánchez-Albavera, 'El Desarrollo Productivo Basado en la Explotación de los Recursos Naturales' (Recursos Naturales e Infraestructura No 86, ECLAC, 2004) 20 (hereafter 'El Desarrollo Productivo Basado').

obstacles and following the guidelines of the Bank, in the 2000s the new concern of these companies was to obtain the 'social licence' of the communities settled in the exploited territories, so that they could operate long-term mining activities in optimal conditions.[78] Furthermore, in 2002 the Bank stated that the benefits in terms of investment, production, exports, and taxes in the Andean states, derived from large-scale mining projects, were not comparable with those coming from small-scale and medium-scale mining, which were not significant from a macro-economic perspective.[79] The interest of the large mining companies in promoting a strategy to gain the support of the communities, added to the Bank's support for large-scale mining projects, with one of its priorities at the beginning of the twenty-first century being addressed to strengthen the so-called 'tripartite' dialogues or a three-way dialogue between governments, communities, and companies.

For the Bank, this dialogue could represent a kind of win-win for the parties involved, who, according to the Bank, would greatly benefit from the so-called 'sustainable mining'[80] aimed to bring development in the regions where mining operations would take place, while mitigating environmental impacts. However, it required a preparatory work with the parties involved to ensure that all of them were willing to contribute to the extractive processes and to extract the maximum possible benefits from them.[81]

The Bank pointed out that the success of a tripartite dialogue process also depended on the governments in each state effectively creating a favourable environment for foreign investors, providing the conditions indicated by the Bank in accordance with the reform policies in the institutional and legal frameworks, designed by this institution since the 1990s.[82] For the dialogue to be effective, and the communities to commit themselves throughout the extractive processes, it was necessary that the governments also made an effort to achieve the required modifications in internal legislations and the reforms to the creation of new and 'modern' mining codes. In this sense, the Bank emphasized the need for governments to comply with the commitment to promote a stable and 'non-discriminatory' legal apparatus with private investors, which guaranteed them legal security of tenure,

---

[78] ibid.
[79] World Bank and IFC, *Large Mines and Local Communities. Forging, Partnerships, Building Sustainability* (Mining and Development, Global Mining, The World Bank Group's Mining Department, 2002) 4 <https://static1.squarespace.com/static/5bb24d3c9b8fe8421e87bbb6/t/5c2939a40e2e72e38 d7dc0e8/1546205607691/Large-mines-local-communities.pdf> accessed 7 June 2023 (hereafter 'Large Mines and Local Communities').
[80] According to the Bank, the so-called sustainable mining will require a specific policy formulation and implementation so that mining becomes a sustainable activity over the long term. This institution states that for mining to be sustainable, attention must be given to the full cycle: mine closure, environmental matters, and follow up activities most be considered at an early stage. A Mining Strategy (n 1) xiii–xiv; 79.
[81] Large Mines and Local Communities (n 79) 4.
[82] ibid 16–15.

through procedures and regulations that restricted the discretion margins of local authorities.

The main purpose of that dialogue was to provide foreign investors with the necessary security regarding the holding of mining resources, so that they could carry out long-term operations; in such a way that the companies felt sufficiently secure with the established contractual terms and with the relationship between them and the governments.[83] For this reason, it was so important to involve and commit the communities and obtain their 'social licence', in order to guarantee the mining operations in the long term.

b. The discourse of 'sustainable development' and responsible mining

The second aspect that was emphasized by the Bank in the early years of the twenty-first century to strengthen and promote foreign investment in mining, was the so-called 'sustainable mining' or 'responsible mining'. The guidelines promoted by the Bank since the 1990s on the responsible use of mining resources in social and environmental terms, was strengthened in the twenty-first century. According to the Bank, the sustainability of mining should be framed on the three pillars of the notion of 'sustainable development': economic growth, environmental sustainability, and social equality.

If the mining industry were capable of harmonizing these three elements, its operations could be considered socially and environmentally acceptable.[84] According to the Bank, under this notion, companies would have to take on the challenge of demonstrating that the benefits that mining activities could bring to the communities were capable of offsetting the costs and impacts that said activities implied. In this regard, the Bank highlighted the Canadian experience, which, according to it, constituted a model to be followed by the Latin American states due to its effectiveness in achieving consensus between the mining industry and the communities under a scheme of 'shared profits'.[85]

The Bank argued that this scheme was viable primarily because, with the opening of a mine and the offer of employment to the members of the community, the consumption of goods and services could be expanded in the region where the mining activities were to be carried out. The environmental concern in the developing of mining activities re-emerged in this period.[86] It was similar to what happened in the 1970s when, parallel to the intensification of extractive activities,

---

[83] Mining Reform and the World Bank (n 15) 20.
[84] ibid.
[85] Mining Reform and the World Bank (n 15) 23. See also Large Mines and Local Communities (n 79) 4–6, 11–14.
[86] ibid (Mining Reform and the World Bank) 23–25.

environmental problems were placed on the world agenda, and the report 'The Limits of Growth'[87] was issued.

Under the notion of sustainable development and following the guidelines of the Bank established in the Mining Strategy for Latin America and the Caribbean, each Latin American state promoted the creation of a new institutional framework in the mining sector, including the objective of protecting the environment in mining activities. The Bank pointed out that the structure that should be established in the mining sector of each state should include at least a Ministry of Mines, a Mining Registry Office, a Geological Investigation Agency, an Environmental Mining Office, and a Mining Inspection Authority.[88] Likewise, taking into account that this new institutional framework was linked to what was called the 'sustainable use of natural heritage', large investors should also try to incorporate environmental criteria into their activities and business management.[89]

This context was also marked by the United Nations Conference on Environment and Development (UNCED), better known as the 'Earth Summit', which had been held in Rio de Janeiro between 3 and 14 June 1992. In this event, the Rio Declaration on Environment and Development[90] (Rio Declaration) was adopted by 172 states and the so- called 'Agenda 21'[91] was approved as a global action plan to promote sustainable development. Likewise, a Declaration of Principles was adopted on the most sustainable management of the world's forests, while the signing of a Framework Convention on Climate Change and the Convention on Biological Diversity was promoted.

The Rio Declaration emphasized the notion of 'sustainable development', which since the end of the 1980s had been considered by the Brundtland Commission[92] as the 'great alternative' to eradicating poverty and to environment protection.[93] In the report 'Our Common Future: Report of the World Commission on Environment and Development' issued on 4 August 1987, that Commission referred to sustainable development as the ability to meet or ensure the needs of the present without

---

[87] See Donella H Meadows and others, *The Limits to Growth: A Report for the club of Rome's Project on the Predicament of Mankind* (Universe Books 1972) <http://www.donellameadows.org/wp-content/userfiles/Limits-to-Growth-digital-scan-version.pdf> accessed 7 June 2023.
[88] A Mining Strategy (n 1) 33–39.
[89] El Desarrollo Productivo Basado (n 77) 45.
[90] United Nations, General Assembly, 'Report of the United Nations Conference on Environment and Development' A/CONF.151/26 Vol 1. 12 August 1992. See https://www.un.org/en/development/desa/population/migration/generalassembly/docs/globalcompact/A_CONF.151_26_Vol.I_Declaration.pdf
[91] United Nations Conference on Environment and Development, Rio de Janeiro, Brazil, 3–14 June 1992. Agenda 21. See https://sustainabledevelopment.un.org/content/documents/Agenda21.pdf
[92] The Brundtland Commission also known as the World Commission on Environment and Development at the United Nations in 1983 as an independent organization to promote sustainable development worldwide and to address environmental and developmental problems. See https://www.un.org/en/academic-impact/sustainability
[93] Arturo Escobar, *La Invención del Tercer Mundo. Construcción y Deconstrucción del Desarrollo* (Grupo Editorial Norma 1998) 363 (hereafter 'La Invención').

compromising the needs of future generations. Based on this definition, it was intended to establish the limits to environmental resources, according to the current state of technology, and the meeting of the basic needs of the population, especially those people who were in a situation of poverty.[94]

In the Declaration approved at the 'Earth Summit' in Rio, it was specifically established that, 'Human beings are at the centre of concerns for sustainable development. They are entitled to a healthy and productive life in harmony with nature' (principle 1) and that states have the sovereign right to exploit their own resources pursuant to their own environmental and developmental policies, and the responsibility to ensure that activities do not cause damage to the environment (principle 2). It was also provided that the right to development must be fulfilled so as to equitably meet developmental and environmental needs of present and future generations (principle 3). Likewise, the importance of 'eradicating poverty' was stressed, as this is one of the essential elements of 'sustainable development'. In this regard, the declaration stated that all states and all people shall co-operate in the essential task of eradicating poverty as an indispensable requirement for sustainable development, in order to decrease the disparities in standards of living and better meet the needs of the majority of the people of the world (principle 5). Moreover, the Declaration stated in principle 12 that:

> States should co-operate to promote a supportive and open international economic system that would lead to economic growth and sustainable development in all states, to better address the problems of environmental degradation. Trade policy measures for environmental purposes should not constitute a means of arbitrary or unjustifiable discrimination or a disguised restriction on international trade. Unilateral actions to deal with environmental challenges outside the jurisdiction of the importing country should be avoided. Environmental measures addressing transboundary or global environmental problems should, as far as possible, be based on an international consensus.

The notion of sustainable development was also reaffirmed during the conferences in New York (1997), Johannesburg (2002), and Rio de Janeiro (2012). In these conferences, the necessity for searching a consensus between production and trade and a sustainable use of natural heritage and the protection of the environment, was confirmed. In this regard, ECLAC explained that it was intended to go beyond the question of environmental protection, achieving a balance between all forms of capital and the achievement of growth, the protection of the natural heritage and a

---

[94] United, Nations. General Assembly 'Report of the World Commission on Environment and Development: Our Common Future' A/42/427, 4 August 1987. See <https://digitallibrary.un.org/record/139811?ln=en#record-files-collapse-header> accessed 21 July 2023.

social equity.[95] In this sense, there was strong pressure on states to incorporate 'sustainable' mining practices, based on technological changes and the new environmental criteria, encouraging them to compete for credits to carry out sustainable mining activities by financial institutions and international organizations.

According to ECLAC, the incorporation of technical progress, as axis of productive transformation strategies, would allow the efficient exploitation of natural advantages that could be exploited within the current state of science and technology, while a greater research capacity should identify new natural advantages.[96] Using the 'sustainable development' notion, a series of factors were defined in order to determine the sustainability of mining policies. These factors included: (i) the profits derived from mining exploration and exploitation activities; (ii) a consensus between public and private interest; (iii) the legal certainty of investors; (iv) local and regional development; (v) the heritage integrity (natural, human, cultural and social); and finally, the social equity.[97]

In this regard, ECLAC pointed out that, although mining should contribute to local and regional development, it should also be taken into account that 'without profits there is no sustainable development'.[98] This highlighted the need for states to design and establish necessary conditions to attract foreign investment in the mining sector, such as those aimed at the maximum reduction of costs, including the incorporation of low fiscal and tax rates on mining operations to make such activities more profitable.

Starting from the idea that 'mining is a factor of progress that favors endogenous development and therefore well-being',[99] it was stressed that the need to achieve a consensus between companies and society, and the public interest and the private interest, by considering the so-called 'patrimonial integrity'. This is the respect for the natural, cultural, human, and social heritage of future generations and an 'adequate administration of negative externalities'.[100]

As noted above, the Bank highlighted the 'Canadian experience' and pointed out that this should be an important model to follow for Latin American states, so that they could achieve sustainable development for the benefit of local communities, based on the development of the mining operations. The Bank also emphasized the element of 'consensus' among all parties involved and also stated that mining companies should actively participate in the supply of goods and services, both in the region where mining activities took place and, in the areas, surrounding the mine.[101]

---

[95] Fernando Sánchez-Albavera, *El desarrollo productivo basado en la explotación de los recursos naturales* 2004 (n 77) 46.
[96] ibid 47–48.
[97] ibid 56–61.
[98] ibid 59–60.
[99] ibid.
[100] ibid.
[101] Large Mines and Local Communities (n 79) 11–14.

The supply of goods and services should include medical services, financial services, restaurants, pastry shops, hotels, food for mine personnel, etc; and, to the extent that an expansion of mining activity is generated, there could also be a greater supply of electrical and plumbing goods and services, vehicle repair or those destined for more complex construction, repair, and assembly projects. Finally, the Bank pointed out that, in the mining towns with a faster growth, the supply of goods and services could expand to the point of including infrastructure services, hospitals, and higher education institutions, in coordination with the public sector administration.[102]

The Bank presented—as a remarkable example—the case of Sudbury in Ontario in Canada, which, according to it, had become an important economic centre and had gone from being a 'simple mining town' to a 'mining metropolis'. According to the Bank, it was likely that this occurred because of the extraction of minerals as the basis of the Sudbury economy, and this activity was accompanied in turn by other economic activities that ranged from financial services to health and education services.[103]

According to the Bank, both in the case of Sudbury and in the case of Saskatchewan, also in Canada, well known for the exploitation of uranium mines, a balance was achieved between environmental protection by the mining industry, the economic growth of the region, and the generation of benefits for the indigenous communities of the region. Therefore, it stated that the states of the Latin American region should follow the example of these successful mining cases. The Bank explained that members of the local communities initially had to carry out jobs considered as unskilled or low skilled jobs, while at the same time they had to provide 'unsophisticated' services inside the mines. However, as the mining activities developed and 'matured', other types of services could gradually be generated in which the communities could also be involved, such as vehicle repair, electrical and welding services, machinery sales, etc.[104]

In the long term, the supply of goods and services to repair and maintain heavy machinery would be expanded, and these services would be expanded at the national level. According to the Bank, both the case of the Candelaria mine in Chile and of Yanacocha in Peru, should also be considered successful models to the extent that they had followed the example of Canada; and as a consequence, there had been a significant increase in purchasing power in those regions, which was reflected in the purchases of local businesses.[105]

The Bank also explained that, in relation to the benefits derived from mining activities for indigenous peoples and communities—who in many cases were settled

[102] ibid.
[103] ibid.
[104] ibid.
[105] Mining Reform and the World Bank (n 15) 22–23.

in the exploited territories—their members could be greatly benefited by acquiring relevant skills for the development of mining activities within their own territories; and they could even get to acquire totally or partially the titles on the mines to give continuity to such activities. In this regard, the Bank recognized that, although initially introducing indigenous people into mining activities could generate social problems such as alcoholism or significant changes in their culture and lifestyle, as well as environmental problems, the governments also had to assume a series of commitments to introduce reforms aimed at the adequate management of this type of processes through the tripartite dialogues, mentioned above, between the mining industry, the governments, and the affected communities.[106]

On this point, the Bank pointed out the following:

> 'The introduction of mining in indigenous areas creates important potential benefits but also a number of challenges. Some of the benefits are the same as those that mining generally brings, including employment, taxation, infrastructure development, and local entrepreneurial development. But indigenous communities also have the possibility of capturing some additional spin-off benefits from the local purchases of mining companies, as indigenous peoples may benefit in the future by systematically developing the relevant mining skills so that they can dominate mining activities in the areas where they come from. Ultimately this should include partial or complete ownership of some mine enterprises. Their geographical proximity to the mineral resources and emotional proximity to the affected people should facilitate this. Nevertheless, it is important to note that the initial stages of the introduction of mining to an indigenous area may also usher in some social problems, as outsiders may bring alcohol and introduce foreign lifestyles. Also, pollution may damage the environment, and traditionally reserved areas may be disturbed. Yet those governments that have established credibility in their commitment to reform and the protection of the environment have proven capable of managing the process, largely by making use of the trilateral dialogue with industry and the affected communities.'[107]

Finally, it is important to note that when the Bank stated that, in order to face the possible negative impacts that the mining activities may cause in the territories where indigenous peoples and other local communities are settled, governments have the duty to have a dialogue with all the parties involved and manage adequately to manage the mining processes. Here, the Bank is alluding to 'management' as a key element of 'sustainable development' and the leading role of the state apparatus in that type of process. Within the institutional framework that, according to the World Bank, must be created in each country in order to develop mining activities

---

[106] ibid.
[107] ibid.

according to the objective of environmental protection, this organization stresses the need to create an Environmental Mining Office that acts as an interface between the mining companies and national environmental authority.[108]

5. Problematizing the Mining Model promoted in the Global South from a Development Critical Perspective

In relation to the role of the state in environmental management, Arturo Escobar refers to the state apparatus as an 'interface between capital and nature',[109] explaining that the process of capitalization of nature that occurs within the framework of the discourse of 'sustainable development', is largely mediated by the state itself. Starting from Karl Polanyi's critique on the self-regulated market,[110] Escobar argues that capitalism not only deteriorates or destroys the social and environmental conditions on which this system is built (including nature and labour), but also the capitalist restructuring takes place at the expense of such conditions.[111]

This author explains that capitalization of nature has been fundamental for capitalism since primitive accumulation and the appropriation of communal territories. Moreover, the history of capital is the history of the exploitation of the conditions of production, including the ways in which capital deteriorates or destroys its own conditions.[112] The threat of capital to the environment or the so-called natural resources, and to indigenous peoples and other local communities in their capacity as contributors of unskilled or low skilled labour for mining activities, constitutes an attempt to restructure the conditions of capital, to reduce costs, and to increase its profits.

According to David Harvey, the revival of forms of land grabbing and accumulation of natural resources through privatization and commodification processes, imply an 'accumulation by dispossession'.[113] This involves in turn primitive forms of capital accumulation and entails the dispossession of various subordinate groups who are subjected to neo-colonial forms of exploitation. Harvey explains that the specific processes of primitive accumulation that Marx[114] describes as the

---

[108] ibid 15.
[109] La Invención (n 93) 336.
[110] Karl Polanyi, *La Gran Transformación. Crítica del Liberalismo Económico* (Quipu Editorial 2007).
[111] La Invención (n 93) 376–77.
[112] ibid 336.
[113] David Harvey, *The New Imperialism* (OUP 2003) 137–82.
[114] In the process of the original accumulation of capital explained by Karl Marx, the use of violent methods typical of colonial projects is indispensable. Marx explains that the processes of original accumulation of capital are prior to capitalist accumulation and constitute the starting point of the capitalist regime of production. Carlos Marx, 'La Llamada Acumulación Originaria' in Carlos Marx, *El Capital. Crítica de la Economía Política* (vol I, Fondo de Cultura Económica 1974, originally published 1867) 607–08.

dispossession of rural and peasant populations or the neo-colonial policies of exploitation are still present and have become more prominent.[115]

In dialogue with other Marxist authors such as Rosa Luxemburg,[116] Harvey refers to the 'non-capitalist forms of production' in the processes of capital accumulation, in which neo-colonial methods prevail.[117] Due to the permanence of these methods over time, Harvey prefers to speak of forms of accumulation by dispossession,[118] arguing that such forms cannot be considered 'exterior' to the capitalist system or 'pre-capitalist'.

It is also important to highlight that technological change is essential for capitalism restructuring as it ensures the availability of raw materials, and cheaper and more disciplined labour. However, such changes also require the commitment of the state in cooperation and intervention actions to sustain capital gains.[119] This is reflected in the shaping of constitutions and domestic legislations and in the enacting of new development plans according to the financial institutions' guidelines above. In this sense, the Bank's discourse on a 'sustainable mining' aimed at implementing large-scale mining projects supposedly compatible with the protection of the environment policies and that mitigate the social impacts within the communities, may result in an effective strategy to legitimize large-scale mining because it involves a promise to reconcile elements that oppose each other and particularly the aspiration 'to reconcile humanity with nature'.[120]

According to Julia Dehm and Usha Natarajan the importance of shaping the domestic legislations is because law has played a crucial role in subordinating the interest of environmental protection to the economic interests. It also shows the dynamics of transnational law and in particular how international law is instrumentalized by powerful economic actors, and the restricted capacity of this normative order to correct serious inequities that are reproduced in the domestic sphere under the gaze of political and legal devices that operate globally. At the same time, this produces a kind of 'regulatory dysfunction' that arises when the regulatory order aimed at protecting the environment seeks to mitigate the damages caused by projects promoted in the name of 'development', as is the case of the large-scale mining projects, but at the same time, the law that protects the foreign investors' interests and that seeks to maintain a model of economic development ends up prevailing.[121]

---

[115] David Harvey, *A Companion to Marx's Capital*. (Verso 2010) 306–07.
[116] Rosa Luxemburg, *The Accumulation of Capital* (Routledge 2003) 432.
[117] David Harvey, 'El "Nuevo" Imperialismo: Acumulación por Desposesión' (2004) 40 Soc Register 111–12.
[118] ibid 113.
[119] La Invención (n 93) 336.
[120] ibid 365.
[121] Julia Dehm and Usha Natarajan, 'Where is the Environment? Locating Nature in International Law' (2019) 3 TWAILR 1–8 <https://twailr.com/wp-content/uploads/2019/08/Natarajan-Dehm-Where-is-the-Environment_Locating-Nature-in-International-Law.pdf> accessed 7 June 2023.

These authors argue that

> Law plays a crucial role in transforming a unified planet into discrete sovereign territories, in converting nature into exchangeable property, in turning interconnected ecosystems into realms of infinite commodification and exchange, and in extracting and conceptually separating an atomized human individual from the intertwined mesh of life. Law not only enables environmental destruction but understands the natural environment in a manner that ensures the impossibility of remedy. To remedy this conceptual dislocation of nature requires an exit from the confines of Western modernity.[122]

Despite the limitations of the notion of 'sustainable development' and its promise to harmonize the different interests that it involves, this concept has ended up legitimizing itself. This is because such notion has become a narrative that rhetorically regulates a political strategy of difference and diversity, a strong discourse functional for the international human rights community in terms of inclusion—poverty, cultural diversity, gender, and indigenous communities—and also a process of integration in the agendas on peace and culture that demand the management and control of mining conflicts in the name of development.[123]

The way of harmonizing the elements of environmental protection, economic growth, and social equity under the umbrella of 'sustainable development' has resulted in practice in assimilating 'other' ways of life to a univocal vision of development guided by the extractivist paradigm, that is in alignment with the logic of commodities speculation in the financial market and that responds to the dominant economic model.[124] From the Bank's policies on mining, it can be inferred that the purpose of joining mining with the notion of 'sustainable development' is mainly to increase consumption based on an economic model that relies on the sustained and permanent extraction of natural resources.

This not only contradicts the idea of protecting the environment, but also denies the limited existence of the planet's resources, without questioning the extractivist paradigm that is strongly connected to the notion of economic development. On this point, Escobar explains that, far from restating the typical concerns of the classical notion of development, such as basic needs, population, resources, technology, institutional cooperation, food security, and industrialism, what sustainable development does is to redistribute and reprioritize those elements.[125]

---

[122] ibid 6–7.

[123] Mirta Alejandra Antonelli, 'Minería Transnacional y Dispositivos de Intervención en la Cultura. La Gestión del Paradigma Hegemónico de la Minería Responsable y el Desarrollo Sostenible' in Maristella Svampa and Mirta Alejandra Antonelli (eds), *Minería Transnacional, Narrativas del Desarrollo y Resistencias Sociales* (Editorial Biblos 2009) 76.

[124] See Eduardo Canel, Uwafiokun Idemudia, and Liisa North, 'North Rethinking Extractive Industry: Regulation, Dispossession, and Emerging Claims' (2010) 30 Can J Dev Stud/Revue Canadienne d'Etudes du Développement 1–2.

[125] La Invención (n 93) 376–77.

The Canadian experience as the model to follow for Latin American states, as promoted by the Bank, is an example of this. As explained above, the Bank argues that such a model brings significant benefits for the indigenous peoples as long as they integrate to the mining projects, and are able to learn the necessary skills to carry out the required activities in the mines including unskilled or low-skilled jobs. At best, these peoples could conserve their territories 'legally' as long as they used them for such activities.

It is also worth recalling that the Bank described the cases of Yanacocha in Peru and of the Candelaria mine in Chile as successful, arguing that the construction of these mines had led to increased consumption in those regions. This understanding of 'sustainable development' is far from harmonizing the elements of economic growth, environmental protection, and social equity, as it tends to prioritize the element of 'economic growth' over the other two elements. This is problematic because it inhibits the ability to imagine 'other' possible worlds and rules out the existence of 'other' ways of living that differ from a way of life that is presented as unique, and that responds to the practical and legal requirements imposed by a hegemonic extractivist economic model. According to other ways of life the relationship with nature may be different and may challenge the economic rationality and the accumulation practices embedded in the hegemonic model.

In this sense, it is problematic that, according to the Bank's notion of sustainable development, it is growth, not the environment, that must be sustained. Furthermore, since poverty is understood not only as a cause, but as an effect of environmental problems, growth is also required for the purpose of eliminating poverty at the same time than environment is protected.[126] Hence the importance of generating, under the discourse of sustainable development, an entire institutional framework or a global 'ecocracy' willing to manage the environment and the human use of the planet, presenting nature and the industrial urban system as compatible under notions of 'responsible mining'. This is problematic, given that what is at stake is the continuity of an economic model based on growth and on a hegemonic notion of development through adequate administrative strategies.[127] The discourses that sustain the worldwide mining model leads key transnational actors to perceive large-scale extractive projects as essential measures to fight poverty, and to recognize in a restricted way the right to participate of local communities as indigenous and afro-descendant peoples.[128] As it was explained above, under this logic the local communities use to be added to the exiting extractive projects and it is expected from them to contribute with their labour force, but not

---

[126] ibid 369.
[127] ibid 364.
[128] Roger Merino, 'Coloniality and Indigenous Territorial Rights in the Peruvian Amazon: A Critique of the Prior Consultation Law' (2015) 38 BPIDW 8.

to question key aspects of those projects such as the scale and its impacts on their social conditions or on environment.

This has led to the promotion of large-scale mining projects at a global level aimed at trying to join the notions of 'responsible mining' and 'sustainable development' under the idea of environmental management and the administration of the planet's natural heritage, and as a strategy oriented towards economic development.[129] The main objective is to try to demonstrate that this type of mining project can contribute to a global transition towards sustainable development. These projects also present themselves as diverse and therefore tend to involve local communities, consumers, suppliers, governments, workers, organizations, indigenous groups, non-governmental organizations, consultants, international organizations, and financial institutions. However, as it was explained above, this type of project does not intend to involve these diverse sectors, or question the current economic and development model, but to interweave the notions of 'responsible mining' and 'sustainable development' with certain administrative strategies. This confirms that, in the framework of management led by the institutions designed under the discourse of sustainable development, what it is intended to be sustained is the growth or expansion of the market, but not the environment.

6. Conclusion

This chapter analyzes the mining model promoted by international insitutions like the World Bank in Latin American states since the 1990s, which sought the collaboration of the states to adapt their legal and institutional frameworks in the domestic sphere, and to remove obstacles to the optimal operation of mining corporations. The analysis of the reforms promoted by the Bank in a context of 'global coloniality' from a critical development perspective, explains how mining policies promoted 'from above' have led to a kind of 'subordinated developmentalism'.

In this context, Global South states, such as Colombia, under the endorsement of their own legislation and their own institutions, have ended up reinserting themselves again and again in a peripheral position within a world-economy, providing raw materials and commodities according to the demands of a global economic system. It has been possible due to some key discourses like the 'sustainable development' notion, that have ended up to legitimate economic activities like large scale-mining projects, in the name of 'development'. This has meant that the current economic model, and the profits derived from it, are sustained, but not the environment.

---

[129] See International Institute for Environment and Development (IIED), *MMSD+10 Reflecting on a Decade on Mining and Sustainable Development* (IIED Discussion Paper, Sustainable Markets, June 2012).

PART IV
THE ROLE OF INTERNATIONAL ECONOMIC LAW

13
International Investment Law

Ursula Kriebaum

1. Introduction

International investment law has developed into a specialized field within the broader context of international law. It is one of a number of subsets of public international law,[1] like human rights law or environmental law that are relevant in the context of sustainable development. International investment law deals with the protection of foreign investments and aims to promote development and to protect foreign investments at the same time. It is widely acknowledged that foreign investment is necessary to achieve sustainable development.[2]

Already in the 1960s, the World Bank pointed to the link between economic development, international cooperation, and private international investment. It believed that the availability of impartial and independent dispute settlement

---

[1] Bruno Simma and Dirk Pulkowsky called it 'special' branch: see Bruno Simma and Dirk Pulkowsky, 'Two Worlds but Not Apart: International Investment Law and General International Law' in Marc Bungenberg and others (eds), *International Investment Law* (Nomos 2015) 361–71, 369. Pierre-Marie Dupuy and Jorge Vinuales spoke of 'two sets of legal regimes belong[ing] to the same legal order, namely international law': Pierre-Marie Dupuy and Jorge Vinuales, 'Human Rights and Investment Disciplines: Integration in Progress' in Marc Bungenberg and others (eds), *International Investment Law* (Nomos 2015) 1762–66, 1766. Rainer Hofmann and Christian J Tams used 'sub-area' of international law: see Rainer Hofmann and Christian J Tams, 'International Investment Law: Situating an Exotic Special Regime within the Framework Of General International Law' in Rainer Hofmann and Christian J Tams, *International Investment Law and General International Law, From Clinical Isolation to Systemic Integration?* (Nomos 2011) 9–16.

[2] See, e.g., Stephan W Schill, 'International Investment Law as Development Law', in Andrea K Bjorklund (ed), *Yearbook on International Investment Law and Policy 2012–2013* (OUP 2014) 329–13, 327 (hereafter Schill, 'International Investment Law as Development Law'); Jorge Viñuales, 'Investment Law and Sustainable Development: The Environment breaks into Investment Disputes', in Marc Bungenberg and August Reinisch (eds), *International Investment Law: A Handbook* (Nomos 2015) 1714 (hereafter Viñuales, 'Investment Law and Sustainable Development'); *Agenda 21: Programme of Action for Sustainable Development* UN Doc A/Conf151/6/Rev1 (UN Conference on Environment and Development, Rio de Janeiro, 3–14 June 1992) para 2.23; 'Monterrey Consensus on Financing for Development' (International Conference on Financing for Development, Monterrey, 18–22 March 2002) para 20 <https://www.un.org/esa/ffd/wp-content/uploads/2014/09/MonterreyConsensus.pdf > accessed 10 June 2023; *Plan of Implementation of the World Summit on Sustainable Development* UN Doc A/Conf199/20 (26 August–4 September 2002), para 4 <http://www.un.org/esa/sustdev/documents/WSSD_POI_PD/English/WSSD_PlanImpl.pdf> accessed 10 June 2023 (hereafter 'Plan of Implementation'); United Nations General Assembly (UNGA), *Transforming Our World: The 2030 Agenda for Sustainable Development* (UNGA Res 70/1, UN Doc A/RES/70/1, 25 September 2015) para 67.

by an international tribunal would lead to an improvement of a country's investment climate. This would lead to more foreign private investment in developing countries.[3]

In 1966, the Convention on the Settlement of Investment Disputes between States and Nationals of Other States (ICSID Convention)[4] entered into force after twenty states had ratified it.[5] The text had been negotiated under the auspices of the World Bank. The Convention establishes the International Centre for Settlement of Investment Disputes (ICSID). It provides a neutral forum to depoliticize the settlement of investor-state disputes by mixed arbitration. 'Depoliticize' means here that interstate confrontations between home-states and host-states of investors are avoided.[6]

Attempts to agree on international rules on substantive protection standards in a multilateral, supra-regional instrument failed several times.[7] This led to the creation of a network of bilateral investment treaties (BITs). In the aftermath of the conclusion of the ICSID Convention, states have concluded over 3,000 BITs that offer mixed arbitration often before ICSID tribunals as a mode of dispute settlement.[8] In more recent times, states have also increasingly concluded bi- or multilateral free trade agreements with investment protection chapters offering investor-state dispute settlement.[9]

In contrast to the ICSID Convention, these treaties include definitions of 'investment'. Furthermore, they contain binding obligations for states concerning their treatment of foreign investments and foreign investors. Typically, among these guarantees are: (1) compensation for expropriations or measures having an equivalent effect, (2) a guarantee of fair and equitable treatment (FET), (3) full protection and security, (4) national treatment, (5) most-favoured-nation (MFN)

---

[3] 'Note by the President to the Executive Directors' (R 61-128, 28 December 1961) in *History of the ICSID Convention*, vol II-1 (ICSID 1968) 4–6.

[4] Convention on the Settlement of Investment Disputes between States and Nationals of Other States (18 March 1965) 4 ILM 524 (entered into force 14 October 1966); the text of the ICSID Convention is available via <https://icsid.worldbank.org/resources/rules-and-regulations/convention/overview> accessed 22 August 2023. See especially Stephan W Schill and others, *Schreuer's Commentary on the ICSID Convention* (3rd edn, CUP 2022) General Bibliography 1732 *et seq*.

[5] On the history of the Convention, see, e.g., Antonio Parra, *The History of ICSID* (OUP 2012).

[6] Ibrahim Shihata, 'Towards a Greater Depoliticization of Investment Disputes: The Roles of ICSID and MIGA' (1986) 1 ICSID Rev 1; Ursula Kriebaum, 'Evaluating Social Benefits and Costs of Investment Treaties: Depoliticization of Investment Disputes' (2018) 33 ICSID Rev 14.

[7] See, e.g., Rudolf Dolzer, Ursula Kriebaum, and Christoph Schreuer, *Principles of International Investment Law* (3rd edn, OUP 2022) 10 *et seq* (hereafter Dolzer, Kriebaum, and Schreuer, *Principles of Investment Law*).

[8] The United Nations Conference on Trade and Development (UNCTAD) homepage provides access to many of the texts of these treaties. See UNCATD, 'International Investment Agreements Navigator' <https://investmentpolicy.unctad.org/international-investment-agreements> accessed 10 June 2023.

[9] The UNCTAD homepage mentions that states have concluded 425 such treaties as of 15 May 2022, of which 333 are in force. On this type of treaties, see e.g. Rainer Hoffmann, Stephan W Schill, and Christian Tams (eds), *Preferential Trade and Investment Agreements: From Recalibration to Reintegration* (Nomos 2013).

treatment, (6) a right to transfer money for investments into and profits and investments out of the country, (7) as well as an umbrella clause which guarantees the observance of commitments of the state vis-à-vis a foreign investor.

Usually, these treaties do not require the exhaustion of local remedies as a prerequisite for the possibility to bring a claim against the host state of the investment. Tribunals may award compensation in case of a lawful expropriation or damages in case of a breach of the investment treaty. The pecuniary obligations imposed by an award are enforceable in all state parties to the ICSID Convention, in case of an ICSID arbitration. Otherwise, if other arbitration rules are agreed upon, awards can be enforced under the New York Convention on the Recognition and Enforcement of Foreign Arbitral Awards.[10]

State parties concluding investment protection treaties always aim to foster economic development. Only more recently, concerns for sustainable development have led to the inclusion of language into investment protection treaties that aims to integrate goals of investment protection and sustainable development.[11] The Brundtland Commission Report 'Our Common Heritage' of 1987 defined sustainable development as 'development that meets the needs of the present without comprising the ability of future generations to meet their own needs'.[12] The concept[13] was further developed in the following years and its multi-faceted aspects today include economic development, environmental protection, as well as social development.[14] Since the notion of sustainable development is itself a concept without an exact meaning, this contribution will focus on those aspects that arise most frequently in the context of investment arbitration: protection of the environment, labour standards and other human rights-related issues and provisions dealing with corruption.

As will be shown in the next section of this contribution, treaty preambles increasingly not only mention development, but sustainable development or particular aspects thereof as object and purpose of the treaty.

---

[10] United Nations Convention on the Recognition and Enforcement of Foreign Arbitral Awards (10 June 1958) 330 UNTS 3 (entered into force 7 June 1959) <http://www.uncitral.org/uncitral/en/uncitral_texts/arbitration/NYConvention.html> accessed 10 June 2023. For an overview of the dispute settlement procedure, see Dolzer, Kriebaum, and Schreuer, *Principles of Investment Law* (n 7) 334 *et seq*.

[11] See Kathryn Gordon, Joachim Pohl, and Marie Bouchard, 'Investment Treaty Law, Sustainable Development and Responsible Business Conduct: A Fact Finding Survey' (OECD Working Papers on International Investment, January 2014).

[12] World Commission on Environment and Development UNGA Res 42/87 (11 December 1987).

[13] There is an ongoing controversial discussion about the normative content and status of sustainable development; Ulrich Beyerlin, 'Sustainable Development' in Max Planck Encyclopedia of Public International Law (OUP 2013) para 15 (hereafter 'Sustainable Development'). The International Court of Justice (ICJ) referred to sustainable development as a concept in its *Gabčíkovo-Nagymaros Project (Hungary v Slovakia* (Judgment) [1997] ICJ Rep 7, para 140. This contribution uses the expression 'concept of sustainable development' here without further discussion of its exact legal status.

[14] See e.g. Beyerlin, 'Sustainable Development' (n 13) para 11.

International investment protection and sustainable development share the common goal to have a rule of law based[15] international system that provides a solid legal basis for investments that have as their ultimate goal (sustainable) development. This alignment between a regulatory environment based on rule of law premises and sustainable development is particularly obvious in the field of environmentally friendly energy production. Investment, including foreign investment, will be indispensable to achieve a transition to more environmentally-friendly technologies. An obvious goal is the sustainability of the energy sector without cutting back living standards or undermining social and environmental protection and potentially undermining the ability of states to fulfil their environmental and human rights obligations. To be able to attract private investment in the green economy, a stable legal framework with a functioning dispute settlement system and enforceable outcomes will be necessary.

At the same time, this system must allow for the necessary regulations by states to balance the various, sometimes competing, interests in the field of economic development, the environment, and human rights; a goal that is inherent in the concept of sustainable development. International investment law may help to generate the financial and technical resources needed to foster the green economy and to create the conditions under which human rights can be realized for the development component of sustainable development.

Out of the many aspects that are relevant in the context of investment law and sustainable development[16] this contribution will present the more recent

[15] The rule of law as essential enabling factor for investment in the context of sustainable development was, for example, explicitly acknowledged in the Plan of Implementation of the World Summit on Sustainable Development, see *Plan of Implementation* (n 2) para 4.

[16] On this issue, see e.g. Nico Schrijver and Friedl Weiss (eds), *International Law and Sustainable Development: Principles and Practice* (Brill 2004); Antony Crockett, 'Stabilisation Clauses and Sustainable Development: Drafting for the Future' in Chester Brown and Kate Miles (eds), *Evolution in Investment Treaty Law and Arbitration* (CUP 2011); Marie-Claire Cordonier Segger, Markus W Gehring, and Andrew Newcombe (eds), *Sustainable Development in World Investment Law* (Kluwer 2011); Elena Blanco and Jona Razzaque (eds), *Natural Resources and the Green Economy: Redefining the Challenges for People, States and Corporations* (Martinus Nijhoff Publishers 2012); Caroline Henckels, 'Balancing Investment Protection and Sustainable Development in Investor-State Arbitration: The Role of Deference' in Andrea K Bjorklund (ed), *Yearbook on International Investment Law & Policy 2012–2013* (OUP 2014) 305; Rahim Moloo and Jenny J Chao, 'International Investment Law and Sustainable Development: Bridging the Unsustainable Divide' in Andrea K Bjorklund (ed), *Yearbook on International Investment Law and Policy 2012–2013* (OUP 2014) 273; Schill, 'International Investment Law as International Development Law' (n 2) 327; Freya Baetens (ed), *Investment Law within International Law: Integrationist Perspectives* (CUP 2013); Roberto Echandi and Pierre Sauvé (eds), *Prospects in International Investment Law and Policy: World Trade Forum* (CUP 2013); Vyoma Jha, 'India's Twin Concerns over Energy Security Climate Change: Revisiting India's Investment Treaties through a Sustainable Development Lens' (2013) 5 TL & D 109; Anne van Aaken, 'Smart Flexibility Clauses in International Investment Treaties and Sustainable Development: A Functional View' (2014) 15 JWIT 827; Anne-Juliette Bonzon, 'Balance Between Investment Protection and Sustainable Development in BITs: The Example of Switzerland' (2014) 15 JWIT 809; Tarcisio Gazzini, 'Bilateral Investment Treaties and Sustainable Development' (2014) 15 JWIT 929; Rainer Hofmann, Christian Tams, and Stephan W Schill (eds), *International Investment Law and Development* (Edward Elgar 2014); Andreas R Ziegler, 'Special Issue: Towards Better BITs?—Making International Investment Law Responsive to Sustainable Development Objectives' (2014) 15 JWIT 803; Viñuales, 'Investment Law and Sustainable Development'

investment treaty practice that contains explicit links and references to sustainable development or certain aspects thereof, like the protection of the environment, labour standards or human rights-related provisions and provisions against corruption. However, many of the investment treaties in force lack explicit references to sustainable development or aspects thereof. Therefore, this contribution illustrates ways developed by tribunals to consider sustainable development-related aspects when interpreting existing treaties. Finally, the contribution deals with the case law on renewable energy disputes and national regulatory policies. It does so to illustrate how tribunals developed criteria in the assessment of the expropriation provision and the FET standard that allow states to benefit from their required regulatory space and provide at the same time for the necessary regulatory stability to foster investment necessary to achieve sustainable development goals.

2. Investment Treaty Language and Sustainable Development

For many years investment protection treaties only rarely included references to sustainable development or components of it such as environment protection, labour rights, or human rights. This has changed in recent years and the inclusion of sustainable development-related issues has become a common practice in investment protection treaties.[17] The United Nations Conference on Trade and

---

(n 2) 1714–38; Gabriele Gagliani, 'The Interpretation of General Exceptions in International Trade and Investment Law: Is a Sustainable Development Interpretive Approach Possible?' (2015) 43 Denver J Int'l Law Policy 559; Claudia S Levy, 'Drafting and Interpreting International Investment Agreements from a Sustainable Development Perspective' (2015) 3 Groningen J Int Law 59; Stephen Hindelang and Markus Krajewski (eds), *Shifting Paradigms in International Investment Law* (OUP 2016); Yulia Levashova, Tineke E Lambooy, and Ige Dekker (eds), *Bridging the Gap between International Investment Law and the Environment* (eleven 2016); Shawkat Alam, Jahid H Bhuiyan, and Jona Razzaque (eds), *International Natural Resources Law and Sustainable Investment: Principles and Practice* (Routledge 2017); Manjiao Chi, *Integrating Sustainable Development in International Investment Law: Normative Incompatibility, System Integration and Governance Implications* (Routledge 2017); Frederico Ortino, 'Investment Treaties, Sustainable Development and Reasonableness Review: A Case against Strict Proportionality' (2017) 30 LJIL 71; Marie-Claire Cordonier Segger and Christopher G Weeramantry (eds), *Sustainable Development Principles in the Decisions of International Courts and Tribunals: 1992–2012* (Routledge 2017); Pia Acconci, 'Sustainable Development and Investment: Trends in Law-Making and Arbitration' in Andrea Gattini, Attila Tanzi, and Filippo Fontanelli (eds), *General Principles of Law and International Investment Arbitration* (Brill/Martinus Nijhoff 2018); Stephan W Schill and Vladislav Djanic, 'Wherefore Art Thou? Towards a Public Interest-Based Justification of International Investment Law' (2018) 33 ICSID Rev 29; Lise Johnson, Lisa Sachs, and Nathan Lobel, 'Aligning International Investment Agreements with the Sustainable Development Goals' (2019) 58 Colum J Transnat'l L 58; Jack Biggs, 'The Scope of Investors' Legitimate Expectations under the FET Standard in the European Renewable Energy Cases' (2021) 36 ICSID Rev 99; Emmanuel T Laryea and Oladapo O Fabusuyi, 'Africanisation of International Investment Law for Sustainable Development: Challenges' (2021) 20 J Int Trade Law Policy 42; Ole K Fauchald, 'International Investment Law in Support of the Right to Development?' (2021) 34 LJIL 181–201.

[17] Kathryn Gordon, Joachim Pohl, and Marie Bouchard, 'Investment Treaty Law, Sustainable Development and Responsible Business Conduct: A Fact Finding Survey' (OECD Working Papers on International Investment, January 2014) 5. They make this statement concerning investment

Development (UNCTAD) investment policy hub shows 2,794 investment protection agreements. 2,574 of these have been mapped. Thirty-nine out of the 2,574 mapped treaties since the beginning of the database contain references to all three of the following sustainable development-related issues: health and environment, corruption, and labour.[18] Out of 302 listed treaties from 1 January 2014 to 16 May 2022, seventy-seven have been mapped and of these seventy-seven treaties, twenty-seven contain references to all three sustainable development-related issues: health and environment, corruption, and labour. Therefore, there is a significant increase in references to sustainable development-linked issues in recent years. This trend towards including references to sustainable development issues, already thoroughly researched and documented in an Organization for Economic Cooperation and Development (OECD) study from 2014,[19] continues.

Reference to sustainable development or components thereof is more common in the preamble of the treaties. The Canada/Burkina Faso BIT is an example for a reference to sustainable development as well as several sustainable development-related issues. It provides the following in its preamble:

> **UNDERSTANDING** that investment is a form of sustainable development that meets present needs without compromising the ability of future generations to meet their own needs and that it is critical for the future development of national and global economies as well as for the pursuit of national and global objectives for sustainable development; ...
> **RECOGNIZING** the undertakings in the *United Nations Convention against Corruption*; ...
> **NOTING** internationally-recognized standards of corporate social responsibility;
> **RECOGNIZING** the right of each Party to adopt or maintain any measures that are consistent with this Agreement and that relate to health, safety, the environment, or public welfare, as well as the difference in the Parties' respective economies;[20]

The Israel/United Arab Emirates (UAE) BIT is an example for a preamble containing references to several components of sustainable development without explicitly mentioning the term itself:

---

protection treaties concluded between 2008 and 2013. See also Siobhan McInerney-Lankford and Manuela C Vasquez, 'International Human Rights Law and International Investment Law: Perspectives on International Legal Coherence' (2022) 16 DRI 45–83, 70 *et seq*.

[18] UNCTAD Investment Policy Hub, 'Mapping of IIA Content' (*UNCTAD*) <https://investmentpolicy.unctad.org/international-investment-agreements/iia-mapping> accessed 23 June 2023.
[19] See Gordon, Pohl, and Bouchard, 'OECD Working Papers on International Investment' (n 17).
[20] Agreement between the Government of Canada and the Government of Burkina Faso for the Promotion and Protection of Investments (signed 20 April 2015, entered into force 11 October 2017) (hereafter 'Canada/Burkina Faso BIT').

Recognizing the growing importance of foreign investments in creating, maintaining and enhancing sustainable economic growth and prosperity for both Parties;

Reaffirming their commitment to protecting investors, consumers, market integrity and financial stability, as well as maintaining all applicable regulatory standards;

Confirming that any kind of investment should be made in good faith;

Acknowledging each Party's right to protect its security, safety, environment and public interests within its territory; ...

Recognizing that these objectives can be achieved without relaxing health, safety and environmental measures of general application; ... [21]

The Austria/Malta BIT can serve as an example for a treaty that contains only a reference to one sustainable development related issue in its preamble, namely, workers' rights: 'REAFFIRMING their commitment to the observance of internationally recognized labour standards, in striving to achieve the objectives of this Agreement.'[22]

Such treaty language in preambles has important interpretative functions. One of them is to establish that sustainable development or components thereof are part of the context and of the purpose of the treaty. Both are relevant for the interpretation of treaty norms as provided for in article 31(1) of the Vienna Convention on the Law of Treaties (VCLT).[23] With regard to investment treaties, this is particularly important in the context of the FET standard and indirect expropriation. Under both standards, legitimate expectations of investors can be of relevance in the assessment of their potential violation. A reference to sustainable development or a component thereof will often bar the emergence of a legitimate expectation that a host State will not take measures to foster these goals that negatively affect the investor.

Such language sends a clear signal that the contracting parties want to reserve policy space to enact public policies in the field of sustainable development. In this context, provisions in the preamble will sometimes correspond with clauses in expropriation definitions that are incorporated into annexes to the investment

---

[21] Agreement between the Government of the State of Israel and the Government of of the United Arab Emirates on Promotion and Protection of Investments (signed 20 October 2020, entered into force 27 December 2021).

[22] Agreement between the Republic of Austria and Malta on the Promotion and Mutual Protection of Investments (signed 29 May 2002, entered into force 1 March 2004, terminated 1 March 2022).

[23] Article 31 of the Vienna Convention on the Law of Treaties (opened for signature 23 May 1969, entered into force 27 January 1980) 1155 UNTS 331 (hereafter 'VCLT'), General Rule of Interpretation: '1. A treaty shall be interpreted in good faith in accordance with the ordinary meaning to be given to the terms of the treaty in their context and in the light of its object and purpose. 2. The context for the purpose of the interpretation of a treaty shall comprise, in addition to the text, including its preamble and annexes: ...'.

protection treaties. The Canada/Burkina Faso BIT is an example for such an approach. Its expropriation definition in Annex I reads:

> The Parties confirm their shared understanding that: ...
> 3. a non-discriminatory measure or series of measures of a Party designed and applied to protect legitimate public welfare objectives, such as health, safety and the environment, does not constitute indirect expropriation, except in rare circumstances, such as when a measure or a series of measures is so severe in the light of its purpose that it cannot be reasonably considered as having been adopted and applied in good faith.[24]

In light of such a clause, only in rare circumstances will measures that are designed and applied to protect sustainable development goals constitute indirect expropriations.[25] The provision mentions the severity of the measure as a condition for such a finding and requires that it is disproportionate in a manner that it could not be considered to have been adopted or applied in good faith.

Clauses that prohibit lowering standards, such as that found in the Preamble of the Israel/UAE BIT, are a reminder to the two state parties that they must not lower standards in the indicated fields to attract foreign investors; but they also can be important for the interpretation of the FET and indirect expropriation provisions of such a treaty. In the presence of such a clause, it will be difficult for a foreign investor to rely on an expectation that the host state would lower standards in these fields. If the host state, contrary to assurances by its state organs, does not lower such standards, an investor will not be able to successfully rely on the FET or expropriation provision of the treaty.

Some treaties contain 'no lowering of standard' clauses in the operative part of the treaty and combine it with a consultation obligation between the parties in case one of the parties considers that the other party has breached it. The Canada/Mongolia BIT contains an example of such a clause:

> Article 15 Health, Safety and Environmental Measures
> The Parties recognize that it is inappropriate to encourage investment by relaxing domestic health, safety or environmental measures. Accordingly, a Party should not waive or otherwise derogate from, or offer to waive or otherwise derogate from, such measures as an encouragement for the establishment, acquisition, expansion or retention in its territory of an investment of an investor. If a Party

---

[24] Canada/Burkina Faso BIT (n 20).
[25] On similar clauses in treaties, see e.g. Ursula Kriebaum, 'CETA—Article 8.12 Expropriation' in Marc Bungenberg and August Reinisch (eds), *CETA Investment Law: Article-by-Article Commentary* (Nomos 2022) 297, 318–21 (hereafter Kriebaum, 'CETA Article-8.12 Expropriation'); Christoph Schreuer and August Reinisch, *International Protection of Investments: The Substantive Standards* (CUP 2020) 100–11 (hereafter Reinisch and Schreuer, *The Substantive Standards*).

considers that the other Party has offered such an encouragement, it may request consultations with the other Party and the two Parties shall consult with a view to avoiding any such encouragement.[26]

There is a difference in the legal consequences on inter-state relations between having such a clause merely in the preamble as opposed to in the operative part of the treaty: the latter creates a direct legal obligation for the states and will also have to be considered as context in the interpretation of the FET or the expropriation provisions of the treaty. However, tribunals also have to take preambular language into consideration when interpreting a FET or expropriation provision. On the other hand, such a clause will not alter the relation between the host state and the investor.

As the case law of investment tribunals shows, the tribunals have for quite some time been sensitive to problems of corruption. In most cases they rely on 'in accordance with host State law' clauses to deal with this issue. Depending on the exact wording of the investment protection treaties, they have declined jurisdiction or denied the admissibility of a claim when they had established that corruption had occurred. They did so even in the absence of an 'in accordance with host State law' clause. More recently, states have also included direct references to the United Nations (UN) Convention on Corruption in the preambles or provisions of BITs.[27] While the provisions do not explicitly state any direct consequences for investors, it is very unlikely that any tribunal would find that an investment acquired by corruption should enjoy the protection of these treaties.[28]

A further possibility for states to foster sustainable development in investment protection treaties is to clarify that they share the expectation that investors in both states will uphold corporate social responsibility and business and human rights

---

[26] Agreement between Canada and Mongolia for the Promotion and Protection of Investments (signed 8 September 2016, entered into force 24 February 2017) (hereafter 'Canada/Mongolia BIT').
[27] See e.g. Canada/Burkina Faso BIT (n 20), preamble; Agreement between Japan and the Republic of Kazakhstan for the Promotion and Protection of Investment (signed 23 October 2014, entered into force 25 October 2015), art 10.
[28] For an overview, see Dolzer, Kriebaum, and Schreuer, *Principles of Investment Law* (n 7) 106–14; see also e.g. Christina Knahr, 'Investments "in Accordance with Host State Law"' in August Reinisch and Christina Knahr (eds), *International Investment Law in Context* (Eleven International Publishing 2008) 27; Andrea Carlevaris, 'The Conformity of Investments with the Law of the Host State and the Jurisdiction of International Tribunals' (2008) 9 JWIT 35; Ursula Kriebaum, 'Illegal Investments' (2010) 4 Austrian YB Int'l Arb 307; Andrew Newcombe, 'Investor Misconduct: Jurisdiction, Admissibility, or Merits?' in Chester Brown and Kate Miles (eds), *Evolution in Investment Treaty Law and Arbitration* (CUP 2011) 187; Stephan W Schill, 'Illegal Investments in Investment Treaty Arbitration' (2012) 11 LPICT 281; Zachary Douglas, 'The Plea of Illegality in Investment Treaty Arbitration' (2014) ICSID Rev 155; Jarrod Hepburn, 'In Accordance with Which Host State Laws?' (2014) 5 JIDS 531; Thomas Obersteiner, '"In Accordance with Domestic Law" Clauses' (2014) 31 J Int Arb 265; Ralph A Lorz and Manuel Busch, 'Investment in Accordance with the Law—Specifically Corruption', in Marc Bungenberg and others (eds), *International Investment Law: A Handbook* (Nomos 2015) 577; Michael Polckinghorne and Sven-Michael Volkmer, 'The Legality Requirement in Investment Arbitration' (2017) 34 J Int Arb 149; Kathrin Betz, *Proving Bribery, Fraud and Money Laundering in International Arbitration* (CUP 2017); Aloysius P Llamzon, *Corruption in International Investment Arbitration* (2nd edn, OUP 2021).

responsibilities. Clauses in treaties vary in this respect. Often treaties highlight that states shall encourage investors to honour the OECD Guidelines for Multinational Enterprises or the UN Guiding Principles on Business and Human Rights. Some of them mention these soft law instruments explicitly[29] others only contain a general reference to them.[30]

However, in exceptional cases, treaties create obligations for investors.[31] The Morocco/Nigeria BIT 2016 is an example of a treaty that does provide for investor obligations in the context of sustainable development. Article 14 requires investors to comply with environmental impact assessment processes and to conduct social impact assessments.[32] Furthermore, investors have to apply the precautionary principle in the context of the environmental impact assessment and its implementation.[33] Article 18(1) contains post-establishment obligations for investors to

---

[29] See e.g. Free Trade Agreement between the European Union and the Repulic of Singapore (signed 19 October 2018, entered into force 21 November 2019), Trade and Investment Promoting Sustainable Development, art 12.11:

> [...] 4. When promoting trade and investment, the Parties should make special efforts to promote corporate social responsibility practices which are adopted on a voluntary basis. In this regard, each Party shall refer to relevant internationally accepted principles, standards or guidelines to which it has agreed or acceded, such as the Organization for Economic Cooperation and Development Guidelines for Multinational Enterprises, the UN Global Compact, and the ILO Tripartite Declaration of Principles concerning Multinational Enterprises and Social Policy. The Parties commit to exchanging information and cooperating on promoting corporate social responsibility.

[30] See e.g. Canada/Mongolia BIT (n 26), Corporate Social Responsibility, art 14:

> Each Party should encourage enterprises operating within its territory or subject to its jurisdiction to voluntarily incorporate internationally recognized standards of corporate social responsibility in their practices and internal policies, such as statements of principle that have been endorsed or are supported by the Parties. These principles address issues such as labour, the environment, human rights, community relations and anti-corruption. The Parties should remind those enterprises of the importance of incorporating such corporate social responsibility standards in their internal policies.

[31] On investor and home-state obligations in the context of foreign investments, see Ludovica C Curzi, *General Principles for Business and Human Rights in International Law* (Brill Nijhoff 2020).

[32] For a critical assessment of corporate social responsibility clauses, see Nicolas Bueno, Anil Yilmaz Vastardis, and Isidore N Djeuga, 'Investor Human Rights and Environmental Obligations: The Need to Redesign Corporate Social Responsibility Clauses' (2023) 24 JWIT 179.

[33] Reciprocal Investment Promotion and Protection Agreement between the Government of the Kingdom of Morocco and the Government of the Federal Republic of Nigeria (signed 3 December 2016, not yet in force) (hereafter 'Morocco/Nigeria BIT 2016') art 14—Impact Assessment:

> '1) Investors or the investment shall comply with environmental assessment screening and assessment processes applicable to their proposed investments prior to their establishment, as required by the laws of the host state for such an investment or the laws of the home state for such an investment, whichever is more rigorous in relation to the investment in question.
> 2) Investors or the investment shall conduct a social impact assessment of the potential investment. The Parties shall adopt standards for this purpose at the meeting of the Joint Committee.
> 3) Investors, their investment and host state authorities shall apply the precautionary principle to their environmental impact assessment and to decisions taken in relation to a proposed investment, including any necessary mitigation or alternative approaches of the precautionary principle by investors and investments shall be described in the environmental impact assessment they undertake.'

maintain an environmental management system and specifies specific standards for resource exploitation.[34] The treaty contains two provisions specifically dealing with human rights issues. Unlike the obligations of investors contained in article 14, article 15 deals with obligations of the state parties, which will however, be relevant context in the interpretation of the investment protection standards in the treaty. Articles 18(2) to 18(4) contain post-establishment obligations of investors to honour core labour standards.

Furthermore, the investor must manage and operate the investment in accordance with human rights standards to which the home or the host state of the investor are parties.[35] Article 17 contains investor obligations in the context of the fight against corruption and specifies what is to be considered as not 'in accordance with host State law', the clause so far used by tribunals to exclude investments obtained by corruption from investment protection.[36] In addition, article 20 provides for civil liability in the home state of the investor for significant damage, personal injuries, or loss of life in the host state.[37]

Similarly, the Netherlands Model BIT 2018 provides in article 7(1), that investors and their investments have to comply with the domestic laws and regulations of the host state including those in the fields of human rights and environmental protection.[38] In article 7(4) it contains a liability in their home state for acts or decisions made in relation to the investment where such acts or decisions lead to significant damage, personal injuries, or loss of life in the host state.[39]

---

[34] ibid art 18—Post-Establishment Obligations:
  '1) Investments shall, in keeping with good practice requirements relating to the size and nature of the investment, maintain an environmental management system. Companies in areas of resource exploitation and high-risk industrial enterprises shall maintain a current certification to ISO 14001 or an equivalent environmental management standard.'

[35] ibid art 18—Post-Establishment Obligations:
  '2) Investors and investments shall uphold human rights in the host state.
  3) Investors and investments shall act in accordance with core labour standards as required by the ILO Declaration on Fundamental Principles and Rights of Work, 1998.
  4) Investors and investments shall not manage or operate the investments in a manner that circumvents international environmental, labour and human rights obligations to which the host state and/or home state are Parties.'

[36] On the issue of corruption, see n 26.

[37] Morocco/Nigeria BIT 2016 (n 33), art 20—Investor Liability: 'Investors shall be subject to civil actions for liability in the judicial process of their home state for the acts or decisions made in relation to the investment where such acts or decisions lead to significant damage, personal injuries, or loss of life in the host state.'

[38] Netherlands model Investment Agreement (2019) Corporate Social Responsibility, art 7:
  '1. Investors and their investments shall comply with domestic laws and regulations of the host state, including laws and regulations on human rights, environmental protection and labor laws.'

[39] ibid art 7(4):
  '4. Investors shall be liable in accordance with the rules concerning jurisdiction of their home state for the acts or decisions made in relation to the investment where such acts or decisions lead to significant damage, personal injuries or loss of life in the host state.'

The Sustainable Investment Facilitation & Cooperation Agreement (SIFCA) is a further example of such an approach. This model BIT, developed for The Gambia, contains an obligation for the investor to submit a declaration of compliance with both the SIFCA and the UN Guiding Principles on Business and Human Rights as a condition for the possibility to submit a dispute to arbitration. The model treaty also requires that investors when they start an arbitration consent to recognize concerns of human rights, environmental protection, sustainability, and investment protection, as interrelated and arising directly from an investment (including for jurisdiction under ICSID). A further requirement for arbitration is consent to the tribunal's jurisdiction over any third-party claims asserted against the investor by natural persons who have suffered the violation of internationally recognized human rights in connection with an investment.[40] In this context, the treaty draft provides for the option to use of the Hague Rules on Business and Human Rights Arbitration[41] that have been specifically developed as a remedy in business and human rights disputes. In this way the so far triangular relationship between the home state, the host state, and the investor that is typical for investment treaties[42] can be supplemented by a possibility to claim against investors for third parties whose human rights are infringed by the investment operation of a foreign investor.[43]

Exception clauses in investment treaties are a further possibility for states to attempt to promote sustainable development objectives by aiming to exclude states' regulatory measures from the scrutiny of investment arbitration.[44] However, they

---

[40] See Robert L Houston, Raja Bose, and Chester Brown, 'Notes From Practice: Announcing the SIFCA Framework—is the Confluence Of Investment Protection with Business and Human Rights the Future of Investment Treaties?' (*Kluwer Arbitration Blog*, 26 November 2021) <http://arbitrationblog.kluwerarbitration.com/2021/11/26/notes-from-practice-announcing-the-sifca-framework-is-the-confluence-of-investment-protection-with-business-and-human-rights-the-future-of-investment-treaties/> accessed 23 June 2023.

[41] For the text of the rules, the commentary to the rules, as well as Q&As, see Center for International Legal Cooperation (CILC) (The Hague), 'The Hague Rules on Business and Human Rights Arbitration' <https://www.cilc.nl/cms/wp-content/uploads/2019/12/The-Hague-Rules-on-Business-and-Human-Rights-Arbitration_CILC-digital-version.pdf> accessed 23 June 2023. See also Ursula Kriebaum, 'The Hague Rules on Business and Human Rights Arbitration', in *Proceedings of the 114th Annual Meeting of the American Society of International Law: Protecting Human Rights Through International Adjudication* (2020) (vol 114, CUP 2021) 149; Bruno Simma and Giorgia Sangiuolo, 'The Hague Rules on Business and Human Rights Arbitration: Some Challenges and Responses' (2022) 28 Southwestern J Int'l L 401.

[42] On the classical distribution of roles between home states, host states, and investors in the context of disputes involving human rights issues in investment arbitration, see Ursula Kriebaum, 'Foreign Investments & Human Rights—the Actors and their Different Roles', in Jansen N Calamita, David Earnest, and Markus Burgstaller (eds), *The Future of ICSID and the Place of Investment Law in International Law* (BIICL 2013) 45–59.

[43] For a discussion of such possibilities, see Martin Jarrett, Sergio Puig, and Steven Ratner, 'Towards Greater Investor Accountability: Indirect Actions, Direct Actions by States and Direct Actions by Individuals' (2023) 14 J Int Dispute Settl 259–80.

[44] See e.g. Catherine Titi, *The Right to Regulate in International Investment Law* (Nomos 2014); Güneş Ünüvar, 'A Tale of Policy Carve-outs and General Exceptions: Eco Oro v Colombia as a Case Study' (2023) J Intl Dispute Settl, <https://doi.org/10.1093/jnlids/idad017> (accessed 23 August 2023).

may at the same time also frustrate development objectives since they may prevent investments in fields like green energy and the fight against climate change in which private investment is needed.[45]

Therefore, there are numerous possibilities for states to adapt their investment protection treaties to fit their individual needs in the context of sustainable development. Given the trend away from short and general treaties to detailed and complex new BITs or investment chapters, this will become a more challenging endeavour. The states will have to carefully balance the various provisions so that they are able to achieve all their different sustainable development goals at the same time.

3. Investment Treaty Cases and Sustainable Development

Many of the cases that deal with facts that concern sustainable development related public concerns like environment protection, human rights, and health concern the regulatory autonomy of host states and involve indirect expropriations and the FET standard.[46] Therefore, the following discussion will focus on those two standards.

Since most existing treaties lack explicit links to sustainable development or aspects thereof it is the task of treaty interpreters to develop ways to consider sustainable development-related aspects through the interpretation of existing treaties.[47] Some tribunals have interpreted the clauses on expropriation and FET in a way that takes into account the regulatory interests of states and provide a rule of law based test to assess whether a compensable expropriation or a breach of the FET standard has occurred.[48]

---

[45] Markus W Gehring and Avidan Kent, International Investment Agreements and the Emerging Green Economy: Rising to the Challenge, in Freya Baetens (ed), *Investment Law within International Law* (CUP 2013) 187–216, 205.

[46] For an analysis of sustainable development related cases see also e.g. Nathalie Bernasconi-Osterwalder, Martin D Brauch, and Stefanie Schacherer, *International Investment Law and Sustainable Development: Key Cases from the 2010s* (IISD 2018).

[47] For a discussion on how tribunals dealt with environmental issues, see e.g. Viñuales, 'Investment Law and Sustainable Development' (n 2) 1714–38.

[48] For an overview of how tribunals dealt with human rights issues arising in investment disputes, see e.g. Ursula Kriebaum, 'Human Rights and International Investment Arbitration', in Thomas Schultz and Frederico Ortino (eds), *Oxford Handbook of International Arbitration* (OUP 2020) 150–85 (hereafter Kriebaum, 'Human Rights and International Investment Arbitration'); Siobhan McInerney-Lankford and Manuela C Vasquez, 'International Human Rights Law and International Investment Law: Perspectives on International Legal Coherence' (2022) 16 DRI 45–83.

a. Evolutive treaty interpretation

Most tribunals, when interpreting treaties, start by invoking article 31 of the VCLT.[49] At times, tribunals also refer to the supplementary means of interpretation contained in article 32 of the VCLT.[50] Tribunals have recognized the validity of the rules on treaty interpretation in the VCLT as part of customary international law.[51] This means that these rules are of general application independently of whether all parties to a treaty have ratified the VCLT.

The appropriate temporal context in which treaty terms must be interpreted is not addressed in the VCLT or in the 1966 International Law Commission (ILC) Articles on the Law of Treaties.[52] However, it is generally accepted that the obligation to interpret a treaty in good faith provided for in article 31(1) VCLT encompasses a duty to establish the appropriate temporal context of a treaty term.[53] There are two possibilities: either to interpret a provision in accordance with the ordinary meaning at the time of the adoption of the treaty or to interpret a provision in line with the ordinary meaning at the time of the interpretation. The issue has gained attention in investment arbitration since some tribunals have referred to the concept of 'contemporaneity', which they understood as static interpretation, when interpreting MFN provisions in investment treaties.[54] The ILC's Study Group on the MFN Clause stated in its Final Report this context:

---

[49] VCLT (n 23), art 31(1) provides: 'A treaty shall be interpreted in good faith in accordance with the ordinary meaning to be given to the terms of the treaty in their context and in the light of its object and purpose'. See e.g. *Siemens v Argentina* [3 August 2004] Decision on Jurisdiction, para 80.

[50] VCLT (n 23) art 32, dealing with supplementary means of interpretation provides:

Recourse may be had to supplementary means of interpretation, including the preparatory work of the treaty and the circumstances of its conclusion, in order to confirm the meaning resulting from the application of article 31, or to determine the meaning when the interpretation according to article 31:

(a) leaves the meaning ambiguous or obscure; or
(b) leads to a result which is manifestly absurd or unreasonable.

[51] *Methanex v United States* [3 August 2005] Final Award on Jurisdiction and Merits, part IV, ch B, para 29 (hereafter '*Methanex v United States*, Award'); *Malaysian Historical Salvors v Malaysia* [16 April 2009] Decision on Annulment, para 56; *Bureau Veritas v Paraguay* [29 May 2009] Decision on Jurisdiction, para 59; *Kiliç v Turkmenistan* [7 May 2012] Decision on Article VII.2 of the Turkey-Turkmenistan Bilateral Investment Treaty, para 6.4; *Micula v Romania* [11 December 2013] Award, para 503 (hereafter '*Micula v Romania*, Award'); *Churchill Mining v Indonesia* [24 February 2014] Decision on Jurisdiction, paras 95, 149; *Itisaluna v Iraq* [3 April 2020] Award, para 61.

[52] For a general analysis of this topic, see e.g. Epaminontas E Triantafilou, 'Contemporaneity and Evolutive Interpretation under the Vienna Convention on the Law of Treaties' (2017) 32 ICSID Review 138–69.

[53] See e.g. International Law Commission (ILC), 'Draft Articles on the Law of Treaties with Commentaries' (1966) UN Doc A/CN4/SER4/1966/Add 1 Draft Articles, art 27, commentary 16. See, however, Christian Djeffal, *Static and Evolutive Treaty Interpretation: A Functional Reconstruction* (CUP 2016) 153.

[54] For the controversial approach to this issue, see e.g. *Wintershall v Argentina* [8 December 2008] Award, para 128; *Urbaser v Argentina* [19 December 2012] Decision on Jurisdiction, para 149; *Daimler v Argentina* [22 August 2011] Award on Jurisdiction, para 220; *Garanti Koza v Turkmenistan* [3 July 2013] Decision on the Objection to Jurisdiction for Lack of Consent, para 57; *UP (formerly Le Chèque*

[W]hether an evolutionary (evolutive) interpretation is appropriate in any given case will depend on a number of factors, including the intention of the parties that the term in question was to be interpreted in an evolutionary (evolutive) way, the subsequent practice of the parties, and the way they themselves have interpreted and applied their agreement.[55]

The ILC, in its Draft Conclusions on the Role of Subsequent Agreements and Subsequent Practice, did not take any position regarding the appropriateness of a more static or a more evolutive approach to treaty interpretation in general.[56] It points to the fact that by applying articles 31 and 32 of the VCLT, it shall be established whether a term should be given a meaning capable of evolving over time.[57] It pointed out that subsequent agreements and subsequent practice may assist in determining whether a term has a meaning that is capable of evolving over time.[58]

Like the ILC, the International Court of Justice (ICJ) also did not make a general statement concerning the appropriateness of a more static or a more evolutive approach to treaty interpretation. It starts from the idea that a treaty has to be interpreted in light of the common intentions of the parties to the treaty at the time of its conclusion as manifested in the treaty's text. However, there are situations where it must be presumed that the parties to a treaty have been aware that the meaning of a term will change over time.[59] In such a situation, the Court presumes that the common intention of the parties was that a provision has to be interpreted with the meaning the term has at the time at which the treaty is to be applied.[60] One of the indicators for the appropriateness of an evolutive interpretation is according to the ICJ the use of 'generic terms'. It said in the Dispute Regarding Navigational and Related Rights:

> Where the parties have used generic terms in a treaty, the parties necessarily having been aware that the meaning of the terms was likely to evolve over time, and where the treaty has been entered into for a very long period or is 'of

---

Déjeuner) and CD Holding Internationale v Hungary [3 March 2016] Decision on Preliminary Issues of Jurisdiction, paras 165–75.

[55] ILC, 'Final Report of the Study Group on the Most-Favoured-Nation Clause', in UN, *Yearbook of the International Law Commission* (vol II, part 2, 2015) 30, 31, paras 176–78 (footnote omitted).
[56] ILC, *Subsequent Agreements and Subsequent Practice in Relation to the Interpretation of Treaties* (Part 1, A/73/10) Commentary 3 to Conclusion 8 (hereafter ILC, 'Subsequent Agreements').
[57] ibid.
[58] ibid Commentary 4 to Conclusion 8.
[59] Paolo Palchetti, 'Interpreting "Generic Terms": Between Respect for the Parties' Original Intention and the Identification of the Ordinary Meaning', in Nerina Boschiero and others (eds), *International Courts and the Development of International Law: Essays in Honor of Tullio Treves* (Springer 2013) 92.
[60] ibid.

continuing duration', the parties must be presumed, as a general rule, to have intended those terms to have an evolving meaning.[61]

Judge Higgins defined 'generic term' as 'a known legal term, whose content the parties expected would change through time'.[62]

Concerning FET provisions that are of great importance in the context of sustainable development, the Tribunal in *Mondev v United States* explicitly mentioned with reference to *Pope and Talbot v Canada* that 'Article 1105 NAFTA incorporated an evolutionary standard, which allowed subsequent practice, including treaty practice, to be taken into account.'[63]

As the Tribunal in *CCFT v US* has found, subsequent practice can also consist in a number of unilateral actions by the state parties to a treaty that are concordant, common, and consistent.[64] The ILC referred to this example in its Draft Conclusions on the Role of Subsequent Agreements and Subsequent Practice.[65] In investment arbitration, we can witness that also model treaties that, by definition, are not binding treaties, have considerable influence on the interpretation of treaties.

An illustrative example of such a case that has a link with sustainable development is the *Methanex v United States*[66] case. The case concerned a Canadian producer of methanol, a key component in methyl tertiary butyl ether (MTBE), which is used to increase oxygen content and to act as an octane enhancer in unleaded gasoline. In 1999, California imposed a ban on the use of MTBE by the end of 2002. It argued that banning MTBE was necessary because the additive is contaminating drinking water supplies, and is therefore posing a significant risk to human health and safety, and the environment. The company argued that the ban was tantamount to an expropriation of the company's investment and therefore a violation of article 1110 of the North American Free Trade Agreement (NAFTA), and that it was enacted in breach of the FET standard contained in article 1105 of the NAFTA.

The NAFTA treaty contains a classical expropriation clause without a definition of an indirect expropriation.[67] In 2004, the United States (US) and Canada

---

[61] Dispute Regarding Navigational and Related Rights (*Costa Rica v Nicaragua*) (Judgment) [2009] ICJ Rep 213, para 66.
[62] *Kasikili/Sedudu Island* (*Botswana v Namibia*) Declaration of Judge Higgins (Judgment) [1999] ICJ Rep 1113, para 2.
[63] *Mondev v United States* [11 October 2002] Award, para 105. Similarly, for an evolutive interpretation of the international minimum standard of treatment enshrined in NAFTA, art 1105, *Chemtura v Canada* [2 August 2010] Award, para 122 (hereafter '*Chemtura v Canada*, Award').
[64] *CCFT v United States* [28 January 2008] Award on Jurisdiction, paras 188–89.
[65] ILC, 'Subsequent Agreements' (n 56).
[66] *Methanex v United States*, Award (n 51).
[67] North American Free Trade Agreement (NAFTA) (opened for signature 17 December 1992, entered into force 1 January 1994, terminated 1 July 2020), art 1110: Expropriation and Compensation

1. No Party may directly or indirectly nationalize or expropriate an investment of an investor of another Party in its territory or take a measure tantamount to nationalization or expropriation of such an investment ('expropriation'), except:

    (a) for a public purpose;

had chosen to refine the scope of protection under the expropriation clause in investment treaties by abstract instructions on how to identify an indirect expropriation and in explicitly providing for regulatory space.[68] Annex B of the US Model BIT that deals with expropriations starts by mentioning that the following provision is intended to reflect customary international law.[69] The Canadian Model BIT 2004 does not contain such an explanation. Both Model BITs of 2004 instruct tribunals to consider the economic impact of a measure, the interference with investment-backed expectations, and the character of the governmental action to establish whether an indirect expropriation has occurred.[70] The US Model BIT 2004 further specifies that *bona fide* regulation for public welfare objectives will normally not constitute an indirect expropriation: 'Except in rare circumstances, non-discriminatory regulatory actions by a Party that are designed and applied to protect legitimate public welfare objectives, such as public health, safety, and the environment, do not constitute indirect expropriations.'[71] The Canadian Model BIT 2004 contains a similar provision in its Annex on Expropriation.[72]

> (b) on a non-discriminatory basis;
> I in accordance with due process of law and Article 1105(1); and
> (d) on payment of compensation in accordance with paragraphs 2 through 6.

[68] The US Model BIT of 1998 still contains the classical expropriation clause.
[69] Annex B Expropriation (1) US Model BIT (2004) <https://ustr.gov/archive/assets/Trade_Sectors/Investment/Model_BIT/asset_upload_file847_6897.pdf> accessed 23 June 2023.
[70] See *Methanex v USA*, Award (n 51) and NAFTA (n 67) art 1110.
[71] Annex B Expropriation of the US Model BIT 2004 reads in this regard:

> The Parties confirm their shared understanding that: 1. Article 6 [Expropriation and Compensation] (1) is intended to reflect customary international law concerning the obligation of States with respect to expropriation. 2. An action or a series of actions by a Party cannot constitute an expropriation unless it interferes with a tangible or intangible property right or property interest in an investment. 3. Article 6 [Expropriation and Compensation] (1) addresses two situations. The first is direct expropriation, where an investment is nationalized or otherwise directly expropriated through formal transfer of title or outright seizure. 4. The second situation addressed by Article 6 [Expropriation and Compensation] (1) is indirect expropriation, where an action or series of actions by a Party has an effect equivalent to direct expropriation without formal transfer of title or outright seizure. (a) The determination of whether an action or series of actions by a Party, in a specific fact situation, constitutes an indirect expropriation, requires a case-by-case, fact-based inquiry that considers, among other factors: (i) the economic impact of the government action, although the fact that an action or series of actions by a Party has an adverse effect on the economic value of an investment, standing alone, does not establish that an indirect expropriation has occurred; (ii) the extent to which the government action interferes with distinct, reasonable investment-backed expectations; and (iii) the character of the government action. (b) Except in rare circumstances, non-discriminatory regulatory actions by a Party that are designed and applied to protect legitimate public welfare objectives, such as public health, safety, and the environment, do not constitute indirect expropriations. <https://ustr.gov/archive/assets/Trade_Sectors/Investment/Model_BIT/asset_upload_file847_6897.pdf> accessed 23 June 2023.

[72] Annex B13(1), Canada Model BIT 2004:

> Expropriation reads in this regard: The Parties confirm their shared understanding that: a) Indirect expropriation results from a measure or series of measures of a Party that have an effect equivalent to direct expropriation without formal transfer of title or outright seizure; b) The determination of whether a measure or series of measures of a Party constitute an indirect expropriation requires a case-by-case, fact-based inquiry that considers, among other factors: i) the economic impact of the measure or series of measures, although the sole fact

Furthermore, unlike the US Model BIT of 1984, the 2004 version contains a reference to sustainable development goals in its preamble:

> *Recognizing* that agreement on the treatment to be accorded such investment will stimulate the flow of private capital and the economic development of the Parties;
> Agreeing that a stable framework for investment will maximize effective utilization of economic resources and improve living standards....
> Desiring to achieve these objectives in a manner consistent with the protection of health, safety, and the environment, and the promotion of internationally recognized labor rights.[73]

The tribunal in *Methanex,* in its decision on the existence of an indirect expropriation, used exactly the criteria that had been formulated in the two Model BITs of Canada and the US with regard to indirect expropriations. However, it did not explicitly rely on the two Model BITs. Therefore, it also did not elaborate whether, since they were the Model BITs of the home and the host state of the investor, it could use them for interpretative purposes. The wording of the Tribunal's decision rather signifies that it considered the rule it applied to be part of customary international law or a general principle of law. It held:

> [A]s a matter of general international law, a non-discriminatory regulation for a public purpose, which is enacted in accordance with due process and, which affects, inter alios, a foreign investor or investment is not deemed expropriatory and compensable unless specific commitments had been given by the regulating government to the then putative foreign investor contemplating investment that the government would refrain from such regulation.[74]

This interpretation of an expropriation clause not containing any language on regulatory space of states has since become quite common in the case law of investment tribunals. Many tribunals dealing with issues related to sustainable development have followed this approach to interpret expropriation provisions in investment treaties.

> that a measure or series of measures of a Party has an adverse effect on the economic value of an investment does not establish that an indirect expropriation has occurred; ii) the extent to which the measure or series of measures interfere with distinct, reasonable investment-backed expectations; and iii) the character of the measure or series of measures; c) Except in rare circumstances, such as when a measure or series of measures are so severe in the light of their purpose that they cannot be reasonably viewed as having been adopted and applied in good faith, non-discriminatory measures of a Party that are designed and applied to protect legitimate public welfare objectives, such as health, safety and the environment, do not constitute indirect expropriation.

---

[73] The Canadian Model BIT 2004 contains an explicit reference to sustainable development in its preamble.
[74] *Methanex v USA*, Award (n 51) part IV, ch D, para 7.

One such example is *Chemtura v Canada*. This case concerned the ban of an agricultural insecticide said to be harmful to human health and the environment. The US investor argued that the prohibition of its sale would amount to an expropriation of its investment under the NAFTA. The Tribunal rejected the claim stating that:

> Irrespective of the existence of a contractual deprivation, the Tribunal considers in any event that the measures challenged by the Claimant constituted a valid exercise of the Respondent's police powers. As discussed in detail in connection with Article 1105 of NAFTA, the PMRA took measures within its mandate, in a non-discriminatory manner, motivated by the increasing awareness of the dangers presented by lindane for human health and the environment. A measure adopted under such circumstances is a valid exercise of the State's police powers and, as a result, does not constitute an expropriation.[75]

The Tribunal in *Philip Morris v Uruguay* can serve as a further example. The case concerned public health and the right to regulate. The Tribunal pointed at the development in the case law of investment tribunals and the inclusion of the right to exercise police powers and to regulate in the US and Canadian Model BITs of 2004 and 2012 as well as in the CETA.[76, 77] It explained that it considered these provisions to reflect the position under general international law.[78]

b. Using systemic integration to take sustainable development goals into account

A method of treaty interpretation that is important in the context of sustainable development issues is that which relies on the principle of systemic integration[79]

---

[75] *Chemtura v Canada*, Award (n 63) para 266.
[76] Comprehensive Economic and Trade Agreement between the European Union and Canada (CETA), Annex 8-A, Expropriation. On these provisions, see e.g. Kriebaum, 'CETA—Article 8.12 Expropriation' (n 25) 292–330.
[77] *Philip Morris v Uruguay* [8 July 2016] Award, para 300 (hereafter '*Philip Morris v Uruguay* Award').
[78] ibid para 301.
[79] Report of a study group of the UN International Law Commission, *Fragmentation of International Law: Difficulties Arising from the Diversification and Expansion of International Law* (UN Doc A/CN.4/L.682, 13 April 2006) para 413 (hereafter ILC, 'Report on Fragmentation'); Campbell McLachlan, 'The Principle of Systemic Integration and Article 31(1)(c) of the Vienna Convention' (2005) 54 ICLQ 279–320 (hereafter McLachlan, 'The Principle of Systemic Integration'); Bruno Simma and Theodore Kill, Harmonizing Investment Protection and International Human Rights: First Steps towards a Methodology, in Christina Binder and others (eds), *International Investment Law for the 21st Century, Essays in Honour of Christoph Schreuer* (OUP 2009) 678–707 (hereafter Simma and Kill, 'Harmonizing Investment Protection and International Human Rights'); Thomas Waelde, Interpreting Investment Treaties: Experience and Examples, in Christina Binder and others (eds), *International Investment Law for the 21st Century, Essays in Honour of Christoph Schreuer* (OUP 2009) 724–81 (hereafter Waelde, 'Interpreting Investment Treaties: Experience and Examples'); Trinh Hai Yen, *The Interpretation of*

of treaty obligations emanating from, for example, human rights treaties, environmental law treaties, or conventions against corruption. The principles of treaty interpretation as provided for in the VCLT offer possibilities to take such treaty obligations into consideration when deciding whether a violation of investment law has occurred.[80]

Article 31(3)(c) of the VCLT requires that in the interpretation of a treaty '[t]here shall be taken into account, together with the context: ... any relevant rules of international law applicable in the relations between the parties'.[81] It is disputed whether sustainable development-related norms are relevant rules in the context of the interpretation of an investment protection treaty. Also, it is not entirely clear what 'applicable in the relations between the parties' means in an investor-state arbitration context.[82] Sustainable development-related norms will obviously be relevant to the interpretation of an investment protection treaty if the preamble of the treaty refers to such rules. Furthermore, if both state parties to a BIT conferring jurisdiction on the tribunal are also parties to a particular sustainable development related treaty, this requirement will also be fulfilled.[83] The situation is more problematic with regard to regional investment protection treaties such as the NAFTA, the Comprehensive and Progressive Agreement for Trans-Pacific Partnership (CPTPP), or the Energy Charter Treaty (ECT). In such context, the additional question arises whether all parties to the regional treaty also must be parties to the

---

Investment Treaties (Brill 2014) 55–61; Romesh J Weeramantry, *Treaty Interpretation in Investment Arbitration* (OUP 2012) paras 3.134, 3.141–3.149; Tarcisio Gazzini, Interpretation of International Investment Treaties (Hart Publishing 2016) 210 *et seq*.

[80] On this issue, see Simma and Kill, 'Harmonizing Investment Protection and International Human Rights' (n 79) 678–707. For various manners, tribunals have dealt with potential human rights issues in investment disputes; see e.g. Kriebaum, 'Human Rights and International Investment Arbitration' (n 48) 150–85.

[81] VCLT (n 23) art 31(3)c.

[82] See e.g. Simma and Kill, 'Harmonizing Investment Protection and International Human Rights' (n 79) 695–703; Waelde, 'Interpreting Investment Treaties: Experience and Examples' (n 79) 774–75; Richard Gardiner, *Treaty Interpretation* (2nd edn, OUP 2015) 310–11; Campbell McLachlan, 'Investment Treaties and General International Law' (2008) 57 ICLQ 361, 371–72; ILC, 'Report on Fragmentation' (n 79) paras 421–23, 461–79; McLachlan, 'The Principle of Systemic Integration' (n 79) 314–15. Oil Platforms Case (*Iran v United States*) (Merits) [2003] ICJ Rep 161, para 41. But see also Oil Platforms Case (*Iran v United States*), Separate Opinion of Judge Buergenthal (Merits) [2003] ICJ Rep 270, paras 22–23; Oil Platforms Case (*Iran v United States*), Separate Opinion of Judge Higgins (Merits) [2003] ICJ Rep 225, paras 45–46.

[83] ILC, 'Report on Fragmentation' (n 79) para 472. For human rights norms, Simma and Kill refer furthermore to the concept of *erga omnes* obligations (Simma and Kill, 'Harmonizing Investment Protection and International Human Rights' (n 79) 678–707, 701); Bruno Simma, 'From Bilateralism to Community Interest in International Law' (1994) 250 Recueil des Cours VI, 216, 293–321; see also Ursula Kriebaum, 'Human Rights of the Population of the Host State in International Investment Arbitration' (2009) 10 JWIT 653; Siobhan McInerney-Lankford and Manuela C Vasquez, 'International Human Rights Law and International Investment Law: Perspectives on International Legal Coherence' (2022) 16 DRI 45, 64–69.

sustainable development-related treaty relied upon. There is no uniform answer to this question.[84]

However, there are examples where tribunals explicitly stated that investment obligations have to be reconciled with obligations emanating from other treaties and used the principle of systemic integration enshrined in article 31(3)(c) of the VCLT when assessing violations of investment protection treaties.

The Tribunal in *SD Myers v Canada*[85] can serve as an example in this regard in the field of environmental law. It first reviewed environmental law agreements in the abstract to establish the obligations of the home and host state of the investor under these agreements.[86] Then it relied on them in the evaluation of violations of the national treatment standard of article 1102 of the NAFTA.[87] In *Chemtura v Canada*, the Tribunal referred to two environmental law treaties when assessing the legitimacy of Canadas ban of lindane.[88]

The *Urbaser v Argentina* case provides an example from the realm of human rights.[89] There, the Tribunal considered Argentina's human rights obligations when interpreting the FET provision of the Argentina-Spain BIT. Concerning the compatibility of the human right to water and investment law obligations, the Tribunal decided that the state is required to fulfil both of them simultaneously:

> [I]ts obligations regarding the population's right to water, and its obligations towards international investors. The Argentine Republic can and should fulfill both kinds of obligations simultaneously. In so doing, the obligations resulting from the human right to water do not operate as an obstacle to the fulfillment of its obligations towards the Claimants.[90]

The Tribunal held when deciding whether Argentina had violated the FET standard that the province had to guarantee the continuation of the basic water supply and that this universal basic human right was a component of the framework of the claimant's legitimate expectations.[91] 'Respondent rightly recalls that the Province had to guarantee the continuation of the basic water supply to millions of Argentines. The protection of this *universal basic human right* constitutes

---

[84] See ILC, 'Report on Fragmentation' (n 79) paras 471–72; Joost Pauwelyn, *Conflict of Norms in Public International Law* (CUP 2003) 257–63; Campbell McLachlan, 'The Principle of Systemic Integration and Article 31(1)(c) of the Vienna Convention' (2005) 54 ICLQ 313–15; Mark E Villiger, *Commentary on the 1969 Vienna Convention on the Law of Treaties* (Martinus Nijhoff 2009) 433, para 25.
[85] *SD Myers v Canada* [13 November 2000] Partial Award.
[86] ibid paras 204–21.
[87] ibid paras 247, 255.
[88] *Chemtura v Canada*, Award (n 63) paras 136–39.
[89] *Urbaser v Argentina* [8 December 2016] Award (hereafter '*Urbaser v Argentina*, Award'); see also e.g. *Tulip v Turkey* [30 December 2015] Decision on Annulment, paras 86–92.
[90] *Urbaser v Argentina*, Award (n 89) para 720.
[91] ibid paras 623–24.

the *framework* within which Claimants should frame their *expectations*.'[92] Since, as we have seen the existence of legitimate expectations is also an important consideration in the decisions on indirect expropriations, these considerations are also valid for this standard.

The tribunal in *Philip Morris v Uruguay* explicitly relied on article 31(3)(c) of the VCLT and took into account customary international law containing a right to the *bona fide* exercise of police powers when assessing whether a compensable expropriation had occurred.[93] It stated in this context:

> As pointed out by the Respondent, Article 5(1) of the BIT must be interpreted in accordance with Article 31(3)(c) of the VCLT requiring that treaty provisions be interpreted in the light of '[a]ny relevant rules of international law applicable to the relations between the parties', a reference 'which includes ... customary international law'. This directs the Tribunal to refer to the rules of customary international law as they have evolved.[94]

Therefore, in using this method, tribunals have the possibility to take sustainable development concerns into account when interpreting substantive protection standards of investment treaties. The method is particularly relevant in the context of the establishment of legitimate expectations that in turn are relevant both for the existence of indirect expropriations and the FET standard.

A procedural tool to take into account sustainable development concerns that tribunals have recently used is to accept jurisdiction for counterclaims.[95] This allows a state to enforce investor obligations in the context of human rights or environmental law. The Tribunal in *Burlington v Ecuador* upheld Ecuador's counterclaim concerning environmental damage based on Ecuadorian environmental law.[96] The Tribunal's jurisdiction to hear the counterclaim did not pose any problem in this case since the investor agreed to an agreement with Ecuador not to contest jurisdiction over the counterclaim.

The Tribunal in *Urbaser v Argentina* accepted jurisdiction over a counterclaim based on human rights but denied that the investor had a positive obligation concerning the right to water. The Tribunal found that under current international law there was no positive obligation on investors to provide access to water based on international human rights law. The acceptance of the bid and the concession

---

[92] ibid para 624 (emphasis added).
[93] *Philip Morris v Uruguay*, Award (n 77) paras 290–301.
[94] ibid para 290 (footnotes omitted).
[95] Arnaud de Nanteuil, 'Counterclaims in Investment Arbitration: Old Questions, New Answers?' (2018) 17 LPICT 374; Andrea K Bjorklund, 'The Role of Counterclaims in Rebalancing Investment Law' (2013) 17 Lewis & Clark L Rev 461.
[96] *Burlington v Ecuador* [7 February 2017] Decision on Counterclaims, paras 159, 889, 1099.

contract could not create such an obligation under international law.[97] Therefore, the counterclaim failed on the merits.

c. Developing a test for the right to regulate

As the case law of investment tribunals illustrates, one of the most challenging issues of the last twenty years was to differentiate between the *bona fide* exercise of the right to regulate and compensable expropriations. Much of the debate on the right to regulate concerned sustainable development issues.

The *Casinos Austria v Argentina* case does not deal with an issue of sustainable development. However, it is important for this field because of its stringent analysis of the rights of host states to exercise their police powers and to regulate. It does so although the applicable BIT between Austria and Argentina of 1994 contains no reference to other goals than economic development and cooperation between the two countries and contains a classic expropriation definition without any reference to regulatory powers of states.[98] Therefore, it is a classic example of a tribunal taking into account these rights and powers when interpreting an investment protection treaty without any specific reference to them in the underlying treaty. The *Casinos Austria* Tribunal relies for this purpose on the *Methanex* Tribunal and later arbitral awards.[99] It points out in this regard, that host states' police powers that imply measures negatively affecting foreign investments without triggering a compensation obligation have long before modern investment treaty arbitration been recognized as part of customary international law.[100] A state's police powers and its right to regulate under customary international law qualify as 'relevant rules of international law applicable in the relations between the parties' in the sense of article 31(3)(c) of the VCLT.[101]

Therefore, tribunals have to take them into account when interpreting the provisions of an investment protection treaty such as the protection against uncompensated expropriation or the FET clause. This encompasses the right to regulate in the public interest and to enforce these regulations against foreign investors without triggering a duty to pay compensation.[102] This is however only valid for reasonable *bona fide*, non-discriminatory regulation.[103] Abusive exercise of these rights triggers a violation of international law.[104]

---

[97] *Urbaser v Argentina*, Award (n 89) para 1212.
[98] Agreement between the Republic of Argentina and the Republic of Austria for the Promotion and Protection of Investments (signed 7 August 1992, entered into force 1 January 1995).
[99] *Casinos Austria v Argentina* [5 November 2021] Award, para 331 (hereafter '*Casinos Austria v Argentina*, Award').
[100] ibid para 332, n 417.
[101] *Philip Morris v Uruguay*, Award (n 77) para 290; *Marfin v Cyprus* [26 July 2018] Award, para 828 (hereafter '*Marfin v Cyprus*, Award'); *Casinos Austria v Argentina*, Award (n 99) para 332.
[102] *Casinos Austria v Argentina*, Award (n 99) para 333.
[103] See e.g. ibid; see also e.g. *Philip Morris v Uruguay*, Award (n 77) para 295.
[104] *Casinos Austria v Argentina*, Award (n 99) para 333.

To distinguish between a measure that is covered by the host state's right to regulate and to exercise its police powers on the one hand, and a measure that is abusive on the other, tribunals have relied on rule-of-law elements, albeit without explicitly referring to the concept: instead they have resorted to rule-of-law elements like good faith, non-discrimination, the prohibition of arbitrariness, and proportionality. The Tribunal in *Casinos Austria v Argentina* relied on a long line of cases and held:

> In order to avoid abuse of the host State's regulatory powers, their exercise must be *bona fide* and in line with principles of international investment law, such as good faith, non-discrimination, and the prohibition of arbitrariness, and result in measures whose impact on investments is proportionate to the interest(s) protected.[105]

The Tribunal in *Marfin v Cyprus* equally relied on rule-of-law elements and decided:

> The Tribunal considers that the economic harm consequent to the non-discriminatory application of generally applicable regulations adopted in order to protect the public welfare do not constitute a compensable taking, provided that the measure was taken in good faith, complied with due process and was proportionate to the aim sought to be achieved.[106]

The *Casinos* Tribunal noted that these limits on the rights to regulate and to exercise police powers exist not only in treaty provisions but also have a basis in customary international law.[107] Furthermore, it points to the fact that the situation will be different, when the host State has made assurances or accepted specific commitments that it would refrain from such regulation.[108]

PL Holdings v Poland is another award that, while not dealing with issues of sustainable development, is relevant here since it refined the proportionality test.[109]

---

[105] ibid para 336. For case law on proportionality, see e.g. Kriebaum, 'CETA–Article 8.12 Expropriation' (n 25) 319–21; Reinisch and Schreuer, *The Substantive Standards* (n 25) 168–70.

[106] *Marfin v Cyprus*, Award (n 101) para 826. The Cyprus-Greece BIT applicable in the case contains a classic expropriation provision without an explicit regulation exception.

[107] *Casinos Austria v Argentina*, Award (n 99) para 336.

[108] ibid para 336, referring, for this purpose, to *Methanex Corporation v United States*, Award (n 51) para 7.

[109] *Marfin v Cyprus*, Award (n 101); *PL Holdings Sàrl v Poland* [28 June 2017] Partial Award (hereafter 'PL Holdings Sàrl v Poland, Partial Award'). On proportionality, see e.g. Ursula Kriebaum, Regulatory Takings: Balancing the Interests of the Investor and the State (2007) 8 JWIT 717–44; Benedict Kingsbury and Stephan W Schill, 'Public Law Concepts to Balance Investors' Rights with State Regulatory Actions in the Public Interest—The Concept of Proportionality', in Stephan W Schill, *International Investment Law and Comparative Public Law* (OUP 2010) 75–104; Gebhard Bücheler, *Proportionality in Investor-State Arbitration* (OUP 2015).

It found that a forced sale of shares amounted to an indirect expropriation.[110] For that purpose, it assessed whether the measures ordered by the authorities were proportionate to the public purpose they sought to achieve.[111] The Tribunal found that the 'principle [of proportionality] is understood in largely similar terms across jurisdictions'.[112] It indicated a number of criteria to assess whether a measure is proportionate:

[A] measure must
    (a) be one that is *suitable* by nature for achieving a legitimate public purpose,
    (b) be *necessary* for achieving that purpose in that no less burdensome measure would suffice, and
    (c) *not be excessive* in that its advantages are outweighed by its disadvantages.[113]

An example for a case involving sustainable development issues where a tribunal applied a proportionality test in the context of the FET standard is *Infinito Gold v Costa Rica*.[114] It concerned the uncertainties over the validity of a 2002 gold mining exploitation concession allegedly granted to the claimant's local subsidiary. After conflicting decisions of Costa Rica's Supreme Court and the state's administrative courts on the cancelation of the concession, the president adopted a moratorium on open-pit mining in 2010. The legislature enacted a ban that took effect in 2011. Of interest here is the finding of a violation of the FET standard through the legislative enactment and the administrative decision implementing the open-pit mining ban. The Tribunal decided that the ban in the abstract was not unfair or inequitable.[115] The legislation had a rational purpose and was therefore also not arbitrary.[116] The Tribunal assumed that the legislation's objective was the protection of the environment despite the absence of an express mention of that goal and despite certain exceptions for small-scale miners that would go against it.[117] It decided that the claimant could not have had a legitimate expectation regarding the stability of the legal order absent a specific assurance.[118] By contrast, it held that the application of the legislative mining-ban on the claimant's project was unfair and inequitable. The claimant was the only project that at the time of the enactment was affected by the ban. The Constitutional Chamber had ruled that the project was environmentally sound. Therefore, the measure was not necessary to achieve the

---

[110] *PL Holdings Sàrl v Poland*, Partial Award (n 109) paras 320–23.
[111] ibid para 354.
[112] ibid para 355.
[113] ibid para 355 (emphasis added).
[114] *Infinito Gold v Costa Rica* [3 June 2021] Award (hereafter '*Infinito Gold v Costa Rica*, Award').
[115] ibid para 560.
[116] ibid para 560.
[117] ibid para 560.
[118] ibid para 515.

goal sought by the ban and constituted an excessive burden for the investor. The Tribunal relied on *AES v Hungary* and required that for a measure to be reasonable:

> [T]here needs to be an appropriate correlation between the state's public policy objective and the measure adopted to achieve it, [and t]his has to do with the nature of the measure and the way it is implemented.[119]
>
> To be reasonable and proportionate vis-à-vis the Claimant (while still capturing future projects that were untested), Parliament could have included a grandfathering provision that protected the Crucitas Project, or could have allowed pending proceedings to continue.[120]

Although adopted in the context of FET, the criteria 'proportionality' and 'reasonableness', applied by the Tribunal, correspond to the tests applied by tribunals in the context of indirect expropriation.

Therefore, we can conclude that even absent treaty provisions explicitly providing for regulatory space connected with sustainable development, it will be possible for investment tribunals to consider legitimate public welfare objectives when deciding whether an indirect expropriation has occurred through a regulation that a host state designed and applied to foster such an objective. Among these public welfare objectives are typical sustainable development issues such as public health, safety, and the environment or human rights concerns. If these regulations have been adopted in good faith, are not arbitrary or discriminatory, complied with due process and result in outcomes whose impact on investments is proportional they will not constitute an indirect expropriation. Considerations of suitability of the measures for achieving the legitimate public purpose invoked, and their necessity for achieving that purpose as well as whether the disadvantages for the investor are not excessive compared to their advantages for the public good are important further guidelines for tribunals when deciding on the proportionality of the host state's measures. A further important element is the existence of specific promises to the investor. Tribunals will take the existence of a specific commitment or a representation to an investor into consideration in the proportionality test. An example for a tribunal explicitly highlighting the importance of specific representations is the *Methanex* case:

> [A]s a matter of general international law, a non-discriminatory regulation for a public purpose, which is enacted in accordance with due process and, which affects, inter alios, a foreign investor or investment is not deemed expropriatory and compensable unless specific commitments had been given by the regulating

---

[119] ibid para 562, quoting *AES v Hungary* [23 September 2010] Award, para 10.3.9 (hereafter '*AES v Hungary*, Award').

[120] *Infinito Gold v Costa Rica*, Award (n 114) para 563.

government to the then putative foreign investor contemplating investment that the government would refrain from such regulation.[121]

4. Lessons Learned from Renewable Energy Cases

By the end of 2021 more than eighty cases arbitrated before investment tribunals concerned disputes related to renewable energy.[122] They have in common that the regulatory environment had been (substantially) changed and investors frequently alleged a violation of the FET standard and in some cases an uncompensated indirect expropriation.[123]

These investments may help to achieve several sustainable development goals like producing environmentally-friendly energy and providing for economic development, but have high upfront costs. Therefore, it is important to develop criteria that allow host states as well as investors to assess when regulatory changes will trigger compensation obligations. Tribunal have developed the following criteria in the context of renewable energy cases.

Dealing with indirect expropriation, tribunals first inquired whether there was a substantial deprivation and then addressed the intensity or severity of the economic impact of the disputed measures.[124] To reach a sufficient severity for an expropriation, a loss of control over the investment or a total or near total loss of its value is required. It is not necessary that the state's measures affect formal ownership.[125] Since the installations usually remained under the control of the investors and the plants were in general still in operation, managed by their original owners, and produced some revenue, tribunals decided that no substantial deprivation had occurred.[126] Therefore, the focus was on the FET standard.

---

[121] *Methanex v United States*, Award (n 51) at part IV, ch D, para 7.

[122] See UNCTAD, 'Investment Dispute Settlement Navigator' <https://investmentpolicy.unctad.org/investment-dispute-settlement> accessed 24 June 2023; only those cases have been counted that have a summary pointing to a renewable energy dispute or where, in case no summary was available, the name of the claimant identified the dispute as renewable energy related.

[123] In a number of cases no claim on indirect expropriation had been raised or it had been subsequently dropped. For an example of the latter situation, see e.g. *Masdar v Spain* [16 May 2018] Award (hereafter '*Masdar v Spain*, Award').

[124] See e.g. *Renergy v Spain* [6 May 2022] Award, paras 993–94 (hereafter '*Renergy v Spain*, Award').

[125] For a recent case, see ibid para 994. For an overview on indirect expropriation, see Dolzer, Kriebaum, and Schreuer, *Principles of Investment Law* (n 7) 153–82; Reinisch and Schreuer, *The Substantive Standards* (n 25) 51–188.

[126] See e.g. *Charanne v Spain* [21 June 2016] Award, paras 461–62 (hereafter '*Charanne v Spain*, Award'); *Isolux v Spain* [12 July 2016] Award, para 826 (hereafter '*Isolux v Spain*, Award'); *Novenergia II v Spain* [15 February 2018] Award, paras 761–62 (hereafter '*Novenergia II v Spain*, Award'); *Foresight/ Greentech v Spain* [14 November 2018] Award, paras 428–31 (hereafter '*Foresight/Greentech v Spain*, Award'); *9REN v Spain* [31 May 2019] Award, paras 370–72; *BayWa v Spain* [2 December 2019] Decision on Jurisdiction, Liability and Directions on Quantum, paras 429–32; *Cavalum v Spain* [31 August 2020] Decision on Jurisdiction, Liability and Directions on Quantum, paras 652–53; *Renergy v Spain*, Award (n 124) paras 1002–04. In most of the Energy Charter Treaty cases, investors alleged an expropriation. Out of all of them, Hober reports only two were tribunals found that an expropriation

The *RWE Innogy v Spain* Tribunal aptly described the problem, which tribunals that have to decide cases concerning regulatory interferences in investments in the renewable energy sector have to solve:

> [R]eference to dictionary definitions scarcely helps it in interpreting the formula *'fair and equitable'*. The terms *'fair'* and *'equitable'* are not in any event particularly difficult to understand as a matter of ordinary meaning: the difficulty, as is very well-known, is how and where to draw the line between what is fair/unfair, equitable/inequitable, in particular in the context of a State's adoption of regulations of general application.[127]

The *Renergy* Tribunal stated in this context that answering the question of where to draw the line between fair and unfair treatment 'requires a balancing exercise, as follows not only from the very concepts of fairness and equity themselves but also from the object and purpose of the ECT'.[128] Where legislative changes are at the centre of the dispute, a tribunal must 'balance the host State's undisputed right to regulate with legitimate interests of an investor who committed resources on the basis of the earlier legal regime'.[129]

These cases show how sometimes different sustainable development goals have to be balanced against each other. In the renewable energy cases, the host states introduced the regulatory changes to deal with economic problems created by the previous subsidizing regimes. These measures can thus be said to have been taken to foster the economic and social well-being of a state. On the other hand, the measures negatively affect environmental protection since they stifle investment in renewable energies and hence the transition from other forms of energy generation to renewable forms of energy generation which is considered essential to cope with the climate crisis. Foreign investors will only be willing to invest in such projects if rule of law criteria like predictability of legal changes will be respected. However, their investments are needed to achieve the transition to renewable energy generation.

To establish criteria for an appropriate balancing between these different sustainable development interests, the *Renergy* Tribunal carefully analysed the case law of arbitral tribunals dealing with renewable energy cases. Therefore, its award provides a very useful overview of the questions tribunals have to answer when

---

had occurred, seeKaj Hober, *The Energy Charter Treaty* (OUP 2020) 287. None of them concerned a renewable energy case.

[127] *RWE Innogy v Spain* [30 December 2019] Decision on Jurisdiction, Liability, and Certain Issues of Quantum, para 440 (hereafter '*RWE Innogy v Spain*, Award'); see also *Saluka v Czech Republic* [17 March 2006] Partial Award, para 297 (hereafter '*Saluka v Czech Republic*, Partial Award'; *Micula v Romania*, Award (n 51) para 504.
[128] *Renergy v Spain*, Award (n 124) para 608.
[129] ibid.

deciding whether changes in the regulatory framework upset the balance between the host state's right to regulate and an investor's expectations of stability based on an earlier legal regime.

As for the applicable test, the *Renergy* Tribunal established first, that the tests applied by previous tribunals varied primarily in terminology rather than in substance. It distilled the following pertinent questions from the case law of tribunals:

i) Did the host state act in a way that, at the time the investment was made, gave rise to legitimate expectations on the part of investors?
ii) Did the investor in question place reliance on those expectations when making its investment?
iii) Did the host state frustrate those expectations with its subsequent behaviour?[130]

With regard to the time factor when legitimate expectations could have been created, the Tribunal confirmed the consistent case law that the existence of a legitimate expectation is to be assessed as at the time when the investment was made.[131] If an investment is made in multiple parts and it is not possible to identify one particular point in time for the making, it will not be possible to focus only on one date for the identification of legitimate expectations. Rather it will be necessary to assess the legitimate expectations at each of those dates separately.[132]

Concerning the assessment of legitimate expectations, the case law requires an objective assessment.[133] This concerns the perspective of the state as well as the perspective of the investor. Concerning the state, as already stated by the Tribunal in *Micula*, an intention to commit itself is not necessary. Rather, what counts is whether the state acted in a manner that would reasonably be understood to create a legitimate expectation.[134]

The Tribunal in *Renergy* recently confirmed this approach:

[I]t is irrelevant which intentions the State pursued when carrying out the actions that objectively gave rise to certain legitimate expectations, in particular

---

[130] ibid para 611.
[131] ibid para 637; see also *Southern Pacific Properties (Middle East) Limited (SPP) v Arab Republic of Egypt* [20 May 1992] Award, paras 82–83; *Saluka v Czech Republic*, Partial Award (n 127) para 329; *Azurix v Argentina* [14 July 2006] Award, para 372; *LG&E v Argentina* [3 October 2006] Decision on Liability, para 130; *Siemens v Argentina* [6 February 2007] Award, para 299; *Enron v Argentina* [22 May 2007] Award, para 262; *BG v Argentina* [24 December 2007] Final Award, para 298; *Duke Energy v Ecuador* [18 August 2008] Award, paras 340, 347, 365; *National Grid v Argentina* [3 November 2008] Award, para 173; *AES v Hungary*, Award (n 119) paras 9.3.8–9.3.12.
[132] Christoph Schreuer and Ursula Kriebaum, At What Time Must Legitimate Expectations Exist? in Jacques Werner and Arif Ali (eds), *A Liber Amicorum: Thomas Wälde—Law Beyond Conventiona Thougt* (CMP 2009) 265, 273, with approval, *Renergy v Spain*, Award (n 124) para 637.
[133] *Renergy v Spain*, Award (n 124) para 638; *Novenergia II v Spain*, Award (n 126) para 652.
[134] *Micula v Romania*, Award (n 51) para 669.

whether the State subjectively sought to commit itself to anything by virtue of those actions.[135]

On the part of the investor, it is equally not the subjective belief that is relevant,[136] but rather the assessment a prudent investor would make of the situation. Therefore, a tribunal will base the assessment of the legitimacy of expectations on the information a prudent investor would have. In case the investor had additional information, tribunals will also consider this.[137]

Tribunals have made it clear that investment treaties neither freeze the law nor provide a permanent 'insurance policy' for foreign investors against changes in the host state's legal framework. For such an effect to be achieved the host state needs to provide a specific commitment to this effect.[138]

Such specific commitments can be found in principle in statements or conduct of the host state and can be explicit or implicit.[139] It is accepted, that stabilization clauses in contracts between host states and investors may, depending on the formulation, amount to a specific commitment to freeze a legal order or parts of it.[140]

By contrast, general legislation cannot create a legitimate expectation that a host state will not make changes in a particular field of legislation. The *Renergy* Tribunal considered this approach to be justified since stabilization clauses in contracts cannot be changed unilaterally, but stabilization commitments in laws are 'just as much subject to change as all the other dispositions of the law in question'.[141] It came to this conclusion after having diligently analysed the allegedly incoherent case

---

[135] *Renergy v Spain* Award (n 124) 638.
[136] ibid para 638; *Charanne v Spain* Award (n 126) para 495; *Isolux v Spain* Award (n 126) para 777; *Antin v Spain* [15 June 2018] Award, para 536 (hereafter '*Antin v Spain*, Award'); *Foresight/Greentech v Spain* Award (n 126) para 354; *RREEF v Spain II* [30 November 2018] Decision on Responsibility and on the Principles of Quantum, para 261; *Suez v Argentina* [30 July 2010] Decision on Liability, para 209; *El Paso v Argentina* [31 October 2011] Award, paras 356, 358, 364 (hereafter '*El Paso v Argentina*, Award'); *Invesmart v Czech Republic* [26 June 2009] Award, para 250; *Saluka v Czech Republic*, Partial Award (n 127) para 304.
[137] *Antin v Spain*, Award (n 136) para 537. See also *Renergy v Spain* Award (n 124) para 638.
[138] ibid; *Antaris v Czech Republic* [2 May 2018] Award, para 360(10) (hereafter '*Antaris v Czech Republic*, Award'); *Charanne v Spain* Award (n 126) para 499; *Electrabel v Hungary I* [30 November 2012] Decision on Jurisdiction, Applicable Law and Liability, para 7.77; *Blusun v Italy* [27 December 2016] Award, para 372; *EDF v Romania* [8 October 2009] Award, para 217; *Plama v Bulgaria* [27 August 2008] Award, para 219; *AES v Hungary*, Award (n 119) paras 9.3.31–9.3.34; *InfraRed v Spain* [2 August 2019] Award, para 366; *RWE Innogy v Spain* Award (n 127) paras 448, 451; *Philip Morris v Uruguay* Award (n 77) para 426; *El Paso v Argentina* Award (n 136) para 372; *Parkerings v Lituania* [11 September 2007] Award, para 332 (hereafter '*Parkerings v Lituania* Award').
[139] *Micula v Romania* Award (n 51) para 669; *Novenergia v Spain* Award (n 126) para 650f; *Antaris v Czech Republic* Award (n 138) para 360(3); *Parkerings v Lituania*, Award (n 138) para 331.
[140] *Renergy v Spain*, Award (n 124) para 640; see also e.g. *Micula v Romania*, Award (n 51) para 529; *Antaris v Czech Republic* Award (n 138) para 360(7); *Stadtwerke München v Spain* [2 December 2019] Award [264] (hereafter '*Stadtwerke München v Spain*, Award'); see also *AES v Hungary*, Award (n 119) para 9.3.25; *Parkerings v Lituania*, Award (n 138) paras 332, 336; *Philip Morris v Uruguay*, Award (n 77) paras 423, 481.
[141] *Renergy v Spain* Award (n 124) para 641, quoting *Masdar v Spain*, Award (n 123) para 504.

law[142] on the matter, which it found not to differ in essential points.[143] Therefore, it considered that general legislation would not create 'Absolute Stability',[144] which would rather require a specific commitment that the legislation will not be changed in the future.[145]

However, the majority in *Renergy* agreed with the well-established case law of investment tribunals that general legislation could engender legitimate expectations of 'Relative Stability'.[146] This means that legislative changes are possible but may not exceed a wide margin of appreciation granted to host states for this purpose. The Tribunal lists a number of different terms used by various tribunals that characterize this standard. Tribunals have qualified such changes that exceed a wide margin of appreciation as: unreasonable, unjustified, unfair, inconsistent, disproportionate, contrary to public interest, fundamental and/or radical, subversive, total, unpredictable, or as suddenly and unexpectedly removing essential features of the previous regulatory framework.[147]

The *Renergy* Tribunal furthermore distilled a list of criteria from existing case law to decide whether changes in the legislation stayed within the acceptable margin of appreciation. They are:

(i) *Magnitude of the change*: The more fundamental the changes to the legislation are, ... the more likely such changes are to exceed the acceptable margin.
(ii) *Economic impact*: The more damaging the legislative changes are to the investor, the more likely they are to exceed the acceptable margin.
(iii) *Abruptness of the change*: The more time a host State gives to the investor to adjust to the new regulatory regime, ... , the more likely it is that Relative Stability is respected; contrariwise, if the regime change even features elements of retroactivity, or at least retrospectivity, this makes the legislative changes more likely to violate legitimate expectations.
(iv) *Change of external circumstances*: The more the legislative changes were triggered by a change of external circumstances, ... the more likely such legislative changes are to remain within the acceptable margin of change.

---

[142] See *Masdar v Spain*, Award (n 123) paras 490–95, 504–10; *RWE Innogy v Spain*, Award (n 127) para 453.
[143] *Renergy v Spain*, Award (n 124) para 640.
[144] ibid para 641.
[145] ibid paras 662, 673, 677–79; see also nn 723–724.
[146] *AES v Hungary*, Award (n 119) para 9.3.73; *Antaris v Czech Republic*, Award (n 138) para 360(7); outside the ECT also *El Paso v Argentina*, Award (n 136) para 402; *Philip Morris v Uruguay*, Award (n 77) para 433. For a different opinion, see the majority in *Stadtwerke München v Spain*, Award (n 140) paras 264, 268–308.
[147] *Renergy v Spain*, Award (n 124) para 642, footnotes omitted.

(v) *Public interests involved*: The more important the public interests involved are, which often coincides with a high level of regulation, the more a diligent investor could have expected change.
(vi) *Prior legislative practice*: The more the measures in dispute depart from the host State's previously established practice in respect of legislative changes, in particular in the same field, the less could a diligent investor have expected those measures and the more likely they are to violate Relative Stability.
(vii) *Stability assurances*: Even if a host State's assurances as to the stability of the regulatory framework do not qualify as specific commitments giving rise to a legitimate expectation of Absolute Stability, the degree to which such assurances were made is still relevant for the question of whether subsequent changes to the regulatory framework exceeded the acceptable margin.[148]

A legislative change, according to the *Renergy* Tribunal, will only violate the requirement of Relative Stability if it exceeds the margin of change that a diligent investor applying all the aforementioned criteria could have foreseen.[149]

Concerning the public interest involved and the obligation to balance them against the interest of the investor, the *Renergy* Tribunal stressed that this is one of the core responsibilities and prerogatives of a state. It would not second-guess the host state's assessment at the time it adopted the legislative changes. It therefore would defer to the state's assessment as long as it is not manifestly unreasonable.[150]

Concerning the balancing of the investor's interest of regulatory stability and the public interest in the regulatory changes, the Tribunal referred to the following statement of the *Antaris* Tribunal:

> The host State is not required to elevate the interests of the investor above all other considerations, and the application of the FET standard allows for a balancing or weighing exercise by the State and the determination of a breach of the FET standard must be made in the light of the high measure of deference which international law generally extends to the right of national authorities to regulate matters within their own borders.[151]

However, a state will narrow the acceptable margin of appreciation of legal changes if it made statements pointing to the need of regulatory stability, which reinforce the legitimate expectations of Relative Stability compared to a situation where it

---

[148] ibid para 681, footnotes omitted.
[149] ibid para 707.
[150] ibid para 901.
[151] ibid para 681(v), referring to *Antaris v Czech Republic*, Award (n 138) para 360(9) (footnote omitted).

only enacted certain incentives or support schemes, for example, renewable energy without giving any assurances of stability.

This 'FET-test', summarized and clarified by the *Renergy* Tribunal, allows for the necessary regulatory space for host states but at the same time secures the required legal stability vital to attract the private investment so much needed to manage the transit from fossil fuels to green energy. It uses a balancing system that corresponds to rule-of-law criteria applied by the European Court of Human Rights in situations of interference with human rights. It shows the necessary deference to the host state as best equipped to assess the priorities of a national legislator in the first place, but provides control against discrimination or abusive legislation. The most important lesson for host states is 'don't promise what you can't keep'. If states feel that they have to make promises to attract investments they should be aware that they will have to deliver.

In this way the *Renergy* Tribunal further contributed to a toolbox of criteria for the balancing between the interest of economic and social prosperity of a host state and the interests of foreign investors. Investors expect to be treated in accordance with the rule of law as manifested in investment law standards as a condition for their willingness to invest in green energy projects. The latter may in the long run also foster economic development and therefore serve this sustainable development goal.

5. Conclusion

The main message of this chapter, intended for sustainable development specialists, is that sustainable development considerations are increasingly present in foreign investment law. This is true for treaty texts as well as for investment disputes and case law dealing with them. Concerns related to sustainable development, like the protection of the environment, health and human rights, and the prevention of corruption, have increasingly permeated foreign investment disputes. Even absent specific references to sustainable development or particular components thereof in treaties, tribunals using the methods provided for in the VCLT have been able to interpret the treaty provisions in a manner that took into account sustainable development related concerns.

This will be especially relevant for 'climate friendly' investments in the renewable energy sector as can be seen from the number of cases that have emerged as a consequence of regulatory changes. As can be seen from the cases decided, these investments have high up-front investment costs and become profitable only after a considerable time. Therefore, they are vulnerable to regulatory changes especially in the subsidies schemes. At the same time, it must be possible for states to adapt their regulatory regimes in accordance with their needs and in accordance with their existing obligations under international law, including under human rights treaties or climate agreements. An effective remedy at the international plane that is capable of controlling whether these changes were not abusive is therefore of pivotal importance. The same is true for the fossil fuel phase-out that may well have impacts that reach the severity required for an expropriation. First cases have already been introduced.[152]

Recent investment awards offer elaborate criteria on how to deal with such regulatory measures, the FET standard and the question of expropriations. Regarding both standards, the existence of specific promises or assurances that can be found in a variety of sources make an important difference for the legitimacy of investors' expectations. The existence of such expectations is highly relevant in the assessment of the existence of an indirect expropriation as well as of a breach of the FET standard. The criteria applied by tribunals to distinguish measures triggering compensation or damages from measures that do not, largely correspond with rule of law criteria.[153]

If applied in a systematic manner, the application of such criteria will foster predictability. This will allow states to exercise their legitimate regulatory power and, at the same time, will provide the necessary regulatory stability to attract investment, which will ultimately be necessary to achieve sustainable development goals.

---

[152] *RWE v the Netherlands*, ICSID Case No ARB/21/4, see Lisa Bohmer, 'The Netherlands is Facing its First ICSID Arbitration, as German Energy Giant RWE Makes Good on Earlier Threats' (*IA Reporter*, 3 February 2021) <https://www-iareporter-com.uaccess.univie.ac.at/articles/the-netherlands-is-facing-its-first-icsid-arbitration-as-german-energy-giant-rwe-makes-good-on-earlier-threats/> accessed 23 August 2023 and International Energy Charter, <https://www.energychartertreaty.org/details/article/rwe-ag-and-rwe-eemshaven-holding-ii-bv-v-netherlands-icsid-case-no-arb214/> accessed 23 August 2023; *Uniper v the Netherlands* ICSID Case No ARB/21/22, see Lisa Bohmer, 'Uniper Lodges Treaty-Based Claim Against the Netherlands' (*IA Reporter*, 27 April 2021) <https://www-iareporter-com.uaccess.univie.ac.at/articles/uniper-lodges-treaty-based-claim-against-the-netherlands/> accessed 23 August 2023 and International Energy Charter, <https://www.energychartertreaty.org/details/article/uniper-se-uniper-benelux-holding-bv-and-uniper-benelux-nv-v-netherlands-icsid-case-no-arb21/> accessed 23 August 2023. For suggestions on how to deal with climate change related regulatory changes, see e.g. David Khachvani, 'Non-Compensable Regulation versus Regulatory Expropriation: Are Climate Change Regulations Compensable?' (2020) 35 ICSID Rev 154–73.

[153] On Rule of Law notions in various fields of international law, see the contributions of August Reinisch, 'The UN Concept of the Rule of Law'; Michael Hahn, 'Challenges for the Rule of Law in the WTO'; Ursula Kriebaum, 'Rule of Law Notions in Human Rights Law'; Marc Bungenberg and Angshuman Hazarika 'Rule of Law in the EU Legal Order'; and Marcin Menkes, 'ICMA, ISDA, Sovereign Debt Restructuring and the Rule of Law' in 3 ZEuS (2019) 337–428; particularly on substantive investment protection standards, see August Reinisch and Stephan W Schill (eds), *Investment Protection Standards and the Rule of Law* (OUP 2023).

14
International Trade and Foreign Investment

Chin Leng Lim

1. Introduction

In keeping with our aim of explaining how international law informs development, this chapter offers a short history and overview of various principles and doctrines which have emerged from trade and investment treaties as well as from soft law instruments. Many of these principles and doctrines are interpretative in nature, and require an understanding of the role of third-party dispute settlement.

Rather than to have been expressed clearly as an issue of colonial reparations we have seen a development agenda play out in the decades following World War II, in the trade and investment spheres, in the guise of principles of non-reciprocity, market access, special and differential treatment, and the incorporation of sustainable development principles into treaty drafting and adjudicative interpretation. Here is a story about preferential trade terms given without the expectation of reciprocity, preferential principles written into treaty and other formal instruments, and writing or reading—meaning drafting and interpreting—sustainable development principles into commercial and investment treaties. All this we call 'international law' and an understanding of its role in development is germane to developmental policy formulation.

Apart from writing new rules into bilateral investment treaties (BITs) and regional trade agreements (RTAs) which will integrate the principles that underpin sustainable development—as these have been derived from the United Nations Conference on Sustainable Development, Rio+20, and the Sustainable Development Goals (SDGs)—into international trade and investment law, so much has depended or relied upon the adjudicative function of tribunals. Specifically, on tribunals taking a more joined-up view of international law than the fragmented regimes of international economic law, and the fragmentary handling of international economic law principles and sustainable development principles, have until now allowed. However, there are broader notions of colonial reparation and decoloniality which are beginning to impinge, again, on what we mean by 'development' and they deserve at least some mention toward the end of this chapter.

Chin Leng Lim, *International Trade and Foreign Investment* In: *The Roles of International Law in Development.*
Edited by: Siobhán McInerney-Lankford and Robert McCorquodale, Oxford University Press. © Chin Leng Lim 2023.
DOI: 10.1093/oso/9780192872906.003.0014

2. Context

Beginning with the Stockholm Declaration of 1972 and Rio Declaration in 1992,[1] sustainability and development have become intertwined. This now is reflected in the way in which development has featured not only in trade but also in the investment sphere. Having said this, the manner in which developmental concerns have featured in trade and investment has traditionally been defined politically by reference to a divide between the Global North and the Global South. Whatever one thinks of that terminology, however limiting this North-South categorization may be, that still is how such concerns are often perceived.

Also coming out of the Rio Conference, in Chapter 2 of Agenda 21, a non-binding document, was recognition of a risk that trade and the promotion of development, as well as the prevention of environmental degradation, might work at cross-purposes. In 2000, the United Nations Millennium Declaration was signed and the Millennium Development Goals (MDGs) were proclaimed. By 2002, at the World Summit on Sustainable Development, participants there noted the need to support the World Trade Organisation's (WTO's) Doha Development Round (Doha Round) which had been launched the previous year.[2] Subsequently, Rio+20 in 2012 launched the process of developing the SDGs which were intended to build upon the MDGs.

However, the Doha Round, to put it delicately, had been moribund for years and this explains the relief with which the limited agreements coming out of the recent twelfth ministerial conference in 2022 were greeted. The last time that a successful major round of global talks was concluded was in 1994, almost three decades previously. In the meantime, trade liberalization had since the 2000s been carried out through a proliferation of RTAs in addition to a more long-standing and continued proliferation of BITs in the absence of a multilateral investment treaty system. The Seattle Ministerial Meeting in 1999 was marked too by anti-globalization protests. However, after '9/11' there was a renewed impetus to launch a fresh round of global trade talks, dubbed the 'Doha Development Round' which then had raised heightened expectations. In 2017, the eleventh WTO ministerial conference saw even an inability to produce a declaration at its conclusion. On the investment front, the Organization for Economic Cooperation and Development (OECD) launched negotiations for a multilateral agreement on investment (MAI) in 1995, but by April 1998, in the midst of the anti-globalization movement, negotiations were discontinued.

---

[1] The Stockholm Declaration was adopted at the 1972 United Nations Conference on the Human Environment, while the Rio Declaration on Environment and Development was adopted at the 1992 United Nations Conference on Environment and Development.

[2] 'A Brief History of Trade, Finance and Sustainable Development' (*IISD*) < https://enb.iisd.org/process/trade_invest-intro.htm> accessed 20 March 2022.

In short, during the 2000s, particularly trade and investment treaty negotiations were then spurred by a shift towards competitive liberalization instead as despondency with multilateral initiatives set in.[3] It was also the age of what international lawyers dubbed 'the death of treaties',[4] in reference to several failures in multilateral treaty negotiations. In this climate there were understandable concerns that developing nations would be unable to band together if they negotiated bilaterally rather than multilaterally, but there were as well other concerns, such as the erosion of developing country preferences and whether, as is discussed further below, RTAs can accommodate special and differential treatment.[5]

3. The Twentieth Century 'Post-War' International Economic Order

a. Different perspectives

One might begin with the design of the post-war international economic order. With the Bretton Woods Agreement, it was felt there was a need to kick-start international trade. And to do so by removing discrimination and replacing import quotas with bound tariffs through an international trade organization (ITO). The ITO was stillborn and its remnant was the 1947 General Agreement on Tariffs and Trade (GATT). Trade was also to be stimulated by facilitating foreign trade payments through current account liberalization, and by stabilizing exchange rates under the International Monetary Fund (IMF).[6] Thus economic liberalism became enshrined in the GATT, although John Ruggie had the insight to see that over a longer, hundred-year period of decline since the nineteenth century, economic liberalism had also become 're-embedded' in various national societies. The New Deal in the United States (the US) and the welfare state in United Kingdom (the UK) came to shape the GATT itself, in a way that made intervention more

---

[3] United States Senate Committee on Finance, 'Statement of Robert B Zoellick US Trade Representative before the Committee on Finance of the United States Senate' (9 March 2004) <https://www.finance.senate.gov/imo/media/doc/030904rztest.pdf> accessed 22 June 2023.

[4] Jeffrey S Lantis, *The Life and Death of International Treaties: Double-Edged Diplomacy and the Politics of Ratification in Comparative Perspective* (OUP 2009); Joel Trachtman, 'Reports of the Death of Treaty Are Premature, but Customary International Law May Have Outlived Its Usefulness' (2014) 108 AJIL Unbound 36.

[5] See e.g. C L Lim, 'Regional Trade Agreements and the Poverty Agenda' in John Linarelli (ed), *Research Handbook on Global Justice and International Economic Law* (Edward Elgar 2013) 101–05 (hereafter 'Regional Trade Agreements').

[6] C L Lim and Bryan Mercurio, 'The Fragmented Disciplines of International Economic Law after the Global Financial and Economic Crisis: An Introduction' in C L Lim and Bryan Mercurio (eds), *International Economic Law after the Global Crisis* (CUP 2015) (hereafter 'Fragmented Disciplines')

favourable in post-war international arrangements than had been the case during the nineteenth century.[7]

Alternatively, one could begin with the views of the new states which had emerged during the United Nations decolonization era from the 1950s to the 1970s, and whose efforts institutions such as the World Bank (the Bank) managed to insulate themselves from.[8] This was even prior to allegations of 'mission creep' taking hold in Washington's international financial institutions (IFIs). With the emergence of the Washington Consensus, we saw conditionality and structural adjustment programmes drawing controversy. The Bank is the foremost development institution internationally in terms of prestige, sway, and resources, and has a central role in co-ordinating activities with other international organizations, aid agencies, and export credit institutions.

The IMF, for its part, plays a similar role in times of sovereign crises. Be that as it may, there has been well-known criticism of the IMF for policy proliferation, opaqueness, and lack of accountability, and being accused of 'killing the patient with its bad medicine'.[9] I have written briefly, elsewhere, about these criticisms and of a 'turn' to the WTO in the 2000s as a developmental organization, as a new platform, akin to forum shopping, but in this case, institutional shopping on the part of developing states; because developing countries have a direct hand in creating market opportunities through negotiating market access and also a hand in shaping trade rules there.[10]

All of this is only a snapshot. The story of building development principles into trade rules, at least from the GATT perspective, began earlier.

b. Non-reciprocity, preferential access, and 'special and differential' treatment

Accommodating developmental differences at the GATT had been defined in terms of (i) not requiring reciprocity for trade concessions granted to developing nations ('non-reciprocity'), (ii) 'preferential market access', and (iii) 'special and differential treatment'.[11] The most visible manifestations of these demands were

---

[7] Andrew T F Lang, 'Reconstructing Embedded Liberalism: John Gerard Ruggie and Constructive Approaches to the Study of the International Trade Regime' in John Gerard Ruggie (ed), *Embedding Global Markets: An Enduring Challenge* (Routledge 2008) 19; John Gerard Ruggie, 'International Regimes, Transactions, and Change: Embedded Liberalism in the Postwar Economic Order' (1982) 36 Intl Orgs 379.

[8] Dimitri Van Den Meerssche, 'International Law as Insulation—The Case of the World Bank in the Decolonization Era' (2019) 21 J Hist Int'l L 459.

[9] Jessica Einhorn, 'The World Bank's Mission Creep' (2001) 80 Foreign Aff 22.

[10] Chin Leng Lim, 'Do International Financial Institutions Repress Development', in Chin Leng Lim, *The Turn to Trade*: Proceedings of the 116th ASIL Annual Meeting (CUP 2008) 231–37.

[11] See Robert E Hudec, *Developing Countries in the GATT Legal System* (reprint edn, CUP 2010) (hereafter 'Developing Countries')

the generalized system of preferences (GSP) and something 'Gattologists' called the 'Enabling Clause'. The Enabling Clause was a relaxation of the GATT's usual conditions for departing from the most-favoured-nation (MFN) rule in article I of the GATT, a rule which requires any more favourable tariff concession made to any GATT-WTO or non-GATT-WTO member state or member to be granted immediately and unconditionally to all member states. The GSP is about preferences granted to developing countries without any accompanying demand for a reciprocal concession and which, at the same time, are not granted to all other contracting states or members. Usually, article XXIV of the GATT will only permit customs unions and RTAs to be formed on condition that barriers toward trade with third countries were not raised, and importantly, that they involve the mutual elimination of duties substantially on all the trade between the members of the customs union or between the RTA parties.[12]

What developing countries wanted—and obtained with the Enabling Clause which essentially was a document waiving contradictory legal entitlements—was non-reciprocal but preferential treatment, i.e. unilateral concessions which the GATT, notwithstanding article XXIV's conditions for departure from article I's MFN rule and notwithstanding article I itself, should permit. Initially, the US refused the Latin American states' request for a GSP, but relented subsequently. Others, most notably the European Union (EU) and Japan, followed with their own generalized systems.

Turning from non-reciprocity and preferential access, other rules which granted special and differential treatment tend to be couched in preambular, uncertain, and insubstantive language in the GATT. At times they create the impression of consisting merely of homilies although, as we shall see, they are not always without substantive treaty effect, commonly granting various flexibilities to developing countries and especially to the least developed countries (LDCs).[13] The following is a quick overview of such language and provisions in the GATT, and also the Marrakesh Agreement.

The first preamble in the 1994 Marrakesh Agreement, which established the WTO, speaks of the members:

[A]llowing for the optimal use of the world's resources in accordance with the objective of sustainable development, seeking both to protect and preserve the

---

[12] For the GATT, see GATT art XXIV:5(b) (the 'shall not be higher or more restrictive' standard or 'external' requirement) and GATT art XXIV:8(b) (the 'substantially all trade' or 'internal' requirement). For the 'parenthetical list problem', concerning a possible prohibition of trade remedy action between RTA members, see also GATT art XXIV:8. See further, for example, C L Lim, 'Free Trade Agreements in Asia and Some Common Legal Problems' in Yasuhei Taniguchi and others (eds), *The WTO in the Twenty-first Century* (CUP 2006). See further Lorand Bartels and Frederico Ortino, *Regional Trade Agreements and the WTO Legal System* (OUP 2006).
[13] See 'Special and Differential Treatment Provisions' (*World Trade Organization*) <https://www.wto.org/english/tratop_e/devel_e/dev_special_differential_provisions_e.htm> accessed 22 June 2023.

environment and to enhance the means for doing so in a manner consistent with their respective needs and concerns at different levels of economic development …

Whereas the second preambular paragraph speaks of their recognition: '[F]urther that there is need for positive efforts designed to ensure that developing countries, and especially the least developed among them, secure a share in the growth in international trade commensurate with the needs of their economic development …'.

As for the substantive provisions, article XVIII of the GATT, which had been written with the developing countries in mind, permits them to have a wider use of protectionist measures,[14] concerning the setting-up and maintenance of new industries and addressing balance-of-payment problems.[15]

Subsequently, part IV comprises articles XXXVI to XXXVIII and is entitled 'Trade and Development'. The late Robert Hudec once called the provisions in part IV 'form without substance'; in other words, that the developing countries received nothing real.[16] He had used as an illustration article XXXVII.1 of the GATT:[17] 'The developed contracting parties shall to the fullest extent possible - that is, except when compelling reasons, which may include legal reasons, make it impossible - give effect to the following provisions …'.

Hudec's view is too sceptical. Article XXXVI states, for example, the GATT contracting states' agreement that '[t]here is need for a rapid and sustained expansion of the export earnings of the less-developed contracting parties' (paragraph 2), and also that '[t]here is need for positive efforts designed to ensure that less-developed contracting parties secure a share in the growth in international trade commensurate with the needs of their economic development' (paragraph 3). That article also recognizes that '[g]iven the continued dependence of many less-developed contracting parties on the exportation of a limited range of primary products, there is need to provide in the largest possible measure more favourable and acceptable conditions of access to world markets …' (paragraph 4). Notably, the Enabling Clause, which allows preferential market access to be given to developing countries notwithstanding GATT's article I's MFN rule, refers explicitly to the aims stated in article XXXVI,[18] or what Bhala calls article XXXVI's identification of

---

[14] See e.g. John H Jackson, *World Trade and the Law of GATT* (Michie 1969) ch 25.
[15] See also 'Decision on Safeguard Action for Development Purposes' (28 November 1979) GATT Decision L/4897; 'Declaration on Trade Measures Taken for Balance-of-payment Purposes' (28 November 1979) GATT Decision L/4904; 'Understanding on the Balance-of-payment Provisions of the General Agreement on Tariffs and Trade 1994 in Annex 1A of the Marrakesh Agreement Establishing the World Trade Organization.'
[16] Developing Countries (n 11) 1, 99.
[17] ibid (Introduction by J. Michael Finger to the New Edition) 1.
[18] GATT art XXIV:7.

'objectives concerning the link between trade and development'.[19] Notice too article XXXVI.8, which states, importantly, that 'The developed contracting parties do not expect reciprocity for commitments made by them in trade negotiations to reduce or remove tariffs and other barriers to the trade of less-developed contracting parties.'

In short, preferential market access and non-reciprocity for the developing countries, although having their political origins in the 1949 Prebisch Report and 1958 Haberler Report,[20] have a firm legal foundation in part IV, specifically, in article XXXVI of the GATT.

Article XXXVII then states the corresponding obligations of the developed GATT contracting states/WTO members, whereas article XXXVIII, which Hudec had highlighted, states in its first paragraph that '[t]he contracting parties shall collaborate jointly, within the framework of this Agreement and elsewhere, as appropriate, to further the objectives set forth in Article XXXVI.' It is not without substance. A GATT-era panel had found the European communities to have acted inconsistently with that provision.[21]

Lest it should be forgotten, article XVIII of the GATT, which concerns 'Governmental Assistance to Economic Development' in its section B (article XVIII: B), allows tariffs, quotas, and other trade restrictions where a GATT contracting state or party 'in rapid process of development'—i.e. a developing country contracting state—experiences 'balance of payments difficulties arising mainly from efforts to expand their internal markets as well as from the instability in their terms of trade'. That provision became the subject of a well-known dispute in the complaint brought by the US against India in the *India—Balance of Payments Measures* case.[22] India lost that case due to the absence of a causal link being demonstrated between the removal of the trade restrictive measures and a recurrence of balance of payments difficulties; and because it failed to persuade the WTO Appellate Body that the panel, by requiring India to use macroeconomic and alternative development policy instruments, would have required India to have altered its own developmental policy.

c. The Doha Development Agenda

In 2001, with the launch of the Doha Development Round, there was a renewed effort to address the concerns of the developing country members of the WTO.

---

[19] Raj Bhala, *International Trade Law: Interdisciplinary Theory and Practice* (Matthew Bender/LexisNexis 2008) 1280.
[20] The latter led to the 1963 Programme of Action.
[21] EC—Refunds on Exports of Sugar (1981) GATT BISD 27S, 69–98.
[22] India-Quantitative Restrictions on Imports of Agricultural, Textile and Industrial Products (22 September 1999) WT/DS90/AB/R.

Apart from the tariff negotiations themselves, on agricultural market access as well as in non-agricultural market access (NAMA), and so on, there was to be renewed rule-making, or at least rule-refinement, not least concerning the rules on special and differential treatment (SDT) which, according to the Doha Ministerial Declaration, should be strengthened and made more effective and operational. The WTO's Committee on Trade and Development (CTD) became entrusted with the task in particular of considering which SDT provisions are, and which ought to become, mandatory. Paragraph 44 of the Ministerial Declaration reads:[23]

> We reaffirm that provisions for special and differential treatment are an integral part of the WTO Agreements. We note the concerns expressed regarding their operation in addressing specific constraints faced by developing countries, particularly least-developed countries. In that connection, we also note that some members have proposed a Framework Agreement on Special and Differential Treatment (WT/GC/W/442). We therefore agree that all special and differential treatment provisions shall be reviewed with a view to strengthening them and making them more precise, effective and operational. In this connection, we endorse the work programme on special and differential treatment set out in the Decision on Implementation-Related Issues and Concerns.

More specific issues in the context of the Doha Round negotiations have also gained prominence. Mention should be made of agricultural subsidies. For developing countries, article 6.2 of the WTO Agriculture Agreement allows them important flexibilities in what is termed the 'development box'.[24] Generally available agricultural subsidies, such as input subsidies to low-income or resource-poor producers, are thus exempt from members' domestic support commitments. Likewise, in the agricultural subsidies debate, the 'Peace Clause' under article 13 of the Agriculture Agreement, has meant immunity for Agriculture Agreement-compliant domestic support schemes and export subsidies from being challenged under the WTO Agreement on Subsidies and Countervailing Measures (the SCM Agreement). India has proposed its retention in the context of the Doha Round but only for the developing countries.[25]

As has been mentioned, with the proliferation of RTAs against the backdrop of a moribund Doha Round, new questions arise now about building in developmental concerns at the level of bilateral and regional treaties,[26] as well as new

---

[23] Ministerial Declaration (20 November 2001) WT/MIN(01)/DEC/1.
[24] In the general parlance of the WTO subsidies regulation regime, only a 'traffic light' terminology of 'green light', 'amber light', and 'red light' subsidies—is used. But a more expansive terminology is to be found in the Agriculture Agreement.
[25] Negotiations on WTO Agreement on Agriculture (15 January 2001) G/AG/NG/W/102.
[26] For example, article 1.3 of the Framework Agreement on Comprehensive Economic Cooperation among the Government of the Republic of Korea and the Member Countries of the Association of Southeast Asian Nations (ASEAN). In other ASEAN free trade agreements, the tendency is towards

concerns about the bargaining position of the smaller developing countries which had benefited from the operation of the GATT's MFN rule. There also are fears about trade diversion caused by RTAs. Imagine two developed economies entering into an RTA which diverts trade previously with a developing country or with developing countries. The proliferation of divergent and complex rules—including but not limited to rules of origin—would also tend to increase the administrative cost for developing country exporters.[27] There also is fear of being left out of RTA formations, be they between developed countries only, between developed and developing countries, or purely between other developing countries. Particularly as such formations grow larger in size, but only encompass particular regions, such as Pacific Rim nations.

d. The 'international standard' of compensation for expropriation and the uncertain outcome of the NIEO

During roughly the same period, in the investment rather than the trade sphere, there was a parallel but distinct attempt at the UN to rewrite the rules of the international economic order. That aspect consisted of the efforts by developing country nations to address the international standard of compensation for expropriation which the industrialized nations upheld in the form of the Hull Doctrine, as well as to resist the growing resort to international arbitration. In effect, the developing countries asserted a doctrine of permanent sovereignty over their natural resources, and declared a 'New International Economic Order' (NIEO) in seeking—amongst other things—to uphold the doctrine that foreign investment disputes should be resolved under their laws and in their domestic courts.[28]

Developing countries generally sought to have their position accepted as a universal rule, indeed to remake the international economic order, through a new majoritarian theory of the formation of customary international law as evidenced in General Assembly resolution-making.[29] Some of the key

---

flexibilities for Cambodia, Myanmar, Lao People's Democratic Republic, and Vietnam (the CMLV countries). See further, e.g., Regional Trade Agreements (n 5) 96.

[27] Jagdish Bhagwati, 'US Trade Policy: The Infatuation with Free Trade Areas' in Jagdish Bhagwati and Anne O Krueger (eds), *The Dangerous Drift to Preferential Trade Agreements* (The AEI Press 1995). See also Jagdish Bhagwati, *Termites in the Trading System. How Preferential Agreements Undermine Free Trade* (OUP 2008).

[28] In other words, for the 'Calvo doctrine', see Carlos Calvo, *Derecho Internacional Teórico y Práctico de Europa y América* (D'Amyot 1868). But the NIEO was not limited to that, and extended broadly to include other issues which were of special economic interest to the developing countries. One of which was the question of succession to state debts.

[29] See further, e.g., C L Lim, 'Neither Sheep nor Peacocks: T O Elias and Post-colonial International Law' (2008) 21 Leiden J I L 295.

resolutions are well-known—the Declaration on 'Permanent Sovereignty over Natural Resources',[30] the 'Declaration on the Establishment of a New International Economic Order',[31] and not least the 'Charter of Economic Rights and Duties of States' of 12 December 1974, adopted by 118 votes to six, with ten abstentions and with a separate vote for its controversial paragraph 2(2)(c).[32]

Their outcome has been uncertain legally. Today the global debate has shifted, however, from uncertain customary international law or contentious claims about custom to treaty laws. In the investment rules sphere that debate now concerns the terms of the latest bilateral investment treaties. Amongst the issues are those of treaty design particularly at the level of the formulation of standards of protection. It involves fear on the part of capitals, including but no longer limited to developing nation capitals, of their shrinking policy space in the face of an expansion of investor and investment protection.

Thus seen, different forums are involved when we compare trade and investment, as have different legal methods, kinds of instrument, and issues been involved. In this regard, the question of the emergence of developmental norms has been defined partly by the fragmented nature of international economic laws which in turn constitute the international economic 'order'.

Another, again different, perspective is to view the role of international law in development, affecting the trade and investment spheres, from the viewpoint of the emergence of a third-generation human right to development.[33] We will have to come back to this view as it also involves asking how trade and investment treaties should be construed, a subject discussed further below. Much could depend upon whether such a right is, or is likely to be construed and framed as a human right in third-party trade and investment dispute settlement. So far, the indication is that WTO panels and the Appellate Body have not shown a tendency to integrate the 'right to development' in that manner, and investment arbitration tribunals too take a cautious albeit informed approach to a systemic, or joined-up, and in any case more rigorous view of international law.

---

[30] *Permanent Sovereignty over Natural Resources* (17 December 1973) UN Doc A/RES/3171 (XXVIII), adopted by a vote of 108 to one, with sixteen abstentions.

[31] *Declaration on the Establishment of a New International Economic Order* (1 May 1974) UNGA Res 3201 (S-VI), adopted without a vote.

[32] *Consideration of the Economic and Social Situation in the Sudano-Sahelian Regional Stricken by Drought and Measures to be Taken for the Benefit of that Region* (4 December 1974) UN Doc A/RES/3281 (XXIX), 104 votes to sixteen, with six abstentions.

[33] See Declaration on Development (4 December 1986) UNGA Res 41/128; Mohammad Ghaebi Reza, 'Realization of the Right to Development: Prospects for Drafting a Convention on the Right to Development' (2015) 14 J Hum Rights 548; Nico Schrijver, 'A New Convention on the Human Right to Development: Putting the Cart Before the Horse?' (2020) 38 NQHR 84 (hereafter 'A New Convention'). For the larger conceptual issue of third-generation people's rights, see Roland Rich, 'The Right to Development: A Right of Peoples?' in James Crawford (ed), *The Rights of Peoples* (OUP 1988).

4. Trade and Development Issues and the GATT/WTO Jurisprudence

Some of the most prominent issues shaping the debate on international trade law and development,[34] and on international investment law and development, have not been located in the design of substantive rules. They are instead closely linked to the adjudicative and interpretative practices and approaches of panels and the WTO Appellate Body as well as of investment treaty tribunals,[35] and these resist easy categorization.

a. Cases involving issues of particular interest to developing country members

First, there were cases in which a developmental dimension had been prominent, meaning that they involved issues which were of particular interest to developing countries. However, the legal issue was not some dispute over a WTO developmental rule. Such was the case with Brazil's claim against the US in respect of cotton subsidies. To this category of cases, brought by developing countries in order to defend their interests, which may have had implications for 'development principles' only as they saw it, we might add *US—Wool Shirts and Blouses* concerning India's complaint under articles 2, 6, and 8 of the Agreement on Textiles and Clothing, and similarly *US—ROOs for Textiles and Apparels*.[36] The latest palm oil disputes brought against the EU's Renewable Energy Directive also have a developmental feel and bring out the tension between 'sustainable development' and 'development'.[37] Similar cases involving China, such as the *Raw Materials* and *Rare Earths* cases,[38] or *US—AD & CVD*,[39] are in a special sub-category due to that country's unusual WTO-plus regime wherein what essentially is a developing country took on more burdensome obligations to gain entry into the WTO.

---

[34] See further, Yong-shik Lee and others (eds), *Law and Development Perspective on International Trade Law* (CUP 2012).

[35] For a different characterization of trade and development disputes, see Tomer Broude, 'Development Disputes in International Trade' in Lee and others (eds), *Law and Development Perspective on International Trade Law* (CUP 2011) 41.

[36] *United States—Measures Affecting Imports of Woven Wool Shirts and Blouses from India* (23 May 1997) WT/DS33/AB/R; *United States—Rules of Origin for Textiles and Apparel Products* (21 July 2003) WT/DS243/R.

[37] See Andrew D Mitchell and Dean Merriman, 'Indonesia's WTO Challenge to the European Union's Renewable Energy Directive: Palm Oil and Indirect Land-use Change' (2020) 12 Trade L & Dev 548.

[38] *China—Measures Related to the Exportation of Various Raw Materials* (22 February 2012) WT/DS394/AB/R; *China—Measures Related to the Exportation of Rare Earths, Tungsten and Molybdenum* (29 August 2014) WT/DS431/AB/R.

[39] *US—Antidumping and Countervailing Duties (China)* (11 March 2011) WT/DS379/AB/R.

b. Cases involving a development principle or goal

Secondly, there have been cases in which a developmental principle or goal became directly involved, such as that involving Brazil's ban on the importation of used and retreaded tyres. In that case, recycling was argued to be detrimental to public health protection under the GATT. Brazil which sought to prevent the importation of retreaded tyres argued that the differential capacity of developing countries to mitigate adverse public health effects ought to be taken into account.[40] Article XX of the GATT states, specifically in paragraph (b), that:

> Subject to the requirement that such measures are not applied in a manner which would constitute a means of arbitrary or unjustifiable discrimination between countries where the same conditions prevail, or a disguised restriction on international trade, nothing in this Agreement shall be construed to prevent the adoption or enforcement by any contracting party of measures: …
> (b) necessary to protect human, animal or plant life or health …

In *Brazil—Retreaded Tyres*, Brazil argued that its ban on retreaded tyres was justified under that provision. In such cases, the WTO Appellate Body's approach, under a 'two-tier' test, is to begin with whether the measure is 'necessary' for the purposes of paragraph (b). If that is answered in the affirmative, one then turns to the *chapeau* to ask whether, notwithstanding that, the measure constitutes a 'means of arbitrary or unjustifiable discrimination between countries where the same conditions prevail, or a disguised restriction on international trade'. Failure in the second part will also render the measure in violation of the GATT.

The developmental issue arose in the following way. As to whether the Brazilian measures were necessary both the Appellate Body and the WTO panel considered whether these measures meant that there will be fewer waste tyres and would thus be a 'material contribution' toward achieving the objective of human health and the environmental protection. The issue was that retreaded tyres are non-biodegradable and stored in landfills where in the tropics they would become breeding grounds for the *Aedes aegypti* mosquito which transmits dengue fever, a common tropical disease.[41] In deciding upon the 'material contribution' point, consideration needed to be given too to possibly less trade restrictive trade measures than the Brazilian import ban on retreaded tyres. The EU's suggestions of alternative measures was however rejected. *Brazil—Retreaded Tyres* was a

---

[40] *Brazil—Measures Affecting Imports of Retreaded Tyres* (17 December 2002) WT/DS332/AB/R (hereafter '*Brazil—Retreaded Tyres,* AB Report').

[41] See further, Marie Wilke, 'Litigating Environmental Protection and Public Health at the WTO: The Brazil—Retreaded Tyres Case' (ICTSD Information Note No 1, September 2010) <https://www.files.ethz.ch/isn/139109/case_brief_brazil_tyres_v51.pdf> accessed 22 June 2023 (hereafter 'Litigating Environmental Protection')

well-known 'environmental' dispute but it has an important development aspect, notwithstanding the fact that the Brazilian measures were ultimately found to be discriminatory.

It was in its consideration of alternative measures that the Appellate Body had also considered that, in applying that requirement, regard should be given to an 'undue burden' upon Brazil. The test of undue burden in turn was to be defined by the prohibitive costs and substantial technical difficulties which the imposing country would face and also the degree of that country's development.[42]

There were other, incidental aspects which raised controversy, not least the point that Brazil's exemption of Southern Common Market (MERCOSUR; Spanish abbreviation) countries under that RTA would not have mattered in the view of the distinguished WTO panel (comprising Mitsuo Matsushita of Japan as Chair, Don McRae of Canada, and Chang-fa Lo of Chinese Taipei) where its trade effects were minimal.[43] The Appellate Body disagreed with the panel, requiring the exemption to fall within the objective of the measure if it is not to be discriminatory.[44]

c. Conservation cases involving sustainable development principles

Finally, there is a broader class of 'conservation' cases, to which *Brazil—Retreaded Tyres* also belongs, and which concern the principle of sustainable development in the preamble to the Marrakesh Agreement, such as the *Shrimp-Turtle* case.[45] That was a landmark decision preceding *Brazil—Retreaded Tyres* which had established the 'two-tier' test. The most significant aspect of the Appellate Body's approach in *Shrimp-Turtle* lay in the prominence it gave to a new method of reading the GATT's provisions in light of the Marrakesh Agreement's preambular reference to 'sustainable development'.

Article XX(g) of the GATT states—rather than, as paragraph (b) does—that nothing in the GATT shall be construed to prevent measures necessary to protect human, animal, or plant life or health—that nothing in the GATT shall similarly prevent the adoption or enforcement of measures '(g) relating to the conservation of exhaustible natural resources if such measures are made effective in conjunction with restrictions on domestic production or consumption . . .'.

The argument raised was that measures relating to the conservation of the sea turtle do not fall within article XX(g) of the GATT. This was since that provision's reference to 'exhaustible natural resources' does not include living things, rather

---

[42] *Brazil—Retreaded Tyres*, AB Report (n 40) 156; Litigating Environmental Protection (n 41) 6.
[43] *Brazil—Measures Affecting Imports of Retreaded Tyres* (17 December 2002) WT/DS332/R [7.288].
[44] *Brazil—Retreaded Tyres*, AB Report (n 40) 233.
[45] WTO, *United States—Import Prohibition of Certain Shrimp and Shrimp Products* (6 November 1998) WT/DS58/AB/R.

than, say, petroleum resources. However, the Appellate Body pointed instead to the Marrakesh Agreement's reference to sustainable development as something which any interpretation of article XX(g) would need to account for. The Appellate Body did not define sustainable development as such. The WTO covered agreements do not do so, but the *Shrimp-Turtle* Appellate Body report is consistent, at any rate, with the definition in the Brundtland Report of 1987, a document which was roughly contemporaneous with the negotiation of the Marrakesh Agreement, and which defines sustainable development in the following manner:[46] 'Humanity has the ability to make development sustainable to ensure that it meets the needs of the present without compromising the ability of future generations to meet their own needs.'

It is perhaps fair to say that, to this extent, the WTO jurisprudence has incorporated the Bruntland Commission's views. If that is correct, then the WTO may be said to uphold the Brundtland Report's view that sustainability and development are inseparable, notwithstanding terms like the 'Doha Development Round' as a reflection of a concept of development that revolves around the demands of the developing countries.[47]

5. Investment Treaties and Investor-State Arbitration

Unlike in the international trade sphere, in the case of investment there is a sense of both developing country and also developed country failures where the issues have revolved around, first, the perceived collapse of the developing countries' effort in the 1970s to construct an NIEO as mentioned earlier. Secondly, there were failures both by developed countries to negotiate and conclude a multilateral agreement on investment (MAI) as well as by developing countries to regulate the conduct of multinational corporations (MNCs) at the global level. However thirdly, there now are on-going efforts to 'rebalance' the content of investment treaties as well as to reform investor-state arbitration/investor-state dispute settlement (ISDS) procedures.

Some of the key UN General Assembly resolutions by which the developing countries asserted permanent sovereignty and the right to development (rather than sustainable development) have already been mentioned. Suffice to say that this did not involve the wealth and natural resource transfer imagined. The arbitrator in the well-known *Texaco* arbitration considered that it was one thing to have permanent sovereignty, but another to argue, as Libya did, on the basis of

---

[46] Gro Harlem Brundtland, *Report of the World Commission on Environment and Development: Our Common Future* (20 March 1987) UN Doc A/42/427 [27].

[47] For the difficulties which lawyers sometimes face with the concept of sustainable development as a legal, rather than a political, concept, see e.g. P Ørebech and others, *The Role of Customary Law in Sustainable Development* (CUP 2005).

UN General Assembly resolution 3171, that in the case of an expropriation the matter of compensation should be determined by the host state under its laws, or that the nineteenth century Calvo doctrine developed to contain armed reprisals against the Latin American nations now represents customary international law.[48] It illustrates the distinction between rights of property or dominium in respect of land, on the one hand, and having sovereignty, jurisdiction, or imperium on the other. There was also a decolonization dimension. By the middle to later part of the twentieth century, the new developing countries in Asia and Africa admittedly were now sovereign and independent, but the oil wells, gold and copper mines, and plantations belonged nonetheless to their rightful owners and any injury to their rights would incur international responsibility in the view of the Western industrialized nations. Moreover, the resolutions just mentioned were considered by the arbitrator to have been no more than *de lege ferenda*.

By then, as the arbitrator in *Texaco* was also to point out, BITs had emerged, beginning with the Abs/Shawcross Draft Convention and the Germany-Pakistan BIT of 1959. Unlike the GATT, absence of a multilateral investment regime meant that investment protection coming out of the ill-fated Third World attempt to establish the NIEO shifted first from protection under customary international law to contractual protection, contracts were seen to have become 'internationalized' (i.e. to be governed by international law as the proper law), and then, secondly, to bilateral treaty protection.[49]

At the multilateral level in 1992 the World Bank Development Committee adopted its Guideline on Foreign Investment. At the OECD, in 1994, the developed countries pushed initially for the negotiation of a MAI but in part due to disagreements between the developed nations themselves, as well as the anti-globalization protests of the 1990s and ostensibly the consequent pressure they exerted on Western governments, that effort was abandoned. Traditionally, developing countries have been resistant to the idea of a multilateral investment treaty and, as had been mentioned, they have been more concerned about the regulation rather than the protection of foreign investment as well as the regulation of MNCs. But developed countries resisted and by 1992 the developing countries had given up on regulating the conduct of MNCs through a multilateral instrument. The most well-known of these proposals was for a Code of Conduct on Transnational Corporations under the auspices of the relatively short-lived United Nations Commission on Transnational Corporations.

By the late 1990s the developing countries, finding themselves competing for capital, had largely abandoned their efforts. What was perceived by Third World

---

[48] *Texaco Overseas Petroleum Co/California Asiatic Oil Co v Government of Libya* (Award on the Merits) (1977) 17 ILM 1, [85] (hereafter '*Texaco*').
[49] See C L Lim, Jean Ho, and Martins Paparinskis, *International Investment Law and Arbitration* (2nd edn, CUP 2021), 10-26 (hereafter 'International Investment Law').

countries as an attempt to shift the idea of a multilateral investment agreement subsequently into the Doha Round Negotiations,[50] in other words into the trade sphere, as a part of the four 'Singapore Issues' (transparency in government procurement, trade facilitation, trade and investment, and trade and competition) was resisted at the Ministerial Conference in Cancún in 2003 by Brazil, India, and China. These nations soon were to emerge as a part of the 'BRICS'[51] diplomatic grouping or association of emerging economies.[52] Tension has long existed between having greater investment protection as well as investment market access on the one hand, and having greater host state control of investment and transfers of technology on the other. That was how the development issue was framed, even if some might object to this use of a North-South framework of analysis.

Thereafter, how principles of sustainable development were addressed in the international law of foreign investment was to shift again. By the 2010s there was revolt, not just in the streets wherein the issue might have been framed in environmental terms or in terms of human rights, but also in the capitals of both developed and developing countries. What had emerged was an official backlash cutting across the traditional North-South divide against both the terms of the thousands of BITs and the device of investor-state arbitration which these treaties typically would provide for.[53] Some Latin American capitals such as Bolivia, Ecuador, and Venezuela denounced the ICSID Convention in 2007, 2010, and 2012, respectively. There also were terminations of India's and Indonesia's BITs, or at least older treaties, while they prepared new model BITs. In India's case its new model BIT of 2015 removed coverage of taxation measures from challenge under investor treaty arbitration, amidst other changes.[54] Thus both on the 'procedural side' (removing recourse to ICSID arbitration) as well as in terms of the 'rebalancing' of substantive treaty protection, various capitals had become part of a broader backlash against investment treaties and investment arbitration.[55] This as has been said is not limited to the adverse reaction in some of the BRICS, including in India and South Africa, or in developing countries alone. Across the Atlantic, in the EU-Canada Comprehensive Economic and Trade Agreement (CETA) between the EU and Canada and in the Transatlantic Trade and Investment Partnership (TTIP)

---

[50] For the account just given, see Muthucumaraswamy Sornarajah, *The International Law on Foreign Investment* (5th edn, CUP 2021) 291–304.
[51] Brazil, Russia, India, China, and South Africa.
[52] Founded in 2006 at the margins of the UN General Assembly's General Debate.
[53] See International Investment Law (n 49) 575 *et seq*. See further Michael Waibel and others (eds), *The Backlash against Investment Arbitration* (Kluwer 2010); Muthucumaraswamy Sornarajah, *Resistance and Change in the International Law on Foreign Investment* (CUP 2015). Sornarajah had served as a member of Ecuador's Presidential Commission on Foreign Investment.
[54] See further Aniruddha Rajput, 'India and Investment Protection' in C L Lim (ed), *Alternative Visions of the International Law on Foreign Investment: Essays in Honour of Muthucumaraswam Sornarajah* (CUP 2016).
[55] ibid.

negotiations between the US and the EU, and also across the Pacific in the Trans-Pacific Partnership (TPP) and later Comprehensive and Progresive Agreement for Trans-Pacific Partnership (CPTPP), 'megaregional' RTAs containing investment chapters were also being 'rebalanced'.

The issues in the case of CETA, TTIP, and the TPP/CPTPP have been substantive, such as the need to take a host state's public welfare measures or regulatory space into account in say discrimination claims, or in claims of unfair and inequitable treatment.[56] Part of the perceived problem was that there is often no equivalent provision to article XX of the GATT's 'General Exceptions' clauses in BITs. Thus tribunals may ignore the environmental protection, conservation, or public health aims of host states. Substantive rebalancing seeks to address this absence of 'general exceptions' clauses in BITs, and thus may also reflect traditional developmental concerns, although such concerns now are shared by developed countries too that have felt the brunt of investment arbitration claims.

There have also been procedural reforms. These involve suggestions of using summary awards and/or adverse cost awards in order to deter frivolous claims in light of the threat posed by overwhelming numbers of claims brought against poor developing countries.[57]

At the multilateral level, the EU's proposal to replace investment arbitration altogether with a two-tier multilateral investment court (MIC) or at least to have the appellate tier accept full-blown appeals against the awards of arbitral tribunals is currently being discussed and debated in UN Commission on International Trade Law's (UNCITRAL's) Working Group III.[58] While it has been the EU which has pushed for a MIC, and therefore the issue is not one that should be seen as one which developing countries are pushing for, there nonetheless is an overlap with developing country critiques of investment arbitration. As we have seen, developing country concerns have their origin in suspicion of arbitration as a device weighted in favour of the oil companies in the Arab oil arbitrations of the 1950s, 1960s, and 1970s.[59]

---

[56] See, for the TPP/CPTPP, C L Lim, 'Finding a Workable Balance Between Investor Protection and the Public Interest' in Benedict Kingsbury and others (eds), *Megaregulation Contested* (OUP 2019) (hereafter 'Finding a Workable Balance').

[57] ibid.

[58] See e.g. C L Lim, 'Reaching for Utopia, Geneva as Inspiration for Investment Disputes?' in Meredith K Lewis and others (eds), *The Post WTO International Legal Order: Utopian, Dystopian and Other Scenarios* (Springer 2020) (hereafter 'Reaching for Utopia'). The author declares his attendance in these meetings.

[59] Amr Shalakany, 'Arbitration and the Third World: Bias under the Scepter of Neo-Liberalism' (2000) 41 Harvard Int'l L J 419.

6. Analysis

Thus, international law addresses development principles within the context of international trade law and the international law on foreign investment's respective treaty frameworks at the multilateral, regional, or bilateral levels. Legal innovation has been more sophisticated in trade law due to the way in which treaty rules have incorporated development principles. The late and very distinguished Robert Hudec was simply too pessimistic. Evidently developmental principles are not only reflected in the way developing country WTO members frame their negotiating demands, but also in the way they frame their trade disputes, while WTO panels and the Appellate Body have at times responded directly. Importantly, in cases like *Brazil—Retreaded Tyres* and in *Shrimp-Turtle*, they have responded to the need to build up and refine developmental principles in the traditional GATT-WTO sense as well as in a Brundtlandian sense of sustainable development.

At first glance, the investment sphere has been less amenable to the kinds of development principles we see in the trade sphere, which border on resource redistribution. While rewriting treaties may reflect the various developmental policies of developing countries in their BIT negotiations, for example, in carving out procurement and tax policies,[60] this has not coalesced, generally speaking, into the kinds of development principles that we see present in the trade law context. For example, in particular sectors or areas of concern, such as in the extractive industries or with respect to privatization programmes. Whereas in the trade sphere similar issues to those that have occurred in investment treaty negotiations are also often played out, even if this can sometimes be controversial under article XXIV of the GATT or GATS article V's conditions for forming an RTA, where entire difficult sectors may be removed from the negotiating table as a result.

Analogous issues do sometimes arise in the investment treaty negotiation sphere. Procurement for example may be a sensitive issue both in the trade and in the investment sphere where investment arbitration may be brought if procurement is not subjected to treaty carveouts. Certainly, in the context of TPP negotiations these kinds of issues were viewed to have become inter-related by negotiators and addressed in a way which cut across traditional divisions, such as that between trade and investment. The question of state-owned enterprises is another example.[61] Still, these depend upon the parties and the dynamics of particular negotiations.

There is a general issue in respect of investment treaties and investment arbitration practice which should be singled out. That has involved questions about how

---

[60] Some others may be more controversial, ranging from the role of state-owned enterprises to racially-based economic policies.
[61] See e.g. Mitsuo Matsushita and C L Lim, 'Taming Leviathan as Merchant' (2020) 19 World Trade Rev 402.

an 'investment' ought to be defined. Must it contribute to the economic development of the host country? This issue involves the well-known 'Salini' problem in ICSID arbitration.[62] Framed in this way, the next question one might ask is how sustainable development can be brought into the definition of an investment. For example, if a purported investment does not qualify as an 'investment' according to some sustainable development criterion, would it be desirable for a tribunal, acting without any explicit guidance in the investment treaty, to say that no arbitration may be brought at all? This would be a very controversial proposition.[63] There is, currently, no such arbitral pronouncement.[64] However, the Morocco-Nigeria BIT of 2016 has drawn recent attention by including in its definition of an 'investment' the need for a contribution to the sustainable development of the host state. 'Sustainable development', however, is left undefined:[65]

> 'Investment'. Investment means an enterprise within the territory of one State established, acquired, expanded or operated, in good faith, by an investor of the other State in accordance with law of the Party in whose territory the investment is made taken together with the asset of the enterprise which contribute sustainable development of that Party and has the characteristics of an investment involving a commitment of capital or other similar resources, pending profit, risk-taking and certain duration.

A closely related issue for adjudicative bodies has to do with the manner in which other rules and principles of international law—including those of sustainable development—should feature when interpreting treaty instruments, including article 25 of the ICSID Convention's reference to the need for an 'investment' in order to bring an ICSID arbitration claim. It involves reading article 31(3)(c) of the

---

[62] *Salini Costruttori SpA and Italstrade SpA v Kingdom of Morocco* (Decision on Jurisdiction) ICSID Case No ARB/00/4 [52]; Emmanuel Gaillard and Yas Banifatemi, 'The Long March towards a Jurisprudence Constante on the Notion of Investment' in Meg Kinnear and others (eds), *Building International Investment Law: The First Fifty Years of ICSID* (Kluwer 2015); Katia Yannaca-Small and Dimitrios Katsikis, 'The Meaning of "Investment" in Investment Treaty Arbitration' in Katia Yannaca-Small (ed), *Arbitration under International Investment Agreements: A Guide to the Key Issues* (2nd edn, OUP 2018) 286 *et seq*.

[63] Naimeh Masumy, 'ICSID Tribunals Fail to Address the Imbalance between Sustainable Development Principles and Investment Protections' (*Investment Treaty News*, 20 December 2021) <https://www.iisd.org/itn/en/2021/12/20/icsid-tribunals-fail-to-address-the-imbalance-between-sustainable-development-principles-and-investment-protections/> accessed 22 June 2023.

[64] See further, Daniela Gómez Altamirano, 'Protecting FDI Contributing to Host Countries' Development: The Rise of the "Forgotten" Salini Criterion as Part of the Definition of Investment' (Columbia FDI Perspectives No 320, 31 December 2021) <https://ccsi.columbia.edu/sites/default/files/content/docs/fdi%20perspectives/No%20320%20-%20G%C3%B3mez%20Altamirano%20-%20FINAL.pdf> accessed 22 June 2023 (hereafter 'Protecting FDI'). It contains also a concise survey of some BITs which have taken this approach, building upon the idea in *Salini v Morocco* (Decision on Jurisdiction, 23 July 2001) ICSID Case No ARB/00/4 [52] that an 'investment' for the purposes of article 25(1) of the ICSID Convention is required to contribute to the economic development of the host state.

[65] Reciprocal Investment Promotion and Protection Agreement between the Government of the Kingdom of Morocco and the Government of the Federal Republic of Nigeria (3 December 2016).

Vienna Convention on the Law of Treaties so as to require reference to other international rules and principles when interpreting any treaty text.[66]

7. Ancillary Developments

Development as a trade or investment law concept has not been framed explicitly as an issue of colonial reparations. Rather, we have seen developmental principles framed in substantive rather than in an adjectival or remedial way, be it in the guise of non-reciprocity, or for some other form of special and differential treatment, or in the incorporation of sustainable development principles into treaty interpretation. Yet debates about colonial redress are not entirely irrelevant and may yet in the future present a further dimension. In the *Chagos Archipelago* request for an International Court of Justice (ICJ) Advisory Opinion, concerning the forced separation by the UK of the Chagos from Mauritius, the ICJ considered that the people of a non-self-governing territory are entitled to exercise their right to self-determination in respect of their whole territory. Therefore, detachment of the Chagos without the freely expressed consent of the Chagos Islanders violates their right to self-determination which the UK, as administering Power, was bound to respect. To date, however, the UK has refused to abide by the Opinion, which although technically non-binding, declares a breach of international law.[67]

Other issues, such as colonial responsibility for acts done during colonization, specifically under principles of succession to state responsibility, are closely related.[68] The issue is especially pertinent to claims of responsibility for acts done

---

[66] See Martti Koskenniemi and others, 'Fragmentation of International Law: Difficulties Arising from the Diversification and Expansion of International Law, Report of the Study Group of the International Law Commission' (13 April 2006) UN Doc A/CN4/L682, especially n 64 in respect of 'self-contained regimes' so-called, such as the trade and investment regimes; Campbell MacLachlan, 'The Principle of Systemic Integration and Article 31(3)(c) of the Vienna Convention' (2005) 54 ICLQ 279.

[67] *Legal Consequences of the Separation of the Chagos Archipelago from Mauritius in 1965* (Advisory Opinion) (2019) ICJ GL No 169.

[68] 'Second Report on Succession of States in Respect of State Responsibility by Pavel Šturma, Special Rapporteur' (6 April 2018) UN Doc A/CN4/719, Annex I, 53, wherein Draft article 6(1) states that: 'Succession of States has no impact on the attribution of the internationally wrongful act committed before the date of succession of States'. Cf article 1 of the Articles on the Responsibility of States for Internationally Wrongful Acts, ILC Yearbook (2001) vol II, part 2, 26–30, which reflects the general principle of non-succession. But answering the question of attribution does not answer the question as to whether the predecessor metropolitan state bears responsibility. In that regard, the remaining paragraphs of draft article 6 envisage the responsibility of the colonial metropolitan power (paragraph 2), but in the case of continuing acts (paragraph 3) that do not preclude the responsibility of the successor state as well (e.g. a post-independence state). See further, Anastasija Kaplane, 'Succession of States in Respect of State Responsibility: Toward Yet Another Vienna Convention?' (RGSL Research Paper No 23, 2020) especially 30–31 <https://www.rgsl.edu.lv/data/publikacijas/kaplane-final.pdf> accessed 22 June 2023. See further, 'Fourth Report on Succession of States in Respect of State Responsibility/by Pavel Sturma, Special Rapporteur' (2020) UN Doc A/CN4/743. For the work of the Institut de Droit International, see Marcelo Kohen, 'La Succession d'Etats en Matière de Responsabilité Internationale/ State Succession in Matters of State Responsibility' in *Yearbook of Institute of International Law* (Tallinn Session, vol 76, Pedone 2015); Marcelo Kohen and Patrick Dumberry, *The Institute of International*

against the colonial people prior to their achievement of independence. Examples include claims for colonial injustice, slavery, genocide, and/or torture.[69]

Still, the issue of redress, and more specifically, that of reparations, have not featured in any explicit manner in trade rules. It also has not featured in a similarly explicit manner in the investment sphere. At best, it is implicit in the positions and demands of developing countries, most notably in debates about the standard of compensation to foreign property owners in post-independence nationalizations. It is also true to say that, at least until recently, developing country demands have been made against GATT as a rich nation's club, and international investment law as that body of rules concerned almost solely with international responsibility for violations of the rights of alien nationals. At the same time, trade and investment laws even now are often viewed as unconnected with developments in the wider international law field. Partly because trade for long belonged to the province of commercial diplomats rather than international lawyers, and international investment arbitration has been as much the domain of commercial arbitration practitioners.

We should not however ignore clear emerging trends. While there is formal recognition of sustainable development in international trade and investment law, or at least of environmental and health policies in international investment arbitration, and recognition too of development principles as a part of the GATT's trade rules, we are now witnessing a decolonial movement unfold.[70] Taking the *Chagos* Advisory Opinion again as an example, the broader international law field is not untouched. At the same time, Philip Alston, a distinguished human rights lawyer, had considered as long ago as in 1979 that a 'right to development' had already come into existence, and he saw it as the next step of the process of decolonisation.[71] Going into the future, all this may need close consideration. In short,

---

Law's Resolution on State Succession and State Responsibility: Introduction, Text and Commentaries (CUP 2019).

[69] See e.g. Andreas Buser, 'Colonial Injustices and the Law of State Responsibility: The CARICOM Claim to Compensate Slavery and (Native) Genocide' (2017) 77 ZaöRV 409; *Mutua et al v Foreign and Commonwealth Office* [2011] EWHC 1913 (QB); [2012] EWHC 2678 (QB); ibid (Kohen and Dumberry) 128–36, discussing article 16 of the IDI's Resolution on State Succession and State Responsibility which states, inter alia, that in the case of newly independent states responsibility shall not pass to it from the metropolitan state, and further that rights arising from such responsibility, be they committed against the predecessor colonial state or its people, do pass to the newly independent state (art 16, paras 2 and 4). For a stark comparison with the current ILC Draft Articles on Succession of States in Respect of State Responsibility, see draft article 8 which does not contain the IDI resolution's express stipulation that rights arising from such responsibility, be they committed against the predecessor colonial state or its people, pass to the newly independent state. See ibid (Sturma's Second Report) Annex I, 53–54 and also the commentary at 33–36.
[70] Walter D Mignolo, *The Darker Side of Western Modernity: Global Futures, Decolonial Options* (Duke University Press 2011); Catherine D Walsh and Walter Mignolo, *On Decoloniality: Concepts, Analytics, Praxis* (Duke University Press 2018).
[71] Philip Alston, 'The Right to Development at the International Level' in René-Jean Dupuy (ed), *The Right to Development at the International Level* (Sijthoff and Noordhoff 1989) 110–11.

no consideration of the role of international law in the areas we have looked at in this chapter can ignore a shift toward building up a body of post-colonial legal principles.

Thus, the proposal for a Convention on the Right to Development now raises questions about its inter-relationship with the current, already complex, treaty regimes for trade and investment sought to be presented here in brief outline only.[72] Article 23 of that Draft Convention is especially noteworthy:[73]

> The provisions of the present Convention shall not affect the rights and obligations of any State Party deriving from any existing international agreements, except where the exercise of those rights and obligations would contravene the object and purpose of this Convention. The present paragraph is not intended to create a hierarchy between the present Convention and other international agreements.

8. Conclusion

I have sought to explain, briefly, the way developmental issues have arisen in trade and investment, the way countries have approached these in their treaty and other behaviour, as well as the way in which adjudicative bodies have looked at them. Preferential market access and non-reciprocity as well as other flexibilities are all reflected in the GATT. Sustainable development is already a treaty concept to be found in the WTO's Marrakesh Agreement. In the case of investment treaties, the new issues are largely interpretative. Such as whether the requirement in article 25 of the ICSID Convention that an 'investment' is required before an arbitration can be brought paves the way for the imposition of a requirement to contribute to the development of the host state. There is no such requirement in the case of non-ICSID arbitration, such as arbitration under the UNCITRAL Rules.[74] A second issue involves new treaty clauses such as that in the Morocco-Nigeria BIT, whilst a third involves greater use of the systemic integration clause in the Vienna Convention on the Law of Treaties.

The concept of 'development' has in a sense only a restricted meaning in the context of trade and investment. One limited to creating exceptions to principles such as trade reciprocity and non-discrimination, or limited to the formulation

---

[72] UNHRC, 'Draft Convention on the Right to Development' (17 January 2020) UN Doc A/HRC/WG2/21/2.

[73] ibid.

[74] For the formulation of bespoke investment arbitration rules elsewhere, see e.g. C L Lim, 'Developments in International Investment Law and Policy in Asia' in Lisa Sachs and others (eds), *Yearbook of International Investment Law & Policy 2019* (OUP 2021).

or reformulation of the legal meaning of 'investment',[75] or one which ekes out an existence as an interpretative principle applied by adjudicatory bodies, and even then only in the guise of 'sustainable development'.[76] The Draft Convention on the Right to Development is the latest thing to unfold which raises again the question of giving greater scope to human rights. The question is not new and concerns a perceived need to integrate labour rights, in addition to environmental and conservation concerns, as well as human rights more broadly, into WTO law.[77] There is a similar question about the mis-treatment thus far of international investment law as a specialised regime that is divorced from other public international law norms, including international human rights norms.[78]

Beginning around 2004, successive US model BITs and comprehensive free trade agreements (FTAs) such as the US-DR-CAFTA, Korea-US FTA, US-Colombia FTA, US-Panama FTA, as well as the TPP/CPTPP, have shown the means of importing labour and environmental concerns into trade and investment treaties.[79] Short of new treaty rules, however, any hope of integrating emerging development principles into international trade and investment law is likely to continue to depend heavily upon the adjudicative function in international economic law. There is some hope of a more joined-up view being taken by adjudicative bodies despite consideration of trade and investment as if they were entirely fragmented.[80] This may be especially true where there is already a broad international consensus, such as a consensus over the SDGs. But not where North/South and post-colonial

---

[75] See further, Morocco's 2019 Model BIT, note 3.3, which defines closely the requirement in article 1 that an investment should make a 'contribution to the development of the host State'. Discussed in Protecting FDI (n 64) 1.
[76] Schrijver citing the World Summit Outcome Document (24 October 2005) UN Doc A/RES/60/1, describes development as encompassing 'sustainability, good governance and the rule of law'; A New Convention (n 33) 90.
[77] See Rachel Harris and Gillian Moon, 'GATT Article XX and Human Rights: What Do We Know from the First Twenty Years?' (2015) 16 Melbourne J I L 1.
[78] Some have addressed this question by asking whether international investment law is within the public international law field at all, whether the former is merely 'influenced' by the latter and vice versa, or asked if public international law is an accurate or appropriate 'paradigm'. See Jürgen Bering and others, 'General Public International Law and International Investment Law—A Research Sketch on Selected Issues' (Institut für Wirtschaftsrecht March 2011) <https://telc.jura.uni-halle.de/sites/default/files/BeitraegeTWR/Heft%20105.pdf> accessed 20 March 2022; Valentina Vadi, *Proportionality, Reasonableness and Standards of Review in International Investment Law and Arbitration* (Edward Elgar 2018) 23–27. The position taken here is that BITs at any rate are treaties; that they concern, to use Sornarajah's Sornarajah's terminology, the 'international law on foreign investment'. Thus, their interpretation becomes a matter of public international law. International investment arbitration is a broader subject. Contractually-based investment arbitration may even belong to an 'international order of contracts', to use René-Jean Dupuy's term in *Texaco* (n 48) or the 'arbitral legal order' to use Daniel Cohen's phrase, rather than to public international law or private international law. But for our present purposes that is quite beside the point. See further C L Lim, 'Development of the Principal Forms from Antiquity to Arbitromania' in C L Lim (ed), *The Cambridge Companion to International Arbitration* (CUP 2021).
[79] Discussed further in Finding a Workable Balance (n 56) 556 *et seq*. It is not limited to US treaties, see e.g. CETA, Annex 8-A where the indirect expropriation rule requires that legitimate public welfare measures such as health, safety, and the environment must be taken into account, amongst other things.
[80] Fragmented Disciplines (n 6) generally.

controversies are still at play. Consensus remains therefore crucial, not least when the role of international courts and tribunals has become itself an object of criticism. However, the prospect of the WTO Appellate Body driving greater coherence is, at least in the short and medium terms, discouraging. That body now faces a crisis whose roots lie in perceptions of the exercise of an overbroad authority. Still, it has not dissuaded those who have proposed a multilateral investment court modelled in many senses upon the WTO dispute settlement system.[81]

In short, the issue today has to do with international law's ability to address three challenges at once. These are the environmental crisis, developmental aspirations, and the ability of international liberal institutions to fashion rules which grant sufficient freedom to states to pursue social and environmental protection through policies that promote public welfare.[82] All of this now takes place within a shifting global order and under intense conditions of global rivalry and competition. Rather than that international law might fail to meet these challenges, it should at least be borne in mind that it is a patient discipline.

---

[81] See further, for the comparison, Reaching for Utopia (n 58) 172, and generally.

[82] John Gerard Ruggie, 'International Regimes, Transactions, and Change: Embedded Liberalism in the Postwar Economic Order' (1982) 36 Int'l Org 379, Andrew T F Lang, 'Reconstructing Embedded Liberalism: John Gerard Ruggie and Constructive Approaches to the Study of the International Trade Regime' in John Gerard Ruggie (ed), *Embedding Global Markets: An Enduring Challenge* (Aldershot 2008); discussed also in Finding a Workable Balance (n 56) 552.

15
The Adequacy of Financing for the Development Agenda

Thomas F McInerney

1. Introduction

Adequate financing is essential to making development progress. Whether mobilized from external or domestic sources, undertaking reforms, and investing in infrastructure and human capacity, requires resources. The ambitions embodied in the Sustainable Development Goals (SDGs) (many of which embody multilateral treaty commitments) and the needs for climate change adaptation and mitigation following the Paris Agreement establish baselines for the resources needed for sustainable development. The Addis Ababa Action Agenda (AAAA) set forth approaches to deliver the requisite financing to meet these objectives.[1]

Yet the development finance landscape is confused and problematic in many respects. There is a level of cognitive dissonance manifest both in terms of the resources being mobilized for the SDGs and the institutional infrastructure to support sustainable development finance. As described more fully below, at the time of writing in August 2022, the resources needed to meet the financing needs of both the Transforming our World: the 2030 Agenda for Sustainable Development (2030 Agenda) and its SDGs and the Paris Agreement on climate change have fallen substantially short. At the same time, the legal and governance infrastructure to support key elements of the financing for development agenda have, with some modest exceptions, largely not improved. We also see that approaches to financing international law, most notably multilateral treaties, fail to provide sufficient and equitable resources. A theme running throughout this chapter is the international community's relatively weak financial response to the major development and environmental challenges facing the world.

---

[1] UN, 'Addis Ababa Action Agenda of the Third International Conference on Financing for Development (Addis Ababa Action Agenda)' (Financing for Development, Third International Conference, 13–16 July 2015) <https://sustainabledevelopment.un.org/content/documents/2051A AAA_Outcome.pdf> accessed 24 June 2023 (hereafter 'AAAA').

The problems that have emerged in the seven years since the AAAA was defined are now likely to be compounded by global macroeconomic conditions caused by the dramatic monetary and fiscal policy expansion undertaken to counter the global COVID-19 demand shocks. Among these issues are inflation due to supply chain disruptions caused by COVID-19 and the Russian attack on Ukraine, subsequent monetary policy tightening, and significant increases in indebtedness in developing countries, much of which is held at variable interest rates, and likely to exacerbate the debt repayment challenges. On top of these problems are significant indications that the global economy is slowing while the US dollar is strengthening, thereby reducing revenues from trade in commodities, increasing the cost of imports, and compounding debt service demands. The recent crisis in Sri Lanka may be a harbinger of problems other countries will soon face, some commentators argue.[2] As such, not only have expectations for increases in development finance at the time the AAAA was concluded not materialized, but the likelihood of a new debt crisis occurring in developing and emerging economy countries in the coming years appears a distinct possibility.[3]

The landscape of development cooperation today reflects increasing fragmentation or, stated more positively, growing pluralism in financing sources and approaches. The changes that have occurred can be understood as parallel to changes to the state and market generally. Broadly speaking, these changes involve a shift in emphasis from state-driven development to private-sector-driven development.[4] Exemplifying these trends are changes in the role of traditional development financing actors. In this context, the work of multilateral development banks (MDBs) has shifted from financing large public works projects to creating the institutional structures for the market economy. To support private actors' participation in development financing, several new financing approaches have emerged.

This chapter begins with an overview of the current landscape for development finance. It then examines some of the legal challenges associated with three thematic areas of particular importance to increasing the resources available for development. These are sovereign debt sustainability, tax law and policy, and the private sector role in development, including the use of environmental, social, and governance (ESG) standards. In the final part, I examine financial considerations in relation to international law, specifically involving multilateral regulatory treaties.

---

[2] Shantayanan Devarajan and Homi Kharas, 'Is the Sri Lankan Debt Crisis a Harbinger' (*Foreign Affairs*, 4 August 2022).

[3] Daniele Balbi, 'Billions in Distressed Debt Threaten Developing Countries' (*Bloomberg*, 8 July 2022) <https://www.bloomberg.com/news/newsletters/2022-07-08/the-big-take-developing-nations-at-risk-of-debt-crisis> accessed 24 June 2023.

[4] Emma Mawdsley, '"From Billions to Trillions": Financing the SDGs in a world "Beyond Aid"' (2018) 8(2) Dialogues Hum Geogr 191–95.

2. Current Development Finance Situation

A starting point for discussing the development finance situation today is the AAAA adopted by United Nations (UN) members in 2015 to support the 2030 Agenda and SDGs. The themes of the AAAA have become a central reference point for efforts to finance achievement of the SDGs. The resulting slogan of moving 'from billions to trillions' reflects general recognition of the magnitude of the challenge.[5]

Following the conclusion of the AAAA, the Paris Agreement was adopted in December 2015.[6] A central pillar of that accord was the need to increase financing for climate change adaptation for developing countries. In keeping with article 4(3) of the UN Framework Convention on Climate Change (UNFCCC), the resources needed to support these efforts should be additional to other development funding.[7]

As described more fully below, development finance currently falls substantially short of the identified need. The shortfall in resources is not marginal but instead more than 75 per cent, although the amount is much greater for developing countries. The role of law, legal instruments, and related institutions in leading to this state of affairs is difficult to say precisely, but, as this chapter will show, the gaps and inadequacies that exist among legal mechanisms suggest that at the very least existing arrangements are maladaptive given the scope and magnitude of the challenge.

Among the sources of financing identified in the AAAA, three were given particular importance: domestic tax mobilization, private sector investment, and official development assistance (ODA). The first source of financing the AAAA emphasizes is domestic resource mobilization.[8] This measure followed trends in development finance since Monterrey in 2002,[9] although the AAAA made it an even stronger priority. As elaborated in the AAAA, national fiscal resources were recognized as not only desirable, but essential to achieving development progress. The second source is private sector investment. In this regard, the AAAA reflected trends in governance and economic policy over the past four decades. There is widespread agreement in development policy discussions that private sector finance is crucial to achieving the SDGs.[10] In terms of the third priority,

---

[5] UN Secretary-General, 'Secretary-General's remarks at World Bank event "Billions to Trillions—Ideas to Action"' (13 July 2015) <https://www.un.org/sg/en/content/sg/statement/2015-07-13/secretary-general's-remarks-world-bank-event-"billions-trillions--> (accessed 23 August 2023).
[6] UN Framework Convention on Climate Change (Paris Agreement) (12 December 2015).
[7] ibid.
[8] AAAA (n 1) paras 20–34.
[9] *Report of the International Conference on Financing for Development* (A/CONF198/11, 18–22 March 2002) ch 1, resolution 1, annex.
[10] See e.g. Christopher McHugh, 'Mobilizing Private Funding of Development Finance' (2021) 57(12) J Dev Stud 1979–2001.

ODA, the AAAA reiterates the longstanding expectation since the 1960s that developed countries should provide aid in the amount of 0.7 per cent of gross domestic product (GDP) per annum.[11] Yet the AAAA recognizes that ODA has a role of 'complementing', not replacing, domestic public resources.[12]

Experience with each of these sources shows shortcomings, problems, and unintended consequences. For ODA, amounts have fallen well short of targets since the beginning, with an average among the Organization for Economic Cooperation and Development (OECD) Development Assistance Committee (DAC) of approximately 0.3 per cent of GDP since 2018. This result is hardly anomalous since in the past sixty years, few donor countries have ever delivered such levels of aid. Mobilization of fiscal resources has also been insufficient, however, as described below, there have been some important efforts in recent years to improve international tax law and policy that suggest possibilities for improvements.

Although the AAAA focused on limitations of ODA to finance development, private investment has fallen far short of the trillions needed. Not only has the private sector contribution fallen short, but an unanticipated twist has occurred: increased private *lending* to developing countries. Were such credit used to support long-term investment that could generate long-term development results, it might be helpful to development aims, but evidence suggests that much has been used by governments to support current consumption or refinance existing debt rather than investment. Without exaggeration, many observers contend that conditions increasingly appear similar to those preceding the Latin American debt crisis of the 1970s and 1980s.[13]

One of the priorities recognized by the AAAA was the need for infrastructure finance. To mobilize such financing the Global Infrastructure Hub was launched between the OECD, World Bank, and the International Monetary Fund (IMF). Results from this initiative have thus far been minimal. The larger story for infrastructure finance has been China's Belt and Road Initiative (BRI). With announced funding of more than US$8 trillion, amounts provided under the BRI dwarf those of other development financing.[14] Infrastructure is a global need and the Chinese response is a massive contribution to addressing the challenge, although debt, environmental, and social sustainability concerns have been raised.[15]

---

[11] AAAA (n 1) para 51.
[12] ibid para 50.
[13] Sydney Maki, 'Historic Cascade of Defaults is Coming for Emerging Markets' (*Bloomberg*, 8 July 2022).
[14] John Hurley, Scott Morris, and Gailyn Portelance, 'Examining the Debt Implications of the Belt and Road Initiative from a Policy Perspective' (CGD Policy Paper 121, Center for Global Development, 4 March 2018).
[15] Johanna A P Lorenzo, 'A Path to Sustainable Development Along the Belt and Road' (2021) 24 J Int'l Econ Law 591–608.

a. Finance shortfalls

A review of the costs of achieving sustainable development objectives in the coming decades exposes both the incredible magnitude of the sums required and the dramatic gap in funds that have been mobilized. In 2014, in preparation for the adoption of the SDGs, the UN Conference on Trade and Development (UNCTAD) issued a report setting forth estimates for the financing needed for the SDGs, including elements related to infrastructure and climate change. At the time, UNCTAD found the cost of the SDGs overall was between US$5 trillion and US$7 trillion, and for developing countries between US$3.3 trillion and US$4.5 trillion per year to 2030.[16] These amounts include US$1.6 trillion to US$2.5 trillion per annum for what UNCTAD refers to as economic infrastructure including power, transportation, telecommunications, and water and sanitation. Food security and agriculture were estimated at US$480 billion per year and social infrastructure comprised of education and health were estimated at US$330 billion and US$210 billion annually, respectively. All of these figures were inclusive of anticipated climate change expenses.

If we examine more recent figures on global infrastructure needs alone, estimates are that approximately 5 per cent of global GDP must be allocated annually. More specifically, according to the G-20 Global Infrastructure Outlook, the investment required in infrastructure globally is US$97 trillion, while projected expenditures are US$79 trillion through 2040.[17] Other studies have estimated the cost of infrastructure globally at US$3.9 trillion annually to 2040, nearly more than UNCTAD's high end estimate on the total annual cost of the SDGs. The Asian Development Bank has estimated that US$1.7 trillion annually must be spent on infrastructure in Asia alone to 2030 for the region to continue to grow, reduce poverty, and address climate change.[18] Yet total investment in infrastructure globally was US$739 billion in 2020 of which US$303 billion was spent in Western Europe and the United States (US).[19] Despite great hopes for private sector contributions to development, in 2020 private sector investment in infrastructure was US$156 billion, with three-quarters going to developed countries.[20]

A portion of the global infrastructure finance required pertains to financing to achieve temperature and adaptation goals of the Paris Agreement. Estimates of

---

[16] UNCTAD, 'World Investment Report 2014: Investing in the SDGs: An Action Plan' (*UNCTAD*)<https://unctad.org/system/files/official-document/wir2014_en.pdf> accessed 24 June 2023.
[17] 'G20 Global Infrastructure Outlook: Forecasting Infrastructure Investment Needs and Gaps' (*Infrastructure Outlook*) <https://outlook.gihub.org/> accessed 24 June 2023.
[18] Asian Development Bank, 'Meeting Asia's Infrastructure Needs' (*ADB*, February 2017) <https://www.adb.org/publications/asia-infrastructure-needs> accessed 24 June 2023.
[19] 'G20 Global Infrastructure Monitor 2021' (*Global Infrastructure Hub*) <https://cdn.gihub.org/umbraco/media/4740/gihub_v10.pdf> accessed 24 June 2023.
[20] ibid.

those amounts are between US$3 trillion to US$6 trillion per year through 2050.[21] The International Panel on Climate Change (IPCC) estimates that the amount of climate finance needed for developing countries must increase by four to eight times until 2030.[22] Yet current spending is only approximately US$630 billion with the majority going to developed countries.[23]

While the amounts needed to finance infrastructure and climate change responses are falling short globally, as the foregoing suggests, the shortfall is even greater for developing countries. The private sector is not coming close to meeting the needs. According to World Bank figures, institutional investors including sovereign wealth funds, pension funds, and mutual funds constitute 0.67 per cent of total global investment in developing countries.[24] Green bonds are only 3 per cent of global bond markets and are mostly issued by developed countries or China.[25]

Although the AAAA anticipated that ODA would be insufficient to meet the cost of the SDGs, donor funds have increased only marginally since 2016. For OECD DAC donors, total ODA was US$157 billion in 2016 and dropped to US$137 billion in 2018.[26] It was not until 2020 that spending exceeded 2016 amounts again. In 2020, total ODA was US$162 billion and in 2021 sums rose again to US$169 billion.[27] One question these shortfalls raise is whether donors are shifting a portion of their aid from development generally to climate change, contravening the additionality principle.[28]

While the shortfalls in funding are palpable, finding precise figures is difficult. While UNCTAD calculated the costs of the SDGs based on relevant infrastructure and climate change expenses, more recent figures are available for both infrastructure and climate change alone. Yet determining the portion of infrastructure expenses related to climate change is often not clear and climate change expenditures involving infrastructure are likewise difficult to distinguish. Double counting is a distinct risk. Further complicating the analysis is the fact that, with financing

---

[21] Prasad Ananthakrishnan and others, 'Mobilizing Private Climate Financing in Emerging Market and Developing Economies' (IMF Staff Climate Note 2022/007, International Monetary Fund, 2022) (hereafter 'Mobilizing Private Climate Financing').
[22] Intergovernmental Panel on Climate Change (IPCC), 'Climate Change 2022: Impacts, Adaptation, and Vulnerability: Summary for Policymakers' (2022).
[23] Mobilizing Private Climate Financing (n 21).
[24] World Bank, 'The Contribution of Institutional Investors: Private Investment in Infrastructure' (*The World Bank*, 2018) <https://documents.worldbank.org/en/publication/documents-reports/documentdetail/674561524549509963/contribution-of-institutional-investors-private-investment-in-infrastructure> accessed 24 June 2023.
[25] Mobilizing Private Climate Financing (n 21).
[26] Jonas Wilcks, Néstor Pelechà Aigües, and Emily Bosch, Organization for Economic Cooperation and Development (OECD), 'Development Cooperation and Funding: Highlights from the Complete and Final 2019 ODA Statistics' (*Development Co-operation Profiles*, 2022) <https://www.oecd-ilibrary.org/sites/401f9a42-en/index.html?itemId=/content/component/401f9a42-en> accessed 24 June 2023.
[27] ibid.
[28] Asa Persson and Aaron Atteridge, 'The Role of Finance for Adaptation' in Eva C H Keskitalo and Benjamin L Preston (eds), *Research Handbook on Climate Adaptation Policy* (Elgar 2019) 365–83.

having lagged identified needs for the first seven years of SDG implementation, the annual costs to close the gap have accrued significantly.

b. Institutional changes

Another major trend in development finance has been the increased number of financing agencies involved. First, is the growth of so-called non-traditional bilateral development donors from the Gulf states and Brazil, Russia, India, China, and South Africa (BRICS) countries. Driven largely by these states, a variety of new multilateral agencies have also emerged such as Asian Infrastructure Investment Bank and New Development Bank.[29] Additional agencies are the development financial institutions (DFIs) of which approximately 450 have been created in both OECD and newer donor states. In the climate change context, numerous new bodies have been created to finance projects particularly around adaptation. These developments have complicated the picture for development finance, particularly in relation to legal and governance standards.

These efforts need to be understood against the background of geopolitical competition between China and Western development institutions.[30] As developed further below, the growing animosity between OECD countries and China is an important factor in today's development finance landscape. Whether or not we are entering a new bipolar world similar to the Cold War, it is clear that such competition is an important driver of development finance activity, which has implications for the achievement of the AAAA.

Finally, innovations have arisen, which hold promise for future development finance efforts, although the results have been modest at this stage. These include the emergence of blockchain technology and cryptocurrencies. Other examples include impact investment, which involves diverse approaches to generating both social impact benefits and financial returns. The most significant development is blended finance, which involves public sector measures to incentivize private sector firms to participate in development-related projects. Below I discuss blended finance in greater depth in relation to private sector finance.

---

[29] Hongying Wang, 'Regime Complexity and Complex Foreign Policy: China in International Development Finance Governance' (2021) 12(S4) Glob Policy 69.

[30] Shivshankar Menon, 'Nobody Wants the Current World Order: How All Major Powers—Even the United States—Became Revisionists' (*Foreign Affairs*, 3 August 2022).

3. Debt Sustainability Challenges Today

A major challenge to meeting the goals of the AAAA is the dramatic increase in debt among developing and emerging economies. The overall ratio of debt to GDP in developing countries rose from 22.8 per cent in 2008 to 30.6 per cent in 2021.[31] Yet much of the share of the overall debt amounts was attributable to China, which grew GDP an average of 10 per cent per year during this time.[32] If China is excluded, the share of external debt to GDP among developing economies rose to 45.6 per cent in 2021.[33] In aggregate, external debt stocks of developing countries rose from US$4.1 trillion in 2009 to US$11.1 trillion in 2021.[34]

Unsurprisingly, the levels of increased indebtedness are having effects on the fiscal space needed to achieve the SDGs in developing countries. Overall, low-income developing economies experienced an increase in the share of government services devoted to debt service from 4.8 per cent in 2012 to 12 per cent in 2020 and 9.7 per cent in 2021.[35] In sub-Saharan Africa, figures rose from 3.4 per cent in 2012 to 15 per cent in 2021.[36]

During this time, an increasing share of debt financing has come from the private sector. In 2000, private creditors provided a total of 43 per cent of all long-term debt of developing economies with commercial banks representing 11 per cent, bond purchasers 27 per cent, and other creditors 5 per cent.[37] By 2009, the overall share of private creditors dropped to 41 per cent, including 30 per cent private bond buyers, 9 per cent commercial banks, and 2 per cent other.[38] By 2020, the share of borrowing from private sources had surged to 62 per cent of which bond issuances were 51 per cent, commercial bank lending 8 per cent, and other, 3 per cent.[39] This result suggests that a growing share of developing country debt is on non-concessional terms, which will add to the burden as economic growth slows.

a. Debt reduction and distressed debt mechanisms

The AAAA articulated several approaches to addressing debt related concerns. As a general proposition, it recognized that 'borrowing is an important tool for financing investment critical to achieving sustainable development' and can be

---

[31] UN Global Crisis Response Group, 'A World of Debt: A Growing Burden to Global Prosperity' (2023), <https://unctad.org/publication/world-of-debt> accessed 10 September 2023.
[32] ibid.
[33] ibid.
[34] ibid.
[35] ibid.
[36] ibid.
[37] ibid.
[38] ibid.
[39] ibid.

useful as a countercyclical measure during economic downturns.[40] Yet it also noted the importance of managing debt sustainably. While referring to the positive influence of the highly-indebted poor countries (HIPC) programme and the Multilateral Debt Relief Initiatives as approaches to reducing over-indebtedness, it acknowledged the challenge of debt sustainability for many least-developing countries (LDCs), small island developing states (SIDS), and some developed countries.

By many accounts, HIPC has been successful in helping countries achieve greater debt sustainability and practising sound debt management. Most countries have graduated from the process leading to the need for a replacement system.[41] Recently, the IMF launched a new system for to assist developing and emerging market economies, the Resilience and Sustainability Trust.[42] A question is whether the new IMF approach will be an improvement.

Notwithstanding the new debt sustainability challenges that are emerging, there is some evidence that efforts of international institutions to improve public sector financial management and debt management practices have put many countries in relatively better positions to respond to debt sustainability concerns. Positive developments include the IMF-World Bank debt sustainability analysis framework.[43] Likewise, capacity building and technical assistance to improve budgeting and expenditure controls have strengthened governments' ability to manage their finances.

But the growth in debt in developing countries is more problematic in light of the lack of good systems for debt relief and addressing debt crises, something SDG target 17.4 sought to address.[44] While borrowing can be a useful means of advancing development, where states accumulate excessive debt, it can be a drain on development by depleting budgetary resources needed to support current spending and investment. Efforts to assist developing countries manage their debt have been undertaken over the years by bilateral and multilateral development agencies, yet remain works in progress.

Early in the COVID-19 pandemic, the G20 developed the Debt Service Suspension Initiative (DSSI) to reduce debt service requirements among seventy-three IDA and UN LDCs.[45] The programme placed a moratorium on debt service payments between 1 May and 31 December 2020 and new repayments began in

---

[40] AAAA (n 1) para 93.
[41] Rumu Sarkar, *International Development Law: Rule of Law, Human Rights & Global Finance* (2nd edn, Springer 2020).
[42] International Monetary Fund (IMF), 'Resilience and Sustainability Trust' (*IMF Live*) <https://www.imf.org/en/Topics/Resilience-and-Sustainability-Trust> accessed 24 June 2023.
[43] World Bank, 'Debt & Fiscal Risks Toolkit' (*The World Bank*) <https://www.worldbank.org/en/programs/debt-toolkit/dsf> accessed 24 June 2023.
[44] SDG Target 17.4: 'Assist developing countries in attaining long-term debt sustainability through coordinated policies aimed at fostering debt financing, debt relief and debt restructuring, as appropriate, and address the external debt of highly indebted poor countries to reduce debt distress.'
[45] World Bank, 'Debt Service Suspension Initiative' (*The World Bank*) <https://www.worldbank.org/en/topic/debt/brief/covid-19-debt-service-suspension-initiative> accessed 24 June 2023.

June 2022. The programme sought to encourage private lenders to participate, however, to date, the private sector has not. Assessments of the programme find that it was useful to mitigate the immediate needs of developing countries during the economic shock caused by COVID-19, however, since the programme did not reduce debt, it has not prevented countries from debt distress today.

Perhaps the most significant shortcoming in sovereign debt has been the lack of any system for sovereign bankruptcy.[46] Although the IMF and individual creditors regularly work with countries facing liquidity and solvency problems, these efforts are ad hoc and entail substantial uncertainty. Former IMF head Anne Kruger sought unsuccessfully to create such a system beginning in 2002.[47] More recently, early in the COVID-19 crisis, the IMF managing director Kristalina Giorgieva made a push for the creation of a sovereign bankruptcy system. This call follows decades of advocacy in policy and economics communities to create such a mechanism.[48]

In the absence of a true sovereign bankruptcy system, in the past decade a number of initiatives have been convened to examine the possibility of creating some frameworks for improving sovereign borrowing. First, the Paris Club retains its position as an important institution for addressing debt crises. It has developed new approaches to promoting transparency and dialogue between sovereign creditors and debtors. The AAAA calls for the development of guidelines for creditor and debtor responsibilities relating to sovereign borrowing and lending.[49] Precedent for such approach can be seen in a UNCTAD expert group, which drafted principles on responsible sovereign borrowing and lending and a subsequent group dealt with the possibility of a workout mechanism.[50] Other relevant examples include the Human Rights Council's adoption of 'Guiding Principles on Foreign Debt and Human Rights' in 2011.[51]

b. Implications of private borrowing shift

The shift in the mix of private sector financing from commercial banks to capital markets raises important concerns regarding debt relief. At a basic level, the use of

---

[46] Barry Herman, 'Toward a Multilateral Framework for Recovery from Sovereign Insolvency', in Martin Guzman, Jose Ocampo, and Joseph Stiglitz (eds), *Too Little, Too Late: The Quest to Resolve Sovereign Debt Crises* (Columbia University Press 2016) 207–22 (hereafter 'Toward a Multilateral Framework').

[47] IMF, A New Approach to Sovereign Debt Restructuring (2002), available at: https://www.imf.org/external/pubs/ft/exrp/sdrm/eng/index.htm

[48] Toward a Multilateral Framework (n 46).

[49] AAAA (n 1) para. 97.

[50] Toward a Multilateral Framework (n 46) 217.

[51] OHCHR, *Guiding Principles on Foreign Debt and Human Rights* (A/HRC/20/23, 10 April 2011) <https://www.ohchr.org/en/documents/reports/ahrc2023-guiding-principles-foreign-debt-and-human-rights> accessed 24 June 2023.

the capital markets as opposed to banks has increased the number of counterparts involved in any debt restructuring processes. This situation is compounded by the fact that bond holders have independent contractual claims to be repaid, which they may use to reject proposed workout arrangements.

In some notable instances such as in Argentina, so-called 'vulture funds' (investors who purchase distressed assets at a discount in the hope of realizing gains after conditions improve) purchase sovereign bonds at a fraction of the principal amount. They then may seek repayment of the entire principal amount typically by refusing to accept the terms of a proposed debt restructuring or rescheduling even if a majority of the other bondholders agree to the terms. In this way, the hold out creditors can effectively demand that the other bondholders make them whole, despite the majority's willingness to accept a debt reduction (haircut) or longer maturity. In some cases, the holdouts effectively may block a debt restructuring.

In response to such fears, efforts have been made to set terms for bond indentures that prevent such holdouts from occurring. The main approach has been to use collective action clauses (CAC). CACs generally provide that if more than 51 per cent of bondholders agree to modify bond terms, they will bind the other bondholders, thus preventing holdouts from occurring. In the past decade, the terms of CACs have become more sophisticated, with the International Capital Markets Association (ICMA) developing an influential model. As practice has become more established, CACs have been increasingly adopted for new sovereign bond issuances. In addition to the use of CACs, several governments have enacted legislation to prevent holdouts. The AAAA expressed concern over holdout creditors and voiced support for the ICMA model as well as legislative approaches.

Given the lack of a sovereign bankruptcy procedure, CACs constitute an important means of facilitating debt restructuring processes. Evidence from nine debt restructuring cases after 2014 suggests that they have more frequently resulted in pre-emptive (i.e. pre-default) restructurings than post-default, which had previously been the more common occurrence.[52] They also appear to have enabled reductions in the time involved in restructurings from 3.5 years on average to 1.2 years on average, allowed sovereigns to re-enter the capital markets more quickly, reduce losses in economic outputs post-restructuring, and eliminate ex-post restructuring litigation with private creditors.[53] While more evidence needs to be gathered, results to date suggest that CACs may be seen, if not as a functional equivalent to an actual sovereign bankruptcy procedure, an important means of facilitating a more orderly and less harmful resolution to sovereign debt problems.

Despite the positive results seen from the use of CACs, many existing bond issues do not include them. Bonds issued before 2014 typically will not have a CAC,

---

[52] IMF, 'The International Architecture for Resolving Sovereign Debt Involving Private-Sector Creditors: Recent Developments, Challenges, and Reform Options' (1 October 2020).
[53] ibid.

however, more recent issuances still may not have included one. This situation means that significant shares of countries facing debt crises may undergo difficult debt restructuring processes.

4. Tax Law and Governance

The conditions for realizing the goal of improving domestic fiscal resources for development have been changing in recent years due to changes in global tax law and regulation. Among these developments are modifications in tax treaties and associated institutions. These initiatives have been led by the OECD/G20 Inclusive Framework on Base Erosion and Profit-Shifting (Inclusive Framework) and UN Committee of Experts on International Cooperation in Tax Matters (UN Tax Committee). Together they provide the basis for further international cooperation to combat abusive tax avoidance, which may have positive effects on fiscal resources in developing countries.

A central aim of these developments has been to reduce tax avoidance by multilateral enterprises. In 2017, the United Nations Model bilateral tax treaty gained a new article 12A covering technical service fees. This clause enables developing countries to withhold taxes on technical service fees, which would normally have been excluded for contractors unless they met the standard for permanent establishment.[54] In addition, both the OECD Model Tax Treaty and the UN Model have had individual clauses strengthened and include new general anti-abuse rules.[55]

The UN Committee of Experts on International Cooperation in Tax Matters (UN Tax Committee) has taken various steps to improve developing countries' ability to negotiate and implement tax treaties. Following a request from the G20 Development Working Group, the IMF, OECD, UN, and World Bank Group developed the Platform for Collaboration on Tax.[56] Regional initiatives within Association of South East Asian Nations, the African Tax Administration Forum, the Caribbean Community, and the East African Community have developed models that their members have used to negotiate treaties.[57] Several developing countries have also renegotiated or reviewed existing bilateral tax treaties. Overall, the changes in bilateral tax treaties have tended to expand the definition of permanent establishment, which in theory could increase the tax base in developing countries, however, these changes have been offset by general reductions in tax withholding rates.[58]

---

[54] Martin Hearson, Joy W Ndubai, and Tovony Randriamanalina, 'The Appropriateness of International Tax Norms to Developing Country Contexts' (2020).
[55] ibid.
[56] ibid.
[57] ibid.
[58] ibid.

Within the OECD, two major treaties have been developed to facilitate tax collection. First is the Multilateral Convention on the Mutual Administrative Assistance (MAA) in Tax Matters developed under the OECD and Council of Europe, but open to all jurisdictions.[59] The MAA is designed to streamline the process whereby countries' tax authorities request information on their taxpayers from foreign jurisdictions. Traditionally, those types of requests could be time consuming or might not be acted upon due to incompatibilities between the regulatory standards of different countries. Under the treaty, these types of requests are supposed to be acted upon automatically. Currently, 146 states and jurisdictions have ratified or otherwise participate in the agreement. Once ratified, the agreement becomes effective between the new entrant and all contracting parties. While the numbers of requests occurring have not been massive, they are happening on a more routine basis, which may mean that countries can crack down on tax evasion.[60]

The second treaty is the Multilateral Convention to Implement Tax Treaty Related Measures to prevent Base Erosion and Profit Shifting (Multilateral Instrument), which was developed to support the OECD/G20 Base Erosion and Profit Shifting (BEPS) project. The Multilateral Instrument is a unique international legal measure because it provided a novel solution to the challenge of amending many different bilateral tax treaties. To do so, it provides that each new party agrees that all outstanding bilateral agreements with other parties are amended in accordance with the Multilateral Instrument. As more parties have ratified the Multilateral Instrument, its standards become more widely applied. Currently, seventy-eight states are parties to the treaty.[61]

Despite these developments, significant gaps and inconsistencies exist in global tax law and governance relevant to development. Of relevance are approaches to tax avoidance among DFIs. DFIs may structure investments in ways that avoid tax by governments in jurisdictions where they undertake private sector investments.[62] To prevent such situations, governments could require disclosure by DFIs. Donor countries could also take steps to ensure coherence between tax policies and development policies.

These developments in tax governance and law are occurring alongside tightening of international anticorruption and money laundering regulation. Tax evasion has been made a predicate offence for money laundering.[63] The synergistic

---

[59] Council of Europe and OECD, 'Multilateral Convention on the Mutual Administrative Assistance (MAA) in Tax Matters: Amended by the 2010 Protocol' (1 June 2011).
[60] OECD, 'Exchanges of Information under Automatic Exchange of Information Standard' (Global Forum on Transparency and Exchange of Information for Tax Purposes, 25 July 2022) <https://www.oecd.org/tax/transparency/documents/AEOI-exchanges.pdf> accessed 24 June 2023.
[61] See OECD website <Home page - OECD> accessed 25 June 2023.
[62] Lauri Finér, 'Tax Avoidance in Development Finance: The Case of a Finnfund Investment', in Krishen Mehta and others (eds), *Tax Justice and Global Inequality: Practical Solutions to Protect Developing Country Revenues* (Zed Books 2022) 180–200.
[63] OECD, 'Principle 7: Make Tax Crimes a Predicate Offense for Money Laundering' in OECD, *Fighting Tax Crime: Ten Global Principles* (Paris 2017), <https://www.oecd-ilibrary.org/sites/bda3dbe6-en/index.html?itemId=/content/component/bda3dbe6-en>

approaches to these legal regimes are enabling tighter enforcement of illicit transactions.[64] Improving law enforcement capabilities to tackle these practices together could further support the tax base in many developing countries.

Despite progress on furthering tax cooperation and closing loopholes, a critical limitation of the reforms in tax law and governance is the fact that much of the system is based on bilateral tax treaties, which were designed with the interests of developed countries in mind.[65]

5. Thinking Critically about the Private Sector Role

Given the emphasis of the AAAA and other policy statements on the private sector role in development finance, it is important to consider the expectations more critically. Three main sets of questions will be addressed. First, is to analyse the reasons for limited private sector investment. Second, are concerns about expectations for ESG investment to further sustainable development. Third, are concerns about business practices generally.

a. Limitations on private sector participation

As described above, the private sector has failed to invest anywhere near the amounts required for the SDGs, infrastructure, or climate change finance. There are many reasons for these shortfalls, which makes it difficult to devise a simple solution. At the heart of the concerns is the nature of business as profit seeking. Measures can be taken to encourage and incentivize private sector investment in development, yet to achieve the scale required, much stronger efforts must be deployed. Put differently, market mechanisms alone will not suffice, instead, legislative and regulatory action will be needed.

There are also structural factors limiting private sector investment. These limits are evident both in terms of portfolio and foreign direct investment (FDI). In terms of portfolio investments, despite the increasing resort of developing economy sovereign borrowers to the capital markets, there are significant limitations for investors. Only between twelve and fifteen emerging market or developing countries have sufficiently large and liquid bond markets needed to enable investors to

---

[64] OECD and World Bank, 'Improving Co-operation between Tax Authorities and Anti-corruption Authorities in Combatting Tax Crime and Corruption' (2018) <Improving Co-operation between Tax Authorities and Anti-Corruption Authorities in Combating Tax Crime and Corruption - OECD> accessed 25 June 2023.
[65] Martin Hearson, *Imposing Standards: The North-South Dimension to Global Tax Politics* (Cornell University Press 2021).

develop diversified bond portfolios. As a result of the limited number of sovereign bond issuers, investor appetite is modest.

FDI in developing countries involves a well-known impediment: uncertain and risky investment climates. This concern is as valid in connection with development-related finance as in other business transactions. Paradoxically, while the development finance needs of developing countries are the greatest, it is precisely conditions of underdevelopment that impede such investment. Countries' ability to raise money from private financial sources is positively correlated to their levels of economic development, particularly standards of governance, regulation, and rule of law. As a result, the countries with the most acute development challenges have the least access to private finance.

Consistent with the market-oriented approach to development finance, over the past decade, new efforts have arisen to overcome these limitations. An influential approach is blended finance. Supported by the creation of a variety of national and multilateral DFIs, blended finance is based on the idea of maximizing the degree of voluntary action by the private sector.

The concept is based on recognition of the comparative advantage of private and public sector financing. Rather than approaching the state as the main driver of development assistance, blended finance seeks to compensate for the failure of the market to meet financing needs. Proponents of blended finance view traditional state-based development finance as crowding out the private sector. In contrast, blended financing is designed to 'crowd in' private sector finance by incentivizing private actors to provide financing. A central element to the approach is for DFIs to assume some of the risks of development projects that lead to business reluctance to invest in developing countries. As such, the incentives used in blended finance are calibrated to the amounts needed to get the private sector to invest but not subsidize that participation by providing amounts beyond what is needed.

To support blended finance, the OECD has adopted a set of five principles, which include (1) ensure a development rationale; (2) increase commercial financing; (3) tailor transactions to local contexts; (4) focus on effective partnerships; and (5) monitor for transparency and results.[66] The OECD Evaluation Network is developing methodologies to measure results from blended finance.[67]

Despite these efforts, there are a number of factors that limit the development impact of blended finance at this stage. First, the amounts involved are relatively modest. The OECD reported that in 2018 to 2019, US$50 billion had been

---

[66] OECD, 'Blended Finance Principles Guidance' (29 September 2020) <https://www.oecd.org/officialdocuments/publicdisplaydocumentpdf/?cote=DCD/DAC(2020)42/FINAL&docLanguage=En> accessed 25 June 2023.
[67] OECD, 'Evaluating Blended Finance and Private Sector Support' <https://www.oecd.org/dac/evaluation/evaluating-private-sector-blended-finance.htm> accessed 25 June 2023.

disbursed as blended finance by development agencies.[68] A second issue is the disproportionate concentration of blended financing in middle income countries. The overall share of blended finance for LDCs and lower income countries (LICs) was 12 per cent in 2018–19. The top five recipients were India, Turkey, China, Brazil, and Argentina. A further problem is sectoral distribution. Approximately 58 per cent of financing is concentrated in the energy and finance sectors. In sum, based on available evidence, blended finance has potential to alter the risk profile of investments in developing countries and thereby encourage investment that might otherwise not be made. Thus far, it falls below levels needed to meet the financing requirements and has not overcome the limited private sector contribution to development, particularly in lower income countries.

The nature of infrastructure transactions entails other specific limitations that hinder private finance. In general, private investors are reluctant to invest in large greenfield projects at scale due to difficulties such as budgeting and delivering on time, and challenges such as forecasting given the lack of operating history.[69] The IMF staff have noted that 'currently, climate projects in [emerging markets and developing economies] do not justify the risks for private sector investment flows'.[70] The appeal of these investments may also be limited as 'these types of projects are most likely to attract a small pool of specialized investors demanding high returns in a developing and relatively illiquid asset class, with debt being the main instrument.'[71]

Despite the potential for green finance, there is widespread acceptance of the need for governments to drive the market if it is ever going to achieve scale. Accounting firm PwC notes that 'scaling this investment up will continue to require government intervention to make the business models work and attract investment, whether through subsidies, tax breaks, or other mechanisms.' The IMF staff have noted that appropriate carbon pricing is an 'indispensable' means 'to incentivize the changes needed' to address climate change.

b. Environmental, social, and governance standards

Over the past twenty years, demands for accountability for environmental and social harms caused by international development and business activity have led to the creation of standards pertaining to such matters. Today, environmental, social,

---

[68] OECD, 'Amounts Mobilized from the Private Sector by Official Development Finance 2018–2019' (August 2021) <https://issuu.com/oecd.publishing/docs/amounts-mobilsed-from-the-private-sector-by-dev-fi> accessed 25 June 2023.
[69] PWC, 'Global Infrastructure Trends: Part 2 Developments in Financing' (*PWC*) <https://www.pwc.com/gx/en/industries/capital-projects-infrastructure/publications/infrastructure-trends/global-infrastructure-trends-financing.html> accessed 25 June 2023.
[70] Mobilizing Private Climate Financing (n 21).
[71] ibid.

and governance standards are typically referred to as 'ESG'. An important change has been the convergence of private sector human rights standards and mechanisms with development institutions.[72] Over the past two decades standards for environmental and social accountability have developed and are applied by bilateral and multilateral donors. Ombuds and accountability mechanisms and environmental and social safeguard policies in international financial institutions (IFIs) are indicative of these changes.

While shortcomings remain, the compliance arrangements have led to improved levels of accountability in many respects. Within the MDBs, compliance ombudsmen and inspection functions have matured into established procedures through which actors affected by development projects can seek redress.

At the same time, the field of corporate social responsibility has evolved through the Guiding Principles on Business and Human Rights (UNGP) and the OECD Guidelines on Multinational Corporations (MNE Guidelines). Both frameworks provide for grievance mechanisms. As DFIs have begun supporting private sector development, new standards are emerging, which reflect norms and values of both the development agencies and the private sector human rights standards.

For multinational enterprises, the system of National Contact Points created by the MNE Guidelines has become a forum for actors contesting corporate activity in host countries to seek redress in firms' home jurisdictions. The creation of monitoring bodies such as the UN High Commissioner for Human Rights (UNHCHR) Working Group on Business and Human Rights has added a new system for reviewing state implementation and application of the UNGPs. Despite creating meaningful approaches to accountability, there are gaps and limitations of such processes, particularly in the development context. Those gaps have become more critical as development policy has emphasized the importance of the private sector role.

A challenge to the observance of high standards for social and environmental sustainability is the increase in development institutions discussed earlier. The so-called non-traditional donors have approached these issues differently and in varying degrees.[73] There is evidence that some new multilateral development banks (AIIB) are instituting environmental and social safeguards policies similar to more established IFIs.[74] Yet bilateral donors appear to have resisted these measures on grounds of 'non-interference' with domestic affairs. To illustrate, the BRI is notable for taking a different approach to sustainability standards, which appears

---

[72] Antonio Morelli, 'International Financial Institutions and their Human Rights Silent Agenda: A Forward-looking View on the "Protect, Respect and Remedy" Model in Development Finance' (2020) 36 Am U Int'l L Rev 51.

[73] Bin Gu, 'MCDF: A New Beacon of Multilateralism in Development Finance' (2020) 23 J Int'l Econ L 665–84.

[74] Asian Infrastructure Investment Bank, 'Environmental and Social Framework' <https://www.aiib.org/en/policies-strategies/framework-agreements/environmental-social-framework.html> accessed 25 June 2023.

less rigorous than MDB standards.[75] Similarly, with the increased emphasis on the role of the private sector to development, applicable standards are still developing.

c. Private finance incentives

While difficult to pinpoint its influence, the emergence of the ESG-investing paradigm appears to have shaped views of the role of the private sector in development finance. If most companies can be seen as supporting ESG then they can be seen as suitable actors for advancing development. Belief in the muscle power of ESG to contribute to sustainable development must be read against claims about the size of the market for ESG investments. Serious questions about how ESG investment is tallied have arisen recently.

Following a whistle-blower tip, on 31 May 2022, German prosecutors raided the Deutsche Bank asset management subsidiary DWS Group on suspicions of overstating its green investment portfolio. That case highlighted a particular problem with the way in which asset managers have been calculating their ESG investment exposure. At issue is the practice of 'ESG integration', whereby portfolio managers in non-ESG funds were told by management to use ESG criteria as risk mitigation tools rather than as criteria for screening and *excluding* non-ESG assets.[76] Accordingly, applying the ESG integration concept, Deutsche Bank claimed that it had €459 billion in ESG assets out of its total portfolio of €793 billion. After the whistle-blower's claims were raised, it dropped the practice.

Yet these practices go beyond one firm. The Global Sustainable Investment Alliance, an ESG industry association, reported that in 2020 total ESG assets under management in major economies amounted to US$35 trillion. A 2022 piece in *The Economist* found that, of this amount, approximately US$25.2 trillion was based on the ESG integration computation.[77] Drawing on figures from the Bank of International Settlements instead of the industry association, *The Economist* has reported that total worldwide ESG investments under management in 2021 were approximately US$2.7 trillion.[78]

Aside from the question of the value of ESG investments, another well recognized issue facing the field is the metrics by which ESG adherence is calculated. Currently, dozens of different ESG frameworks are in use. A study of six frameworks found that they used 709 different metrics across sixty-four categories with

---

[75] Hongsong Liu, Yue Xu, and Xinzhu Fan, 'Development Finance with Chinese Characteristics: Financing the Belt and Road Initiative' (2020) 63(2) Revista Brasileira de Política Internacional 1; Lorenzo Jap, 'A Path Toward Sustainable Development Along the Belt and Road' (2021) 24(3) J Int'l Econ L 591.
[76] Henry Tricks, 'In Need of a Clean-up', *The Economist* (London, 23 July 2022).
[77] ibid.
[78] ibid.

only ten categories common to all.[79] In response, efforts are underway to standardize ESG disclosure. The International Sustainability Standards Body, modelled on financial accounting standard setting organizations, has developed frameworks for standardizing ESG disclosures.[80] In the climate change context, the US Securities and Exchange Commission has put forward draft regulations on how firms should disclose their climate risks.[81]

In addition to these concerns about measurement, recent indications suggest that faith in ESG investment as a vehicle for international development have more fundamental problems. Many of the concerns were catalogued in a 2021 piece by Tariq Fancy, formerly head of ESG at BlackRock, the world's largest asset manager.[82] Fancy wrote a devastating account of the inherent contradictions in the ESG paradigm that arise from the fiduciary obligations of both asset managers and corporate boards and officers. Fiduciary duties require these actors to keep safe the assets they hold. The entire ESG paradigm has been based on the assumption that companies that choose sustainable business practices will be more profitable. According to Fancy, the research is ambiguous on this point and in any event the positive evidence for the claim is not robust.

His proposed solution is for governments to regulate in ways that make it more costly for business to choose unsustainable practices. I have made similar arguments elsewhere on the importance of regulation over voluntary corporate social responsibility (CSR) measures.[83] The issue has particular importance in the development context as many developing countries are in need of governance and regulatory improvements. To the extent that ESG proponents contend that voluntary corporate decisions are the answer to the major ESG issues (of which the SDGs are increasingly considered a baseline), they are deflecting attention from the need to improve domestic law and regulation that might mandate firms to follow ESG criteria. A major contradiction of these voluntary efforts is the fact that in many countries, business continuously lobbies against tighter regulation. Empirical research that Fancy co-authored supported the view that if citizens believe the private sector is acting to prevent environmental or social harm, they perceive less need for government action. Advocates for ESG investment rebuff those claims, arguing that they seek to use ESG to complement rather than supplant government regulation. Yet is noteworthy that among the many repeated references to business

---

[79] ibid 2.
[80] IFRS, 'International Sustainability Standards Board' (*IFRS*) <https://www.ifrs.org/groups/international-sustainability-standards-board/> accessed 25 June 2023.
[81] US Securities and Exchange Commission, 'The Enhancement and Standardization of Climate Risk Disclosure for Investors' <https://www.sec.gov/rules/proposed/2022/33-11042.pdf> accessed 25 June 2023.
[82] Tariq Fancy, 'The Secret Diary of a Sustainable Investor' (*Medium*, August 2021) <https://medium.com/@sosofancy/the-secret-diary-of-a-sustainable-investor-part-1-70b6987fa139> accessed 25 June 2023.
[83] Thomas F McInerney, 'Putting Regulation Before Responsibility' (2007) 40 Cornell Int L J 171.

contributing to development in the AAAA, little attention is given to the need to regulate companies better.

Scrutiny of ESG is also growing from a different angle, namely the regulatory and enforcement communities. Following the German raid on DWS, in the US, the Securities and Exchange Commission (SEC) has sued Goldman Sachs based on ESG-related claims. The SEC has created a unit dedicated to countering fraudulent greenwashing claims. In the United Kingdom, the Advertising Standards Agency is scrutinizing ESG marketing and the Financial Conduct Authority starting to scrutinize ESG practices.[84] Overall, it appears that these actions may lead to more rigour in company disclosures around ESG, which could lead to demands for better regulation to promote ESG priorities.

d. The private sector as a reliable development partner

There is a troubling legal paradox raised by the so-called 'Wall Street' consensus[85] on the central role of the private sector in development. That is, how do we reconcile these expectations with the evidence of substantial amounts of corporate malfeasance and misfeasance that occur regularly? Every year, as the seasons pass, widespread instances of fraud and corruption in the private sector emerge and we gaze on as the regulators slap impressive penalties—or often not—on individual firms. What is difficult to assess is whether we are only scratching the surface or the regulators are catching the really bad actors. What is clear, however, is that now that most major multinational corporations (MNCs) now have compliance programmes, legal violations are still commonplace. A deeper question is whether regulatory enforcement is adequate and whether firm-level compliance is the best way to structure regulatory enforcement models particularly around fraud and corruption. Put simply, does management-based regulation rely on unduly optimistic views of firms' propensity to comply?

Studies of the impact of compliance programmes on corporate conduct suggest that, at best, they generate marginal reductions in non-compliance. A review of compliance practices across multiple regulatory topics concluded that evidence for positive impact of compliance systems was limited.[86] As such, should private sector participation in development be based on existing approaches to firm level self-regulation as sufficient or should enhanced regulatory enforcement be a precondition?

---

[84] Harriet Agnew, 'Are Green-themed Funds all They're Cracked Up to Be?' *Financial Times* (London, 21 February 2022).
[85] Celine Tan, 'Private Investments, Public Goods: Regulating Markets for Sustainable Development' (2022) 23 EBOR 241–71.
[86] Christine Parker and Vibeke L Nielsen, 'Corporate Compliance Systems' (2009) 41(1) Admin Soc 3.

If corporate malfeasance is as widespread as evidence suggests it is, should expectations for business' role in financing development change? In considering this question, we should also take into account the fact that corporate fraud, corruption, and malfeasance rates today are occurring *after* the significant shift towards management-based regulatory standards. Viewed in this context, the deleterious role of the private sector in undermining standards of governance through their violations of law is difficult to square with the idea of business as a partner in development without requiring consistent adherence to international and domestic legal standards.

6. Financing Issues Affecting International Law

As one of the principal sources of international law, treaties provide a good basis for analysing applicable financial requirements. Among treaties, multilateral treaties are particularly relevant, because in many cases they involve significant operational aspects that require financing. Financing of multilateral treaties implicates many of the challenges affecting development finance generally, yet also involves specific concerns deriving from their legal nature. To illustrate these challenges, I will first describe the main approaches to financing multilateral treaties. Next, I will describe some of the challenges arising from these approaches, particularly the practice of donor earmarking of their contributions and the disparities in financing that arise due to heterogeneous financing mechanisms.

a. Treaty financing models

The main approaches to treaty financing are similar to those followed by international organizations. Three main models exist: assessed contributions, voluntary contributions, and trust funds.[87] Assessed contributions are used to finance treaty activities in two principal fashions. First involve treaties which assess all member parties for a portion of the costs. The assessments typically follow the scale adopted by the UN General Assembly. The second approach occurs in international organizations which support multilateral treaties as part of their overall responsibilities. Examples include the International Labour Organization, the UNHCHR, and the Food and Agriculture Organization. In those organizations, the member parties contribute to the regular budget of the organization per the assessment scale, with a portion of the budget allocated to treaty-related activities such as meetings of the conferences of parties (COPs), capacity building and technical assistance, and

---

[87] Thomas F McInerney, *Strategic Treaty Management: Practice and Implications* (CUP 2015) (hereafter 'Strategic Treaty Management').

general administrative support. Typically, these regular budgets do not cover all of the costs of treaty activities. Assessed contributions constitute the regular budgets (also called core budgets), which are set pursuant to organizations' strategic or work plans.

The second main approach to treaty financing is voluntary contributions. Over the past two decades, increasing shares of intergovernmental organization (IGO) and treaty budgets are derived from voluntary contributions, which are referred to as extrabudgetary to distinguish them from the budgets approved by the organizational or treaty governing bodies. Voluntary contributions can be used to fund most types of treaty activities, but have gradually come to include matters traditionally funded by core contributions.

The third type of treaty finance involves trust funds. Often these are established under the auspices of an international financial institution or IGO, which act as trustees. Trust funds receive voluntary contributions, often based on a replenishment model, whereby a multiyear budgetary framework is put forward by the trust fund secretariat to which individual donor states make pledges. The pledged funds are pooled and spent in accordance with the budgetary framework.

b. Voluntary contribution concerns

As recognized in many discussions of IGO financing, the shift to voluntary funding has pernicious effects on the effectiveness and legitimacy of the institutions. One driver of this shift has been member state insistence on zero nominal growth budgets for many organizations. Over time this practice has eroded the core budgets of treaties and IGOs responsible for treaties.

Another important effect of voluntary funding is to enable donors to specify what their contributions will finance. In some cases, donors make voluntary grants to programmes or areas of work that are reflected in strategy or work plans. Expenditures are then made by the treaty bodies or IGOs to deliver on those workplans and strategies. This approach gives the staff some degree of control to respond to priorities that may contribute to the effectiveness of treaties overall. Increasingly, however, funds are earmarked for specific purposes donors select. As a result, rather than acting upon plans and strategies set by governing bodies (e.g. COPs) overall, the secretariats respond to the priorities set by individual donors.

When earmarking occurs in IGOs with broad mandates, the specification of activities by individual donors may not be injurious to the effectiveness or legitimacy of the organization. In contrast, when it occurs in relation to legal instruments, different concerns arise. Treaties generally have more specific mandates than IGOs. In many cases, parties are scrutinized for compliance with an agreement. In this context, earmarking of contributions is in tension with the legal obligations.

Evidence form treaties in diverse areas confirms this fear. The UNHCHR has responsibility for managing all of the key UN Human Rights treaties. Gradually, regular budgetary contributions have declined as a percentage of the overall revenues. In 2022, only one-third of the budget is regular with the remainder voluntarily funded. Of these extrabudgetary resources, only 37 per cent were unearmarked. According to UNHCHR, 'the level of earmarking remains high and makes it more difficult for the Office to effectively implement the [OHCHR Management Plan]', which 'means reduced flexibility, higher transaction costs and constraints on the effective response to emerging needs'.[88]

These statements were confirmed by a 2017 UN Office of Internal Oversight Services (OIOS) evaluation. It found that earmarking was a significant funding challenge for the office. The report noted that the proportion of unearmarked funding had decreased from 54 per cent in 2013 to 47 per cent in 2014 and 37 per cent in 2015 and 2021.[89]

Similar findings were made by an independent evaluation of the Global Program of the UN Office on Drugs and Crime (UNODC) to support implementation of UN Convention Against Corruption (UNCAC). The evaluators concurred with UNODC senior management's assertion that delivering results-based management priorities would be feasible if the office received commensurate financial means and was 'in the position to put the funds where they are needed'.[90] The evaluators found that a majority of funds to the programme were earmarked and time bound. More worrisome was the observation that 'it is the donors who in the end, based on their national interests and priorities, decide where the money goes and how it is used'.[91] They also found that the programme management's ability to 'plan long-term and build on accomplishments' was constrained due to the short-term directives of donors. 'Strategic planning, priority setting, and building on the organization's comparative advantages' were compromised as a result. Similar conclusions were reached in a separate independent evaluation of UNODC as a whole by the Multilateral Organization Performance Assessment Network in 2019, which was favourably referenced by the above-mentioned independent evaluators.[92]

---

[88] UNHCHR, 'OHCHR Funding and Budget' <https://www.ohchr.org/en/about-us/funding-and-budget> accessed 25 June 2023.

[89] UN Office of Internal Oversight Services (OIOS), *Evaluation of the Office of the High Commissioner for Human Rights*, UN Economic and Social Council (E/AC51/2017/19, 17 March 2017) (hereafter 'Evaluation of the Office of High Commissioner').

[90] UNODC, 'Independent In-depth Evaluation: Global Program to Prevent and Combat Corruption through Effective Implementation of the United Nations Convention on Corruption in Support of Sustainable Development Goal 16' (June 2021) 26, <https://www.unodc.org/documents/evaluation/indepth-evaluations/2021/Mid_term_Evaluation_Report_GLOZ99.pdf> accessed 25 June 2023.

[91] OIOS, 'Evaluation of the Office of High Commissioner' (n 89).

[92] Multilateral Organization Performance Assessment Network, 'Assessment of Office of the High Commissioner for Human Rights' (April 2019) <https://www.mopanonline.org/assessments/ohchr2017-18/OHCHR Report.pdf> accessed 25 June 2023.

c. Funding competition and imbalances

In addition to problems arising from earmarking voluntary contributions, another concern is competition for donor funds between different instruments and the imbalances in funding provided for different treaties. The resources available to multilateral treaties affect the underlying regulatory effectiveness of treaties. There are several manifestations of this problem.

The availability of trust funds for certain treaties is one illustration of the imbalances that may occur between different treaties. To put it in context, the financial imbalances between different treaty regimes can be considered a product and cause of fragmentation in international law. On one level, different treaty bodies compete with one another for access to funds. The decision to provide much greater funding for some treaties over others puts those agreements on superior footing than other treaties.

Discrepancies in funding can also be illustrated simply in reference to the relative size of funding available for different treaties. Consider the incredibly small portion of the UN budget devoted to human rights, despite the centrality of human rights to the purpose of the organization overall. Only 3 per cent of the UN regular budget goes to human rights. While already under limited resources, Human Rights Council mandates to OHCHR have increased. A review by OIOS of forty-five resolutions randomly selected (out of one hundred) showed that they all requested UNHCHR to implement the decision based on existing resources. Of course, the cost of implementing different treaties may differ, but it seems reasonable base funding allocations on grounds that reflect the legal or regulatory considerations.

The Global Environmental Facility (GEF) illustrates how imbalances can arise through different funding mechanisms. According to the GEF charter, specified treaties are eligible for financing of projects carried out at the national level. Two cases illustrate the challenge. The first concerns the biodiversity-related conventions. The GEF has been designated as the funding mechanism for the Convention on Biological Diversity (CBD), which includes the Nagoya and Cartagena protocols. In addition to the CBD, six other biodiversity-related treaties have been agreed. These include the Ramsar Convention, Convention on International Trade in Endangered Species (CITES), the Convention on Migratory Species, the International Plant Protection Convention, the International Treaty on Plant Genetic Resources for Agriculture, and the World Heritage Convention.

These other biodiversity-related treaties must seek resources for activities that further the CBD. To the extent that many aspects of the other six conventions are consistent with the CBD, there is no necessary substantive issue. The situation does put the CBD in a privileged position, however. While one can argue that certain treaties like the CBD or UNFCCC have greater importance or larger mandates and thus deserve greater emphasis, the situation seems unfair and hard to defend on principled or effectiveness grounds.

One can see the challenge treaty bodies face here. A resolution from the CITES COP illustrates the parties' frustration. It refers to efforts of the CITES Secretariat to 'facilitate access to the Global Environmental Facility (GEF) funding for GEF-eligible projects relevant for CITES' and to continue to closely collaborate with the GEF Secretariat, the Secretariat of the CBD and the Biodiversity Liaison Group on the issue of gaining access to GEF funding'. It also invited the GEF Council to take note of resolutions and decisions of the CITES COP in developing the next GEF Biodiversity Strategy. The CITES COP also decided to convey to the CDB COP it taking into account CITES' objectives and priorities in support of the Aichi Targets in the CBD Strategic Framework and to relate this information to the GEF. This does not seem an optimal approach.

A similar situation is evident in the chemicals and wastes field. The GEF provides financing for projects related to the Stockholm Convention on Persistent Organic Pollutants and the Minimata Convention on Mercury, but not the Basel Convention on Hazardous Wastes or Rotterdam Convention on Pesticides. The sense of this approach is difficult to understand given that the Basel, Rotterdam, and Stockholm Conventions have merged many of their administrative and governance functions as a way to create synergies and economize on costs. There does not appear to be any substantive rationale for this imbalance.

Competition is also evident in treaty bodies' posture in relation to other treaties. Even if the allocation of funds is not a zero-sum game, each treaty body may implicitly seek to have their cause moved to the top of the pile in the donors' inboxes. At the national level, governments charge different ministries with responsibility for specific treaties. This situation may pit officials in one ministry against one another. The problem of imbalances in funding can be seen within specific organizations. It may reflect both substantive and geographic differences. For UNHCHR, as funding from central offices has been reduced, field offices have had to do more fundraising as found by OIOS in its evaluation. This situation may lead to some country offices or regions having more funding than others, which may not correspond to the level of need or priority the human rights issue deserves.[93]

The common thread connecting these diverse cases is the fact that decisions about which treaties receive funding and in what amounts is often a function of political vicissitudes, power imbalances, or accident rather than any dispassionate evaluation of the relative regulatory, governance, or development importance of particular legal instruments.

Consistent with the findings of the OIOS evaluation of UNHCHR, one approach to managing these choices better is through strategic planning and priority

---

[93] OIOS, 'Evaluation of the Office of High Commissioner' (n 89) 25.

setting.[94] The utility of such approaches derives from an overall understanding of the relevant needs and purpose of specific treaties. Ear-marking of contributions undermines those approaches.

7. Conclusion

The logic of including a financial framework to support the 2030 Agenda and SDG implementation was premised on the understanding that significant resources would be necessary to accomplishing the international community's ambitions. Seven years into process, it is clear the amounts that have been raised have been dramatically lower than hoped. The AAAA made clear that national resources were to be an essential source of financing, yet the greatest hopes were placed on the private sector. For reasons described in this article, those expectations appear substantially unrealistic.

Not only have overall amounts of private finance fallen far below the forecasted needs but what resources have been mobilized from the private sector appear to have gone to the countries that are most economically well off. That conclusion would be problematic enough were it not for the fact that the greatest financial needs are in the poorest countries. A further limitation is the fact that what investment has been mobilized has been concentrated in economic and climate adaptation infrastructure needs. The role of the private sector as a trusted development partner is belied by the complete failure of any firms to participate in the DSSI during the COVID-19 global public health emergency. While infrastructure to prevent climate-related disasters arguably could benefit the most vulnerable people in developing countries, it is abundantly clear that the agenda of 'leave no one behind', has not been advanced by private sector investment. Nor does available evidence suggest that it can be.

The other main candidate for the private sector's contribution to sustainable development, ESG, has likewise been shown lacking. First, the amount of true ESG investment is approximately one per cent of global portfolio investment. While it is possible that amounts could be increased over time, structural limitations of financial markets suggest that it is unlikely to ever generate the horsepower needed to drive the major economic and political transformations needed to accomplish the SDGs.

An obvious implication of this assessment of the private sector contribution to development finance is that governments must do more. Efforts to expand the tax base in developing countries is an important part of the agenda, but reality quickly brings us to the proverbial chicken-and-egg problem. Without economic growth

---

[94] Strategic Treaty Management (n 87).

to expand the tax base (making the pie bigger), better tax law and governance will only maximize returns from a limited set of resources. Compounding that problem is the structure of the international tax system based on bilateral tax treaties, which fosters tax competition that leads to reduced marginal tax rates. The constraints on domestic resource mobilization also makes governance reforms needed for FDI more difficult to achieve.

Expanding ODA is another needed step, yet the strain of COVID-19 countercyclical fiscal policies and subsequent monetary tightening will place upward limits on available financing. At the same time, as the climate crisis becomes daily front page news, governments will increasingly shift portions of their aid to climate change adaptation and mitigation, notwithstanding additionality commitments.

All of these considerations lead to an unpleasant set of conclusions. Increasingly, it appears that a two-tiered world is emerging, whereby developed countries and larger middle-income countries can gain access to resources needed to address their major development concerns, particularly around infrastructure and climate finance. For these countries, private investment will indeed be a significant factor in their efforts. Even though their expenditures will likely continue to lag the full amounts needed, they will achieve some approximation of the needed measures.

For the most vulnerable countries, including LDCs, SIDS, and lower middle income countries available financing will fall far short of what is required. China's BRI will likely provide needed financing for infrastructure, however, debt sustainability challenges have been raised in regards to those transactions. The evidence of the limited impact of private finance on these poorer countries should be sufficient now to discard the illusion that the private sector can close the gap for climate or infrastructure investment. Social development, a core of the 'leave no one behind' agenda, will require significant aid. This focus may help overcome the existential doubts about the utility of ODA when confronting the massive development needs that exist.

Given the critical role of multilateral treaties within the SDGs, the fragmented financial arrangements and unbalanced allocation of resources between different agreements presents another challenge. It is not at all clear that funding for the multilateral treaties underlying the SDGs is being applied in proportion to the relative importance of those instruments to sustainable development.

The urgency of addressing the priorities in the SDGs is becoming more apparent given the current crises facing the world. Food shortages, inflation, supply chain disruptions, and growth slowdowns will all affect state resources for development. Recessions in developed markets are likely to reduce the appetite for the private sector to engage in development related projects.

Ultimately, the incredible shortfall in the estimated financial needs for the SDGs will have to factor in the deliberations about the post-2030 sustainable development agenda. It is one thing to develop stretch goals, but another to advance a financial plan for the goals which falls short by 75 per cent or more. This conclusion is not to say that the underlying goals are not appropriate—many are rooted in international law, after all—but that much more realistic planning will be required to put these goals into action.

16
Responsibilities and Public-Private Partnerships in Infrastructure

Humberto Cantú Rivera[*]

1. Introduction

Infrastructure has traditionally been a pivotal aspect of the economy, playing a central role in economic and social development. In general terms, infrastructure creates employment and incentivizes public and private investment in projects that contribute to social development, and in some cases, infrastructure itself is a pre-condition to economic and social development, contributing to conditions that lead to social well-being. This is the case when infrastructure projects focus on solving different types of public deficiencies, such as a lack of infrastructure to provide education, health, water, or sanitation services; access to the internet; or housing, among others. Indeed, it is important to note that infrastructure is not just about constructing buildings, airports, or roads. Instead, it should be understood as 'a sophisticated network linking multiple infrastructure assets and corridors to streamline the movement of goods, data and people, for commercial, economic and social benefit'.[1]

Infrastructure has also traditionally been a focus of public service and investment. However, as the private sector has assumed more public duties and involved itself in financing different types of infrastructural projects, its development has become more widespread as new sources of financing and expertise that would otherwise not be easily accessible, become available. This has been enhanced by the United Nations' (UN) call to promote private engagement in issues that would normally be the focus of state action, in an effort to contribute to sustainable development.[2] Yet, despite the growing involvement of both public and private sectors in infrastructural development, international legal scholarship has only recently— and scarcely—begun to address the issue.[3]

---

[*] Professor, Faculty of Law and Social Sciences and Director, Human Rights and Business Institute of the University of Monterrey (UDEM, Mexico), LLD, Université Panthéon-Assas Paris II.
[1] UN General Assembly, *Transforming our World: The 2030 Agenda for Sustainable Development* (A/RES/70/1, 25 September 2015) (hereafter '2030 Agenda').
[2] ibid.
[3] Some recent examples include Michael B Likosky, *Law, Infrastructure, and Human Rights* (CUP 2006); Emma Palmer, 'Regulating Infrastructure: Human Rights and the Sustainable Development

Indeed, beyond international economic law and international financial institutions, there has been a relatively modest engagement of academia on the role of international law vis-à-vis infrastructure. While this chapter does not set out to cover the many areas of international law that may intersect with infrastructure and development, it aims to contribute to this topic by analysing two of the main branches of international law that have started to explore the relationship with infrastructure, while also addressing the more traditional question of responsibility. In that regard, section 2 addresses the inherently complex position of infrastructure between the need to achieve economic and social development, and the perceived 'limitations' it may face in relation to international human rights law. Furthermore, section 3 covers the distinction between state obligations and business responsibilities, taking into consideration the particular characteristics of infrastructure and the specific challenges presented by public-private partnerships in international law, especially from the angle of business and human rights.

2. Infrastructure in International Law: Between Development and Human Rights?

Infrastructure is a concept that links different disciplines, particularly given that it involves economic, environmental, and social dimensions. However, within international law, it has become a reference point that revolves primarily around economic development and its implications for society. In this regard, there are two basic approaches to infrastructure: first, that it is necessary to promote economic development that consequently yields social benefits; and second, that the focus of infrastructure should respond to human needs rather than exclusively economic considerations.

This implies that there are two questions that are being considered, both of which are the focus of the present section: first, should infrastructure be understood only from a strict point of view focused on economic development without further considerations? Or, second, should infrastructure be planned on the basis of satisfying human needs, particularly human rights? The traditional approach of infrastructure has occurred in the context of (economic) development, although recent initiatives have brought it closer to a position where it has an inextricable relation with sustainability; and yet, it has been a consideration within international human rights law for the past thirty years, where the relationship between infrastructure development and its impact on different human rights—and notably economic, social, and cultural rights—has been a subject of constant analysis. This

---

Goals in Myanmar' (2021) 21(3) HRL Rev 588; see also Lisa Clarke, *Public-Private Partnerships and Responsibility under International Law: A Global Health Perspective* (Routledge 2016).

section addresses both themes, in an effort to locate infrastructure between the distinct concepts of development and human rights.

a. Infrastructure in the context of development

Infrastructure has traditionally been understood as a pre-condition to development, particularly when the latter is considered exclusively from an economic perspective. Indeed, without infrastructure, goods and services cannot be provided, making it a backbone of human society and the economy.[4] However, for all its economic relevance, it should also be perceived as an instrument aimed at promoting and enhancing social and environmental benefits.

This discursive transition from a purely economic focus to one that is more integral and that encompasses environmental and social considerations, reveals an important gap in the way in which different areas of international law understand the role of infrastructure. On the one hand, it is clear that the link with the concept of development and its expansion towards sustainability posit an understanding of infrastructure that revolves around putting people and the environment in the centre. On the other hand, the challenge of securing changes in other areas of international law that have been intrinsically linked to development, most notably trade and investment, highlight how the conceptual and normative frameworks within which infrastructure is understood challenge the possibility of ensuring a uniform transition towards sustainability. It is between these two extremes that this section addresses how infrastructure is perceived.

The turn of the millennium and the rise in prominence of sustainability marked a change in the landscape of development, especially through the need to integrate social and environmental considerations to development projects, and particularly in relation to infrastructure. With the adoption of the Millennium Development Goals[5] (MDGs) to combat poverty, the inclusion of non-economic concerns to infrastructural projects became more prevalent—or at least more visible. In the last report on the MDGs in 2015, for example, infrastructural needs were mentioned in relation to education, health, water, and the internet, highlighting their relevance

---

[4] OHCHR, 'Baseline Study on the Human Rights Impacts and Implications of Mega-Infrastructure Investment' (2017) 9.

[5] The Millennium Development Goals (MDGs), which were in place between 2005 and 2015, and were the predecessors to the Sustainable Development Goals (SDGs), focused on eight thematic priorities: eradicating extreme poverty and hunger; achieving universal primary education; promoting gender equality and empowering women; reducing child mortality; improving maternal health; combating HIV/AIDS, malaria, and other diseases; ensuring environmental sustainability; and forging a global partnership for development. The MDGs were developed as a result of the adoption of the UN Millennium Declaration; see UN General Assembly, *United Nations Millennium Declaration* (A/RES/55/2, 8 September 2000).

for creating economic opportunities and delivering basic social services.[6] These elements, and the fundamental role that infrastructure plays for the economy and society, led to a fuller integration of the issue into the sustainable development agenda, marking a clear step forward towards its inclusion in international instruments and policy-making efforts.

The adoption of the Sustainable Development Goals[7] (SDGs) in 2015 by the UN General Assembly facilitated such an integration. In particular, SDG 9 calls relevant stakeholders to build resilient infrastructure, promote inclusive and sustainable industrialization, and foster innovation.[8] The specific targets in relation to that SDG revolve around the social and environmental dimensions of sustainability, as part of an over-arching strategy to link them with the economic focus of infrastructure and industry. For instance, there are references to developing infrastructure to support economic development and human well-being, to upgrading infrastructure to make it environmentally sound, and particularly to facilitate infrastructural development in developing countries through financial, technological, and technical support.[9]

Other SDGs also address the issue of infrastructure. Goal 2, which focused on ending hunger, achieving food security, improving nutrition, and promoting sustainable agriculture, refers to the need to increase investment in rural infrastructure.[10] Goal 5, on achieving gender equality and empowering all women and girls, also refers to the issue, with a focus on recognizing and valuing the unpaid care and domestic work through the provision of public services, infrastructure, and social protection policies.[11] Goal 7, on ensuring access to affordable, reliable, sustainable, and modern energy for all, also makes reference to the issue, through the promotion of investment in energy infrastructure[12] and the expansion of infrastructure and upgrade technology in developing countries.[13] As a series of targets related to different objectives, this expanded focus on the role of infrastructure shows its cross-cutting nature and relevance to achieving a type of sustainable development that puts people and their needs in the centre.

Yet, one important aspect that needs to be considered is the role of international law in relation to infrastructure and development. While the SDGs represent the multilateral and political perspective on sustainability, the *mise en oeuvre*

---

[6] United Nations, 'The Millennium Development Goals Report 2015' (2015) <https://www.un.org/millenniumgoals/2015_MDG_Report/pdf/MDG%202015%20rev%20(July%201).pdf> accessed 25 June 2023.
[7] 2030 Agenda (n 2).
[8] ibid Goal 9.
[9] ibid.
[10] ibid Goal 2.a.
[11] ibid Goal 5.4.
[12] ibid Goal 7.a.
[13] ibid Goal 7.b.

(implementation) of infrastructure projects, regardless of their sustainable character, depends largely on (private) contracting between states and international financial institutions, or is a consequence of international trade and investment agreements.[14] This can have an important impact on the characterization of infrastructure as 'sustainable', as the inclusion of social and environmental perspectives have traditionally faced significant obstacles when transferred to international economic instruments or to other private development tools.

In the context of international financial institutions, for example, and particularly of multilateral development banks, there has been growing recognition of, and alignment with, international social and environmental standards as part of their sustainability strategies. For example, the World Bank's private sector arm, the International Finance Corporation, included in its 2012 Policy on Environmental and Social Sustainability specific references to human rights and focused on preventing harm to people and planet, enhancing sustainability and promoting positive development outcomes.[15] In the Americas, the Inter-American Development Bank highlights in its Environmental and Social Policy Framework the need to respect human rights as part of its commitment to environmental and social sustainability.[16] The '2009 Safeguard Policy Statement' of the Asian Development Bank also makes reference to the need to protect the rights of people likely to be affected or marginalized by the development process.[17]

However, critics such as Jessica Evans argue that, 'IFIs [International Financial Institutions] do very little to encourage or support governments to protect their people from corporate abuse, shy away from human rights due diligence, and … fail to ensure remedy for abuse.'[18] Indeed, in many cases the IFIs only refer to specific human rights (such as labour, indigenous peoples, and, in some cases, resettlement) and rarely recognize the relevance of human rights and environmental due diligence as a central component of their safeguard policies, or as a contractual requirement to be included in agreements and executed for specific development projects. The same can be said of international trade and investment agreements where, despite progress on labour rights and environmental protection in recent

---

[14] See Andria Naudé-Fourie, 'SDG 9: Build Resilient Infrastructure, Promote Inclusive and Sustainable Industrialization and Foster Innovation' in Jonas Ebbeson and Ellen Hey (eds), *The Cambridge Handbook of the Sustainable Development Goals and International Law* (CUP 2022) 231–57. For a general perspective on the role of private international law in relation to the SDGs, see Vivienne Bath, 'SDG 9: Industry, Innovation and Infrastructure' in Ralf Michaels, Verónica Ruiz Abou-Nigm, and Hans van Loon (eds), *The Private Side of Transforming our World: UN Sustainable Development Goals 2030 and the Role of Private International Law* (Intersentia 2021) 283–316.

[15] International Finance Corporation, 'International Finance Corporation's Policy on Environmental and Social Sustainability' (1 January 2012) paras 9, 12.

[16] Inter-American Development Bank, 'Environmental and Social Policy Framework' (2020) para 1.3.

[17] Asian Development Bank, 'Safeguard Policy Statement' (2009) para 14.

[18] Jessica Evans, 'The Record of International Financial Institutions on Business and Human Rights' (2016) 1(2) Bus Hum Rights J 327.

examples, most of them routinely ignore conceptual and practical elements that could lead to more sustainable investment and trade practices,[19] including investor obligations and public-interest regulation, and access to remedy for persons affected by development projects.[20] Without a more systematic integration of these environmental and social safeguards and obligations in the normative structures of international trade and investment agreements, it will be challenging for development projects to consider such elements beyond discourse, and fully include them in the planning and execution of infrastructure development.

The evolution of the idea of development under international law towards sustainability presents inherent conceptual challenges. In particular, it highlights the need to adapt the concept of development to a role that is more closely aligned with international human rights and environmental standards,[21] and that has been strongly advocated by the international human rights community. Within this context, the topic of infrastructure has progressively become more visible, especially in light of the different contact points that it shares with human rights in general, and with many economic, social, and cultural rights in particular.

b. Infrastructure in international human rights law

Infrastructure was not originally an explicit area of focus of international human rights law, despite the inherent links between development projects and their impact on human rights. However, as globalization became the prevalent economic model and different international financial institutions started to promote infrastructure development in the Global South, the issue became much more apparent.[22] Indeed, infrastructure is a pre-condition of social and economic development, making it a precondition for the realization of human rights. And yet, infrastructure presents inherent risks to human rights and these need to be properly

---

[19] See, for example, the United States-Mexico-Canada Agreement (USMCA), the successor to the North American Free Trade Agreement (NAFTA), where there are explicit references to labour and environmental standards, but where responsible business conduct and other relevant elements are merely presented in a recommendatory nature. USMCA, 'Protocol Replacing the North American Free Trade Agreement with the Agreement between the United States of America, the United Mexican States, and Canada' (30 November 2018) (entered into force 1 July 2020).

[20] See Nicolas M Perrone, 'Bridging the Gap between Foreign Investor Rights and Obligations: Towards Reimagining the International Law on Foreign Investment' (2022) 7(3) Bus Hum Rights J 375; General Assembly, *Human Rights-Compatible International Investment Agreements: Report of the Working Group on the Issue of Human Rights and Transnational Corporations and other Business Enterprises* (A/76/238, 27 July 2021) para 3.

[21] Humberto Cantú Rivera, 'Avanzar Hacia el Cumplimiento del ODS 9: sobre la Vinculación de la Infraestructura, la Industria y la Innovación con el Respeto a los Derechos Humanos' in Eduardo Ferrer Mac-Gregor and Nuria González Martín (eds), *Emergencia Sanitaria por Covid-19: Agenda 2030 para el Desarrollo Sostenible (II)* (IIJ-UNAM 2021) 65–70.

[22] See John Gerard Ruggie, *Just Business: Multinational Corporations and Human Rights* (W W Norton 2013) xv–ff (hereafter 'Just Business').

understood and addressed to ensure the protection and full realization of human rights.

International and regional human rights systems have addressed this issue in different ways. For instance, the UN human rights system has led different efforts to facilitate the understanding of the human rights obligations of states in the context of infrastructure development, notably through the work of UN Special Procedures and UN treaty bodies. Within them, there has been a particular focus on the issue from economic, social, and cultural rights mandate-holders, where infrastructure development is often crucial to contribute to their progressive realization. For example, the Special Rapporteur on the Right to Adequate Housing has addressed this issue in several reports, starting with its 2009 report on mega events. While tracing the roots of infrastructure development in the context of the Olympic Games, she noted how a shift took place in the 1980s to promote involvement of the private sector for urban infrastructure renewal and real-estate investments.[23] While the positive economic effects are well known, the Special Rapporteur argued that the impacts of mega events on the enjoyment of the right to adequate housing are unclear, particularly considering the recurring allegations of 'mass forced evictions and displacement for infrastructural development and city renewal, reduced affordability of housing as a result of gentrification, sweeping operations against the homeless, and criminalization and discrimination of marginalized groups'.[24]

The Special Rapporteur on the Human Rights to Safe Drinking Water and Sanitation has consistently referenced infrastructure in the annual reports submitted to the UN Human Rights Council or General Assembly. When addressing megaprojects, for example, he stated that:

> The human rights to water and sanitation are relevant not only to national planning exercises in the water sector but should also be considered in other national development planning and infrastructure development involving projects that may have an impact on water availability and quality, among other elements of the normative content of the rights. It is important that water and sanitation, in particular the impact on access to those services, are considered when it comes to strategies and plans of action, even in a seemingly unrelated sector such as infrastructure development.[25]

---

[23] Human Rights Council, *Report of the Special Rapporteur on Adequate Housing as a Component of the Right to an Adequate Standard of Living, and on the Right to Non-discrimination in this Context, Raquel Rolnik* (A/HRC/13/20, 18 December 2009) paras 2–3.
[24] ibid para 6.
[25] General Assembly, *Report of the Special Rapporteur on the Human Rights to Safe Drinking Water and Sanitation* (A/74/197, 19 July 2019) para 48.

The issue has also been addressed in the context of the right to education, where the Special Rapporteur on the Right to Education has elaborated on the role of the private sector in educational infrastructure, particularly given that investment through public-private partnerships may be necessary to improve educational quality. A recent report stated that '[o]utsourcing non-educational services allows the private sector to provide services at costs that Governments can rarely match.... It must be recognized, however, that the provision of non-educational services and constructing educational establishments in accordance with agreed norms and standards is a factor in quality education.'[26] In addressing education in the digital age in a separate report, the Special Rapporteur noted that the cost of investing in technological infrastructure to contribute to the realization of the right to education was one of the barriers that needed to be addressed, but cautioned against facilitating unregulated private investment, as it could exacerbate disparity in the access to quality education.[27]

Beyond economic, social, and cultural rights, other UN Special Rapporteurs have also addressed the impact that infrastructure development can have on the respect, protection, and fulfilment of human rights of vulnerable groups or at-risk populations. For example, in a 2003 report on the impact of large-scale or major development projects on indigenous peoples' rights, the Special Rapporteur on the Rights of Indigenous Peoples observed that whenever such developments occur in areas occupied by indigenous peoples,

> their communities will undergo profound social and economic changes that are frequently not well understood, much less foreseen, by the authorities in charge of promoting the projects. Large-scale development projects will inevitably affect the living conditions of indigenous peoples. Sometimes the impact will be beneficial, very often it is devastating, but it is never negligible.[28]

Indeed, as will be explored below, the Inter-American Court of Human Rights has grappled with these very issues in several cases involving violations of the right to free, prior and informed consultation and consent in the context of development projects undertaken in the territory of indigenous peoples, leading to the development of an extensive jurisprudence on State due diligence obligations vis-à-vis the role of non-State actors in development.

---

[26] General Assembly, *Report of the Special Rapporteur on the Right to Education* (A/70/342, 26 August 2015) para 63.

[27] Human Rights Council, *Report of the Special Rapporteur on the Right to Education* (A/HRC/32/37, 6 April 2016) paras 36–38.

[28] Commission on Human Rights, *Report of the Special Rapporteur on the Situation of Human Rights and Fundamental Freedoms of Indigenous People, Rodolfo Stavenhagen, submitted in accordance with Commission Resolution 2001/65* (E/CN4/2003/90, 21 January 2003) para 7.

The Special Rapporteur on Human Rights Defenders has also shed light on the issue of development and infrastructure projects, and especially on the role of private security companies and their impact on human rights. In this regard, one of the reports identifies several lines of action that companies involved in development projects should take vis-à-vis their private security forces, including assessing the risk of their involvement for potentially affected communities; the need to ensure that they receive adequate training and have mechanisms to report and investigate any allegation of abuse; and particularly, developing their work in line with relevant international standards, including the Voluntary Principles on Security and Human Rights and the International Code of Conduct for Private Security Service Providers.[29]

UN human rights treaty bodies have also explored the topic of infrastructure. For example, the Committee on the Rights of Persons with Disabilities has addressed the issue of accessibility in infrastructure, recalling that there is an obligation to ensure access to all newly designed, built or produced objects, infrastructure, goods, products, and services, which is different from the obligation to remove barriers and ensure access to existing services open to the general public.[30] This implies taking measures from the design phase to promote equality and non-discrimination in practice.

Other UN agencies and programmes have also considered the critical role of infrastructure for the realization of human rights. In the field of disaster-risk reduction, for instance, the Child Rights and Business Principles (CRBP) developed jointly by UN International Children's Emergency Fund (UNICEF), Global Compact, and Save The Children touch upon the issue through Principle 7, focused on the business responsibility to respect and support children's rights in relation to the environment and to land acquisition and use.[31] Related to this, UNICEF has focused much of its work in some natural disaster-prone regions to the development of resilient infrastructure jointly with the private sector.[32] The UN Special Rapporteur on the Right to Development has also briefly addressed the issue, focusing part of a report on the need to involve persons with disabilities and their organizations in disaster planning and response, so that they can be contemplated and their needs met in terms of access to physical infrastructure

---

[29] General Assembly, *Report of the Special Rapporteur on the Situation of Human Rights Defenders* (A/68/262, 5 August 2013) para 60.

[30] Committee on the Rights of Persons with Disabilities, *General Comment No 2 (2014). Article 9: Accessibility* (CRPD/C/GC/2, 22 May 2014) para 24.

[31] UNICEF, Global Compact, and Save The Children, 'Children's Rights and Business Principles' (2012) Principle 7.

[32] See, for example, Tamara Plush and Jen Stephens, UNICEF, 'Every Country Protected; Every Child Resilient' (2022), where the authors explain the importance of child-centred, disaster-risk reduction efforts, particularly in the development of resilient infrastructure <https://www.unicef.org/media/120636/file/UNICEF%20DRR%20in%20Action%20-%20Every%20country%20protected.%20Every%20child%20resilient.pdf> accessed 25 June 2023.

relevant for those situations.[33] In addition, Principle 5 of the CRBP addresses the responsibility of business to ensure that products and services are safe and that they support children's rights through them, which refers to the importance of taking steps to maximize accessibility and availability of products and services that are essential to children.[34] In practice, this has also translated into efforts to foster sustainable and accessible infrastructure and urban planning that is adapted to the needs of children.[35] These examples highlight the growing concern about infrastructure development for human rights, and the need to capitalize on opportunities that it may bring to foster human rights realization and ensure equality and non-discrimination.

A different approach has been adopted by regional human rights systems, reflecting the distinct functions they perform compared to UN treaty bodies and special procedures. In the context of the Inter-American Human Rights System, for example, the Inter-American Court of Human Rights has made indirect references to infrastructure development in several judgments related to extractive and commercial activities. In these decisions they have consistently recalled states' obligations to prevent, investigate, sanction, and redress any human rights violations that may occur as a result of such projects.

While several early cases focused on indigenous peoples' right to property in the context of infrastructure development,[36] more recent cases have focused on the impact of development projects and extractive industries on different human rights, and their implications in relation to the human rights obligations of the state. In *Saramaka*, for example, the Court explicitly defined three safeguards that should be taken into account by the state in relation to the impacts of economic activities (logging and mining) on the rights of indigenous peoples: ensure the effective participation of the members of the indigenous people regarding any development or investment plan within their territory; guarantee that any benefits resulting from the project will be shared with them; and the obligation to supervise prior environmental and social impact assessments prior to the granting of any concession.[37]

---

[33] General Assembly, *Report of the Special Rapporteur on the Right to Development* (A/74/163, 15 July 2019) para 43.

[34] ibid Principle 5.

[35] See, for example, Sudeshna Chatterjee and others, 'Evaluation of UNICEF Work for Children in Urban Settings' (UNICEF, 2020). Also, Sudeshna Chatterjee, 'How UNICEF could Engage with Urban Planning to Address Issues of the Environment and Unplanned Urban Growth' (*Global Development Commons*, 2021) <https://gdc.unicef.org/resource/how-unicef-could-engage-urban-planning-address-issues-environment-and-unplanned-urban> accessed 25 June 2023.

[36] See, generally, Humberto Cantú Rivera, 'Towards a Global Framework on Business and Human Rights, Indigenous Peoples, and their Right to Consultation and Free, Prior and Informed Consent' in Claire Wright and Alexandra Tomaselli (eds), *The Prior Consultation of Indigenous Peoples in Latin America: Inside the Implementation Gap* (Routledge 2019) 27–40; see also, *Case of Kichwa Indigenous People of Sarayaku v Ecuador* [27 June 2012] (Merits and Reparations) Judgment (I/A Court HR) Series C No 245, where the state defended its power to determine the need for infrastructure development in the context of oil activities affecting indigenous peoples' territory.

[37] *Case of the Saramaka People v Suriname* [28 November 2007] Preliminary Objections (Merits, Reparations, and Costs) Judgment (I/A Court HR) Series C No 172 [129].

In *Kaliña and Lokono Peoples*, where the construction of a highway as part of a mining project had an impact on different rights of the indigenous community that inhabited the area, including on the right to food,[38] the Court reiterated its position on the three safeguards, while also highlighting that businesses operating in the area must pay special attention when human rights are violated, particularly by identifying and assessing any human rights impacts that may be caused by their operations and activities.[39]

The Inter-American Commission on Human Rights (IACHR) has also touched upon the topic of infrastructure or development projects, notably in its 2015 thematic report on indigenous peoples and afro-descendent communities in the context of extraction, exploitation, and development activities,[40] which it understands as 'any activity that can affect the lands, territory, or natural resources of any indigenous peoples or afro-descendent community, especially any proposal related to the exploration of natural resources'.[41] While not departing from the bases established by the Inter-American Court in its jurisprudence (such as the safeguards of consultation and consent, prior impact assessments and benefit sharing), and recognizing that development activities can contribute to overcoming poverty and inequality and promoting economic development processes and productive investment,[42] the Commission underscored how development cannot occur at the expense of indigenous peoples and afro-descendent communities' rights.[43]

To some extent, the approach of both human rights systems reveals the explicit concerns that exist under international human rights law in relation to development projects, and particularly infrastructure and natural resources extraction. It also reveals tensions, particularly if the notion of development is limited to economic outputs: is the state free to define alone when and how development takes place, as it has been commonly argued before the Inter-American Court of Human Rights? Should the state and the companies with which it promotes development be held liable for adverse human rights impacts? What is the role of international law in this regard? The next section addresses some of these concerns, particularly

---

[38] *Case of the Kaliña and Lokono Peoples v Suriname* (Merits, Reparations, and Costs) Judgment (I/A Court HR) Series C No 309 [92]. While it was not addressed explicitly by the Court, such an impact can be derived from the following section of the judgment:

> Regarding the adverse impact of the mining operations in the nature reserve, the hunting and fishing activities, which were traditional in the area, have declined considerably. In this regard, the noise and vibrations caused by the trucks and the dynamite explosions, the contamination of land and streams, and the destruction of fruit-bearing trees caused the wildlife to flee that the indigenous peoples hunted and fished to feed the members of the local communities. Also, access to the area of the mining concessions was prohibited to the indigenous peoples and to any other unauthorized person.

[39] ibid paras 225–26.
[40] IACHR, 'Indigenous Peoples, Afro-descendent Communities, and Natural Resources: Human Rights Protection in the Context of Extraction, Exploitation, and Development Activities' (2015).
[41] ibid para 12.
[42] ibid para 15.
[43] ibid para 23.

in light of how the two notions have evolved under the logic of the obligations of states and the responsibilities of business enterprises in the field of human rights.

3. Infrastructure and the Roles of States and Businesses: From Dichotomy to Convergence?

The issue of the responsibility of non-state actors under international law, and particularly under international human rights law, has seen a profound shift in the past two decades.[44] The debate on business and human rights in the early 2000s and its evolution over the following years, led to a distinction between state duties and business responsibilities that to a large extent served as a functional dichotomy. The failure of one of the early projects on the topic at the UN, among other factors, prompted the effort to expand existing state duties under international law to private actors. While a distinction is workable in most cases, the UN initiatives did not expressly address the scenario of where states and businesses become partners for the execution of a given project, which happens to occur often in the context of infrastructure development. This section traces the development of distinct duties and responsibilities between states and business enterprises, prior to addressing the situation of a convergence between public and private actors.

a. State duties versus business responsibilities: A functional dichotomy

It is a truism to say that states should regulate the activities of business enterprises; after all, not only do international and regional conventions include state duties to ensure human rights vis-à-vis non-state actors,[45] but the main international instruments addressing the relationship between economic activities and human rights also recognize the existence of a state duty to protect human rights, including through legislation, regulation, and adjudication.[46] While that framing may be minimal compared to the more expansive approach to state duties developed by UN human rights treaty bodies through their interpretive function,[47] where duties

---

[44] See, for example, Surya Deva, 'The UN Guiding Principles on Business and Human Rights and its Predecessors: Progress at a Snail's Pace?' in Ilias Bantekas and Michael Ashley Stein (eds), *The Cambridge Companion to Business & Human Rights Law* (CUP 2021) 145–72.

[45] Human Rights Committee, *General Comment No 31: The Nature of the General Legal Obligation imposed on States Parties to the Covenant* (CCPR/C/21/Rev1/Add13, 29 March 2004) para 8.

[46] Human Rights Council, *Guiding Principles on Business and Human Rights: Implementing the UN 'Respect, Protect and Remedy' Framework* (A/HRC/17/31, 16 June 2011) Principle 1 (hereafter 'UNGPs').

[47] See, for example, Human Rights Committee, *General Comment No 31: The Nature of the General Legal Obligation imposed on States Parties to the Covenant* (CCPR/C/21/Rev1/Add13, 29 March 2004); Committee on Economic, Social and Cultural Rights, *General Comment No 3: The Nature of States Parties' Obligations (art 2, para 1, of the Covenant)* (E/1991/23, 1990).

to respect and fulfil are also clearly recognized, it does highlight a specific facet of the role(s) that states play in the context of economic activities: that of monitoring and regulating business activities, whether public or private.

There is also growing international recognition on the responsibilities of business enterprises in the field of human rights, a movement that was spearheaded by the UN Guiding Principles on Business and Human Rights (UNGPs) and unanimously endorsed by the Human Rights Council in 2011. It has since become a global standard of expected business conduct, with what was originally a declarative international framework,[48] on the expectation that businesses should respect human rights increasingly being introduced in domestic legislation[49] and considered in regional frameworks,[50] thus paving the way for human rights-oriented regulation of business activities.

The UNGPs are organized around three main pillars, that highlight the state duty to protect human rights in the context of business activities; the responsibility of business enterprises to respect human rights in their activities and business relationships; and the need to ensure more effective access to remedy for persons or groups whose rights have been adversely impacted by business activities. In this respect, the UNGPs posit a dichotomy: that states have specific obligations under international human rights law regarding business activities, and that businesses have a non-legal responsibility vis-à-vis the human rights impacts they may cause, contribute to, or be linked to. They are presented as separate sets of duties and responsibilities, albeit interconnected. However, it also makes clear that there may be different approaches to this question depending on the formal nature of the business actor involved, particularly considering the role that the state plays as an economic or business actor itself.

Indeed, within the stream of the state duty to protect human rights, the UNGPs call for a tri-dimensional approach to the question of the role of the state as an economic actor, recognizing its important role as a market force and its evident position to influence business behaviour. The first one relates to the question of public procurement, where it is aptly mentioned that states, as a major economic actor that purchases goods and services, have a duty to establish specific conditions that incentivize business respect for human rights.[51] A second scenario revolves around

---

[48] By 'declarative', we refer to the non-legally binding character of the instrument, which has also been referred to as 'non-voluntary'. In that regard, see Michael K Addo, 'The Mandate of the UN Working Group on Business and Human Rights: Preliminary Thoughts' in Humberto Cantú Rivera (ed), *The Special Procedures of the Human Rights Council* (Intersentia 2015) 85–101.

[49] At the time of writing, domestic legislation that 'hardens' human rights due diligence has been adopted by France, Germany, Switzerland, The Netherlands, and Norway, while other states have introduced legislation on modern slavery or transparency requirements.

[50] European Commission, *Proposal for a Directive of the European Parliament and of the Council on corporate Sustainability Due Diligence and amending Directive (EU) 2019/1937* (COM/2022/71 Final, 23 February 2022); see also IACHR, *Business and Human Rights: Inter-American Standards* (CIDH/REDESCA/INF1/19, 1 November 2019).

[51] UNGPs (n 46), Principle 6. See also Olga Martin-Ortega and Claire Methven O'Brien, 'Public Procurement and Human Rights: Interrogating the Role of the State as Buyer' in Olga Martin-Ortega

the issue of privatization of public services,[52] where the state allows the private sector to intervene in the provision of public goods, and where regulation should be reinforced. A third aspect of the economic dimension of state activities relates to state-owned enterprises, where the distinction between public and private—and the corresponding responsibilities—becomes blurred,[53] but where the focus lies on leading by example. These three dimensions of the economic role of the state are presented as part of an existing State duty to protect human rights, founded in international human rights law and therefore presumed mandatory.

Furthermore, the UNGPs have also established a clear responsibility to respect that applies to all business enterprises, regardless of ownership, size, or sector of operation. Such a responsibility, framed in the sense of avoiding causing harm, entails different positive steps, namely identifying and assessing actual or potential impacts to stakeholders, acting upon those results, and communicating with relevant stakeholders around measures taken to prevent, address, or redress any situation that may entail an adverse human rights impact.[54] One key element of such a responsibility is that it exists regardless of what states do (or fail to do) to address the issue through normative or regulatory measures, as it rests on and reflects societal expectations regarding business conduct.[55]

The separation of duties and responsibilities presented by the UNGPs was not only a functional decision to secure political support from different stakeholders regarding the state of international human rights law on the issue; it also facilitated the framing of the roles that were to be played by states and businesses, functioning as a pedagogical reminder of the bases of human rights as a series of state duties to respect freedoms and ensure the realization of other rights, notably where state intervention is necessary.[56] And yet, that dichotomy between states and business

and Claire Methven (eds), *Public Procurement and Human Rights: Opportunities, Risks and Dilemmas for the State as Buyer* (Edward Elgar 2019) 2–21 (hereafter 'Public Procurement and Human Rights').

[52] UNGPs (n 46), Principle 5. See also Humberto Cantú Rivera, 'Guiding Principle 5: The Content of the State Duty to Protect in the Context of Privatization' in Barnali Choudhury (ed), *The UN Guiding Principles on Business and Human Rights: A Commentary* (Edward Elgar 2023) 42–48 (hereafter 'Guiding Principle 5').

[53] UNGPs (n 46), Principle 4. On the topic of state-owned enterprises, see also Human Rights Council, *Report of the Working Group on the Issue of Human Rights and Transnational Corporations and other Business Enterprises* (A/HRC/32/45, 4 May 2016); for critical perspectives, see Judith Schönsteiner, 'Inter-American Elements for a Systemic Approach to State-Owned Enterprises' Human Rights Obligations' (2022) 7(3) Bus Hum Rights J 397; Larry Catá Backer, 'The Human Rights Obligations of State-Owned Enterprises(SOEs): Emerging Conceptual Structures and Principles in National and International Law and Policy' (2017) 51 Vand J Transnat'l L 827; María Isabel Cubides Sánchez, 'Empresas Públicas: Cerrando la Brecha de Impunidad entre el Deber de Proteger y el Deber de Respetar los Derechos Humanos' in Humberto Cantú Rivera (ed), *El Tratado Sobre las Empresas y los Derechos Humanos: Perspectivas Latinoamericanas* (Tirant Lo Blanch 2022) 171–93.

[54] UNGPs (n 46), Principles 17–22. See also Robert McCorquodale and others, 'Human Rights Due Diligence in Law and Practice: Good Practices and Challenges for Business Enterprises' (2017) 2(2) Bus Hum Rights J 195.

[55] Just Business (n 22) 90 ff.

[56] Olivier De Schutter, *International Human Rights Law: Cases, Materials, Commentary* (3rd ed, CUP 2019) 291–606.

highlights a choice that may ignore a different and more nuanced reality, especially in the context of infrastructure development, where public-private partnerships are a particularly relevant and common model to secure public goods and development with a direct involvement of the private sector.[57]

This necessarily entails an important challenge, as states are required under international human rights law to adopt normative frameworks to address business conduct in their territory or within their jurisdiction, and to regulate effectively the way that businesses conduct their operations, particularly to promote compliance with international and domestic human rights standards. In the context of privatization of public services,[58] and in the context of public procurement,[59] the state tends to enjoy a preeminent role vis-à-vis the private sector, where it can impose its requirements on any contractor desiring to receive public funds and leverage its influence to ensure (or at least promote) a human rights-based approach to development. And yet, the joint participation of public and private parties for infrastructure development implies that the dichotomy posited by the UNGPs may not necessarily be applicable in this context, begging the question of what duties or responsibilities apply in the context of public-private partnerships.

b. The limits of the functional dichotomy: Duties or responsibilities in the context of public-private partnerships?

Public-private partnerships (PPP) have become an increasingly common approach to infrastructure development in developed and developing countries, and their aim is to secure private investment and promote technology transfer to address public issues or concerns. The World Bank defines PPPs as 'a long-term contract between a private party and a government entity, for providing a public asset or service, in which the private party bears significant risk and management responsibility, and remuneration is linked to performance'.[60] Regardless of the different nomenclatures they receive and their focus and scope, they tend to have a 'whole-life approach' to maximize the efficiency of service delivery.[61] PPPs have been used in relation to the provision of many public goods and services, including

---

[57] There has been growing concern over this issue across different UN Special Procedures. See, for example, Human Rights Council, *Report of the Special Rapporteur on the Right to Development* (A/HRC/45/15, 8 July 2020) paras 85–86, where the Special Rapporteur recalls the scope of the duty to ensure human rights in the context of public-private partnerships, including the need for robust oversight measures.

[58] Guiding Principle 5 (n 52).

[59] See, generally, Public Procurement and Human Rights (n 51).

[60] World Bank, 'Public-Private Partnerships Reference Guide' (version 3, 2017) <https://ppp.worldbank.org/public-private-partnership/sites/ppp.worldbank.org/files/documents/PPP%20Reference%20Guide%20Version%203.pdf> accessed 25 June 2023.

[61] ibid 6.

in education, water and sanitation, transport,[62] or even access to the internet; and among a range of benefits, such as the improvement of operational efficiency and budgetary certainty, fostering competitiveness, and securing long-term value for money through risk-transfer to the private sector during the life cycle of the project, have been identified as some of the most relevant ones.[63]

However, for all the benefits they bring and their regular use by states to foster innovation and development, the nature and operation of PPPs has not received sufficient attention in the vast and growing literature on business and human rights. In this sense, the fundamental question of what happens to the 'functional dichotomy' when states and businesses partner up deserves scrutiny, particularly with respect to the role of the state in the context of a very close nexus with businesses, on the applicable duties of states in relation to the governance of the PPP, and in relation to access to remedy. Can a 'functional dichotomy' as posited by the UNGPs operate under such a scenario, or are the clear delineations and distinctions between duties and responsibilities challenged and surpassed by the economic and development needs of the state?

The UNGPs do not make any reference to PPPs. This is especially relevant because PPPs are not identical to privatization, and they may be different than public procurement,[64] considering the different levels of long-term involvement in projects by both states and businesses. Conceptually, public procurement implies 'the buying by the public sector of the goods, services and works it needs to carry out its functions',[65] while privatization is defined as a process through which the private sector becomes responsible for activities traditionally performed by the government.[66] PPPs are different in several respects from both public procurement and privatization, starting from the fact that they are not conceived as an administrative

---

[62] United Nations Office of the High Representative for the Least Developed Countries, Landlocked Developing Countries and Small Island Developing States (UN-OHRLLS), 'Developing Successful Public-Private Partnerships (PPPs) for Increased Transport Connectivity: Case Studies, Experiences and Learning Materials: Draft' (2021) <https://www.un.org/ohrlls/sites/www.un.org.ohrlls/files/training_materials_ppps_botswana_9_oct.pdf> accessed 25 June 2023.

[63] The World Bank, 'Government Objectives: Benefits and Risks of PPPs' (2022) <https://ppp.worldbank.org/public-private-partnership/overview/ppp-objectives> accessed 25 June 2023.

[64] Johun Lee and Kim, 'Traditional Procurement Versus Public-Private Partnership: A Comparison of Procurement Modalities Focusing on Bundling Contract Effects' (ADB Economics Working Paper Series, No 560, 2018) 2:

> In a traditional procurement, the competent authority selects a private firm to design and build a project. After financing the project, the government can either manage and operate a facility itself or select an operator to do this. In a PPP project, the whole implementation process is granted to a single entity.

Despite this differentiation by Lee and Kim, doctrine on the subject seems to classify public-private partnerships either as a form of public procurement or as a form of privatization; we take a different conceptual view on the issue. See Darrin Grimsey and Mervyn Lewis, 'Public Private Partnerships and Public Procurement' (2007) 14(2) Agenda 171; John Kitsos, 'Privatisation and Public Private Partnerships: Defining the Legal Boundaries from an International Perspective' (2015) 10(1) EPPPL 17.

[65] Public Procurement and Human Rights (n 51) 2.

[66] Guiding Principle 5 (n 52).

tool to purchase goods or services per se, nor do they necessarily imply the renunciation by the government over a specific good or service it must provide. Instead, in many cases, PPPs imply a sort of 'temporary privatization', whereby through a long-term contractual relationship based on trust and equity between the parties, the government invites private investment for the development of infrastructure of a higher quality than what it could achieve on its own for a fraction of the cost, where the operator will receive reasonable financial benefits over a long period of time, and where the risks deriving from the project are shared between government and investor.[67] This provides a different conceptual basis in relation to public procurement and privatization, precisely because the relationship between the parties is based on coordination rather than subordination.

Guiding Principle 5 makes an indirect reference to the issue, stating that when states contract with or legislate for businesses to provide services, they should exercise adequate oversight.[68] Perhaps the closest reference can be found in the commentary to Guiding Principle 4: 'the closer a business enterprise is to the State, or the more it relies on statutory authority or taxpayer support, the stronger the State's policy rationale becomes for ensuring that the enterprise respects human rights.'[69] However, neither of these provisions reflect the reality of PPPs, whereas partners, governments, and businesses are in a situation of quasi-equality, with a common goal to address a public issue, although with clearly established benefits for the private party undertaking public duties. And yet, the commentary to Guiding Principle 5 sets forth the obligation of the state to clarify the expectation that businesses respect human rights, whether through law or contract[70] which, regardless of the specificities of PPPs, highlights the need for the state to have a leading role when involving the private sector in infrastructure development through a PPP.

Thus, the general approach of the UNGPs on the role of the state in relation to private parties provides a useful starting point. There are three aspects that merit particular attention: the inclusion of human rights requirements in the formalization of the partnership; the integration of human rights due diligence[71] in the

---

[67] Francisco Javier Treviño Moreno, *Asociaciones Público Privadas* (2nd edn, Porrúa 2020) 57–58 (hereafter '*Asociaciones Público Privadas*').
[68] UNGPs, Guiding Principle 5 (n 52).
[69] UNGPs, Guiding Principle 4 (n 53), Commentary.
[70] UNGPs, Guiding Principle 5 (n 52), Commentary.
[71] OHCHR, 'The Corporate Responsibility to Respect Human Rights: An Interpretive Guide' (2012) 6:

> In the context of the Guiding Principles, human rights due diligence comprises an ongoing management process that a reasonable and prudent enterprise needs to undertake, in the light of its circumstances (including sector, operating context, size and similar factors) to meet its responsibility to respect human rights.

> The UNGPs present the human rights due diligence process as a standard of conduct that requires taking different steps, including undertaking human rights impact assessments, taking action in relation to any risks or impacts that may exist, communicating with relevant stakeholders, and taking appropriate measures to provide or contribute to remedy for harms caused.

governance of the PPP; and finally, the focus on access to remedy. Each of these elements is crucial and needs to be considered in advance, taking into account that in practice, the negotiations for the PPP agreement will normally entail discussions over the privileges for the private party engaging in the partnership (which may include tax incentives, profits from the operation of the built infrastructure, and even protection from legal liability), but also that there will most likely exist a lack of awareness around human rights in general or the requirements and standards set forth by the UNGPs in particular.

The role of the state vis-à-vis its private partner is potentially the most complex part of the equation, considering that the state and the public interest may benefit from the infrastructure project being developed by the private party, but also that the particularly close nexus between them may inhibit adequate regulation or scrutiny required to fulfil the state's human rights obligations. In this regard, state obligations and capacity to regulate in relation to PPPs are different from privatization and public procurement, because the state has potentially less control or leverage over its counterpart if specific conditions are not defined from the outset of the project. To a large extent, the only way such a dilemma can be overcome is if the corresponding regulatory agency is fully aware and capable of implementing its human rights obligations from the start of the negotiations with the private contractor—that is, from the design stage of the project—which could provide a solid basis for the inclusion of human rights as part of the contractual obligations underpinning the PPP. In this sense, contractual clarity regarding the procedural and substantive human rights obligations of the private investor could prevent future problems resulting from the adverse environmental and human rights impacts deriving from the project, and stipulate that just as with other commercial and performance indicators, preventing human rights impacts may entail other incentives and beneficial considerations for the investor.

In this complex scenario of proximity, a key entry point is the insertion of the corporate responsibility to respect human rights in the governance framework of the PPP, particularly through the explicit requirement of human rights due diligence processes that demand from the private party to identify and manage the human rights impacts and risks that may be associated with or derive from the infrastructure project. Whether the PPP is created through a joint venture or other form of commercial entity, one key element of the negotiation should be to ensure that sustainability and human rights are adequately represented and considered in the governance structure of the PPP, and that they have an equal footing to commercial and other considerations. This, in addition to adequate oversight and reporting, should be understood as implicit in state obligations that exist under international human rights law, and which are framed by the UNGPs as part of the state duty to protect human rights.[72]

---

[72] See also *Asociaciones Público Privadas* (n 67) 178, arguing for the alignment of the structure and adjudication of PPPs with the UNGPs.

Potentially, the most significant challenge in this context will be that of access to remedy, considering the proximity between the parties and the potential difficulty in identifying the scope of their respective responsibilities. As experience has shown in relation to projects where there has been a public-private nexus, under international law the state can be responsible for human rights violations resulting from its omissions vis-à-vis the conduct of private parties.[73] And yet, a key element that is often overlooked is the liability of the private counterpart for its direct involvement in the environmental or human rights adverse impact, which in most circumstances will be left to national jurisdictions. Here again, the design of the PPP can provide a useful roadmap for all relevant stakeholders, including the partners and other external parties that may have a legal or legitimate interest as a result of an adverse impact. Thus, the contractual provisions should establish clear limitations to the protections from legal liability that may be agreed during the negotiation phase, especially where environmental or human rights impacts are foreseeable and preventable. This would shift the burden to prevent impacts onto the private party, creating an incentive to take matters seriously under risk of legal liability.

Another element which could be necessary to comply with the UNGPs is the establishment of an operational-level grievance mechanism for the PPP that fulfils the effectiveness criteria set forth by UNGP 31.[74] While it may not yet be a dominant trend within the business and human rights discourse, the duty of the state to provide effective access to remedy could be interpreted in the broad sense to also include non-judicial (and even non-state based) mechanisms.[75] Considering that the state has a stake in the partnership, its international obligation could be fulfilled through the requirement and oversight of such a mechanism within the PPP, that facilitates prevention and reparation, and that contributes to the reinforcement of a remedy ecosystem as articulated by the UN Working Group on Business and Human Rights.[76]

Public-private partnerships are a different version of the state-business nexus under the UNGPs, that require further analysis and consideration as a result of the inherent proximity between public and private parties. As such, while the functional dichotomy set forth by the UNGPs in relation to State duties and corporate responsibilities provides an initial basis to differentiate between the two, it offers

---

[73] *Case of Ximenes Lopes v Brazil* [4 July 2006] (Merits, Reparations, and Costs) Judgment (I/A Court HR) Series C No 149; *Case of Vera Rojas et al v Chile* [1 October 2021] (Preliminary Objections, Merits, Reparations, and Costs) Judgment (I/A Court HR) Series C No 439.

[74] UNGP 31 stipulates that operational-level grievance mechanisms should be legitimate, accessible, predictable, equitable, transparent, rights-compatible, a source of continuous learning, and based on engagement and dialogue.

[75] Human Rights Council, *Improving Accountability and Access to Remedy for Victims of Business-related Human Rights Abuse through Non-state-based Grievance Mechanisms: Report of the United Nations High Commissioner for Human Rights* (A/HRC/44/32, 19 May 2020) para 1.2.(d).

[76] General Assembly, *Report of the Working Group on the Issue of Human Rights and Transnational Corporations and other Business Enterprises* (A/72/162, 18 July 2017).

only a limited roadmap for cases where the possibility of control or leverage by the state is greatly reduced. This calls for a new appraisal of converging duties and responsibilities, that should be based on existing practice and international legal obligations, that facilitate a dialogue between domestic and international law, and between rules and practice.

4. Conclusion

Infrastructure has been essential for economic and social development, as well as for the fulfilment of different human rights, particularly economic, social, and cultural rights. Indeed, it is through the construction of schools, hospitals, roads, airports, databases, and the fulfilment of other needs that the state fulfils a range of international human rights obligations. Considering the limited economic and technical capacity that certain developing states may face, the private sector has gained prominence as a business partner that can contribute its resources and know-how to advance infrastructure development. However, the duties and responsibilities under international law are unclear, particularly when states and businesses join forces through public-private partnerships, reducing the potential leverage or influence the state may exert over its business partner.

The evolving field of business and human rights may offer a starting point and some insights into how states could still use some of their regulatory and contracting powers to incentivize more responsible conduct by its business partners, notably through governance and remedy mechanisms established by law or through contractual provisions in the context of the public-private partnership. With the use of these safeguards, the likelihood of infrastructure development becoming more sustainable can increase, which has the potential to contribute to sustainable development and the respect and protection of human rights.[77]

---

[77] See OHCHR and Heinrich Böll Stiftung, 'The Other Infrastructure Gap: Sustainability. Human Rights and Environmental Perspectives' (2018).

17
The Rule of Law in Investment—A Condition for Development?

*Farouk El-Hosseny**

1. Introduction

Compliance with international obligations should generally bring peace and development. Yet, the fraternity of states continues to consistently flout those obligations, and in the absence of compulsory global adjudication and enforcement mechanisms, the preceding statement may require reinforcing, particularly at the time of writing of this chapter as the drums of inter-state warfare between Russia and Ukraine become increasingly deafening.

They also need reinforcing because, on the domestic plane, despotic regimes are gaining prominence, ignoring the rule of law, yet somehow convinced that development will not be adversely affected; to the contrary.[1] What Milton Friedman calls the 'Miracle of Chile',[2] this author calls the 'Pinochet Curse':[3] the idea that an authoritarian regime can systemically violate the broader, overarching, principles of the rule of law which inexorably encompass human rights—whilst prioritizing political stability and carving out the narrow aspect of judicial and administrative protection of private property rights—and nonetheless achieve economic success and development.[4] This uninspiring model has been—and continues to be—followed by authoritarian regimes around the world.[5]

---

* Farouk El-Hosseny (PhD, Leiden University) is an international arbitration practitioner based in London, United Kingdom. The views expressed in this chapter are solely his own and not those of his employer. The author thanks Ionut Rus and Laure Dupain for their research assistance.
[1] See e.g. Mark Fathi Massoud, 'International Arbitration and Judicial Politics in Authoritarian States' (2014) 39 Law Soc Inq 1, 1–4 (hereafter 'International Arbitration and Judicial Politics').
[2] Donald G Richards, 'The Political Economy of the Chilean Miracle' (1997) 32 Lat Am Res Rev 139.
[3] Augusto Pinochet Ugarte, President of Chile (1974–1990), having seized power in a 1973 coup from the left-wing, democratically-elected former president, Salvador Allende.
[4] The importance of property rights, in particular in incentivizing investment and trade is addressed in Stephen Haggard and others, 'The Rule of Law and Economic Development' (2008) 11 Annu Rev Polit Sci 205, 207 (hereafter 'The Rule of Law and Economic Development'). According to recent studies, political stability is the single most valued factor by foreign investors (49.4 per cent), followed by macroeconomic stability (49 per cent) and the legal and regulatory environment (42 per cent); see Ben van der Merwe, 'War and Peace and FDI' (*Investment Monitor*, 18 December 2020) <https://www.investmentmonitor.ai/global/war-and-peace-and-fdi> accessed 25 June 2023 (hereafter 'War and Peace and FDI').
[5] See e.g. International Arbitration and Judicial Politics in Authoritarian States (n 1) 1–4.

Farouk El-Hosseny, *The Rule of Law in Investment—A Condition for Development?* In: *The Roles of International Law in Development*. Edited by: Siobhán McInerney-Lankford and Robert McCorquodale, Oxford University Press.
© Farouk El-Hosseny 2023. DOI: 10.1093/oso/9780192872906.003.0017

Fortunately, however, empirical studies suggest that the institutionalization of, and improvements in, the (domestic) rule of law promote development and enhance human capabilities—to adopt Amartya Sen and Martha Nussbaum's terminology.[6] Internationally, the United Nations (UN) General Assembly's UN Declaration on the Rule of Law at the National and International Levels unequivocally recognizes the strong interlinkage between the rule of law in both its domestic and international conceptions, on the one hand, and development on the other.[7] The same is true in the UN's 2030 Agenda for Sustainable Development,[8] the Venice Commission of the Council of Europe's Rule of Law Checklist,[9] and, more recently, the draft Convention on the Right to Development.[10]

Based on this evidence and these statements, if a state decides to invade the territory of another sovereign state, or to arbitrarily expropriate the assets of nationals of that other state, it is violating the rule of international law and, as a result, adversely

---

[6] Boettke and Subrick argue that: '... the rule of law will increase the level of development, and the level of development will lead to improvements in human capabilities', see Peter Boettke and J Robert Subrick, 'Rule of Law, Development, and Human Capabilities' (2003) 10 Sup Ct Econ Rev 109, 111–12 (hereafter 'Rule of Law, Development, and Human Capabilities'), citing Amartya Sen, *Development as Freedom* (OUP 1999) 275 (hereafter 'Development as Freedom'); Martha Nussbaum, *Women and Human Development: The Capabilities Approach* (CUP 2000).

[7] UN General Assembly Resolution 67/1, 'Declaration of the High-level Meeting of the General Assembly on the Rule of Law at the National and International Levels' (Sixty-seventh, 30 November 2012) 7 <Declaration of the High-Level Meeting of the General Assembly on the Rule of Law at the National and International Levels : (un.org)> accessed 25 June 2023 (hereafter 'Declaration of the High-level Meeting of the General Assembly') ('We are convinced that the rule of law and development are strongly interrelated and mutually reinforcing, that the advancement of the rule of law at the national and international levels is essential for sustained and inclusive economic growth, sustainable development, the eradication of poverty and hunger and the full realization of all human rights and fundamental freedoms, including the right to development, all of which in turn reinforce the rule of law, and for this reason we are convinced that this interrelationship should be considered in the post-2015 international development agenda'); see also Simon Chesterman, 'An International Rule of Law?' (2008) 56 Am J Comp Law 331, 358–59 (hereafter 'An International Rule of Law'); see also Kenneth Keith, 'The International Rule of Law' (2015) 28 LJIL 403, 406–07.

[8] UN General Assembly Resolution 70/1, 'Transforming Our World: the 2030 Agenda for Sustainable Development' (25 September 2015) <https://documents-dds-ny.un.org/doc/UNDOC/GEN/N15/291/89/PDF/N1529189.pdf?OpenElement> accessed 28 August 2023 ('8. We envisage a world of universal respect for human rights and human dignity, the rule of law, justice, equality and non-discrimination; of respect for race, ethnicity and cultural diversity; and of equal opportunity permitting the full realization of human potential and contributing to shared prosperity [...] 9. We envisage a world in which every country enjoys sustained, inclusive and sustainable economic growth and decent work for all. A world in which consumption and production patterns and use of all natural resources—from air to land, from rivers, lakes and aquifers to oceans and seas—are sustainable. One in which democracy, good governance and the rule of law, as well as an enabling environment at the national and international levels, are essential for sustainable development [...] Goal 16 [...] 16.3 Promote the rule of law at the national and international levels and ensure equal access to justice for all').

[9] European Commission for Democracy Through Law (Venice Commission), 'Rule of Law Checklist' (2016) <https://www.venice.coe.int/images/SITE%20IMAGES/Publications/Rule_of_Law_Check_List.pdf> accessed 25 June 2023.

[10] Human Rights Council, Working Group on the Right to Development, *Revised Draft Convention on the Right to Development* (A/HRC/WG2/23/2, 16–20 May 2022) <https://www.ohchr.org/sites/default/files/2022-04/A_HRC_WG_2_23_2_AEV.pdf> accessed 25 June 2023 ('Recognizing that good governance, accountability and the rule of law at all levels, including the national and international levels, and the realization of the right to development are mutually reinforcing').

affecting development within its jurisdiction and potentially beyond it. In other words, when, for example, the principles of the United Nations Convention on the Law of the Sea (UNCLOS) are faithfully implemented, and inter-state awards are respected, the rule of law is upheld and development is thus enhanced.

When they are not, development is adversely affected, especially in the wake of live territorial disputes and armed conflict.[11] The peaceful settlement of the *Bay of Benghal* dispute between India and Bangladesh is one prime example; whilst China's refusal to participate in, and accept the outcome of, the *South China Sea Arbitration* provides a converse example.[12] Compliance with UNCLOS—and adjudication by way of arbitration or at the International Tribunal for the Law of the Sea (ITLOS) —paves the way for the creation of Joint Development Zones (JDZs) which enable states jointly to explore and exploit natural resources such as offshore oil and gas fields, thus creating cross-border unitization and development, instead of conflict.[13]

It is difficult not to see, therefore, how the violation of the core requirements of the rule of (international) law (i.e. non-arbitrariness, consistency, and predictability)—as enshrined in international treaties, including international investment agreements (IIAs)[14]—adversely affects development. Yet, in the context of the investment treaty regime, numerous detractors have vehemently questioned its legitimacy and, at times, its very existence. In particular, some argue that the investor-state dispute settlement (ISDS) arbitration process contained in IIAs can curtail host-states' ability to regulate in the public interest, trigger so-called 'regulatory chills' (i.e. 'the possibility that investment treaties discourage states from adopting legitimate regulatory measures in practice')[15] and ultimately undermine

---

[11] For empirical data on the increased opportunity costs stalling economic development in the context of territorial disputes, see Hoon Lee and Sara McLaughlin Mitchell, 'Foreign Direct Investment and Territorial Disputes' (2012) 56 J Confl Resolut 675–76, 684–85; see also, more generally, David Carter and others, 'International Law, Territorial Disputes, and Foreign Direct Investment' (2019) 63 Int Stud Q 58–59, 60, 63 (hereafter 'International Law, Territorial Disputes, and Foreign Direct Investment') (notably discussing data suggesting that Russia's violation of Ukraine's sovereignty as a result of its annexation of Crimea in 2014 has had an adverse impact on investors' willingness to remain or enter the Russian market); War and Peace and FDI (n 4).

[12] Salman Khurshid and Zafar Khurshid, 'State-State Arbitration and its Role in Entrenching the Rule of Law in the International Legal Community' in Gourab Banerji and others (eds), *International Arbitration and the Rule of Law: Essays in Honour of Fali Nariman* (Permanent Court of Arbitration 2021) 29, 30–34 (hereafter 'State-State Arbitration'), citing *Bay of Bengal Maritime Boundary Arbitration between Bangladesh and India (Bangladesh v India)* [7 July 2014] PCA Case No 2010-16 UNCLOS Final Award; *The South China Sea Arbitration (The Republic of Philippines v The People's Republic of China)* [12 July 2016] PCA Case No 2013-9 UNCLOS Final Award. In respect to the latter arbitration, however, the position has changed as a result of the President Duterte government in the Philippines changing course; see Alvin Camba, 'Inter-state Relations and State Capacity: the Rise and Fall of Chinese Foreign Direct Investment in the Philippines' (2017) 3 Palgrave Commun 14.

[13] Constantinos Yiallourides, 'Joint Development of Seabed Resources in Areas of Overlapping Maritime Claims: An Analysis of Precedents in State Practice' (2019) 31(2) USF Mar LJ 129, 130–33.

[14] IIAs include free trade agreements (FTAs) with investment chapters as well as bilateral investment treaties (BITs).

[15] Jonathan Bonnitcha and others, *The Political Economy of the Investment Treaty Regime* (OUP 2017) 239 (hereafter 'The Political Economy of the Investment Treaty Regime').

sustainable development and—even—the rule of law.[16] Some have even argued that ISDS has an adverse effect on the green energy transition as it '... could lead to states refraining from, or delaying, measures to phase out fossil fuels' and robustly tackling climate change.[17] Indeed, a recent Organization for Economic Cooperation and Development (OECD) consultation has found that 'there are reasons to believe "regulatory chill" is a legitimate concern when it comes to climate policy'.[18]

This chapter will make the case that, by focusing on the core requirements of the rule of international law and adhering to them, states create the necessary—or at the very least auspicious—conditions for development. First, a definition of the rule of international law will be proposed, where the interlinkage between the domestic and international dimensions of the rule of law will also be addressed. The debate surrounding the benefit of IIAs and ISDS—as tools of global governance—will be discussed, including an overview of the relevant data and the arguments opposing proponents and detractors of the investment treaty regime. The focus will then shift to publicly available ISDS jurisprudence where the adverse effect on investment of the flouting of the rule of law is articulated in practical terms by reference to principles that are relevant to both the domestic and international realms. This will be followed by concluding remarks.

2. Defining the Rule of International Law

Much ink has been spilled, at times with controversy, in attempting to define the rule of law, not only in its domestic iteration,[19] but also in its international one,[20] with some even questioning whether the latter concept even exists.[21] One may also vehemently debate its function, i.e. whether it is primarily concerned with the coordination of inter-state interactions or the protection of individual and state

---

[16] For an overview of those concerns, see Farouk El-Hosseny, *Civil Society in Investment Treaty Arbitration: Status and Prospects* (Brill Nijhoff 2018) 56–60.

[17] Kyla Tienhaara and others, 'Investor-state Disputes Threaten the Global Green Energy Transition' (2022) 376(6594) Science 701, 701; see also Human Rights Council, 'Right to Development in International Investment Law' (A/HRC/EMRTD/5/CRP2, 1 March 2022) 5 <https://www.ohchr.org/sites/default/files/2022-03/A_HRC_EMRTD_5_CRP2.pdf> accessed 25 June 2023.

[18] Anne van Aaken and Tomer Bourde, 'Ways of Reforming International Investment Agreements to Make them More Compatible with Climate Change Goals' in OECD, *Investment Treaties and Climate Change* (January–March 2022) 11 <https://www.oecd.org/investment/investment-policy/OECD-investment-treaties-climate-change-consultation-responses.pdf> accessed 25 June 2023.

[19] An International Rule of Law? (n 7) 340–42.

[20] State-State Arbitration (n 12) 23; Noora Arajärvi, 'The Core Requirements of the International Rule of Law in the Practice of States' (2021) 13 HJRL 173, 175 (hereafter 'The Core Requirements of the International Rule of Law').

[21] James Crawford, *Chance, Order, Change: The Course of International Law* (Hague Academy of International Law 2014) 345–53 (hereafter 'Chance, Order, Change: The Course of International Law'); An International Rule of Law? (n 7) 358; The International Rule of Law and the Idea of Normative Authority (n 37) 232.

autonomy from the arbitrary interference of international institutions.[22] As explained by Robert McCorquodale, the definition exercise might amount to 'defying gravity'.[23]

For present purposes a deliberately narrow, perhaps simplistic but practical, definition of the 'rule of international law' or the 'international rule of law' will be drawn from the Report on Strengthening and Coordinating United Nations Rule of Law Activities, i.e. it is the 'full implementation of the obligations set forth in the Charter of the United Nations and in other international instruments':[24]

> At the international level, the rule of law accords predictability and legitimacy to the actions of States, strengthens their sovereign equality and underpins the responsibility of a State to all individuals within its territory and subject to its jurisdiction. *Full implementation of the obligations set forth in the Charter of the United Nations and in other international instruments,* including the international human rights framework, is central to collective efforts to maintain international peace and security, effectively address emerging threats and ensure accountability for international crimes.[25]

The international rule of law is thus the 'rule of law in international relations' which the community of states is '[c]onvinced of the need to strengthen' as part of their commitment to the 'UN Decade of International Law'—it is 'the respect for the rule of law between states in their dealings with each other'.[26] This principle is

---

[22] The Core Requirements of the International Rule of Law (n 210 176; Carmen E Pavel, 'The International Rule of Law' (2020) 23(3) Critical Review of International Social and Political Philosophy 332, 334.

[23] McCorquodale defines the 'international rule of law' as follows: 'the definition of the international rule of law comprises legal order and stability, equality of application of the law, the protection of human rights through access to justice, and the settlement of disputes before an independent legal body. The international rule of law is not defined by reference to the national institutional arrangements of some democratic, industrialized states, and it is broad enough to include all the participants in the international system within its scope, and not just states'; see Robert McCorquodale, 'Defying Gravity: Defining the International Rule of Law' (2016) 65(2) ICLQ 277, 277–78 (hereafter 'Defying Gravity: Defining the International Rule of Law').

[24] The difficulty of course is that the Charter does not refer to the concept of the 'rule of law'. For a discussion, see Bardo Fassbender, 'What's in a Name? The International Rule of Law and the United Nations Charter' (2018) 17 Chinese JIL 761, 762 *et seq*. For another simplistic definition, albeit one that applies to the domestic realm, see Joseph Raz, 'The Rule of Law and its Virtue' in Joseph Raz (ed), *The Authority of Law: Essays on Law and Morality* (Clarendon Press 1979), 212 (' "the rule of the law" means literally what it says: the rule of the law. Taken in its broadest sense this means that people should obey the law and be ruled by it').

[25] UN General Assembly, 'Strengthening and Coordinating United Nations Rule of Law Activities: Report of the Secretary-General' (Sixty-eighth Session, A/68/213, 29 July 2013) 3 (emphasis added) <https://digitallibrary.un.org/record/756020?ln=en> accessed 28 August 2023, cited in Defying Gravity: Defining the International Rule of Law (n 23) 287; see also The Core Requirements of the International Rule of Law (n 20) 179.

[26] UN General Assembly Resolution 44/23, 'United Nations Decade of International Law' (Forty-fourth Session, 17 November 1989) <https://digitallibrary.un.org/record/82103?ln=en> accessed 27 June 2023; quoted in Ruwantissa I R Abeyratne, 'The United Nations Decade of International Law' (1992) 5(3) Int J Politics Cult Soc 511, 511; Sundhya Pahuja, *Decolonising International Law: Development,*

equally reflected in the 2012 UN Declaration on the Rule of Law at the National and International Levels, where the General Assembly reaffirmed its 'solemn commitment to the purposes and principles of the Charter of the United Nations, international law and justice, and to an international order based on the rule of law, which are indispensable foundations for a more peaceful, prosperous and just world'.[27] To quote Thomas Bingham, the international rule of law consists of 'rules internationally agreed, internationally implemented, and if necessary, internationally enforced'.[28]

Enforcement—a quintessential aspect of any legal order, for which legality in and of itself is insufficient[29]—is entrusted to the International Court of Justice (ICJ) as well as numerous other international courts and ad hoc tribunals, including most notably those administering inter-state disputes and investor-state disputes.[30] Indeed, James Crawford explains that compliance with international arbitration decisions 'contributes to the maintenance of the rule of international law'.[31] But enforcement is the Achilles heel of the rule of international law. With the exception of ISDS, which enables successful claimants to pursue the global enforcement of monetary damages awards against respondent states' assets that are not employed *iure imperii* (i.e. 'by the right of the sovereign'; in other words, assets that are employed for state sovereign purposes, such as diplomatic functions or consular services), the absence of compulsory jurisdiction and/or binding enforcement mechanisms in inter-state and international human rights disputes constitutes an unsurmountable lacuna.[32]

As mentioned, there is evident interlinkage and complementarity between the international and national dimensions as recorded in the 2012 UN Declaration on the Rule of Law at the National and International Levels.[33] The UN General

Economic Growth and the Politics of Universality (CUP 2011), 177; see also UN General Assembly Resolution 60/1, '2005 World Summit Outcome' (Sixtieth Session, 24 October 2005) 134(a) <https://www.un.org/en/development/desa/population/migration/generalassembly/docs/globalcompact/A_RES_60_1.pdf> accessed 27 June 2023 ('Reaffirm our commitment to the purposes and principles of the Charter and international law and to an international order based on the rule of law and international law, which is essential for peaceful coexistence and cooperation among States').

[27] Declaration of the High-level Meeting (n 7).
[28] Thomas Bingham, 'The Rule of Law in the International Order' (Annual Grotius Lecture, British Institute for International and Comparative Law, 18 November 2008) <https://www.biicl.org/newsitems/109/lord-bingham-delivers-annual-grotius-lecture-on-the-rule-of-law-in-the-international-order> accessed 27 June 2023 (hereafter 'The Rule of Law in the International Order').
[29] Defying Gravity: Defining the International Rule of Law (n 23) 289.
[30] State-State Arbitration (n 12) 24; An International Rule of Law? (n 7) 359.
[31] Chance, Order, Change: The Course of International Law (n 21) 348–49.
[32] Tellingly, or rather unfortunately, referring to the recent ICJ ruling in *Ukraine v Russian Federation*, Bloomberg describes it as 'unlikely to carry any real-world ramifications yet'; see Cagan Koc, 'UN Court Orders Russia to Suspend Military Action in Ukraine' (*Bloomberg*, 16 March 2022) <https://www.bloomberg.com/news/articles/2022-03-16/hague-court-orders-russia-to-suspend-military-action-in-ukraine?srnd=premium-europe&sref=dWW9TlvL> accessed 27 June 2023, citing *Allegations of Genocide under the Convention on the Prevention and Punishment of the Crime of Genocide (Ukraine v Russian Federation)*, Order of 16 March 2022 (ICJ) GL No 182 [2022].
[33] See Declaration of the High-level Meeting of the General Assembly (n 7).

Assembly's Millennium Declaration resolved to 'strengthen respect for the rule of law in international and in national affairs and in particular to ensure compliance by member states with the decisions of the ICJ, in accordance with the Charter of the United Nations, in cases to which they are parties'.[34] Referring to ISDS jurisprudence, Crawford articulates the link between the two in the following terms:

> It is not too much to say that in many of these areas the role of international law is to reinforce, and on occasions to institute, the rule of law internally. For example, in an investment protection dispute between a Singaporean company and Myanmar, if the applicable law is international law, *the criterion of liability is a certain set of standards more or less indistinguishable from those of the rule of law*, such as *absence of arbitrary conduct, judicial independence and non-retrospectivity*.[35]

Crawford then points to the often-cited judgment of the ICJ in *Elettronica Sicula SpA (ELSI) (United States v Italy)* where it defined arbitrariness as 'not so much something that is opposed to a rule of law, as something opposed to *the* rule of law'.[36] Non-arbitrariness is one of the many examples where the international and national dimensions of the rule of law converge, blurring the lines between the two.[37] An extensive study of state declarations and ICJ jurisprudence identified non-arbitrariness as one of the minimum, core, requirements of the rule of law, along with consistency and predictability.[38]

The 2021 Rule of Law Index of the World Justice Project—which is solely concerned with the domestic sphere—reflects non-arbitrariness in three of its sub-factors: sub-factors 4.3 and 8.7 ('Due process of the law and rights of the accused') and 4.6 ('Freedom from arbitrary interference with privacy is effectively guaranteed').[39] In fact, a violation of any of the Index's eight factors[40] of (1) 'Constraints on Government Powers'; (2) 'Absence of Corruption'; (3) 'Open Government'; (4) 'Fundamental Rights'; (5) 'Order and Security'; (6) 'Regulatory Enforcement';

---

[34] UN General Assembly Resolution 55/2, 'United Nations Millennium Declaration' (*UNHCHR*, 8 September 2000) 9 <https://www.ohchr.org/EN/ProfessionalInterest/Pages/Millennium.aspx> accessed 27 June 2023, cited in Defying Gravity: Defining the International Rule of Law (n 23) 287.

[35] Chance, Order, Change: The Course of International Law (n 21) 349 (emphasis added), citing *Mondev International Ltd v United States of America* [11 October 2002] ICSID Case No ARB(AF)/99/2 Award; *Yaung Chi Oo Trading Pte Ltd v Government of the Union of Myanmar* [31 March 2003] ASEAN ID Case No ARB/01/1 Award (emphasis added).

[36] Chance, Order, Change: The Course of International Law (n 21) 50 citing *Elettronica Sicula SpA (ELSI), United States v Italy* [1989] GL No 76 Merits Judgment (ICJ Report 15) 76.

[37] Kostiantyn Gorobets, 'The International Rule of Law and the Idea of Normative Authority' (2020) 12 HJRL 227, 229, 235.

[38] The Core Requirements of the International Rule of Law (n 20) 175.

[39] 'The World Justice Project Rule of Law Index 2021' (*The World Justice Project*, 2021) 15, 17, 19 <https://worldjusticeproject.org/sites/default/files/documents/WJP-INDEX-21.pdf> accessed 27 June 2023.

[40] ibid 15.

(7) 'Civil Justice'; and (8) 'Criminal Justice', may very well constitute a breach of a state's international obligations, particularly under IIAs.[41]

Notwithstanding the apparent contribution of IIAs and ISDS to the international rule of law, as already explained, many voices argue that they can curtail host-states' ability to regulate in the public interest, trigger 'regulatory chills'. In his dissenting opinion in *Bilcon v Canada*, Donald McRae opined that: 'a chill will be imposed on [Canadian] environmental review panels which will be concerned not to give too much weight to socio-economic considerations or other considerations of the human environment in case the result is a claim for damages under NAFTA Chapter 11'.[42] The concern, therefore, is that IIAs and ISDS (and the damages awards resulting therefrom) might curtail states' ability to adopt measures in the public interest, including measures aimed at promoting and protecting human rights and the environment, which would ultimately undermine sustainable development and the rule of law—as discussed directly below.

3. The Concern Arising from Regulatory Chills

There is a wealth of economic studies that show that there is a direct positive link between improvement in the domestic rule of law and economic growth, with one study showing that an improvement by one rank in the Rule of Law Index may raise

---

[41] To give but a few examples, for factor (1) 'Constraints on Government Powers', see *RosInvest Co UK Ltd v The Russian Federation* [12 September 2010] SCC Case No 079/2005, Award (where the claimant alleged that 'judges who ruled in favour of Yukos were removed from the case or the bench, those who ruled against were awarded the Order of Friendship and the Medal for Service to the Fatherland'); for factor (2) 'Absence of Corruption', see *Chevron Corporation and Texaco Petroleum Company v The Republic of Ecuador (II)* [30 August 2018] PCA Case No 2009-23 Second Partial Award on Track II (where the tribunal found a treaty violation based, inter alia, on the finding that a domestic judge had acted corruptly in exchange for a bribe); for factor (3) 'Open Government', see *Ascom Group SA, Anatolie Stati, Gabriel Stati and Terra Raf Trans Trading Ltd v Republic of Kazakhstan (I)* [19 December 2013] SCC Case No 116/2010 Award (where the claimants had filed complaints with relevant authorities concerning inspections by several Kazakh agencies, but 'no help was forthcoming'); for factor (4) 'Fundamental Rights', see *Ronald S Lauder v The Czech Republic* [3 September 2001] (UNCITRAL) Award (where the tribunal found that the state had violated the prohibition on discriminatory measures by refusing to award a German company a licence to operate a television station); for factor (5) 'Order and Security', see *American Manufacturing & Trading, Inc v Republic of Zaire* [21 February 1997] ICSID Case No ARB/93/1 Award (where the respondent state was found responsible for having failed to protect AMT's property during riots); for factor (6) 'Regulatory Enforcement', see *Waguih Elie George Siag and Clorinda Vecchi v Arab Republic of Egypt* [1 June 2009] ICSID Case No ARB/05/15 Award (where the tribunal held that the respondent state taking the investor's property was not based on public interest grounds); for factor (7) 'Civil Justice', see *Loewen Group, Inc and Raymond L Loewen v United States of America* [26 June 2003] ICSID Case No ARB(AF)/98/3 Award (where the claimant alleged that it had been subject to 'local prejudice' before domestic courts); for factor (8) 'Criminal Justice', see *Ahmadou Sadio Diallo (Republic of Guinea v Democratic Republic of the Congo)* [2010] Judgment Merits (ICJ Rep)639 (where the ICJ found the expulsion of Diallo was not decided 'in accordance with law' and constituted a violation of the African Charter on Human and Peoples' Rights).

[42] *Bilcon of Delaware Inc et al v Government of Canada* [10 March 2015] PCA Case No 2009-04 (UNCITRAL) *Dissenting Opinion of Prof Donald McRae* [48] [51].

the annual growth rate by a 0.5 percentage point; in other words, there is a positive correlation between the two.[43] Some of these studies have focused on the effectiveness of the judiciary, the predictability of its decision making and the enforceability of contracts so as to construct indexes that capture the fairness and predictability of a legal framework.[44] Indeed, better protection of property rights and a framework that reduces uncertainty about the future—two pillars of Friedrich Hayek's conception of the rule of law—enhance development and human capabilities.[45]

One might therefore assume that the same holds true for the link between the rule of law internationally (particularly through the enactment and implementation of IIAs and enforcement by way of ISDS) and development (particularly through the increase of foreign direct investment (FDI) flows, widely recognized as 'a key component of most states' long-term development strategies').[46] Even vehement critics of the current system, such as Sornarajah, do concede that 'there is no doubt' that FDI benefits developing host-states.[47] Proponents of the current ISDS regime are of the position that it promotes the international rule of law, including by protecting foreign investors from arbitrary state action.[48] Charles Brower argues, for example, that the current system benefits developing states, pointing to evidence that:

> [F]oreign direct investment increases national income and employment and accelerates development and modernization, including by establishing valuable tangible assets within the host country, promoting the development of human capital, facilitating the acquisition of technical knowledge, and creating network effects that create opportunities for future market access abroad.[49]

---

[43] Rule of Law, Development, and Human Capabilities (n 6) 113–14, citing Robert Barro, *Determinants of Economic Growth: A Cross-Country Empirical Study* (MIT Press 1997) 26–28; Xavier Sala-i-Martin, 'I Just Ran Two Million Regression' (1997) 87 Am Econ Rev 178, 178–83; Daniel Kaufmann and others, 'Governance Matters' (World Bank, Policy Working Research Paper 2196, October 1999); see also The Rule of Law and Economic Development (n 4) 208–09; Jonathan Bonnitcha, 'Assessing the Impacts of Investment Treaties: Overview of the Evidence' (International Institute for Sustainable Development, September 2017) 10 <https://www.iisd.org/publications/assessing-impacts-investment-treaties-overview-evidence> accessed 27 June 2023 (hereafter 'Assessing the Impacts of Investment Treaties').
[44] Peter Boettke and J Robert Subrick, 'Rule of Law, Development, and Human Capabilities' (n 6), 113–14.
[45] Rule of Law, Development, and Human Capabilities (n 6) 112, 126, citing F A Hayek, *The Road to Serfdom* (University of Chicago Press 1944) 72.
[46] International Law, Territorial Disputes, and Foreign Direct Investment (n 11) 59.
[47] M Sornarajah, 'A Law for Need or a Law for Greed?: Restoring the Lost Law in the International Law of Foreign Investment' (2006) 6 IEAs 329, 331, 333.
[48] The Political Economy of the Investment Treaty Regime (n 15) 233.
[49] Charles Brower and Sadie Blanchard, 'What's in a Meme? The Truth about Investor-State Arbitration: Why It Need Not, and Must Not, Be Repossessed by States' (2014) 52 Columbia J Transnat'l L 689, 701–03.

The thrust of proponents' proposition has proved to be polemical, however. It is not widely accepted, specifically by detractors of the ISDS regime. These critics question whether the enactment of IIAs necessarily results in a net positive impact for host-states and, by extension, development, particularly in its desirable, sustainable, form.[50] Whilst IIAs could, in principle, trigger progressive administrative and judicial reform that is conducive to the domestic rule of law, it is argued that there is no empirical data to substantiate that proposition in practice.[51] Moreover, they point to evidence suggesting that IIAs could lead to greater loss of policy space, particularly for developing countries compared to developed ones—in other words, faced with the threat of ISDS, host-states may be prone to abandoning preferred regulatory measures, including those aimed at protecting the environment, human rights and public health.[52] Others point to the absence of clear-cut evidence that IIAs have a positive impact on increasing FDI flows.[53] Even if such a correlative link exists, commentators caution against 'strong claims about the macroeconomic effects of investment protection provisions in investment treaties', given that little is known 'about *how* and *why* investment treaties affect different types of investments in different types of host states'.[54]

Of particular interest, detractors point to the potential adverse impact that IIAs, and particularly ISDS, might have on the domestic rule of law. Specifically, it is argued that:

(i) as a 'parallel legal system' that ISDS is only available to a certain class of foreign investors, 'ISDS potentially reduces incentives for host governments to strengthen domestic governance and judicial systems';[55]
(ii) ISDS prevents domestic judicial and administrative systems from developing domestic law and expertise in investment-related matters;

---

[50] Lise Johnson and others, 'Investor-State Dispute Settlement: What Are We Trying to Achieve? Does ISDS Get us There?' (*Columbia Center on Sustainable Investment*, 11 December 2017) <https://ccsi.columbia.edu/news/investor-state-dispute-settlement-what-are-we-trying-achieve-does-isds-get-us-there> accessed 27 June 2023 (hereafter 'Investor-State Dispute Settlement'); Assessing the Impacts of Investment Treaties (n 43) 15.

[51] ibid (Assessing the Impacts of Investment Treaties) 6; Mavluda Sattorova, 'Do Developing Countries Really Benefit from Investment Treaties? The Impact of International Investment Law on National Governance' (*Investment Treaty News*, 21 December 2018) <https://www.iisd.org/itn/en/2018/12/21/do-developing-countries-really-benefit-from-investment-treaties-the-impact-of-international-investment-law-on-national-governance-mavluda-sattorova/> accessed 27 June 2023 (hereafter 'Do Developing Countries Really Benefit from Investment Treaties?').

[52] Assessing the Impacts of Investment Treaties (n 43) 11; see Farouk El-Hosseny, *Civil Society in Investment Treaty Arbitration: Status and Prospects* (Brill Nijhoff 2018), 56–60.

[53] Jonathan Bonnitcha, 'Assessing the Impacts of Investment Treaties: Overview of the Evidence' (n 43), 11; Investor-State Dispute Settlement (n 50). The consensus is that analysis of the data is considered 'quite complex', see International Law, Territorial Disputes, and Foreign Direct Investment (n 11) 63.

[54] The Political Economy of the Investment Treaty Regime (n 15) 178.

[55] Some even suggest that ISDS 'can unwittingly help illiberal regimes continue to repress domestic judiciaries and curtail both the rule of law and human-rights-promotion activities'; see International Arbitration and Judicial Politics in Authoritarian States (n 1) 3.

(iii) the opaqueness of ISDS 'can prevent governments ... from understanding or seeking to internalize any of the principles or guidance that might emanate from ISDS decisions';

(iv) ISDS 'can create incentives' for host-governments to prioritize the concerns of foreign investors over those of their constituencies; and

(v) as a typically quite costly process, and one that often leads to the payment of significant damages to foreign investors, 'ISDS diverts often scarce resources away from public budgets—budgets that could be used to strengthen institutions and courts—to individual claimants'.[56]

Notwithstanding the above, even detractors agree that the overall data suggests that there is a positive correlative link between IIAs and FDI.[57] Indeed, a recent analysis suggests that the entry into force of a BIT between two states can increase FDI flows by 42 per cent.[58] Correlation is not sufficient to establish causation or conditionality, however. It would be tenuous to exploit the current data to form substantiated conclusions as to either the positive macroeconomic effects of IIAs (including ISDS) on host-states or their enhancement of the rule of law.[59]

4. The Case for Symbiosis

Given the imperfection of the data, and putting to one side the legitimacy of the criticisms surrounding the illegitimacy of ISDS (in respect to which there is broad consensus for the need for systemic reform),[60] attention ought to be shifted to the

---

[56] Investor-State Dispute Settlement (n 50); International Arbitration and Judicial Politics in Authoritarian States (n 1); Benjamin K Guthrie, 'Beyond Investment Protection: An Examination of the Potential Influence of Investment Treaties on Domestic Rule of Law' (2013) 45 NYU JILP 1151; Tom Ginsburg, 'International Substitutes for Domestic Institutions: Bilateral Investment Treaties and Governance' (Illinois Law and Economics Working Paper Series, Working Paper No NE06-027, 2006); Lise Johnson and Lisa Sachs, 'Investment Treaties, Investor-State Dispute Settlement and Inequality: How International Rules and Institutions Can Exacerbate Domestic Disparities' (Columbia Center on Sustainable Investment, April 2019) <https://scholarship.law.columbia.edu/cgi/viewcontent.cgi?article=1074&context=sustainable_investment_staffpubs> accessed 27 June 2023; see also Do Developing Countries Really Benefit from Investment Treaties? (n 51).

[57] Although Bonnitcha points to evidence that suggests that the increase in FDI flows does not necessarily impact a broad range of sectors; rather, it concerns the extractive sectors and others associated with high sunk costs, suggesting 'that investment treaties are more effective in attracting the types of FDI that are less beneficial from a host country perspective'; see Assessing the Impacts of Investment Treaties (n 43) 15.

[58] Henk L M Kox and Hugo Rojas-Romagosa, 'How Trade and Investment Agreements Affect Bilateral FDI: Results from a Structural Gravity Model' (2020) 43(12) The World Economy 3203, 3223; see also Muhammad Zubair Mumtaz and Zachary Smith, 'Do Bilateral Investment Treaties Promote Foreign Direct Investment Inflows in Asian Countries?' (2018) IPRI Journal 78.

[59] The Political Economy of the Investment Treaty Regime (n 15) 178.

[60] The UNCITRAL Working Group III identified three types of concerns pertaining to: (i) the lack of consistency, coherence, predictability, and correctness of arbitral decisions by ISDS tribunals; (ii) arbitrators and decision-makers; and (iii) cost and duration of ISDS cases, see UNCITRAL, 'Draft Report of Working Group III (Investor-State Dispute Settlement Reform) on the Work of its Thirty-sixth Session'

complementarity between the substantive principles in IIAs (as articulated and applied in ISDS), the rule of law and the effect on foreign investment and, by extension, development.

The international law on investment is—critically—described as follows:

> A network of over 3,000 partially overlapping treaties governs international investment. These investment treaties grant international legal protection to foreign investors from certain types of adverse action by the governments of the host states in which they invest. Crucially, it is normally possible for foreign investors to enforce these legal protections through international arbitration.[61]

IIAs are described as international instruments that seek to advance the following objectives, which include the promotion of the rule of law:

> (1) promote investment flows; (2) depoliticize disputes between investors and states; (3) promote the rule of law; and (4) provide compensation for certain harms to investors—objectives of varying degrees of importance to multinational enterprises, home states, host states, and other stakeholders.[62]

First and foremost, indeed, the international law on investment—in its over 3,000 treaties—enshrines a number of common and often recurring principles such as non-discrimination, the protection against unlawful expropriation, full protection and security, and fair and equitable treatment (FET).[63] These closely track the principles of the rule of law.[64] They are in fact in symbiosis as will be explained directly below.

Corruption is one, if perhaps not the main, example of that symbiosis. It is anathema to the rule of law—both domestic and international—and, of course, development.[65] In his seminal treatise, *Development as Freedom*, Sen explains that: 'The prevalence of corruption is rightly regarded as one of the major stumbling blocks in the path to successful economic progress and that "[a] high level of corruption can make public policies ineffective and can also draw investment and

---

(A/CN9/964, Advance Copy, 6 November 2018) 8, 40 <https://uncitral.un.org/sites/uncitral.un.org/files/draft_report_of_wg_iii_for_the_website.pdf> accessed 27 June 2023.

[61] Assessing the Impacts of Investment Treaties (n 43) 1.
[62] Investor-State Dispute Settlement (n 50).
[63] According to UNCTAD, there are currently 3,301 BITs and treaties with investment provisions, of which 2,566 are in force; see UNCTAD, 'International Investment Agreements Navigator' <https://investmentpolicy.unctad.org/international-investment-agreements> accessed 27 June 2023. On common standards of protection, see The Political Economy of the Investment Treaty Regime (n 15) 93–95.
[64] ibid (The Political Economy of the Investment Treaty Regime) 112.
[65] For an empirical analysis on the adverse effects of corruption on economic development, see The Rule of Law and Economic Development (n 4) 210–13.

economic activities away from productive pursuits toward the towering rewards of underhanded activities".[66]

That symbiosis clearly transpires in ISDS jurisprudence. The tribunal in *Metal-Tech Ltd v Uzbekistan*—where the investor was found to have paid bribes to secure an exploitation and export licence for copper and molybdenum deposits—found that the investor's corrupt acts prevented the tribunal from exercising jurisdiction under the Israel-Uzbekistan bilateral investment treaty (BIT).[67] Notably, the *Metal-Tech* tribunal clearly articulated its function as a tool for the promotion of the rule of law in the following terms: 'The idea, however, is not to punish one party at the cost of the other, but *rather to ensure the promotion of the rule of law, which entails that a court or tribunal cannot grant assistance to a party that has engaged in a corrupt act*.'[68]

Arbitrariness has the same undesired effects. In *Casinos Austria et al v Argentina*, a case heard under the Austria-Argentina BIT concerning investigations into the claimants' investments—and the ultimate revocation of their gaming licence—by the state's gaming regulatory agency (ENERJA) in breach of Argentine law, the majority held that Argentina violated the BIT. Relying on the ICJ's definition of arbitrariness in *ELSI*,[69] the majority found that 'arbitrariness requires a qualitatively significant breach, an abuse of power, that imposes harm on a foreign investor contrary to the rule of law'.[70] Interestingly, in a subsequent passage blurring the lines between the domestic and international realms, the tribunal found that ENREJA's breaches 'were arbitrary and not in accordance with the requirements of the rule of law under international law'.[71]

The issue of arbitrariness arose as well in *Philip Morris and Abal Hermanos v Uruguay*.[72] The case concerned Uruguay' successful attempts to restrict the marketing of tobacco pursuant to the World Health Organization's Framework Convention on Tobacco Control[73] for public health reasons through two legislative measures: the first precluded tobacco manufacturers from marketing more than one variant of cigarettes per brand family (the 'Single Presentation Requirement'); and the second increased the size of mandatory graphic health warnings on cigarette

---

[66] Development as Freedom (n 6) 275.
[67] *Metal-Tech Ltd v Republic of Uzbekistan* [4 October 2013] ICSID Case No ARB/10/3 Award 389.
[68] ibid (emphasis added).
[69] James Crawford, *Chance, Order, Change: The Course of International Law* (n 22), 50 citing *Elettronica Sicula SpA (ELSI), United States v Italy*, Judgment, Merits, ICJ GL No 76, [1989] ICJ Rep 15, 76.
[70] *Casinos Austria International GmbH and Casinos Austria Aktiengesellschaft v Argentine Republic* [5 November 2021] ICSID Case No ARB/14/32 Award of the Tribunal 371.
[71] ibid 395 (emphasis added).
[72] *Philip Morris Brands Sàrl, Philip Morris Products SA and Abal Hermanos SA v Oriental Republic of Uruguay* [8 July 2016] ICSID Case No ARB/10/7 Award (hereafter '*Philip Morris Brands Sàrl, Philip Morris Products SA and Abal Hermanos SA v Oriental Republic of Uruguay*').
[73] WHO, *Framework Convention on Tobacco Control* (WHO FCTC) (adopted on 21 May 2003, entered into force on 27 February 2005).

packages, such that these would cover 80 per cent of all cigarette packages (the '80/80 Regulation').[74] The majority held that both the Single Presentation Requirement and 80/80 Regulation 'were a valid exercise by Uruguay of its police powers for the protection of public health. As such, they cannot constitute an expropriation of the Claimants' investment' under the Switzerland-Uruguay BIT.[75] Specifically, the majority was of the view that the challenged measures were 'taken *bona fide* for the purpose of protecting the public welfare, must be non-discriminatory and proportionate'.[76] Gary Born dissented, finding that there were contradictory decisions on the part of Uruguay that adversely affected the claimants' investment, and that these 'do not reflect the rule of law', which he states 'implies regularity, stability, and lack of arbitrariness' in breach of the BIT's FET standard.[77]

The question is thus not whether IIAs (and ISDS) prevent states from regulating in the public interest; rather, they regulate *how* they do so.[78] Sitting under the Cyprus-Hungary BIT, the tribunal in *ADC Affiliate and ADC & ADMC Management Limited v Hungary*—a case that concerned the unlawful takeover of the investor's airport investments by the state—held that the rule of law sets the boundaries for host-state action in the public interest in the following terms:

> The Tribunal cannot accept the Respondent's position that the actions taken by it against the Claimants were merely an exercise of its rights under international law to regulate its domestic economic and legal affairs. *It is the Tribunal's*

---

[74] *Philip Morris Brands Sàrl, Philip Morris Products SA and Abal Hermanos SA v Oriental Republic of Uruguay* (n 72) 286, 307. For a more detailed discussion, see Farouk El-Hosseny and Ezequiel Vetulli, '*Amicus* Acceptance and Relevance: The Distinctive Example of *Philip Morris v Uruguay*' (2017) 64 NILR 73, 87–88.

[75] *Philip Morris Brands Sàrl, Philip Morris Products S.A. and Abal Hermanos S.A. v. Oriental Republic of Uruguay* (n 73), 286, 307.

[76] ibid 305.

[77] *Philip Morris Brands Sàrl, Philip Morris Products SA and Abal Hermanos SA v Oriental Republic of Uruguay* [8 July 2016] ICSID Case No ARB/10/7 Concurring and Dissenting Opinion of Gary Born 51, 133.

[78] To give but one example, the WTO General Agreement on Trade in Services (GATS) allows Member States to take certain measures to protect the public order and interest as exceptions to their obligations under the GATS, notably subject to those measures not constituting 'a means of arbitrary or unjustifiable discrimination between countries where like conditions prevail' as follows:

> Subject to the requirement that such measures are not applied in a manner which would constitute a means of arbitrary or unjustifiable discrimination between countries where like conditions prevail, or a disguised restriction on trade in services, nothing in this Agreement shall be construed to prevent the adoption or enforcement by any Member of measures: (a) necessary to protect public morals or to maintain public order; (b) necessary to protect human, animal or plant life or health; (c) necessary to secure compliance with laws or regulations which are not inconsistent with the provisions of this Agreement including those relating to: (i) the prevention of deceptive and fraudulent practices or to deal with the effects of a default on services contracts; (ii) the protection of the privacy of individuals in relation to the processing and dissemination of personal data and the protection of confidentiality of individual records and accounts; (iii) safety; ....'

See also GATS, *Marrakesh Agreement Establishing the World Trade Organization* (Annex 1B, 1869 UNTS 183, 33 ILM 1167, art XIV, 15 April 1994); see also art XIV *bis*.

understanding of the basic international law principles that while a sovereign State possesses the inherent right to regulate its domestic affairs, the exercise of such right is not unlimited and must have its boundaries. As rightly pointed out by the Claimants, *the rule of law, which includes treaty obligations, provides such boundaries*. Therefore, when a State enters into a bilateral investment treaty like the one in this case, it becomes bound by it and the investment-protection obligations it undertook therein must be honoured rather than be ignored by a later argument of the State's right to regulate.[79]

The same is true for non-retrospectivity.[80] In *Cairn Energy and Cairn UK Holdings v India*, the investors successfully impugned the assessment of capital gains taxes pursuant to the application of India's Income Tax Act (1961) with retroactive effect, so as to cover indirect asset transfers by non-residents.[81] The *Cairn* tribunal interpreted India's obligation to accord FET to the investors under the India-United Kingdom BIT through the lens of the Venice Commission's Rule of Law Checklist and the UN's various pronouncements on the rule of law (thus relying on both its domestic and international iterations), holding that 'the principle of legal certainty (and its corollaries, stability and predictability) provides significant guidance when determining whether retroactive taxation is compatible with the FET standard' under the BIT; in other words, under international law.[82] Whilst acknowledging that taxation serves a laudable public purpose and thus recognising India's sovereign right to regulate, the tribunal found that a public purpose cannot justify the retroactive application of new tax legislation, noting that '[i]t does not require a long explanation that accepting such a system would erode the legal certainty and the rule of law'.[83] The *Cairn* tribunal ultimately concluded that India's conduct was 'grossly unfair' in breach of its obligations under the India-United Kingdom BIT in the following terms:

> *By retroactively applying, without a specific justification, a new tax burden on a transaction that was not taxable at the time it was carried out, the Respondent [State] deprived the Claimants of their ability to plan their activities in consideration of the legal consequences of their conduct, in violation of the principle of legal certainty, which the Tribunal considers to be one of the core elements of the FET standard, and of the rule of law more generally.* In the words of the ICJ in *ELSI*, this unjustified retroactivity is 'not so much something opposed to a rule of

---

[79] *ADC Affiliate Limited and ADC & ADMC Management Limited v Republic of Hungary* [2 October 2006] ICSID Case No ARB/03/16 Award 423 (emphasis added).
[80] James Crawford, *Chance, Order, Change: The Course of International Law* (n 22), 349 (emphasis added).
[81] *Cairn Energy PLC and Cairn UK Holdings Limited (CUHL) v Government of India*, [21 December 2020] PCA Case No 2016-7 (UNCITRAL) Award.
[82] ibid 1742–45, 1757.
[83] ibid 1760.

law, as something opposed to the rule of law', and 'shocks, or at least surprises, a sense of juridical propriety'. Having considered the full factual record of this case, the Tribunal finds that the retroactive taxation of the CIHL Acquisition was, to quote Waste Management II, 'grossly unfair'. The Tribunal thus concludes that the Respondent breached its obligation under Article 3(2) of the BIT to accord the Claimants' investments FET.[84]

There is a plethora of examples from ISDS jurisprudence such as the ones above that show that when host-states violate core requirements of the rule of law, such as non-arbitrariness and non-retrospectivity, they harm investments within their jurisdictions and, as a result, breach their international law obligations. Drawing on the ISDS tribunals' analyses above, it is not difficult to see that corruption, arbitrariness, and retrospectivity can only have adverse effects on investments within host-states' jurisdiction and, by logical extension, development. Nor is it difficult to acknowledge that, by censuring corruption, arbitrariness, and retrospectivity, ISDS tribunals contribute to the protection and promotion of the rule of law—in both the international and domestic realms.

But the international rule of law is not a one-way street: cases such as *Metal-Tech v Uzbekistan* categorically confirm that foreign investors are equally bound by its principles. They cannot, on the one hand, engage in corrupt and/or criminal acts such as bribery and money laundering,[85] infringe human rights, or destroy the environment in the context of their investments[86] and, on the other, attempt to seek international protection against host-state action aimed at redressing the harm caused by their acts and omissions. The international rule of law does not, therefore, solely concern states—it is to be respected by all relevant actors,[87] including non-state actors such as foreign investors, as shown here.

5. Conclusion

Even if at times inescapably chimerical, the rule of international law is a 'virtue', to adopt Crawford's term.[88] It is undoubtedly more palpable in the domestic realm. Yet, even there, the data does not categorically suggest that 'the rule of law is a

---

[84] ibid 1816 (emphasis added).
[85] For example, see *Valeri Belokon v Kyrgyz Republic* [24 October 2014] UNCITRAL Award; as set aside by the Paris Court of Appeal (a judgment upheld by the Court of Cassation); see Paris Court of Appeal (Pole 1—First Chamber) Judgment No 15/01650, 21 February 2017; French Court of Cassation, Judgment No 338 FS-P+B, 23 March 2022. More generally, on illegality, see Zachary Douglas, 'The Plea of Illegality in Investment Treaty Arbitration' (2014) 29(1) ICSID Review 155.
[86] For a discussion on the consequences specific to violations of human rights and environmental harm, see Farouk El-Hosseny and Patrick Devine, 'Contributory Fault under International Law: A Gateway for Human Rights in ISDS?' (2020) 35 ICSID Review 105.
[87] Defying Gravity: Defining the International Rule of Law (n 23) 299, 301–02.
[88] Chance, Order, Change: The Course of International Law (n 21) 353.

fundamental correlate of economic development'—in other words, there is a link of utility, not conditionality, between the two.[89] The same holds true internationally.

Although links are at best correlative, not causal, a case for symbiosis can still be made. The argument made in this chapter is that—what Bingham calls—the 'rule of the jungle' on the international plane can only adversely affect development.[90] Conversely, a faithful and full implementation of international obligations—including once internalized through systemic reform—will inexorably be conducive to development.

There is significant tension between the idea that, on the one hand, international investment law—as enshrined in IIAs and enforced by way of ISDS—triggers regulatory chills and, on the other, that IIAs and ISDS are conducive to the international rule of law and, by extension, development. The practical approach proposed in this chapter is entirely independent from the often legitimate, but at times hypothetical, criticisms of IIAs in general, and ISDS in particular, on the premise of regulatory chills. Although (again) legitimate, the criticism risks at times being too myopic, overlooking the lessons that can be learnt from the rich body of publicly available jurisprudence which, as a strict matter of fact, contributes to the rule of international law. As shown by the majority in *Philip Morris v Uruguay*,[91] tribunals unequivocally recognize state police powers and their right (and duty) to regulate in the public interest. It is not about whether or not that right can be exercised—it is about *how*. Indeed, the body of treaties and cases is a treasure trove for those policymakers seeking to enhance the rule of law and, by extension, development.

By looking at the specific instances of inconsistency of prior state measures with the rule of international law, they have at their disposal a practical toolkit to uphold the virtues of the rule of law and—ultimately—enhance development. There is therefore a valuable opportunity to tap into that jurisprudence and internalize those principles in practical terms. The onus is on states to implement and fulfil the aspirations set forth in the myriad of laudable UN General Assembly declarations cited in this chapter by putting them into practice. If not acted upon, these will only be hortatory, if not hollow, statements.

---

[89] Rule of Law, Development, and Human Capabilities (n 6) 114; on utility, see The Rule of Law and Economic Development (n 4) 221.
[90] The Rule of Law in the International Order (n 28).
[91] *Philip Morris Brands Sàrl, Philip Morris Products S.A. and Abal Hermanos S.A. v. Oriental Republic of Uruguay* (n 73), 286, 307.

PART V
CONCLUSIONS

18
The Relevance of International Law to Sustainable Development

Siobhán McInerney-Lankford and Robert McCorquodale

1. Regime Interaction

The thread running through the chapters of this book is the enduring and multifaceted relevance of international law to all aspects of sustainable development. Far beyond analysing the legal dimensions of development, which are recognized in each of its chapters, this book makes a bolder argument about the centrality of international law to sustainable development, in both structural and substantive terms.

Whether international law is assessed in relation to the formation of norms and rules of development law, the evolution of development policy and procedures, the financing of development projects, or in trade, investment, or investment dispute resolution, it plays a foundational role in sustainable development. The role and relevance of international law has both normative and operational dimensions; it is manifest in substantive rules and norms, as well as in processes and procedures.

At the heart of the book's approach is an appraisal of regime interaction in the context of development. Regime interaction and fragmentation are challenges in this context, as is the fundamental question of 'how different elements of international law and governance interact'.[1] Each chapter addresses how a particular specialized branch of international law relates to development and vice versa. In this respect, each one examines—either directly or indirectly—how a particular area of sustainable development interacts with public international law, and how the rules of international law shape aspects of development and help to advance the attainment of the Sustainable Development Goals (SDGs). Conversely, certain chapters address how development law and policy have had formative influences in creating new international law.

As an international law text, this book is concerned with three types of regime interaction relevant to sustainable development: substantive; formal; and institutional. First, from a substantive perspective, the book addresses the interaction

---

[1] Margaret Young, *Regime Interaction in International Law: Facing Fragmentation* (CUP 2015) 11.

Siobhán McInerney-Lankford and Robert McCorquodale, *The Relevance of International Law to Sustainable Development* In: *The Roles of International Law in Development*. Edited by: Siobhán McInerney-Lankford and Robert McCorquodale, Oxford University Press. © Siobhán McInerney-Lankford and Robert McCorquodale 2023. DOI: 10.1093/oso/9780192872906.003.0018

between general international law and specialized regimes as they relate to sustainable development. This is evident in the interplay of norms underpinning the international rule of law and sustainable development, and the triangular relationship between development, international law, and human rights. This interaction is also evident in the debates about international policy coherence and the need to tackle the fragmentation of international law in the context of development. It is also extant in arguments in favour of coherence between development and international law and, in particular, for arguments that rely on the principle of systemic integration derived from article 31(3)(c) of the Vienna Convention on the Law of Treaties (VCLT) related to the interpretation of treaties. This provides that '[t]here shall be taken into account, together with the context: ... (c) any relevant rules of international law applicable in the relations between the parties'.

Second, from a more formal perspective, this book is concerned with the interaction of norms that are qualitatively distinct and that emanate from different sources. On the one hand, there are norms derived from treaties (or customary international law) which are legally binding; on the other hand, there are norms derived from non-legal forms of policy or regulation, such as goals, declarations, frameworks, and agendas for action. This is significant because the broad category of 'development law' is dominated by non-binding instruments, which makes the appraisal of this interaction at the level of form more complex. This 'formal interaction' is exemplified in the interplay between development goals, such as the SDGs and a large number of treaties.

Third, this book concerns the institutions responsible for different regimes within the international system. This is reflected in the division of labour among international actors established with different legal mandates and competences, which often have 'custodial' responsibilities for particular treaties or issues. In an increasingly interconnected world where global problems and development challenges span a wide range of issues and require coordinated action and specialized interventions across extended time periods and vast geographic areas involving thousands (sometimes millions) of people, international actors must work together to be effective in their responses. In doing so, they must understand their respective roles and responsibilities and work collaboratively in partnerships that reflect their distinct but complementary roles.

For example, Arnold Pronto's chapter tackles the fundamental question of the claim of relevance or value-added of law in development practice, interrogating the role and utility of law, and international law, for sustainable development. Pronto asks, what, in the context of sustainable development, is the promise of the law? In answering this, he points to the role of law in managing complexity, including contradictory policy imperatives, of which the SDGs are a paradigmatic example. Pronto argues that law provides both the framework and discourse narrative for managing complexity, usually by constraining the actions of states and other actors in pursuit of predictable and desirable outcomes.

2. International Law and Development Law

The chapters in the book emerge with different perspectives on the broader appraisal of the relationship of international law to sustainable development: some approaches are more critical, others more sanguine.

a. Critical voices

The fragmentation of international law[2] and international policy coherence[3] are recurring themes in several chapters, as are calls for greater accountability for development processes and outcomes, including for international legal accountability judged against binding rules of international law derived from treaties and customary international law.

Some chapters challenge the politics and assumptions underpinning notions of development and the international legal order. Other chapters point to the limitations attendant on the financing necessary for development or to meet the SDGs, and reveal a desire for development to be far more ambitious and grounded in its actions to combat racism and racial discrimination in development. Still, others point to the general neglect of international law in development policy and practice or, at least the latter's failure to adopt a systematic approach to international law. Some chapters note that, despite points of convergence and confluence, significant disconnects and dissonance exist between international law and aspects of development, including where development actors have created elaborate policy and procedural frameworks that are analogous to international law, but are lacking in certain crucial respects.

These debates emerge clearly in some chapters. For example, the chapter by Thomas McInerney (no relation to the editor) tackles the issue of financing for development, resource mobilization for the multilateral treaties relevant to sustainable development and the specific concerns arising from their legal nature. He analyses the institutional infrastructure needed to support sustainable development finance, noting that the resources needed to meet the financing needs of the SDGs and the Paris Agreement on climate change have so far fallen substantially

---

[2] Martti Koskenniemi and Päivi Leino, 'Fragmentation of International Law? Postmodern Anxieties', 15 Leiden JIL 553, 560–61 (2002); see also Bruno Simma, 'Self-Contained Regimes' (1985) 15 NYBIL 111, 135 ('The question whether treaty subsystems on the protection of human rights constitute "self-contained regimes", is a very controversial one.... [T]he views put forward in favor of such a qualification are both unconvincing and dangerous for the effectiveness of international human rights law.').

[3] For example, the 2008 Accra Agenda for Action provided 'Gender equality, respect for human rights, and environmental sustainability are cornerstones for achieving enduring impact on the lives and potential of poor women, men, and children. It is vital that all our policies address these issues in a more systematic and coherent way.' The 2011 UN Guiding Principles on Business and Human Rights also emphasize the need to ensure policy coherence (e.g. Principles 8, 9, and 10).

short. Chin Leng Lim offers a critical perspective of international law, development, trade, and foreign investment in his chapter. He does so by analysing how international law informs development, through the principles and doctrines which have emerged from trade and investment treaties, as well as from soft law instruments. Recalling enduring North/South and post-colonial controversies, he presents a sceptical appraisal of the concept of 'sustainable development' as having only a restricted meaning in the context of trade and investment, which is reflected in treaties as well as in the interpretative jurisprudence of adjudicative bodies. Lim's chapter addresses the problem of fragmentation in international investment law treated as a specialized regime divorced from other norms of public international law norms, including international human rights.

Harum Mukhayer's chapter offers a critical appraisal of the issue of racial discrimination as a substantive area of international law that has begun to influence development, but where, due to the complex history of development vis-à-vis race and colonialism, the constructive and corrective influence of international law in development has yet to be realized. She argues persuasively that even if the principles of equality and non-discrimination are incipient in development policy and practice, international law and development have yet to meet the challenge of ending racism expressly or to reflect the nuance of lived experiences of racism everywhere.

The chapter by Ximena Sierra-Camargo analyzes mining policies promulgated by insitutions like the World Bank in Latin America in the 1990s, which she argues encouraged states to adapt their legal and institutional frameworks to facilitate the optimal operation of mining corporations. She presents a deeply critical view of the underlying assumptions and objectives of such reforms, and the problematic model of sustainable development that prioritized the rights of private investors over the interests of communities, the environment, and long-term poverty reduction goals. Her analysis challenges the policy prescriptions of international financial institutions and the impact these have had on the constitutional and legislative frameworks of the affected developing country to the potential detriment of sustainble development itself. Similarly, Bakary Kanté's chapter notes the urgent need for action on climate change, especially from the perspective of Africa, and the need for development policies to address its impacts. He particularly notes the potential of existing law to address the climate challenge and its impacts, which could be used much more in development strategies.

b. Positive perceptions

A different set of approaches is evident in chapters that adopt a more positive perspective on the relationship between international law and development. These chapters tend to view the relationship as complementary and as evidencing the potential for mutual reinforcement. Among these are chapters that see the SDGs as examples of a *rapprochement* and which underscore coherence between international law rules and sustainable development. Some chapters argue for the potential, and need, for a synergistic relationship between international law and the SDGs, and some point to elements of 'additionality' in the SDGs with respect to the existing body of international law (including soft law measures). These chapters argue that international law and development are converging in substantive ways that yield positive results and promote sustainable development.

For example, Sandra Fredman's chapter provides a nuanced analysis of the positive relationship between the international law rules and principles relating to gender, with SDG 5. She notes the respective shortcomings of the SDGs, such as weakness of qualitative dimensions of substantive gender equality and their accountability mechanisms, and of human rights, such as the substance of human rights still contested, particularly in relation to women in poverty. From this, she makes a compelling argument for the need for both structures to work together in a synergistic manner to achieve substantive gender equality and to deliver on the ambitious promises of the SDGs. Fredman further argues that both the SDGs and human rights should be deliberately imbued with the perspective of substantive gender equality. The chapter by Laurence Boisson de Chazournes, Mara Tignino, and Haoua Savadogo on the human right to water in sustainable development embodies an argument in favour of legal and policy coherence. The authors acknowledge the importance of the body of soft law on the right to water for the consolidation of this right under general international law, but also argue that the United Nations (UN) 2030 Agenda on Sustainable Development brings a new and important dimension to the right, particularly in its introduction of monitoring at the global level and other innovative dimensions introduced by the interplay of the right to water with SDG 6 on access to water.

Ursula Kriebaum's chapter analyses the shared goals of international investment law and sustainable development: each aims to establish a rule-of-law-based international system that creates a solid legal basis for investments that have as their ultimate goal (sustainable) development. She notes this alignment in the area of foreign investment in green energy, which will be indispensable to achieving a transition to green technologies in developing countries, and which will ultimately serve sustainable goals. She contends that sustainable development considerations are increasingly integrated into foreign investment law and observes this in the texts of investment treaties as well as in the case law of investment disputes. From a different viewpoint, Farouk El-Hosseny's chapter offers structural argument for the positive and symbiotic relationship between the international rule of law and sustainable development. He explores whether respect for the international rule of law, which he defines as 'international rights and obligations set forth in treaties, as enforced by international courts and tribunals, including most notably investment treaty tribunals', results in a 'regulatory chill' or is in fact conducive to development.

Drawing on data and the principles articulated by international courts and tribunals primarily concerned with investment matters, he argues that adverse impacts result from states failing to abide by their obligations in relation to other states, be it in the context of maritime boundary or border disputes or disputes with investors who are nationals of other states.

c. Interchanges

A third group of chapters appraise the current and potential interchange between international law rules, institutions, and processes, with sustainable development. Among these are the chapters analysing labour, human rights generally, the UN human rights treaty bodies, and protections for internally displaced persons, as well as the chapter on infrastructure.

For example, Anganile Willie Mwenifumbo, Harumi Fuentes Furuya, and Marie-Joseph Ayissi consider the work of the UN treaty bodies which have a mandate to supervise the implementation of human rights obligations of states under their respective treaties, and their crucial role in guiding states in their efforts to achieve the SDGs. The chapter examines the treaty bodies' use of their procedural and substantive mandates to help ensure that states' efforts to meet the SDGs also comply with the obligations under UN human rights law treaties. In their chapter, Katerina Tsotroudi and Jordi Agustí Panareda chart the synergies between international labour standards and sustainable development, and examine the mutual relevance of international labour standards to the SDGs, particularly SDG 8 on Decent Work and Economic Growth. This chapter considers the experience of mainstreaming international labour standards in the International Labour Organization's (ILO's) development activities. It assesses the opportunities of integration, while also offering a critical appraisal of the tensions, legal and political challenges and risks extant in mainstreaming the normative-operational integration. Among the challenges, they cite the need for systematic monitoring and evaluation and the need to address a tendency towards technical over-specialization of staff, which may lead to narrowly perceived mandates preventing international labour standards being mainstreamed across functions. They also note the risk of ticking the 'normative box' or including superficial references without specific focus and 'depth' in project proposals. A further set of challenges relates to partnerships, which are needed not only for funding, but also for policy coherence across the UN.

Jan Wouters and Michiel Hoornick's chapter analyses what they characterize as a 'triangular relationship' between human rights, international law, and sustainable development. They argue that, while their respective agendas may operate separately from each other, the fulfilment of human rights and the achievement of sustainable development are integrally connected. They assess how the SDGs reference international law and the degree to which the SDGs themselves (as well as their targets and indicators) are becoming part of public international law and influencing it in different ways. Further, the chapter by Duygu Çiçek, Paige Casaly, and Vikram Raghavan provides an in-depth analysis of the dynamic interplay between the World Bank's work on forced displacement and international law and institutions. Their chapter details how the norms and principles of international refugee law, humanitarian law, and human rights law (among others) have been integrated into the World Bank's development strategies, policies, and operations relating to forced displacement. It also describes the institutional cooperation between the World Bank and the UN High Commissioner for Refugees (UNHCR). They argue that the World Bank's forced displacement policies, practice, projects, and partnerships could contribute to greater global policy coherence and more sustainable development outcomes while also contributing to, and strengthening, the existing and emerging international norms and standards relating to forced displacement.

Taking a comparative approach, Humbert Cantú Rivera deals with development projects relating to infrastructure within a state and notes that the private sector has gained prominence as a business partner in this area. He notes that, in these instances, including when states and business join forces through public-private partnerships, the obligations and responsibilities under international law are unclear. He proposes that the rapidly developing field of business and human rights can offer a valuable framework for showing how a state could still use some of its regulatory and contracting powers to incentivize more responsible conduct by its business partners, so that infrastructure development can become more sustainable and accountable while protecting and respecting human rights.

3. Conclusion

What unifies all the chapters in this book is the sense that international law can, does, and should influence development and that development law itself is an emerging field of international law that should continue to be shaped within the normative and interpretative framework of general international law. An additional operational argument extrapolated from this overall theme is one in favour of international law due diligence as a process or tool to ensure that the relevant and applicable rules of international law are assessed, known, and taken into account by development actors as they create and interpret development policy and procedure.

In this, the argument is not that development actors should enforce a type of international law conditionality, but rather that they should adopt a more systematic and comprehensive approach to relevant and applicable international law rules. They should ensure they are aware of what international law rules govern the areas in which they operate, especially whether they are elaborating policies and procedures or undertaking development activities in particular spheres. An overarching normative proposition underpinning this book is that development does not occur in a legal vacuum and that its goals can be met more effectively and sustainably through greater and more systematic reliance on international law.

Index

For the benefit of digital users, indexed terms that span two pages (e.g., 52–53) may, on occasion, appear on only one of those pages.

Tables are indicated by *t* following the page number

2030 Agenda
  forced displacement 255–56
  international labour standards 128–30
  international law
    broad development of 70–71
    references to 67–68
  legal instrument 68–70
  policy instrument 68–70
  sustainable development agenda 82–84
  treaty bodies 82–84, 102–6
  see also sustainable development

accountability
  concept of 16
  corporate 13, 211–17
  development policies 3–4, 11–12
  legal accountability, definitions of 16n.7, 17–18
Addis Ababa Action Agenda (AAAA) 363, 364, 365–66, 368, 369, 370–71, 372, 373, 376, 381–82, 388
Advancing the Decent Work Agenda in North Africa (ADWA) 119–20
African Charter on Human and Peoples' Rights (ACHPR) 62–63, 65, 164, 236, 237
African Development Bank (AfDB) 74, 185, 236, 250–51
African Vaccine Acquisition Task Team (AVATT) 191
African Vaccine Acquisition Trust (AVAT) 191–93
Alliance for Water Stewardship (AWS) 213
apartheid 126, 172, 178–81
  see also race discrimination
arbitrariness
  definition of 417, 423
  prohibition of 13
Areas Beyond National Jurisdiction (ABNJ) 230–31
Articles on Responsibilities of International Organisations (ARIO) 7
Asian Development Bank (ADB) 185, 367, 395

Asian Infrastructure Investment Bank (AIIB) 185, 192, 369

Banjul Charter *see* African Charter on Human and Peoples' Rights (ACHPR)
Base Erosion and Profit Shifting project (BEPS) 375
Bilateral Investment Treaties (BITs) 215–16, 306, 313, 316, 317, 318n.51, 320–22, 323, 324–25, 339, 340, 348, 353, 354–55, 357n.64, 361–62, 413n.14, 422n.63, 423, 424–25
biological diversity *see* Convention on Biological Diversity (CBD)
Black Lives Matter (BLM) 175–76, 176n.88, 181, 194
  conceptual context 174–76
  see also race discrimination
Brazil, Russia, India, and China (BRIC) 353–54, 369
Bretton Woods agreement 245, 277, 341–42
Brundtland Commission *see* World Commission on Environment and Development
'but for' test 167

Call to Action for Human Rights (C2A) 129–30, 133n.103
Calvo Doctrine 347n.28, 352–53
Cambodia, Myanmar, Lao People's Democratic Republic, and Vietnam Committee on the Protection of the Rights of All Migrant Workers and Members of Their Families (CMW) 80n.3, 81n.8, 89, 90–91, 93–94, 98, 104, 106, 107
capital accumulation 10, 275n.9, 276, 298–99
capital markets 282, 372–73, 376–77
  see also International Capital Markets Association (ICMA)
capitalism 298
  sustainable development and 10
Carbon Dioxide (CO_2) 221

CEPAL *see* Economic Commission for Latin America and the Caribbean (ECLAC)
CESCR *see* Committee on Economic Social and Cultural Rights (CESCR)
Child Rights and Business Principles (CRBP) 399–400
children 85, 86–87, 90, 91, 92–93, 94–96, 99–100, 103–4, 113, 144–45, 154–55, 156, 157–58, 191, 196, 206, 209, 210, 245, 399–400
  child labour *see* International Programme on the Elimination of Child Labour (IPEC); International Programme on the Elimination of Child Labour and Forced Labour (IPEC+)
  emergency fund *see* UNICEF (United Nations International Children's Emergency Fund)
  see also Child Rights and Business Principles (CRBP); Committee on the Rights of the Child (CRC)
Chlorofluorocarbons (CFCs) 221
civil and political rights 91–94
  civil rights and fundamental freedoms 92–94
  participation in political, economic, and public life 92
  see also human rights; International Covenant on Civil and Political Rights (ICCPR)
Clean Development Mechanism (CDM) 234, 235
climate change 13, 221–42
  climate litigation 240–41
  concepts and principles 229–34
    common but differentiated responsibilities 233–34
    environmental harm, prevention of 230–31
    intergenerational equity 233
    polluter pays principle 232–33
    precautionary principle 231–32
    transboundary pollution, prevention of 230–31
  constitutional law 236–39
    procedural rights 239
    substantive rights 237–38
  context 221–22
  ecological functions of property 227
  ecological sustainability and resilience 227
  environmental rule of law 225–29
  gender equality 227
  in dubio pro natura 227
  indigenous and tribal peoples 228
  intergenerational equity 227
  international environmental law 234–36
    Kyoto Protocol 235
    Paris Agreement 235–36
    UNFCCC 234
  intragenerational equity 227
  legal responses to 225–34
    overview 241–42
    statutory law 239–40
  minority and vulnerable groups, participation of 228
  non-regression principle 228
  obligation to protect nature 227
  progression principle 228
  right to environment 227
  right to nature 240–27
  rights of nature 227
  sustainable development, impact on 222–24
    economic impact 224
    environmental impact 222–23
    social impact 223–24
  see also environmental law; Green Climate Fund (GCF); Intergovernmental Panel on Climate Change (IPCC); nature; United Nations Framework Convention on Climate Change (UNFCCC)
Coalition for Epidemic Preparedness Innovations (CEPI) 191
Collective Action Clause (CAC) 373–74
Committee on the Application of Standards (CAS) 116n.35
Committee on Economic Social and Cultural Rights (CESCR)
  COVID vaccination 105
  gender equality 150–51
  General Comments 99
  High-Level Political Forum 88, 106
  human rights framework 83, 159–60
  joint HRC statement 103
  'leave no-one behind' pledge 104
  poverty reduction 96–97
  reproductive health and rights 99, 153
  social security protection 96–97
  sustainable development goals 89–91, 94, 102, 104, 107, 152–53, 207
  treaty bodies 81n.8
  water, right to 201
  work and employment 97
  see also General Comment 22 on reproductive rights (GC22)
Committee on the Elimination of Racial Discrimination (CERD) 65–66, 81n.8, 88, 99, 101, 106, 108, 188–89
Committee on Enforced Disappearances (CED) 81n.8
Committee of Experts on the Application of Conventions and Recommendations (CEACR) 112–13, 116n.35, 117n.39, 122n.63, 128–29, 134n.107

INDEX 441

Committee on Freedom of Association (CFA) 125
Committee on the Rights of the Child (CRC) 65–66, 81n.8
Committee on the Rights of Persons with Disabilities (CRPD) 83, 84n.26, 89, 93, 94, 95–96, 97, 98, 99–101, 102, 103, 105, 106, 107, 253, 399
Committee on Trade and Development (CTD) 345–46
common but differentiated responsibilities 233–34
  principle of 233, 234, 235
Comprehensive Economic and Trade Agreement (CETA) 323, 354–55, 361n.79
Conferences of Party (COP) 383–84
  CITES 387
conflict 12, 17–18, 264–65
  armed 103–4, 139, 155–56, 203–4, 222, 243, 244n.7, 253, 255, 413
  definition of 31n.93
  displacement and 249–50
  land and 223, 266
  mining 300
  Post Conflict Fund (World Bank) 247, 248
  social and environmental 275n.9
  types of 22
  see also Fragility, Conflict, and Violence (FCV)
Convention against Torture and other Cruel, Inhuman or Degrading Treatment or Punishment (CAT) 61–62, 80n.3
Convention on Biological Diversity (CBD) 293, 386–87
Convention on the Elimination of All Forms of Discrimination against Women (CEDAW) 61, 80n.3, 84, 86n.43, 92, 97–98, 99, 100–2, 103, 104, 105–6, 139–41, 152–53, 154, 159n.80, 201–2, 208n.106, 253n.51
Copenhagen Accord 2009 (COP17) 61n.8
Corporate Water Stewardship 213–14
corruption 9–10, 32, 307, 309–10, 313–14, 315, 323–24, 337, 375–76, 382, 383, 385, 417–18, 422–23, 426
  see also United Nations Convention against Corruption (UNCAC)
countervailing measures *see* SCM Agreement (Agreement on Subsidies and Countervailing Measures)
Country Programme Outcomes (CPOs) 121
COVAX (COVID-19 Vaccines Global Access) 189n.178, 191–93
COVID-19 pandemic
  care workers, effect on 143

development financing 187
disability specific impacts 105, 107
economic recovery 108, 135, 136t
economic shock 371–72
fiscal policies 389
gender equality, effect on 139, 142, 143
Gender Response Tracker 158
human rights law 155–56, 164
inflation and 364
International Labour Organization (ILO) 118, 122, 124
'leave no one behind' principle 105
private sector investment 388
race discrimination, effect of 165, 188–93
  AVAT 191–93
  COVAX 191–93
  early phase 190
  global response 191–93
  racialized effects 188–89, 192–93, 194
  vaccine discrimination 188–89
sovereign bankruptcy system 372
TRIPS waiver 189
water, right to 202–3
World Bank financing 192
see also COVAX (COVID-19 Vaccines Global Access); Debt Service Suspension Initiative (DSSI); Strategic Preparedness and Response Program (SPRP)
Crisis Response Window (CRW) 249
customary international law 7–8, 36, 38, 49–52, 63–64, 70–71, 162n.5, 178–79, 217, 230, 252, 269n.131, 318, 320–22, 326, 327, 347–48, 352–53, 432

Danish Institute for Human Rights (DIHR) 65n.33, 86n.40
Debt Service Suspension Initiative (DSSI) 371–72, 388
debt sustainability *see* financing
Decent Work Country Programmes (DWCPs) 116–17, 121, 127
development 9–11
  accountability and 15–16
    legal accountability 15–20
  concept of 339, 352, 358, 360–61, 392–93, 396
  definitions 9, 72
  economic growth and 9
  environmental areas 12
  financing and 13, 363–90
    context 363–64
    current situation 365–69
    finance shortfalls 367–69
    institutional changes 369
  fragmentation 20–23
  human rights aspects of 11

442 INDEX

development (*cont.*)
  humanitarian areas 12
  industrialization and 9
  international law and development practice
      development practice 46–56
      context 46–47
      definition 48–53
      overview 56
    law 23–32
      international legal regimes 28–32
    policy *see* development policies
    regime interaction 20–23
    rule of law and 13, 411–27
  sustainable *see* sustainable development
  trade and *see* foreign investment
development assistance 73, 185
  see also Official Development Assistance (ODA)
Development Assistance Committee (DAC) 366
Development Cooperation (DC) 28–29, 73, 121, 364
Development Finance Institutions (DFI) 369, 375, 377, 379
development policies
  accountability 3–4, 11–12
  bilateral institutions 3–4
  decision-making approaches 6
  global development 6–7
  international human rights obligations, impact of 59–66
  international law 3–4
  market-based approaches 6
  multilateral institutions 3–4
  race discrimination 176–87
    anti-racism 181–84
    apartheid 178–81
    development practice 184–87
    multilateralism 181–84
disability 18, 99–100, 133n.105, 157, 205–6, 207–8, 210, 211
  COVID-19 pandemic, impact of 107
  disability-rights indicators 83–84, 100
  discrimination of the grounds of 207–8n.97
  stigma and stereotypes 93
  UN Special Envoy 105
  see also Committee on the Rights of Persons with Disabilities (CRPD)
disappearances 129
  enforced 136t
  see also International Convention for the Protection of All Persons from Enforced Disappearance (ICPED)
discrimination
  concept of 142–43, 169, 181–82
  definition of 208
  direct vs. indirect 181–82
  racial *see* race discrimination
  water, right to 207–11
  women, against *see* Convention on the Elimination of All Forms of Discrimination against Women (CEDAW)
  see also Committee on the Elimination of Racial Discrimination (CERD); International Convention on the Elimination of Racial Discrimination (ICERD); non-discrimination
displacement, forced *see* forced displacement; Global Program on Forced Displacement (GPFD)
dispute settlement 30, 113, 305–6, 308, 339, 348, 361–62
  see also Investor-State Dispute Settlement (ISDS)
'do no harm' principle 38–39
Doha Development Agenda 345–47
drugs *see* United Nations Office on Drugs and Crime (UNODC)
due diligence 177, 185, 189, 192, 193–94, 212, 216, 263, 264, 395–96, 398, 403n.49, 407–8, 437
  concept of 36–37
  development context 14–45
  environmental and social policies 29
  international law 32–35
    definition of 35–39
  legal accountability and 29–30
  principle of 36

ecological sustainability *see* climate change
Economic Commission for Latin America and the Caribbean (ECLAC) 280–82, 289–90, 294–95
economic development 9, 12, 76, 117–18, 119, 120n.54, 128–29, 134, 202, 205–6, 235, 239–40, 245n.10, 246–47, 262, 280n.30, 300, 307, 308, 322, 327, 337, 344–45, 357n.64, 377, 392–93, 394, 401, 413n.11, 422n.65, 426–27
  see also development
Economic and Financial Organisation (EFO) 168–69
economic order *see* New International Economic Order (NIEO)
economic prospects *see* Global Economic Prospects Report (GEP)
Economic and Social Council (ECOSOC) 126
economic, social and cultural rights 94–98
  economic and social benefits 96–97

education 96
health 95–96
poverty reduction 94–95
social security and protection 96–97
work and employment 97–98
see also human rights
education 9–10, 23, 136t, 196, 296, 367
   forced displacement 248, 252n.44, 255, 261, 266–67
   gender equality and 139, 147, 150–51, 154, 157
   human rights law 60n.3, 67n.40, 71, 77, 78
   public-private partnerships (PPPs) 391, 393–94, 398, 405–6
   Treaty Bodies (TBs) 86–87, 89, 94–95, 96, 100, 104, 106, 107
employment *see* work and employment
enforced disappearances 85, 136t
   see also Committee on Enforced Disappearances (CED)
Environmental Health and Safety Guidelines (EHSGs) 29
Environmental Impact Assessment (EIA) 314–15
environmental law 13, 20–21, 33–34, 46–47, 226, 231–32, 269n.132, 305, 325, 326
   on climate change 234–36
   'no harm', principle of 231
   prevention of environmental harm, principle of 230
      see also climate change; United Nations Environment Assembly (UNEA); United Nations Environment Programme (UNEP)
Environmental Law Institute (ELI) 237n.44
Environmental and Social (E&S) Policy 185, 192, 263
Environmental and Social Commitment Plan (ESCP) 192
Environmental and Social Framework (ESF) 185, 187, 244n.7, 263–65
   economic vs. 393
   forced displacement 263–65
      safeguards 395–96
   IFI safeguard policies 378–80
   sustainability 395
Environmental, Social, and Governance (ESG) 378–80
Environmental and Social Standard (ESS) 41–42, 125–26, 133, 192, 263–64
epidemic preparedness *see* Coalition for Epidemic Preparedness Innovations (CEPI)
Equal Pay International Coalition (EPIC) 119–20, 129, 136t

'equal pay for work of equal value'
   principle of 97–98
equality
   concept of 36
   gender *see* gender equality
   norms 31
   principle of 109
equitable treatment *see* Fair and Equitable Treatment (FET)
equity 19–20
   concept of 332
   contractual 406–7
   intergenerational 227, 229, 233, 242
   intragenerational 227
   social 9–10, 12, 294–95, 301
   vaccine 105, 188–89
erga omnes 61–62, 162–63, 185, 193
   concept of 17–18, 324n.83
European Bank for Reconstruction and Development (EBRD) 126n.76, 177
European Commission (EC) 176, 181
European Convention on Human Rights and Fundamental Freedoms (ECHR) 19–20, 62–63, 68, 164, 172–73, 181, 240
expropriation
   definition of 311–12, 327
   indirect expropriation, definition of 320–22

Fair and Equitable Treatment (FET) 311, 317, 320, 325–26, 327, 329–30, 331, 422
   definitions of 332
   test for 337
fairness 233–34, 418–19
   concept of 332
financial assistance 3–4
financial law 13
financing
   development agenda 363–90
      context 363–64
      current situation 365–69
      finance shortfalls 367–69
      institutional changes 369
   debt sustainability 370–74
      debt reduction 370–72
      distressed debt mechanisms 370–72
      private borrowing shift, implications of 372–74
   forced displacement 258–61
      global concessional financing facility 259
      IDA Window for Host Communities and Refugees 259–61
   international law issues 383–88
      funding competition and imbalances 386–88
      treaty financing models 383–84
      voluntary contribution concerns 384–85

financing (cont.)
  private sector role 376–83
    environmental, social, and governance standards 378–80
    incentives 380–82
    participation, limitations on 376–78
    reliable development partner, as a 382–83
    tax law and governance 374–76
Food and Agricultural Organization (FAO) 148n.29, 179–80
forced displacement 13, 243–72, 436–37
  bank activities, evolution of 245–49
    early approach 245–46
    Global Program for Forced Displacement 249
    internal displacement, gradual engagements with 248
    UNHCR partnerships 246–47
  bank policies and procedures 262–65
    Environmental and Social Framework (ESF) 263–65
    'fragility, conflict, and violence' policy 262–63
  context 243–44
  development approach to 249–51
    coordination with other organizations 250–51
    development and forced displacement 250
  financing mechanisms 258–61
    global concessional financing facility 259
    IDA Window for Host Communities and Refugees 259–61
  international law dimensions 258–68
  international law norms and bank policies and practice 268–72
  legal norms and principles 251–55
    international human rights law 254–55
    international humanitarian law 255
    international instruments 251–52
    international law on IDPs 253–54
    international refugee law 251–53
    regional instruments 252–53
  refugee policy reform and Member State dialogue 265–68
    analytics and diagnostic tools 265–66
    bank-financed operations 266–68
  sustainable development 255–58
    Agenda 2030 255–56
    Global Compact on Migration 256–58
    Global Compact on Refugees 256–58
    SDGs 255–56
  see also Global Program on Forced Displacement (GPFD)
foreign investment 13, 339–62
  analysis 356–58
  ancillary developments 358–60
  context 339–41
  Doha Development Agenda 345–47
  GATT/WTO jurisprudence 349–52
    conservation cases 351–52
    developing country members, issues of interest to 349
    development principle or goal, cases involving 350–51
    sustainable development principles 351–52
  'international standard' of compensation for expropriation 347–48
  NIEO, uncertain outcome of 347–48
  investment treaties 352–55
  investor-state arbitration 352–55
  'post-war' international economic order 341–45
    non-reciprocity 342–45
    perspectives 341–42
    preferential access 342–45
    'special and differential' treatment 342–45
  overview 360–62
'fragility, conflict, and violence' (FCV) policy 262–63
fragmentation 20–23
Framework Convention on Tobacco Control (FCTC) 423n.72
freedom(s)
  of action 53
  from arbitrary interference with privacy 417–18
  of assembly 83
  of association 111, 112–13, 114, 117, 119–20, 125, 126, 127n.77, 129, 133–34, 136t
  conditions of 111
  development as 422–23
  of expression 83, 112–13, 239
  fundamental 67n.40, 75–76, 92–94, 122, 162, 164, 165n.18, 208, 412n.7
  of movement 252n.44, 261
  from poverty 177
  of religious belief and thought 141, 170, 252n.44
  from slavery or servitude 112–13
  of thought 112–13
  threats to 252
  from violence and harassment 112–13, 253
full and prior informed consent 76
Fundamental Principles and Rights at Work (FPRW) 119, 120–22, 133
fundamental rights see civil and political rights; human rights

G20 371–72, 374, 375
  see also Base Erosion and Profit Shifting project (BEPS)

gender equality 10, 12, 139–61
  climate change 227
  context 139–42
  international human rights law 152–56
  resourcing 156–60
  substantive 142–51
    demands 156–60
    four-dimensional approach 142–45
    measurements 147–51
    SDGs 145–47
  synergies 160–61
General Agreement on Tariffs and Trade (GATT) 278, 341–45, 346–47, 353, 355, 356, 359–60
  trade and development issues 349–52
    conservation cases 351–52
    developing country members, issues of interest to 349
    development principle or goal 350–51
    sustainable development principles 351–52
General Agreement on Trade in Services (GATS) 424n.78
General Comment 22 on reproductive rights (GC22) 153
Generalized Scheme of Preferences (GSP) 74, 124–25, 342–43
generic term, definition of 320
Global Compact on Migration (Migration Compact) 256–58
Global Compact on Refugees (Refugees Compact) 256–58, 266–67, 270
Global Concessional Financing Facility (GCFF) 258, 259, 262, 266–68, 269, 270–71
Global Economic Prospects Report (GEP) 188
Global Environmental Facility (GEF) 386, 387
Global North 6, 9, 60–61, 71–72, 194, 275–76, 340, 433–34
Global Program on Forced Displacement (GPFD) 249
Global South 6–7, 9, 13, 65n.30, 188–89, 194, 273, 274, 275–76, 275n.9, 277–82, 340, 396–97
  development critical perspective 298–302
globalization 6–7, 340, 353, 396–97
good faith 13, 19, 141, 311, 311n.23, 312, 318, 318n.49, 321–22n.72, 328, 330, 357
good governance principles 74, 114, 225, 361n.76, 412n.8
Governing Body (GB) 111, 127n.82, 167
Green Climate Fund (GCF) 185
Greenhouse Gases (GHGs) 221

health rights 95–96, 139
High Level Panel of Experts (HLPE) 203n.66
High-level Panel Forum on Sustainable Development (HLPF) 67, 69, 85–86, 87–88, 106, 107, 108, 109, 140
Highly-Indebted Poor Countries (HIPC) 370–71
Hull Doctrine 347
human dignity 71, 196, 237–38, 412n.8
  principle of 240–41
human rights
  abuses 8, 216, 217
  approaches *see* Human Rights Based Approach (HRBA)
  concept of 392–93
  corporate responsibility 8
  development and 11
  development policies 59–66
  international obligations 59–66
  legal issues 12
  SDGs and 59–66
  sustainable development and 12
  treaty bodies *see* Treaty Bodies (TBs)
  see also civil and political rights; Danish Institute for Human Rights (DIHR); economic, social and cultural rights; European Convention on Human Rights and Fundamental Freedoms (ECHR); Institute for Human Rights and Business (IHRB); Inter-American Commission on Human Rights (IACHR); International Bill of Human Rights (IBHR); International Human Rights Law (IHRL); National Human Rights Institutions (NHRI); Office of the High Commissioner on Human Rights (OHCHR); United Nations Guiding Principles on Business and Human Rights (UNGPs); United Nations High Commissioner for Human Rights (UNHCHR); United Nations Working Group (UNWG); Universal Declaration on Human Rights (UDHR)
Human Rights Based Approach (HRBA)
  added value of 75–76
  housing, right to 76–77
  nationality, right to 76–77
  requirement for 76–77
  sustainable development and 12, 71–78
    addressees 39
    'international law due diligence,' definition of 35–39
    international legal coherence 32–43
    legal basis 32–34
    limitations of 77–78
    policy application 42–43
    policy content 41–42

446 INDEX

Human Rights Based Approach (HRBA) (cont.)
  policy interpretation 42–43
  purpose 34–35
  sphere of application 39–43
  treaty interpretation 39–41
Human Rights Committee (HRC) 81n.8, 166

ICCPR see International Covenant on Civil and Political Rights (ICCPR)
ICESCR see International Covenant on Economic, Social and Cultural Rights (ICESCR)
Identification for Development (ID4D) 77
IGPRA see Pakistan Income Generating Project for Refugee Areas (IGPRA)
in dubio pro natura 227
indigenous and tribal peoples 228
  see also United Nations Declaration on the Rights of Indigenous Peoples (UNDRIP)
infrastructure 13, 392–402
  concept of 392
  development 393–96
  human rights 396–402
  states and businesses, roles of 402–10
    functional dichotomy 402–5
    PPPs 405–10
  see also Public-Private Partnerships (PPPs)
Institute for Human Rights and Business (IHRB) 203n.67
Integrated Water Resources Management (IWRM) 204
intellectual property (IP) rights 189
  trade-related aspects of see TRIPs Agreement
Inter-Agency and Expert Group on SDG Indicators (IAEG-SDGs) 210–11
Inter-American Commission on Human Rights (IACHR) 401
Inter-American Convention on Human Rights (ACHR) 62–63
Inter-American Development Bank (IADB) 125–26, 395
intergenerational equity 242
  climate change 227, 233
  principle of 233
Intergovernmental Panel on Climate Change (IPCC) 63–64, 367–68
internally displaced persons (IDPs) 243n.1, 248, 268, 436
  international law on 253–54
  see also forced displacement
International Bank for Reconstruction and Development (IBRD) 25n.61, 244n.6, 245n.10, 273n.1, 282–83
International Bill of Human Rights (IBHR) 163–64

International Capital Markets Association (ICMA) 373
International Centre for Settlement of Investment Disputes (ICSID) 244n.6
International Committee of the Red Cross (ICRC) 5n.10
International Convention for the Protection of All Persons from Enforced Disappearance (ICPED) 80n.3
International Convention on the Elimination of Racial Discrimination (ICERD) 27, 61–62, 92, 108, 163–64, 165, 166, 168, 174–75, 178–79, 180, 253n.51
International Council on Metals and the Environment (ICME) 278
International Court of Justice (ICJ) 4–5, 17–18, 61–62, 169n.41, 178, 307n.13, 319, 358, 416
International Covenant on Civil and Political Rights (ICCPR)
International Covenant on Economic, Social and Cultural Rights (ICESCR) 62–63, 68n.47, 80n.3, 83, 85n.35, 86n.41, 163, 200, 206, 253n.51
International Development Association (IDA) 244n.6, 245n.10, 282–83
  see also Window for Host Communities and Refugees (WHR)
International Finance Corporation (IFC) 121n.60, 124, 126n.76, 243–44, 277n.15, 278, 288, 291n.79
International financial institutions (IFIs) 5, 24–25, 342, 378–79, 396–97
International Human Rights Law (IHRL) 12, 15n.4, 21–22, 34, 35, 61–62, 63, 64, 78, 113, 139–40, 142, 162, 169, 171, 174–75, 180–81, 326–27, 392–93, 402, 403–5, 408
  effectiveness of 15n.2, 433n.2
  forced displacement 254–55
  gender equality 152–56
  infrastructure in 396–402
international humanitarian law 253n.51, 254
  forced displacement 255
International Institute for Environment and Development (IIED) 302n.129
International Investment Agreements (IIAs) 276, 413–14, 417–18, 419, 420, 421–22, 424, 427
International Labour Conference (ILC) 111, 121–22
International Labour Organization (ILO) 110–14, 116–17, 136t
  dialogical standards-based approach 139–40
  establishment 172–73
  gender equality 152–53, 154–55, 157, 158, 159

integrated standards-setting 115–17
operational mandate 115–17
racial discrimination 183, 184
standards *see* International Labour Standards (ILS)
International Labour Standards (ILS) 67–68, 436
  2030 Agenda 128–30
  DC programmes and partnerships 123–26
  flexibility 115
  integrated standards-setting 115–17
  landmark cases 126–28
  'lifecycle' 115–17
  normative-operational integration 130–35
  operational mandate 115–17
  political declarations 119–23
  SDG indicators, custodianship of 136*t*
  social dialogue 115–17
  sustainable development 123–26
  technical cooperation 117–30
  trade and investment 123–26
  tripartism 115–17, 119–23
  UN development system 128–30
international law
  challenge for 53–56
  customary international law 7–8
  development and 14–15
  development policies 3
  dialogical standards-based approach 110–14
  financing issues 383–88
    funding competition and imbalances 386–88
    treaty financing models 383–84
    voluntary contribution concerns 384–85
  Global North/South 6–7
  human-rights based approach (HRBA)
    added value of 75–76
    nationality, right to 76–77
    need for 76–77
    ousing, right to 76–77
    sustainable development, limitations to 77–78
  importance of 3
  institutional bodies 5–6
  international organizations and 5
    ILO 110–14
  international personality 4–5
  investment law 13
  jus cogens 7
  non-governmental organizations 5–6
  non-state armed groups 5–6
  principles of 13
  rights and duties 4–5
  roles of 4–8, 11–12
  rule of law and 414–18

  scope of 8
  'soft' 7–8
  sustainable development and *see* sustainable development
  terrorist activities 5–6
  treaties and 3
  UN organisation 4–5
International Law Commission (ILC) 20–21, 27n.79, 30–31, 63–64, 111, 115n.31, 116n.35, 119, 122, 124–25n.70, 318
International Monetary Fund (IMF) 5, 187, 341–42, 366, 371, 374, 378
International Organizations (IOs) 4, 5, 7, 8, 342
  development practice 21, 23, 24–25, 29, 35, 39–40n.142, 48–49, 50, 51–52, 55
  human rights 59, 60, 63–64, 69, 70–71
  labour law 110, 111n.2, 134
  racial discrimination 168–69, 171–72, 176, 185
  water rights 204–5, 206–7
  World Bank 273, 274, 288, 294–95, 302
International Programme on the Elimination of Child Labour (IPEC) 123–24, 132n.102
International Programme on the Elimination of Child Labour and Forced Labour (IPEC+) 123–24
International Telecommunications Union (ITU) 179–80
international trade law *see* United Nations Commission on International Trade Law (UNCITRAL)
International Trade Organizations (ITOs) 341–42
International Tribunal for the Law of the Sea (ITLOS) 36–37, 413
International Union for Conservation of Nature (IUCN) 226
intertemporal law, principle of 178
intragenerational equity 227
investment law 13, 305–38
  agreements *see* International Investment Agreements (IIAs)
  context 305–9
  disputes *see* International Centre for Settlement of Investment Disputes (ICSID)
  'investment', definitions of 306–7, 356–57
  overview of 337–38
  renewable energy cases 331–37
    abruptness of change 335
    economic impact 335
    external circumstances, change of 335
    magnitude of change 335
    prior legislative practice 336
    public interests involved 336
    stability assurances 336

investment law (cont.)
  sustainable development 317–31
    evolutive treaty interpretation 318–23
    investment treaty language 309–17
    right to regulate, test for 327–31
    systemic integration and SDGs 323–27
  trade and foreign investment *see* foreign investment
Investment Project Financing (IPF) 192n.197, 263n.94
investment treaties 352–55
  see also investment law
investor-state arbitration 352–55
Investor-State Dispute Settlement (ISDS) 352, 413–14, 416–17, 418, 419–22, 423, 424, 426, 427

Joint Development Zones (JDZs) 413
Joint Implementation (JI) 234
Joint Monitoring Programme (JMP) 205, 207, 209
jus cogens 7, 185
justice, conceptions of 144

labour rights 12, 24n.58, 65n.33, 74, 98, 124, 126, 128–29, 136t, 146, 309–10, 360–61, 395–96
labour standards *see* International Labour Organization (ILO); International Labour Standards (ILS)
League of Nations 164–65, 168–73, 195
  principles of 170
Least Developed Countries (LDCs) 60–61, 343, 370–72, 377–78, 389
Leave No One Behind (LNOB) principle 85–86, 98, 105, 109, 133n.103, 205–6, 208, 243–44, 255, 389
legal certainty 225, 274, 280, 284, 295
  principle of 425–26

maritime law *see* International Tribunal for the Law of the Sea (ITLOS)
Members of the European Parliament (MEP) 182
MERCOSUR 351
metals *see* International Council on Metals and the Environment (ICME)
meteorology *see* World Meteorological Organization (WMO)
Methane (CH) 221
Methyl Tertiary Butyl Ether (MTBE) 320
migration 101–2, 104, 136t, 203–4, 207–8, 211, 222, 251, 271–72
  see also Global Compact on Migration (Migration Compact)

Millennium Development Goals (MDGs) 23, 24, 60–61, 80, 84–85, 207–8, 340, 393–94
mining reforms *see* World Bank
minority groups 77, 96, 228
Monitoring and Evaluation (M&E) 131, 132, 436
MOPAN *see* Multilateral Organisation Performance Assessment Network (MOPAN)
Multilateral Agreement on Investment (MAI) 340, 352
Multilateral Development Banks (MDBs) 5, 11, 12, 125–26, 133–34, 185, 187, 250–51, 259, 269, 270, 364, 379–80, 395
Multilateral Environmental Agreements (MEAs) 234
Multilateral Investment Agreement (MIA) 353–54, 355
Multilateral Investment Guarantee Agency (MIGA) 244n.6
Multilateral Organisation Performance Assessment Network (MOPAN) 123n.66, 130n.93
Multinational Corporations (MNCs) 352, 353, 379, 382
Mutual Administrative Assistance (MAA) 375

NAFTA *see* North American Free Trade Agreement (NAFTA)
NAMA *see* Non-Agricultural Market Access (NAMA)
National Human Rights Institutions (NHRI) 70, 105
Nationally Determined Contributions (NDC) 234, 236, 241–42
nature
  conservation *see* International Union for Conservation of Nature (IUCN)
  obligation to protect 227
  right to nature 240–27
  rights of nature 227
  see also climate change; environmental law
needs, concept of 9
New International Economic Order (NIEO) 65n.30, 341–45, 352
  non-reciprocity 342–45
  perspectives 341–42
  preferential access 342–45
  'special and differential' treatment 342–45
  trade and foreign investment 347–48
Nitrous Oxide (NOx) 221
Non-Agricultural Market Access (NAMA) 345–46
non-discrimination 13, 109, 163, 164–65, 176, 180–81, 185, 195, 205–6, 208
  see also discrimination

INDEX   449

non-governmental organizations (NGOs) 5–6, 21, 72–73, 142, 158–59, 213, 302
non-interference principle 36
non-reciprocity 342–45, 360
non-refoulement principle 252, 254–55
non-regression principle 228
non-succession principle 358–59n.68
North American Free Trade Agreement (NAFTA) 278, 320–22, 323, 324–25, 396n.19, 418

OECD *see* Organization for Economic Cooperation and Development (OECD)
Office for Internal Oversight Services (OIOS)
Office of Hawaiian Affairs (OHA)
Office of the High Commissioner on Human Rights (OHCHR)
Official Development Assistance (ODA)
Organisation of the Petroleum Exporting Countries (OPEC)
Organization for Economic Cooperation and Development (OECD)
  blended finance 377–78
  Development Assistance Committee (DAC) 366, 368
  development financing 187, 369
  Evaluation Network 377
  Global Infrastructure Hub 366
  Guidelines for Multinational Enterprises 313–14, 379
  Guiding Principles 212n.134, 216n.175, 232
  MAA in Tax Matters 375
  Model Tax Treaty 374
  multilateral agreement on investment (MAI) 340, 353
  Platform for Collaboration on Tax 374
  Private Finance for Sustainable Development (PF4SD) Conference 211n.130
  regulatory chill 414
  sustainable development study (2014) 309–10
  see also Base Erosion and Profit Shifting project (BEPS)
Organization of African Unity (OAU) 252, 258
oversight services *see* Office for Internal Oversight Services (OIOS)

pacta sunt servanda principle 19, 26, 32–33
Pakistan Income Generating Project for Refugee Areas (IGPRA) 246–47nn.18–19
petroleum resources 351–52
  see also Organisation of the Petroleum Exporting Countries (OPEC)
Policy Outcomes (POs) 121

political declarations 28, 108, 118, 119–23
Polluter Pays Principle (PPP) 230n.22, 232–33, 242
pollution *see* climate change
postal union *see* Universal Postal Union (UPU)
poverty 17–18
  causes of 73
  environmental law and 222, 235–36, 301–2
  extreme 60, 183, 393n.5
  freedom from 177
  gender equality and 141–42, 145, 160–61, 435
  infrastructure and 401
  MDGs and 393–94
  racial discrimination and 188, 190, 192–93
  reduction of 60–61, 74, 77, 86–87, 94–95, 96–97, 106, 121n.60, 122, 136t, 202, 255
  relative poverty, definition of 259n.82
  SDGs and eradication of 23, 89, 94, 98, 294, 300
  UN Special Rapporteur on Extreme Poverty 18
  'Voices of the Poor' report 11
  water rights 203–4
  World Bank 274, 278, 293–94
  see also Highly-Indebted Poor Countries (HIPC)
precautionary principle 229, 231–32, 234, 314–15
preferential access 342–45
private sector 77–78, 152, 160, 437
  development agenda 364, 365–66, 367, 368, 369, 371–73, 375, 376–83, 388–89
  environmental, social, and governance standards 378–80
  incentives 380–82
  participation, limitations on 376–78
  Public-Private Partnerships (PPPs) 391, 395, 397, 398, 399–400, 403–7, 410
  reliable development partner, as a 382–83
  water rights 198, 201, 211–12, 216, 218
  World Bank mining reforms 12P17, 279, 282–83, 285, 286, 289–90
  see also financing
privatization
  definition of 406–7
Programmatic Structural Adjustment Credits (PSACs) 288
Programmatic Structural Adjustment Loan (PSALs) 288
Programme and Budget (P&B) 121, 126n.76
progression principle 228
project financing *see* Investment Project Financing (IPF)
proportionality test 328–31

property 173, 205–6, 418n.41
  access to 97, 145
  ecological functions of 227
  exchangeable 300
  immoveable 252n.44
  intangible 321n.71
  intellectual *see* intellectual property (IP) rights
  looting of 243
  mining titles 285–87
  private 10, 285, 411
  rights 6–7, 321n.71, 352–53, 400–1, 411, 418–19
  value of 285
Public-Private Partnerships (PPPs) 212–13, 391–410, 437
  definition (World Bank) 405–6
  duties vs. responsibilities 405–10
  see also infrastructure

race discrimination 12, 17n.14, 162–95, 433
  concept of 169
  conceptual context 168–76
    Black Lives Matter, impact of 174–76
    general 168–69
    historical perspectives 169–72
    lived experiences 172–74
    race and colour 169–72
    race, conceptions of 195
  context 162–65, 193–95
  COVID-19 pandemic, effect of 188–93
    AVAT 191–93
    COVAX 191–93
    early phase 190
    global response 191–93
  definition of 165–68
    race, definitions of 194
  development policy 176–87
    anti-racism and multilateralism 181–84
    apartheid 178–81
    development practice 184–87
  inequality and 188–93
  prohibition of 61–62
  race, definition of 165–68
  see also Black Lives Matter (BLM); Committee on the Elimination of Racial Discrimination (CERD); International Convention on the Elimination of Racial Discrimination (ICERD)
racism 164, 176, 192, 193
  anti-racism movements 165, 168, 175, 177, 180–84, 186, 187, 189, 193, 194, 433, 434
  definition of 165–68
  institutional and structural 175, 176, 186

Red Cross *see* International Committee of the Red Cross (ICRC)
Refugee Organization (IRO) 245–46n.11
Refugee Policy Review Framework (RPRF) 261, 266
refugees 192, 245, 248–49, 250, 260, 261–62, 263, 264–65, 266–68, 271–72
  Afghan 246–47
  Cartagena Declaration 253
  'climate' 223, 238
  definition (1951 Convention) 251–53
  financing mechanisms 258
  German 245–46
  IDA Window for Host Communities and Refugees 259–61
  international law 251–53
    humanitarian protection 255
    international instruments 251–52
    protection framework 254–55
    regional instruments 252–53
  Pakistan 246
  policy reform and dialogue with Member States 265–68
    analytics and diagnostic tools 265–66
    bank-financed operations 266–68
  see also forced displacement; Global Compact on Refugees (Refugees Compact); internally displaced persons (IDPs); United Nations High Commissioner for Refugees (UNHCR); Window for Host Communities and Refugees (WHR)
Regional Trade Agreements (RTAs) 124–25, 339, 340–41, 342–43, 346–47, 354–55
regulatory chills 413–14, 418–21, 427, 435–36
relief and rehabilitation *see* United Nations Relief and Rehabilitation Administration (UNRRA)
renewable energy 69–70, 72, 308–9, 331–37, 349
  abruptness of change 335
  economic impact 335
  external circumstances, change of 335
  magnitude of change 335
  prior legislative practice 336
  public interests involved 336
  stability assurances 336
reproductive rights *see* General Comment 22 on reproductive rights (GC22)
rights
  concept of 73
rule of law 3, 54, 73, 82, 114, 152, 317, 332, 337, 338, 361n.76, 377
  concept of 415n.24
  definition of 225, 414–18, 435–36
  development and 13, 222, 411–27

environmental 225–29, 238, 239, 242, 308
  importance of 3
  international law and 30–31, 414–18, 431–32, 435–36
  investment law 411–27
  regulatory chills 418–21
  symbiosis, case for 421–26

SCM Agreement (Agreement on Subsidies and Countervailing Measures) 346
SDG Indicators 72, 114, 129, 136*t*, 149–50, 208, 210–11, 256n.61
  see also Inter-Agency and Expert Group on SDG Indicators (IAEG-SDGs)
Security Council *see* United Nations Security Council (UNSC)
social security and protection 97–98, 122, 129, 157, 252n.44, 393–94
  rights 86–87, 96–97, 104, 112–13, 136*t*
  standards 124, 136*t*
soft law 7–8, 24–26, 43, 50–52, 62–63, 67–68, 89, 91, 109, 189, 230, 232, 255, 313–14, 339, 433–35
  definition 7–8
  soft international law 7–8
  sustainable development and 10, 11
Southern Common Market *see* MERCOSUR
'special and differential' treatment 339, 341, 342–46, 358
Special Mandate Holders (SMHs) 65n.32
special regimes 21, 22–23, 27–28, 29, 30, 43
  definition of 20–21
Standards Review Mechanism (SRM) 112n.5, 115n.31, 132
State-Owned Mining Enterprises (SOEs) 278–79, 282–83
State sovereignty
  concept of 36
  principle of 171–72
statistics *see* United Nations Statistics Division (UNSD)
Strategic Preparedness and Response Program (SPRP) 191
Strengthening Labour Relations and its Institutions in Egypt (SLARIE) 120n.54
structural adjustment *see* Programmatic Structural Adjustment Credits (PSAC); Programmatic Structural Adjustment Loan (PSAL)
Subcommittee on Prevention of Torture (SPT) 81n.8
subsidies 9, 158, 277, 279, 337–38, 346–47, 349, 378
  see also SCM Agreement (Agreement on Subsidies and Countervailing Measures)

sustainable development
  2030 Agenda for *see* 2030 Agenda
  capabilities approach 11
  capital accumulation and 10
  capitalism and 10
  climate change, impact of 222–24
    economic impact 224
    environmental impact 222–23
    social impact 223–24
  concept of 9, 24, 25–26, 59–60, 128–29, 307n.13, 308, 352n.47, 360, 433–34
  corporate concentration 10
  critiques of focus on 10
  definitions of 9–10, 59–60, 202, 307, 351–52
  export-oriented growth 10
  forced displacement
    Agenda 2030 255–56
    Global Compact on Migration (Migration Compact) 256–58
    Global Compact on Refugees (Refugees Compact) 256–58
    recent developments 255–58
  goals *see* Sustainable Development Goals (SDGs)
  human development and 9
  human dislocation 10
  human rights-based approach (HRBA) 12, 71–78
    address*ees* 39
    'international law due diligence,' definition of 35–39
    international legal coherence 32–43
    legal basis 32–34
    limitations of 77–78
    policy application 42–43
    policy content 41–42
    policy interpretation 42–43
    purpose 34–35
    sphere of application 39–43
    treaty interpretation 39–41
  international labour standards 123–26
  international law, role in 11–12
    critical voices 433–34
    development law 433–37
    interchanges 436–37
    overview 437–38
    positive perceptions 434–36
    regime interaction 431–32
    relevance 431–38
  investment treaty cases 317–31
    evolutive treaty interpretation 318–23
    language 309–17
    right to regulate, test for 327–31
    systemic integration and SDGs 323–27

452 INDEX

sustainable development (*cont.*)
  limitations, concept of 9
  mining sector 292–98
  needs, concept of 9
  outcomes 11
  principles 238, 351–52
  rights language 11
  soft law and 10
  treaty bodies
    agenda 81–88
    high-level political forum 106–8
  water, importance of 202–4
  World Bank 9–10
  see also climate change; environmental law; High-level Panel Forum on Sustainable Development (HLPF)
Sustainable Development Goals (SDGs) 3–4, 23, 46–47, 59, 66n.38, 80–81, 114, 139, 196, 201, 243–44, 339, 363, 393n.5, 431
  forced displacement 255–56
  human rights and 71–78
    impact 59–66
    standards 84–88
  ILO custodianship 136*t*
  international law, relationship to 67–71
  investment law 308–9, 312, 320–22, 331, 332, 338
  substantive gender equality 145–47
    measurements 147–51
  systemic integration and 323–27
  see also 2030 Agenda
Sustainable Investment Facilitation & Cooperation Agreement (SIFCA) 316
systemic integration principle 40–41, 43–44, 323–24, 325, 431–32

tax law 364, 366, 375, 376, 388–89
  governance and 374–76
  permanent establishment, definition of 374
  see also financing
technical assistance operations 3–4, 12, 14, 38–39, 41, 117n.39, 118, 159–60, 168–69, 191, 206, 288, 371, 383–84
Technical Cooperation (TC) 114, 117–30
telecommunications *see* International Telecommunications Union (ITU)
territorial integrity
  concept of 36
Theory of Change 132
third-generation people's rights 348n.33
tobacco control *see* Framework Convention on Tobacco Control (FCTC)
torture 136*t*, 178, 254–55, 358–59
  see also Convention against Torture and other Cruel, Inhuman or Degrading Treatment or Punishment (CAT); Subcommittee on Prevention of Torture (SPT)
trade law 13, 20–21, 189, 349, 356
  see also foreign investment
trade-related aspects of intellectual property *see* TRIPs Agreement
Transatlantic Trade and Investment Partnership (TTIP) 354–55
Treaty Bodies (TBs) 12, 62–63, 65–66, 80–109, 140–41, 384, 386, 387, 397, 399, 400, 402–3, 436
  2030 Agenda 82–84, 102–6
  approaches 80–81
  case-by-case approach 90–91
  CEDAW 89–90
  CESCR 89–90
  CMW 90–91
  concluding observations 88–91
  CRC 89–91
  CRPD 90–91
  general comments/recommendations 99–102
  holistic approach 89–90
  international treaties, definition of 17n.15, 25n.62
  normative framework 81–88
  sustainable development agenda 81–106
    high-level political forum 106–8
    human rights standards 84–88
  see also civil and political rights; economic, social and cultural rights; United Nations Treaty Bodies (UNTBs)
Tripartite Working Group (TWG) 112n.5, 115n.31
TRIPs Agreement 189
'two-tier' test 350, 351

UNCITRAL *see* United Nations Commission on International Trade Law (UNCITRAL)
UNCTAD *see* United Nations Conference on Trade and Development (UNCTAD)
undue burden 351
UNESCO 183, 184, 201n.50
  see also World Water Assessment Programme (WWAP)
UNICEF (United Nations International Children's Emergency Fund) 136*t*, 191, 205, 207n.96, 209, 399–400
  see also Joint Monitoring Programme (JMP)
United Nations (UN) 46, 63
  Charter 44, 162–63, 415–17
  climate change, perspectives on 221
  decolonization era (1950s-1970s) 342
  development system 77–78, 128–30, 132
  establishment 4

INDEX 453

global concessional financing facility 259
infrastructure 391
Mar del Plata Water Conference 198–99
Member States 23, 25n.62, 196
Millennium Declaration 200, 340
Model bilateral tax treaty 374
purposes and principles of 5–6
Secretary General 225
Special Envoys 105
Special Rapporteur on Extreme Poverty 18
specialized agencies 111
see also 2030 Agenda; High-Level Political Forum (HLPF); Sustainable Development Goals (SDGs); Treaty Bodies (TBs); Economic Commission for Latin America and the Caribbean (ECLAC)
United Nations Commission on International Trade Law (UNCITRAL) 355, 360, 421–22n.60
United Nations Commission on Transnational Corporations 353
United Nations Conference on Environment and Development (UNCED) 199, 232, 234, 293
United Nations Conference on the Human Environment 198
United Nations Conference on Sustainable Development 339
United Nations Conference on Trade and Development (UNCTAD) 278, 306nn.8–9, 309–10, 367, 368–69, 372, 422n.63
United Nations Convention against Corruption (UNCAC) 313, 385
United Nations Convention on the Elimination of All Forms of Discrimination against Women (CEDAW) *see* Convention on the Elimination of All Forms of Discrimination against Women (CEDAW)
United Nations Convention on the Law of the Sea (UNCLOS) 67–68, 230–31, 412–13
United Nations Convention relating to the Status of Refugees 251–52
United Nations Declaration on the Rights of Indigenous Peoples (UNDRIP) 186–87
United Nations Development Programme (UNDP) 64n.28, 74, 179–80, 197
United Nations Economic and Social Council *see* Economic and Social Council (ECOSOC)
United Nations Educational, Scientific and Cultural Organization (UNESCO) 183, 184

United Nations Environment Assembly (UNEA) 226
United Nations Environment Programme (UNEP) 63–64n.21, 225, 237n.44, 278
United Nations Framework Convention on Climate Change (UNFCCC) 60–61n.7, 63–64n.21, 67–68, 221n.3, 223–24, 231–32, 233, 234, 235, 293, 365, 386–87
United Nations General Assembly (UNGA) 7–8, 24, 26, 65–67, 70–71, 163–64, 179–80, 199–201, 211–12, 243–44, 255, 256–57nn.66–67
United Nations Guiding Principles on Business and Human Rights (UNGPs) 7–8, 15n.3, 212n.133, 216, 316, 379, 402n.44, 403, 433n.3
United Nations High Commissioner for Human Rights (UNHCHR) 71, 379, 383–84, 385, 386, 387
United Nations High Commissioner for Refugees (UNHCR) 63–64n.21, 77, 193, 244, 245–46n.11, 256–57, 260–61, 262, 264–65, 266, 270–71, 436–37
  partnerships on forced displacement issues 246–47, 250, 252
United Nations International Children's Emergency Fund *see* UNICEF (United Nations International Children's Emergency Fund)
United Nations Monetary and Financial Conference 245
United Nations Office on Drugs and Crime (UNODC) 385
United Nations Population Fund (UNFPA) 150
United Nations Relief and Rehabilitation Administration (UNRRA) 245–46
United Nations Secretary-General (UNSG) 12, 65–66, 105, 129–30
United Nations Security Council (UNSC) 40, 67n.40, 179, 180n.116
  resolutions 5–6, 180
United Nations Treaty Bodies (UNTBs) *see* Treaty Bodies (TBs)
United Nations Water 204–5
United Nations Working Group (UNWG) 113–14
United States-Mexico-Canada Agreement (USMCA) 396n.19
Universal Declaration on Human Rights (UDHR) 24, 44, 67–68, 71, 73, 80n.3, 86–87, 108, 152, 162–63, 239, 254
Universal Periodic Review (UPR) 66, 74
Universal Postal Union (UPU) 179–80

454 INDEX

USMCA *see* United States-Mexico-Canada Agreement (USMCA)

Vaccination Readiness Assessment Framework (VRAF) 191n.195
Vaccine Introduction Readiness Assessment Tool (VIRAT) 191n.195
Vienna Convention on the Law of Treaties (VCLT) 19, 39–41, 311, 357–58, 360, 431–32
violence *see* conflict; Fragility, Conflict, and Violence (FCV)
Voluntary National Reviews (VNRs) 67, 69, 87–88, 108, 109
vulnerable groups 27, 188–89, 248, 263n.98, 272, 398
  participation of 228

Washington Consensus 277
water
  corporate accountability and 211–17
  discrimination and 207–11
  resources *see* Integrated Water Resources Management (IWRM)
  right to 12, 196–218
    definition of 197
    recognition of 198–202
  SDG 6 (moving boundaries), interfaces with 204–17
  sustainable development, importance for 202–4
  see also World Water Assessment Programme (WWAP)
Water Supply, Sanitation and Hygiene (WASH) 205, 214n.146
well-being 6, 68n.47, 111, 146–47, 221–22, 227, 237, 241–42, 295, 332, 391, 394
  principle of 168–69
Window for Host Communities and Refugees (WHR) 258, 259–61, 268, 269, 270–71, 272
women *see* Convention on the Elimination of All Forms of Discrimination against Women (CEDAW); gender equality
work and employment 94, 97–98
World Bank (WB)
  Group *see* World Bank Group (WBG)
  mining reforms 13, 273–302
    constitutional shaping 284–85
    context 273–76
    development critical perspective 298–302

foreign investment 285–89
Global South 277–82
guidelines for legislative reform 285–89
historical context 282–89
local communities, social licence of 290–92
overview 302
responsible mining 292–98
strategies 289–98
sustainable development, discourse of 292–98
see also Environmental and Social Framework (ESF); Environmental and Social Standard (ESS); forced displacement; Vaccination Readiness Assessment Framework (VRAT)
World Bank Group (WBG) 176, 182–84, 187, 191, 194, 250, 282–83, 374
World Commission on Environment and Development
  'Our Common Future' report 9, 14n.1, 293–94
  sustainable development, concept of 59–60
World Health Organisation (WHO) 190, 197, 423–24
  see also Framework Convention on Tobacco Control (FCTC); Monitoring Programme (JMP); Vaccine Introduction Readiness Assessment Tool (VIRAT)
World Humanitarian Summit 12
World Meteorological Organization (WMO) 63–64n.21
World Trade Organisation (WTO) 278, 342
  Agriculture Agreement 346
  Appellate Body 345, 348, 350–52, 356, 361–62
  Committee on Trade and Development (CTD) 345–46
  COVID-19 waiver of TRIPs 189
  dispute settlement system 361–62
  Doha Development Round 340, 345–46, 352
  GATT *see* General Agreement on Tariffs and Trade (GATT)
  human rights 360–61
  Marrakesh Agreement 343–44, 360
  Ministerial Conference 119, 189, 340
  special and differential treatment 346
  subsidies regulation regime 346n.24
  see also Committee on Trade and Development (CTD); General Agreement on Trade in Services (GATS); SCM Agreement (Agreement on Subsidies and Countervailing Measures)
World Water Assessment Programme (WWAP) 206n.86